FORENSIC PRACTITIONER'S GUIDE TO THE INTERPRETATION OF COMPLEX DNA PROFILES

FORENSIC PRACTITIONER'S GUIDE TO THE INTERPRETATION OF COMPLEX DNA PROFILES

PETER GILL
Oslo University Hospital
Forensic Genetics Research Group
Oslo, Norway

University of Oslo
Department of Clinical Medicine
Oslo, Norway

ØYVIND BLEKA
Oslo University Hospital
Forensic Genetics Research Group
Oslo, Norway

OSKAR HANSSON
Oslo University Hospital
Forensic Genetics Research Group
Oslo, Norway

CORINA BENSCHOP
Netherlands Forensic Institute
Division of Biological Traces
The Hague, The Netherlands

HINDA HANED
University of Amsterdam
Institute of Informatics
Amsterdam, The Netherlands

Academic Press is an imprint of Elsevier
125 London Wall, London EC2Y 5AS, United Kingdom
525 B Street, Suite 1650, San Diego, CA 92101, United States
50 Hampshire Street, 5th Floor, Cambridge, MA 02139, United States
The Boulevard, Langford Lane, Kidlington, Oxford OX5 1GB, United Kingdom

Copyright © 2020 Elsevier Inc. All rights reserved.

No part of this publication may be reproduced or transmitted in any form or by any means, electronic or mechanical, including photocopying, recording, or any information storage and retrieval system, without permission in writing from the publisher. Details on how to seek permission, further information about the Publisher's permissions policies and our arrangements with organizations such as the Copyright Clearance Center and the Copyright Licensing Agency, can be found at our website: www.elsevier.com/permissions.

This book and the individual contributions contained in it are protected under copyright by the Publisher (other than as may be noted herein).

Notices

Knowledge and best practice in this field are constantly changing. As new research and experience broaden our understanding, changes in research methods, professional practices, or medical treatment may become necessary.

Practitioners and researchers must always rely on their own experience and knowledge in evaluating and using any information, methods, compounds, or experiments described herein. In using such information or methods they should be mindful of their own safety and the safety of others, including parties for whom they have a professional responsibility.

To the fullest extent of the law, neither the Publisher nor the authors, contributors, or editors, assume any liability for any injury and/or damage to persons or property as a matter of products liability, negligence or otherwise, or from any use or operation of any methods, products, instructions, or ideas contained in the material herein.

Library of Congress Cataloging-in-Publication Data
A catalog record for this book is available from the Library of Congress

British Library Cataloguing-in-Publication Data
A catalogue record for this book is available from the British Library

ISBN: 978-0-12-820562-4

For information on all Academic Press publications
visit our website at https://www.elsevier.com/books-and-journals

Publisher: Stacy Masucci
Acquisitions Editor: Elizabeth Brown
Editorial Project Manager: Susan Ikeda
Production Project Manager: Punithavathy Govindaradjane
Designer: Christian Bilbow

Typeset by VTeX

Contents

About the authors	*xv*
Contributors	*xvii*
Foreword	*xix*
Preface	*xxi*
List of websites and resources	*xxv*

1. Forensic genetics: the basics — **1**

1.1. Short tandem repeat (STR) analysis — 2
    1.1.1. Historical development of multiplexed systems — 3
1.2. Development and harmonization of European National DNA databases — 4
    1.2.1. Development of the European set of standard (ESS) markers — 5
1.3. Hardy–Weinberg equilibrium — 6
    1.3.1. Measuring deviation from Hardy–Weinberg equilibrium — 8
    1.3.2. Extension to multiple alleles in STRs — 10
1.4. Quality assurance of data — 11
1.5. Recap: the laws of statistics — 12
    1.5.1. Effect of conditioning on probabilities — 13
1.6. The likelihood ratio — 14
1.7. Simple mixtures interpretation: the basics — 15
    1.7.1. Nomenclature — 15
    1.7.2. Minimum number of contributors — 15
    1.7.3. Interpretation of two-contributor mixtures — 17
    1.7.4. Step 1: condition the number of contributors — 18
    1.7.5. Step 2: state the alternative propositions — 18
    1.7.6. Step 3: evaluate the probability of the evidence under the defense proposition — 18
    1.7.7. Step 4: evaluate the probability of the crime-stain evidence under the prosecution proposition — 19
    1.7.8. Step 5: calculate the likelihood ratio — 20
    1.7.9. Step 6: report the likelihood ratio — 20
1.8. Three allele mixtures — 21
    1.8.1. Calculation of the likelihood ratio — 21
1.9. Two allele mixtures — 23
1.10. Multiple contributors — 24
1.11. Automating calculations with a computer program — 24
    1.11.1. Two-contributors — 24
    1.11.2. Recap — 27
    1.11.3. Extension to three or more contributors — 27
1.12. The effect of population sub-structuring — 29
    1.12.1. What is a population? — 29
    1.12.2. Genetic drift — 31
    1.12.3. Common ancestry — 32

v

vi Contents

1.12.4. A computer simulation to illustrate effects of genetic drift	35
1.12.5. Extension to multi-allelic systems (STRs)	36
1.12.6. Balding and Nichols F_{ST}	37
1.13. Simulation studies to show the effect of genetic drift and F_{ST} corrections	39
1.13.1. Details of the experiment	39
1.14. Sampling error correction	41
1.15. European Network of Forensic Science Institutes (ENFSI) evaluation of STR markers	42
1.15.1. Hardy–Weinberg tests	43
1.15.2. F_{ST} estimation	44
1.15.3. What F_{ST} to apply in casework?	45
1.16. Relatedness: kinship analysis	46
1.16.1. Effect of relatedness on the likelihood ratio calculation	46
1.16.2. Formal treatment and extension to mixtures	47
1.17. A brief introduction to the software approaches used to interpret mixtures	49
1.18. Summary	52
Notes	53

2. Empirical characterization of DNA profiles	**55**
2.1. Heterozygote balance	55
2.1.1. Peak height or peak area	55
2.1.2. Definitions	55
2.1.3. Methods to visualize data	56
2.1.4. The use of guidelines	56
2.1.5. Heterozygote balance summary	60
2.1.6. Characterization of heterozygote balance with *STR-validator*	60
2.2. Stutters	62
2.2.1. Characterization of stutters	62
2.2.2. Effect of number of STR repeats on the stutter size	63
2.2.3. Interpretation challenges with stutters	65
2.2.4. Stutters summary	66
2.2.5. Characterization of stutters with *STR-validator*	66
2.3. The Clayton guideline: a binary model to interpret simple mixtures	70
2.3.1. Step 1: identify the presence of a mixture	70
2.3.2. Step 2: identify the potential number of contributors to a sample	73
2.3.3. Step 3: determine the approximate ratio of the components in the mixture	74
2.3.4. Step 4: determine the possible pairwise combinations for the components of the mixture	76
2.3.5. Step 5: compare with reference samples	82
2.4. Characterization of massively parallel sequencing (MPS) kits using *STR-validator*	86
2.5. Summary	88

3. Allele drop-out and the stochastic threshold	**89**
3.1. What causes allele drop-out?	89
3.1.1. A mathematical model showing the relationship of heterozygote balance and drop-out	92

Contents   **vii**

3.2.	Stochastic thresholds and drop-out	93
3.3.	National DNA databases and low-template DNA crime stains	94
3.4.	Definition of drop-out and extreme drop-out	95
3.5.	Towards a meaningful definition of the low-template-DNA (T) threshold	96
3.6.	Historical development of probabilistic evaluation of drop-out	98
3.7.	Introducing probability of drop-out	99
	3.7.1. The defense proposition	100
	3.7.2. The prosecution proposition	100
3.8.	A method to calculate probability of drop-out and the stochastic threshold	102
	3.8.1. Experimental design and data collection	102
	3.8.2. An explanation of logistic regression	103
3.9.	Using *STR-validator* to plot drop-out characteristics	105
3.10.	Summary	107
	Notes	110

4. Low-template DNA   **111**

4.1.	Historical	111
4.2.	The consensus method explained	112
	4.2.1. Contamination vs. drop-in	115
4.3.	Statistical analysis	118
4.4.	Working with replicates	118
	4.4.1. An example to assess the strength of the evidence of three replicates	119
4.5.	Degradation	122
	4.5.1. Pre-PCR quantification and characterization of degradation	123
4.6.	Summary	127
	Note	128

5. *LRmix* model theory   **129**

5.1.	Background	129
5.2.	Model description	130
5.3.	Theoretical considerations	131
5.4.	Replicate probability	133
	5.4.1. Drop-out and drop-in: definitions	133
	5.4.2. Drop-out and drop-in: formalization	134
	5.4.3. Example 1	135
	5.4.4. Example 2	136
5.5.	Genotype probability	137
	5.5.1. Determining the genotypes for the unknowns	137
	5.5.2. Correcting for population sub-structuring	141
	5.5.3. Example 3	142
	5.5.4. Calculating genotype probabilities for relatedness	143
	5.5.5. Example with relatedness in mixtures	146
5.6.	Full example for calculating LR	146
5.7.	Summary	149
	Notes	150

viii Contents

6. **A qualitative (semi-continuous) model: *LRmix Studio*** **153**
6.1. Interpretation of a major/minor DNA mixture, where the minor contributor is evidential 153
    6.1.1. Case circumstances 153
    6.1.2. Exploratory data analysis 154
    6.1.3. The propositions 154
    6.1.4. Sensitivity analysis 157
    6.1.5. Calculation of levels of drop-out using an empirical method 158
    6.1.6. Non-contributor analysis 163
    6.1.7. How the LR is used in a statement 166
6.2. A case with two suspects 167
    6.2.1. Case circumstances 167
    6.2.2. Exploratory data analysis 167
    6.2.3. Minimum number of contributors 167
    6.2.4. Non-contributor tests 168
    6.2.5. Formulation of propositions and exploratory data analysis 169
6.3. Considerations of the ISFG DNA commission 174
    6.3.1. Formulation of propositions: summary 174
6.4. An example of a replicate analysis 175
6.5. Relatedness 177
6.6. Summary 178
Notes 179

7. **The quantitative (continuous) model theory** **181**
7.1. Introduction 181
7.2. Towards a quantitative model 181
    7.2.1. An example using the "MasterMix" Excel spreadsheet program 185
    7.2.2. Using the information across loci 190
7.3. Likelihood ratio estimation using probabilistic models 191
    7.3.1. The normal distribution model 192
    7.3.2. Step 1: calculation of expected peak heights 192
    7.3.3. Step 2: calculate the weighting 193
    7.3.4. Step 3: combine weightings with probability of genotype given the proposition 194
    7.3.5. Estimating the parameters of the normal distribution: maximum likelihood estimation (MLE) 196
7.4. Recap 198
7.5. The Gamma model 199
    7.5.1. Gamma distribution 199
    7.5.2. Model for one contributor 200
    7.5.3. Reparameterization 201
    7.5.4. An example 201
7.6. Drop-out for the gamma model explained 205
    7.6.1. The Q allele 206
    7.6.2. Comparison of the Excel spreadsheet with *EuroForMix*: a summary 210
7.7. Deconvolution 212
7.8. Degradation 215

Contents ix

7.8.1.	Demonstration with a spreadsheet	219
7.8.2.	Recap	219
7.9.	Stutter	220
7.9.1.	Recap: taking account of peak height expectations using mixture proportions M_x	222
7.9.2.	The full stutter model	223
7.9.3.	A worked example showing the impact of stutter in *EuroForMix*	223
7.9.4.	Combining stutter and degradation in the same model	226
7.9.5.	Using a spreadsheet model to illustrate stutter	226
7.9.6.	Dealing with forward and complex stutters	234
7.10.	The drop-in model	235
7.10.1.	Estimating lambda using *EuroForMix*	236
7.10.2.	Characterization of drop-in	236
7.11.	Summary	237
Notes		238

8. *EuroForMix*   **239**

8.1.	*EuroForMix* theory	239
8.2.	Interpretation using *EuroForMix*	239
8.3.	Theoretical considerations	240
8.4.	Model features	240
8.5.	An example	241
8.5.1.	ENFSI exercise 1: a major/minor profile, where the minor component is evidential	241
8.5.2.	Reference samples	243
8.5.3.	Preliminary assessment of the evidence	243
8.5.4.	Model specification	244
8.5.5.	The MLE fit tab	246
8.5.6.	Model selection	248
8.5.7.	Model validation	251
8.5.8.	Probability-probability, PP-plots	251
8.5.9.	LR sensitivity	254
8.5.10.	Model fitted peak height tab	255
8.5.11.	Non-contributor analysis	255
8.5.12.	Deconvolution	257
8.6.	ENFSI exercise 2: illustration of the advantage of using the quantitative model	258
8.6.1.	Case circumstances	258
8.6.2.	Effect of removing the conditioned suspect from the analysis	261
8.7.	A complex case: robbery	263
8.7.1.	Case circumstances	263
8.7.2.	Analysis	263
8.7.3.	*EuroForMix* analysis	266
8.8.	Relatedness calculations	268
8.8.1.	Results and discussion	271

x Contents

8.9.	Important updates to *EuroForMix*	272
8.10.	A summary of the interpretation process	274
	Notes	275

9. Validation — 277

9.1.	Context	277
9.2.	Avoiding the black-box	278
9.3.	Model validation	279
	9.3.1. Conceptual validation	279
	9.3.2. Operational validation	280
9.4.	Defining benchmarks for LR-based models	281
	9.4.1. Software validation	281
9.5.	Validation study of *LRmix Studio* and *EuroForMix*	282
	9.5.1. NGM DNA profiles	283
	9.5.2. PPF6C DNA profiles	283
	9.5.3. Replicates	284
	9.5.4. Stutter filter	284
	9.5.5. Allele frequency database	285
9.6.	Design of experiments	285
	9.6.1. Experiments using NGM profiles	285
	9.6.2. Experiments using PPF6C profiles	285
9.7.	Method	286
	9.7.1. Defining characteristics of the models	286
9.8.	Comparison of *LRmix Studio* and *EuroForMix* when the POI was the true contributor	287
9.9.	Comparison of *LRmix* and *EuroForMix* when the POI was not a true contributor	288
9.10.	Characterization of false positive results	290
	9.10.1. NGM results	290
	9.10.2. PPF6C results	291
9.11.	Characterization of false negative results	293
9.12.	LR values as a function of allele drop-out	294
	9.12.1. NGM results	294
	9.12.2. PPF6C results	296
9.13.	Comparing the performance of two or more different models using ROC plots	296
9.14.	Comparison of the stutter model in *EuroForMix* versus GeneMapper stutter filter	297
9.15.	Calibration of the likelihood ratio	299
9.16.	Further comparative studies between different software	302
9.17.	Defining guidelines for using probabilistic genotyping software in forensic casework	304
9.18.	Summary	306
	Notes	308

10. Development and implementation of *DNAxs* — 309

The DNAxs Team

10.1.	DNA expert system	309
	10.1.1. Functionalities of *DNAxs*	310

10.2.	*LoCIM-tool*	310
10.3.	*DNAStatistX*	315
	10.3.1. Similarities and differences between *EuroForMix* and *DNAStatistX*	316
	10.3.2. Optimizer to estimate parameters	317
	10.3.3. Number of optimizer iterations	319
	10.3.4. Overall versus dye-specific detection threshold	320
	10.3.5. Model validation	321
	10.3.6. *DNAxs* software testing	323
10.4.	An exemplar case analyzed with *DNAxs-DNAStatistX* and *EuroForMix*	324
	10.4.1. Analysis using *DNAxs-DNAStatistX*	324
	10.4.2. Comparison of the exemplar using *EuroForMix*	332
10.5.	Summary	337

11. Investigative forensic genetics: *SmartRank, CaseSolver* and *DNAmatch2* — **339**

11.1.	National DNA databases	339
11.2.	When is evaluative reporting appropriate?	341
11.3.	A cautionary tale	342
11.4.	Current methods used to compare crime stains with national DNA databases	342
	11.4.1. Prüm inclusion rules	343
	11.4.2. Prüm matching rules	343
	11.4.3. CODIS inclusion and matching rules	344
11.5.	Limitations of traditional national DNA databases: introducing "*SmartRank*"	344
11.6.	Experimental details to test efficiency of *SmartRank*	345
	11.6.1. *SmartRank* performance	346
11.7.	*SmartRank* versus CODIS	347
	11.7.1. Specifying a likelihood ratio threshold and a top ranked candidate list	349
	11.7.2. Limitations	350
11.8.	*SmartRank* exercise	352
11.9.	Using *EuroForMix* for database searching	354
11.10.	*CaseSolver*: an expert system based on *EuroForMix*	356
	11.10.1. Method	358
	11.10.2. Mixture comparison	359
	11.10.3. Model parameters	362
11.11.	Demonstration using a real case example	362
	11.11.1. Case circumstances	362
	11.11.2. Importing data to CS	364
	11.11.3. Comparing references to mixtures	365
	11.11.4. Viewing the results	366
	11.11.5. Deconvolution	367
	11.11.6. Relatedness searches	368
	11.11.7. Advanced options	369
	11.11.8. More detailed summary of results	370
	11.11.9. Searching a large fictive national DNA database	373
11.12.	The need for new digital tools in forensic genetics: improving efficiency of searching large DNA databases	374

xii Contents

11.12.1. Why use a stepwise strategy to extract candidate matches?	378
11.12.2. The flexibility of CS	378
11.12.3. Searching large national DNA databases	379
11.12.4. Using *DNAmatch2* to search large databases and as a contamination search engine	380
11.12.5. Future improvements for estimating the number of contributors	382
11.13. Summary	382
Notes	383

12. Interpretation, reporting, and communication   **385**

12.1. Early methods used to express the value of the evidence and their limitations	385
12.2. An outline of the important principles to interpret scientific evidence	387
12.3. Propositions	388
12.4. Scope of the forensic scientist as an investigator or evaluator	389
12.5. Hierarchy of propositions	390
12.6. Formulation of propositions to avoid bias	393
12.7. Activity level propositions	394
12.8. The prosecutor's fallacy and prior probabilities	395
12.8.1. Prior odds can be updated	397
12.9. Avoidance of the prosecutor's fallacy	397
12.10. Database searches	399
12.11. Statement writing	400
12.12. The use of the verbal scale and the "weak evidence effect"	401
12.13. Using terms like "inconclusive" and "excluded" as expressions in statements	403
12.14. Conditioning and the application to DNA mixtures	404
12.15. The effect of relatedness on the likelihood ratio	406
12.16. Assigning the number of contributors	407
12.17. Non-contributor tests	407
12.17.1. The "two suspect" problem	411
12.18. Summary	416
Notes	417

13. Interpretation of complex DNA profiles generated by massively parallel sequencing   **419**

Peter Gill, Rebecca Just, Walther Parson, Chris Phillips, Øyvind Bleka

13.1. Introduction	419
13.2. SNP analysis	420
13.3. Number of contributors	421
13.4. Effect of choosing the wrong number of contributors	421
13.5. Comparison of quantitative and qualitative methods	422
13.6. Limitations	422
13.7. The effect of uncertainty of the number of contributors on the likelihood ratio	425
13.8. Summary	425
13.9. Short tandem repeats	427

	13.9.1. Nomenclature	427
13.10.	Historical perspective: lessons of the past	429
13.11.	STR-MPS stutters	431
	13.11.1. Extension to LUS+ nomenclature	433
13.12.	Characterization of stutters with MPS	435
13.13.	MPS programming using *EuroForMix*	437
	13.13.1. Automated conversion of sequence into RU/LUS/LUS+ nomenclature	437
13.14.	Demonstration of likelihood ratio calculations using *EuroForMix*	440
	13.14.1. Analytical threshold (AT)	440
	13.14.2. Rules for stutter filtering	440
	13.14.3. Noise	442
	13.14.4. Experimental summary	442
13.15.	Automating the interpretation strategy	442
	13.15.1. *EuroForMix* analysis	444
	13.15.2. Stutter filter effect	446
13.16.	Information gain: measuring the effect of the stutter filter and different nomenclatures	446
	13.16.1. Information gain: comparing stutter filter vs no stutter filter	449
13.17.	Summary	450
Notes		451

A. Formal descriptions of the genotype probabilities — **453**

A.1.	Extending the F_{ST}-formula to mixtures	453
A.2.	Relatedness	454
	A.2.1. Formulae for relatedness	454
	A.2.2. Extension with the F_{ST}-formula	455
	A.2.3. Specific relatedness formulae F_{ST}-correction	456

B. Formal description of the probabilistic models — **459**

B.1.	Definitions	459
B.2.	Extension to parameterized statistical models	460
	B.2.1. The likelihood for parameterized statistical models	460
	B.2.2. LR calculations for parameterized statistical models	461
B.3.	Mathematical details of the probabilistic models	462
	B.3.1. The contribution from assumed genotypes	462
	B.3.2. Mathematical details of the qualitative model	463
	B.3.3. Inference of the drop-out parameter	464
	B.3.4. Mathematical details of the quantitative model	465
	B.3.5. The gamma distribution	466
	B.3.6. Model for a single contributor	466
	B.3.7. Model for multiple contributors	468
	B.3.8. Model for allele drop-out	470
	B.3.9. Model for allele drop-in	471
	B.3.10. Model for multiple replicates	472

B.3.11. Model for backward-stutters		472
B.3.12. Estimating the LR in *EuroForMix*		473
B.4. Deconvolution		475

Bibliography — 477
Index — 497

About the authors

Peter Gill is professor of forensic genetics at the Department of Forensic Sciences, Oslo University Hospital and the Department of Clinical Medicine, Oslo University, Norway. He has 38 years experience as a forensic scientist, working primarily as a researcher, but he also has substantial experience reporting cases to courts. He has led and participated in numerous interpretation workshops. He has more than 200 coauthored publications, with more than 20,000 citations in the literature. He is chair of the International Society for Forensic Genetics (ISFG) DNA Commission and is recipient of the scientific prize (2013) of the ISFG.

Øyvind Bleka is a research scientist at the Department of Forensic Sciences at Oslo University Hospital, where he develops statistical applications within forensic science (genetics). He has developed the software *EuroForMix*, *CaseSolver*, and *dnamatch2*, used for DNA comparison. In addition, he works with developing methods for age estimation, mainly focusing on techniques based on DNA-methylation. His background is a masters degree in statistics and data analysis and a PhD degree in forensic statistics.

Corina Benschop is a research scientist employed at the Netherlands Forensic Institute since 2005. She has a background in molecular biology and a PhD degree in forensic genetics. Primarily, Corina performs and supervises research studies regarding the interpretation of complex DNA profiles. She is involved in the development and validation of methods (e.g., *LoCIM*, *LRmix Studio*, *SmartRank*, *DNAxs*, *DNAStatistX*), implementation into forensic casework, defining guidelines for best practice, and providing training in various (international) mixture interpretation workshops.

Oskar Hansson is head of the reporting officers and research unit at the Department of Forensic Sciences, Oslo University Hospital, Norway. He has 18 years experience from forensic genetics, working primarily with laboratory development, public procurement, validation, and implementation of new methods. His background is in molecular biology and programming and a PhD degree in forensic genetics. He has provided training in various international mixture interpretation and validation workshops. Oskar has developed, and maintains, the *STR-validator* R package, which in 2019 averaged in excess of 500 monthly installs.

Hinda Haned is professor of data science by special appointment at the University of Amsterdam. Her research focuses on researching and developing solutions for best practices for safe and responsible AI. Hinda has developed and is still maintaining the *forensim*

R package, she has also designed and co-developed the *LRmix Studio* and *SmartRank* open-source software. Hinda is also currently working as a principal scientist at Ahold Delhaize (Zaandam, The Netherlands).

Contributors

Peter Gill

Øyvind Bleka

Oskar Hansson

Corina Benschop

Hinda Haned

Chapter 10: Development and implementation of *DNAxs*

The DNAxs Team
Netherlands Forensic Institute, The Hague, The Netherlands

Chapter 13: Interpretation of complex DNA profiles generated by massively parallel sequencing

Rebecca Just
National Biodefense Analysis and Countermeasures Center, Fort Detrick, MD, United States
DNA Support Unit, Federal Bureau of Investigation Laboratory, Quantico, VA, United States

Walther Parson
Institute of Legal Medicine, Medical University of Innsbruck, Innsbruck, Austria
Forensic Science Program, The Pennsylvania State University, University Park, PA, United States

Chris Phillips
Forensic Genetics Unit, Institute of Forensic Sciences, University of Santiago de Compostela, Santiago de Compostela, Spain

Foreword

Professor Peter Gill and his collaborators have put together *a tour de force text* as a legacy to their united efforts over the past few decades in advancing the theory and practice of forensic DNA evidence interpretation. Collectively, this team of authors has over 90 years of experience in forensic DNA research and casework and written more than 250 research articles in the field. They regularly conduct informative training courses on the topics covered in this book. The authors have also developed and made available open-source software, including *STR-validator, LRmix Studio, EuroForMix, CaseSolver,* and *SmartRank* to aid DNA interpretation in forensic casework. These programs are highlighted throughout the book and an accompanying website.

This book can assist forensic practitioners in understanding the models underlying probabilistic genotyping software (PGS) systems. Much of the information contained herein grew out of the European Forensic Genetics Network of Excellence (https://www.euroforgen.eu/), which was funded by the European Union from 2012–2017. In addition, the material in this book builds on recommendations made in multiple DNA Commissions of the International Society for Forensic Genetics (ISFG). These ISFG DNA Commissions, led by Professor Gill over the past two decades, have provided important recommendations for DNA interpretation efforts worldwide.

Their book describes important principles and the value of empirical data and simulations to inform probabilistic models used in modern DNA interpretation. Readers are introduced to short tandem repeat (STR) markers, population genetics, and probability theory in the introductory chapter, and then taken through factors that influence STR typing (Chapter 2), stochastic effects and methods to calculate the probability of drop-out (Chapter 3), methods to cope with low-level DNA and degraded DNA (Chapter 4), theory and qualitative models for semi-continuous PGS systems *LRmix* and *LRmix Studio* (Chapters 5 and 6), use of peak heights with the quantitative continuous PGS system *EuroForMix* (Chapters 7 and 8), software validation experiments (Chapter 9), development of an expert system (Chapter 10), investigative tools (Chapter 11), and important guidance on interpreting, reporting, and communicating DNA results (Chapter 12). The last chapter (Chapter 13) covers cutting-edge research on massively parallel sequencing, and involves three additional authors (Rebecca Just, Walther Parson, and Chris Phillips). Two appendices describe mathematic details for genotype probabilities and probabilistic models under various scenarios. A bibliography lists 362 references.

Peter Gill has been at the forefront of forensic DNA method development and interpretation since his seminal 1985 *Nature* paper with Alec Jeffreys, which launched the field. Three of his book co-authors performed their PhD research with Professor Gill, and have continued to be important contributors in forensic genetics. The authors'

xix

commitment to the forensic genetics community is such that proceeds from the book, which might rightly be received as royalties for their countless hours in creating this text, will instead be donated to ISFG for use in future training events and education of other scientists.

On behalf of the ISFG Executive Board and members of our society, which represents over 1300 members from 84 countries, we thank the authors for their generosity and the creation of this guide to lead forensic practitioners through the challenges of interpreting complex DNA profiles.

John M. Butler
ISFG President
April 2020

Preface

That a belief, however necessary it may be for the preservation of a creature, has nothing to do with truth, one can see, for example, in the fact that we have to believe in time, space, and motion, but without feeling constrained to grant them absolute reality.

On Truth and Untruth: Selected Writings
Friedrich Nietzsche

When DNA profiling technology was introduced in the mid to late 1980s, there was an early recognition that interpretation was challenging. Often, parts of the DNA profile were missing, because of the poor quality of the material analyzed; mixtures of two or more contributors were often encountered in the crime-stain evidence. The crime stain and the reference samples from persons of interest (POIs), such as suspects or victims, were not perfect "matches", i.e., either there were mismatches, where extra alleles were present in the crime stain that did not match a known individual, or else there were alleles present in the person of interest that were absent in the crime stain. It quickly became apparent that the classical approaches of interpretation using methods, such as random man not excluded (RMNE), were over-simplistic. Consequently, there were significant risks associated with either understating or overstating the value of the evidence. Without a coherent method to interpret evidence, this culminated in some cases that were successfully challenged in court, in particular, a high-profile case in 1987, the People v. Castro (New York,USA), there was a successful challenge to the DNA evidence. This led to controversy known as the "DNA wars", where the issues were strongly debated by academics, practitioners, and lawyers. This discourse led to self-examination and invigorated efforts to improve interpretation methodology.

The advent of DNA profiling in the mid to late 1980s coincided with a parallel revolution in the interpretation of evidence framework, which was rooted in the likelihood ratio approach. This endeavor laid the foundation blocks to enable the interpretation of complex DNA profiles.

The progression of forensic genetics is strongly motivated to increase the sensitivity of the technique. The development of low-template DNA analysis at the turn of the last century came with a set of new challenges. Practitioners had to deal with notions of allele "drop-out" (alleles in the POI that did not "match" the crime-stain evidence) and "drop-in" (extra alleles from the environment). To accommodate these phenomena, laboratories devised complicated rulesets to decide whether a sample could or could not be interpreted. The problem with such rulesets is that they are always unsatisfactory; they involve the use of thresholds, which are set in an arbitrary way. If you make a rule that says you can interpret your sample if the allele peak heights are above a certain threshold

x, then what happens if the sample is just a fraction below the threshold? Is it really logical to have such a sharp cut-off point? "Probabilistic genotyping" is based upon likelihood ratios and continuous probabilities: there is no need to make all or nothing decisions on whether to report crime-stain evidence based on subjective thresholds. The adoption of this technology reduces the need for subjective rule-making, thereby improving standards of tests.

For many years now, the authors have designed and carried out training courses for practitioners. This book charts the progression of ideas and theories that were used to develop the field. The first application of the likelihood ratio method applied to mixtures was carried out by Ian Evett and colleagues in 1991. At the turn of the century, to accommodate low-template DNA profiles, incorporating ideas from John Buckleton, the likelihood ratio was extended to include a statistical evaluation of "drop-out" and "drop-in". But these formulae were limited to simple case examples, and were very time-consuming to derive by hand. At this point, it became clear that computer programs would be required to carry out the extensive calculations that were needed. An algorithm called *LoComatioN.* was developed by James Curran in 2005, which was able to include drop-out, drop-in, and multiple contributors in likelihood ratio calculations. Based on this work, Hinda Haned, as part of a PhD investigation, developed a statistical package called *Forensim* that incorporated the mixture interpretation module *LRmix*. Later, *LRmix* was adopted by the Netherlands Forensic Institute (NFI), which developed a Java package *LRmix Studio* and a database search engine *SmartRank*, with improved graphics and reporting facilities. These were widely adopted by laboratories in Europe, and beyond. In 2012 the Euroforgen network-of-excellence was created with a European grant awarded to the authors respective laboratories. This funding was used to facilitate the next generation of probabilistic genotyping software. As the main focus of his PhD project, in 2015, Øyvind Bleka built a software package called *EuroForMix*, which was based upon the theory of Robert Cowell and colleagues— the "gamma model". This new generation of software was able to take account of allele peak heights. Two associated packages included *CaseSolver* and *dnamatch2*, the former software was designed to interpret complex cases, where the practitioner is confronted with numerous case stains and suspects, the latter is a database search engine. Both packages utilize the functionality of *LRmix* and *EuroForMix*. Oskar Hansson, as part of his PhD project, developed a software package *strvalidator*. This software is suited to speeding up the validation and characterization of STR multiplex systems, according to ENFSI and SWGDAM recommendations. The most recent innovation is from the NFI. In 2019 the DNAxs team of the NFI developed *DNAStatistX*, a module within the software suite *DNAxs*, which has the same functionality as *EuroForMix*, but is Java based and has some important differences that are discussed in the *DNAxs* chapter of the book. Current research described in the final chapter of the book shows how crime-stain evidence mixtures, analyzed by massively parallel sequencing, both SNPs and STRs, can be evaluated using *EuroForMix*.

The book describes the chronological history of the interpretation of complex DNA profiles, i.e., mixtures of two or more individuals, where the samples are often partial and degraded. The various methods are described in sufficient detail so that the material will be useful to a wide range of individuals, ranging from those studying for degrees in forensic science to the experienced practitioner. To facilitate learning, the software code has been converted into a series of exemplar Excel spreadsheets, which can be downloaded from the book's website. The reader can use these spreadsheets to help understand the formulae and principles behind probabilistic genotyping. We start with the earliest historic example *Mastermix*, which is non-probabilistic; it illustrates the principle of selecting genotypes based on their allelic peak heights. This spreadsheet was used as part of the binary method of interpretation, where the "Clayton guidelines" were used to include/exclude various genotype combinations. Ian Evett and colleagues (1998) developed a probabilistic method based upon the normal distribution assumption of allele peak heights. *EuroForMix* assumes that peak heights are gamma distributed. Both the normal and gamma distribution models are provided as Excel spreadsheet examples. In relation to *LRmix Studio*, *EuroForMix*, and allied software, the reader is able to download data from case examples discussed in the text.

Recommendations of the DNA Commission of the International Society of Forensic Genetics (ISFG) on the evaluation of evidence, co-authored with Tacha Hicks and the members of the DNA commission, are discussed to provide guidance about formulating propositions, case reporting, and avoiding pitfalls, such as the prosecutor's fallacy.

All of the methods described in this book are supported by open-source software along with demonstrations that we use on training courses. Open-source software is fully transparent, and there are no restrictions on use. Both software and data can be downloaded via links from the book's website. This includes additional information— links to user manuals and teaching videos.

This book not only supports the community of users of our software, but many of the principles that we discuss are generalized, for example, we discuss the principles of interpretation in some detail, which is applicable to users of all other software solutions. In keeping with our open-source philosophy and non-profit ethos, all of the royalties that arise from sales of this book are donated to the International Society for Forensic Genetics (ISFG), in recognition of their continued support, to generate funds to support non-commercial training programmes.

The authors are supported by their respective institutions who provide the resources to enable the basic research, development, training, and support of software to be carried out, with some help from grants provided by the European Council, and scientific societies.

List of websites and resources

A list of websites, where software, data, user manuals, and teaching resources detailed in this book can be downloaded:

The book's website: https://sites.google.com/view/dnabook/
Contains the data and Excel spreadsheets for all of the examples described in the book.

The R project for statistical computing: https://www.r-project.org/
The R-program can be downloaded from this website.

forensim: http://forensim.r-forge.r-project.org/
Developed and maintained by Hinda Haned. An R-version of *LRmix* can be downloaded. Also an R-version of "Mastermix".

***LRmix Studio* and *SmartRank*:** https://github.com/smartrank/lrmixstudio.git
Developed by Hinda Haned and Jeroen de Jong. Maintained by the Netherlands Forensic Institute (NFI). The programs listed are written in Java.

***EuroForMix, CaseSolver, dnamatch2, seq2lus*:** http://www.euroformix.com/
Developed and maintained by Øyvind Bleka, Oslo University Hospital. Programs listed are written in R and C++.

***DNAxs/DNAStatistX*:**
Maintained by the Netherlands Forensic Institute (NFI). The programs listed are written in Java. https://www.forensicinstitute.nl/research-and-innovation/european-projects/dnaxs

strvalidator: https://sites.google.com/site/forensicapps/strvalidator
Developed and maintained by Oskar Hansson, Oslo University Hospital. Program written in R.

CHAPTER 1

Forensic genetics: the basics

The interpretation of forensic genetic evidence is based upon probability. Probability is expressed as a number that is somewhere between zero and one, representing two extremes: a probability of zero means that something is impossible, whereas a probability of one means that something is certain. In practice, a probability is never exactly zero or one—it is usually somewhere between the two extremes.

In forensic genetics, a probability is usually equated to the "frequency" of observation of particular "type". Before the DNA era, probabilities were applied to blood groups. One of the first used for forensic typing was the ABO grouping that was credited to the Austrian scientist Karl Landsteiner, who identified the O, A, and B blood types in 1900.

The inheritance of the ABO blood groups follows the laws of Mendelian genetics. Chromosomes are inherited in pairs. There are two genes, one is inherited from the mother and the other from the father. The genes are inherited via gametes, i.e., sperm of the father and the eggs (ova) of the mother. To ensure that the offspring only has a single pair of genes per cell, the gametes only contain a single copy.

Some basic definitions follow:

Gene: The gene is a stretch of DNA positioned on a chromosome. The gene may have a function, such as producing proteins that determine eye colour. However, genes that are currently analyzed in forensic science are sometimes described as "junk DNA" since they have no known function, although this idea has been challenged.

Locus: Describes the position of a gene on a chromosome, commonly expressed by a universal identifier, such as D22S11.

Allele: Genes of forensic interest are *variable*; this means that there are different versions of genes, where the DNA code differs.

Therefore for the blood group ABO gene, which is positioned chromosome 9 at the band/locus 9q34.2, which means the long (q) arm of chromosome 9 at position 34.2. Over recent years, the human genetics community has compiled two human genome assemblies called GRCh37 and GRCh38. Both are references in human genome databases, such as the NCBI Genome Browser http://www.ncbi.nlm.nih.gov. Because it is the most up-to-date, GRCh38 is recommended by the DNA Commission of the ISFG [1]. The molecular location of the ABO gene is between 133,250,401 to 133,275,201 base pairs on chromosome 9: https://ghr.nlm.nih.gov/gene/ABO# location. It comprises three common different alleles, namely A, B, and O. In diploid

Forensic Practitioner's Guide to the Interpretation of Complex DNA Profiles
https://doi.org/10.1016/B978-0-12-820562-4.00009-2

Copyright © 2020 Elsevier Inc.
All rights reserved.   1

cells, there are six possible combinations called *genotypes* that are observed in the population. These are AA, AB, AO, BO, OO, BB, and they are described as mutually exclusive to the individual, meaning that a person can only have one genotype, but mutually inclusive with respect to the population, meaning that any given individual selected from the population must have one of these genotypes.[1]

Alleles A and B are both *dominant* to allele O. If a person has an AO or BO genotype, the "O" is masked, which results in the person being "typed" as A or B, respectively. The masked O allele is called *recessive*. Dominant alleles mask the genotype of the person. People are classed as being A, B, or O *phenotypes*, where a phenotype can be expressed by more than one genotype.

With conventional DNA profiling, we do not need to worry about phenotypes, because we deal with well defined genetic sequences.

The variability of the gene forms the basis of its usefulness to discriminate *between* individuals. Usually, the aim is to associate crime-stain evidence to some specific individual, typically a suspect who may have been apprehended. He/she may be described as the "questioned individual", or the "person of interest" (POI). Note that the POI is not always the suspect, sometimes he/she may be a victim, for example, where a body fluid stain is found on the clothing of the suspect.

1.1. Short tandem repeat (STR) analysis

Short tandem repeats (STRs) are blocks of tandemly repeating DNA sequences found throughout the human genome. Forensic laboratories usually use four base pair repeats, because shorter sequences were much more prone to artefacts known as stutters. For a comprehensive review of STRs currently used in casework, the reader is referred to [2] and the NIST STRBase website https://strbase.nist.gov/index.htm, which lists sequences of common and rare alleles. Refer to Parson et al. [1], supplemental materials, for full details of sequences using up-to-date recommendations of the ISFG DNA commission.

There are three kinds of repeat sequences defined by Urquhart et al. [3]. "Simple" repeats contain units of identical length and sequence; "compound" repeats comprise two or more adjacent simple repeats; "complex" repeats may contain several repeat blocks of variable unit length, along with variable intervening sequences.

Simple repeat example

The STR HUMTH01 locus is an example of a simple AATG sequence ranging between three to 14 repeats, and it is written shorthand as $[AATG]_a$, where $a =$ the number of repeats. A common microvariant allele is observed that consists of a single base deletion of the seventh repeat in the 10 allele, which results in a partial repeat of just three bases. It is signified as $[AATG]_6$ ATG $[AATG]_3$, and the nomenclature follows as HUMTH01 9.3.

Compound repeat example

HUMVWA is an example of a compound repeat locus[2] $[TCTA]_a$ $[TCTG]_b$ $[TCTA]_{0-1}$, where the final sequence is either not observed or observed once.

Complex repeat example

D21S11 is a highly polymorphic locus with a compound structure of several intervening sequences $[TCTA]_a$, $[TCTG]_b$, $[TCTA]_c$, TA $[TCTA]_d$, TCA $[TCTA]_e$, TCCATA $[TCTA]_f$.

Repeat unit nomenclature is standardized for capillary gel electrophoresis (CE) applications. This enables universal comparisons between laboratories and national DNA databases to be achieved. The nomenclature used is based upon the number of repeat sequences [4].

Existing designation systems that are universally applied to national DNA databases are based upon the repeating structure of "typical" reference alleles that were discovered and characterized in the early to mid 1990s. All new allelic variant designations must fit within the scheme, regardless of sequence, and are strictly conditioned upon the number of bases that are counted in the fragment length. Comparisons are made against an allelic ladder. This means that the length of the STR repeat, and its correspondence to the reference sequenced repeat does not necessarily hold. Let us suppose that there is a deletion of a single base in the flanking region of an amplicon in an allele 27 variant; though the repeating structure may be identical to that listed, the allelic designation must change to 26.3. Consequently, this allele designation no longer reflects the repeat structure of the reference sequence.[3]

With the introduction of massively parallel sequencing (MPS), the issue of nomenclature has achieved new prominence [1]. Whereas the sequence information is generally hidden from view with conventional CE applications, with MPS, this information is available. This results in the observation of polymorphisms, where there are sequence differences between alleles, though the STR fragment sizes are identical. With CE, all of these polymorphisms would be classed together, whereas with MPS they can be separated, with the resulting increase in discriminating power. There is continued discussion on nomenclature in relation to MPS in Chapter 13.9.1. The main aim is to devise a new nomenclature to maximise the benefits of MPS, whilst at the same time retaining back-compatibility with existing CE repeat unit nomenclature.

1.1.1 Historical development of multiplexed systems

Short tandem repeat (STR) analysis was introduced into forensic casework about 25 years ago. The ability to combine several markers to form multiplexes and to subsequently visualize the results by automated fluorescent sequencing made national DNA databases feasible. The first example was launched in 1995 by the UK Forensic Science Service (FSS). In total there have been three iterations of multiplexes.

Early multiplexes consisted of relatively few loci based on simple STRs. The four locus "quadruplex" was the first multiplex to be used in casework, and was developed by the Forensic Science Service (FSS) [5]. Because it consisted of just four STRs, there was a high probability of a random match—approximately 1 in 10,000. In 1995 the FSS re-engineered the multiplex, producing a 6 locus STR system combined with the amelogenin sex test [6]. This acquired the name "second generation multiplex" (SGM). The addition of complex STRs, D21S11 and HUMFIBRA/FGA [7], which have greater variability than simple STRs, decreased the probability of a random match to about 1 in 50 million. In the UK, the introduction of SGM in 1995 facilitated the implementation of the UK national DNA database (NDNAD) [8]. As databases become much larger, the number of pairwise comparisons increases dramatically, so it became necessary to ensure that the match probability of the system was sufficient to minimize the chance of two unrelated individuals matching by chance (otherwise known as an adventitious match). Consequently, as the UK NDNAD grew in its first four years of operation, a new system known as the AmpF/STR SGM Plus [9], with average match probability of 10^{-13} was introduced in 1999. This system comprised 10 STR loci with amelogenin, replacing the previous SGM system. To ensure continuity of the DNA database, and to enable the new system to match samples that had been collated in previous years, all six loci of the older SGM system were retained in the new AmpF/STR SGM Plus system.

1.2. Development and harmonization of European National DNA databases

Harmonization of STR loci was achieved by collaboration at the international level. Notably, the European DNA profiling group (EDNAP) carried out a series of successful studies to identify and to recommend STR loci for the forensic community to use. This work began with an evaluation of the simple STRs HUMTH01 and HUMVWFA31 [10]. Subsequently, the group evaluated D21S11 and HUMFIBRA/FGA [11]. Recommendations on the use of STRs were published by the ISFG [4].

Most, if not all, European countries have legislated to implement national DNA databases that are based upon STRs [12]. In Europe, there has been a drive to standardize loci across countries to meet the challenge of increasing cross-border crime. In particular, a European Community (EC) funded initiative led by the ENFSI group was responsible for co-ordinating collaborative exercises to validate commercially available multiplexes for general use [13]. National DNA databases were introduced in 1997 in Holland and Austria; 1998 in Germany, France, Slovenia, and Cypus; 1999 in Finland, Norway, and Belgium; 2000 in Sweden, Denmark, Switzerland, Spain, Italy, and Czech Republic; 2002 in Greece and Lithuania; 2003 in Hungary; 2004 in Estonia and Slovakia [14].

A parallel process has occurred in Canada [15,16] and in the US [17]), where standardization was based on thirteen STR loci, known as the Combined DNA Index System (CODIS) core loci.

An FBI-sponsored CODIS core loci working group recommended an expanded set of loci from the thirteen in use in 2011 [18,19]. There followed an extensive validation study, which resulted in the recommendation that seven new loci were to be adopted [20], resulting in 20 CODIS core loci to be implemented by 2017. The additional seven loci included the five new European ESS markers, plus D2S1338 and D19S433 (see next section). This resulted in comparability of the CODIS core and expanded ESS to have 15 DNA loci in common [21].

1.2.1 Development of the European set of standard (ESS) markers

Based on the initial EDNAP exercises and recommendations by ENSFI and the Interpol working party [22], four loci were originally defined as the European standard set (ESS) of loci—HUMTH01, HUMVWFA31, D21S11, and HUMFIBRA/FGA. The identity of these loci was dictated by their universal incorporation into different commercial multiplexes that were utilized by member states. By the same rationale, three additional loci were added to this set—D3S1358, D8S1179, and D18S51. These loci are the same as the standard set of loci identified by Interpol for the global exchange of DNA data.

A subsequent expansion of ESS loci was motivated by the Prüm treaty of 2005 [23], that was signed by Austria, Germany, France, Spain, Belgium, Luxembourg, and the Netherlands (many more states have since signed). This treaty promoted cross-border cooperation by agreement to exchange information, including DNA profiling databases, to be made available for pan-European searches. Clearly, the relatively high combined random match probability of the original ESS loci (approximately 10^{-8}) was not sufficient to enable comparisons to be made without unacceptable risk of chance (adventitious) matches (Chapter 12.10). In addition, since the development of the original multiplexes, a significant number of new STRs had been discovered, and it was shown that "mini-STRs" had improved potential to analyze compromised (degraded) DNA samples, because of their short amplicon size [24]. To meet the challenges, discussions began in Europe in 2005, within the ENFSI organization. Collaborative experimentation confirmed that "mini-STRs" showed the expected efficacy [25] to analyze degraded DNA. In consultation with manufacturers of multiplex kits, a list of candidate ESS markers were published [26] and revised [27], so that the final list of five additional loci were D10S1248, D12S391, D22S1045, D1S1656, and D2S441, making a grand total of 12 ESS loci, with a probability of chance match roughly equal to 10^{-15}. The new loci were officially adopted by the European Commission [28] and Interpol in 2010; this led to development of a series of new multiplexes by the major companies (Promega, Life Technologies, and Qiagen). See Fig. 1.1. Practically speaking there are sixteen loci, since D16S539, D19S433, D2S1338, and SE33 are all included European multiplexes in addition to the ESS markers. A complete list of multiplex kits and their loci can be accessed from the NIST website https://strbase.nist.gov/multiplx.htm.

New biochemistry has simultaneously increased the sensitivity of tests, to the extent that the once controversial low-level or low-template (LT-) DNA analysis is considered to be routine (Chapter 4). However, this is not without challenge. LT-DNA profiles tend to be complex mixtures, with problems of "missing alleles", known as drop-out. This book will explain how statistical methods, based on likelihood ratio (LR) estimation, have been critical to improve the interpretation of evidence.

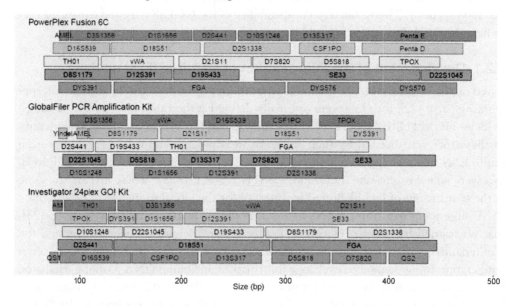

Figure 1.1 Commonly used multiplex kits showing ESS and CODIS loci relative to molecular weights (bp) using different dye markers.

1.3. Hardy–Weinberg equilibrium

There is a fundamental principle that underpins all population genetics: the Hardy–Weinberg equilibrium, named after two scientists who simultaneously discovered the formula in the early 1900's [29].

To illustrate, consider a simple example that comprises two alleles: *a* and *b*, respectively. These two alleles are found in three alternative diploid combinations (genotypes) *aa*, *ab*, and *bb* respectively: two alleles the same are called homozygotes *aa*, *bb* whereas two different alleles, *ab* are heterozygotes.

Suppose we sample a population of $n = 100$ individuals and observe $20aa$, $45ab$, and $35bb$ individuals. It is relatively straight forward to express the genotype observations in terms of frequencies as this is simply

$$\underbrace{20/100}_{aa} + \underbrace{45/100}_{ab} + \underbrace{35/100}_{bb}$$
$$= 0.2aa + 0.45ab + 0.35bb = 1.$$

It is a law of probability that the sum of all possible outcomes is one. It also follows that the larger the sample size, the better the frequency estimate will be. International Society for Forensic Genetics (ISFG) DNA commission recommendations [30] suggest that a sample size of at least 500 is desirable, although for small discrete populations that are difficult to access, a smaller sample size will suffice.

Next, the number of alleles in the population is calculated. This is achieved by counting the number of alleles in the observed data. In the example, there are two alleles (and three genotypes). For a homozygote aa, there are two a alleles, whereas for a heterozygote ab, there is one a allele.

The total number of a and b alleles is twice the number of individuals (n).

There are $20aa$ homozygotes, or $20 \times 2 = 40a$ alleles. There are $45ab$ heterozygotes, or $45a$ alleles and $45b$ alleles. So, in total, there are $40 + 45 = 85a$ alleles. To find the proportion, we divide by $2n$, hence $p_a = 85/(2 \times 100)$

$$p_a = 0.425.$$

The same calculation is carried out for allele b: $p_b = (70 + 45)/(2 \times 100)$

$$p_b = 0.575$$

and

$$p_a + p_b = 1.$$

Once the allele frequencies are estimated, this information can be used to calculate the expectation that an individual chosen at random will be a particular genotype. The expected genotype proportions are calculated by applying the Hardy–Weinberg equilibrium formula, which describes the relative probabilistic expectations of the genotype proportion in genotypes aa, ab, bb.

The Hardy–Weinberg formula is important, because it is the basis of the *product rule*. This relies upon a law of probability, which states that the probability of two independent events occurring together can be estimated by multiplying their individual probabilities. The probability of genotype aa is therefore $p_a \times p_a = p_a^2$, and the probability of genotype bb is derived in the same way as $p_b \times p_b = p_b^2$.

Heterozygote genotype *ab* can occur in two different ways: There are two chromosome strands, which can be labeled $c1$ and $c2$. Therefore there are two alternative arrangements whereby an individual can be *ab*, either state 1: $\{c1, a\}$ and $\{c2, b\}$, or state 2: $\{c1, b\}$ and $\{c2, a\}$. When there are alternative states to consider, where only one can be true, the addition rule is applied to calculate the probability. Hence the probability that an individual is heterozygote is $\underbrace{p_a \times p_b}_{\text{State 1}} + \underbrace{p_b \times p_a}_{\text{State 2}} = 2p_ap_b$.

Writing the Hardy–Weinberg expectation in full, there are three genotypes: $p_a^2 + 2p_ap_b + p_b^2$. As before, the sum of the probabilities always equals one.

The Hardy–Weinberg formula holds true if

1. There is no migration in or out of the population.
2. There is no natural selection that favours the survival of individuals with certain alleles.
3. The population is assumed to be randomly mating, without inbreeding and is very large.
4. There is no mutation of alleles.
5. Generations are non-overlapping.

In practice, it is difficult to fulfill the Hardy–Weinberg assumptions, because populations are not discrete or static; there is often much migration, immigration, and interbreeding between different populations. Furthermore, because populations are finite, there is always some inbreeding. The effect of inbreeding is to increase the level of homozygosity (the Wahlund effect [31]), and this means that the multiplication rule used to estimate genotype frequencies is not strictly valid. The implications and solution is examined in greater detail in Section 1.12.

Continuing with the above example, given that the probabilities of allele $a = 0.425$ and allele $b = 0.575$, the Hardy Weinberg expectations are

$$
\underbrace{p_a^2}_{\substack{0.425^2=0.18 \\ observed=0.2}} + \underbrace{2p_ap_b}_{\substack{2\times0.425\times0.575=0.49 \\ observed=0.45}} + \underbrace{p_b^2}_{\substack{0.575^2=0.33 \\ observed=0.35}}
$$

The number of expected *aa*, *ab*, *bb* genotypes is recovered by multiplying their expected frequencies by n (Table 1.1). Note that the observed and expected genotype frequencies are close, but not exactly the same. It is usual to see small deviations of this kind.

1.3.1 Measuring deviation from Hardy–Weinberg equilibrium
Chi-square test

The chi-square statistic tests the null hypothesis, which basically states that there is no difference between the observed and expected results. It is calculated as follows

(Table 1.1):

$$\chi^2 = \sum \frac{(o-e)^2}{e} \tag{1.1}$$

where o = observed data and e = expected data

Table 1.1 Chi-square statistic to test for deviation from Hardy–Weinberg equilibrium.

Genotypes	aa	ab	bb	Total
expected genotype frequencies	0.18	0.49	0.33	1
no. observed	20	45	35	100
no. expected	18	49	33	100
$(o-e)^2$	4	16	4	24

$$\chi^2 = \frac{4}{18} + \frac{16}{49} + \frac{4}{33} = 0.67 \tag{1.2}$$

The result is compared to a chi-square distribution table, e.g., https://www.itl.nist.gov/div898/handbook/eda/section3/eda3674.htm, to determine if it is "significant" or not, with one degree of freedom. In this case, the statistic would need to exceed 3.84 to reject the null hypothesis at a significance level of $\alpha = 0.05$.

If a result is significant at a chosen level, then the null hypothesis is rejected. Traditionally, the significance level (α) chosen by biologists is $\alpha = 0.05$. However, this rationale has been criticized, because there is no scientific reason to choose this arbitrary level to make a binary decision. If a sample shows significance at $\alpha = 0.05$, this means that there is an expectation that 1 in 20 identically arranged experiments, where the same population is repeatedly sampled would be expected to fail the test (even if the underlying population was in HW equilibrium). This is not the same as saying that the "sample is not in HW equilibrium". This becomes an issue if there are large numbers of tests carried out; in 100 independent tests about five would fail if a significance level of 0.05 was applied, because of predictable sampling effects. One way to account for this is by application of the Bonferroni correction. This correction compensates by reducing the overall significance to α/m, where α is the desired overall significance level and m is the number of tests carried out. For example, if there are $m = 20$ tests with a desired $\alpha = 0.05$, then the Bonferroni correction would test each individual hypothesis at $\alpha = 0.05/20 = 0.0025$, making it less likely that any individual test will fail the null hypothesis.

Fisher's exact test

As a rule of thumb, chi-square tests are not considered appropriate if any of the expected values are less than five. This will be true for the majority of tests that will be carried out by forensic scientists in relation to collecting frequency databases of STRs, because we deal with rare alleles, which will have low expectation of being observed, even in large population surveys. Consequently, an alternative test, Fisher's exact test, is usually employed to test HW deviation. This formula is exact, because it tests for all possible permutations of the data and uses factorials denoted by an exclamation mark (!). A factorial is an integer multiplied by all the numbers below it, so factorial $4! = 4 \times 3 \times 2 \times 1 = 24$. The formula estimates Pr(genotype counts | allele counts)[4] under HW equilibrium:

$$Pr(n_{aa}, n_{ab}, n_{bb} | n_a, n_b, \text{HWE}) = \frac{n!}{n_{aa}! n_{ab}! n_{bb}!} \times \frac{2^{n_{ab}} n_a! n_b!}{(2n)!} \tag{1.3}$$

Raw programming of these formulae lead to huge numbers that lead to errors. An R-package, "HardyWeinberg" is available: https://cran.r-project.org/web/packages/HardyWeinberg/HardyWeinberg.pdf. This package can be easily utilized to carry out the necessary calculations using the "HWExact" function. The chi-square test is also accommodated under the "HWChisq" function.

Exact tests are important in the quality assurance of frequency databases, and this is described in more detail in Section 1.15.

1.3.2 Extension to multiple alleles in STRs

Whereas single nucleotide polymorphisms described in Section 1.3 are described by two alleles, all of the autosomal STR systems currently in use have many more alleles per locus. A compilation of allele frequency databases can be directly accessed from the "STRs for identity ENFSI reference database" (STRidER): https://strider.online/ [32]. For example, HUMTH01 has eight alleles listed; FGA has 24 alleles listed.

The extension to multiple alleles and loci is straight forward. A list of all possible genotypes can be obtained by listing the alleles sequentially in the first row and column of Table 1.2. The genotypes, comprised of two alleles, are designated by their intersections in the table. This process is also known as *pairwise comparison*. The diagonal lists the homozygotes, and the rest of the table lists the heterozygotes. The probabilities of the genotypes are calculated using the product rule, as previously shown, with heterozygotes multiplied by a factor of two. Therefore the probability of genotype $Pr(7, 6) = 2 \times p_7 \times p_6$. The number of possible genotypes (n_G), given the number of alleles n_A, can be calculated as

$$n_G = \binom{n_A + 1}{2} = \frac{(n_A + 1) \times n_A}{2} \tag{1.4}$$

where $\binom{x}{y} = \frac{x!}{(x-y)! y!}$ is the binomial coefficient giving the number of outcomes to select y elements out of x elements (unordered with replacement). There are eight alleles in

HUMTH01, hence there are a total of 36 genotypes, which is the number of elements in the lower triangular matrix, plus the number of elements of the diagonal of Table 1.2.

Pairwise comparison is an important part of computer programming, which will be discussed in detail in Section 1.11. All possible genotype combinations are easily listed, hence the probabilities of the genotypes are also easily generated by multiplying their allele frequencies together.

Table 1.2 Depiction of all possible 36 genotypes for HUMTH01 using pairwise comparisons of eight alleles.

Alleles	5	6	7	8	9	9.3	10	10.3
5	5,5							
6	6,5	6,6						
7	7,5	7,6	7,7					
8	8,5	8,6	8,7	8,8				
9	9,5	9,6	9,7	9,8	9,9			
9.3	9.3,5	9.3,6	9.3,7	9.3,8	9.3,9	9.3,9.3		
10	10,5	10,6	10,7	10,8	10,9	10,9.3	10,10	
10.3	10.3,5	10.3,6	10.3,7	10.3,8	10.3,9	10.3,9.3	10.3,10	10.3,10.3

1.4. Quality assurance of data

It is desirable to carry out statistical tests to demonstrate if HW expectations are satisfied (Section 1.3) as a step to demonstrate if the data are independent, so that they can be properly utilized in strength of evidence calculations using the product rule.

On behalf of the European Network of Forensic Science Institutes (ENFSI) group, Welch et al. [13] assessed a series of 26 European populations. Association studies both within and between loci were carried out using methods based on Fisher's exact test (Section 1.3.1), as described by [33]. It was found that deviation from HW expectations was most commonly observed with compromised data, rather than for genetic reasons, primarily because of accidental incorporation of duplicate samples into datasets; close relatives that shared a large number of the same alleles; transcription errors. Once the duplicates and other errors were verified with the participating laboratory and subsequently removed from the datasets, it was concluded that they did not significantly differ from Hardy–Weinberg equilibrium after Bonferroni adjustment. Population substructure (inbreeding) is accommodated by application of a correction factor using F_{ST}, otherwise known as theta (θ), (discussed in detail in Section 1.12).

This collection of European population data was made accessible by the European Network of Forensic Science Institutes (ENFSI) on STRbASE, now superseded by STRidER (STRs for identity ENFSI Reference database) [32] https://strider.online/. It has an integrated approach to assuring the quality of submitted data before acceptance.

In support of STRidER, the International Society for Forensic Genetics (ISFG) has published guidelines [30]. The recommendations are summarised by the following:
1. The minimum requirements are 15 autosomal STR loci, typed from 500 samples.
2. The geographical origin of the database is stated.
3. Methods of analysis stated, STR typing kit used.
4. Information on data analysis and handling.
5. Datasets must pass STRidER QC tests before they can be published in FSI: Genetics.

When databases are submitted, the data are examined for duplicates, close relatives, and transcription errors. Once data have been verified, statistical tests are carried out to show if the data conform to Hardy–Weinberg expectations. STRidER actively accepts new databases (Fig. 1.2) and is working towards collections of data generated by new generation sequencing (NGS).

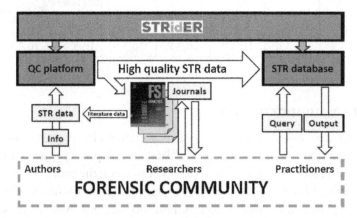

Figure 1.2 Figure taken from [32]. The STRidER work flow, showing the integration of the QC platform and the STR database, resulting in high quality data in FSI: genetics publications. Reproduced from [32] with permission from Elsevier.

1.5. Recap: the laws of statistics

Before progressing further to explain mixture interpretation, it is necessary to recap two fundamental laws of statistics:

The product rule: The probability that two *independent* alleles both occur together is defined by the multiplication rule, so the probability (*Pr*) of observing a genotype, *ab*, where *a* is on chromosome strand *c*1 and *b* is on chromosome strand *c*2, is $p_{ab} = p_a \times p_b$, and the probability of the alternate arrangement is $p_{ba} = p_b \times p_a$, i.e., $p_{ba} = p_{ab}$.

We do not know the chromosomal arrangement of alleles, but one or the other must be true, they cannot both be true at the same time. The probability of either genotype ab or genotype ba (events A or B) is subject to the addition rule.

Addition rule: When two events, A and B, are mutually exclusive, the probability that A **or** B will occur is the sum of the probability of each event.

We continue with the example. Genotype ab is observed and the chromosomal arrangement is unknown, hence the probability that the order is ab or ba is $p_{ab} + p_{ba}$. Combined with the multiplication rule, $p_{ab} = 2 \times p_a \times p_b$.

Independent/dependent: If the occurrence of event A changes the probability of event B, then events A and B are dependent. On the other hand, if the occurrence of event A does not change the probability of event B, then events A and B are independent.

Conditional probability: The probability that event A occurs, given that event B has occurred, is called a conditional probability. The conditional probability of event A, given event B, is denoted by the vertical symbol $Pr(A|B)$.

Complement: The complement of an event is the event of it not occurring. The probability that event A will not occur is denoted by $Pr(\bar{A})$, and if there is a binary choice available, e.g., either allele a or allele b is observed in a population, then the probability of allele b can be calculated from allele a as: $p_b = 1 - p_a$.

Basic maths:
- When "+" (plus) is used, this means "OR"
- When "×" (times) is used, this means "AND"

1.5.1 Effect of conditioning on probabilities

An urn contains 20 red balls (r) and 50 white (w) balls and 30 green (g) balls.
1. The probability of drawing either a red ball or a white ball is $Pr(r \text{ OR } w) = w + r$: $0.20 + 0.50 = 0.7$ (or 7 in 10).
2. The probability of drawing one red ball and one white ball together is $Pr(r \text{ AND } w) = r \times w$: $0.20 \times 0.50 = 0.10$ (or 1 in 10).

Changing the question, changes the probability. Let us draw a ball. Say this is white. Now what is the chance of drawing a red ball *given* that the first is white?

Notice that the total number of balls in the urn is now 99, since one has been withdrawn. There are now 20 red balls, 49 white balls, and 30 green balls, a total of 99. The removal of a white ball has now increased the chance of drawing either a red or a green ball, hence the probability of drawing another white ball is 49/99; the chance of drawing a red ball is 20/99, and the probability of drawing a green ball is 30/99.

Therefore the chance of drawing a red ball, given that we have drawn a white ball, is $Pr(r|w) \times Pr(w)$. Note that since the drawn ball was white, we know that the event w has happened, so that $Pr(w) = 1$, hence $Pr(r|w) = 20/99 = 0.202$.

1.6. The likelihood ratio

The likelihood ratio is a statistic used to quantify the relative goodness of fit between two statistical models or hypotheses, calculated by taking the ratio of their corresponding *conditioned* probabilities.

In any criminal case, there is the crime-stain evidence E, and a person of interest (POI) who may be a suspect (S) or a victim (V). For example, the prosecution may seek to establish the strength of evidence to support the contention that the suspect was a contributor to the crime stain. The defense will put forward an alternative explanation— the suspect is innocent and consequently an unknown individual is the contributor. These two alternative hypotheses are called *propositions*.

We follow a standard format that is used to interpret evidence in all casework. The evidence (E) is evaluated relative to alternative pairs of propositions. Usually, these are formulated as follows:

H_p (the prosecution proposition): The crime-stain evidence is from the suspect.

H_d (the defense proposition): The crime-stain evidence is from an unknown (unrelated) individual.

For each of these propositions, we are interested in quantifying the following *conditioned* probabilities: $Pr(E|H_p)$, the probability of the evidence if the crime stain originated from the suspect (the prosecution proposition), and $Pr(E|H_d)$ the probability of the evidence if the crime stain originated from an unknown (unrelated) individual (the defense proposition). These two probabilities are then used to formulate the likelihood ratio (LR), which is written as

$$LR = \frac{Pr(E|H_p)}{Pr(E|H_d)} \tag{1.5}$$

The top part of the fraction is called the *numerator* and the bottom part is called the *denominator*.

The LR is very flexible, and it can be used to compare many different kinds of possible propositions, including multiple individuals and victims. For example, suppose that the crime stain is a vaginal swab from a rape victim. Clearly, there is an expectation that female DNA from victim's vaginal cells will be present, and these may provide a DNA profile in admixture with the sperm DNA from the assailant. Hence the victim is conditioned in both the numerator and denominator, and by assuming that the crime-stain is a two-person mixture, the propositions change to

H_p: The crime-stain evidence is from the victim and the suspect;

H_d: The crime-stain evidence is from the victim and an unknown (unrelated) individual.

Importantly, an unknown individual (or several) assigned in any of the propositions are always assumed to belong to a population (i.e., they can be pretended to be drawn randomly). The conditional probabilities as presented above will then be based on how often different data types will occur for individuals in the assumed population.

The *LR* is used in statement writing for court-going purposes; an example is provided in Chapter 6.1.7.

1.7. Simple mixtures interpretation: the basics

1.7.1 Nomenclature

We use a simple nomenclature throughout. An alphabetic notation is used relative to the molecular weight of the alleles. For example, if an individual has the alleles "8" and "9", we say that the individual has the *genotype* (8,9). The notation is given in order of the molecular weight, where "8" is the smallest and "9" is the largest allele. In general situations, we only use an alphabetic conversion, such that '*a*' corresponds to the allele with smallest molecular weight, '*b*' corresponds to the second smallest molecular weight, etc. For mixtures, i.e., profiles with more than one contributor, there will be several genotypes combined. For instance, a mixture can be comprised of two individuals having the genotypes (8,9) and (7,7). The corresponding alphabetic conversion for these would then be *bc* and *aa*, which we simply denote as *bc, aa*. Additional examples are illustrated in Table 1.3.

Table 1.3 Examples of alphabet nomenclature used to describe mixture genotypes. There are two alleles per contributor. The alphabetic conversion follows low to high molecular weight. If the locus is homozygote, then each allele is the same.

Example	Contributor 1	Contributor 2	Alphabetic conversion
1	4,6	5,7	*ac, bd*
2	8,9	7,7	*bc, aa*
3	7,7	3,3	*bb, aa*
4	4,8	5,9	*ac, bd*
5	5,7	5,6	*ac, ab*

1.7.2 Minimum number of contributors

So far we have discussed the principles of genetics in relation to single, non-mixed samples. However, the reality of casework is that many crime stains are mixtures of two or more individuals. To interpret such data, it is necessary to decide the number of contributors to condition on. The easiest way to do this is by using the allele counting method [34]. For example, with a two-person mixture, there are five possible kinds of allelic combinations:

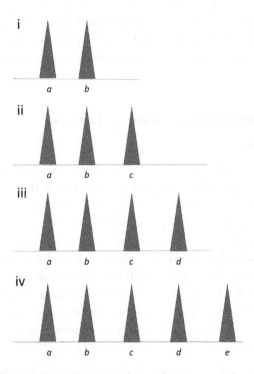

Figure 1.3 Depiction of 2–5 alleles in 4 separate electropherograms. (i) has two alleles and is a minimum single person contributor, but this does not exclude possibility of two contributors, which may be type *ab*, *ab*. (ii) and (iii) have 3–4 alleles, respectively, which implies a minimum two-persons contributing. If both contributors are heterozygous, then there is masking in (ii), i.e., one of the alleles must be shared between two contributors. (iv) has five alleles, and must be a minimum three-person contributors.

1. If both contributors are heterozygote (*ab*, *cd*) and have different alleles to each other, then there are four alleles present.
2. If both contributors are heterozygote and one allele is the same (*ab*, *bc*), then there are three alleles present, because one is shared between the two individuals (allele *b*) and is said to be masked.
3. If both contributors are heterozygote (*ab*, *ab*) and share the same alleles, then just two are present, because two alleles are masked.
4. If one contributor is homozygote, then three alleles are present if the combination is (*aa*, *bc*) or two alleles if one is shared (*aa*, *ab*).

5. Finally, if both contributors are homozygote, then two alleles are present if the combination is (aa, bb), but just one allele is observed if both contributors are the same (aa, aa).

A typical two-person mixture will be represented by a number of loci showing variation in the number of alleles that are present, ranging between one and four. Because of masking, we can never be 100% sure of the absolute number of contributors, but we can assess the minimum number of contributors (nC_{min}) from the locus/loci that have the greatest number of alleles: If HUMTH01 has three or four alleles, then this suggests that the minimum number of contributors is two. If there are five or six alleles, then this suggests a minimum number of three contributors (Fig. 1.3). A simple formula can be used to estimate nC_{min}:

$$nC_{min} = \frac{N_{alleles}}{2} \tag{1.6}$$

If the answer is a fraction, e.g., $nC_{min} = 3/2 = 1.5$, then it is rounded up to the nearest integer, i.e., $nC_{min} = 2$.

This is a brief introduction to the number of contributors problem. This basic method is simple in practice to use, and it works well for full profiles. However, it does not take account of artefacts, such as stutters or drop-in, introduced in later chapters. Consequently, the method may over-estimate the true number of contributors. The expansion to multiple loci is described in Chapter 2.3.2.

1.7.3 Interpretation of two-contributor mixtures

Everything that follows is now positioned in the likelihood ratio framework described in Section 1.6 and follows that originally described by Evett et al. [35]. For simplicity, we consider a single locus at a time (in reality there will be 15 or more to consider), but once the theory for a single locus has been grasped, the extension to multiple loci is straightforward for STR profiles.

Suppose that a crime has been committed and a blood stain is retrieved from the crime-scene. It is analyzed and reveals a DNA profile, which is a mixture of a minimum of two contributors, because there are between 2 and 4 alleles at each of the loci (Eq. (1.6)).

A suspect has been apprehended, and on typing a reference sample from a buccal scrape, it is found that two of his alleles at a locus, which we designate ab, "match"[5] the crime-stain evidence (Fig. 1.4). This means that there are two alleles present in the crime stain (cd) that do not match. A logical assessment of the evidence uses the likelihood ratio approach described in Section 1.6, where two alternative propositions are examined: one for the prosecution (H_p) and one for the defense (H_d).

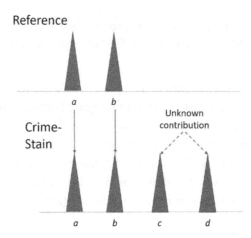

Figure 1.4 Depiction of an electropherogram, where the crime stain has four alleles, two match the reference sample.

1.7.4 Step 1: condition the number of contributors

To form propositions, we need to be able to assign a number of contributors. In Chapter 12.14 there is a much more extensive discussion on how this is achieved with respect to the propositions formulated.

First we condition on the number of contributors (Section 1.7.2). There are two contributors,[6] one of whom is proposed by the prosecution to be the suspect.

1.7.5 Step 2: state the alternative propositions

The *prosecution* proposition (H_p) is as follows: the DNA comes from the suspect and one unknown individual.

The *defense* proposition (H_d) is the following: the DNA comes from two unknown unrelated individuals.

1.7.6 Step 3: evaluate the probability of the evidence under the defense proposition

This is where the idea of conditioning becomes important. To avoid the fallacy of the transposed conditional, or the prosecutor's fallacy (Chapter 12.8), we must evaluate the probability of the evidence ***if***[7] if it comes from two unknown contributors. The conditional word ***if*** acts as a verbal separator of the two elements under consideration—namely the evidence and the proposition. In mathematical notation, this is written $Pr(E = abcd | G_S, H_d, I)$, where G_S is the genotype of the suspect and I is the background information, e.g., allele frequencies.

The defense says that the defendant is innocent as the DNA profile has come from two unknown individuals.

If the evidence is from any two random individuals from the subset of alleles in the crime stain, then we can formulate a list of all of the possible combinations of genotypes that give rise to pairs of individuals as follows:

1. *Make a list of all the alternative genotype combinations*

   Given a four-allele crime stain, for each individual there are six possible genotypes: ab, ac, ad, cd, bd, bc. The genotype of contributor 2 under H_p consists of the two alleles not found in contributor 1. The complete complement of genotypes is listed in Table 1.4.

Table 1.4 All possible genotype pairs for two contributors, each with two different alleles.

Contributor 1	Contributor 2
ab	cd
ac	bd
ad	bc
cd	ab
bd	ac
bc	ad

2. *Assign probabilities to each of the possible pairs of genotypes*

   For the next step, probabilities are assigned to each genotype per contributor, from the Hardy–Weinberg expectation. This is $2p_a p_b$ and $2p_c p_d$ for row 1, for example. To calculate the probability $Pr(E = abcd | G_S, H_d, I)$, we need to multiply the columns together, because we want to calculate the probabilities of contributor 1 "and" contributor 2 genotypes (Table 1.5). The product in each row becomes $4p_a p_b p_c p_d$. Only one of the rows can be true, because the list of genotype combinations is mutually exclusive. The "or" word is necessary to describe mutual exclusivity between alternative events, hence the final column is summed to provide the probability $Pr(E = abcd | G_S, H_d, I) = 24 p_a p_b p_c p_d$.

1.7.7 Step 4: evaluate the probability of the crime-stain evidence under the prosecution proposition

If it is true that the defendant contributed to the crime stain, then we expect to observe genotype ab with certainty, $Pr = 1$. However, there are two unaccounted alleles from an unknown person. From Table 1.4, the first row is ab, cd. No other combinations of the genotypes are possible. The probability of ab, given it is from the defendant, equals one. The probability of $cd = 2p_c p_d$.

The *conditional* expression for the numerator for the likelihood ratio is $Pr(E = abcd | G_S, H_p, I) = 1 \times 2p_c p_d$

Table 1.5 Probabilities of genotype combinations for two different alleles from two contributors. G_1 is the genotype for contributor 1, and G_2 is the genotype for contributor 2.

$Pr(G_1)$	$Pr(G_2)$	**Product** $Pr(G_1) \times Pr(G_2)$
$2p_ap_b$	$2p_cp_d$	$4p_ap_bp_cp_d$
$2p_ap_c$	$2p_bp_d$	$4p_ap_bp_cp_d$
$2p_ap_d$	$2p_bp_c$	$4p_ap_bp_cp_d$
$2p_cp_d$	$2p_ap_b$	$4p_ap_bp_cp_d$
$2p_bp_d$	$2p_ap_c$	$4p_ap_bp_cp_d$
$2p_bp_c$	$2p_ap_d$	$4p_ap_bp_cp_d$
	Total sum =	$24p_ap_bp_cp_d$

1.7.8 Step 5: calculate the likelihood ratio

The final stage is to calculate the likelihood ratio:

$$LR = \frac{Pr(E = abcd | G_S, H_p, I)}{Pr(E = abcd | G_S, H_d, I)} \tag{1.7}$$

Substituting the formulae for numerator and denominator, we obtain

$$LR = \frac{2p_cp_d}{24p_ap_bp_cp_d} \tag{1.8}$$

Canceling p_cp_d, as shown, gives

$$LR = \frac{1}{12p_ap_b} \tag{1.9}$$

As an example, if the frequency of all alleles $a, b, c, d = 0.1$, then for the above example, the $LR = 8.3$. Compare this with the example of a single (non-mixture) profile: if an ab crime-stain matches the defendant, then $LR = 50$ ($\frac{1}{2p_ap_b}$), i.e., the strength of evidence of a mixture is greatly reduced, because of the uncertainty introduced by the additional alleles in the crime stain that do not match the defendant. Also see [36], Table 5, for a list of formulae for various mixtures and conditioning.

1.7.9 Step 6: report the likelihood ratio

The strength of evidence is always calculated as a likelihood ratio, and a typical statement puts the likelihood ratio into words as follows:

"I have evaluated the proposition that Mr. X is a contributor to the crime stain Y compared to the alternative proposition that Mr. X is not a contributor to crime stain Y. These conditions are as follows:

a) Mr. X and an unknown person are both contributors to the sample.
b) Two unknown persons are both contributors to the sample.

The evidence is 8.3 times more likely to obtain if the first proposition (a) is true, compared to the alternative described by (b)."[8]

Refer to Chapter 12.11 for details about statement writing.

1.8. Three allele mixtures

We now consider a more complex mixture with three alleles (*abc*) contributed by two individuals. The suspect reference sample is type *ab*. As before, the defense proposes that the crime stain originates from two unknown individuals. A list is compiled of all 12 possible pairwise genotype combinations (Table 1.6), and their probabilities are calculated as shown in Table 1.7.

Table 1.6 Pairwise genotype combinations showing three alleles shared between two contributors.

Contributor 1	Contributor 2
aa	*bc*
bb	*ac*
cc	*ab*
ab	*ac*
ab	*bc*
bc	*ac*
bc	*aa*
ac	*bb*
ab	*cc*
ac	*ab*
bc	*ab*
ac	*bc*

1.8.1 Calculation of the likelihood ratio

The final stage is to calculate the likelihood ratio. The defense proposition calculation is shown in Table 1.7 as $Pr(E = abc | G_S, H_d, I) = 12 p_a p_b p_c (p_a + p_b + p_c)$. If the suspect with genotype *ab* is contributor 1, then the unknown contributor, assigned as contributor 2, must have at least one *c* in order to describe the evidence. This corresponds to the three following genotypes: *ac*, *bc*, or *cc*. Consequently, the probability of the evidence under the prosecution proposition is

$$Pr(E = abc | G_S, H_p, I) = p_c^2 + 2 p_a p_c + 2 p_b p_c \tag{1.10}$$

Forensic Practitioner's Guide to the Interpretation of Complex DNA Profiles

Table 1.7 Probabilities of genotype combinations for two contributors with three shared alleles. G_1 is the genotype for contributor 1, and G_2 is the genotype for contributor 2.

$Pr(G_1)$	$Pr(G_2)$	Product
p_a^2	$2p_bp_c$	$4p_a^2p_bp_c$
p_b^2	$2p_ap_c$	$2p_ap_b^2p_c$
p_c^2	$2p_ap_b$	$2p_ap_bp_c^2$
$2p_ap_b$	$2p_ap_c$	$4p_a^2p_bp_c$
$2p_ap_b$	$2p_bp_c$	$4p_ap_b^2p_c$
$2p_bp_c$	$2p_ap_c$	$4p_ap_bp_c^2$
$2p_bp_c$	p_a^2	$2p_a^2p_bp_c$
$2p_ap_c$	p_b^2	$2p_ap_b^2p_c$
$2p_ap_b$	p_c^2	$2p_ap_bp_c^2$
$2p_ap_c$	$2p_ap_b$	$4p_a^2p_bp_c$
$2p_bp_c$	$2p_ap_b$	$4p_ap_b^2p_c$
$2p_ap_c$	$2p_bp_c$	$4p_ap_bp_c^2$
	Total sum $=$	$12p_ap_bp_c(p_a+p_b+p_c)$

To calculate the *LR*, we substitute the formulae from Eq. (1.10) into the numerator and sum of products from Table 1.7 into the denominator:

$$LR = \frac{Pr(E=abc|G_S, H_p, I)}{Pr(E=abc|G_S, H_d, I)} = \frac{p_c^2 + 2p_ap_c + 2p_bp_c}{12p_ap_bp_c(p_a+p_b+p_c)} \tag{1.11}$$

Canceling p_c in both the numerator and denominator gives

$$LR = \frac{p_c + 2p_a + 2p_b}{12p_ap_b(p_a+p_b+p_c)} \tag{1.12}$$

Now suppose that the suspect is homozygote *aa*. The denominator is unchanged. However, the unknown contributor can only be a *bc* heterozygote, and so $Pr(E|G_S, H_p, I) = 2p_bp_c$

From this the *LR* is

$$LR = \frac{2p_bp_c}{12p_ap_bp_c(p_a+p_b+p_c)} \tag{1.13}$$

Canceling $p_{p_bp_c}$ in the numerator and the denominator gives

$$LR = \frac{1}{6p_a(p_a+p_b+p_c)} \tag{1.14}$$

1.9. Two allele mixtures

Under the defense proposition, a two-allele mixture, $E = ab$, from two contributors may arise from one of three different situations:

1. Two similar heterozygotes, e.g., ab and ab;
2. Two different homozygotes, e.g., aa and bb;
3. A homozygote and a heterozygote, e.g., aa and ab.

There are seven possible genotype combinations (Table 1.8).

Table 1.8 Pairwise genotype combinations showing two alleles shared between two contributors.

Contributor 1	Contributor 2
aa	bb
aa	ab
bb	ab
ab	ab
bb	aa
ab	aa
ab	bb

The denominator $Pr(E|G_S, H_d, I)$ is calculated from the combinations of genotypes listed in Table 1.9.

Table 1.9 Probabilities of genotype combinations for two contributors with two shared alleles. G_1 is the genotype for contributor 1, and G_2 is the genotype for contributor 2.

$Pr(G_1)$	$Pr(G_2)$	Product
p_a^2	p_b^2	$p_a^2 p_b^2$
p_a^2	$2p_a p_b$	$2p_a^3 p_b$
p_b^2	$2p_a p_b$	$2p_a p_b^3$
$2p_a p_b$	$2p_a p_b$	$4p_a^2 p_b^2$
p_b^2	p_a^2	$p_a^2 p_b^2$
$2p_a p_b$	p_a^2	$2p_a^3 p_b$
$2p_a p_b$	$2p_b^2$	$2p_a p_b^3$
	Total sum $=$	$2p_a p_b(3p_a p_b + 2p_a^2 + 2p_b^2)$

If the suspect is homozygote (aa), then the unknown is either ab OR bb, hence

$$Pr(E = ab|G_S, H_p, I) = 2p_a p_b + p_b^2 \tag{1.15}$$

To calculate the LR, we substitute the formulae from Eq. (1.15) into the numerator and sum of products from Table 1.9 to the denominator:

$$LR = \frac{Pr(E = ab|G_S, H_p, I)}{Pr(E = ab|H_d)} = \frac{p_b(2p_a + p_b)}{2p_a p_b(2p_a^2 + 3p_a p_b + 2p_b^2)} \tag{1.16}$$

Canceling p_b in both the numerator and denominator gives

$$LR = \frac{2p_a + p_b}{2p_a(2p_a^2 + 3p_a p_b + 2p_b^2)} \tag{1.17}$$

If the suspect is heterozygote ab, then the numerator $Pr(E|H_p)$ has three alternatives for the unknown, either ab OR aa OR bb, hence

$$Pr(E|G_S, H_p, I) = 2p_a p_b + p_a^2 + p_b^2 = (p_a + p_b)^2 \tag{1.18}$$

Substituting the formulae from Eq. (1.18) into the numerator and Table 1.9, the total sum of the products into the denominator, the LR becomes

$$LR = \frac{(p_a + p_b)^2}{2p_a p_b(2p_a^2 + 3p_a p_b + 2p_b^2)} \tag{1.19}$$

1.10. Multiple contributors

The previous sections illustrate the basic method to calculate likelihood ratios for simple two person mixtures. However, real crime-stain samples are often composed of more than two contributors. For example, if three are considered, the problem becomes much more complex, because the number of possible genotype combinations under H_d increases exponentially. Imagine a mixture of three heterozygotes ab, cd, ef. Under H_d, there are now 144 possible genotype combinations, which is unmanageable using the spreadsheet method that was used in Section 1.8.1. Generalized formulae are listed by Weir et al. [36].

Even for relatively simple cases, hand calculations are already becoming much too intensive for routine use, and they are subject to manual errors. Consequently, this highlights the need for computer programs, or expert systems to remove this burden, at the same time removing the quality problems associated with manual calculations.

1.11. Automating calculations with a computer program

1.11.1 Two-contributors

In Section 1.8.1, likelihood ratios are derived by formulae. These are complex, and each genotype combination requires a different formula, which is dependant upon the conditioning used. Adding more than two contributors considerably increases the range of formulae required, so that it is impractical to hard code them into a computer program. An alternative method is needed. Computers are very good at carrying out repetitive tasks using simple rule-sets on large amounts of data. The trick is to identify the rule-sets and to organize data into matrices, which may be huge, and multi-dimensional—too large and tedious to examine by eye, but perfect for a computing environment.

The importance of pairwise comparisons was explained in Section 1.3.2 (Table 1.2). This principle is extended here. Consider a locus that has four known alleles. There are ten possible genotypes and 100 possible two-person genotype combinations that can be represented in a two-dimensional matrix (Table 1.10).

Table 1.10 Pairwise comparisons of all possible genotype combinations for a two-person mixture with a locus with four possible alleles. Colour coding used to show number of unique alleles per cell, reflecting the appearance in the electropherogram: Grey = one allele; white = two alleles; green = three alleles and red = four alleles.

Genotypes	aa	ab	ac	ad	bb	bc	bd	cc	cd	dd
aa	aa,aa	aa,ab	aa,ac	aa,ad	aa,bb	aa,bc	aa,bd	aa,cc	aa,cd	aa,dd
ab	ab,aa	ab,ab	ab,ac	ab,ad	ab,bb	ab,bc	ab,bd	ab,cc	ab,cd	ab,dd
ac	ac,aa	ac,ab	ac,ac	ac,ad	ac,bb	ac,bc	ac,bd	ac,cc	ac,cd	ac,dd
ad	ad,aa	ad,ab	ad,ac	ad,ad	ad,bb	ad,bc	ad,bd	ad,cc	ad,cd	ad,dd
bb	bb,aa	bb,ab	bb,ac	bb,ad	bb,bb	bb,bc	bb,bd	bb,cc	bb,cd	bb,dd
bc	bc,aa	bc,ab	bc,ac	bc,ad	bc,bb	bc,bc	bc,bd	bc,cc	bc,cd	bc,dd
bd	bd,aa	bd,ab	bd,ac	bd,ad	bd,bb	bd,bc	bd,bd	bd,cc	bd,cd	bd,dd
cc	cc,aa	cc,ab	cc,ac	cc,ad	cc,bb	cc,bc	cc,bd	cc,cc	cc,cd	cc,dd
cd	cd,aa	cd,ab	cd,ac	cd,ad	cd,bb	cd,bc	cd,bd	cd,cc	cd,cd	cd,dd
dd	dd,aa	dd,ab	dd,ad	dd,ad	dd,bb	dd,bc	dd,bd	dd,cc	dd,cd	dd,dd

This summarizes all genotype combinations that were described in Section 1.7.6 (Table 1.4). If a crime stain consists of four alleles (*abcd*), then all of the combinations are illustrated in red; if three alleles are present, e.g., *abc*, then the possible genotypes are found in the green cells. A computer can easily select the genotypes by using some simple rule-sets:

H_d assessment

1. If all of the unique alleles present in the crime stain, are found in the cell, with no non-matching alleles—and this applies to each cell—then the genotype combination is selected.
   - If the crime-stain profile is *abc*, there are three alleles, hence each green cell in Table 1.10 is compared to see if all are present. For example, genotype combination *ab, ac* is selected, whereas *ab, dd* is not, because allele *c* is missing in the latter. The selection of cells will mirror the list in Table 1.6, and these are taken forward to calculate the probability of evidence under H_d shown in Table 1.7.

2. If a cell is selected, then the genotype probability is automatically calculated using simple programmed rule-sets dependant upon the alleles:
   - Homozygotes are calculated as p_a^2 or p_b^2 or p_c^2
   - Heterozygotes are calculated as $2p_ap_b$ or $2p_ap_c$ or $2p_bp_c$
   - For example, considering genotype combination ab, ac, where ab is from contributor 1 and ac is from contributor 2

$$Pr(E|ab, ac) = 2p_ap_b \times 2p_ap_c = 4p_a^2p_bp_c$$

   - It is necessary to take into account the possibility of genotypes originating from the alternate contributors ($ab, ac \Rightarrow ac, ab$ in the example above), which gives the same expression as above, multiplied by a factor of two:

$$Pr(E|ab, ac \text{ or } ac, ab) = (2p_ap_b \times 2p_ap_c) + (2p_ap_c \times 2p_ap_b) = 8p_a^2p_bp_c$$

   - The list of 12 genotypes that would be selected for a crime stain abc from Table 1.10 is exactly the same, as shown in Table 1.6; the associated probabilities are listed in Table 1.7.
   - If the two genotypes are the same, e.g., heterozygote ab, ab or homozygote aa, aa, then the factor of two is omitted, since both contributors have identical genotypes, and there is no reverse order in the table. All these genotypes are listed along the diagonal in Table 1.10.

H_p assessment

When the suspect is conditioned, then the procedure is as follows:

1. Assign contributor 1 as the suspect.
2. If the reference genotype is type ab, then cells from row 2 (Table 1.10) are selected if they include all alleles found in the crime stain.
   - For example, if the crime stain is four alleles (a, b, c, d), then cell ab, cd is selected (i.e., the unknown contributor is type cd). We do not consider genotype combination cd, ab, since we condition that suspect is contributor 1.
   - If the crime sample is three alleles (abc), as per the previous example, then cells $ab, ac; ab, bc; ab, cc$ are selected: the genotype of the unknown contributor is type ac, or bc, or cc.
3. When cells are selected, then the probabilities of the unknown contributors are calculated using Hardy–Weinberg expectations. The probability of the known individual, under a given proposition, is assigned $Pr = 1$.
   - If the known suspect genotype is ab and the crime stain is $abcd$, then $Pr(E = abcd|G_S, H_p, I) = 1 \times 2p_cp_d$
   - If the known genotype is ab and the unknown genotype is either ac, or bc, or cc, then $Pr(E = abcd|G_S, H_p, I) = 1 \times (2p_ap_c + 2p_bp_c + p_c^2)$

- Because the suspect is assigned to be a specific contributor, there is no alternative to consider, as with the H_d calculation. The same rationale applies if there is conditioning on a known individual in the denominator (typically this would be a victim who would be assigned as contributor 2).

The likelihood ratio is formulated as previously described in Section 1.8.1, by dividing the H_p numerator by the H_d denominator. This gives the same results using formulae. Although computers do not derive formulae, they are useful to work through large tables of data, such as that illustrated in Table 1.10, using simple rule sets that are easily programmed, as described above.

1.11.2 Recap

The following procedure is carried out.
1. For each locus all possible genotypes are listed.
2. A matrix is prepared that shows pairwise comparisons of all possible genotypes, and this gives a matrix of all possible two-contributor genotype combinations, as shown in Table 1.10.
3. The set of unique alleles in the crime stain are compared to the set of unique alleles in each cell of the matrix. If there is not a match, then the probability assigned to the genotype combination is zero.
4. If there is a match between the unique alleles in the reference sample compared to the matrix, then the probability of the cell is calculated by multiplying the allele probabilities, per contributor, according to HW expectations, and then multiplying the results.
5. Under the H_p proposition, the suspect is contributor 1. A conditioned victim is contributor 2.
   - The probability of the known individual, suspect and/or victim, is assigned $Pr = 1$.
6. If the contributor is unknown under the proposition, then the genotype combination is tested per contributor. If the contributor is known under the proposition, then there is no alternate genotype combination to consider.
7. The probabilities across all genotype combinations are summed under H_p and H_d to provide the same, as described in Section 1.8.1.

1.11.3 Extension to three or more contributors

It was previously noted that the methodology in Section 1.7 was realistically restricted to just two individual contributors, because the number of different pairwise combinations increases exponentially, and it becomes very difficult to derive the necessary formulae. However, the expansion to more than two contributors is accomplished by adding new dimensions to the matrix.

Suppose that the crime stain is proposed as three contributors. Table 1.10 is expanded to incorporate a new dimension, so it becomes a three-dimensional cube (Fig. 1.5). The third dimension incorporates all possible genotypes of the third contributor. To form the cube, it is necessary to replicate Table 1.10 ten times, one for each genotype list in the row/column headers.

In the first sheet, the first and second contributors are listed exactly as described for Table 1.10 in the first and second dimensions of the cube. The third dimension corresponds to the third contributor. If there are 10 possible genotypes at a locus, this results in the third dimension of 10 different layers, where each layer corresponds to the third contributor genotype. In the first layer, the third contributor is assigned as *aa*, the second layer is *ab*, the third is *ac*, and so on, until each of the possible three contributor genotypes has been assigned in each of the 10 layers.

The procedure to assign probabilities is exactly the same as described in Section 1.11.1. For example, if the crime stain is a three-person mixture with alleles *a*, *b*, *c*, then each cell in the cube is examined to see if they "match" the unique alleles in each cell. Hence, in the first layer, genotype *aa, ab, ac* is a match, whereas *ad, ab, ac* is not.

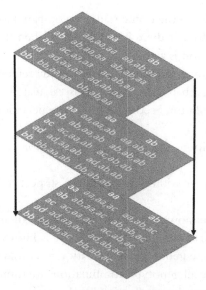

Figure 1.5 Three-dimensional comparison of three contributors, where the crime stain has four alleles. Only a small portion of the table is shown. The first and second contributor genotypes listed in the first row/column are replicated in each layer. The third contributor is the same genotype within each layer, but different between the layers. The first genotype combination is *aa, aa, aa* in the top layer; this becomes *aa, aa, ab* in the second layer and *aa, aa, ac* in the third.

Probabilities are assigned in exactly the same way as previously described: one of the genotype combinations considered is *aa, ab, ac*, for which $Pr = p_a^2 \times 2p_a p_b \times 2p_a p_c$. Under H_d, all alternative combinations are included—instead of two, there are now six to consider (all will be found in the extended cube structure illustrated in Fig. 1.5):

$$aa, ab, ac$$
$$aa, ac, ab$$
$$ab, aa, ac$$
$$ab, ac, aa$$
$$ac, aa, ab$$
$$ac, ab, aa$$

Each genotype combination has the same probability, which are summed together: $Pr = 6(p_a^2 \times 2p_{ab} \times 2p_{ac})$. Suppose that under H_p a suspect is conditioned as contributor 1, and he/she is type aa, then the alternatives to include are aa, ab, ac and aa, ac, ab and $Pr = 2(2p_{ab} \times 2p_{ac})$.

The exercise is repeated for all possible genotype combinations, too numerous to do by pen and paper; their probabilities are summed, as outlined for the simpler two-contributor examples in Section 1.11.1.

The extension to four or more contributors is exactly the same (but impossible to illustrate, because each contributor adds a new dimension to the array). Fortunately, computers are adept at solving multi-dimensional problems like this, but the exercise shows that the computing power required increases exponentially with each contributor added, and this results in a limitation of the methods that we discuss in later chapters.

The illustrations so far have only considered likelihood ratios at a single locus with four alleles. Modern multiplexes have at least 15 loci, with many more alleles to consider, hence the exercise described above will be carried out sequentially many times, one per locus. The likelihood ratios are multiplied together to provide an overall strength of evidence calculation for the complete crime-stain profile, conditioned upon the various prosecution and defense propositions.

1.12. The effect of population sub-structuring

1.12.1 What is a population?

A "population" is a broad term. It refers to a group of interbreeding individuals within a defined geographical location. Populations may also be defined by traits, such as religion or ethnic background if this separates them from others. Populations are said to be stratified or hierarchical, consisting of sub-groups, or sub-populations. These hierarchical divisions are somewhat arbitrary, but taking the UK population as an example, first the populations can be divided into broad ancestral groups: White Caucasian, Afro-Caribbean, Asian. These populations can be subdivided further, e.g., Scotland, Wales,

North England, and Southern England. The next level could include counties, and finally villages. These sub-populations are to some extent isolated from each other, which means that individuals within a sub-population will tend to breed preferentially with each other, rather than with members of different sub-populations. The more distant sub-populations are from each other, the less likely it is that they will interbreed. An idealised example would be a series of rural villages before the days of motorized transport. Whereas there was communication between villages and some intermarriages, it was more likely that individuals within the same village would marry each other, rather than individuals in an adjacent village. It was highly unlikely that an individual located in Cornwall would marry someone from the Shetland Isles, which is some 1,000 km distant. A degree of genetic isolation will tend to cause differences between sub-populations in terms of their allele frequencies, because of *random genetic drift*: where random mating alone causes changes in allele frequencies over generations. If the population size is small and isolated, genetic drift can lead to complete loss of heterozygosity such that all members of the population can become homozygous at a given locus. This is known as *fixation*.

1.12.1.1 Mutation

Once fixation occurs, genetic drift stops unless a mutation event occurs. The larger the population, the more likely it is that mutations will occur, and some of these will spread throughout populations and eventually become common. The effect of mutation introduces genetic diversity into the population and counters the effect of genetic drift. The mutation must be non-deleterious, otherwise natural selection will act to remove it from the population. The mechanism of mutation followed by genetic drift is responsible to produce the variants currently observed in STRs. Mutation rates of STRs are high compared to SNPs; for example, using the PowerPlex 21 kit (20 autosomal loci), Zhang et al. [37] observed a mutation rate of 0.3% in D12S391; the average was estimated to be 1.246×10^{-3} per meiosis in Chinese Han individuals. This contrasts with an average mutation rate of 2.5×10^{-8} [38] per nucleotide per generation. The high mutation rate of STRs is the reason why they are highly polymorphic in populations.

1.12.1.2 Migration

Migration between sub-populations results in gene-flow, so that genes can spread across populations over time. Over the past 200–300 years, there has been much population movement into cities, which has resulted in the development of cosmopolitan populations without the clear boundaries that may be defined by rural villages—as movement increases, random mating extends beyond the sub-population boundaries, then they lose their separate identities and effectively coalesce. Populations that are close together have the greatest similarities. The greatest differences between populations occur between continental groups (Europe and Africa), because they are much more isolated from each other. Gene flow is an important mechanism for transferring genes across populations; this also counters the effect of genetic drift.

1.12.2 Genetic drift

A population, which we call the *total* population, consists of a number of separate sub-populations. The effect is greatest when sub-populations are completely isolated from each other; there is no migration between them, no mutation, and no natural selection. A further assumption is that the sizes of the sub-populations are the same and do not change from one generation to the next. Although these criteria are somewhat unrealistic, the assumptions are nevertheless useful to provide a basic explanation about the genetic diversity within and between sub-populations and the total population. This leads to a discussion about the use of correction factors to prevent the over-estimation of strength of evidence of crime-samples.

In any sub-population, the frequency of alleles will alter per generation as a result of random sampling of gametes from parents, but in the total population, defined as a collection of sub-populations, the average allele frequency across all sub-populations will remain relatively constant. Genetic drift can cause allele frequencies to fluctuate considerably between isolated populations.

To illustrate, we follow examples based on Hartl et al. [39], Chapter 4. Suppose there are four isolated sub-populations in a total population that undergoes random genetic drift. We consider an example with a locus of two alleles with frequencies a and b, respectively. They start with frequencies $p_a = p_b = 0.5$, and under HW expectation $p_{aa} = 0.25$; $p_{ab} = 0.5$; $p_{bb} = 0.25$. Genetic drift causes allele frequencies to diverge between sub-populations. Eventually, over a number of generations, fixation occurs, where two populations have allele $p_a = 1$ and two have allele $p_b = 1$. If a sample is taken across all four sub-populations in equal proportions (because they are treated as a single total population of interest), then the allele probabilities are unchanged: $p_a = p_b = 0.5$. Under HW expectations, the relative genotype frequencies are unchanged, but because fixation has occurred, there is excess homozygosity present in all of the sub-populations: either $p_{aa} = 1$ or $p_{bb} = 1$ and $p_{ab} = 0$, hence there are no heterozygotes at all. Consequently, the population does not fulfill HW expectations and if applied to calculate genotype frequencies, would greatly under-estimate the probabilities of homozygotes in the population [39], Chapter 4.

This deficiency of heterozygotes across sub-populations that are combined into a single total population is called the *Wahlund effect*. It is intimately connected to the reduction in heterozygosity caused by inbreeding. The smaller the population and the more isolated it is, the more likely it is that individuals will share common ancestors.

1.12.3 Common ancestry

To measure the effect of common ancestry, there are a number of different *fixation indices*, or F statistics [40]. We are primarily interested in the statistic F_{ST}, which is a measure of population differentiation due to population structure. One way to estimate this statistic is by measuring the overall reduction in average expected heterozygosity in sub-populations, defined by HW $2p_ap_b$ expectation, relative to that of the total population:

$$F_{ST} = \frac{H_T - H_S}{H_T} \qquad (1.20)$$

- H_T is the average expected heterozygosity of individuals in the total population considered to be a single randomly mating population under HW expectations.
- H_S is the average heterozygosity among individuals within sub-populations under HW expectations:

$$H_S = \frac{\sum\limits_{i=1,...,K} (H_i \times n_i)}{\sum\limits_{i=1,...,K} n_i} \qquad (1.21)$$

where i is the ith sub-population; there are K sub-populations in total, each of size n_i individuals, and H_i is the expected heterozygosity.

F_{ST} can alternatively be expressed in terms of probability of identity by descent (IBD):

$$F_{ST} = \frac{f_0 - f_1}{1 - f_1} \qquad (1.22)$$

where f_0 is the probability of identity by descent of two different genes drawn from the same population, f_1 is the probability of identity by descent of two genes drawn from two different populations [41].

Two alleles that are the same type are either identical by descent or identical by state. If the latter, then a mutation event has occurred at some point in a lineage, where allele a has randomly mutated from a progenitor allele b. If compared to a genotype from a separate lineage that also has allele a, they may appear the same type, but they do not originate from a common ancestor. In STRs, mutations occur at a rate of 1.2×10^{-3} [37] and tend to be step-wise; this means that allele HUMTH01 8 will tend to mutate one tandem unit to either allele 7 or allele 9. The effect of mutation is to reduce F_{ST}, since a newly mutated allele is no longer IBD, and genetic diversity is increased in the population.

A simplified illustration of alleles that are IBD is provided in Fig. 1.6. A common ancestor is the mother of two children. Per individual, for each generation, the probability that a gene is inherited from the common ancestor is halved (this is the same probability as flipping a coin for heads or tails). At the fourth generation this probability

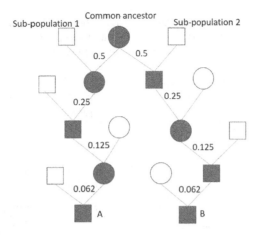

Figure 1.6 Individuals A and B inherit genes from a common ancestor. At each generation, there is a loss of 50% of genes due to random assortment from each parent. After four generations, ancestors A and B will have inherited 6.2% of genes from the common ancestor, and of these will share 0.38% of genes between them.

has reduced to 0.062. Because the genes that are inherited are random, the probability that these two ancestors will share the same gene is $0.062 \times 0.062 = 0.0038$. This simple illustration does not take into account genes from other common ancestors who are more remote. The effect is additive. In addition, if there are several children per generation, then there are more opportunities for a given gene to be preserved in a sub-population. Closely linked genes will be inherited together, because of lack of recombination between them. Each cluster of genes can have a different ancestral origin. The levels of common ancestry are always greater in sub-populations compared to the overall total population.

The average genotype frequencies across sub-populations can be calculated by applying F_{ST} to homozygotes *aa* and heterozgotes *ab*:

$$\textit{aa:} \ p_a^2 + p_a p_b F_{ST} \tag{1.23}$$

$$\textit{ab:} \ 2p_a p_b - 2 p_a p_b F_{ST} \tag{1.24}$$

Note the formulae show that $F_{ST} > 0$ has the effect of increasing the frequency of homozygotes, whilst decreasing the frequency of heterozygotes, compensating for the Wahlund effect discussed in Section 1.12.2. It is also important to reiterate that whereas the individual sub-populations are in HW equilibrium, it is the combined total population, which is not in HW equilibrium, that requires the F_{ST} adjustment—not the sub-populations themselves. The steps necessary to calculate F_{ST} are provided in Box 1.1.

34   Forensic Practitioner's Guide to the Interpretation of Complex DNA Profiles

Table 1.11 Extreme example discussed in Section 1.12.2. There are four sub-populations, where fixation has occurred in sub-populations 1,2 for allele a and sub-populations 3,4 for allele b so that frequencies of each are either 0 or 1. There are no heterozygotes. Allele frequencies measured across the four sub-populations to form the total population gives $p_a = p_b = 0.5$. In the total population, under HW expectations, heterozygosity, $H_T(p_{ab}) = 2 \times p_a^2 \times p_b^2 = 0.5$, is greatly over-estimated. However, application of $F_{ST} = 1$ (Eq. (1.24)) corrects the over-estimate so that $p_{ab} = 0$, hence $p_{aa} = p_{bb} = 0.5$.

	Allele frequencies		Calculated from HW	
Sub-population	allele a	allele b	$1 - H_S$	$H_S(p_{ab})$
1	1	0	1	0
2	1	0	1	0
3	0	1	1	0
4	0	1	1	0
Total population (average)	0.5	0.5	HW expectation $= 0.5$	
H_T without $F_{ST} = 2 \times 0.5 \times 0.5 = 0.5$			H_T with $F_{ST} = 0.0$	

Box 1.1 Steps to calculate F_{ST}

1. For each sub-population, calculate allele frequencies p_a and p_b
2. Calculate the the average allele frequencies (p_a and p_b across sub-populations)
3. Calculate heterozygosity for the total population: $H_T = 2 \times p_a \times p_b$
4. Calculate heterozygosity $H_{S(1,...,K)}$ for each sub-population, where there are K sub-populations
5. Calculate H_S as the average heterozygosity across sub-populations using Eq. (1.21)
6. $F_{ST} = \frac{H_T - H_S}{H_T}$

With the extreme example described in Section 1.12.2, there are four sub-populations, where alleles p_a and p_b are fixed in two populations each (Table 1.11). If the four populations are combined in equal proportions in a population database to form the total population, then their allele frequencies are $p_a = p_b = 0.5$. Estimates of p_{aa}, p_{ab}, p_{bb} are calculated from HW expectations as $0.25 : 0.5 : 0.25$, respectively. However, in the sampled total population, there are no heterozygotes observed, hence there is homozygous excess recorded, and the sample clearly does not conform to HW expectations. With knowledge of the sub-populations, F_{ST} can be calculated from Eq. (1.20), as $F_{ST} = \frac{H_T - H_S}{H_T} = \frac{0.5 - 0}{0.5} = 1$. When $F_{ST} = 1$ is now applied to Eq. (1.23), the frequency of homozygote genotypes $(1 - H_T)$ is revised to $p_{aa} = p_{bb} = 0.5^2 + 0.5 \times 0.5 \times 1 = 0.5$, and heterozgosity is revised to $H_T = 0$ when Eq. (1.24) is applied. Sub-populations are essentially invisible, their presence may be inferred by departures from HW equilibrium observed in a total population. This is obvious with the extreme example described above, because of complete absence of heterozygotes in the observed total population. However, in typical forensic collections of population data, deviations from HW equilibrium are usually too minor to detect. Match probabilities can be compensated using

F_{ST} corrections applied to the total population database, i.e., the dataset used for frequency estimation. F_{ST} is usually informed from analysis of discrete datasets, which are from defined geographical areas (Section 1.15).

Table 1.12 There are four sub-populations. All follow HW expectations. The total population gives allele frequencies $p_a = p_b = 0.5$. There is heterozygote deficiency in the total population, which is compensated by F_{ST}. Two different calculations are shown that follow Eq. (1.20) and (1.29) in parentheses (the latter is the preferred Balding equation).

Sub-population	Allele frequencies		Calculated from HW		
	allele a	allele b	$1 - H_S$	H_S	p_{aa}
1	0.55	0.45	0.5050	0.4950	0.3025
2	0.45	0.55	0.5050	0.4950	0.2025
3	0.53	0.47	0.5018	0.4982	0.2809
4	0.47	0.53	0.5018	0.4982	0.2209
Total population (average)	0.5	0.5	$1 - H_T = 0.5$	HW expectation $= 0.25$ with $F_{ST} = \textbf{0.251 (0.258)}$	

In Table 1.12, a more realistic example is shown (compared to the extreme described in Table 1.11). Again, there are four sub-populations, whose allele frequencies diverge. The average allele frequencies of the total population are $p_a = p_b = 0.5$, as in the extreme example. Under HW expectations, the genotype probabilities are also the same as previously described. Average $H_S = 0.4966$, illustrating that $H_T = 0.5$ is an over estimate of heterozygosity. F_{ST} is calculated as $\frac{0.5 - 0.4966}{0.5} = 0.0068$. This level of F_{ST} is much more in keeping with that expected from typical cosmopolitan populations, and the effect is consequently small. The genotype probability of aa, bb with $F_{ST} = 0.0068$ is $p_{aa} = p_{bb} = 0.5^2 + 0.5 \times 0.5 \times 0.0068 = 0.2517$. A calculation using the Balding and Nichols F_{ST} Eq. (1.29) [42], described in Section 1.12.6, gives a slightly higher value of 0.258.

1.12.4 A computer simulation to illustrate effects of genetic drift

The effects of genetic drift can be illustrated by computer simulation [43]: A total of 50 sub-populations were created from the starting generation of a locus with two alleles. For each sub-population, a new generation was simulated by random sampling of the binomial$(2n, p_A)$ distribution, where $2n = 1000$ independent alleles, and $p_A = p_B = 0.5$. This procedure is the same as counting the number of heads from a coin flipped 1000 times. The new allele frequency for the new generation is $p_A = n_A/2n$, $p_B = 1 - n_A/2n$. This new allele frequency then forms the basis for a recursive calculation to generate the next p_A value, which is sampled to form the next generation size $2n$ per sub-population.

For each generation, the mean p_A across sub-populations was calculated to provide the total population allele frequency along with H_T and H_S parameters to calculate F_{ST} using Eq. (1.20), described in Section 1.12.3.

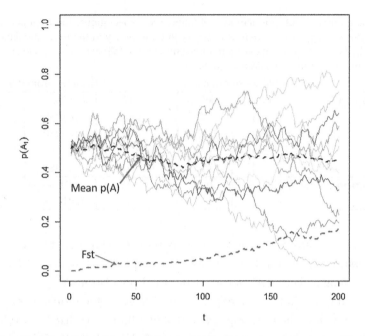

Figure 1.7 Genetic drift showing 11 out of 50 independent loci, where zero generation $p_A = 0.5$. The mean p_A is shown for the total population (average of sub-populations), along with F_{ST}. The simulation was run for $t = 200$ generations (x-axis).

In Fig. 1.7, for the sake of clarity, only results from 11 of the sub-populations are shown. The mean p_A is based on the average across all 50 sub-populations. Whereas the sub-population allele frequencies are notably divergent, the mean p_A of the total population estimate remains approximately unchanged at $p_A \approx 0.5$. As the sub-populations diverge, F_{ST} steadily increases, until eventually fixation is reached for the majority at about 2000 generations (not shown).

1.12.5 Extension to multi-allelic systems (STRs)

So far we have only discussed genetic drift and F_{ST} in relation to binary allelic systems. Fortunately, the extension to multi-allelic systems of STRs is straightforward. Following [44,45], Eq. (1.20) can be rewritten in terms of homozygosity, rather than heterozygosity. The reason to do this is that homozygosity can be defined in terms of allele frequencies. If h is homozgosity and H is heterozygosity, then $h = 1 - H$. Plugging

Forensic genetics: the basics **37**

this into F_{ST} Eq. (1.20) gives

$$G_{ST} = \frac{h_s - h_T}{1 - h_T} \qquad (1.25)$$

where S are sub-populations, and T is the total population; there are I types of allelic variants in the total population. Per locus, the h_T parameter is estimated as the sum of $i = 1, ..., I$ mean allele frequencies squared $(\bar{p}_i^2)$. Here we continue to use the term F_{ST} instead of G_{ST}, as they are considered to be equivalent.

$$h_T = \sum_{i=1}^{I} \bar{p}_i^2 \qquad (1.26)$$

where $\bar{p}_i^2$ is the mean frequency of allele i across K sub-populations:

$$\bar{p}_i^2 = \frac{1}{K} \sum_{k=1}^{K} p_{ki} \qquad (1.27)$$

h_S is the within sub-population measure of homozygosity, given by the summation of $i = 1, ..., I$ allele frequencies squared per sub-population k, summed across all sub-populations $(k = 1, ..., K)$:

$$h_s = \frac{1}{K} \sum_{k=1}^{K} \sum_{i=1}^{I} p_{ki}^2 \qquad (1.28)$$

These formulae are easily programmed (example provided on the book's website), and can be used to measure F_{ST} in simulated and actual population surveys, as described in the next section.

1.12.6 Balding and Nichols F_{ST}

Balding and Nichols [42] refined the F_{ST} correction formula for forensic purposes. In a crime stain, alleles are observed. A suspect is found who matches. The defense alternative is that the suspect is innocent, and the donor is from the same sub-population. Since the forensic database compiles data across sub-populations, the Wahlund effect suggests that using match probabilities derived from Hardy–Weinberg expectations are prejudicial to the defense, because they under-estimate match probabilities. If allele a is observed in a crime stain, then the same allele is more likely to be found in a reference sample, and the conditioning should reflect this. Following this logic, they derived two different formulae, which are in common use: one for homozygotes and the other for heterozygotes. The conditioning is explicit in each. What is the probability of observing alleles a and b in a suspect? Given that the same alleles are observed in the crime stain and the suspect is innocent, the donor of the crime stain is another person who is from the same sub-population as the suspect. θ is F_{ST}; p_a and p_b are probabilities of alleles a and b, respectively.

Homozygotes:

$$Pr(aa|aa) = \frac{[2\theta + (1-\theta)p_a][3\theta + (1-\theta)p_a]}{(1+\theta)(1+2\theta)} \qquad (1.29)$$

Heterozygotes:

$$Pr(ab|ab) = \frac{2[\theta + (1-\theta p_a][\theta + (1-\theta)p_b]}{(1+\theta)(1+2\theta)} \qquad (1.30)$$

Note that if $F_{ST} = 0$, then the two formulae give p_a^2 and $2p_ap_b$, respectively.

The extension to multiple loci is straightforward. Once the F_{ST} correction has been applied individually to each locus, the results are multiplied together to provide a probability that is conditioned on the assumption of population sub-structuring.

This approach has been very widely adopted and is standard practice. Buckleton et al. [46] have carried out the largest survey of data from 250 papers in the forensic literature. They suggest that values around 0.01–0.03 to be appropriate for the majority of "broad geographic groups", although levels of 0.01–0.02 are often used by laboratories. For more isolated groups, or those with significant inbreeding, such as Inuit or North American Indian, larger values $F_{ST} = 0.05$ are considered appropriate. In general, the effect of population sub-structure is small, especially in cosmopolitan populations, but it is good practice to incorporate the parameter into calculations, because of the valid criticism of the product rule violation if ignored.

Now, if these previously isolated sub-populations come together and they suddenly undergo random mating, then this has the effect of decreasing the homozygosity, and the heterozygosity consequently increases. Within the first generation of two sub-populations, which are fixed for allele a and b respectively, described in Table 1.11, 50% of the individuals will be heterozygote ab. With modern cosmopolitan populations, advanced communication, travel, and mobility of individuals undoubtedly act to minimize effects of sub-structuring in these populations.

Populations of interest that are typically represented in databases used by forensic scientists consist of many millions of individuals. With large populations, the frequencies of alleles tend to be stable. Within European white Caucasians, the differences between countries are relatively small. An example is provided by the European Network of Forensic Science Institutes (ENFSI) study, where F_{ST} was shown to be < 0.004 [13]. The practical impact is low within white Caucasian populations of Europe.

1.12.6.1 Extension to mixtures

The formulae from Section 1.12.6 can be expanded to calculate the genotype probability for multiple contributors, where sub-population structuring is accounted for. See Chapter 5.5.2 and Appendix A for theory and examples.

1.13. Simulation studies to show the effect of genetic drift and F_{ST} corrections

The biggest concern is that match probabilities will be under-estimated if a database is used that comprises several unknown sub-populations. It is often impractical to carry out actual sampling of such populations, but we can usefully use computer simulation to work out the practical effect in real casework.

1.13.1 Details of the experiment

The allele frequencies of the ESX17 Promega kit are used as the "starting population" (generation zero). To create the first generation, a total of 2,500 individuals or 5,000 gametes are simulated, each with specific alleles, randomly drawn so that their proportions reflect the allele frequency proportions. A total of 50 sub-populations, each with 2,500 individuals are simulated. Because of stochastic effects of random number generation, no two populations will have the same composition of alleles, hence frequencies will vary between them.

For each of these 50 sub-populations, allele frequencies are determined and recorded. Those of the "total population" are calculated from the means across all sub-populations, as described in Section 1.12.3 (the total population consists of equal numbers of each of the sub-populations). Using these allele frequencies, a new population is simulated. This process is continued until a desired F_{ST} is reached in the next generation. F_{ST} varies between loci and is generation dependent. Once achieved, the allele frequency data were stored, to be used in calculations that followed.

To demonstrate the effect of genetic drift, a sub-population was selected at random, then a genotype was selected at random using allele frequencies calculated for the same population. Next, the likelihood ratio was calculated: a) using the allele frequencies of the chosen sub-population (giving LR_a) and b) the average allele frequencies of the total population (giving LR_b). To ensure a good spread of likelihood ratios, partial profiles were simulated by choosing at random between 4–16 loci. The two LR values, LR_a and LR_b, were stored. Next, the procedure was repeated except that the total population LR_b was adjusted using the Balding/Nichols correction (Eqs. (1.23), (1.24)); no adjustment made to the reference sub-population LR_a. The whole process was repeated to choose 1000 random genotypes in total, using randomly chosen alleles from a randomly chosen sub-population: the results were plotted (Fig. 1.8).

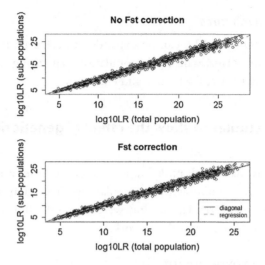

Figure 1.8 Comparison of likelihood ratios obtained without and with $F_{ST} = 0.01$ correction. The red line is the 45° diagonal ($x = y$), and the green dashed line is the calculated regression.

If data points (Fig. 1.8) fall below the red diagonal line, then the x-axis LR_b given by the total population frequency database is anti-conservative, compared to the LR_a from the sub-population of origin on the y-axis. The majority of data fall below the red diagonal ($x = y$) line when the F_{ST} correction is *not* applied. The regression line is completely below the red diagonal ($x = y$) line. In the second plot, where the Balding/Nichols correction is applied, the majority of data are above the red diagonal ($x = y$), as is the green regression line. This illustrates that the F_{ST} correction performs well in compensating for the effect of genetic drift between isolated sub-populations.

A close-up view showing $log_{10}LR = 4 - 9$ is provided in Fig. 1.9. If $LR = 10^{25}$ is misreported as $LR = 10^{30}$, it is unlikely to have much impact, since the numbers are so large and exceed an upper-reporting threshold employed by some jurisdictions, such as the UK, where an $LR > 10^9$ is not reported. However, when LRs are a few thousands or millions, then over-estimation might make a difference to jury decisions. At this level, where $F_{ST} = 0.01$, the effect of ignoring the parameter may cause an anti-conservative bias of more than an order or a magnitude. However, this is largely rectified by application of the F_{ST} correction (although, in some cases, there can still be a bias of approximately one order of magnitude). The F_{ST} correction compensates the effect of genetic drift, so that the red diagonal ($x = y$) and the regression lines are almost coincident. There will naturally be a distribution of points either side, which will be conservative and anti-conservative in equal measure.

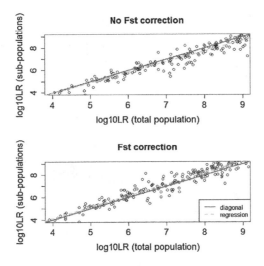

Figure 1.9 Comparison of likelihood ratios obtained without and with $F_{ST} = 0.01$ correction. $F_{ST} = 0.01$, where $log_{10}LR = 4 - 9$. The red line is the 45° diagonal ($x = y$), and the green dashed line is the calculated regression.

1.14. Sampling error correction

The anti-conservative reporting of likelihood ratios for some of the outliers in Fig. 1.9 can be compensated by introducing a sampling error correction. A typical frequency database consists of c.200–500 individuals randomly sampled. If the underlying population is resampled, then we will observe different frequency estimates for each data collection. This is known as *sampling error*: for rare alleles in a population ($p < 0.01$), there is a good chance that they will not be sampled. Eventually, during live casework, some of these missing rare alleles are encountered for the first time. Some of these alleles are extremely rare. They are collated by the NIST website: https://strbase.nist.gov/var_tab.htm. Because rare alleles are not observed in the frequency database, their notional allele frequency is $0/2n = 0$, where $n =$ no. of individuals. Zeros cannot be used in calculations. One solution is to add all alleles observed in a given casework sample into the frequency database, so this means that all observed allele frequencies are increased by $Pr = 1/2(n+1)$, so the minimum allele frequency is also $p_{min} = 1/2(n+1)$, i.e., in a database of $n = 200$ individuals $p_{min} = 0.0025$ [13]. Another method in common use introduces a minimum allele frequency of $5/2n$ [47]. There is no real consensus on any particular sampling correction that should be used (See Buckleton et al. [48], Chapter 6, for a review of methods). However, it is not a good idea to be too conservative as this may grossly understate the strength of evidence in a case. Fig. 1.10 shows that choosing an $F_{ST} = 0.02$, which is higher than the actual $F_{ST} = 0.01$ in the population, in combination with a sampling error correction of $1/2(n+1)$ performs well, with only a few anti-conservative datapoints.

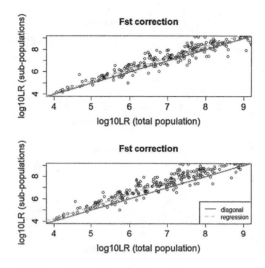

Figure 1.10 Comparison of likelihood ratios obtained with $F_{ST} = 0.01$ (upper pane) and 0.02 corrections (lower pane). A sampling error correction of 1/400 is added to each allele frequency. The red line is the 45° ($x = y$) diagonal, and the green dashed line is the calculated regression.

In cosmopolitan populations typically encountered in casework, F_{ST} is of the order $F_{ST} = 0.001$: a correction of $F_{ST} = 0.01$ along with a sampling error correction of $1/2(n + 1)$ seems to work well (Fig. 1.11, because all of the data points are coincident with or above the red diagonal [$x = y$] line).

1.15. European Network of Forensic Science Institutes (ENFSI) evaluation of STR markers

A comprehensive review of European populations was undertaken by the ENFSI group in 2011–12. This survey involved analysis of 26 different populations from across Europe, and it was carried out to support the introduction of new multiplexes that incorporated the European standard set (ESS) of twelve STR loci. The multiplexes that were evaluated as a part of this survey were Promega Powerplex ESX-16, ESX-17, and ESI-16,17 kits, and Applied Biosystems AmpFlSTR NGM.

To carry out analysis, it is first necessary to detect errors within datasets. Whereas most laboratories submitted complete genotypes, for legal (privacy) reasons, some laboratories could only submit shuffled datasets, whereby the alleles within each locus were randomly assorted. This had no effect on the allele frequencies of the dataset, but negated their inclusion in population genetics and concordance studies, since the original genotypes were unknown. The most common errors were duplication of samples, which were detected using software designed to detect duplicates and close matches that may indicate accidental inclusion of relatives. Another reason for discrepancies was

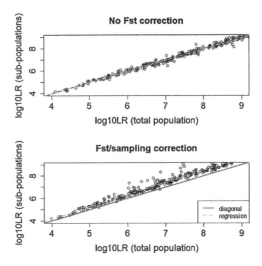

Figure 1.11 The base population $F_{ST} = 0.001$. Comparison of likelihood ratios obtained with no F_{ST} correction (upper pane) vs. $F_{ST} = 0.01$ correction and sampling correction $1/2(n+1)$, where $2n = 200$ (lower pane). The red line is the 45° diagonal ($x = y$), and the green dashed line is the calculated regression.

non-concordance between different multiplexes used. Most laboratories submitted data analyzed with two different multiplexes, hence there was an opportunity to check for differences (discordances) between them. The majority were attributed to simple transcription errors. For example, an 18.3 allele at D1S1656 typed as 18.8; a 29 allele at D21S11 typed as 20; a 22 allele at FGA typed as 12, and at amelogenin, an XX genotype was mistranscribed as XY. The total number of discordances detected represented less than 0.05% of the data. When detected, laboratories were contacted and further work carried out to verify the correct allele designations before continuing any further analysis.

The second kind of discordance occurs because of the presence of primer-binding site mutations, which are sequence differences within the primer-binding region. The primer cannot bind, and this prevents amplification of the allele. Since different kits use different primers, a mutation will be detected in one kit, but not in the other. This typically leads to one kit giving a homozygote and the other a heterozygote (Fig. 1.12).

Because genetic analyses test for excess homozygosity, it is important to resolve discordances beforehand.

1.15.1 Hardy–Weinberg tests

After the data had been "cleaned" and discrepancies resolved, Hardy–Weinberg (HW) tests were carried out for each locus within each population using freely available software, Arlequin [49], which uses a test analogous to Fisher's exact test, based on the

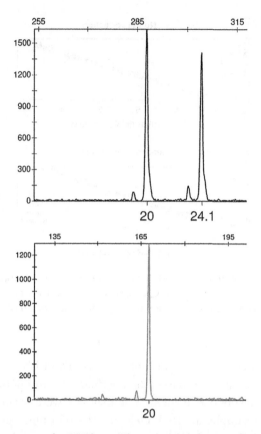

Figure 1.12 Discordance seen at the FGA locus. The top panel shows a 20, 24.1 heterozygote genotype using the ESX-17 kit. The bottom panel revealed allele 20 only, using the ESI-17 kit, since the 24.1 failed to amplify, because of a primer-binding site mutation.

algorithm outlined by Guo and Thompson [50]. Hardy–Weinberg expectations were also evaluated using genetic data analysis (GDA) software for comparison. This method is also based on Fisher's exact tests, as described by Weir [51]. Balding [52], Chapter 5, goes into detail about these tests for the interested reader. He also comments that the HW test is "not crucial for forensic work". Deviation can be attributed to sampling effect, especially if sample sizes are small. The application of the F_{ST} correction mitigates the anti-conservative effect of sub-structuring and takes account of HW deviation, because of population sub-structuring. HW tests are still recommended for practitioners to use, however, primarily because they can be used to detect genotyping errors.

1.15.2 F_{ST} estimation

Provided that populations were shown as far as possible to be error-free, they were forwarded to the next stage of testing to determine the differentiation between populations (sub-structure) as described previously (Section 1.12.5), using the GDA software [51].

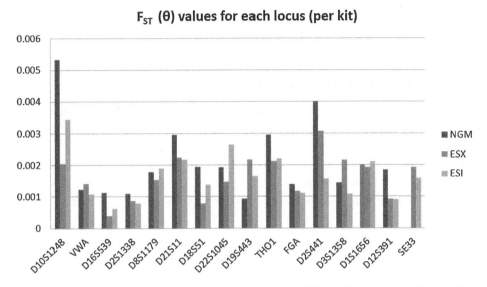

Figure 1.13 $F_{ST}(\theta)$ values for each locus using NGM, ESI, and ESX STR kits. Reprinted from [13] with permission from Elsevier.

The highest F_{ST} observed was 0.005 (NGM, D10S1248). All other F_{ST} values were less than 0.004 (Fig. 1.13). The NRC report [53] published in 1996 recommended the use of F_{ST} correction $= 0.01$ and 0.03 for smaller isolated populations. Application of the Nichols and Balding $F_{ST} = 0.01$ correction, along with a sampling correction is conservative (Fig. 1.11) for population groups, where the underlying F_{ST} is around 0.001. It is recommended that local population databases are collected for given jurisdictions, but it is also possible to use a combined European database for white Caucasian individuals [13], so long as an F_{ST} correction is applied to take account of the sub-population allele diversity.

1.15.3 What F_{ST} to apply in casework?

Forensic databases are typically collected from local geographical populations subdivided according to their geographical ancestry. The criteria are typically broad-brush. For example, in the UK, white Caucasian databases are collected from individuals across the entire country; databases labeled as "Asian" or "Chinese" may have broad ancestry originating from entire continents. The ENFSI study showed that across Europe, sub-structuring measured by F_{ST} was generally less than 0.004, and this has a relatively small effect. However, if the suspect and the alternative perpetrator originate from a sub-population that is not represented by the forensic database collection, then F_{ST} may be under-estimated. Balding [52], page 97, suggests that values of $F_{ST} = 0.02$ should be used in large well-mixed populations, 0.03 for large minority groups, and 0.05 for small minority groups. If perpetrator and suspect are not from the same sub-population, then a smaller value of 0.01 is justified, since they will have little coancestry. Buckleton et al. [46] advise similar ranges to use in casework based on a large survey.

1.16. Relatedness: kinship analysis

The value of the evidence is critically dependent upon the propositions that are put forward by the defense and the prosecution. If these arguments are altered in any way, then the likelihood ratio is also altered and recalculation is required.

This issue of relatedness was first discussed by Ian Evett in 1991 [54], and the following is adapted from that paper.

Consider a crime stain with only a single contributor so that the competing propositions are:

H_p: The DNA is from Mr. S.
H_d: The DNA is from an individual who is unrelated to Mr. S.

With a single contributor, with no ambiguity in the evidence and reference profiles, the calculation of the value of the evidence is straightforward. The numerator, $Pr(E|H_p) = 1$. Ian Evett then asks:

"What is the denominator? This is the probability of the observed crime-stain type if someone else had left it. The problem is what we mean by "someone else". It is recognized that there is no burden on the defense to provide any details of this alternative scenario, and so, in the absence of any other information, it is universal convention to consider this hypothetical alternative person as one selected at random from the population...Given these conditions, the likelihood ratio is therefore the inverse of the observed relative frequency of the type of the crime stain. The relationship in this case is a simple one, though it is important to remember that in other situations it may not be nearly so simple."

Ian Evett continues his exposition (now paraphrasing): It may be suggested that the alternative defense proposition is that the alternative explanation is that a sibling (for example) could have left the stain-material. The propositions that form the likelihood ratio have now changed to the following:

H_p: The DNA is from Mr. S.
H_d: The DNA is from a sibling of Mr. S.

1.16.1 Effect of relatedness on the likelihood ratio calculation

If we take a simple example, where there are two alleles denoted a and b at a locus, where their respective probabilities are p_a and p_b in a relevant population have been ascertained to be 1% each (to make the point that it is assumed they are both rare alleles), then the likelihood ratio calculation, assuming that the DNA under H_d is from an unrelated individual, then the LR is calculated as follows:

$$LR = \frac{1}{2 \times p_a p_b} \tag{1.31}$$

$$LR = \frac{1}{2 \times 0.01 \times 0.01} \tag{1.32}$$

$$LR = 10,000 \tag{1.33}$$

However, if the propositions are changed to

H_p: The DNA is from Mr. S.
H_d: The DNA is from a sibling of Mr. S.

Because there is a 50% probability that a sibling will inherit a given allele from a given parent, the likelihood ratio is calculated[9]:

$$LR \approx \frac{1}{0.5 \times 0.5} \tag{1.34}$$

$$LR \approx 4 \tag{1.35}$$

This change in the likelihood ratio from $LR = 10,000$ to $LR = 4$ may seem to be surprising, but it is simply a reflection of the fact that if the propositions are changed, we will get different answers, and the differences can be dramatic.

For further examples, e.g., parent/child/cousin relationships, see Chapter 5.5.4, Chapter 5 for comprehensive details, and Appendix A.2 for relatedness (kinship) formulae.

1.16.2 Formal treatment and extension to mixtures

A comprehensive list of kinship analysis programs can be found at http://www.cstl.nist.gov/strbase/kinship.htm. A classic example of kinship analysis is paternity testing; other uses include the identification of missing persons and disaster victim identification. When mixtures are considered, where the contributors are believed to be related, propositions of the following type may be considered:

H_p: The evidence is a mixture of the victim and her untyped grandfather.
H_d: The evidence is a mixture of the victim and an unknown, unrelated individual.

Another type of scenario involves mixtures, where someone related to the questioned contributor is considered as an alternative contributor:

H_p: The evidence is a mixture of the victim and a suspect.

H_d: The evidence is a mixture of the victim and an untyped brother of the suspect.

Common to both scenarios is that one of the relatives is untyped. Fung and Hu [55] have derived kinship coefficients for cases with pairwise relationships like the two examples above. However, when there are more than two related contributors involved, another approach must be taken. In Egeland et al. [56] (which includes information on open software implementation), the problem of mixtures with related contributors was treated in generality with the use of pedigrees to describe relationships. This approach also allows for different family relationships to be specified under the opposing propositions, such as the following:

H_p: The evidence is a mixture of two typed individuals, who are siblings, and their untyped brother.
H_d: The evidence is a mixture of two typed individuals, who are half siblings, and their untyped father.

The open-source package *relMix* [57] https://cran.r-project.org/web/packages/relMix/index.html is able to calculate the *LR*s from propositions that describe multiple related contributors, such as those given above. The software is similar to *LRmix Studio*, so that it cannot use allele peak heights or stutter in the model. But it incorporates drop-out.

It is not so difficult to model relationships between pairs of individuals, and this has been implemented in the programs *likeLTD* [58], *TrueAllele* [59] and *STRmix* [60], see Table 3 in Steele and Balding [61].

The later versions of the probabilistic genotyping software *LRmix Studio* (Chapter 6) and *EuroForMix* (Chapter 8) now support the possibility to specify that one of the unknown contributors under H_d is related to an individual having a known genotype. This kind of specification is very useful to evaluate propositions, such as "a sibling of the suspect is a contributor the evidence". Other relationships would typically be parent-child, uncle/aunt-nephew/niece, 1st-order cousins, grandparent-grandchild, half-siblings, etc.

The correction to take relatedness into account is carried out by adjusting the genotype probabilities of the unknowns; the other parts of the model remain the same. In the previous section it was shown how F_{ST}-correction can be implemented to take into account sub-structuring of the allele frequencies. The additional information that an unknown individual is related to a specific known individual introduces further restrictions on the genotype probabilities.

Once the relatedness-formula has been applied for one unknown contributor, it is easy to extend to multiple unknown contributors as before (Chapter 5.5.4), since these are assumed to be be unrelated to all other contributors.

1.17. A brief introduction to the software approaches used to interpret mixtures

The different models used for mixture interpretation are typically classified into three groups:

I   Binary models
II Qualitative, or semi-continuous models
III Quantitative, or continuous models

Binary models are described in Chapter 2.3. Empirical methods employing heterozygote balance and mixture proportions were used to either discard or select genotype combinations to calculate the value of the evidence. *LoCIM-tool* (Chapter 10.2) is an empirical method used to infer major contributor genotypes. Binary models are generally not suited to mixtures with more than two contributors or low template profiles.

In qualitative (semi-continuous) models, peak heights may be used to inform the model parameters in an informal way (e.g., if there are distinct major/minor contributors to a mixture), otherwise peak heights are ignored. They can be used with multiple contributors and low template DNA. In contrast, quantitative (continuous) models incorporate peak heights fully, and can include stutters, because they utilize more information, they are the most powerful methods available.

The classical models labeled as I are described in detail in Chapter 2.3 and by Buckleton et al. [48], pp. 231–253, whereas Steele and Balding [61] review software with emphasis on models II and III. Coble and Bright [62] also provide a useful historical overview of probabilistic genotyping methods and provide a list of software. Chapters 5 and 6 discuss the theory and practice of qualitative (semi-continuous) models in detail; Chapters 7 and 8 describe the quantitative (continuous) theory and practice.

In general, when it comes to statistical evaluation of forensic DNA samples, there are two main approaches: the *LR* approach, or calculation of the probability of exclusion (PE), or its converse, the probability of inclusion (PI), also termed random man not excluded (RMNE). The latter is discussed in some detail in Chapter 11.

The preferred approach, according to the ISFG DNA commission [63], is to calculate the likelihood ratio (*LR*). However, whereas the computation of summary statistics, such as the RMNE, is straightforward, the complexity of likelihood ratios requires the use of specialized software to analyze complex DNA profiles. Although the theory to support the use of *LR*s has been available for several years [64–66], the introduction was slow, but is now gaining momentum.

A number of software, dedicated to the interpretation of low template DNA mixtures, have been introduced over the last decade [67,68,59,60,69,70]. These software are anchored in a likelihood-ratio framework, but they all use different probabilistic models, and rely on different distributional assumptions (see Steele and Balding [61] for a review). Table 1.13 gives an overview of some of the available software (either open-source or commercial), and Table 1.14 further describes the different approaches for mixture interpretation.

Table 1.13 Summary of some of the available mixture interpretation software.

Software	Approach	License	Ref
CeesIT	Continuous	(a)	[73]
DNAmixtures	Continuous	Open-source[b]	[74]
DNAStatistX	Continuous	Open-source	[75]
DNA-view mixture solution	Continuous	Commercial	(c)
eDNA	Continuous	(d)	(d)
EuroForMix	Continuous	Open-source	[76]
Genoproof	Continuous	Commercial	[77]
Kongoh	Continuous	Open-source	[78]
Lab Retriever	Semi-continuous	Open-source	[79]
LikeLTD v.6	Continuous[e]	Open-source	[80]
LiRa	Semi-continuous/continuous[f]	Commercial	[69]
LoCIM-tool	Empirical	Open-source	[81]
LRmix/LRmix Studio	Semi-continuous	Open-source	[68]
MaSTR	Continuous	Commercial	[82]
STRmix	Continuous	Commercial	[60]
TrueAllele	Continuous	Commercial	[83]

(a) *Ceesit* license is "no cost to local, state and federal forensic DNA laboratories or entities pursuing research, forensic validation or education for non-commercial purposes" but a full license is required for commercial use;

(b) *DNAmixtures* is a free of charge open-source R package, however it requires the HUGIN commercial software to run;

(c) *DNA-view*: http://dna-view.com/ and http://dna-view.com/downloads/Mixture%20Solution% 20poster.pdf;

(d) *eDNA*: http://ednalims.com/probabilistic-genotyping/. Freely available web-based software available to consortium members. Bullet uses *LRmix* and Bulletproof uses *EuroForMix*. Each program has a custom built graphical user interface;

(e) *LikeLTD* also has a semi-continuous model [84];

(f) *LiRaHT* is available as a continuous model: https://cdnmedia.eurofins.com/european-west/media/1418957/lgc_lira_fact_sheet_en_0815_90.pdf.

Of the continuous models listed in Table 1.13, *DNAmixtures, DNAView Mixture Solution, DNAStatistX, LikeLTD, LiRaHT,* and *EuroForMix* are all anchored in the gamma model (Chapter 7), but there are differences between all encoded software assumptions. *CEESIt* uses a normal distribution. *Kongoh* estimates peak height distributions by using the Monte Carlo simulation based on experimental data to consider allele- or locus-specific effects. *STRmix* and *TrueAllele* are both commercial solutions, based on a Bayesian approach through specifying prior distributions on the unknown model parameters. They use Markov chain Monte Carlo (MCMC) methods [71,72] to calculate marginalized likelihood expressions by simultaneously sampling over the discrete set

Table 1.14 Advantages and disadvantages of the main interpretation approaches. Reproduced from [85] with permission from Elsevier.

Model	Advantages	Disadvantages
Binary	Easy to use and to implement	Cannot be used for LT DNA
Qualitative (Semi-continuous)	Can be used for LTDNA Makes fewer assumptions than continuous models	Model-parameters have to be estimated Does not make use of peak heights Implementation requires specialised software
Quantitative (Continuous)	Make use of peak heights Can be used for LTDNA	Numerous parameters need to be estimated Implementation requires specialised software Require calibration for different STR kits and different conditions (e.g. PCR cycle no.)
Empirical	Simple to implement in casework	Require calibration for different STR kits and different conditions (e.g. PCR cycle no.) Can only be used to extract major profiles Cannot be used for weight of the evidence

of genotypes for the unknown contributors specified in the model and the unknown parameters. *MaSTR* and *GenoProof Mixture* also employ MCMC in their calculations.

1.18. Summary

The application of DNA analysis to forensic casework in 1985 transformed the field. The variability of individual loci was much greater than that found with conventional protein-coding loci that were utilized pre-1985. From the inception, it took another decade to develop multiplexed short tandem repeat (STR) loci that were to form the backbone of national DNA databases. The main challenge was to standardize loci that were in common between different jurisdictions, so that cross-border comparisons of data could be facilitated. These efforts have largely been successful. To date there have been several iterations to develop sets of standard loci, largely driven by European and North American laboratories. Current multiplex systems accommodate at least 16 loci, and some systems have more than 20 loci. Innovations in biochemistry have made these changes possible.

The interpretation of evidence is rooted in population genetics theory. The fundamental principle that underpins this is the Hardy–Weinberg equilibrium. The inheritance of genes follows laws of probability that enable probability estimates to describe the "rarity" of a DNA profile. Such calculations rely upon the Hardy–Weinberg equilibrium assumption of "independence", i.e., that populations are very large, randomly interspersed, and randomly mating. However, such assumptions are rarely justified—populations are structured into "sub-populations"; the frequencies of their alleles differ. To compensate, the F_{ST} statistic is used as a measure of population differentiation due to population structure, and this parameter is used to correct strength of evidence calculations so that they are not anti-conservative. It is routine practice for laboratories to carry out population surveys so that the reference database is relevant to a given local population. There are initiatives to collate such data to provide community databases that can be accessed, for example, STRidER acts as a platform that is used as a repository that is subject to rigorous quality control before release.

The likelihood ratio (*LR*) is fundamental to all aspects of interpretation of forensic evidence. The calculation of the *LR* is a comparison of two alternative propositions (usually one is put forward by the defense and the other by the prosecution). The probability of the evidence is calculated for each proposition, and the values are compared by dividing one value by the other to give an indication of the "strength of the evidence" in favour of a given proposition.

Likelihood ratios are very flexible. In particular, they can be used to evaluate DNA mixtures, which are the subject of much of the material to be found in subsequent chapters. The early genetics theory applied to mixtures is described, limited to two-contributors. The calculations are very complex. The need for computer algorithms to take over the burden of calculation are described, and there is a demonstration of the principle of extension of multiple contributors. A list of software available to carry out analysis of mixtures is provided. Finally, extension of the theory to relatedness (kinship) tests is introduced.

Notes

1. This is an oversimplification since there are several sub-types of A, O, B so that in total there are six alleles that are common in the human population. In addition there are numerous rare alleles that will be sometimes be encountered. The list of alleles must be continually updated to ensure that the 'inclusivity' rule is not violated.
2. Note that the reverse sequence is listed in STRBase.
3. STRBase https://strbase.nist.gov/STRseq.htm reports such an example with TPOX where a deletion in the flanking region converted an 11 allele to a 10.3 allele. The visualisation depended on the multiplex kit used. Whereas PowerPlex 1.1 and Identifiler were unaffected, PowerPlex 2.1 and PowerPlex 16 products were affected because the primer binding sites were further away from the repeat structure.
4. See Section 1.5 for explanation of the conditional bar, |, used in this formula.
5. The term 'match' must not be confused with 'identity'. This is not the intention as we don't know if the two alleles have originated from the suspect.
6. It is necessary here to condition on an absolute number of contributors. Later, it may be necessary to evaluate the strength of evidence if three (or more) contributors are proposed. There should be some dialogue between prosecution and defense to agree this point.
7. The words *if* and *given* are both conditioning terms that are interchangeable.
8. This number is very small as we consider just one locus here.
9. Note that this formula is a simplification that ignores the allele frequencies. The exact equation is: $LR = \frac{4}{1+p_a+p_b+2p_ap_b}$.

CHAPTER 2

Empirical characterization of DNA profiles

To interpret results, it is necessary to characterize loci by their key features, namely heterozygote peak balance, inter-locus balance, stutter ratio, and the stochastic threshold. See validation recommendations of the "Scientific Working Group on DNA Analysis Methods (SWGDAM)" [86] and European Network of Forensic Science Institutes (ENFSI) DNA working group guidelines [87].

2.1. Heterozygote balance

There is considerable information in peak heights, which are used to interpret mixtures. But before we can do this, it is necessary to understand the characteristics and behavior of profiles that are from single individuals. In this respect, the characterization of heterozygote peak balance is vital.

2.1.1 Peak height or peak area

The electropherogram representation of an allele can be quantified either in terms of its area, or height. In principle, it does not matter which is used, so long as there is consistency. However, the current universal practice is to use peak height.

2.1.2 Definitions

There are two common definitions of heterozygote balance: the high molecular weight allele peak height divided by the low molecular weight allele peak height (Eq. (2.1)) [88–90] (the converse may also be used [91,92]). The alternative method (Eq. (2.2)) calculates the smaller peak height divided by the larger peak height (irrespective of molecular weight of the allele) [93–97]:

$$H_b' = \frac{\phi_{HMW}}{\phi_{LMW}} \tag{2.1}$$

$$H_b = \frac{\phi_{smaller}}{\phi_{larger}} \tag{2.2}$$

where ϕ is the peak height; HMW and LMW refer to the high and low molecular weight allele, respectively; $\phi_{smaller}$ and ϕ_{larger} represent the smaller and larger peak heights in RFU. Whereas H_b' can assume any value, H_b is restricted to values that are always ≤ 1.

Forensic Practitioner's Guide to the Interpretation of Complex DNA Profiles
https://doi.org/10.1016/B978-0-12-820562-4.00010-9

Copyright © 2020 Elsevier Inc.
All rights reserved. **55**

Eq. (2.2) has been criticized as wasting information about the ordering of the alleles [88,98], but is often used for pragmatic simplicity. Both formulae ignore the repeat number difference between alleles.

2.1.3 Methods to visualize data

There are a number of different ways to visualize data, showing the distribution of heterozygote balance. Box-whisker plots were used by [91] (Fig. 2.1). These plots are easily generated using the R package *strvalidator*, which is available, along with a user manual and tutorials at https://sites.google.com/site/forensicapps/strvalidator.

The data are divided into quartiles. The box contains 50% of the data. The line down the middle of the box is the median (the 50 percentile), and the edges of the box represent the second and third quartiles, respectively, (or they can be called the 25 and 75 percentiles). The first and fourth quartiles are represented by the whiskers, and the outliers are points shown as dots that are outside the main body of the distribution.

Underneath the box-plot, an alternative representation is the scatter plot that includes the peak height on the y-axis. A comparison of the two plots shows the outliers correspond to alleles with very low peak heights, whereas the main body of the data is delineated by the whiskers in the box plot.

The third method is the histogram, where the frequency of data are represented by the y-axis.

2.1.4 The use of guidelines

Analyses of data using methods outlined above have shown that, for good quality profiles, the heterozygote balance tends to fall within limits. Pragmatic guidelines of $0.6 < H'_b < 1.6$ (Eq. (2.1)) and $H_b \geq 0.60$ (Eq. (2.2)) have generally been adopted as a loose definition of a good quality profile with balanced heterozygote alleles. However, primer-binding site (Fig. 1.12) and somatic mutations can produce outliers. There is a direct relationship between quantity of DNA and allele peak height. Consequently, as the average peak height decreases, the variance of heterozygote balance increases [99,100] (Fig. 2.2), and this results in extreme values, where $H_b < 0.6$, i.e., heterozygotes are said to be *imbalanced*. This imbalance is a feature that is expected as allele peak heights approach the "stochastic threshold" discussed in Chapter 3.2. Indeed, it can be so extreme that an allele may completely fail to amplify, and this is known as "allele drop-out". Consequently $H_b \approx 0$ [88,101].

Notice in Fig. 2.1 that the median (50 percentile) is slightly displaced, so $H'_b < 1.0$. This means that shorter DNA fragments are preferentially amplified as the PCR is more efficient. The effect is that peak height decreases as the length of the amplified DNA fragment increases. Sample inhibition and degradation is common in casework samples,

Empirical characterization of DNA profiles   57

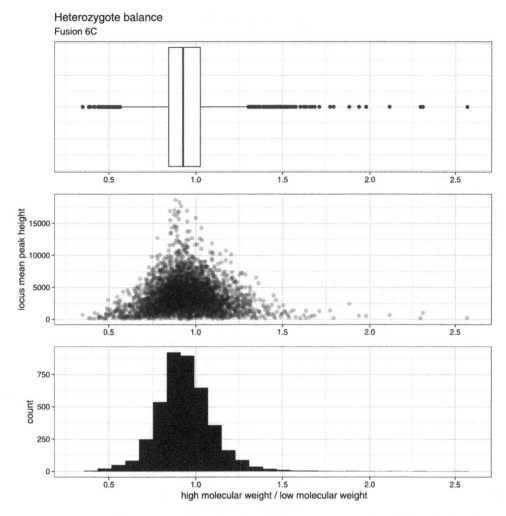

Figure 2.1 An example comparing data using three different representations: a) Box-whisker plot at the top; b) A scatter plot in the middle; c) A histogram in the bottom panel. The x-axis represents the H'_b method of calculation. The y-axis in the scatter plot is the mean peak height of the two alleles. Note that the peak imbalance increase as they get smaller. The y-axis in the histogram shows counts in each bin. Note that extreme imbalance is rare.

so that high molecular weight alleles may drop-out completely. Tvedebrink et al. [89] showed a significant relationship between the difference in repeat units and the heterozygote balance in roughly half of the loci tested using two different kits. Kelly et al. [88] found that for each unit increase in repeat difference, the natural logarithm of the heterozygote peak balance $log_e(H'_b)$ decreased by 3% on average. Leclair et al. [102] observed reduced median values and higher variability in casework samples compared

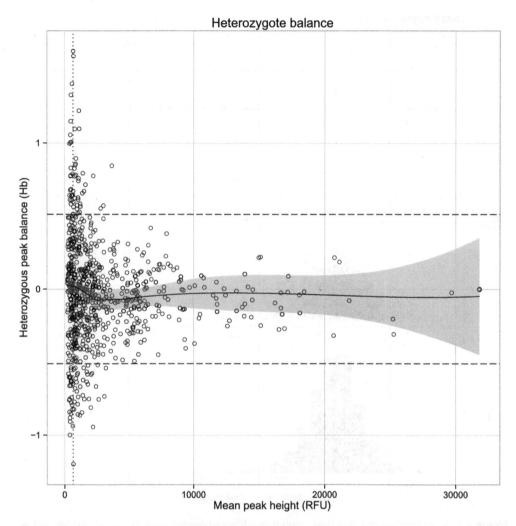

Figure 2.2 Data generated from AB3500xl analyzer. Plot of average peak height vs. natural logarithm of H_b (764 data-points), showing increased variance as the stochastic threshold ($T = 634$ RFU) is approached (vertical dotted line). Data are the same used for the drop-out plot in Fig. 3.10, except that data below the analytical threshold $AT = 200$ RFU have been removed. The two horizontal dashed lines are the 0.6 H_b guideline that is used to interpret conventional DNA profiles. The y-axis is the natural logarithm of H_b to achieve symmetry. Analysis of data carried out using the heterozygote balance module of R package *strvalidator* (version 1.3), plot created using *ggplot2* (version 1.0) with the default loess regression smoothing. Reproduced from [85] with permission from Elsevier.

to reference database samples, where the latter were higher quality. The phenomenon of more efficient amplification of low molecular weight DNA is closely related to "degradation", described in Chapter 4.5.

Empirical characterization of DNA profiles 59

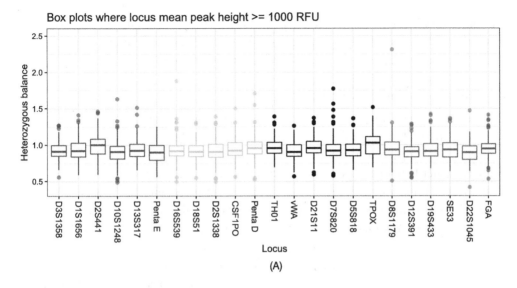

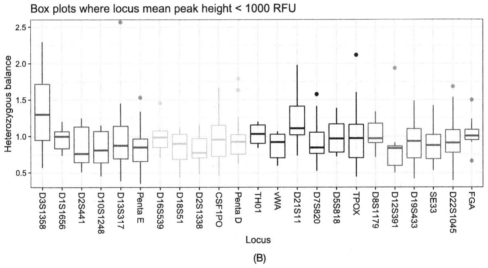

Figure 2.3 A comparison of heterozygotes from 23 loci of Fusion 6C showing the distributions of heterozygote balance using the H'_b method of calculation. The ranges for the bottom panel (B) are much greater than the top panel (A).

Because heterozygote balance is essentially a product of the relative numbers of molecules that are randomly pipetted into the PCR mix (Chapter 3.1), it is not surprising to find that no locus dependencies have been observed [88]. There is no effect of using different genetic analyzers of the same or different models [101,103,93], or using different multiplex systems [90,89,93]. Furthermore, it has been shown that the

60 Forensic Practitioner's Guide to the Interpretation of Complex DNA Profiles

distributions of heterozygote balance for mixed and non-mixed stains for casework and artificial samples, created using pristine (extracted) DNA, are very similar [104]. So this means that such studies can be used to aid the interpretation of mixtures.

2.1.5 Heterozygote balance summary

1. For high quality DNA, it is unusual to observe an imbalance of heterozygotes, where the peak height of the allele having the lowest signal is less than 60% of the size of its companion (the allele that has the largest signal). This guideline is useful to interpret DNA profiles that are well represented (Fig. 2.3).
2. However, imbalance will be observed as the mean peak height decreases. The peak height is associated with DNA quantity so that imbalance is observed with "low-template" DNA, which is discussed in detail in Chapter 4. In fact, the allele may be missing altogether, allele drop-out; this is discussed in detail in Chapter 3. The 60% guideline therefore has limitations. Its use is with well-represented DNA profiles, where the quantity is sufficient, so that the phenomena associated with low-template DNA are not an issue.
3. Amplification of high molecular weight alleles is less efficient than low molecular weight alleles; this is why the median $H'_b < 1$.

2.1.6 Characterization of heterozygote balance with *STR-validator*

STR-validator has a module to characterize heterozygote balance (Fig. 2.3). The samples amplified should be single source and could target the optimal amount of input DNA, or be of varying amounts. Begin with analyzing the samples in a genotyping software, e.g., GeneMapperID-X. The "genotypes table" or equivalent is exported as a text file. The exported file must contain information about sample names, marker names, dyes, allele designations, and allele peak heights. Start R and load the *strvalidator* package with the command *library(strvalidator)*. Open its graphical user interface with the command *strvalidator()*. Import the data from the *Workspace* tab using the *Import* button. Perform the characterization following the steps outlined below:

1. Select the *Balance* tab, and click the button *Calculate* intra-locus balance (heterozygote balance) located in the *intra-locus and inter-locus balance* group. The *calculate heterozygote balance* window opens (Fig. 2.4).
2. Select the dataset containing the imported sample data in the first drop-down menu. The kit used is automatically suggested, and will be the default kit when plotting the result.
3. Select the reference dataset containing the known profiles in the second drop-down menu.
4. There are two pre-processing options to remove sex markers and quality sensors from the data before analysis.

5. Select the preferred definition of heterozygote balance in the drop-down menu *Define Hb as*. Available options are *High molecular weight / low molecular weight*, *Low molecular weight / high molecular weight*, *Smaller peak / larger peak*.
6. There are checkboxes that control matching of sample names from the reference dataset to sample names in the dataset to be analyzed. Use the *check subsetting* button to verify correct settings.
7. The post-processing option *Calculate average peak height* calculates for each sample the average peak height, the total peak height, the number of observed and expected peaks, and the profile proportion. Unchecking this option will reduce the computation time.
8. Click the *Calculate* button to proceed with the analysis. The window closes when finished. Process information is written to the R console. The result is a data table that for each sample contains the sample name, marker name, dye, the difference in repeat units between the two alleles, their peak heights, marker mean peak height, and the heterozygote balance.

Figure 2.4 Screenshot from *STR-validator* showing options for the calculation of heterozygote balance.

The resulting table can be used to calculate summary statistics using the *summarize* button. It is possible to specify the quantile to be calculated with a spin button and a radio button toggles the calculation of global statistics across all markers, or locus (marker) specific statistics. The result is a data table with marker names (only the latter case), number of heterozygote values summarized (n), minimum and maximum values, the mean and standard deviation, and the result of the specified quantile.

There are various plots that can be created using the result table. The window is opened by the *Plot* button. It is possible to customize the plot title, the x and y axis titles, and the visual appearance and layout. Values can be transformed into natural logarithms. The heterozygote balance can be plotted against the mean locus peak height, the average profile peak height, by the difference in repeat units, or by marker (exemplified in Fig. 2.3). Plots can be exported as images, or *ggplot* objects that can be modified manually in R.

2.2. Stutters

Stutter peaks complicate DNA mixture interpretation and are therefore important to characterize [105]; low-level alleles may be confused with stutters. Stutters are artefacts caused by mispairing of the DNA strands during the PCR [106]. The phenomenon is often referred to as the "strand slippage model" or "slipped strand mispairing/displacement model" (Fig. 2.5), and is a natural mechanism for DNA sequence evolution [107]. Stutters appear as smaller peaks that are usually shorter ($n-1$ repeat unit) than the original parent allele (otherwise known as backward stutter) [108,105,109], or they can be longer by $n+1$ [110,111], and these are known as forward stutter. Bright et al. [112] characterize forward stutters as being much rarer than backward stutter, and the stutter ratio much lower (average was < 4%). Double backward/forward (complex) stutters ($n \pm 2$ repeats) can also be observed, but these are much lower in intensity compared to the common $n-1$ form. Dimeric STRs are particularly prone to multiple stutters [113], to the extent that they would render interpretation to be particularly problematic for forensic use, hence this is why they were never used in casework. Tetrameric and pentameric STRs were adopted instead, as these stutter much less than dimerics.

2.2.1 Characterization of stutters

Stutters are always much smaller than the parent allele. Stutter peak size is characterized by the stutter ratio (S_R), or less commonly the stutter proportion (S_x),

$$S_R = \frac{\phi_S}{\phi_A} \tag{2.3}$$

$$S_x = \frac{\phi_S}{(\phi_A + \phi_S)} \tag{2.4}$$

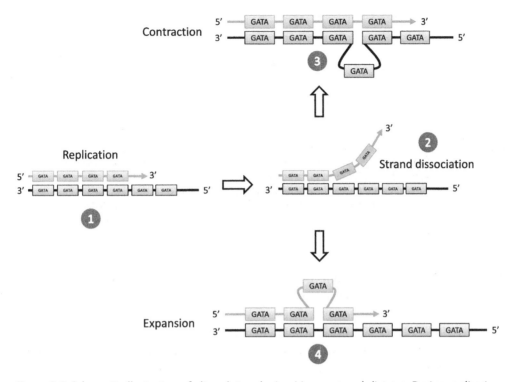

Figure 2.5 Schematic illustration of *slipped-strand mispairing* or *strand slippage*. During replication, the DNA sequences are associated, and the DNA polymerase can recognize and bind to the 3' end of the DNA strand, allowing it to synthesize an identical complementary copy (1). Sometimes the strands will dissociate, the DNA polymerase complex falls off, and replication stops (2). When the two DNA strands pair up again, they will align correctly most of the time (1). Sometimes, because of the repeated sequences (GATA), the strand will mispair to create a shorter "copy" (3) or more rarely a longer copy (4). These faulty copies are called *stutters* in general, and *backward stutter* (3) and *forward stutter* (4) in particular. The direction of the DNA strands is denoted 5' and 3'. Reproduced from [114].

where ϕ_S is the height of the stutter peak, and ϕ_A is the height of the parent allelic peak.

2.2.2 Effect of number of STR repeats on the stutter size

The general trend is that increased stutter is observed with increasing number of repeats for the parent allele [89,102,97,111,117]. However, there are microvariant alleles (e.g., alleles 15.3, 16.3, 17.3 in D1S1656 and 9.3, 10.3 in TH01), and sequence variants (e.g., in SE33) interrupting the number of consecutive repeats of the same type. Fig. 2.6 shows stutter ratios for two markers from the Fusion 6C kit. Marker D1S1656 shows two parallel trends, one for normal variants and one for microvariants. The x.3 alleles arise from a TGA insertion typically found after four full TAGA repeats [2].

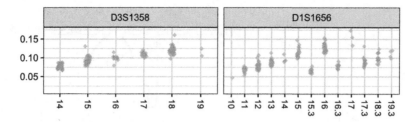

Figure 2.6 Backward stutter data for markers D3S1358 and D1S1656 for the Fusion 6C kit. The example shows that stutter ratios (y-axis) increase by increasing number of repeats (x-axis). Marker D1S1656 show two parallel trends, one for normal variants and one for microvariants. The x.3 alleles arise from a TGA insertion, typically after four full TAGA repeats [115]. This insertion interrupts the uniform repeat stretch, and the observed stutter ratios of the microvariants are comparable to alleles four repeats shorter, i.e., 11 and 15.3 stutters are approximately the same. *Illustration: cropped plot created using STR-validator* [116]. Reproduced from [114].

This insertion interrupts the uniform repeat stretch, and the observed stutter ratios of these microvariants are comparable to alleles four repeats shorter, i.e., the 11 and 15.3 stutters are approximately equivalent. Consequently, the longest uninterrupted repeat stretch (LUS) is a better predictor than the total number of repeats [89,118,106,119]. In a clever and highly controlled study using synthetic STR fragments, Brookes et al. [120] confirmed these findings. Furthermore, they showed that high content of the base pair AT in the synthetic fragments increased the stutter ratio. This is explained by the lower bond strength: there are two hydrogen bonds in an AT base pair compared to three in a GC base pair. However, the finding was contradicted by analysis of reference data. Nevertheless, it is well established that the repeat sequence is important and that the degree of stutter formation differ between loci [102,97,111].

Taylor et al. [121] noted that the LUS model poorly explained stutter ratios of SE33. A better model, termed "the multi-sequence model" was devised, where all repeat sequences were considered as contributing to stutter, after subtracting a factor of x repeats, which is defined as "the number of repeats before stuttering begins". This system does not differentiate between repeats, it considers them as a whole.

The stutter ratio is also affected by the size of the repeat unit, hence the trinucleotide repeat locus D22S1045 is expected to show higher stutter ratios than tetranucleotide repeat loci [111]. The lower levels of forward stutters compared to backward stutters may be caused by structural limitations within the *Taq* enzyme, or the higher energy requirement for a forward shift to occur [113]. Leclair et al. [102] found similar stutter ratios in casework and database samples. Optimizing PCR conditions by lowering the annealing and extension temperatures has been shown to decrease the heights of stutter peaks [122]. At low template levels, the stutter ratio gradually increased as the peak height of the parent allele decreased towards the analytical threshold (AT). This can be explained by the additive effect of stutter with background noise peaks [89,102].

Mixture interpretation becomes more difficult when stutters need to be considered [105], especially when a person's contribution is similar in height to stutters of a major contributor; it is difficult to differentiate stutters from true alleles with absolute certainty. However, by using massively parallel sequencing (MPS) systems instead of current standard length based CE systems (Chapter 13.11), it is sometimes possible to distinguish the difference, because of sequence variations [123].

2.2.3 Interpretation challenges with stutters

Considerable efforts have been made to model stutter characteristics. [89,118,109]. Simulations of stutter formation were demonstrated by Gill et al. [124] and Weusten et al. [125]. Stutters complicate mixture interpretation.

For single source profiles, there is no complication from stutters, because the major allele is always much larger in peak height, and they can be safely discounted. This is not necessarily the case when mixtures are examined, because the allele peaks belonging to minor contributors may be similar in heights to stutters, which means that they cannot be easily distinguished (Fig. 2.7).

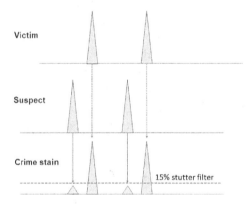

Figure 2.7 Illustration of a mixture of victim with a suspect. Under the prosecution proposition, the suspect has contributed the two minor alleles in the crime stain. If these are in stutter positions of the major contributor (victim), then the defense proposition will be that they are stutters. They could also be a combination of allele and stutter. If a stutter filter is applied, then both minor alleles will be removed from the EPG.

2.2.3.1 Filters applied by software

Software, such as open-source OSIRIS https://www.ncbi.nlm.nih.gov/osiris/ and commercial GenemarkerHID https://softgenetics.com/, have filters that can be set to flag heterozygote imbalance using the 60% guideline discussed in Section 2.1.4. Stutter filters can be customized to remove stutter from the electropherogram. Stutter positions $n-1, n-2, n+1$ can be accommodated. For example, a global filter (e.g., 15% of the

66 Forensic Practitioner's Guide to the Interpretation of Complex DNA Profiles

parent allele) can be set for all $n-1$ stutters, but it is also possible, and preferable, to set the filters per locus (since different loci have different propensity to stutter). Allele specific filters can be used to account for reduced stutter expected for $x.3$ microvariants in loci, such as D1S1656 (Fig. 2.6). In general, stutter filters are set to capture peaks that are $\pm$3SDs above the mean expected S_R (Eq. (2.3)).

2.2.4 Stutters summary

Stutters associated with tetrameric STRs have the following characteristics:

1. The most common and pronounced stutter is one repeat unit ($n-1$) shorter than the parental allele. These are known as simple backward-stutters.
   a. Backward stutters commonly have a 95th percentile $S_R \leq 0.15$ (Eq. (2.3)) [97, 108].
   b. Stochastic effects, especially associated with low-template samples, can produce outliers. In addition, somatic mutations are often found in stutter positions, and this may contribute to abnormally high peaks [126,127]. These effects can be investigated by replicate studies to determine if they are reproducible.
2. Simple forward stutters are one repeat unit ($n+1$) greater than the parent allele.
   a. They are usually much smaller than simple back-stutters.
3. Complex stutters can be both backward ($n-2$) or more repeat units and forward ($n+2$) or more repeat units. Intermediate stutters may be observed at some loci (e.g., two base-pairs shorter in D1S1656 and SE33), but to a much lesser extent —these complex stutters are observed with high signals, where samples may be over-amplified [90,100,128,117,129].
   a. Complex stutters are much lower in peak height compared to simple backward and forward stutters.
   b. Software can be used to filter stutters from EPGs. These filters can use global parameters, or can be customized per marker (in some software even per marker and allele).
4. Often stutters will appear in pairs if the genotype is heterozygote (one for each allele).
5. They may appear below the threshold of detection limit.
6. There is a tendency for stutter ratios to increase relative to the number of longest uninterrupted repeat sequences (LUS).

2.2.5 Characterization of stutters with *STR-validator*

STR-validator has a module to characterize stutters. The samples amplified should be single-sourced, and could either target the optimal amount of input DNA or be of varying amounts. Begin with analyzing the samples in a genotyping software, e.g., GeneMapperID-X. Make sure that the stutter filter is turned off. Export the "geno-types table" or equivalent as a text file. The exported file must contain information about sample names, marker names, allele designations, and allele peak heights. Start R, and load the *strvalidator* package with the command *library(strvalidator)*. Open its graphical user interface with the command *strvalidator()*. Import the data from the *Workspace* tab using the *Import* button. Perform the characterization following the steps outlined below:

1. Select the *Stutter* tab, and click the button *Calculate*. The *Calculate stutter ratio* window opens (Fig. 2.8).
2. Select the dataset containing the imported sample data in the first drop-down menu. The kit used is automatically suggested, and will be the default kit when plotting the result.
3. Select the reference dataset containing the known profiles in the second drop-down menu.
4. Use the *Check subsetting* button to verify correct matching of sample names from the reference dataset to sample names in the dataset to be analyzed.
5. Specify the analysis range using the two spin buttons for backward and forward stutters located in the options group.
6. Select the preferred *Level of interference within the given range*. The default is *no overlap between stutters and alleles*. Other levels may be used to explore the impact of additive effects on the stutter ratio.
7. There is a customizable table to *Replace "false" stutters*. False stutter types are a consequence of the stutter calculation, which is based on repeat units (i.e., "true allele" repeats − "stutter peak" repeats). The current implementation, however, does not "understand" repeats; it is merely a numeric calculation. This gives, e.g., -1 for an allele 10 with stutter at position 9, whereas an allele 20 with stutter at position 19.2 becomes -0.8. The latter is by default corrected to -0.2.
8. Click the *Calculate* button to proceed with the analysis. The window closes when finished. Process information is written to the R console. The result is a data table that for each stutter contains sample name, marker name, the true allele and its peak height, the stutter and its peak height, the calculated stutter ratio, and type of stutter.

The resulting table can be used to calculate summary statistics using the *summarize* button. It is possible to specify the quantile to be calculated with a spin button, and a radio button toggles the calculation of global statistics across all markers, locus (marker) specific statistics, or stutter specific statistics. The result is a data table with marker names, type of stutter, number of unique alleles, number of stutters, the mean and standard deviation, the result of the specified quantile, and the maximum observed ratio.

There are various plots that can be created using the result table. The window is opened by the *Plot* button. It is possible to customize the plot title, the x and y axis titles, and the visual appearance and layout. The stutter ratio can be plotted against the true allele designation (exemplified in Fig. 2.6) or the true allele peak height. Plots can be exported as images, or *ggplot* objects that can be modified manually in R.

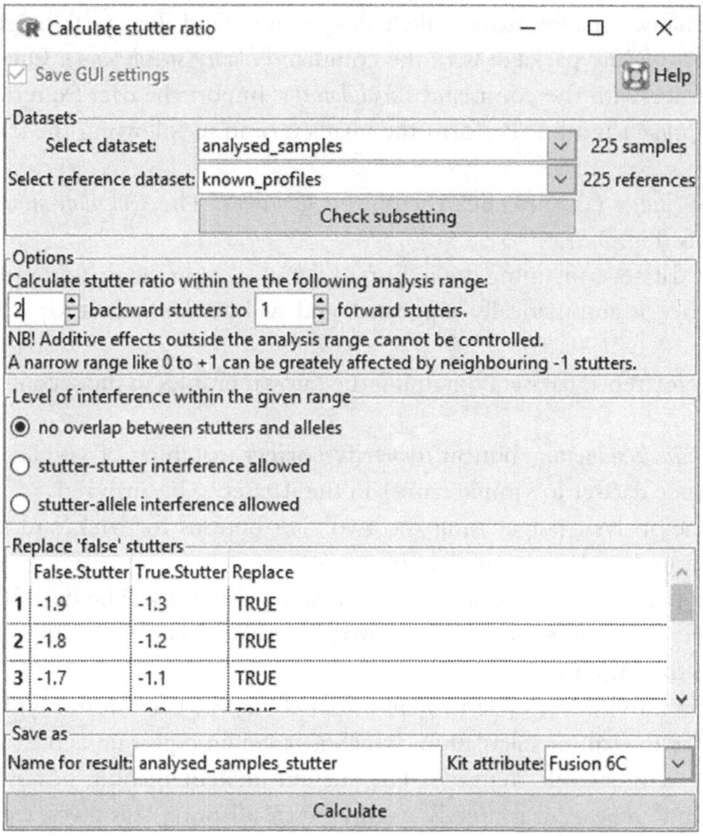

68 Forensic Practitioner's Guide to the Interpretation of Complex DNA Profiles

Figure 2.8 Screenshot from *STR-validator* showing options for the calculation of stutter ratio.

Using *STR-validator*, as described above, an internal validation of the Promega Fusion 6C kit was undertaken. Analysis of 225 single contributor crime-stained extracts (175 males and 50 females) was carried out. Quantification was carried out using the short fragment of QF Trio, and amplified with target amounts 0.5 and 1.0 ng using 30 and 29 cycles, respectively, with 24 seconds injection time on 3500xL Genetic Analyzers. The results were analyzed twice with GeneMapperID-X 1.2, first using current ESX17 Fast settings and manual editing artefacts to create "references", then using an analytical threshold of 50 RFU and no stutter filter to create the dataset to be analyzed in *STR-validator*. We collected stutter data for $n - 2$, $n - 1$, $n + 1$ repeats and -2 bp stutters. *STR-validator* provides a comprehensive analysis of stutter numbers and stutter ratios per locus (Table 2.1 shows the stutter ratio summary; the full table is available on the website associated with this chapter).

In general, $n - 1$ stutters were common, and ratios were $S_R < 0.2$; however, there was a lot of variation between loci, the maximum observed ratio ranging between 0.05

Table 2.1 95th percentile stutter ratios for Promega Fusion 6C kit. The colors represent the various dyes attached to loci.

Marker	−1 stutter	+1 stutter	−2 stutter
D3S1358	0.128	0.018	0.013
D1S1656	0.134	0.031	0.021
D2S441	0.076	0.019	0.017
D10S1248	0.137	0.018	0.016
D13S317	0.086	0.018	0.005
Penta E	0.067	0.011	0.025
D16S539	0.110	0.022	0.019
D18S51	0.146	0.033	0.041
D2S1338	0.130	0.050	0.049
CSF1PO	0.110	0.023	0.010
Penta D	0.035	0.211	NA
TH01	0.042	0.040	NA
vWA	0.132	0.065	0.019
D21S11	0.121	0.027	NA
D7S820	0.093	0.009	NA
D5S818	0.091	0.024	NA
TPOX	0.057	NA	NA
D8S1179	0.106	0.025	0.029
D12S391	0.156	0.013	0.021
D19S433	0.120	0.032	0.016
SE33	0.150	0.031	0.085
D22S1045	0.134	0.076	0.014
DYS391	0.090	0.034	0.014
FGA	0.119	0.022	0.019
DYS576	0.124	0.048	0.039
DYS570	0.125	0.020	0.027

and 0.2. The occurrence of $n + 1$ stutters was also common, but the stutter ratios were much lower ($S_R < 0.05$). The exception was D22S1045, which has three base pair repeats, and the stutter ratio is $S_R < 0.1$. In contrast, $n - 2$ stutters were rare, stutter ratios were comparable to $n + 1$ stutters. At locus SE33, -2 bp stutters were common (12 observations), and stutter ratios were $S_R < 0.08$, but they were also occasionally observed at compound repeating loci D19S433 and FGA.

Stutter size increases with the number of repeats, as discussed in Section 2.2.2, but microvariants disrupt this trend. Stochastic effects are observed at low amounts, but stutter rates are not affected much by increased amounts of DNA. Negligible differences were observed between 29 and 30 cycles (1 and 0.5 ng).

2.3. The Clayton guideline: a binary model to interpret simple mixtures

The Clayton guideline [94] was the first protocol proposed as a means to empirically assess a mixture. It builds on the heterozygote balance and stutter guidelines outlined above. The term *guideline* is used in preference to *rule*, for the simple reason that there are always exceptions to a rule. All guidelines have limitations and experimentation is necessary to define them. Even though the guideline is more than 20 years old, it is still relevant, because it is useful for practitioners to empirically evaluate an EPG before carrying out probabilistic genotyping. The Clayton guideline consists of a series of well-defined steps that are moderated by limitations discussed below. It is called a "binary model", because all or nothing decisions are made to keep or reject a genotype from the analysis (Chapter 1.17). Only two-person mixtures are considered.

2.3.1 Step 1: identify the presence of a mixture
2.3.1.1 a) By the presence of extra alleles

A mixture may be identified by the presence of extra allelic peaks. No more than two alleles per locus are expected from a single contributor. It follows that if more are visualized, then a mixture must be present. Stutters (Section 2.2) appear in allelic positions, but are generally lower than 15% the size of the parent peak. This guideline can be used to filter stutters from the main profile. However, this cannot be done if the person of interest is also low level, i.e., if alleles and stutters are approximately the same in peak height.

2.3.1.2 b) Identify the presence of a mixture by peak imbalance

Suppose that we prepare a mixture of equal proportions of two known individuals of genotypes *aa* and *ab*, respectively. Because of "masking", where both contributors share allele *a*, there are three parts *a* to one part *b*. Consequently, the locus shows marked imbalance (Fig. 2.9).

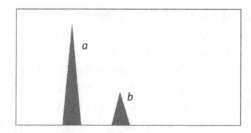

Figure 2.9 A mixture of two contributors in equal proportions, where the genotypes are *ab*, *aa*. This locus shows marked imbalance, where allele peak *a* is three times the size of allele peak *b*, i.e., $\phi a : \phi b = 3 : 1$.

Stochastic effects also lead to heterozygote imbalance (discussed in Chapter 3). Provided that the profiles are well represented, and from quantities of DNA > 500 pg, box-whiskers plots (Fig. 2.3) show that the heterozygote balance $H_b > 0.6$ (Eq. (2.2)); this has become a commonly used threshold guideline to indicate whether a heterozygote is imbalanced or not. If $H_b < 0.6$, then it may be regarded as imbalanced. In the example illustrated in Fig. 2.9, $H_b = 1/3$, i.e., considerably less than the 0.6 guideline. It can be inferred that masking is responsible for this (Chapter 1.7.2). The $H_b > 0.6$ guideline only applies to well-represented DNA profiles, which are above the stochastic threshold (discussed in Chapter 3.2) and cannot be used for low-template profiles, where there is marked expectation of heterozygote imbalance and allele drop-out.

2.3.1.3 Genetic mutations affect the number of alleles visualized

There are two kinds of genetic mutation that can result in extra alleles at a locus without the need to propose an additional contributor to a crime stain [130–132].

The first is type 1: somatic mutation. This is caused by a mutation event during embryogenisis, where an allele mutates; typically this is a step-wise mutation that results in a $n \pm 1$ repeat difference, so that it occurs in exactly the same position as a stutter. In the example shown in Fig. 2.10, the affected alleles are types 26.2 and 27.2. Without further investigation, we do not know which of these is the original progenitor allele; the sum of peak heights of these two alleles approximates the size of the third allele (type 17). Because somatic mutations occur during embryonic development, not all tissues will show identical mutations. Note that a $n - 1$ mutation event will produce an allele coincident with the back-stutter position of the progenitor allele. Consequently, it is possible that some large stutters are actually a combination of stutter and somatic mutation. It is possible for some tissue types to be devoid of somatic mutation. Hair has a higher rate, because of rapid cell division in the follicles [130].

The second kind of mutation is type 2: trisomy. This condition is easier to identify. It results from gene duplication. As it is present in the germ cell, all of the cells of an individual are affected. Consequently, the observed alleles are approximately the same height (Fig. 2.10). Trisomy is most commonly observed in XY chromosomes. For example, Klinefelters syndrome is XXY, and the amelogenin X peak height is twice the size of the Y. Triallelic loci are rare; see the NIST website for a comprehensive, up-to-date list of examples http://cstl.nist.gov/biotech/strbase/tri_tab.htm. There are 272 reported examples at core STR loci, 65 at other common STR loci, and 64 at Y-STR loci listed when the site was accessed on 8/2/2019. Both somatic and trisomy mutations are rare, but there is considerable variation between loci. For example, TH01 appears particularly stable. Crouse et al. [131] genotyped 10,000 individuals at three loci (CFS1PO, TH01, and TPOX), finding 19 trisomies, where 18 of these were at the TPOX locus. Overall, the mutation rate is lower than 0.1% per profile, which indicates that it is unlikely that triallelic patterns will be exhibited at more than one locus; in combination with the peak height characteristics described, this can be used as a useful diagnostic.

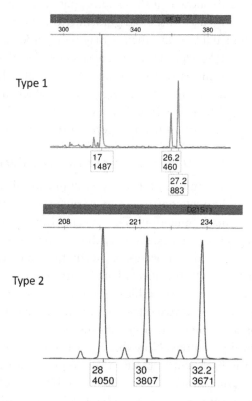

Figure 2.10 Two types of genetic aberration can lead to increased number of alleles. Type 1 somatic mutation is characterized by three alleles of unequal size. Type 2 trisomy, characterized by three alleles the same size.

2.3.1.4 Other genetic causes of heterozygote imbalance

Another cause of genetic imbalance is mutation at the primer-binding site [133–135] (Chapter 1.15). If this occurs at the 3' end, then PCR amplification is completely inhibited resulting in a "null" allele. If the mutation occurs elsewhere within the primer, the binding efficiency of the primer will be affected, because annealing and melting temperatures are reduced. This will decrease the efficiency of amplification, resulting in a reduced peak-height of the affected allele. If the mutation causes complete suppression of an allele, then it will result in excess homozygosity in populations, i.e., the population will not conform to HW expectations (Chapter 1.3). Of course, the reference sample and the crime stain will still match within the laboratory, but if the crime stain and reference sample is analyzed at different laboratories with different multiplexes, then a mismatch may occur. If primer-binding site mutation is a possibility then it is easily tested by using alternative primers to test the samples. This is usually achieved by using a test kit from a different manufacturer. The precise primer sequences and their locations are proprietary, hence not available to view, but different commercial companies utilize different sets of primers in their kits.

Once primer-binding site mutations are identified, it can be rectified by manufacturers either adding a new primer that recognizes the mutation, or by building redundancy into the primer. This requires adding a universal nucleobase, for example, inosine, that can pair with any other base, thereby preventing the need to build two specific primers per mutation [136].

2.3.1.5 Recognizing and dealing with rare genetic phenomena

Primer-binding site mutations, trisomy, and somatic mutations are rare. Because of this, it is unlikely that more than one event will be observed in a given crime-stain profile. If a mutation event is suspected, it is always preferable to carry out further biochemical analysis for confirmation, rather than to speculate on causes. To summarize, for somatic or trisomy mutations, check the reference samples for consistency; for primer-binding site mutations, analyze the sample using a different set of primers.

2.3.2 Step 2: identify the potential number of contributors to a sample

A profile from a single contributor is easily recognized as individual loci will be restricted to showing one allele (homozygote) or two alleles (heterozygote). On the other hand, a two-person mixture will typically have a maximum of four alleles at a locus. If the same allele is shared between two contributors, e.g., (*ab* and *ac*), then allele *a* is said to be masked, because there is a contribution from both individuals and just three alleles are visualized (Chapter 1.8). If the genotypes are the same in each contributor *ab*, then only two alleles are visualized.

Consequently, for two contributors there is a maximum of four alleles at a given locus; for three contributors, there is a maximum of six, but this is dependent upon all of the contributors being heterozygote, with no overlap of alleles between them. As the number of contributors increases, the chance of the masking effect also increases, hence this results in under-estimation. However, from an inspection of an EPG, it is possible to estimate the minimum number of contributors from the locus or loci that show the maximum number of alleles L_{max}:

- If three or four alleles are observed at one or more loci, then the DNA profile is a mixture of two or more individuals.
- If the profile shows five or six alleles at one or more loci, then it is a mixture of three or more individuals, and so on.

So the minimum number of contributors (nC_{min}) is

$$nC_{min} = ceiling\frac{L_{max}}{2} \qquad (2.5)$$

where "*ceiling x*" is the least integer that is greater than or equal to x. The method is known as the maximum allele count (MAC).

Box 2.1   Estimating *actual* numbers of contributors

To estimate the *actual* number of contributors, the MAC method is inefficient for complex mixtures, because of the masking effect [137,132]. Alternatives are suggested by Biedermann et al. [138], using a Bayesian network; Haned et al. [139] used a maximum likelihood estimator, taking into account population sub-structure, and showed that this method gave more accurate results compared to the MAC method. Swaminathan et al. [140] have developed a free tool NOC*It* https://lftdi.camden.rutgers.edu/provedit/software/, which calculates an *a posteriori* probability. A training set of data is used to calibrate the model, which is able to take into account peak heights, allele frequencies, allele drop-out, and stutter. Accuracy was 83% for experimental samples between one to five contributors, a marked improvement over existing methods. Machine learning methods [141] also show improved accuracy—estimated at 85% for two to five contributors.

2.3.3 Step 3: determine the approximate ratio of the components in the mixture

In the following, we consider a simple two-contributor mixture. Taking peak height into consideration, a mixture can be classified as one of three categories:

1. An even mixture, which is well represented, where both contributors are approximately the same quantity.
2. A minor/major mixture, where one contributor is notably higher in proportion compared to the other.
3. A low-template mixture, where both contributors are low-level.

If experimental mixtures are prepared in specific ratios, e.g., 1:2; 1:4, etc., then these ratios are approximately reflected across all loci [142]. This is a guideline that can be used to interpret simple DNA profiles.

In simple mixtures of two individuals, the mixture ratio is best assessed from loci with four alleles *abcd*. If the peak heights of all four alleles are similar, then the mixture ratio is $M_r = 1{:}1$. Alternatively, peak heights conditioned on the minor or the major contributor can be expressed as a proportion $M_x = 0.5$.

A minor/major profile is shown in Fig. 2.11. The conditioned minor genotype is 14, 17 and the conditioned major is 16, 18. The mixture ratio (M_r) is calculated as

$$M_r = \frac{(\phi_{14} + \phi_{17})}{(\phi_{16} + \phi_{18})} \qquad (2.6)$$

where ϕ is the peak height. The mixture proportion, conditioned on the minor genotype 14, 17 can be calculated in the following manner:

$$M_x = \frac{(\phi_{14} + \phi_{17})}{(\phi_{14} + \phi_{16} + \phi_{17} + \phi_{18})} \tag{2.7}$$

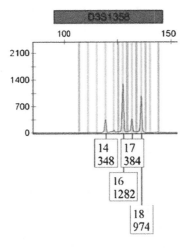

Figure 2.11 Four alleles showing, a mixture of two individuals, who are clear major/minor contributors.

The proportion of the mixture attributed to the alternate major genotype 16, 18 is $(1 - M_x)$.

From the example shown in Fig. 2.11, we can calculate the mixture minor:major ratio from Eq. (2.6):

$$M_r = \frac{348 + 384}{1282 + 974} = 0.325 : 1$$

The mixture proportion of the minor contributor is calculation from Eq. (2.7):

$$M_x = \frac{348 + 384}{348 + 1282 + 384 + 974} = 0.245$$

The proportion of the major contributor is $(1 - M_x) = 0.755$. The next question to consider is whether the minor alleles could be paired with any of the major alleles, assuming that they were from the same contributor. Can alleles 14 and 16 be paired (Fig. 2.11)? The $H_b > 0.6$ guideline is used for this assessment. Since $M_r \ll 0.6$, it is unlikely that a major allele can be paired with a minor allele, and is therefore discounted.

If the mixture is male/female, the next step is to evaluate the evidence in support of which is minor, and which is major. Table 2.2 compares the expected "dosage" or peak heights of X and Y alleles, from the amelogenin locus, for given mixture ratios.

76 Forensic Practitioner's Guide to the Interpretation of Complex DNA Profiles

Table 2.2 A table showing the mixture ratio relative to the dosage, and ratio of X,Y alleles observed. Reproduced from [94] with permission from Elsevier.

Mixture ratio		Dosage of alleles observed		Ratio of peak heights X:Y
Male (XY)	Female (XX)	X	Y	X:Y
10	1	12	10	1.2:1
5	1	7	5	1.4:1
4	1	6	4	1.5:1
3	1	5	3	1.6:1
2	1	4	2	2:1
1	1	3	1	3:1
1	2	5	1	5:1
1	3	7	1	7:1
1	4	9	1	9:1
1	5	11	1	11:1
1	10	21	1	21:1

In the example, $M_r = 0.245$, i.e., an approximate 1:3 or 3:1 male:female mixture. The table shows that expected peak ratios are X:Y = 1.6:1 if male(major):female(minor), and X:Y = 7:1 if female(major):male(minor). These differences are quite large. If the contributors are both male, then the expected X:Y ratio will be 1:1.

2.3.4 Step 4: determine the possible pairwise combinations for the components of the mixture

Once M_r or M_x have been ascertained, along with an indication of whether the minor/major components can be assigned to male/female contributors, the next step is to evaluate each locus in turn to determine which genotypes are best supported by the evidence, and to identify those that are less well supported. To do this, all possible genotype combinations are listed exactly as described in Chapter 1. Beginning with the four-allele example shown in Fig. 2.11, all possible combinations follow from Table 1.4 and are listed in Table 2.3. From the previous section, the evidence best supports the 14,17/16,18 minor/major option. The process of deciding the best-favored genotype combinations is known as *deconvolution*. Note that the remaining genotype options crossed out in Table 2.3 are regarded as options that are less well supported. They are not definitive exclusions as such, as there is a finite probability that one of these may be the true genotype. The aim of probabilistic genotyping (described in subsequent chapters) is to quantify this (albeit small) probability so that it may be properly factored into likelihood ratio calculations. For the purpose of this exercise, the crossed-out options are not considered further.

It is more difficult to assign minor/major contributors to three-allele mixtures. From Chapter 1.8, there are two types of three-allele mixtures:

Table 2.3 All possible genotype pairs for two contributors at D3S1358 locus, each with two different alleles. The less well-supported genotypes are crossed out. The genotypes in bold are the complements of the first three listed.

Minor	Major
~~14,16~~	~~17,18~~
14,17	16,18
~~14,18~~	~~16,17~~
~~17,18~~	**~~14,16~~**
~~16,18~~	**~~14,17~~**
~~16,17~~	**~~14,18~~**

1. One contributor is homozygote *aa*, and the second is heterozygote *bc*. The corresponding expectations for allele peak height ratios for given contributor mixture ratios are provided in Table 2.4.
2. An allele is shared between two heterozygote contributors, e.g., *ab, bc*. The corresponding expectations for allele peak height ratios for given contributor mixture ratios are provided in Table 2.5.

In Fig. 2.12, the TH01 alleles 6, 7, 9.3 are represented by peak height ratios of 1:3.7:4.1. The mixture ratio was calculated earlier as approximately 1:3 or 3:1. If one of the peaks was homozygote (*aa, bc*), then the corresponding expectation of peak height ratios ($a:b:c$), from the look-up table (Table 2.4) is 6:1:1, or 2:3:3. Conversely, if there is a shared allele, *a*, in a mixture *ab, ac*, from Table 2.5, the expected ratios are 4:3:1 or 4:1:3 (see Table 2.6). This is closest to the observed ratios of TH01 peak heights, where allele $a = 6$, $b = 7$, $c = 9.3$. But the peak height difference between the two major (7:9.3) alleles is 3.7:4.1, which is insufficient to select one of these as the shared (*b*) allele. Consequently, the minor contributor is either 6,7 or 6,9.3, which leaves 7,9.3 as the major contributor. (Table 2.7).

An alternative calculation can be carried out using M_x. The allele peak height proportions are calculated as shown in Table 2.8.

In Fig. 2.13, the proposed minor/major contributor alleles are listed as shown. The expected allele proportions are calculated by dividing M_x and $1 - M_x$ by two. Because allele 7 is shared between the contributors, the proportions of each are summed— a shared allele will always sum to 0.5. The *expected* peak height proportions for alleles 6, 7, 9.3 are 0.12, 0.5 and 0.38, respectively. Now we repeat the exercise for the other

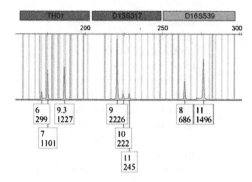

Figure 2.12 An electropherogram showing three loci: a mixture of two individuals who are clear major/minor contributors.

Table 2.4 Mixture ratio compared to expected ratio of peak heights for a three-allele locus, where the first contributor is homozygote.

Mixture ratio		Ratio of peak heights
aa	bc	a:b:c
10	1	20.1:1
5	1	10.1:1
4	1	8.1:1
3	1	6.1:1
2	1	4:1:1
1	1	2:1:1
1	2	1:1:1
1	3	2:3:3
1	4	1:2:2
1	5	2:5:5
1	10	1:5:5

possible combination of alleles: minor 6, 9.3; major 7, 9.3. These calculations are shown in Fig. 2.14.

The expected allele peak height proportions for alleles 6,7 and 9.3 are 0.12, 0.38 and 0.5, respectively. The differences between the two calculations are quantified in Table 2.9.

To summarize, two alternative genotype combinations are explored: minor;major 6, 7;7, 9.3 and 6, 9.3;7, 9.3. The allele proportions conditioned upon the respective genotypes M_x and $1 - M_x$ are calculated using Figs. 2.13, 2.14. The observed and expected peak height proportions are listed in Table 2.9. The expected peak heights are calculated from the proportions, e.g., expected peak height of allele 6, $\phi_{6(expected)} = 0.12\times$ sum of

Table 2.5 Mixture ratio compared to expected ratio of peak heights for a three-allele locus, where both contributors are heterozygotes.

Mixture ratio		Ratio of peak heights
ab	ac	a:b:c
10	1	11.10:1
5	1	6.5:1
4	1	5.4:1
3	1	4.3:1
2	1	3:2:1
1	1	1:1:1
1	2	3:1:2
1	3	4:1:3
1	4	5:1:4
1	5	6:1:5
1	10	11:1:10

Table 2.6 A summary of best supported genotype ratios from the three-allele TH01 mixture.

Mixture ratio		Ratio of peak heights
aa	bc	a:b:c
3	1	6.1:1
1	3	2:3:3
ab	ac	a:b:c
3	1	4.3:1
1	3	4:1:3

observed peak heights $= 315$. Next, the differences between observed and expected peak heights are calculated giving the *residual*, i.e., residual $=$ observed peak height − expected peak height (to avoid negatives the sign of the residual is ignored as we are only interested in absolute differences). Note that this definition differs from the residual sum squared (RSS) method used in later chapters.

The residual is calculated for each genotype combination. This shows that the 6, 9.3;7, 9.3 genotype combination has the lower of the two options considered, indicating that the evidence provides greater support for this genotype. Using residuals enables the various genotype options to be ranked in order. The calculations illustrated above can be extended to all possible genotype combinations listed in Table 2.7, but this would be time-consuming. To demonstrate, consider the 6, 6;7, 9.3 genotype combination (Fig. 2.15). The 6, 6 minor genotype is very unlikely, as the residual for allele 6 $= 431$

Table 2.7 All possible genotype pairs for two contributors at TH01 locus, each with two different alleles. The less well-supported genotypes are crossed out. The genotypes in bold are the complements of the first six listed.

Minor contributor	Major contributor
~~6,6~~	~~7,9.3~~
~~7,7~~	~~6,9.3~~
~~9.3,9.3~~	~~6,7~~
~~6,7~~	~~6,9.3~~
6,7	7,9.3
~~7,9.3~~	~~6,9.3~~
7,9.3	**6,6**
6,9.3	**7,7**
6,7	**9.3,9.3**
~~6,9.3~~	~~6,7~~
~~7,9.3~~	~~6,7~~
6,9.3	7,9.3

Table 2.8 Calculation of TH01 allele proportions.

Allele	6	7	9.3	Sum
peak height	299	1101	1227	2627
proportion	0.11	0.42	0.47	1

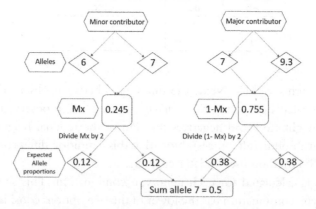

Figure 2.13 Calculation of expected peak height proportions for TH01 6, 7;7, 9.3.

and the total absolute residual = 763, which ranks this combination below the others in the table. It is not "excluded" as such, but there is poor support for this option.

Empirical characterization of DNA profiles 81

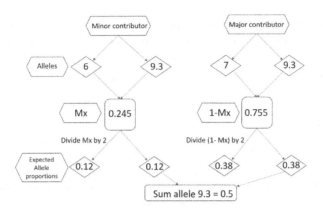

Figure 2.14 Calculation of expected peak height proportions for TH01 6, 9.3;7, 9.3.

Table 2.9 TH01, calculation of residuals from observed and expected peak heights from Figs. 2.13, 2.14, 2.15. There is poor support for the option shown in red (medium grey in print version) type, because the sum of the absolute residuals is high.

	Allele proportions			Peak heights			Residuals			Sum of residuals
Alleles	6	7	9.3	6	7	9.3	6	7	9.3	
Observed proportions	0.11	0.42	0.47	299	1101	1227				
6,7;7,9.3 expected	0.12	0.5	0.38	315	1313	998	16	212	229	**457**
6,9.3;7,9.3 expected	0.12	0.38	0.5	315	998	1313	16	103	86	**205**
6,6;7,9.3 expected	0.24	0.38	0.38	730	998	998	431	103	229	763

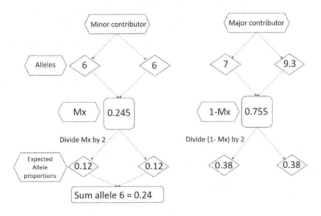

Figure 2.15 Calculation of expected peak height proportions for TH01 6, 6;7, 9.3.

Using the empirical methods outlined, it is possible for the practitioner to discount the majority of possible genotype combinations. A calculation of the summed absolute value of the residuals can be used to rank the genotype combinations, where the top

82 Forensic Practitioner's Guide to the Interpretation of Complex DNA Profiles

rank is the genotype that has the best support. This process shows how deconvolution can be carried out using quantifiable methods. The ideas expounded here were the first steps towards using the power of computers to carry out probabilistic calculations on all possible genotype combinations, ultimately circumventing the need for empirical evaluation.

2.3.4.1 D13S317

This locus is also a three-allele mixture; the ratios of alleles 9, 10, 11 are approximately 10:1:1. The evidence supports homozygote 9 (major contributor) and heterozygote 10, 11 (minor contributor). It is extremely unlikely that allele 9 could be paired with either 10 or 11, because of the wide discrepancy in allele peak heights. Consequently the evidence supports minor 10, 11; major 9, 9 (expectation of 3:1 mixture is allele peak height ratio of 5:1:1),

2.3.4.2 D16S539

This locus is a two-allele mixture. The peak height ratio is approximately 1:2.2, so it is unlikely that the mixture is two 8, 11 heterozygote contributors, because $H_b < 0.6$. If the contributors are a homozygote with a heterozygote, the imbalance is because of the masking effect. The expectations of peak height ratios are the same as for the XY chromosome (Table 2.2). For a 3:1 mixture ab, bb, the expectation is $a : b = 1.6:1$; for a 1:3 mixture the expectation is 7:1. The latter is discounted, because there is a wide discrepancy between observed vs. expected peak heights. The 1.6:1 ratio is not discounted. Here allele $a = 11$, and allele $b = 8$. If the option is true, then allele 11 will be divided between minor and major contributors. Approximately 686 RFU is paired with allele 8, and the remaining $1496 - 686 = 810$ RFU is the contribution from the minor homozygote 11 (Table 2.10, Fig. 2.16); hence the best supported minor/major genotype is 11, 11;8, 11. A second possibility is that there are two homozygote contributors, namely 8, 8;11, 11, where the minor/major expected ratios are 1:3, recall that the observed ratio was 1:2.2.

The proportions of alleles 8 and 11 are calculated (Table 2.11). The two alternative genotype combinations, 11, 11;8, 11 and 8, 8;11, 11, are tested using the M_x method, following the protocol described for TH01, (Figs. 2.17, 2.18). The observed and expected proportions of the alternative genotype combinations are listed in Table 2.12. From the sum of the absolute value of the residuals, the evidence favors the 11, 11;8, 11 minor/major alternative, but there is little difference between the two, hence both should be included to calculate the likelihood ratio.

2.3.5 Step 5: compare with reference samples

It is important that interpretation of evidence is carried out without the knowledge of the reference sample. Only after a list of deconvolved genotypes has been prepared can

Table 2.10 All possible genotype pairs for two contributors at D16S539 locus, each with two different alleles. The less well-supported genotypes are crossed out. The genotypes in bold are the complements of the first three listed.

Minor contributor	Major contributor
8,8	11,11
~~8,8~~	~~8,11~~
11,11	8,11
~~8,11~~	~~8,11~~
~~11,11~~	**8,8**
8,11	**8,8**
8,11	**~~11,11~~**

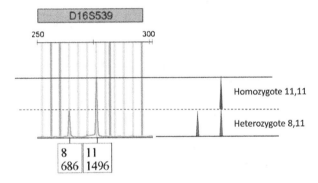

Figure 2.16 D16S539 locus. A mixture of two alleles showing how the minor homozygote and the major heterozygote are deconvolved on the right hand side of the figure. The 11 allele is proposed as shared between the two contributors; the alleles peak heights are additive.

Table 2.11 Calculations of D16S539 allele proportions.

Allele	8	11	Sum
peak height	686	1496	2182
proportion	0.31	0.69	1

the reference profiles be compared. A tabulated list of results is shown in Table 2.13. The deconvolved minor and major contributors are shown, and compared with the reference profiles. In this example, the first ranked genotype for each locus, from step 4, matches the reference sample of the suspect.

Next follows a calculation of the likelihood ratio. If the suspect is the minor contributor under the prosecution proposition, together with an unknown major contributor, and there are two unknown contributors under the defense proposition, then the *LR*

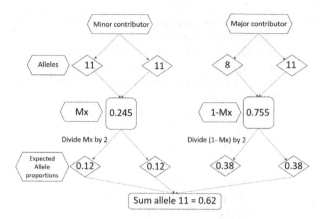

Figure 2.17 Calculation of peak height proportions of the D16S539 11, 11;8, 11 genotypes. The 11 allele is proposed as shared between the two contributors; the alleles peak heights are additive.

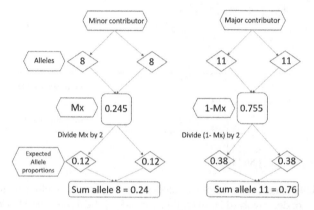

Figure 2.18 Calculation of peak height proportions of the D16S539 8, 8;11, 11 genotypes.

Table 2.12 Residuals analysis of locus D16S539 genotype combinations.

	Allele proportions		Peak heights		Residuals		Sum of residuals
Alleles	8	11	8	11	8	11	
Observed proportions	0.31	0.69	686	1496			
11,11;8,11 expected	0.38	0.62	829	1353	143	143	**286**
8,8;11,11 expected	0.24	0.76	524	1658	162	162	**324**

is calculated per locus, as shown in the table. The procedure is identical to that described in Chapter 1.7, except that genotype combinations that are not supported by the evidence have been excluded from this calculation.

This reduces the number of genotype combinations under H_d, which in turn reduces the probability of the evidence $Pr(E|H_d)$, thereby increasing the overall LR. If a single

Table 2.13 Genotypes selected by deconvolution. The likelihood ratio formulae for each of these genotypes is shown.

Locus	Minor contributor	Major contributor	Reference (minor)	Reference (major)	$Pr(E\vert H_d)$	$Pr(E\vert H_p)$	$LR = \frac{Pr(E\vert H_p)}{Pr(E\vert H_d)}$
D3S1358	14,17	16,18	14,17	16,18	$4p_{14}p_{17}p_{16}p_{18}$	$2p_{16}p_{18}$	$\frac{1}{2p_{14}p_{17}}$
TH01	6,7 6,9.3	7,9.3 7,9.3	6,9.3	7,9.3	$4p_6p_7^2p_{9.3}$ $4p_6p_{9.3}p_7p_{9.3}$	$2p_7p_{9.3}$	$\frac{1}{2p_6(p_7+p_{9.3})}$
D13S317	10,11	9,9	10,11	9,9	$2p_{10}p_{11}p_9^2$	$2p_9^2$	$\frac{1}{2p_{10}p_{11}}$
D16S539	11,11 8,8	8,11 11,11	11,11	8,11	$2p_{11}^3p_8$ $p_8^2p_{11}^2$	$2p_8p_{11}$	$\frac{1}{p_{11}(p_{11}+0.5p_8)}$

86 Forensic Practitioner's Guide to the Interpretation of Complex DNA Profiles

genotype combination is deconvolved then the LR converges to be the same as for the suspect's DNA profile calculated as a single (unmixed) profile ($1/2p_ap_b$). There are two examples shown in Table 2.13 for D8 and D13 loci.

2.4. Characterization of massively parallel sequencing (MPS) kits using STR-validator

STR-validator (version 2.2) does not have dedicated modules or functions to analyze massively parallel sequencing (MPS) data (described in Chapter 13). However, many of the current functionalities, e.g., stutter and heterozygote balance calculations, will work with MPS data after minor manual modifications.

1. Open the kit definition file *kit.txt* in a spreadsheet software. Manually add the following:
   a. The marker name in column *Marker*.
   b. Alleles in column *Allele*. For the basic functions it is not necessary to add all possible alleles. Simply add "1" as the allele on a single row for each marker.
   c. The dye color in column *Color*. The color is used by plot functions to split the data in panes, i.e., rows, and control the default color for data points. Use any of the supported colors (currently "blue", "green", "purple", "red", and "yellow"). For example, autosomal markers can be assigned one color, and SNP markers another.
   d. A short name for the kit definition in column *Short.Name*. Avoid special characters, since they may not be supported. The short name will show up in drop-down menus.
   e. Indicators for sex markers (i.e., markers located on the X or Y chromosome) in column *Sex.Marker*. Use the values *TRUE* or *FALSE*.
   f. Indicators for quality sensor (i.e., internal controls that are not part of the DNA profile) in column *Quality.Sensor*. Use the values *TRUE* or *FALSE*.

   All other columns in the kit definition can be left empty or filled with the value *NA*. It is possible to create multiple customized kit definitions. One can define subsets of markers, e.g., separate definitions showing only female markers, only SNP markers, and so on.

2. The MPS result file, e.g., the Excel file generated by the universal analysis software, must be reformatted in a way that is supported by *STR-validator* (i.e., a tab separated text file or a data frame in R). This must be done using customized scrips, e.g., in R. Table 2.14 show an example suitable for *STR-validator*.

3. Rename the *Counts*, *Reads*, or similar column to *Height*. This can be done before importing the data, using a text editor or spreadsheet software (be aware of automatic date formatting that may corrupt the data). A safer way is to first import the data into *STR-validator* and then do the following:
   a. Select the *Tools* tab, and click the *Columns* button.

Table 2.14 Example of MPS data formatted in a way readable to *STR-validator*. The column *Marker.System* is not required, but may be useful to create subsets of the data, e.g., here aSTR = autosomal STR, ySTR = Y-chromosome STR, xSTR = X-chromosome STR.

Sample.Name	Marker	Allele	Height	Dye	Marker.System
SampleID	AMEL	X	147	B	aSTR
SampleID	AMEL	Y	326	B	aSTR
SampleID	CSF1PO	8	21	B	aSTR
SampleID	CSF1PO	9	514	B	aSTR
SampleID	CSF1PO	11	27	B	aSTR
SampleID	CSF1PO	12	356	B	aSTR
SampleID	DYF387S1	36	37	G	ySTR
SampleID	DYF387S1	37	266	G	ySTR
SampleID	DYF387S1	38	30	G	ySTR
SampleID	DYF387S1	39	263	G	ySTR
SampleID	DXS10074	16	104	R	xSTR
SampleID	DXS10074	17	862	R	xSTR

    b. Select the MPS data as *dataset* and specify the column containing reads as *column 1*. Type "Height" in the field *Column for new values*. If the data in *STR-validator* is stored as numeric values, select, e.g., the action "*", and type the number "1" in the field *Fixed value* (i.e., multiply the data with 1, which will result in identical data). If the data are stored as characters, select the action "&", and leave the field *Fixed value* empty (i.e., concatenate the data with an empty string, which will result in identical data).

The column will now be recognized by *STR-validator* and used in calculations. Fig. 2.19 shows an example of MPS data analyzed by *STR-validator*.

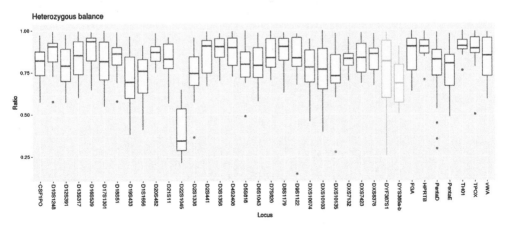

Figure 2.19 Example of MPS peak balance observed using *ForenSeq DNA signature prep kit* for all markers, where two peaks are expected.

2.5. Summary

1. Empirical evaluation of evidence, where allele peak heights are taken into consideration can only be carried out with well-represented DNA profiles.
2. A well-represented profile is defined as one which is above the stochastic threshold (discussed later in Chapter 3.2).
3. The methods shown here are restricted to two-person contributors to a mixture.
4. Characterization of heterozygotes, stutters, and genetic artefacts, such as trisomy, are needed to understand mixtures.
5. With well-represented profiles, heterozygotes are balanced, such that the $H_b > 0.6$ guideline can be used to make decisions about whether alleles can be paired to infer that they are from a given contributor.
6. The mixture ratio (or proportion) can be estimated from four-allele loci, and the (approximate) value applied across all loci.
7. A masked allele consists of contributions from two individuals; the peak heights are additive.
8. With information about the mixture ratio, it is possible to infer genotype combinations and exclude others. This process is called deconvolution.
9. Deconvolution is easiest with minor/major mixtures, where the minor contributor $M_r < 0.6$.
10. Deconvolution may result in more than one genotype combination. They can be ranked in order of the alternatives that are best supported by the evidence.
11. Deconvolution must be carried out before knowledge of the reference samples.
12. The LR can be calculated from the deconvolved genotype combinations. Provided that the evidence supports a "match", the value of the LR is usually much larger compared to that calculated if peak heights are not taken into consideration.

CHAPTER 3

Allele drop-out and the stochastic threshold

In Chapter 2, the discussion centered primarily on well-represented profiles. To interpret mixtures, it is necessary to understand the characteristics of samples that are *not* mixtures. Heterozygote balance is pivotal to this discussion. With well-represented DNA profiles, alleles from a single contributor will show balance > 60% of the peak height of the major allelic peak. When the quantity of DNA is reduced, this guideline breaks down, so that extreme imbalance may be observed, ultimately leading to complete disappearance of the allele from the electropherogram. This is known as allele drop-out. It is extremely important, because

- The crime stain no longer provides a complete match to the reference sample.
- Interpretation of minor contributors of mixtures becomes problematic as the formulae in Chapter 1.7 no longer apply.

An example is shown in Fig. 3.1 using ESX 17. The reference sample is a complete profile (500 pg DNA) in the top panel. The lower panel is a profile from less than 20 pg of DNA. The peak heights of the alleles are much smaller; the entire locus is missing at VWA. At locus D21S11, allele 31.2 is missing. In this example, there would be an apparent mismatch between crime stain (D21S11-type 29 homozygote) compared to the reference sample, where D21S11 is heterozygote 29, 31.2. In this chapter, we develop the theory to deal with the apparent ambiguities caused by drop-out.

3.1. What causes allele drop-out?

If there is a reasonable quantity of DNA, there are thousands of DNA molecules in a tube from an extracted sample. On the other hand, if the sample is low-template, there are just a few molecules, maybe ten, or even lower. If the volume of the DNA sample is ·100 μl, and 25 μl are removed by pipette to carry forward for PCR amplification, then three quarters of the DNA remain behind. Now take an extreme example: Suppose that there is just one molecule of DNA in a sample extract of 100 μl and 25 μl are removed by pipette. Sometimes the molecule is captured, but there is a probability of 0.75 that it will *not* be captured by pipette. There is nothing to PCR, and there will be allele drop-out. Now suppose that there are two molecules in the extract, which are different alleles, designated a and b, of a single locus. After pipetting an aliquot, there are now four possible outcomes, which will be visualized in the EPG, either alleles a and b (no drop-out); a (drop-out of b); b (drop-out of a); or none (drop-out of both a and b).

Forensic Practitioner's Guide to the Interpretation of Complex DNA Profiles
https://doi.org/10.1016/B978-0-12-820562-4.00011-0

Copyright © 2020 Elsevier Inc.
All rights reserved.   **89**

90 Forensic Practitioner's Guide to the Interpretation of Complex DNA Profiles

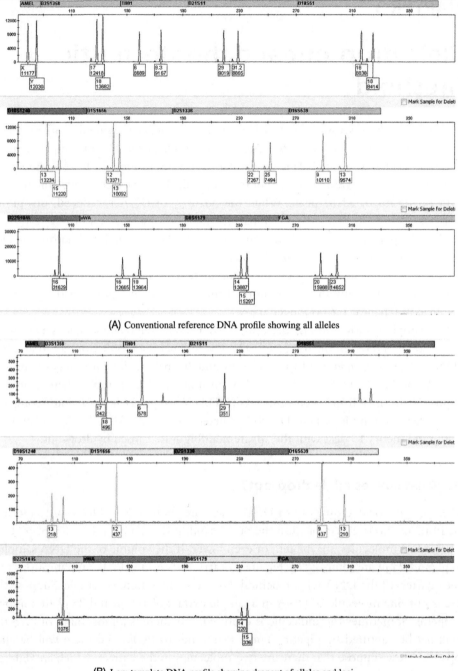

(A) Conventional reference DNA profile showing all alleles

(B) Low-template DNA profile showing dropout of alleles and loci

Figure 3.1 (A) Conventional ESX 17 profile compared with (B) low template profile from the same individual.

There are usually more than one or two molecules available for analysis. The more molecules there are, the greater the probability that a specific allele type will be captured by pipetting, and the lower the probability that drop-out will occur.

Definition of drop-out: The phenomenon of allele drop-out is an extreme form of heterozygote imbalance that is characteristic of low-template or partial DNA profiles [34,143,144], and is specifically defined as an allelic signal that falls below the analytical threshold (AT) [144]—this is the level where signals from alleles and background noise cannot be differentiated (Fig. 3.4).

In the literature, a number of different terms have been used to describe the "minimum distinguishable signal" [145]. The analytical threshold seems to be standard and is the term adopted here. Bregu et al. [145] review the various methodologies that can be used to determine the AT, usually based upon determination of the level that is three or more standard deviations above the baseline noise. Mönich et al. [146] suggest a method based upon log-normal distribution of noise. *STR-validator* has implemented multiple methods to estimate the AT, which can be explored simultaneously. Negative controls or DNA containing samples are both supported. Known alleles and surrounding noise can automatically be filtered from the calculations.

Insufficient molecules to generate a PCR signal result from insufficient template; alternatively, the sample may contain inhibitors to the PCR enzyme, preventing efficient amplification [147].

Heterozygote imbalance (Fig. 3.2) occurs, because different numbers of molecules are captured when the sample is pipetted. This is known as the *stochastic* effect. Stochastic is defined by the Oxford English dictionary as: "Having a random probability distribution or pattern that may be analyzed statistically but may not be predicted precisely."

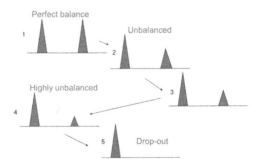

Figure 3.2 Illustration of heterozygote balance. Perfect balance (1) is achieved if there are the same number of molecules for each allele present in the pipetted extract. The heterozygote becomes unbalanced if unequal numbers of molecules are captured (2) leading to highly unbalanced (3 and 4), and finally allele drop-out (5), where no alleles are recovered (or there are insufficient to exceed the AT).

3.1.1 A mathematical model showing the relationship of heterozygote balance and drop-out

From a sample containing a large number of DNA molecules, a single locus is chosen that is heterozygous: a total of seven molecules are randomly drawn. Each molecule is an allele that may be either type a or type b; the probability of selecting either a or b is 0.5 (the same as a coin toss). There are eight different alternative combinations of a, b molecules shown in Table 3.1, and the corresponding heterozygote balance (H_b) is calculated as described in Chapter 2.1.2:

$$H_b = \frac{\phi_{smaller}}{\phi_{larger}} \tag{3.1}$$

where smaller and larger refer to the respective peak heights of the heterozygote. For example, if there are 6 a alleles and 1 b allele, then $H_b = 1/6 = 0.14$.

A different probability is needed to answer the question: "How likely is it that we will observe this heterozygote balance indicated by a specific combination of a, b molecules?" This probability is provided by the binomial distribution B (Table 3.1), where $H_b \sim B(n, p)$; the symbol $\sim$ means "has distribution"; n and p are parameters that describe the number of molecules and the probability of selecting a particular allele, respectively.

Table 3.1 Demonstration of expected distribution of heterozygote balance if seven alleles are recovered from a sample (each selection of a or b is $p = 0.5$). The table shows heterozygote balance conditioned on the given number of a, b alleles shown. The binomial probability is the probability of observing a given number of molecules: e.g., 7 a and 0 b alleles.

No. of a alleles	No. of b alleles	Heterozygote balance	Binomial probability
7	0	0	0.008
6	1	0.14	0.054
5	2	0.29	0.164
4	3	0.42	0.273
3	4	0.42	0.273
2	5	0.29	0.164
1	6	0.14	0.054
0	7	0	0.008

For low template samples, the pre-selection of target DNA molecules as an aliquot from an extraction has a critical effect on the heterozygote balance. In Fig. 3.3, aliquots forwarded for PCR were taken from extracts containing between 1–100 molecules of each allele of a heterozygote. Whether drop-out occurs is critically dependent upon the number of molecules in the original sample extract. The fewer molecules that are present, the greater the probability of drop out [124,148].

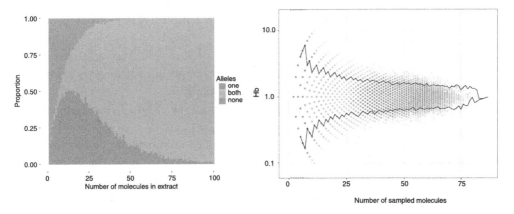

Figure 3.3 Binomial simulations (1000x) of the low-template pre-selection of alleles and the effect on heterozygote balance for a small aliquot proportion of 0.05. *Left:* An aliquot was taken from DNA extracts containing 1–100 molecules of each allele. The proportion when none (locus drop-out), one (allele drop-out), or both alleles were obtained was plotted by the number of molecules in the DNA extract. *Right:* An aliquot was taken from DNA extracts containing 10–600 molecules of each allele. The heterozygote balance was plotted by the total number of sampled molecules. The solid line indicates the 5th and 95th percentile. Reproduced from [114].

3.2. Stochastic thresholds and drop-out

The stochastic threshold, measured in peak height (RFU), was designed as a guideline to decide whether a locus could be considered to be well-represented. Defined as conforming to expectations of heterozygote balance, where there was an unlikely possibility of allele drop-out occurring [143]. The definition was particularly pertinent to homozygotes, since these exist as single alleles. The question is whether the single allele peak is a definitive *aa* genotype, or whether it is an *a, F* genotype, where '*F*' represents an allele that may have dropped out. '*F*' also includes allele *a* if drop-out has not happened, hence its allele frequency becomes $p_F = 1$. Laboratories used different sets of rules[1] to interpret conventional, high-template (HT) vs low-template (LT)-DNA samples, hence it was considered important to decide how to distinguish between the two kinds of DNA.

Consequently, a stochastic or homozygote threshold (T) serves as an approximate delineation between an LT single peak that is evaluated as $2p_a p_F$ versus a conventional profile evaluated as p_a^2; it is dependant on DNA STR typing kit, amount of template, PCR and CE settings.

Fig. 3.4 represents all possible heterozygote states, dependent upon whether alleles are considered to be low- or high-template; the latter is "conventional". There are two thresholds, the analytical threshold (AT) and the stochastic threshold (T); these will be set to values such as 50 RFU for AT and 150 RFU for T^2. To summarize:
1. When alleles are above T, then the sample is high-template (HT). No drop-out has occurred. The alleles should be well balanced.
2. When both alleles are between T and AT, then no drop-out has occurred, but the locus is considered low-template, hence extreme variation of heterozygote balance is expected outside the guidelines used for high template.
3. One allele is between T and AT; the other is below AT. This allele is dropped out, even if it is visible below the AT.
4. Only one allele is between T and AT. It is either a homozygote or heterozygote with allele drop-out.
5. The final example is *extreme drop-out*. Here there is an allele above T, which is high-template. There is an allele below the AT, which has dropped out. This profile could be treated wrongly as a "conventional" (HT) homozygote.

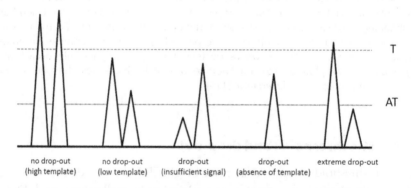

Figure 3.4 High-template profiles usually have well balanced heterozygote peaks and no drop-out. Low-template profiles are characterized by the risk of drop-out. They may well show complete genotypes with no drop-out, but usually with increased imbalance. Upon analysis, this can lead to three types of drop-out: insufficient number of molecules to generate a signal above the AT; complete dropout, which is the absence of a molecule in the PCR reaction, and extreme drop-out with one allele above the stochastic threshold (T) and one below the AT. Reproduced from [114] with permission from Oskar Hansson.

3.3. National DNA databases and low-template DNA crime stains

Laboratories have guidelines about what kinds of DNA profiles can be searched against national DNA database, dependent upon the number of alleles observed and the quality of the profile. Gill et al. [143] describes the reasons for using a stochastic threshold. If the donor has a heterozygote genotype, $g = (ab)$ and the crime-stain (E) appears as a homozygote genotype, $E = a$, either the suspect is excluded, and the donor is type (ab), or the alternative explanation is that allele b has dropped out. A crucial part of the decision-making process is whether $E = (aa)$ or $E = (aF)$, where "F" matches any allele, including a, when searched against the national DNA database (NDNAD), i.e., it is used as a "wild card". If a crime stain appears to be a homozygote, it is usually compared against the pre-determined stochastic threshold T. Historically, the level of T was typically set at 150 RFU peak height with systems like SGM plus run on the 3700 ABI genetic analyzer.

In the following, we explore the implications in terms of observed drop-out rates and the false inclusion/exclusion risks associated with a given threshold T. If the allele peak height is greater than T, then the crime-stain locus is designated as a homozygote (aa); if it is below T, then it is designated as (aF). When a statistical assessment of the strength of evidence is carried out, F is incorporated as a neutral event, which leads to a likelihood ratio of $LR = 1/2p_a$. Buckleton and Triggs [149] show that this treatment was not necessarily conservative, especially when the height/area of the surviving or present allele approached T (Section 3.7).

The threshold T is determined experimentally. If it was set too high, then the number of samples that could be downloaded onto the database would be unnecessarily restricted, because (aa) genotypes would be typed as (aF). This is not an error as such, since the (aa) combination is implicit in the F designation. However, if the crime stain is an (aa) homozygote, then an increased number of false inclusions would occur since any a-combination would match.

Conversely, if T is set too low, it is possible that an (aa) designation could be erroneously provided. This would result in potential false exclusions, where the suspect (if present on the database) would fail to match the crime stain.

To summarize, there are two competing issues with the decision about where the stochastic threshold (T) should be placed:

1. If T is too high, then needless invocation of "F" means that the probability of a match is increased, and there is much greater likelihood of a chance match on the NDNAD (false inclusion).
2. If T is set too low, a false exclusion may result if a heterozygote (ab) is mis-designated as a homozygote (aa).

i.e., reducing risk of false inclusions increases the risk of false exclusions, and vice versa.

A table of consequences that may arise are given in Table 3.2.

3.4. Definition of drop-out and extreme drop-out

When there is sufficient DNA present (typically 500 pg or more), then PCR amplification will produce well-balanced heterozygous profiles [108,91]. When smaller amounts

96 Forensic Practitioner's Guide to the Interpretation of Complex DNA Profiles

Table 3.2 A table of consequences: the 'F' designation is used whenever allele a is below an arbitrarily designated low-level-DNA threshold. The worse case scenario occurs when the crime stain is type a and the offender is type (ab), because a mismatch can occur on the NDNAD, and therefore the offender (assuming that he is on the database) may not be detected. The table is reproduced from [143] with permission from Elsevier.

Crime-stain phenotype	Offender genotype	Applied designation	NDNAD consequence	NDNAD risks	LR (court reporting consequence)
a	ab	aF	Match	False inclusion	$1/2p_a$ (can be anti-conservative)
a	ab	aa	No Match	False inclusion	No match
a	aa	aF	Match	False inclusion	$1/2p_a$ (conservative)
a	aa	aa	Match	None	p_a^2
ab	ab	ab	Match	None	$1/2p_ap_b$
FF	aa	FF	No information	Cannot be loaded	LR=1
FF	ab	FF	No information	Cannot be loaded	LR=1

of DNA are analyzed, the heterozygote balance is more variable. To report an allele, it must be above a certain level known as the analytical threshold (AT). Below this threshold, the background noise may mask the presence of an allele. Typically, a default AT is approximately 50 RFU for systems utilizing the AB3100/3130 automated sequencer, but is raised to about 200 RFU for the more sensitive AB3500 instrument. Given a heterozygous donor with genotype $g = (ab)$, we define drop-out to be the event, where the affected allele in the crime-stain is below the AT. We define extreme allele drop-out to be the event, where the affected allele in the crime stain is below the AT, and the present allele is above T (Fig. 3.5).

Allele drop-out is just an extreme form of reduced heterozygote balance (H_b); the probability of drop-out increases as the amount of DNA analyzed decreases.

3.5. Towards a meaningful definition of the low-template-DNA (T) threshold

To determine the T threshold, we are specifically concerned with the event, where the donor $g = (ab)$, and the crime stain is $R = a$, and a is the present allele. It is implicit under this definition that probability $Pr(R = a|g = (ab), H_p)$, conditional on the prosecution proposition (H_p), can only be non-zero if drop-out of allele b is possible. Conversely, under H_d, the proposition that the locus is an (aa) homozygote, i.e., there

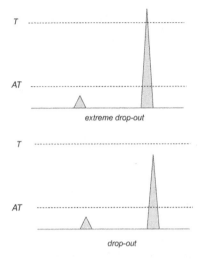

Figure 3.5 When drop-out occurs, one of the alleles is below the limit of detection (AT) threshold. With extreme drop-out, the present allele is above the low template threshold T. Reproduced from [143], with permission from Elsevier.

is no drop-out, is entirely valid. A formal statistical treatment can be used to assess the strength of evidence, but to do this it is necessary to include the probability of allele drop-out, p_D. Buckleton and Triggs [149] point out that when p_D goes to one, the LR goes to zero (exclusion) if the size of the present allele approaches T.

A crude definition of the stochastic threshold (T) follows: In a population of individuals having n heterozygote genotypes (for one marker), given a heterozygote (ab), and drop-out of either a or b, the T threshold is the maximum observed peak height of the present allele (i.e., the allele that has not dropped out, so it appears to be a homozygote). Consequently, the perceived purpose of T is to define the transition point between the conventional high-template versus the low-template-DNA profile, relative to the size of the present allele. According to this definition, the threshold, $T = x$ (RFU), where a present allele is of type a with associated height of y_a, so that $y_a < T$, means that drop-out is possible, and the genotype is designated as (aF). If $y_a > T$, then drop-out is deemed to be not possible, and the genotype is designated as (aa). But we must now consider whether this "all or nothing approach" based on a threshold or "cut-off" point is realistic. The problem is illustrated in Fig. 3.6. If we choose a threshold of 150 RFU, this means that the profile is high template, conventional, i.e., not low-template, whereas if the peak is 1 RFU lower, it suddenly becomes low-template. This sudden change in a binary classification over 1 RFU is illogical, because the *probability of drop-out* flips from 0 to 1, and is called the falling-off-the-cliff-effect.

Figure 3.6 An illustration of the falling-off-the-cliff-effect. There is a sudden change of definition of low-template vs conventional DNA over 1 RFU.

3.6. Historical development of probabilistic evaluation of drop-out

In 2009–2010 there was a debate in the journal Forensic Science International (FSI): Genetics, where the distinction between low-template and conventional DNA profiling was discussed [150]. Proponents who wished to distinguish between low-template and conventional DNA, based on sample quantity, claimed that low-template analysis was not robust, and its use should be restricted to investigative analysis [151]. A cut-off of 200 pg DNA was proposed to delineate between the two categories. This is an example of the falling-off-the-cliff-effect. A DNA sample with 200 pg is acceptable, where as one with 199 pg is not. The way forward is to avoid the debate completely by building probabilistic models, where the probability of a drop-out event is measured relative to the increasing size of the present peak. The cut-off is avoided, because the shift from conventional to low-template is gradual, part of a continuum. Adoption of probabilistic definitions removes the need to categorize. Instead, a universal method is introduced that can be applied to interpretation of all DNA profiles, regardless of the quantity of the sample, or its quality.

When it comes to assessing the strength of evidence of a DNA profile, if the crime stain is a low-template single allele a, then $Pr(E|H_d) = p_a^2$. If the reference sample from the suspect shows two alleles (ab), then there is no longer a match (Fig. 3.7). The evidence can only be justified under the prosecution proposition if drop-out *has* happened with a probability of one. However, the defense can argue two possibilities to explain the evidence. If drop-out *has not* occurred, then the true donor is homozygote $Pr(E|H_d) = p_a^2$. Alternatively, if drop-out *has* happened, then the donor has any allele, other than a and $Pr(E|H_d) = 2p_a p_b$. Putting the likelihood ratio together gives

$$LR = \frac{1}{\underbrace{p_a^2}_{\text{no drop-out}} + \underbrace{2p_a(1-p_a)}_{\text{drop-out}}} \quad (3.2)$$

Simplifying the formula,

$$LR \approx \frac{1}{2p_a - p_a^2} \quad (3.3)$$

Eq. (3.3) is known as the *2p* rule, and it was the first probabilistic attempt to deal with the phenomenon of drop-out. Strictly, the denominator should be reduced by p_a^2, but for simplicity, this was not carried out.

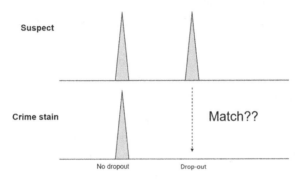

Figure 3.7 A comparison of a reference profile from a suspect compared to a crime stain that exhibits drop-out under the prosecution proposition.

3.7. Introducing probability of drop-out

A theory to incorporate drop-out into probabilistic calculations was introduced by Gill et al. [142]. The example from the previous section is continued using a crime-stain type $E = a$ and reference sample from a suspect, which is type (ab). We will keep using p_D as an abbreviation of the allele drop-out probability. It is informative to make a table to list the various possibilities, Table 3.3, where g is the genotype that is possible under the defense proposition.

Table 3.3 Evaluation of a crime stain profile $E = a$ and $S = ab$. M_j is the genotype or collection of ordered alleles that we consider as having contributed to the crime stain. Here, for simplicity, we do not distinguish between probability of drop-out for homozygotes vs. heterozygotes.

Proposition	g	$Pr(g)$	$Pr(E\|g)$	Products
1	(aQ)	$2p_a(1-p_a)$	$(1-p_D)p_D$	$2p_a(1-p_a) \times (1-p_D)p_D$
2	(aa)	p_a^2	$(1-p_D)$	$p_a^2 \times (1-p_D)$
			Sum of products	$Pr(E\|H_d)$ =sum of above

3.7.1 The defense proposition

Proposition 1: If drop-out has occurred, g is designated aQ, where 'Q' is any allele *except* for a. The probability $Pr(g)$ is in the third column and is the same as described for the denominator of Eq. (3.2) in the previous section. In the next column, $Pr(E|g)$, the probability of drop-out is considered. Allele a *has not* dropped out with probability $1 - p_D$, whereas allele Q *has* dropped out with probability p_D. Next, these probabilities are multiplied together to form the "Products" column.

Proposition 2: If drop-out *has not* occurred, then the genotype is (aa) with $Pr(g) = p_a^2$. There is no drop-out, hence $Pr(E|g) = 1 - p_D$, and these two probabilities are multiplied together in the "Products" column.

Finally, the probability of the evidence under H_d is calculated from the sum of products.

Note that the elements under $Pr(g)$ are the same as described in Eq. (3.2).

3.7.2 The prosecution proposition

The prosecution proposition is that the suspect is type (ab). This is "Proposition 1" statement in Table 3.3. Allele a has not dropped out, whereas allele b has, hence the combined probability is $(1 - p_D)p_D$. As with previous examples, $Pr(g) = 1$, because we condition upon the genotype of the suspect: (aQ).

Forming the likelihood ratio: The likelihood ratio is formulated from the sum of products in Table 3.3:

$$LR = \frac{Pr(E|H_p)}{Pr(E|H_d)}$$
$$= \frac{(1 - p_D)p_D}{[2p_a(1 - p_a) \times (1 - p_D)p_D] + [p_a^2 \times (1 - p_D)]} \tag{3.4}$$
$$= \frac{p_D}{p_a[2(1 - p_a) \times p_D + p_a]}$$

In Eq. (3.4), if $p_D = 1$ is substituted then Eq. (3.3), $LR = 1/2p_a - p_a^2$, is recovered. Up until now (Section 3.6), the numerator of the likelihood ratio, the prosecution proposition is assigned a probability of one. However, this exercise shows that p_D is in the numerator, and its value must be less than one when low-template samples are analyzed. This means that it is not neutral to ignore probability of drop-out. A plot of the "2p" rule vs. Eq. (3.4) Fig. 3.8A, where $p_a = p_b = 0.2$ shows that it is anti-conservative when $p_D < 0.5$. When $p_D < 0.05$, the $LR < 1$. It follows that it is particularly inadvisable to use the 2p rule when the present allele is above the stochastic threshold T, because this equates to $p_D \approx 0$, which results in the strength of evidence being strongly in favor of the defense proposition (Fig. 3.8B). The evidence is more likely if the donor to the crime stain is homozygote, i.e., it is clearly unreasonable to postulate drop-out if the surviving allele was a peak that was well above the background so that the expectation of drop-out would be low [149].

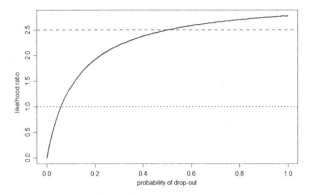

(A) Comparison of *LR*s calculated using the '2p' rule, without p_D (red dotted line) vs. eq. (3.4), which includes probability of drop-out. Black dotted line shows LR=1, the point of neutrality. When the line dips below, it favours the defence proposition of exclusion. In this example $p_a = p_b = 0.2$

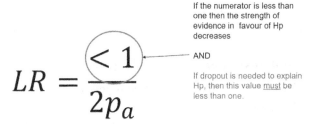

(B) The '2p' rule. If allele drop out, using the parameter p_D, is taken into account, the numerator (prosecution proposition) is less than one, and as a result the strength of evidence in favour of the prosecution proposition must decrease.

Figure 3.8 Relationship of the 2p rule and probability of drop-out.

Fig. 3.9 Illustrates a phenotypic homozygote (i.e., could be a heterozygote, where one allele has dropped out), where the size gradually changes between T and the AT [34].

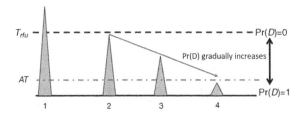

Figure 3.9 Alleles 1–4 are phenotypic homozygotes of decreasing size. The probability of allele drop-out p_D increases as the size of the surviving peak decreases.

3.8. A method to calculate probability of drop-out and the stochastic threshold

The stochastic threshold is often determined by experimentation, and is set to an arbitrary level, where it is highly unlikely that a drop-out event occurs if an allele is above the designated threshold. This enables a homozygote to be designated with a high degree of confidence. If a single allele at a locus, denoted as a, appears below the stochastic threshold, it is designated (aF), where 'F' signifies that "any allele", including a, may be present.

However, previous sections show that the stochastic threshold (T) cannot be thought of in absolute terms of a cut-off because of the falling-off-the-cliff-effect. Nevertheless, it is possible to apply $T = x$ RFU if qualified by a risk analysis. This can be accomplished by considering a population of n heterozygotes, genotype (ab), and drop-out of either a or b, then T is the peak height that will not be exceeded by the present (surviving) allele, with a certain probability. This probability (in terms of risk) is determined by the database users, prosecuting authorities, and not by the scientist. In practice, users will want a very low risk of error, which would reduce the number of useful profiles, i.e., those that could be reported to the national DNA database (NDNAD).

3.8.1 Experimental design and data collection

Data collected to determine setting T should be representative of the crime-stain samples used in the NDNAD. As a starting point, data can be generated in the laboratory, which represent low-template-DNA profiles, where extreme allele drop-out occurs.

By way of example, the ISFG DNA commission [63] described an experimental regime that employed a series of dilution experiments, either a body fluid, or more usually for practical reasons, extracted and purified DNA. It is important to use dilutions that are in the critical region, where extreme allele drop-out is, or is not occurring.

Considering a heterozygote, there are three possible outcomes (we use a notation in parentheses, where 1 means drop-out, and 0 means no drop-out):

1. Two alleles are present (0,0).
2. One allele is present, and the other is absent: (1,0) or (0,1).
3. Both alleles are absent—locus drop-out (1,1).

The experiment was designed so that the data produce all three types of events. This is easiest to achieve if the laboratory runs a pilot study to determine a range of concentrations of DNA that produce all three states within the same experiment.

We are interested in the peak heights of the alleles. An allele is deemed to have dropped out if it is below the AT of 50 RFU (for example). To carry out the experiment, it is useful to lower the detection limit threshold on the sequencing instrument to, e.g., 30 RFU, because this extends the curve and improves the probability of drop-out, p_D, estimation below the AT.

Table 3.4 (A) Raw dataset showing allele designation and its recorded peak height (RFU). (B) Allele peak height 1 from (A) shown with the drop-out state of allele 2 decided by *AT* of 50 RFU. The table is reproduced from [63] with permission from Elsevier.

Sample no.	Allele designation 1	Allele peak height 1	Allele designation 2	Allele peak height 2
1	17	135	25	193
2	11	30	13	80
3	29	157	30	160
4	14	30	16	142
5	13	319	14	117
6	6	150	9.3	36
7	21	56	23	30

(A)

Sample no.	Allele peak height 1	Drop-out state 2
1	135	0
2	30	0
3	157	0
4	30	0
5	319	0
6	150	1
7	56	1

(B)

A small subset of seven observed heterozygote loci is shown from a dataset of 496 loci (in total) from a validation exercise of the SGM plus kit (Table 3.4A):

Step 1: Taking each row in Table 3.4A, an allele is designated "1" if its partner has dropped out (< 50 RFU), or "0" if it has not dropped out (≥ 50 RFU). We only do this for the first allele in the table.

Step 2: Make a new table showing the peak height of allele 1 and the drop-out state of allele "2" (Table 3.4B).

3.8.2 An explanation of logistic regression

Ordinary linear regression models use the formula

$$y = a + bx$$

where y is the dependent variable (which could be the drop-out indicator of the allele of interest), and x is the explanatory variable (the height of the partner allele in RFU).

Note that y has a linear relationship to x; a and b are the linear model parameters, where a is the intercept, and b is the gradient of the slope.

In the example shown in Table 3.4B, the dependent variable (y) is binary, either zero or one, so it cannot be used in a linear regression model. In this example, the *probability of allele drop-out* (p_D), is the dependent variable; the analysis employs *logistic regression*. This method works by calculating odds $p/(1-p)$, where p is some probability. For example, suppose we take a subset of data between 125 RFU–175 RFU and wish to calculate the odds of drop-out; we carry out experimentation, if 25 out of 100 loci exhibit drop-out ($p = 0.25$), this is translated into odds: $0.25/0.75 = 0.33$. Conversely, the odds of no drop-out is $0.75/0.25 = 3$.

These two numbers are asymmetrical, but applying natural logarithms regains this symmetry, since $log_e(0.33) = -1.099$, and $log_e(3) = 1.099$; the odds of drop-out vs. no drop-out are of opposite signs. Taking the natural logarithm of odds is known as the logit function, and the logistic regression formula is essentially the same as the linear regression formula, where $y = logit(p_D)$:

$$log_e \left[\frac{p_D}{1 - p_D} \right] = a + bx \tag{3.5}$$

After rearrangement, the model is usually expressed as

$$p_D = \frac{1}{1 + e^{-(a+bx)}} \tag{3.6}$$

In the open-source software, R, the following commands can be used:

```
fit = glm(y~x, family=binomial)
summary(fit)
```

where y is the binomial response p_D and x is the covariate (peak height RFU). An example plot is shown in Fig. 3.10.

It is informative to plot the logistic regression using log p_D on the y-axis, since this gives a straight-line relationship, and can be used to evaluate the risks at very low probabilities. For example, the risk of drop-out if there is a single allele at 250 RFU is $p_D = 4 \times 10^{-4}$. Because we have extended the estimation of the curve to 30 RFU, we can comfortably estimate the lower limit of drop-out, $p_D = 0.45$ at the $AT = 50$ RFU.

Allele drop-out and the stochastic threshold   105

Box 3.1   Using R code to plot logistic regression
The following script can be run in R to generate a graph.

```
# Prepare data in 2 columns with first column = peak height and col-
umn 2=binary response variable
# Save into .csv format and run the code to generate summary statis-
tics and plot
dat<-read.table(file="LogisticTableR.csv",sep=",",
header=TRUE)
x=dat[,1]
y=dat[,2]
data1=cbind.data.frame(x,y)
mod1 = glm(y x, family = binomial,data=data1)
summary(mod1)
plot(x,y,ylab="Probability of drop-out",xlab="size (Peak Height)",
                                         xlim=c(0,300),pch=20)
curve(predict(mod1,data.frame(x=x),type="resp"),
add=TRUE)
```

The logistic regression model has been widely used to provide an understanding of drop-out [152–154,93,155].

Finally, we note that the logistic regression model applies to heterozygotes only. The estimation is different for homozygotes, but we do not consider it further here, since Buckleton [149] showed that under the condition, where the evidence is allele a and the suspect is (aa), there is no anti-conservative issue with reporting p_a^2. The issue relates solely to the evidence being a and the suspect being (ab), where anti-conservativeness is a possibility with the 2p rule.

3.9. Using *STR-validator* to plot drop-out characteristics

STR-validator has a module to characterize drop-out. Select the *Drop-out* tab and click the button *Calculate* to open the window for drop-out analysis. There are drop-down menus to select a dataset and a reference dataset, respectively. The number of samples are shown next to the drop-down menus. The *Check subsetting* button opens up a separate window listing the reference samples and matching samples in the dataset. It is important that each sample is analyzed with the correct reference. In the *Options* group is a checkbox to ignore case in sample names. Drop-out is defined as an allele with a peak height lower than the *AT*. The lowest peak height in the dataset is automatically suggested as the *AT*. There are four ways to score drop-out alleles:
- Score drop-out relative to the low molecular weight allele
- Score drop-out relative to the high molecular weight allele

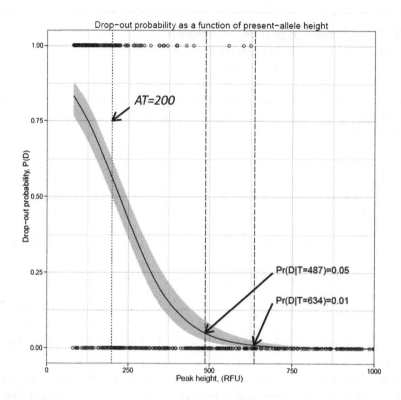

Figure 3.10 Estimation of the stochastic threshold by logistic regression of known heterozygotes from the AB3500xl analyzer. In this example, the analytical threshold (*AT*) is set at 200 RFU with this instrument. The stochastic thresholds corresponding to $p_D = 0.01$ and 0.05 are at 634 and 487 RFU, respectively. The same data were used to generate Fig. 2.2. Analysis of data carried out using the drop-out module of the R package *strvalidator* (version 1.3), plot customized using *ggplot2* (version 1.0). Reproduced from [85] with permission from Elsevier.

• Score drop-out relative to a random allele
• Score drop-out per locus

The first three options are recommended by [63], whereas the last option is included for experimental purposes. The first three options may discard many drop-out events, whereas the experimental option catches all drop-out events. On the other hand, the recommended options can score events below the AT, whereas the experimental option cannot. The effect of the scoring method on the accuracy of the predicted drop-out probabilities is not extensively studied. Multiple scoring methods can be selected. The function is executed by clicking the *Calculate* button. This will create a new data frame with the specified name and save it in the workspace.

The *Model* button opens a new window (Fig. 3.11) to model the drop-out probability based on the result from a drop-out analysis. There is a drop-down menu to select a dataset to model. There are options to print the model parameters, mark the stochastic threshold at a specified probability of drop-out, include the underlying observations, and to calculate a specified prediction interval. A conservative estimate of the stochastic threshold can be calculated from the prediction interval—the risk of observing a drop-out probability greater than the specified threshold limit, at the conservative peak height, is less than a specified value (e.g., $1 - 0.95 = 0.05$). To evaluate the goodness of fit t-value for the logistic regression the Hosmer–Lemeshow test is used [156]. A value below 0.05 indicates a poor fit. Alternatives to the logistic regression method are discussed in [157,111]. Additional settings to customize the plot are available in the expandable groups *Data points*, *Axes*, and *X labels*. Clicking the *Plot predicted drop-out probability* button will open up a separate plot window and draw the predicted probabilities for a range of peak heights (Fig. 3.11). The plot window can be resized. Changing the plot settings and clicking the plot button will update the plot window.

There are currently four heatmap plot options: *Average peak height*: to plot drop-out events and sort by average peak height; *Amount*: to plot drop-out events and sort by amount; *Concentration*: to plot drop-out events and sort by concentration; *Sample*: to plot drop-out events and sort by sample name. There are two other plot options: *ecdp* to plot the empirical cumulative distribution, and *Dotplot* to plot by marker. Clicking a plot button will open up a separate window, and will draw the plot (Fig. 3.12).

From the data, we can compute a probability of extreme allele drop-out, denoted by the term $(p_D, x > T)$, where $x =$ peak height, for any putative (T) as shown in Fig. 3.10.

3.10. Summary

When low levels of DNA are analyzed, the interpretation of DNA profiles are complicated, because of stochastic effects leading to imbalanced heterozygotes. An extreme form of heterozygote imbalance leads to the disappearance of one or both alleles and this is called allele drop-out. The higher the peak heights, or the greater the quantity of DNA, the lower the probability of drop-out. The stochastic threshold is the peak height level that corresponds to a probability of drop-out that is very low, so that if the practitioner observes a single allele at a locus, then it may be inferred that drop-out of a second (hidden) allele is unlikely to have occurred.

The stochastic threshold can be defined by estimating the probability of allele drop-out (e.g., $p_D = 0.05$) relative to peak height, determined by logistic regression of a series of samples of varying quantity, as recommended by the ISFG DNA Commission [144] (Fig. 3.10). A risk analysis associated with choice of p_D to designate T is provided by Gill et al. [143], and demonstrated by Kirkham et al. [95]. Alternative ways to estimate the T have been published: empirical cumulative distribution of peak heights from single heterozygote peaks [111]; peak height of the largest observed single heterozygote allele [90,158], and variance of heterozygote peak balance [159]. Butler [160], page 95,

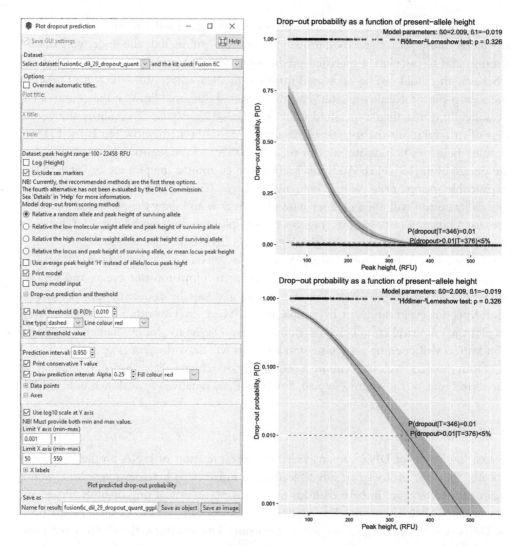

Figure 3.11 The *STR-validator* "Plot drop-out prediction" window (left) to visualize the regression model and the stochastic threshold. In this example, the axes are customized to Log_{10} scale. This produces a linear relationship, which are usually easier to read at small probabilities (bottom) compared to the default normal plot (top). Plots produced using *strvalidator* (version 2.2).

compares stochastic thresholds between the ABI 3130 and ABI 3500 instruments (the latter is much more sensitive).

The probability of drop-out has been shown to be locus-dependent [154,153]. It is also affected by the *AT* [161,162]. Although drop-out and allele length have been shown to correlate [162], it was also suggested by Lohmueller et al. [162] that logistic regressions, based on average drop-out estimation, resulted in robust *LRs*. This relation-

Allele drop-out and the stochastic threshold 109

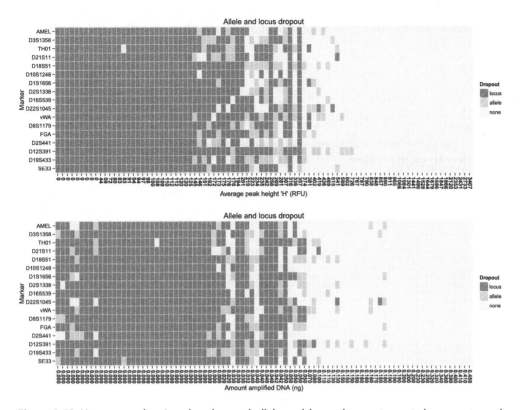

Figure 3.12 Heat maps showing the observed allele and locus drop-out events by average peak height (top) and by amount amplified DNA (bottom). One column represents the result from one sample, and there is one row for each locus. There is no specific order for ties. The amount of DNA was estimated from duplicate runs using Quantifiler Duo. Detection threshold to define drop-out was set to $AT = 200$ RFU. Average peak height was calculated using peak heights down to 80 RFU. Original colors were replaced to improve printed version. Reproduced from [116] with permission from Elsevier.

ship also held true with data from different STR multiplex systems [162]. However, the differences can be quite large between capillary electrophoresis instruments [95,158]; utilization of different numbers of PCR cycles has a significant effect [89,153].

Drop-out probability has been modeled by Gill et al. [143], who used the peak height of the surviving heterozygote peak as a predictor. Tvedebrink et al. [163] used the average peak height of the profile instead, arguing that this has lower variability than using a single peak observation [154]. Both methods rely upon empirical data. There are also simulation-based approaches that estimate the probability of drop-out using the crime scene profile and stated propositions. Balding et al. [70] used a simulated annealing algorithm to maximize the probability of evidence (i.e., using maximum likelihood estimation (MLE)), whereas Haned et al. [68] used Monte-Carlo simulations to generate a distribution of drop-out probabilities that would result in the observed number of alleles.

Notes

1. Typically, the 'consensus method' would be used to interpret low-template profiles as described in Chapter 4.2.
2. Laboratories will set these values according to their validation studies for given protocols. There will be some inter-laboratory variation.

CHAPTER 4

Low-template DNA

4.1. Historical

Forensic scientists are always motivated to increase the sensitivity of their methods. When PCR multiplexing was first introduced in 1995, PCR was generally limited to 28 cycles. Findlay et al. [164] demonstrated that single cells (buccal) could be successfully analyzed by amplifying DNA samples utilizing 34 PCR cycles using the AmpFlSTR SGM Plus multiplex system. However, there was a draw-back. Compared with conventional analysis, the interpretation was not straightforward—additional alleles (known as drop-in products) were occasionally observed; the size of stutter artefacts was enhanced; missing alleles, known as allele drop-out, were common. Increasing the sensitivity of PCR by raising the number of cycles was used to increase the range of evidence types available to analysis. A few examples of this rapid expansion to analyze all kinds of "trace" evidence included the following:

Wiegand and Kleiber [165], who analyzed epithelial cells transferred from an assailant after strangulation using 30–31 cycles of PCR. Van Hoofstat et al. [166] analyzed fingerprints from grips of tools with 28–40 cycles analysis of STRs from telogen hair roots, and hair shafts in the absence of the root was reported [167–169].

Enhancement of sensitivity was quickly adopted by anthropologists and forensic scientists to identify ancient DNA from bones ([170–172]. Gill et al. [173] used 38–43 cycles to analyze STRs from 70 year old bone from the Romanov family. Schmerer et al. [174,175] and Burger et al. [176] analyzed STRs from bone thousands of years old (60 and 50 PCR cycles respectively). Some authors used modified PCR methods, for example, a nested primer PCR strategy was used by Strom and Rechitsky [177]. This utilized a first round amplification with 40 cycles, with subsequent analysis of a portion with a further 20–30 cycles. This method was used to analyze DNA from charred human remains and minute amounts of blood. Modern multiplexes operate with a much more efficient biochemistry, so that the number of PCR cycles is reduced to 30. Now it is routine to analyze DNA from bones recovered from mass disasters and has led to the founding of major laboratories, such as the Internal Commission on Missing Persons (ICMP) laboratory in the Hague, Netherlands.

For a comprehensive review of the literature relating to trace DNA evidence, the reader is referred to Van Oorschot et al. [178].

All methods used to analyze low quantities of DNA suffered from the same basic disadvantages of stochastic (random) effects described in Chapter 3. If present in low copy-number, a DNA molecule will be delivered in variable quantities as a result

Forensic Practitioner's Guide to the Interpretation of Complex DNA Profiles
https://doi.org/10.1016/B978-0-12-820562-4.00012-2

Copyright © 2020 Elsevier Inc.
All rights reserved. **111**

of sampling variation. This leads to the preferential amplification of alleles. There are therefore several consequences that cannot be avoided:

- Locus drop-out, i.e., a whole locus fails to amplify.
- Allele drop-out may occur, because one of a pair of alleles at a heterozygote locus fails to be amplified to a detectable level.
- Heterozygote imbalance, as described in Section 3.1.
- Stutters may increase in size relative to the progenitor allele.
- Allele drop-in results in additional alleles "contaminating" the sample.

DNA profiles may not fully represent the source. Tarbelet et al. [179] originally suggested a method of replicated analyzes that comprised a rule that an allele could only be scored if observed at least twice in replicate samples. This theory was expanded by Gill et al. [142], who adopted Tarbelet's duplication rule. Later on, the introduction of new software solutions that incorporate the drop-in/drop-out probabilities into calculations [144] superseded the need to derive consensus sequences, and this approach was much to be preferred as it was able to take direct account of drop-in, drop-out, peak heights, and stutter, thereby taking account of much of the information available in the electropherogram (Chapters 6 and 8).

Low-template analysis was considered to be quite controversial when it was first introduced in the year 2000. Challenges included the lack of reproducibility, the uncertainty of the meaning of the evidence, and the impact of contamination. This culminated in a trial in 2007, "The Omagh Bombing trial", where the defendant was found "not guilty" and the judge criticized the use of low-template DNA (https://judiciaryni.uk/sites/judiciary/files/decisions/Queen%20v%20Sean%20Hoey.pdf). This led to temporary suspension of the method by UK authorities, but after review it was quickly reinstated: http://news.bbc.co.uk/1/hi/uk/7341251.stm. Instead of being called "low-copy-number", it was "re-branded" as "low-template" LT-DNA analysis, and since then it has become normal routine. LT-sensitivity is standard in the latest generation of multiplexes. In addition, sensitivity is increased by new biochemistry that reduces the effect of inhibitors on PCR. The Omagh trial demonstrated the need to ensure that the interpretation resided within a coherent framework—the DNA result, by itself, does not provide information of the activity, which requires some knowledge about "how" or "when" the profile was transferred. As time has progressed, it has become more apparent that DNA can easily transfer between objects and people. Interpretation at activity level is a challenge that needs to be addressed, and this is discussed further in Chapter 12.5.

4.2. The consensus method explained

The consensus method of interpretation was an early innovation to interpret low-template DNA. It was developed at the Forensic Science Service (UK) in response to a requirement to extend DNA analysis to "high volume crime", in particular burglary, theft of vehicles, etc., where items, such as steering wheels, were swabbed and submitted to the laboratory for analysis. Although Gill et al. [142] had developed a theoretical framework to interpret data that exhibited drop-out and drop-in, it was not ready for use in the year 2000, hence an alternative (less-than-ideal) strategy had to be found. The last sentence in the paper prophetically declares:

"Ultimately these guidelines will be superseded by expert systems utilising the Bayesian principles described in this paper."

The consensus method developed from the observation that single alleles could be recovered from empty tubes that were utilized as negative controls. These were included with every set of case samples analyzed.

An early example of results from 30 negative controls are shown in Fig. 4.1.

Negative controls showed evidence of spurious bands that were quite common observations. In Table 4.1, there were nine instances where no drop-in events were observed; fourteen examples of single alleles; six examples with two alleles, and one example with three alleles.

The drop-in probability p_C can be easily estimated per sample per locus from

$$p_C = \frac{n}{N \times L} \tag{4.1}$$

where p_C = probability of drop-in; n = number of observed drop-in events; N = the number of negative control samples; L = number of loci.

Hence, in the example (Table 4.1) there are a total of $n = 24$ drop-in events; $N = 30$; $L = 10$ STR loci:

$$p_C = \frac{24}{30 \times 10} = 0.08 \tag{4.2}$$

The recorded drop-in level was very high; it was an early experiment and highlighted the need for stringent precautionary measures to be adopted to minimize levels of contamination and drop-in. Later, a level of $p_C = 0.05$ was adopted as the default value for probabilistic genotyping software. However, by current standards, this value is also somewhat high. System and laboratory process have been much improved over the past twenty years so that much lower drop-in values, in the region $p_C = 0.001$, would now be typical. This analysis does not take account of peak height; it is revisited in Chapter 7.10 to describe how *EuroForMix* incorporates this information.

Drop-in events tend to be random and can occur at any locus. As a result, it is unlikely that a drop-in allele will be duplicated in a set of replicates. Here a replicate is always defined as two or more samples taken from a *single* DNA extract that are taken forward to separate PCRs. Stochastic effects cause differences in the number of molecules retrieved, along with their allelic identities (Chapter 3). Table 4.2 shows an example of the consensus method.

114 Forensic Practitioner's Guide to the Interpretation of Complex DNA Profiles

Table 4.1 A compilation of spurious alleles found in 30 replicate negative controls (AMPFlSTR SGM plus) from Table 1 of [142]: Amelo: amelogenin; THO: HUMTH01; D21: D21S11; D18: D18S51; D8: D8S1179; VWA: HUMVWFA31/A; FGA: HUMFIBRA/FGA; D19: D19S433; D16: D16S539; D2: D2S1338; D3: D3S1179. Reproduced from [142], with permission from Elsevier.

Sample	Amelo	D19	D3	D8	THO	VWA	D21	FGA	D16	D18	D2
1	–	–	–	–	–	–	–	–	–	–	–
2	–	–	15	–	–	–	–	–	–	–	–
3	–	–	–	–	–	–	–	–	–	–	–
4	–	–	17	–	–	–	–	–	–	–	–
5	–	–	–	–	–	–	–	–	–	–	–
6	–	–	–	–	–	–	–	–	–	–	–
7	–	14	–	–	–	–	–	–	–	–	–
8	X	–	–	13	–	–	–	–	–	–	–
9	–	–	14	–	–	–	–	–	–	–	–
10	X	–	–	–	–	–	–	–	–	–	–
11	X	–	–	–	–	16	–	–	–	–	–
12	–	–	–	–	–	–	–	–	–	–	–
13	–	13	–	–	–	–	–	–	–	–	–
14	–	–	–	–	–	–	–	–	–	–	–
15	–	–	16	–	–	–	–	–	–	–	–
16	–	–	–	15	–	–	–	–	–	–	–
17	X	15	–	–	–	–	–	–	–	–	–
18	X	14	–	14	–	–	–	–	–	–	–
19	–	–	–	–	–	–	28	–	–	–	–
20	–	–	–	–	–	–	–	–	–	13	–
21	–	–	–	–	–	–	33.2	–	–	–	–
22	–	–	–	–	–	–	–	–	–	–	–
23	–	–	–	10	–	–	25 27	–	–	–	–
24	–	–	–	–	–	–	–	–	–	–	–
25	–	–	15	–	–	–	–	–	–	–	–
26	–	–	–	–	–	–	–	–	–	–	–
27	X	–	–	10	–	–	–	–	–	–	–
28	–	15	–	–	–	–	–	–	–	–	–
29	–	–	15	–	–	16	–	–	–	–	–
30	–	15	–	–	–	–	–	–	–	–	–
+ ve	X Y	14 15	15 17	11 12	6 7 9.3	16 17	28 31.2	23 25	11 13	12 13	17 22
– ve	–	–	–	–	9.3	–	–	–	–	–	–

Consider two replicates R_1 and R_2 that have provided different DNA profiles (Table 4.2). A comparison is shown with the suspect's reference profile in the bottom row. The "F" designation (where F signifies any allele) was used to signify a potential dropout event, for example, in replicate R_2, locus TH01, the second allele could be "6" if

Table 4.2 An example of the consensus method, where two replicate analyzes (R_1, R_2) are analyzed. Alleles must be reproduced to be scored in the consensus profile, otherwise the "F" designation is used. Reproduced from [142], with permission from Elsevier.

Sample	Amel	VWA	TH0	D8	FGA	D21	D18	D19	D3	D16	D2
R_1	X,Y	16,19	6,7	12,14	20,24	28,30	12,F	13,17	15,16	11,13	17,20
R_2	X,Y	16,19	6,F	12,14	20,24,25	28,30	12,F	13,17	15,16	11,13	17,20
Consensus	X,Y	16,19	6,F	12,14	20,24	28,30	12,F	13,17	15,16	11,13	17,20
Suspect	X,Y	16,19	6,7	12,14	20,24	28,30	12,12	13,17	15,16	11,13	17,20

it was homozygote, or any other allele if heterozygote. At locus FGA, there are three alleles: 20, 24, 25, hence one must be a drop-in event if there is just one contributor. Because allele "25" is not present in R_1, it does not appear in the consensus. The only difference between the consensus and reference in this example is at TH01, where a drop-out event of allele 7 is recorded, and D18, where the F designation is provided. The 2p rule (Chapter 3.7) was used whenever the F designation appeared.

Benschop et al. [180,181] compared different methods of generating consensus profile results ranging from $n =$ two to six amplifications. These methods included that, as described above, alleles reproduced in two or more replicates were included in the consensus. The "$n/2$" method included alleles detected in at least half of the replicates. It was shown that the most efficient method for accuracy and database searches was the $n/2$ method and the optimal number of replicates (n) was four (assuming sufficient sample was available). The authors also compared results with the composite method, where all alleles in all replicates were combined. This resulted in profiles with drop-in alleles present and "less perfectly matching loci", and was not recommended for routine use. Conversely, Buckleton et al. [182] found that the composite method was acceptable, provided that the probabilities of drop-out and drop-in were small, and the analysis was carried out using the generalized statistical theory described in Section 4.4.1.

4.2.1 Contamination vs. drop-in

It is important to distinguish between contamination and drop-in. Both are detected by negative controls, but their causes and effects are different [63]:

1. Contamination is an event, where a spurious DNA profile is obtained, originating from a laboratory source, most likely from a person actually working in the laboratory, or from a crime scene investigator collecting the pieces of evidence. For this reason many laboratories insist that workers and visitors to sensitive parts of laboratories provide a DNA sample. This is compared with both control and case-work samples to determine whether a traceable contamination event has occurred. Because alleles from a contamination are from the same source, they are said to be *dependent*. Contamination is usually low-level and partial. The following is a summary of contamination causes:

a. Transfer from scientists and police investigators: skin flakes or saliva spray from talking. This is minimized by good laboratory practice—gowns and face-masks. Elimination databases of scientists and police investigators are compared to discover inadvertent transfer of DNA. A study by Fonneløp et al. [183] demonstrated that contamination of evidence bags by police and staff working in laboratories was of particular concern. Education is important to make sure that all staff members are aware of the need to take particular care when handling evidence by taking precautionary measures, such as those outlined by ENFSI [184] and the UK forensic science regulator [185].

b. Reagent contamination: plasticware may be contaminated during the manufacturing process. Sterile does not equate to DNA-free, because methods used to sterilize plasticware primarily used for medical use, eg., gamma irradiation, destroys bacteria and viruses, but does not destroy DNA. An efficient method to destroy potential contaminating DNA on plasticware employs ethylene oxide [186–188], but this chemical is too dangerous for routine laboratories to use, hence this process is best applied at manufacturing source. Any reagent may be potentially contaminated at manufacturing source. The major scientific societies, ENFSI and SWGDAM, recognized this to be an issue of concern, and jointly published guidelines to encourage manufacturer databases to check for spurious profiles [189]. In practice, it has proven difficult to persuade manufacturers to comply, primarily because of data protection rules. The UK Forensic Science Service previously held a manufacturer contamination database until its closure. This has now been adopted by ICMP with support from ENFSI DNA database management review and recommendations [190]. In 2016 an ISO standard for forensic DNA-grade products [191] was launched and has been adopted by some manufacturers. However, it has been criticized as insufficient by Vanek et al. [192] on the grounds that the standard "specifies requirements for the production of products used in the collection, storage, and analysis of biological material for forensic DNA purposes, but does not set specifications for consumables and reagents used in post-amplification analyses."

c. Contamination may arise from another sample that has been processed in the laboratory. For example, in the case of wrongful arrest of Adam Scott [193], pp. 21–25, contamination of samples occurred when a CE microtitre plate was inadvertently reused. In the case of Queen v. Farah Jama [193], pp. 27–30, the contamination occurred in a medical examination room; samples had been taken from the same suspect the previous day and somehow managed to contaminate samples from an unrelated case. The exact mechanism of transfer was never discovered though. The UK regulator has published guidance to prevent contamination in custodial facilities and medical examination rooms [194].

2. Drop-in is a consequence of single alleles from fragmented DNA from different individuals [195]. This DNA is mobile in aerosol and is present in household dust

[196]. If a DNA fragment falls into an open tube it will be amplified. If two DNA fragments fall into an open tube, both will be amplified, but they are probably from two different individuals. These alleles are treated as *independent*. The distinction is important, because probabilistic genotyping models that take account of drop-in assume independence of alleles in the calculations, hence this does not accommodate contamination, which can instead be incorporated into a standard *LR* analysis as an unknown contributor in both numerator and denominator.[1]

Regardless of how well a laboratory is organized, drop-in and contamination are unavoidable. Both will occur. The purpose of monitoring with negative controls is to estimate the levels of both occurrences. This knowledge is important for quality control monitoring of the laboratory; it is described further by Gill and Kirkham [197]. The negative control does not give assurance about whether there is contamination or drop-in within a particular sample. So the absence of drop-in or contamination in the negative control does not mean that the entire batch of samples is completely free of either. It is an error to use a clean negative control result as evidence that contamination has not occurred in a sample, such a test does not exist.

Drop-in and contamination events tend to be low in peak height, so that the larger the allele peaks, the less likely it is to be a contamination or drop-in event [197]. For quantitative probabilistic models, this peak height relationship can be modeled using an exponential distribution (described further in Chapter 7.10).

A question that often arises is how many drop-in events can be reasonably assumed to be drop-in as opposed to "contamination". Following the same method of Taylor et al. [121], Hansson et al. [195] plotted the observed number of peaks per profile, defined as relative occurrence, and superimposed the fitted Poisson distribution with rate parameter $\lambda = 0.437$. Poisson is a discrete probability distribution that expresses the probability of a given number of events occurring in a fixed interval if these events occur with a known constant rate, defined by λ, and are independent of each other. The "plot contamination" function in *STR-validator* was used to create Fig. 4.1. The plot shows the observed relative occurrence of peaks per profile from 1061 negative controls extracted from the 228 crime sample batches, using the PowerPlex ESX 17 Fast kit. The fitted Poisson distribution shows the expectation for independent events. The point where the drop-in peaks no longer fit the Poisson distribution (independence model) delineates drop-in contamination from gross contamination. In the example, the Poisson distribution is fitted to 0–3 alleles, but does not explain the observation of four or more alleles. Consequently, the drop-in parameter may be reasonably applied to three drop-in events, i.e., from three different contributors. Anything more is regarded as contamination, where the alleles are *dependent*, i.e., such alleles are best treated to be from a single contributor.

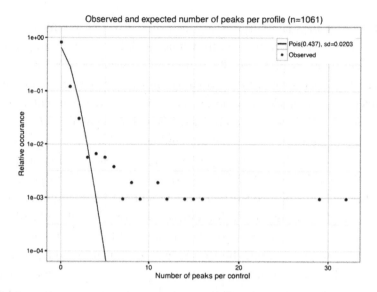

Figure 4.1 Plot of the observed number of peaks per profile for 1061 negative controls extracted from the 228 crime sample batches. The fitted Poisson distribution shows the expectation for independent events. Reproduced from [195] with permission from Elsevier.

4.3. Statistical analysis

A generalized statistical theory to take account of drop-out, drop-in, and stutter was provided by [142]. This paper laid the ground-work for the basic theory, and was used to justify the consensus model, which was intended as an interim measure. Readers interested in a full statistical analysis are referred to the paper. The following is a simplified explanation that expands Chapter 3.7.

4.4. Working with replicates

There has been some discussion in the literature about the merits of carrying out replicate analysis [180,181,80]. The practice originally arose from the empirical "consensus" method described in Section 4.2. With this protocol, only alleles that were reproduced could be reported. It was noted that drop-in events were essentially random and unlikely to be reproducible (so they would not be reported). The problem with the empirical method was that it did not take account of all the available information, and its use to interpret mixtures was constrained. There is no restriction or absolute requirement for probabilistic models to use replicates. Sometimes there is insufficient DNA to carry out replication. If there is sufficient DNA, then replication is possible, but of course increases the costs of the test. From a purely scientific point of view, replicate analyses are always useful, because they can be used to corroborate test results. But if very small amounts of DNA are available, the downside is that a test itself may be compromized if dilution results in excessive allele drop-out. Whether replication is carried out or not is a decision that depends on the quantity of material available.

Replicate samples are prepared from single extracts, which are split into at least two different portions before PCR analysis. If low-template, then the replicates will differ, because of stochastic effects discussed in Chapter 3. Likelihood ratios can either be analyzed per replicate, or a single combined LR, known as a joint probability, can be provided that encompasses all replicates.

Haned et al. [68] explain

"Once the genotypes of the unknown individuals are derived, conditioned on the data observed in the three replicates, the replicate probabilities can be multiplied together. However, this is different from simply deriving the LR for each replicate separately, and taking the product, since the replicates are simultaneously conditioned on the genotypes of the hypothesised contributors."

4.4.1 An example to assess the strength of the evidence of three replicates

Consider the crime-stain evidence that was analyzed three times, and three different genotypes were observed at the D18S511 locus: $R_1 = 12$; $R_2 = 16$; $R_3 = 12, 16$ and the suspect $S = 12, 16$.

Evaluation of the evidence proceeds using the likelihood ratio framework described in Chapter 1.6.

Either:
H_p: The DNA from replicates R_1, R_2, R_3 came from the suspect S.
or:
H_d: the DNA from replicates R_1, R_2, R_3 came from an unknown (unrelated) person.

To assess the strength of the evidence, where drop-out and drop-in events are possible we need to include two parameters to represent the probability of these respective events: The allele drop-out probability p_D and the drop-in probability p_C. The probabilities of *no drop-out* and *no drop-in* are $(1 - p_D)$ and $(1 - p_C)$, respectively, abbreviated to $p_{\overline{D}}$ and $p_{\overline{C}}$. Since homozygotes have two copies of the same allele, this double dose means that it is less likely to drop-out compared to an allele of a heterozygote. If a homozygote drops out, then this is approximated by p_D^2 [65]. However, Balding and Buckleton [198] state that a better estimate is provided by the formula $0.5 \times p_D^2$.

If drop-out occurs, then we do not know the allele's identity, because it is not observed— it could be any allele other than those that are already visualized in the crime stain. To allow for this, a virtual allele called "Q" was introduced [65]. In this example, the probability of Q is $p_Q = 1 - p_{12} - p_{16}$. The advantage of using Q in this way, is that it simplifies the calculations, which is important when mixtures are analyzed.

120 Forensic Practitioner's Guide to the Interpretation of Complex DNA Profiles

The alternative would be to cycle through every possible allele at a locus: for each replicate, under H_d it would be necessary to carry out probabilistic calculations of all of the 18 possible pairwise combinations listed in STRidER, that must include allele 12 for R_1, and allele 16 for R_2. For R_1 combinations 9,12; 10,12; 11,12; 12,13 etc are all required in the calculation. Using the Q designation (ignoring drop-in for the time-being) simplifies this to just three combinations to consider: $Q, 12$; $12,12$; $12,16$. Taking account of drop-in requires H_d considerations of $12, Q$; $16, Q$, and Q, Q. The latter is true if alleles 12 and 16 are both drop-in events.

The formulae necessary to make the LR calculation can be built up as shown in Table 4.3. Here g is the conditioned genotype of the donor, which is under consideration, and $Pr(g)$ is the probability of observing the genotype g. R_i is the replicate genotype, and $Pr(R_i|g)$ is the probability of the replicate R_i when conditioned on genotype g.

The steps are as follows:

- Step 1: Assess the reasonable random man genotypes from the information in the replicates. List these in the column g, enumerated as $g_1, g_2, \ldots$ etc.
- Step 2: Calculate $Pr(g)$ in the second column
- Step 3: Calculate $Pr(R_i|g)$ in columns R_1, R_2, and R_3
- Step 4: Calculate the products of each row
- Step 5: Sum the products
- Step 6: The numerator is the product $Pr(R_i|g)$ corresponding to the probability of observing replicate R_i, given the genotype of the suspect. In the example (Table 4.4), this appears as part of the term at the right hand side of the second row corresponding to the genotype 12,16, but without the frequency terms.

Table 4.3 A format to illustrate the calculation of the LR.

g	$Pr(g)$	R_1	R_2	R_3	**Calculation**
g_1	$Pr(g_1)$	$Pr(R_1|g_1)$	$Pr(R_2|g_1)$	$Pr(R_3|g_1)$	Product of this row
g_2	$Pr(g_2)$	$Pr(R_1|g_2)$	$Pr(R_2|g_2)$	$Pr(R_3|g_2)$	Product of this row
g_3	$Pr(g_3)$	$Pr(R_1|g_3)$	$Pr(R_2|g_3)$	$Pr(R_3|g_3)$	Product of this row
					Sum of this column

In the following example from [142], for simplicity, we consider that homozygote and heterozygote genotypes have equal probabilities of drop-out. In Chapter 5, we describe separate drop-out probabilities for each type.

For each replicate, we need to apply the drop-out and drop-in probabilities, where we condition on the g genotype. For example, $R_2 = 16$ given $g = 12, 12$ can only be explained if allele 12 has dropped out *and* allele 16 has dropped in. Though $12, 12$ is a homozygote genotype, for simplicity, we assign the drop-out probability with p_D (instead of p_D^2, in keeping with the description in [142]. Whenever an allele drops in, we apply the population frequency of that allele to the calculation, giving probability $p_C p_{16}$ (we assume drop-in to be random, hence the probability of a particular allele appearing is its frequency in the population). Converting words into a formula gives $p_D p_C p_{16}$, which is multiplied by the adjacent rows in Table 4.4 to provide the product in the final column (multiplication is used, because all of the events described in a given row are conditioned on the genotype g). This is repeated for all rows in Table 4.4, which are multiplied together to give the formula in the final column. The sum of the final column provides the (marginalized) probability of the evidence conditioned on proposition H_d being true; this is called the "law of total probability" (the same formula is used separately for both propositions, H_p and H_d, to construct the LR). When conditioning on the suspect, only the term $p(R_i|g)$ is calculated, where $g = S = (12, 16)$, since the genotype of the suspect is known (hence no allele frequencies are used).

The following is a summary of the above in a number of steps:

1. Under the prosecution proposition H_p, it is clear that if the suspect with genotype (12,16) contributed the crime stain, then there is drop-out in R_1 and R_2. If H_p is true, then in R_1 the 16 allele must have dropped out; for R_2, the 12 allele has dropped out, and there is no drop-out or drop-in in the R_3 replicate. The absence of alleles in the first two replicates must reduce the probability of the evidence.

2. Conversely, if H_d is true, then all of the different possible genotypes of an unknown individual are listed under the first column, g, in Table 4.4.

3. Consider $g = (12,12)$: The first replicate is $R_1 = 12$; the evidence is explained if there is no (homozygote) drop-out, and no drop-in (contamination): $p_{\overline{D}} p_{\overline{C}}$.

4. The second replicate is $R_2 = 16$; the evidence is explained if there is a (homozygote) drop-out of allele 12 with probability p_D (a better estimate would be p_D^2, but we are being consistent with [142], where no distinction was made between homozygote and heterozygote drop-out).

5. The third replicate is $R_3 = 12, 16$; the evidence is explained if there is no (homozygote) drop-out of allele 12 and a drop-in of allele 16: $p_{\overline{D}} p_C p_{16}$.

6. Repeat for all genotypes in the g column.

The next step is to tabulate the results and derive a formula [142]. Ignoring the Q terms for simplicity (these will be small if p_D is small) this was shown to be

$$LR = \frac{1}{2p_{12}p_{16}[1 + \frac{p_{12}p_{16}p_C^2}{p_D p_{\overline{D}}^2 p_{\overline{C}}^2}]} \tag{4.3}$$

Provided that p_C is small (< 0.3), the LR can be approximated to the inverse match probability of the suspect's genotype:

$$LR \approx \frac{1}{2p_{12}p_{16}} \tag{4.4}$$

Such simplifications are often not possible, however, which is why each case needed separate consideration.

Table 4.4 Calculation of the likelihood ratio for an example, where three replicates show evidence of spurious alleles and drop-out. The summation of the products gives the probability of the evidence under H_d. The probability of the evidence under H_p is provided in red (medium grey in print version) type for $g = 12, 16$. For simplicity, p_D is used to define probability of drop-out for both homozygotes and heterozygotes. The main purpose of the demonstration is to illustrate the complexity of simple examples, and the consequent need for software to take over the burden of calculation.

g	$Pr(g)$	$R_1(12)$	$R_2(16)$	$R_3(12, 16)$	**Products**
12, 12	p_{12}^2	$p_{\overline{D}}p_{\overline{C}}$	$p_D p_C p_{16}$	$p_{\overline{D}}p_C p_{16}$	$p_{\overline{D}}^2 p_{\overline{C}} p_D p_C^2 p_{12}^2 p_{16}^2$
12, 16	$2p_{12}p_{16}$	$p_D p_{\overline{D}} p_{\overline{C}}$	$p_D p_{\overline{D}} p_{\overline{C}}$	$p_{\overline{D}}^2 p_{\overline{C}}$	$2p_{\overline{D}}^4 p_{\overline{C}}^3 p_{\overline{D}}^2 p_{12} p_{16}$
16, 16	p_{16}^2	$p_D p_C p_{12}$	$p_{\overline{D}}p_{\overline{C}}$	$p_{\overline{D}}p_C p_{12}$	$p_{\overline{D}}^2 p_{\overline{C}} p_D p_C^2 p_{12}^2 p_{16}^2$
12, Q	$2p_{12}p_Q$	$p_{\overline{D}}p_D p_{\overline{C}}$	$p_{\overline{D}}^2 p_C p_{16}$	$p_{\overline{D}}p_D p_C p_{16}$	$2p_{\overline{D}}^4 p_{\overline{C}} p_D^2 p_C^2 p_{12} p_Q p_{16}^2$
16, Q	$2p_{16}p_Q$	$p_{\overline{D}}^2 p_C p_{12}$	$p_{\overline{D}}p_D p_{\overline{C}}$	$p_{\overline{D}}p_D p_C p_{12}$	$2p_{\overline{D}}^2 p_{\overline{C}} p_D^4 p_C^2 p_{12}^2 p_Q p_{16}$
Q, Q	p_Q^2	$p_{\overline{D}}^2 p_C p_{12}$	$p_{\overline{D}}^2 p_C p_{16}$	$p_{\overline{D}}^2 p_{\overline{C}}^2 p_{12} p_{16}$	$p_{\overline{D}}^6 p_{\overline{C}}^4 p_Q^2 p_{12}^2 p_{16}^2$
					Denominator is sum of above

In conclusion,

- The formulae are very complicated even for simple cases, which means that it would be impracticable to carry out calculations by hand.
- This is why short-cut generalizations were needed to "make do". But the interpretation was restricted to simple DNA profiles—mixtures were problematic.
- The method shown is logical and can be expanded to incorporate stutters, making the formulae even more complicated.
- It was clear from an early stage that computer software was a necessity to progress the research to a stage that the theory could be utilized by practitioners.

4.5. Degradation

Forensic samples are often compromized due to exposure to environmental factors, such as humidity, bacteria, and ultraviolet light [199].

Degradation is a consequence of random DNA cleavage (refer to the exhaustive review by [200] for details on mechanizms and consequences of degradation). Usually, there are multiple copies of DNA in an extracted sample, but degradation reduces the number of fragments available for PCR; if there are too few, this leads to allele drop-out, discussed in Chapter 3.1.

A recent study found no evidence of protected regions in the DNA molecule when coverage was examined with massive parallel sequencing (MPS) [201]. It makes no difference whether one or more places on the DNA fragment of interest are degraded, as the fragment will fail to amplify no matter where, or how often, the DNA is broken. Consequently, longer DNA fragments are affected more than shorter DNA fragments, and this leads to the classic "ski-slope" profile of the EPG (Fig. 4.2). In forensic DNA samples, where multiple copies of DNA are usually present, degradation causes an increased imbalance, possibly leading to drop-out of alleles [202] (discussed in Chapter 3.1). Bright et al. [203] models degradation by an exponentially decreasing curve. A similar method is described for *EuroForMix* in Chapter 7.8. Exponential curve fitting is used to measure degradation characteristics of a DNA profile *post-PCR*.

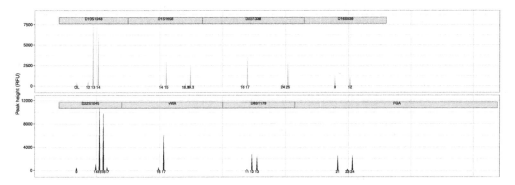

Figure 4.2 Typical ski-slope degradation pattern from ESX 17. Reproduced from [195] with permission from Springer.

4.5.1 Pre-PCR quantification and characterization of degradation

Before PCR, quantification of an extract is carried out to indicate the optimum amount that is forwarded to PCR. Typically, 0.5–1 ng is recommended to ensure a full, well-balanced profile from a single contributor. A degraded sample has less DNA available at high molecular weight, compared to low molecular weight alleles. If there is a lower level of DNA at high molecular weight, then the amount forwarded to PCR may be adjusted upwards to compensate.

Modern human real-time DNA quantification kits, e.g., QuantifilerTrio DNA Quantification Kit and PowerQuant System, have the ability to measure the degree of degradation for each sample [204–207]. This is accomplished by adding a second longer target to measure the total human DNA. Usually a 200–300-base pair fragment (x_2) is generated from the longer target, whereas the shorter one generates a 70–150-base pair fragment (x_1).

The greater the degradation, the greater the difference between the quantification values for each target moiety. This difference is used to calculate a *degradation index*: $DI = \frac{c_{x_1}}{c_{x_2}}$, where c_{x_1} and c_{x_2} are the DNA quantities (c) of the small and large targets, respectively. The *DI* is a simple indicator of size-dependent quantities that are present in a crime sample. After calibration against the generated DNA profiles, the operator can use the information to decide how to process the sample. The calculated *DI* differs between QuantifilerTrio and PowerQuant, because their target sizes are different.

The next step is to calculate a parameter that is independent of the kit used: the *degradation parameter Pr(deg)* is the probability that a single base pair is degraded (Box 4.1).

Box 4.1 Derivation of probability of degradation $Pr(deg)$

Probability of drop-out of a single copy of DNA can be characterized by Eq. (4.5), assuming independence between the base pairs of the copy, to estimate the chance of cleavage of a molecule of x bases:

$$p_D = 1 - (1 - Pr(deg))^x \qquad (4.5)$$

where p_D is probability of drop-out. We can write the probability that a fragment of size x is intact (i.e., not degraded) and available for amplification:

$$p_{\overline{D}} = 1 - p_D = (1 - Pr(deg))^x \qquad (4.6)$$

However, it is necessary to evaluate the probability of cleavage of DNA as a function of n copies of DNA ($Pr(D_n)$). This is defined by the binomial probability in Eq. (4.7):

$$Pr(D_n) = 1 - (1 - p_D)^n \qquad (4.7)$$

We make the same assumptions as [208], and use a constant probability of cleavage across the fragment sequence. Similar to [208], we assume a log-linear relationship between concentration $c(x)$, fragment length x, and the probability of no degradation. Using natural logarithms,

$$log(c(x)) = log(H) + log(1 - Pr(deg))x \qquad (4.8)$$

where H is the allele peak height. From this follow Eqs. (4.9), (4.10):

$$log(1 - Pr(deg)) = \frac{log(c(x_2)) - log(c(x_1))}{x_2 - x_1} \qquad (4.9)$$

$$Pr(deg) = 1 - e^{\frac{log(c(x_1))/log(c(x_2))}{x_1 - x_2}} \qquad (4.10)$$

where $x_1 < x_2$ and $c(x_2) \leq c(x_1)$. We can formalize this as the probability of 5' cleavage of the affected base.

Hansson et al. [148] provides examples of DNA extracts from degraded tissue samples that were quantified using two different quantification kits with capability to measure degradation.

Given $Pr(deg)$, the number of intact fragments of any length can be estimated. Fig. 4.3 shows the probability of intact fragments as a function of their length, for different values of the degradation parameter using Eq. (4.6).

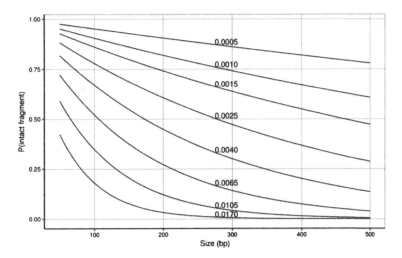

Figure 4.3 Probability of intact fragment available for amplification as a function of fragment length for different values of the degradation parameter (0.0005-0.0170) are shown. Reproduced from [148] with permission from Springer.

To simulate degradation, the probabilities that each allele (i.e., fragment length) is complete, and therefore available for PCR amplification, is calculated. Then a population of post-PCR DNA molecules are generated by simulation.

This was performed using the R package *pcrsim* version 1.0 http://cran.r-project.org/web/packages/pcrsim/index.html. The package was developed based on the simulation functions in forensim [209]. Both packages are implementations of "A graphical simulation model of the entire DNA process" [124]. In *pcrsim*, the PCR efficiency is assumed to be constant across cycle number, which has previously been demonstrated to be true for the first 10 to 15 cycles [210,211]. In reality, PCR efficiency declines towards the plateau phase, mainly because of product inhibition of the DNA polymerase enzyme [212]. However, for STR analysis of low-template samples, the plateau phase is never reached in practice [213]. The authors showed that for each increase in number of PCR cycles from 30 to 35, the allele peak height increase was approximately constant, coinciding with ideal amplification. Hence, the application of a constant PCR efficiency per cycle is a realistic approximation. Some published values of the PCR efficiency are 0.82 [124], 0.85 [214], and 0.82–0.97 [215]. Here we used a PCR efficiency $pcr_{ef} = 0.90$.

The number of intact molecules that are retrieved post PCR are calculated from the binomial

$$N_{intact} = Bin(N_{molecules}, p_{\overline{D}}) \tag{4.11}$$

where $N_{molecules}$ is the simulated number of molecules of each allele after PCR amplification, and N_{intact} is the number of intact molecules. To illustrate, we simulate degradation of a fragment of 300 bases, 1 ng total DNA, corresponding to 167 haploid copies (Fig. 4.4) using the binomial distribution $Bin(N = 167, p_{\overline{D}} = 0.05)$.

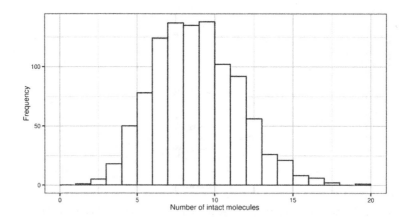

Figure 4.4 1000 simulations N = 167 copies of a 300 bp fragment with $p_{\overline{D}}$ = 0.05 probability of being intact, corresponding to approximately $Pr(deg)$ = 0.0099. The range of intact fragments is 1–19, which may fail to produce sufficient PCR product to trigger a signal. Reproduced from [148] with permission from Springer.

This results in a population of intact fragments that can be amplified, but with this particular example, where $p_{\overline{D}} = 0.05$, there are between 1 and 19 undegraded copies derived from 1 ng. A DNA fragment will only be visualized if there are sufficient molecules present to trigger the capillary electrophoresis machine's charged coupled device (CCD) camera. For 28 cycles, approximately 30 haploid copies (approximately 90 pg) are required before sufficient PCR product is available to trigger a signal [216], whereas for 34 cycles, just one molecule (approximately 3 pg in a haploid cell) is needed to produce sufficient signal [217].

When degraded DNA is analyzed, system optimization cannot be considered without a concurrent consideration of the effect of PCR cycle number. We repeated the simulation with a smaller fragment size of 100 bases (Fig. 4.5). Using the same degradation parameters, a fragment that is just 100 bases has a chance of 37% of surviving. Consequently, a nanogram of DNA from diploid cells will have between 44 and 83 intact molecules of each allele (approximately 264 to 498 pg). The threshold is always exceeded even at 28 cycles.

The number of PCR cycles is a key factor to consider if degraded DNA can be analyzed. If the probability of degradation per base pair is used as a metric, rather than degradation indices, the measure becomes kit-independent. With knowledge of the degradation parameter the resulting characteristics of the DNA profiles can be predicted by simulation as shown.

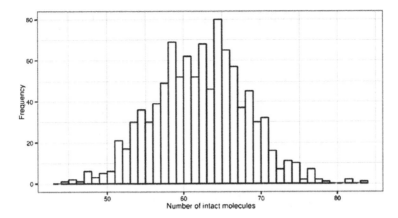

Figure 4.5 1000 simulations $N = 167$ copies of a 100 bp fragment with $p_{\bar{D}} = 0.37$ probability of being intact, corresponding approximately to $Pr(deg) = 0.0099$. The range of intact fragments is 44–83, which normally results in sufficient PCR product to trigger a signal. Reproduced from Hansson et al. [148] with permission from Springer.

4.6. Summary

The previous chapter introduced the concept of stochastic effects leading to allele drop-out and heterozygote imbalance. This chapter traces the early methods used to deal with the interpretation of low-template DNA, starting with the "consensus" method, where replicate tests of a single extract are carried out—only duplicated alleles are reported. This method was restricted to simple profiles and was somewhat *ad-hoc*. The concept of drop-in was introduced. These are spurious alleles, distinct from "contamination". Whereas the former are derived from different individuals, the latter are multiple alleles derived from a single individual. The distinction is important to probabilistic models, because drop-in alleles are treated as independent events, whereas contamination alleles are dependent events, and are treated as coming from a single individual. The number of drop-in alleles that can realistically be attributed to a profile is restricted by the expectation of a Poisson distribution fit to the number of drop-in alleles observed in negative controls for a given multiplex system.

A statistical theory was introduced that combined probabilities of drop-in and drop-out, applied to replicates. The formulae produced are very complex and difficult to derive by hand. Clearly, the next step is to develop computer algorithms to take over the burden of calculation, and this is described in the next chapter.

Degradation of samples is commonly observed in crime samples, since DNA cleaves into shorter fragments that may consequently be unavailable for PCR. Degradation is recognized in the EPG as a classic "ski-slope", where the higher molecular weight fragments are more likely to be degraded compared to the low molecular weight loci, i.e., the probability of drop-out varies across the molecular weight range—the greater the degradation, the greater the probability of drop-out. Real-time DNA quantification kits have the ability to measure the degree of degradation for each sample tested by measuring the quantity of DNA present at two different molecular weights. This information can be used to estimate the *degradation parameter*, which is the probability that a single base pair is degraded. This information can be used to predict the degradation pattern of a given sample, and helps the practitioner decide how much sample to analyze by CE to obtain an optimal result.

Note

1. It isn't possible to distinguish between an unknown individual that arises as part of the crime-event and a laboratory or investigator contamination, unless the individual is held on the elimination database. The *LR* calculation is valid regardless of the origin of the unknown contributor.

CHAPTER 5

LRmix model theory

5.1. Background

In Chapter 4, a basic theory to interpret LT-DNA profiles was introduced that used the concepts of drop-out and drop-in probability, and the use of consensus profiles to calculate the joint probability of the evidence. In Chapter 1.12.6, the Balding and Nichols F_{ST} correction [42] was introduced to take account of population sub-structuring. It was previously noted that the theory was too complex for hand calculation, and could only realistically be achieved using computer algorithms.

This chapter describes the theory that brings together the above concepts, programmed by Hinda Haned into an R-package [218], called *Forensim* [209], dedicated to facilitate the statistical interpretation of forensic DNA evidence. A detailed description of *Forensim* is provided in the package tutorial, available from: http://forensim.r-forge.r-project.org/. Here we introduce the theory that was used to create one particular module of *Forensim*, namely *LRmix* [219], which was the precursor to *LRmix Studio*, described in the next chapter. *LRmix* facilitates the calculation of likelihood ratios of LT-DNA samples with drop-out, drop-in, any number of contributors, and replicates. It was programmed following the model proposed by [220,65], where drop-out and drop-in parameters were introduced to take these events into account.

To evaluate the strength of evidence, the likelihood ratio approach, described in Chapter 1.6, is used. Recall that two alternative propositions are put forward by the prosecution (H_p) and defense (H_d). The value of the evidence is then expressed in terms of a likelihood ratio, measuring the relative weight of each proposition and the *LR* is written as

$$LR = \frac{Pr(E|H_p)}{Pr(E|H_d)} \tag{5.1}$$

where E is the DNA profile of the crime scene evidence. H_p is the proposition of the prosecution, typically of the following form: the suspect is the donor to the crime scene profile, whereas H_d is the proposition of the defense, usually of the form: an unknown person is the donor of the crime scene profile.

To evaluate the value of the evidence, a probabilistic model, termed as the drop-out/drop-in model, was introduced. Along with successive enhancements, it was described in several publications [65,220,221,68].

This probabilistic model was originally implemented in the *likEvid* function, written in the R language and is available in the *Forensim* package for the R statistical software[1] [209]. *likEvid* is written in R, but calls a series of functions written in C code. This

---

Forensic Practitioner's Guide to the Interpretation of Complex DNA Profiles
https://doi.org/10.1016/B978-0-12-820562-4.00013-4

ensures faster calculations in the R environment. To make this function of *Forensim* more accessible to reporting officers, a Tcl/Tk user-friendly interface was prepared, called *LRmix*, also available in the *Forensim* package.

This chapter outlines the statistical theory and provides a detailed description of the probabilistic model. The links between the different components of the model, and its implementation within *LRmix* are described. This model was taken forward to *LRmix Studio*, described in the next chapter, where detailed case examples are described.

5.2. Model description

The theory to calculate the likelihood ratio of simple mixtures was provided earlier in Chapter 1.7–1.11. Incorporation of allele drop-out theory into the *LR* was introduced in Chapter 3.7, and drop-in was introduced in Chapter 4.2.1. Replicate analysis, combining probabilities of drop-in and drop-out was introduced in Chapter 4.4 (where replicates are two or more samples from a single extract).

This section describes how the *LRmix* model calculates the *LR*, where these components are included.

The first step of the analysis is to specify the prosecution and the defense propositions. Propositions are not restricted to single persons. Table 5.1 provides examples of different sets of typical propositions that may be applied.

Table 5.1 Examples of H_p and H_d propositions.

H_p: The suspect is the donor.
H_d: An unknown person is the donor.
H_p: The suspect and the victim are the donors.
H_d: Two unknowns are the donors.
H_p: The suspect and three unknowns are the donors.
H_d: Four unknowns are the donors.

In Table 5.2 a crime scene sample is shown for four out of a total of 15 loci, from three different replicate tests. The corresponding DNA profile of a suspect is provided in Table 5.3.

The DNA profile of the person of interest (a suspect or a victim) is only analyzed once. An example is given in Table 5.3.

Given a pair of alternate propositions, such as those stated above in Table 5.1, likelihood ratios are calculated for every locus of a given profile. The overall *LR* is easily obtained by taking the product of the per-locus *LRs*:

$$LR = \frac{Pr(E_1|H_p)}{Pr(E_1|H_d)} \times \ldots \times \frac{Pr(E_L|H_p)}{Pr(E_L|H_d)} \tag{5.2}$$

Table 5.2 Example of a crime-scene DNA profile, at four loci and three replicates R_1, R_2, R_3.

Sample	Marker	Allele1	Allele2	Allele3
R_1	D3S1358	14	15	16
R_1	VWA	16	19	21
R_1	D16S539	9	10	11
R_1	D2S1338	20	23	24
R_2	D3S1358	14	15	16
R_2	VWA	16	19	21
R_2	D16S539	9	10	11
R_2	D2S1338	20	23	24
R_3	D3S1358	15	16	17
R_3	VWA	16	19	21
R_3	D16S539	9	10	11
R_3	D2S1338	20	23	24

Table 5.3 DNA profile of a suspect. Only four loci are shown.

Sample	Marker	Allele1	Allele2
suspect	D3S1358	15	17
suspect	VWA	16	21
suspect	D16S539	9	10
suspect	D2S1338	23	24

where E_L is the profile of the DNA evidence at locus L. For example, in Table 5.2, $E_{VWA} = \{16, 19, 21; 16, 19, 21; 16, 19, 21\}$, where the three replicates are separated by the semi-colon.

5.3. Theoretical considerations

In this section, we only consider one locus for clarity. Building on the example described in Chapter 4.4.1, following Curran et al. [220], the calculation of interest is given in Eq. (5.3): this is the joint probability of observing the DNA profiles of n replicates at locus l, $E = (R_1, R_2, ..., R_n)$, conditioned on the known and the unknown genotypes, as specified by a given proposition (H):

$$Pr(R_1, ..., R_n | H) = Pr(R_1, ..., R_n | T, V, x) \qquad (5.3)$$

- $R_1, ..., R_n$ are the replicates of the DNA profile at locus l.

- T is the list of genotypes from the profiled individuals that are conditioned under the given proposition H. For example, the suspect and the victim are profiled (their genotypes are known exactly), and conditioned under H.

- V is the list of genotypes from the profiled individuals that are known to be non-contributors under the given proposition H. All the profiled individuals that are among the hypothesized contributors under the prosecution proposition, but not under the defense proposition, become known non-contributors under H_d. For instance, a suspect who is a contributor under H_p becomes a known non-contributor under alternative proposition H_d. We define this set, because observing these genotypes may alter how likely it is to see a given genotype for the unknown.

- x is the number of unknown contributors to the DNA profile under the given proposition H. For example, if the H_p proposition states the DNA profile to be a mixture of DNA from the suspect and one additional person, who is unknown, $x = 1$. The model will then account for this source of uncertainty by cycling through all possible genotypes for this unknown person, as shown in Table 4.4, in the previous section.

By definition, the x unknown individuals could have any set of genotypes u (combined genotype if more than one unknown). We denote U to be the set of possible (combined) genotypes for the x unknown individuals. If there is just one replicate, R_i ($i = 1, ..., n$), Eq. (5.3) can be written as follows:

$$Pr(R_i \mid T, V, x) = \sum_{u \in U} \underbrace{Pr(u \mid T, V)}_{\text{Genotype prob.}} \underbrace{Pr(R_i \mid T, u)}_{\text{Replicate prob.}} \tag{5.4}$$

This is the general formula to sum over all the possible genotypes of the unknown contributors (as already illustrated in Chapter 1). Eq. (5.4) helps to decompose the probability calculations into two components, that can be calculated separately: the replicate probability $Pr(R_i \mid T, u)$ and the genotype probability $Pr(u \mid T, V)$. We now extend this formula by considering all the n replicates. The replicates $R_1, ..., R_n$ are independent when conditioning on the genotype, therefore Eq. (5.4) can be extended to

$$Pr(R_1, ..., R_n \mid T, V, x) = \sum_{u \in U} Pr(u \mid T, V) \prod_{i=1}^{n} Pr(R_i \mid T, u) \tag{5.5}$$

Note that the replicate probability only depends on the genotypes of the assumed contributors $g = (T, u)$, and the set V is ignored. Throughout this chapter we assume that the genotype set $g = (g_1, ..., g_K)$ consists of the genotype of K contributors, where K is number of unknown contributors x, plus the number of genotypes in T.

Note that in cases where there are no unknown individuals $x = 0$, $U = \varnothing$ (i.e., an empty set) and Eq. (5.5) simplifies to Eq. (5.6):

$$Pr(R_1, ..., R_n | T) = \prod_i Pr(R_i | T) \tag{5.6}$$

Since $Pr(T|V) = 1$, the genotype probability is only calculated when there are unknown genotypes in g. In general, unknown individuals have not been profiled, and these need to be factored in as part of the genotype probabilities in the model as presented in Eqs. (5.4) and (5.5). In all cases, the replicate probability has to be calculated.

These replicate and genotype probabilities are evaluated for every possible combined genotype element $g = (T, u)$, where all the genotypes of the unknowns u in the set U must be considered. If there are no unknown contributors ($x = 0$), then the genotype probability is one.

In the following sections, additional information is given about how to calculate the probability of replicates when drop-out and drop-in are taken into account.

5.4. Replicate probability

Replicates were introduced in Chapter 4, and an example to assess the strength of evidence of replicates for a given genotype was outlined in Chapter 4.4.1. In this section, we will define a probabilistic model specified in *LRmix*.

The probabilistic model defines how likely a given replicate is, conditioned on the genotypes of the assumed contributors under H (including the known and unknown donors) and the unknown parameters. The "drop-out probability" (Chapter 3.7) is considered along with "drop-in probability" discussed in Chapter 4.2.1.

The total probability formula provided in Eqs. (5.4) and (5.5) specify the $Pr(R_i | T, u)$ term. Here the replicate(s) are compared to the genotype(s) of T (known contributors) and u (the unknown contributors). For simplicity, the combination of these two sets are defined as g, i.e., $g = (T, u)$. Therefore the probability of replicate R_i must be defined for each combination of g, given as $Pr(R_i | g)$.

5.4.1 Drop-out and drop-in: definitions

A drop-out is an allele that is not detected in the crime-sample profile, because of a low quality or quantity of DNA (this is discussed in further detail in Chapter 3). Although present in the sample, the allele will not be detected if it is below the analytical threshold (AT).

Drop-in is discussed in detail in Chapter 4. A drop-in event is an allele that is detected in the crime-sample profile, although it is not related to the crime-sample. Drop-in occurs because of DNA fragments present in the laboratory environment (e.g., plasticware, house-dust). Drop-in can be considered as a case of mild contamination,

134 Forensic Practitioner's Guide to the Interpretation of Complex DNA Profiles

where one or two alleles, not related to the sample being analyzed, appear in the profile of the trace. If two or more drop-in alleles occur they are considered to be independent events arising from two or more individuals (Chapter 4.2.1).

Allele drop-out and drop-in probability parameters were previously introduced in Chapter 4.2.1 as examples. We define the model parameters (as used in *LRmix*) as follows:

1. d_k is the probability that contributor k drops out with an allele from a heterozygote genotype (same probability for both alleles).
2. d'_k is the probability that contributor k drops out with both its alleles from a homozygote genotype.
3. p_C is the probability of one drop-in event of one locus.

5.4.2 Drop-out and drop-in: formalization

Here we formalize the method that was described and demonstrated in Chapter 4.4.1, to calculate a likelihood ratio for a single donor and show its extension to mixtures. Drop-out and drop-in are considered to be stochastic events, they may occur in just one replicate, but not in the other(s). Following Haned et al. [68], drop-out and drop-in alleles are treated as independent across replicates. To facilitate the calculation of the replicate probability, based on the drop-out and drop-in probabilities, the information provided by each replicate R_i ($i = 1, ..., n$) and a particular genotype combination g, is partitioned into three disjoint sets:

- No drop-out/drop-in set: $A_i = R_i \cap g$; this is the set of alleles that did not drop out or drop in; these alleles are both in g and R_i;
- Drop-out set: $B_i = g \setminus (R_i \cap g)$; this is the set of dropped out alleles (whether in one or several copies); these alleles are in g, but not in R_i;
- Drop-in set: $C_i = R_i \setminus (R_i \cap g)$; this is the set of alleles that have dropped-in, these are alleles in R_i, but not in g.

In addition to these sets, we also define the drop-out probability for a particular allele a, being one of the alleles in the given genotype combination $g = (g_1, ..., g_K)$:

$$D_a(g) = \prod_{k=1}^{K} \left[d_k^{\mathbb{I}(g_k \text{ heterozygote including allele } a)} \right] \left[d_k'^{\mathbb{I}(g_k \text{ homozygote as } a,a)} \right] \tag{5.7}$$

where $\mathbb{I}(x)$ is one if x is true, and zero otherwise. Remember that $d_k^0 = 1$ means there is no drop-out, and conversely $d_k^1 = d_k$ corresponds to a drop-out event. Therefore the formula is the multiplication of all the drop-out parameters d_k (d'_k if homozygote) over all contributors having the specific allele a. This is calculated only for the unique alleles present in the combined genotypes g. Note that $D_a(g)$ is equivalent to the "p_D" allele drop-out probability notation, as used in the formulae in Chapter 4.4.1.

Illustration

If $g = (11, 11; 11, 12)$, then using formula in Eq. (5.7) gives $D_{11}(g) = d'_1 d_2$ and $D_{12}(g) = d_2$. Using this definition, for every genotypic combination g, the replicate probability is defined by the following equations:

A. If $C_i \neq \varnothing$ (i.e., at least one drop-in)

$$Pr(R_i|g) = \underbrace{\left[\prod_{a \in A_i} (1 - D_a) \right]}_{\text{No drop out/in}} \underbrace{\left[\prod_{a \in B_i} D_a \right]}_{\text{Drop-out}} \underbrace{\left[\prod_{a \in C_i} p_C p_a \right]}_{\text{Drop-in}} \tag{5.8}$$

B. If $C_i = \varnothing$ (i.e., no drop-in)

$$Pr(R_i|g) = \underbrace{\left[\prod_{a \in A_i} (1 - D_a) \right]}_{\text{No drop out/in}} \underbrace{\left[\prod_{a \in B_i} D_a \right]}_{\text{Drop-out}} \underbrace{\left[(1 - p_C) \right]}_{\text{Drop-in}} \tag{5.9}$$

where D_a is the drop-out probability for allele a, defined as a function of the drop-out probabilities d_k or d'_k for each donor k, using Eq. (5.7), and p_C is the drop-in probability.

For every replicate i, sets A_i, B_i and C_i are defined for a given genotype combination g, and the joint probability for the n replicates is obtained by multiplying the probabilities for each replicate as defined in Eq. (5.5).

The drop-out parameter d_k (if k has heterozygote genotype) or d'_k (if k has homozygote genotype) is assigned per donor k, under each proposition. Thus under H_p, if there are two donors, the suspect and one unknown individual, there are two drop-out parameters, one for the suspect, and one for the unknown. Each one of these parameters applies to both alleles of a given donor. Note that although the model described here allows different drop-out rates to be applied for different loci, the current casework implementation of the model requires these parameters to remain the same for all loci.

In Appendix B.3.2, an alternative way to present Eqs. (5.8) and (5.9) are provided in the situation when $d'_k = d_k^2$ (this simplifies the formula).

In the following, calculations for the replicate probability are carried out.

5.4.3 Example 1

In this example, we consider replicates $R_1 = \{11, 12, 13\}$ and $R_2 = \{11, 12\}$, and a combination G_1 of the known and unknown genotypes $G_1 = (11,11;12,12;13,14)$. We define the drop-out parameters per contributor k as d_k for a heterozygote genotype, and d'_k for a homozygote genotype. Based on this, we calculate the allele drop-out probabilities for each unique allele found in G_1 using Eq. (5.7):

136   Forensic Practitioner's Guide to the Interpretation of Complex DNA Profiles

- Allele 11: $D_{11} = d_1'$ (donor 1 has homozygote genotype)
- Allele 12: $D_{12} = d_2'$ (donor 2 has homozygote genotype)
- Allele 13: $D_{13} = d_3$ (donor 3 has heterozygote genotype)
- Allele 14: $D_{14} = d_3$ (donor 3 has heterozygote genotype)

For every replicate R_i, we define the alleles in the sets A_i, B_i, and C_i, and the corresponding parameters for every allele in these sets:

Set	Replicate R_1	Replicate R_2
A_i	$\{11, 12, 13\}$	$\{11, 12\}$
B_i	$\{14\}$	$\{13, 14\}$
C_i	$\varnothing$	$\varnothing$

Following Eq. (5.9), the replicate probabilities for this example are the following:

$$Pr(R_1, R_2 | g) = \left[(1 - p_C) \prod_{a \in A_1} (1 - D_a) \prod_{a \in B_1} D_a \right] \left[(1 - p_C) \prod_{a \in A_2} (1 - D_a) \prod_{a \in B_2} D_a \right]$$

$$= \left[(1 - p_C)(1 - D_{11})(1 - D_{12})(1 - D_{13})D_{14} \right] \left[(1 - p_C)(1 - D_{11})(1 - D_{12})D_{13}D_{14} \right]$$

$$= \left[(1 - p_C)(1 - d_1')(1 - d_2')(1 - d_3)d_3 \right] \left[(1 - p_C)(1 - d_1')(1 - d_2')d_3^2 \right]$$

$$= (1 - p_C)^2 (1 - d_1')^2 (1 - d_2')^2 (1 - d_3)d_3^3 \tag{5.10}$$

5.4.4 Example 2

In this example, we consider the genotype combination $G_2 = (11, 11; 12, 12; 12, 14)$ and the same replicates as in Example 1: $R_1 = \{11, 12, 13\}$, and $R_2 = \{11, 12\}$. Note that in this example, donor 2 and 3 in the genotype G_2 set have the shared allele 12.

To calculate the allele drop-out probabilities for the unique alleles found in G_2 using Eq. (5.7), we get:

- Allele 11: $D_{11} = d_1'$ (donor 1 has homozygote genotype)
- Allele 12: $D_{12} = d_2' d_3$ (donor 2 has homozygote genotype, donor 3 has heterozygote genotype)
- Allele 14: $D_{14} = d_3$ (donor 3 has heterozygote genotype)

The drop-out parameters remain the same as in Example 1. For every replicate i, we define the sets A_i, B_i, and C_i as follows:

Set	Replicate R_1	Replicate R_2
A_i	$\{11, 12\}$	$\{11, 12\}$
B_i	$\{14\}$	$\{14\}$
C_i	$\{13\}$	$\varnothing$

Applying Eqs. (5.8) and (5.9), the replicate probability is

$$Pr(R_1, R_2|G_2) = \left[\prod_{a \in A_1}(1 - D_a) \prod_{a \in B_1} D_a \prod_{a \in C_1} p_C p_a \right] \left[(1 - p_C) \prod_{a \in A_2}(1 - D_a) \prod_{a \in B_2} D_a \right]$$
$$= \left[(1 - D_{11})(1 - D_{12})D_{14}p_C p_{13} \right] \left[(1 - p_C)(1 - D_{11})(1 - D_{12})D_{13}D_{14} \right]$$
$$= \left[(1 - d_1')(1 - d_2' d_3)d_3 p_C p_{13} \right] \left[(1 - p_C)(1 - d_1')(1 - d_2' d_3) \right]$$
$$= p_C(1 - p_C)p_{13}(1 - d_1')^2(1 - d_2' d_3)^2 d_3^2 \tag{5.11}$$

This section defines and illustrates the replicate probabilities. In the next section, the genotype probabilities are defined and illustrated. In the last section, a simple example is shown, where these two terms are combined to calculate the likelihood ratio.

5.5. Genotype probability

The set of genotypes for the K contributors, $g = (g_1, ..., g_K)$ consists of the set of known genotypes T, and the set of unknown genotypes u, such that $g = (T, u)$. Since the genotypes of T are known $Pr(T|V) = 1$, the probability of observing the genotype set g becomes

$$Pr(g|T, V) = Pr(T|V)Pr(u|T, V) = Pr(u|T, V) \tag{5.12}$$

When the number of unknown contributors for a certain proposition H is greater than one, (i.e., $x > 0$), the genotype probability term $Pr(u|T, V)$ from Eqs. (5.4) and (5.5) must be calculated. This is the probability of observing a certain combination of genotypes for the unknown(s) u, based on the information provided by the profiles in the set of known contributors T, and known non-contributors V. The details of the calculations are given below, but first, it is necessary to explain how the possible genotypes for the unknowns are derived.

5.5.1 Determining the genotypes for the unknowns

Since the genotype of the unknown individuals are unknown, we need to calculate the total probability $Pr(R_1, ..., R_n|T, V, x)$, where all possible genotype combinations are considered (as presented in Eqs. (5.4) and (5.5)).

If a locus has m alleles in the population, then there are $\binom{m+1}{2} = \frac{(m+1)!}{2!(m-1)!} = \frac{(m+1)m}{2}$ ways of choosing two alleles among these m alleles to form a genotype[2] (also see Chapter 1.11 for some simple examples). This corresponds to the number of combinations of choosing two elements among m, unordered with replacement [220]. For example, at locus FGA, 20 alleles were observed in the Dutch population, thus at this locus, there are 210 distinct/unique genotypes.

138 Forensic Practitioner's Guide to the Interpretation of Complex DNA Profiles

If there is a single unknown, there are $\binom{m+1}{2}$ possible genotypes for him/her. If there is more than one unknown, we have to consider all the combinations of x genotypes among the $\binom{m+1}{2}$ genotypes that are possible at a given locus, which would be $\binom{m+1}{2}^x$ number of combinations in total.

Throughout this section, it is assumed that the drop-out probability parameters are the same for the unknown contributors. It is possible to calculate the sums in Eqs. (5.4) and (5.5), without traversing all the $\binom{m+1}{2}^x$ combinations for unknown genotypes.[3] For example, if a locus has only two alleles, 13 and 14, then there are three possible genotypes: 13,13; 14,14, and 13,14 (here we do not consider allele drop-out). With two unknown individuals ($x = 2$), and three possible genotypes for each of the unknowns, there are six unique unordered combinations for two individuals (the number of ways of choosing two unordered genotypes among three with replacements). Table 5.4 outlines these unique possibilities.

Table 5.4 Possible genotype combinations at a virtual locus with two alleles 13 and 14. Note that the order in which the genotypes are assigned to the unknown individuals is arbitrary.

Combination	Unknown 1	Unknown 2
u_1	13,13	13,13
u_2	13,13	13,14
u_3	13,14	13,14
u_4	13,14	14,14
u_5	14,14	14,14
u_6	13,13	14,14

Note that Table 5.4 is not exhaustive, because it ignores the ordered possibilities 13,14; 13,13, although the converse is listed: 13,13; 13,14. However, to consider all the possible genotypes of the unknowns, this means that both combinations have to be accounted for. Table 5.5 gives the exhaustive list of possibilities.

For this example, there are nine possible genotype combinations for the two unknowns. If the order of the combined genotypes does not matter to the calculations, i.e., if the inner part of the sum in Eq. (5.4) and (5.5),

$$Pr(u|T, V) \prod_{i=1}^{n} Pr(R_i|T, u) \tag{5.13}$$

is identical regardless of whether $u_2 = \{13, 13; 13, 14\}$ or $u_2' = \{13, 14; 13, 13\}$ is evaluated; then the calculation is only required for one of these options. Nevertheless, a permutation factor, indicating the number of ordered possibilities for the certain ordered genotype combination, needs to be taken into account for correct calculation of

Table 5.5 Exhaustive list of all the possible genotype combinations at a virtual locus with two alleles 13 and 14. Note that the combinations that were ignored in Table 5.4 above are highlighted here.

Combination	Unknown 1	Unknown 2
u_1	13,13	13,13
u_2	13,13	13,14
u_2'	13,14	13,13
u_3	13,14	13,14
u_4	13,14	14,14
u_4'	14,14	13,14
u_5	14,14	14,14
u_6	13,13	14,14
u_6'	14,14	13,13

$Pr(R_1, ..., R_n | T, V, x)$. Hence the calculations can be carried out by only considering the unique unordered genotype combinations, provided that we include the permutation factor. For every genotype combination, the permutation factor is simply the number of permutations with replacements of that given genotype combination (gives the number of ordered possibilities). Thus for a given combination, if there are k_1 genotypes of type 1, and k_2 genotypes of type 2, and so on, the permutation factor is given by $\frac{x!}{k_1!...k_J!}$, where J is the number of unique genotypes, and k_j is the number of genotypes being of type j.

For example, with the ordered combined genotypes in Table 5.4, there is a total of $J = 3$ genotypes available for the $x = 2$ unknowns 13, 13; 13, 14; 14, 14. If the second combination U_2 is considered, we see that 13, 13 and 13, 14 appear once, and there are no observations of 14, 14. Thus $k_1 = 1, k_2 = 1, k_3 = 0$, giving the factor $\frac{2!}{1!1!0!} = 2$ permutations. Repeating for all combinations in Table 5.4, the following Table 5.6 is obtained:

Consequently, by taking into account the permutation factor, Eq. (5.5) can be modified to

$$Pr(R_1, ..., R_n | T, V, x) = \sum_{u \in U'} \frac{x!}{\left(\prod_{j=1}^{J} k_j!\right)} Pr(u | T, V) \prod_{i=1}^{n} Pr(R_i | T, u) \qquad (5.14)$$

where U' is the set of all possible unordered combined genotypes (as opposed to set U from Eqs. (5.4) and (5.5), which considered all the ordered combined genotype outcome).

Table 5.6 Extension of Table 5.4 with permutation factors.

Combination	Unknown 1	Unknown 2	Permutation factor
u_1	13,13	13,13	$\dfrac{2!}{2!0!0!} = 1$
u_2	13,13	13,14	$\dfrac{2!}{1!1!0!} = 2$
u_3	13,14	13,14	$\dfrac{2!}{0!2!0!} = 1$
u_4	13,14	14,14	$\dfrac{2!}{1!0!1!} = 2$
u_5	14,14	14,14	$\dfrac{2!}{0!0!2!} = 1$
u_6	13,13	14,14	$\dfrac{2!}{1!0!1!} = 2$

Using the permutation factor, as mentioned above, is very useful to reduce computational effort when the number of unknown contributors increases. However, this is only possible if the parameters for each of the unknown contributors are the same. This means that if different parameters are assumed for the different unknown contributors (such as the drop-out parameter), the full ordered combined genotype outcome has to be considered (e.g., as applied to quantitative models, such as *Euro-ForMix*).

Determining the genotypes for the unknowns when relatedness is conditioned

In Chapter 1.16, it was demonstrated that likelihood ratios are critically dependent upon the propositions formulated. The standard format will assign unknown/known individuals as unrelated to a person of interest (POI). However, this is not compulsory. For example, the defense may put forward a proposition that the DNA is from a sibling of the POI. In the previous section, the calculation of unique pairs of genotype combinations (instead of going through all possible permutations) was only possible if it was assumed that none of the unknown individuals were related to any of the known profiled individuals, such as victim(s) and/or suspects(s).

If relatedness is assumed between an unknown individual and a profiled person, for example, suppose that one of the unknown individuals is assumed to be the brother of a (profiled) suspect, all the genotype permutations have to be considered in Eq. (5.5). This means that we can no longer use the unique combinations, as described above. In the previous example, all the genotypes in Table 5.5 would have to be considered if relatedness was conditioned between an unknown and a known profiled person.

5.5.2 Correcting for population sub-structuring

The probability of any genotype combination is simply that of its expected frequency in the target population.

For instance, for a homozygote genotype 13,13, the genotype probability is p_{13}^2, and for a heterozygote genotype 13,14, the probability is $2p_{13}p_{14}$. These estimates of the genotype frequencies from the allele frequencies follow the Hardy–Weinberg equilibrium (HWE) expectations (Chapter 1.3). This model assumes that the individuals are not related.

Following HWE expectations, probabilities for rare and common genotypes are calculated from population allele frequencies. Consequently, if there was a rare allele in the DNA profile, and the suspect happens to have this allele, then the value of the evidence would shift quite strongly towards the prosecution proposition of inclusion. However, the frequencies of the alleles observed at different loci are estimates. Therefore it is possible that the rarity of a profile could be the result of a bad sampling strategy, or a result of sampling the wrong population: a profile could be very rare in the whole Dutch population, but more common in the suspect's (undefined) sub-population. The effect of population sub-structuring is further discussed in Chapter 1.12.

To correct for population sub-structuring, a correction is applied to allele frequencies. This correction is called the θ or F_{ST} correction (Chapter 1.12.6). θ is a measure of the subdivision of human populations (sub-structuring), it translates the extent to which allele frequencies in sub-populations can differ from the frequencies of the population as a whole. Usual values are between 0.01 and 0.05 for human populations. The θ correction is applied through a "sampling formula" [222] (formula also provided in Appendix A). For every allele a in a given genotype combination u (from set U), the sampling formula is defined as follows:

$$Pr(u|T, V) = 2^h \prod_{a \in u} \frac{m_a \theta + (1 - \theta)p_a}{1 + (m_+ - 1)\theta} \tag{5.15}$$

where, for every element (allele) a of (combined) genotype u^4, m_a is the number of alleles of type a in the sets T and V, in addition to the previously visited ones in the set u. Furthermore, $m_+ = \sum_b m_b$ (for each increment of a), and h is the number of heterozygote genotypes in set u, and p_a is the frequency of allele a. Importantly, if $\theta = 0$ in Eq. (5.15), the Hardy–Weinberg estimates are recovered:

$$Pr(u|T, V) = 2^h \prod_{a \in u} p_a \tag{5.16}$$

To illustrate the calculation of the genotype probability using the sampling formula, two examples are given below.

5.5.2.1 Example 1

In this example, we consider the genotype combination $u_2 = (13, 13; 13, 14)$, $T = \varnothing$ and $V = \varnothing$.

For every element (allele) in u_2, we apply the formula in Eq. (5.15), and we multiply by the permutation factor. The sampling formula goes through the genotype combination u_2 allele per allele, as indicated by the blue (black in print version) boxes below:

- $\boxed{13}, 13; 13, 14$
  - no alleles of type 13 have been sampled yet $\rightarrow m_{13} = 0$
  - no alleles in T nor $V \rightarrow m_+ = 0$
  - If we apply the formula, we obtain p_{13}
- $13, \boxed{13}; 13, 14$
  - one allele of type 13 has been sampled already $\rightarrow m_{13} = 1$
  - one allele has been sampled (previous steps) $\rightarrow m_+ = 1$
  - If we apply the formula, we obtain $\theta + (1 - \theta)p_{13}$
- $13, 13; \boxed{13}, 14$
  - two alleles of type 13 have been sampled already $\rightarrow m_{13} = 2$
  - two alleles have been sampled (previous steps) $\rightarrow m_+ = 2$
  - If we apply the formula, we obtain $\dfrac{2\theta + (1 - \theta)p_{13}}{1 + \theta}$
- $13, 13; 13, \boxed{14}$
  - no alleles of type 14 have been sampled yet $\rightarrow m_{14} = 0$
  - three alleles have been sampled (previous steps) $\rightarrow m_+ = 3$
  - If we apply the formula, we obtain $\dfrac{(1 - \theta)p_{14}}{1 + 2\theta}$

To obtain the probability, we multiply the probabilities obtained at each iteration:

$$Pr(u_2 = (13, 13; 13, 14) | T = \varnothing, V = \varnothing) = 4p_{13}(\theta + (1 - \theta)p_{13})\frac{2\theta + (1 - \theta)p_{13}}{1 + \theta}\frac{(1 - \theta)p_{14}}{1 + 2\theta}.$$

Note that we multiply by four, this is the product of the permutation factor of two, and the correction for the heterozygote genotypes (h in Eq. (5.15)).

5.5.3 Example 3

In this second example, we consider the genotype combination $u_2 = (13, 13; 13, 14)$, $T = (11, 12)$, and $V = \varnothing$. Before we start the sampling formula, we have $m_{11} = 1$ and $m_{12} = 1$ and so $m_+ = 2$. We start with the first allele 13 (the order does not matter):

- $\boxed{13}, 13; 13, 14$
  - no alleles of type 13 have been sampled yet $\rightarrow m_{13} = 0$
  - two alleles in $T \rightarrow m_+ = 2$
  - Applying the formula, we obtain $\dfrac{(1 - \theta)p_{13}}{1 + \theta}$

- 13,$\boxed{13}$;13,14
  - one allele of type 13 has been sampled already $\rightarrow m_{13} = 1$
  - three alleles have been sampled (previous step) $\rightarrow m_+ = 3$
  - Applying the formula, we obtain $\dfrac{\theta + (1 - \theta)p_{13}}{1 + 2\theta}$
- 13,13;$\boxed{13}$,14
  - two alleles of type 13 have been sampled already $\rightarrow m_{13} = 2$
  - four alleles have been sampled (previous steps) $\rightarrow m_+ = 4$
  - If we apply the formula, we obtain
    $$\dfrac{2\theta + (1 - \theta)p_{13}}{1 + 3\theta}$$
- 13,13;13,$\boxed{14}$
  - no alleles of type 14 have been sampled yet $\rightarrow m_{14} = 0$
  - five alleles have been sampled (previous steps) $\rightarrow m_+ = 5$
  - If we apply the formula, we obtain $\dfrac{(1 - \theta)p_{14}}{1 + 4\theta}$

Thus we can write

$$Pr(u_2 = (13, 13; 13, 14)|T = (11, 12), V = \varnothing) =$$
$$4\frac{(1 - \theta)p_{13}}{1 + \theta} \frac{\theta + (1 - \theta)p_{13}}{1 + 2\theta} \frac{2\theta + (1 - \theta)p_{13}}{1 + 3\theta} \frac{(1 - \theta)p_{14}}{1 + 4\theta}$$

Here again, note that we multiply by four, this is the product of the permutation factor of two, and the correction for the heterozygote genotypes. The above examples are easily extended to multiple known/unknown individuals.

5.5.4 Calculating genotype probabilities for relatedness

In Chapter 1.16, it was demonstrated that likelihood ratios are critically dependent upon the propositions formulated. The standard format will assign unknown/known individuals as unrelated to a person of interest (POI). However, the defense may put forward a proposition that the DNA is from a sibling of the POI.

When relatedness is conditioned, the genotype probabilities of the unknown (unprofiled) relatives no longer follow Eqs. (5.15) and (5.16). Indeed, in this case, one of the unknowns is related to a profiled person, such as a suspect, the genotype probabilities depend not only on the allelic frequencies in the population, and θ, but also on the probabilities of *identity by descent* (IBD), which describe the probabilities that two related individuals share alleles from a common (recent) ancestor, as discussed in Chapter 1.12.3. See Appendix A.2 for more details about the corresponding relatedness for different IBD values to appreciate how the relatedness formulae can be generalized using the IBD values.

The genotype probabilities for unknown unprofiled individuals, given the profile of their relative(s), have been extensively discussed in the forensic literature [223,48,70]. In the following, we describe the same formulae used by these authors. Note that we only describe a situation where one of the unknowns is assumed to be related to one of the profiled individuals (in set T or V).

Remember that under a given proposition, there may be x unknown contributors. In the previous sections, we assumed that those unknowns were unrelated to the profiled individuals, and we used Eqs. (5.15) and (5.16), to determine their probabilities. We now consider a situation, where among the x unknowns, there might be one relative to a given profiled person in set T or V.

The vector of unknown genotypes u (an element in outcome U), can be split into two independent set of genotypes: $u = (z, q)$, where z is the genotype of the unknown relative, and q is the genotype(s) of the unrelated unknown(s). We choose z as the genotype of the first unknown in the u combination (the placement in which the considered relatedness of the unknown does not matter).

From this, the probability for the unknown genotype set can be factorized as

$$Pr(u|T, V) = Pr(z, q|T, V) = Pr(z|T, V)Pr(q|T, V, z) \qquad (5.17)$$

Eq. (5.17) translates that when u is collapsed into the first genotype of the related unknown, z, and the genotypes of the remaining unrelated unknowns q, we can compute the probability for the relative and the probability of the remaining unknowns independently, and then take the product, provided we account for the profile of the first unknown when computing the latter probability.[5]

The probability for the unrelated unknown genotypes $Pr(q|T, V)$ is obtained as before by applying Eq. (5.15), where each allele a in q is iterated as before, but now where m_a is the number of alleles of type a in the sets z; T and V in addition to the previously visited ones in the set q (for each increment of a).

In *LRmix Studio* and *EuroForMix*, we only consider relatedness under the H_d proposition, where z is the genotype of an unknown relative of a typed individual, which we define as t_{rel}. In *LRmix Studio*, this typed related individual is the specified person of interest (POI) under the H_p proposition, which becomes a known non-contributor under H_d (hence part of the V set). In *EuroForMix*, the related individual can be considered to be any of the individuals defined in V or T.

Notice that if there is no need to correct for population sub-structure ($\theta = 0$), then the genotype of the unknown relative depends only on the genotype of the typed relative t_{rel}:

$$Pr(z|T, V) = Pr(z|t_{rel}) \qquad (5.18)$$

The unknown relative z can be related to different degrees to t_{rel}. Here we consider the most relevant relationships for forensic casework:
- Parent/child
- Siblings

- Half-siblings
- Cousins
- Uncle/Nephew
- Grandparent/Grandchild

The genotype probabilities for the unrelated unknowns are defined by Eq. (5.15), however, the genotypic probabilities of z, given t_{rel}, are defined by Table 5.7 when $\theta = 0$.

Table 5.7 Conditional probabilities for the genotype z of an unknown unprofiled individual, given the genotype of the profiled relative t_{rel}. The probabilities are given for $\theta = 0$.

t_{rel}	z	Parent/child	Siblings	Cousins	Half-sibs., Uncle/Nephew Grandparent/ Grandchild
12, 12	12, 12	p_{12}	$\dfrac{(1 + p_{12})^2}{4}$	$\dfrac{p_{12}(1 + 3p_{12})}{4}$	$\dfrac{p_{12}(1 + p_{12})}{2}$
	13, 13	0	$\dfrac{p_{13}^2}{4}$	$\dfrac{3p_{13}^2}{4}$	$\dfrac{p_{13}^2}{2}$
	12, 13	p_{13}	$\dfrac{p_{13}(1 + p_{12})}{2}$	$\dfrac{p_{13}(1 + 6p_{12})}{4}$	$\dfrac{p_{13}(1 + 2p_{12})}{2}$
	13, 14	0	$\dfrac{p_{13}p_{14}}{2}$	$\dfrac{3p_{13}p_{14}}{2}$	$p_{13}p_{14}$
12, 13	12, 12	$\dfrac{p_{12}}{2}$	$\dfrac{p_{12}(1 + p_{12})}{4}$	$\dfrac{p_{12}(1 + 6p_{12})}{8}$	$\dfrac{p_{12}(1 + 2p_{12})}{4}$
	12, 13	$\dfrac{(p_{12} + p_{13})}{2}$	$\dfrac{1 + p_{12} + p_{13} + 2p_{12}p_{13}}{4}$	$\dfrac{p_{12} + p_{13} + 12p_{12}p_{13}}{8}$	$\dfrac{p_{12} + p_{13} + 4p_{12}p_{13}}{4}$
	12, 14	$\dfrac{p_{14}}{2}$	$\dfrac{p_{14}(1 + 2p_{12})}{4}$	$\dfrac{p_{14}(1 + 12p_{12})}{8}$	$\dfrac{p_{14}(1 + 4p_{12})}{4}$
	14, 14	0	$\dfrac{p_{14}^2}{4}$	$\dfrac{3p_{14}^2}{2}$	$\dfrac{p_{14}^2}{2}$
	14, 15	0	$\dfrac{p_{14}p_{15}}{2}$	$\dfrac{3p_{14}p_{15}}{2}$	$p_{14}p_{15}$

General formulae for calculating $Pr(z|T, V)$, when $\theta > 0$, can be found in Appendix A.2.2. Examples of specific probabilities for parent/child, siblings, cousins, uncle/nephew, half-siblings, and grandparent/grandchild relationships can be found in Appendix A.2.3.

It is worth mentioning that *LRmix Studio* considers an approximation for $Pr(z|T, V)$ when $\theta > 0$, and the set T is not empty under H_d (i.e., when there are conditional contributors)[6]:

$$Pr(z|T, V) \approx Pr(z|t_{rel}) \tag{5.19}$$

146 Forensic Practitioner's Guide to the Interpretation of Complex DNA Profiles

meaning that the alleles of other genotypes as specified in the sets T and V, in addition to t_{rel}, are not taken into account.

5.5.5 Example with relatedness in mixtures

In this section, we will calculate the genotype probability $Pr(u|H)$ for the following proposition:

H: An unknown (untyped) brother of the suspect $t_{rel} = (13, 13)$ (known non-contributor) and an unknown unrelated individual are contributors to the evidence $E = \{13, 14\}$.

If we consider the two contributing individuals under H as unrelated, we can follow the illustration in Chapter 1.9 to obtain Table 5.8, which lists the genotype probabilities for the different genotype combinations (here we do not consider the possibility of allele drop-out).

We now continue evaluating H, where one of the unknown individuals is, in fact, the brother of a profiled suspect, having genotype (13,13), and the second unknown individual is unrelated to the suspect. Note that, since all permutations of the genotypes among the two unknowns are considered in case of relatedness (as listed in Table 5.8), it is equivalent to choosing either the first or the second unknown as the relative to the suspect. We follow Eq. (5.17) to factorize the genotype probability as

$$Pr(u|H) = Pr(z|t_{rel})Pr(q|t_{rel}, z) \qquad (5.20)$$

where z is the genotype of the unknown individual assumed to be a brother of the suspect with genotype $t_{rel} = (13, 13)$.

Using the formula in Table 5.7, we obtain Table 5.9, which gives the genotype probabilities when $\theta = 0$. Table 5.10 gives the genotype probabilities when $\theta > 0$. In Appendix A.2.3, we provide both general and specific relatedness formulae when $\theta > 0$.

5.6. Full example for calculating LR

In this section, calculations for a simple single-locus example are illustrated, with a DNA-profile (evidence) with a single donor. At a given locus, the replicates show alleles as follows: $R_1 = \{13\}$ and $R_2 = \{13, 14\}$. The hypotheses to be evaluated in the likelihood ratio are:

- H_p: The suspect with genotype 13, 14 contributes to the evidence.
- H_d: An unknown person, unrelated to the suspect, contributes to the evidence.

To reduce the complexity of the calculations, it is assumed that the considered locus shows only three alleles in the Dutch population, 12, 13, and 14, with frequencies p_{12}, p_{13}, and p_{14}, respectively. The drop-out and drop-in parameters are defined in Section 5.4.1.

Table 5.8 Exhaustive list of all the possible genotype combinations along with the genotype probabilities, for two unknowns (unrelated to the suspect), for a virtual locus with two alleles 13 and 14.

Combination	Unknown 1	Unknown 2	$Pr(u\|T, V)$
u_1	13,13	13,13	$p_{13}^2 \times p_{13}^2$
u_2	13,13	13,14	$p_{13}^2 \times 2p_{13}p_{14}$
u_2'	13,14	13,13	$2p_{13}p_{14} \times p_{13}^2$
u_3	13,14	13,14	$2p_{13}p_{14} \times 2p_{13}p_{14}$
u_4	13,14	14,14	$2p_{13}p_{14} \times p_{14}^2$
u_4'	14,14	13,14	$p_{14}^2 \times 2p_{13}p_{14}$
u_5	14,14	14,14	$p_{14}^2 \times p_{14}^2$
u_6	13,13	14,14	$p_{13}^2 \times p_{14}^2$
u_6'	14,14	13,13	$p_{14}^2 \times p_{13}^2$

Under H_p:

Since there are no unknown contributors under H_p, the genotype probability is one. The replicate probabilities are given in Eqs. (5.21) and (5.22):

$$Pr(R_1 = \{13\}|T = \{13, 14\}) = d_1(1 - d_1)(1 - c) \tag{5.21}$$

$$Pr(R_2 = \{13, 14\}|T = \{13, 14\}) = (1 - d_1)^2(1 - c) \tag{5.22}$$

The joint replicate probability is the product of Eqs. (5.21) and (5.22):

$$Pr(R_1, R_2|T) = \{13, 14\}) = d_1(1 - d_1)^3(1 - c)^2 \tag{5.23}$$

Since there are no unknowns under H_p, the probability of the evidence is simply the product of the replicate probabilities:

$$Pr(E|H_p) = d_1(1 - d_1)^3(1 - c)^2 \tag{5.24}$$

Under H_d:

Under H_d, there is one unknown, and one known non-contributor (the suspect) with genotype 13,14. Thus $x = 1$, $T = \varnothing$, and $V = \{13, 14\}$. The first step of the analysis, regardless of the profile of the evidence, is to derive the possible genotypes for the unknown individual. The considered locus has three distinct alleles in the Dutch population (12, 13, and 14). Thus there are six possible genotypes: 12,12; 13,13; 14,14; 12,13; 12,14, and 13,14. The unknown could have any of these genotypes. Thus set U

148 Forensic Practitioner's Guide to the Interpretation of Complex DNA Profiles

Table 5.9 Exhaustive list of all the possible genotype combinations along with the genotype probabilities ($\theta = 0$) for an unknown brother of a suspect with genotype 13,13, and for an unrelated unknown.

Combination	Unknowns		$Pr(u\|H)$
	Brother of Suspect	**Unknown**	
u_1	13,13	13,13	$\dfrac{(1+p_{13})^2}{4} \times p_{13}^2$
u_2	13,13	13,14	$\dfrac{(1+p_{13})^2}{4} \times 2p_{13}p_{14}$
u_2'	13,14	13,13	$\dfrac{p_{14}(1+p_{13})}{2} \times p_{13}^2$
u_3	13,14	13,14	$\dfrac{p_{14}(1+p_{13})}{2} \times 2p_{13}p_{14}$
u_4	13,14	14,14	$\dfrac{p_{14}(1+p_{13})}{2} \times p_{14}^2$
u_4'	14,14	13,14	$\dfrac{p_{14}^2}{4} \times 2p_{13}p_{14}$
u_5	14,14	14,14	$\dfrac{p_{14}^2}{4} \times p_{14}^2$
u_6	13,13	14,14	$\dfrac{(1+p_{13})^2}{4} \times p_{14}^2$
u_6'	14,14	13,13	$\dfrac{p_{14}^2}{4} \times p_{13}^2$

contains six possible genotypes. Table 5.11 (below) gives the genotypic probabilities for these six genotypes, when $\theta = 0$ and when $\theta \neq 0$.

The next step is to derive the replicate probabilities for every possible genotype of the unknown individual using the formulae in Eqs. (5.8) and (5.9). Table 5.12 gives these probabilities.

Applying the formula in Eq. (5.5), and combining the terms in Tables 5.11 and 5.12, the probability of the evidence under H_d when $\theta = 0$:

$$Pr(E|H_d) = d_1^2 p_C^3 p_{13}^2 p_{14} \times p_{12}^2 + (1 - d_1')^2 p_C p_{14}(1 - p_C) \times p_{13}^2 + d_1'(1 - d_1')p_C^2 p_{13}^2 \times p_{14}^2$$
$$+ d_1^2(1 - d_1)^2 p_{14}p_C(1 - p_C) \times 2p_{12}p_{13} + d_1^3(1 - d_1)p_C^2 p_{13}^2 \times 2p_{12}p_{14}$$
$$+ d_1(1 - d_1)^3(1 - p_C)^2 \times 2p_{13}p_{14}.$$

The *LR* is obtained by taking the ratio of the probabilities:

$$LR = d_1(1 - d_1)^3(1 - p_C)^2 / [d_1^2 p_C^3 p_{13}^2 p_{14} \times p_{12}^2 + (1 - d_1')^2 p_C p_{14}(1 - p_C) \times p_{13}^2$$
$$+ d_1'(1 - d_1')p_C^2 p_{13}^2 \times p_{14}^2 + d_1^2(1 - d_1)^2 p_{14}p_C(1 - p_C) \times 2p_{12}p_{13}$$
$$+ d_1^3(1 - d_1)p_C^2 p_{13}^2 \times 2p_{12}p_{14} + d_1(1 - d_1)^3(1 - p_C)^2 \times 2p_{13}p_{14}] \tag{5.25}$$

Table 5.10 Exhaustive list of all the possible genotype combinations along with the genotypic probabilities ($\theta > 0$) for an unknown brother of a suspect with genotype (13,13), and for an unrelated unknown.

Combi.	Unknowns		$Pr(u|H)$
	Brother	**Unrelated**	
u_1	13,13	13,13	$\dfrac{1}{4}\left(1+\dfrac{2(2\theta+(1-\theta)p_{13})}{1+\theta}+\dfrac{(2\theta+(1-\theta)p_{13})(3\theta+(1-\theta)p_{13})}{(1+\theta)(1+2\theta)}\right)\times$ $\dfrac{(4\theta+(1-\theta)p_{13})(5\theta+(1-\theta)p_{13})}{(1+3\theta)(1+4\theta)}$
u_2	13,13	13,14	$\dfrac{1}{4}\left(1+\dfrac{2(2\theta+(1-\theta)p_{13})}{1+\theta}+\dfrac{(2\theta+(1-\theta)p_{13})(3\theta+(1-\theta)p_{13})}{(1+\theta)(1+2\theta)}\right)\times$ $2\dfrac{(4\theta+(1-\theta)p_{13})(1-\theta)p_{14}}{(1+3\theta)(1+4\theta)}$
u_2'	13,14	13,13	$\dfrac{(1-\theta)p_{14}}{2(1+\theta)}\left(1+\dfrac{2\theta+(1-\theta)p_{13}}{1+2\theta}\right)\times\dfrac{(3\theta+(1-\theta)p_{13})(4\theta+(1-\theta)p_{13})}{(1+3\theta)(1+4\theta)}$
u_3	13,14	13,14	$\dfrac{(1-\theta)p_{14}}{2(1+\theta)}\left(1+\dfrac{2\theta+(1-\theta)p_{13}}{1+2\theta}\right)\times 2\dfrac{(3\theta+(1-\theta)p_{13})(\theta+(1-\theta)p_{14})}{(1+3\theta)(1+4\theta)}$
u_4	13,14	14,14	$\dfrac{(1-\theta)p_{14}}{2(1+\theta)}\left(1+\dfrac{2\theta+(1-\theta)p_{13}}{1+2\theta}\right)\times\dfrac{(\theta+(1-\theta)p_{14})(2\theta+(1-\theta)p_{14})}{(1+3\theta)(1+4\theta)}$
u_4'	14,14	13,14	$\dfrac{(1-\theta)p_{14}(\theta+(1-\theta)p_{14})}{4(1+\theta)(1+2\theta)}\times 2\dfrac{(2\theta+(1-\theta)p_{13})(2\theta+(1-\theta)p_{14})}{(1+3\theta)(1+4\theta)}$
u_5	14,14	14,14	$\dfrac{(1-\theta)p_{14}(\theta+(1-\theta)p_{14})}{4(1+\theta)(1+2\theta)}\times\dfrac{(2\theta+(1-\theta)p_{14})(3\theta+(1-\theta)p_{14})}{(1+3\theta)(1+4\theta)}$
u_6	13,13	14,14	$\dfrac{1}{4}\left(1+\dfrac{2(2\theta+(1-\theta)p_{13})}{1+\theta}+\dfrac{(2\theta+(1-\theta)p_{13})(3\theta+(1-\theta)p_{13})}{(1+\theta)(1+2\theta)}\right)\times$ $\dfrac{(1-\theta)p_{14}(\theta+(1-\theta)p_{14})}{(1+3\theta)(1+4\theta)}$
u_6'	14,14	13,13	$\dfrac{(1-\theta)p_{14}(\theta+(1-\theta)p_{14})}{4(1+\theta)(1+2\theta)}\times\dfrac{(2\theta+(1-\theta)p_{13})(3\theta+(1-\theta)p_{13})}{(1+3\theta)(1+4\theta)}$

5.7. Summary

This chapter unifies the concepts previously discussed to frame and develop the theory behind the *LRmix* model. *LRmix* is a qualitative model that takes account of drop-out, drop-in, and any number of contributors. However, it does not explicitly model allele peak heights, stutter, or degradation, which is reserved for quantitative (continuous) models, which are further discussed in subsequent chapters. We further summarize the main concepts tackled in this chapter:

1. The *LRmix* model is based upon the likelihood ratio formulation.

Table 5.11 Genotype probabilities under H_d.

Genotype	$Pr(u \mid T, V)$	
u	$\theta = 0$	$\theta > 0$
12,12	p_{12}^2	$\dfrac{(1-\theta)p_{12}(\theta + (1-\theta)p_{12})}{(1+\theta)(1+2\theta)}$
13,13	p_{13}^2	$\dfrac{(\theta + (1-\theta)p_{13})(2\theta + (1-\theta)p_{13})}{(1+\theta)(1+2\theta)}$
14,14	p_{14}^2	$\dfrac{(\theta + (1-\theta)p_{14})(2\theta + (1-\theta)p_{14})}{(1+\theta)(1+2\theta)}$
12,13	$2p_{12}p_{13}$	$2\dfrac{(1-\theta)p_{12}(\theta + (1-\theta)p_{13})}{(1+\theta)(1+2\theta)}$
12,14	$2p_{12}p_{14}$	$2\dfrac{(1-\theta)p_{12}(\theta + (1-\theta)p_{14})}{(1+\theta)(1+2\theta)}$
13,14	$2p_{13}p_{14}$	$2\dfrac{(\theta + (1-\theta)p_{13})(\theta + (1-\theta)p_{14})}{(1+\theta)(1+2\theta)}$

Table 5.12 Replicate probabilities for the genotypes of the unknown, where $g = u$. The allele drop-out probabilities from the heterozygote and homozygote genotypes are d_1 and d_1', respectively (evaluating only one contributor).

g	$Pr(R_1 = \{13\} \mid g)$	$Pr(R_2 = \{13, 14\} \mid g)$	$Pr(R_1, R_2 \mid g)$
12,12	$d_1' p_C p_{13}$	$d_1' p_C^2 p_{13} p_{14}$	$d_1'^2 p_C^3 p_{13}^2 p_{14}$
13,13	$(1 - d_1')(1 - p_C)$	$(1 - d_1') p_C p_{14}$	$(1 - d_1')^2 p_C p_{14}(1 - p_C)$
14,14	$d_1' p_C p_{13}$	$(1 - d_1') p_C p_{13}$	$d_1'(1 - d_1') p_C^2 p_{13}^2$
12,13	$d_1(1 - d_1)(1 - p_C)$	$d_1(1 - d_1) p_{14} p_C$	$d_1^2(1 - d_1)^2 p_{14} p_C (1 - p_C)$
12,14	$d_1^2 p_C p_{13}$	$d_1(1 - d_1) p_C p_{13}$	$d_1^3(1 - d_1)(p_C p_{13})^2$
13,14	$d_1(1 - d_1)(1 - p_C)$	$(1 - d_1)^2(1 - p_C)$	$d_1(1 - d_1)^3(1 - p_C)^2$

2. The model is able to accommodate replicate DNA profiles by analysis of their joint probabilities.

3. Drop-out is an allele that is not detected in a crime-sample profile, because it is of low quality or quantity. Drop-in arises from fragments of extraneous DNA "contaminating" a sample profile, considered as independent events. A probabilistic approach to define drop-out and drop-in is adopted and illustrated by a number of examples.

4. Population sub-structuring is accounted for using the θ-correction, this approach is illustrated by examples.

5. Examples of likelihood ratio calculations that include relatedness in the propositions are provided.

Notes

1. http://forensim.r-forge.r-project.org/.
2. Note that the order of the alleles within the genotypes does not matter, thus genotype a, b is equivalent to genotype b, a.

3. Note that this would not be possible to implement for a quantitative model since each unknown contributor has a different mixture proportion parameter.
4. The formula goes through the (combined) genotype vector u, allele per allele.
5. The conditioning on z matters only if $\theta > 0$.
6. Also in the situation that t_{rel} is not the only element in V.

CHAPTER 6

A qualitative (semi-continuous) model: *LRmix Studio*

The methods described in the previous chapter were programmed into two open-source software packages. The first version was published in the *forensim* R package by Hinda Haned http://forensim.r-forge.r-project.org/. It was later further enhanced by Hinda Haned and Jeroen de Jong (NFI). This software is known as *LRmix Studio*, which is programmed in Java and has a friendly user-friendly interface. This is a *qualitative* model. It does not take account of peak height or stutter directly, however, it models important phenomena, such as drop-out and drop-in indirectly. The software is free and open-source. The software is available from https://github.com/smartrank/lrmixstudio.git. The reader is referred to the manual that can be downloaded from the website; it is available within the software (it needs to be read in parallel with this chapter). The data used for the examples described are available at the book's website https://sites.google.com/view/dnabook/.

6.1. Interpretation of a major/minor DNA mixture, where the minor contributor is evidential

In Chapter 2.3, the interpretation of major/minor profiles was discussed. It is possible to carry out analyses using pen and paper, but the process is lengthy, and it is difficult to avoid manual calculation errors. Here the principles are expanded, instead of using empirical guidelines, drop-out and drop-in (Section 4.2) theory are encoded as described in the previous chapter. Consequently, the whole process is automated. The analysis must be placed in the context of the case circumstances to establish the alternative propositions put forward by the prosecution and the defense. The data used for this analysis are provided on the book's website in the "Major_minor" folder.

6.1.1 Case circumstances

A woman was murdered by being stabbed with a knife, which was recovered at the crime scene. It was identified as the murder weapon, and a DNA profile was obtained from the handle. Based upon a witness report, a suspect was arrested and reference sample was obtained from him. At this stage, it is useful to formulate propositions (it may be necessary to alter them once the results of the DNA analysis are known). There

Forensic Practitioner's Guide to the Interpretation of Complex DNA Profiles
https://doi.org/10.1016/B978-0-12-820562-4.00014-6

is a prior expectation that DNA from the victim is present on the knife. There is also prior expectation of the perpetrator DNA being present on the knife handle.

The electropherogram was generated (Fig. 6.1) and the data loaded into *LRmix Studio* as described in the user-manual https://github.com/smartrank/lrmixstudio/blob/master/docs/manual/manual.pdf.

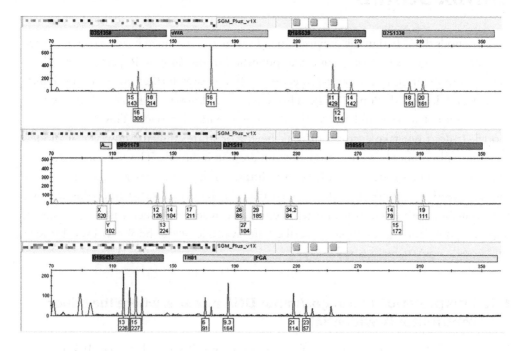

Figure 6.1 Case EPG.

6.1.2 Exploratory data analysis

It is easy to explore the allelic data before any calculations are carried out. Once loaded, the data are compared in a compilation shown under the profile summary tab (Fig. 6.2).

The compilation shows that there is a maximum of four alleles observed per locus in the crime stain, which suggests a simple two-person mixture, using the counting method described in Chapter 1.7.2 and Eq. (1.6). All of the victim's alleles are represented in the crime sample. Loci D2S1338, TH01, and FGA are partially represented in the crime stain; under the prosecution proposition allele drop-out has occurred.

6.1.3 The propositions

Given that the bloody knife was recovered from the crime scene and was identified as the murder weapon, there is an expectation that the victim's DNA would be present.

A qualitative (semi-continuous) model: *LRmix Studio*

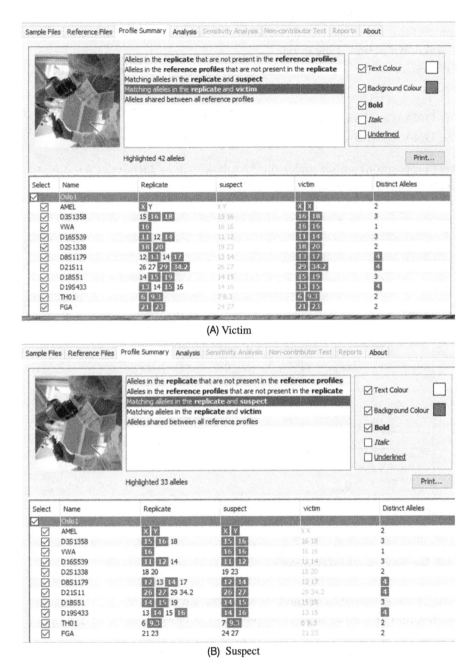

Figure 6.2 Profile summary screenshot from *LRmix Studio* for the major minor example, comparing profiles from (A) Victim and (B) Suspect with the crime-stain (Replicate).

Consequently, this is conditioned under both the alternative propositions. The prosecution contend that the suspect is the donor to the sample, whereas the defense contend that an unknown person is the donor.

The strength of the evidence is determined from a consideration of the alternate propositions:

H_p: The DNA is a mixture of the victim and the suspect.
H_d: The DNA is a mixture of the victim and an unknown person.

These propositions are set under the "Analysis" tab in *LRmix Studio* using the tick boxes. The number of unknown contributors is set under each proposition (Fig. 6.3). The "Drop-out Probability" is the "per-donor" drop-out probability parameter (d_k), as defined in Chapter 5.4.1 (notice that the unknown contributors under a specific proposition use a common drop-out probability parameter). For the time being the Drop-out Probability values are ignored.

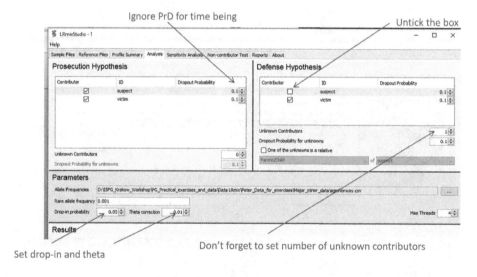

Figure 6.3 The "Analysis" tab in *LRmix Studio*.

In the "Parameters" section, the following data are input:
1. The location of the file is input by pressing the browse button to the right of the bar.
2. The default "Rare allele frequency" is provided (0.001 in this example).
3. The "Drop-in" probability is provided, either from data or from a default (0.05 in this example).
4. A "Theta correction" is provided (0.01 in the example).

6.1.4 Sensitivity analysis

In the sensitivity analysis tab (Fig. 6.4), the tick-boxes at the top give a "Vary Drop-out" option for "Suspect", "Victim", and "Prosecution Unknown Contributors". The victim option is left unticked, because a) The alleles of the victim are fully represented in the crime stain, b) the victim is conditioned under H_p and H_d. If the conditions of a) and b) are not fulfilled, then the box would be ticked.

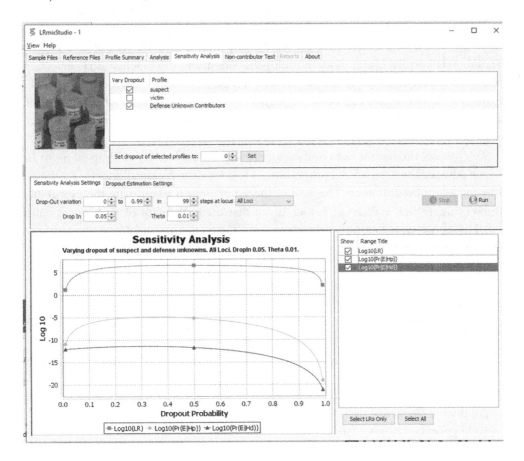

Figure 6.4 The "Sensitivity Analysis" tab in *LRmix Studio*.

Ensure that the "Sensitivity Analysis Settings" tab is selected. Then press "Run". The model applies a drop-out probability parameter d for the "ticked" contributors (here the suspect and unknown contributors). The drop-out probability parameter d is varied between zero and one in steps of 0.01 (x-axis), because we have deselected the victim's tick box in the "Vary drop-out" section, the drop-out probability parameter for the victim equals zero across the entire range (i.e., $d_2 = 0$ under H_p, and $d_1 = 0$ under

H_d). The $log_{10}LR$ is calculated across the range of drop–out probabilities for d (Fig. 6.4). The corresponding $log_{10}Pr(E|H_p)$ and $log_{10}Pr(E|H_d)$ can also be plotted (optional).

The next step is to estimate the "Plausible range of drop–out probabilities" (i.e., finding plausible values for the common drop–out probability parameter d).

6.1.5 Calculation of levels of drop-out using an empirical method

From Gill et al. [124], for low template DNA, in the absence of degradation, it is reasonable to assume that the chance of allele drop-out is independent of the locus. Note that if significant degradation has occurred, then high molecular weight loci will be affected preferentially. Using modern multiplex conditions, the biochemistry/detection system will distinguish a single copy of DNA if it is present in the PCR sample [195]. We provided a method used in an earlier model (*LoComatioN*) to estimate d by simulation, based on the assumption that d is constant across all loci [65]. The following approach is also described in a more general framework in Appendix B.3.3.2.

We consider the number of contributors K and the probability of drop-in p_C to be fixed in advance for a considered proposition. Here U of the K contributors are assumed to be unknown contributors. The goal of the simulations is to estimate the probability of observing in total x alleles at L loci, given that the probability of drop-out is equal to d. That is, we wish to estimate $Pr(x|d, p_C, K)$. Given that p_C and K are constant, this becomes $Pr(x|d)$. Furthermore, we will use this distribution to provide a distribution of d, given the observed x, $Pr(d|x)$.

There are several parts to the simulation:

1. Specify the value of d.
2. Generate $1000 \times U$ random DNA profiles[1] and combine them with the profile of the known contributors to obtain $1000 \times K$ profiles.
3. Randomly drop out alleles of the $1000 \times K$ profiles with the selected drop-out value d.
4. Generate allele drop-in with probability p_C (the specific allele is drawn from the population frequency data).
5. 1000 generated profiles are constructed as a result.
6. Count the total number of total alleles, y for each of the generated profiles.
7. Count the number of situations (out of 1000), where $y = x$ alleles (same as the observed).
8. Repeat steps 1–7 for the next value of d.

We estimate $Pr(x|d)$ by counting the number of x situations from the 1000 iterations (for each of the given values of d).

The process is illustrated in Fig. 6.5. There are 33 alleles observed in a crime-stain evidence, conditioned on three contributors. Profiles of the suspect and victim are available. The drop-out probability parameter and the unknown contributors are unknown.

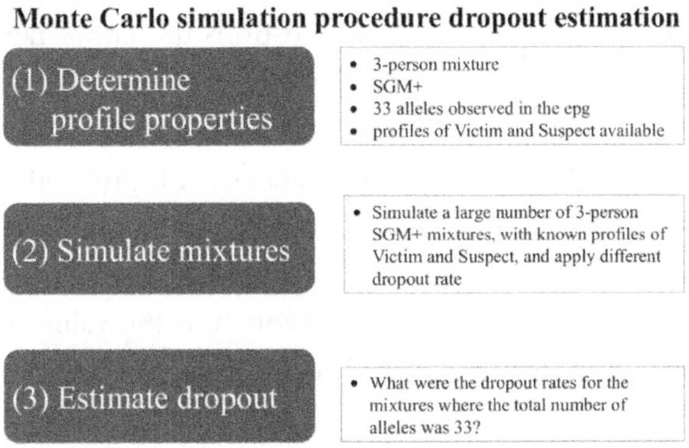

Monte Carlo simulation procedure dropout estimation

(1) Determine profile properties
- 3-person mixture
- SGM+
- 33 alleles observed in the epg
- profiles of Victim and Suspect available

(2) Simulate mixtures
- Simulate a large number of 3-person SGM+ mixtures, with known profiles of Victim and Suspect, and apply different dropout rate

(3) Estimate dropout
- What were the dropout rates for the mixtures where the total number of alleles was 33?

Figure 6.5 Illustration of the simulation process. A large number, e.g., 1000, simulations are carried out to generate three person mixtures, without drop-out. For each simulated profile, the drop-out rate is varied in steps of 0.01 between 0 and 0.99, the distributions of recovered allele numbers (x) are recorded per step.

In the first step, 1000 random DNA profiles are generated, without applying drop-out ($d = 0$), and the number of total alleles are counted for each simulation. The results are represented as a density histogram in Fig. 6.6.

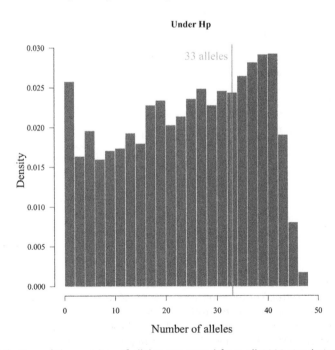

Figure 6.6 Distribution of the number of alleles generated from all 1000 simulations is plotted. No drop-out has been applied.

Furthermore, a drop-out value d is selected from the entire range (0.01–0.99) in steps of 0.01. For a given choice of d, the alleles in each of 1,000 randomly generated profiles are randomly dropped out with probability d. Also, for each of the loci in each of the generated profiles, alleles are randomly drawn with probability p_C, and possibly added to the corresponding profile. Finally, the distribution of 33 alleles can be plotted for each value of d used in the simulations, to provide $Pr(d|x = 33)$. The 5 and 95 percentiles can be calculated from the distribution, and the value that gives the most conservative LR is reported (Fig. 6.7). The process is repeated for H_d.

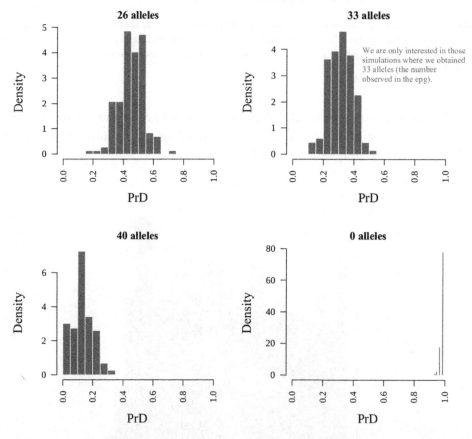

Figure 6.7 Once the simulations are complete for every value of d, density histograms are prepared, showing examples of the $Pr(d|x)$ distribution for $x = 26, 33, 40, 0$. The distribution for $x = 33$ is the one we are interested in, since this represents the observed value of $x = 33$ alleles in the EPG. Note that the larger the value of x, the more the distribution is shifted to the left, indicating that the plausible range of d decreases (the fewer alleles, the higher the level of drop-out must be to explain x and K).

In a different example (Fig. 6.8) described by [65], the effect of varying K is tested. Probability of drop-out is simulated for a profile of 32 alleles using two different conditions: $K = 2$, or $K = 3$. Because there is an expectation of many more alleles to be observed with three contributors, this shifts the distribution of drop-out to the right, i.e., higher levels of drop-out are expected. The "plausible range" is defined by the 5–95 percentiles of the distribution, $F(d|x = 32)$. For two persons, $F(d|x = 32) = 0.95$ corresponds to $d = 0.16$, and for three persons $d = 0.37$; LRmix Studio calculates the likelihood ratios relative to $F(d|x = 32) = 0.95$, and 0.05, the most conservative value, is reported (Fig. 6.9).

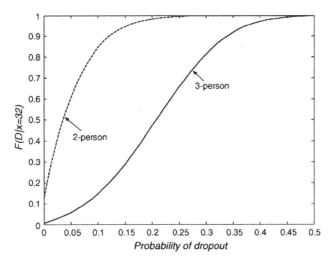

Figure 6.8 The cumulative distribution function (cdf) $F(d|x = 32)$ for a profile with 32 alleles. The solid line is the cdf for d, assuming that there are three ($K = 3$) contributors to this mixture, whereas the dashed line is the cdf for d, assuming that there are two ($K = 2$) contributors. The y-axis tells us the probability that d is smaller than the value on the x-axis. For example, if a vertical line from the x-axis is drawn at the point 0.16 to where it hits the dashed line, and a horizontal line to the y-axis, it hits at about 0.95. We interpret this as, assuming only two people contributed to this mix, we are 95% sure that the true value of d is less than 0.16. Figure reproduced from [65] with permission from Elsevier.

The simulations are carried out separately under the prosecution and defense propositions (Fig. 6.10)—the value that gives the most conservative LR is reported ($d = 0.03$ in this case). To carry out the next step in the calculation, this value is selected as shown in the sensitivity analysis screen under "Set drop-out of selected profiles to: 0.03" (Fig. 6.9). Press the "Set" button and switch to the "Analysis" screen. The drop-out probability parameter d values have been automatically transferred to the suspect (H_p), and unknowns under H_d (Fig. 6.11). Press the "Run" button to finally provide an

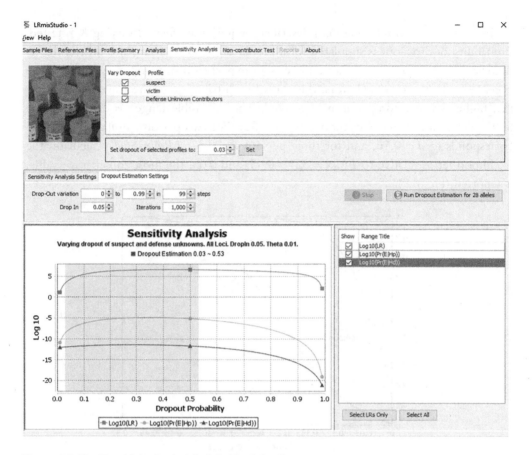

Figure 6.9 The "Sensitivity Analysis" tab in *LRmix Studio*.

LR along with a list of *LR*s for individual loci. Note that three loci (D2S1338, TH01, and FGA) in the example give low *LR*s < 0.1. Examination of the profile shows that drop-out has occurred under H_p at each of these loci. Nevertheless, the overall *LR* = 3005 supporting the prosecution proposition that the mixture is DNA from the suspect and victim (it is usual practice to round the value down, so that *LR* = 3000 would be reported).

	Dropout Probability	
Hypothesis	Minimum (5%)	Maximum (95%)
Prosecution	0.09	0.53
Defense	0.03	0.52
Overall	0.03	0.53

Figure 6.10 From the *LRmix Studio* Report. Results of drop-out sensitivity simulations, showing minimum and maximum drop-out probabilities calculated from 5 and 95 percentiles.

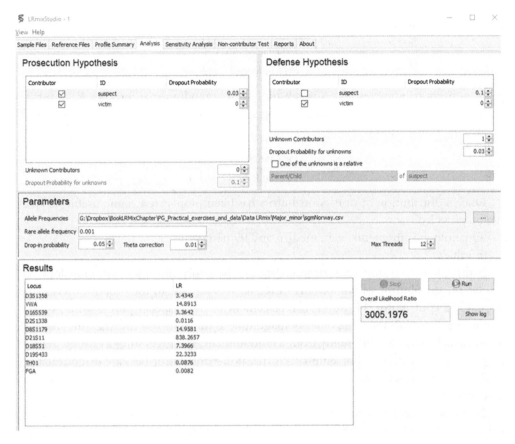

Figure 6.11 Completed analysis showing propositions tested, drop-out and drop-in probabilities, with resultant likelihood ratios per locus, and the overall value.

6.1.6 Non-contributor analysis

Gill and Haned [224] proposed using non-contributor tests to investigate the robustness of a case specific *LR*. These tests are based on the "Tippett test", originally described by Colin Tippett for analysis of paint flakes from vehicles [225] and promoted by Evett and Weir [226] pp. 213–215. Later the test was introduced for DNA profiling on a specific *per case* basis by Gill et al. [221]. The test is used to indicate the probability of misleading evidence in favor of the prosecution. The idea is to replace the profile of the questioned contributor (POI), e.g., the suspect, by a number of random profiles, and for each random profile the likelihood ratio is recomputed. Consider a simple *LR* calculation with two contributors, where S is the questioned contributor (e.g., suspect), V is the victim in the numerator and denominator, and U is an unknown unrelated person in the denominator:

$$LR = \frac{Pr(Evidence|S + V)}{Pr(Evidence|U + V)} \tag{6.1}$$

In non-contributor testing, S is substituted by n random man profiles $R_{1..n}$, where n is usually a large number ≥ 1000, and this gives a distribution of random man LRs if the defense proposition is true:

$$LR_n = \frac{Pr(Evidence|R_n + V)}{Pr(Evidence|U + V)} \tag{6.2}$$

Once a distribution of non-contributors has been propagated, some useful statistics can be provided:
- Quantile measurements, e.g., median and 99 percentile,
- p-values.

If the LR of the suspect is large enough to be easily distinguished, and does not overlap the distribution of random man LRs, it gives support to the proposition that the suspect is a contributor. However, if replacement of the suspect's profile with random profiles results in LRs the same order of magnitude as the observed LR, then the suspect's profile data behaves no differently from a random man, and gives support to the defense proposition of exclusion. The emphasis is that non-contributor tests are diagnostic tests to assist the interpretation, and to understand any limitations of the observed LR that may prevail.

Non-contributor tests are an optional aide that assist the understanding of the case-specific likelihood ratio [68]. To carry out the tests in *LRmix Studio*, switch to the "Non-contributor Test" screen. The parameters and propositions are taken from those applied in the Analysis tab. The non-contributor test consists of calculating the LR obtained when replacing the profile of the person of interest by the profile of a simulated random person.

This is carried out n times, choosing a different random person each time, and n is the number of iterations defined by the user. The output of the test is a distribution of n (log_{10}) likelihood ratios, which are represented as a barplot (Fig. 6.12) as follows:
- The case-specific $log_{10}LR$, obtained with the person of interest, is displayed in red (medium grey in print version);
- The minimum, the maximum, the 1st, the 50th, and the 99th percentiles of the obtained distributions are displayed in grey.

With the example shown, the maximum observed $log_{10}LR$ is -5.667; the 99th percentile is -9.595, and the median is -20.088. These values are well below the observed $log_{10}LR = 3.478$, giving confidence that the model is robust, as it will demonstrably assign low (exclusionary) LRs to random persons.

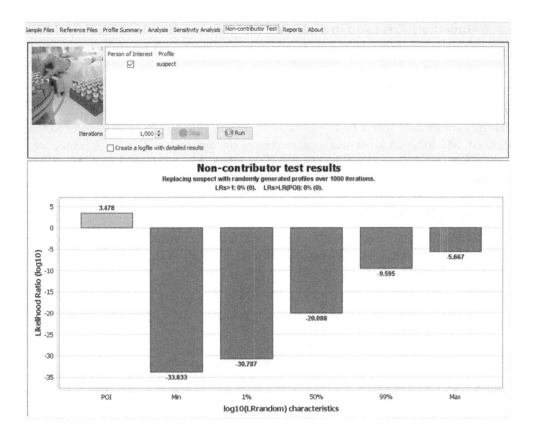

Figure 6.12 Non-contributor test showing percentile results.

Box 6.1 What is the ideal sample size for non-contributor tests?

The risk of a false positive match increases with the number of contributors tested. How often an observed $LR = z$ or more occurs is accommodated by $Pr(LR > z|H_d) < 1/z$ [227]. In other words, we do not expect to see more than N/z chance matches, where N is the number of non-contributor tests. In the example $LR = 3000$ implies that in a sample size of 3000 non-contributors, we might expect to find an individual that gives an LR the same order of magnitude. If we found more than this, then we may conclude that the model is not robust. Therefore when carrying out non-contributor tests, it is useful to test the $Pr(LR > z|H_d) < 1/z$ relationship by evaluating z non-contributors. In the example, when 3000 non-contributors were tested, the highest $log_{10}LR = -4$. The limitation is the time taken to carry out the computation, so this is not realistic for $LR = 1$ bn, for example, but it is possible to carry out 1 m simulations—this takes approximately ten minutes. If the number of non-contributors tested is high enough, then false positive LRs will be observed that may exceed the observed value. This has implications for reference database searches; the latter are discussed in Chapter 11.

166   Forensic Practitioner's Guide to the Interpretation of Complex DNA Profiles

6.1.7 How the LR is used in a statement

To prepare a court-going statement, the following format can be used:

A statement of understanding

From information received from my colleague, Mr. Thomas of the Birmingham Laboratory, I understand that a knife was recovered from the apartment belonging to the deceased, Ms. Jones. A knife was recovered from the apartment. The knife handle was tested, and a mixture of DNA was found. This DNA may have come from Ms. Jones and from Mr. Smith.

Conditioning the statement

My interpretation and conclusions are based on the information available at the time of this examination. Should this information change, I will need to reappraise the propositions considered. This reappraisal is more effective if carried out in advance of any trial.[2]

Purpose

To determine whether or not there is any support for the proposition that the DNA on the knife handle came from Mr. Smith. In particular, to interpret the results of the DNA analysis undertaken in this case.

Statement of findings

STR profiles have been obtained from the knife handle, and from reference buccal samples taken from Mr. Smith and Ms. Jones. There is a mixture of two persons DNA. I have compared this DNA with the reference samples of Mr. Smith and Ms. Jones.

State the alternative propositions

To assess the significance of the above findings I have considered two propositions:
(a) Mr. Smith and Ms. Jones have contributed to the sample.
(b) Ms. Jones and an unknown person unrelated to either of them have contributed to the sample.

Consider the alternatives

The probability of the evidence is 3000 times more likely if the first proposition (a) is true, compared to the alternative described by (b).

If non-contributor tests have been carried out, then an optional addition to aid understanding is the following:

The likelihood ratio has been subjected to a performance test. To do this, we replace Mr. Smith with a random unrelated individual, and we repeat the measurement of the likelihood ratio. We do this a total of 1000 times, with a different random individual each time. When this was carried out, the maximum of the likelihood ratios observed was less than 0.00001.

Note: Never use a statement like: "The probability **that** the DNA came from Mr. Smith and Ms. Jones is 3000 times more likely..." as this is an example of the prosecutor's fallacy. To prevent this, we must always include the conditioning statement: use the "IF" word to describe a likelihood ratio to avoid this trap.

The next case example illustrates how non-contributor tests can be useful to show that the models used to interpret evidence are robust.

6.2. A case with two suspects

The data for this case can be downloaded from folder "Two_Suspect_Case" on the book's website https://sites.google.com/view/dnabook/.

6.2.1 Case circumstances

A female victim has been assaulted. Two suspects S_1 and S_2 were arrested and accused of the assault. The evidence is a swab taken from an exposed area of skin of the victim, where she has been repeatedly struck and bruised. Inspection of the EPG indicated a minimum three-person mixture. Reference samples were available from all three individuals.

6.2.2 Exploratory data analysis

This EPG (Fig. 6.13) is classified as low template of three or more individuals, since there are multiple alleles per locus that fall within the criterion of the low-template zone (between the AT and the stochastic threshold (T)). We expect drop-out may occur, but the profiles appear to be well represented.

The initial propositions from the case circumstances are set:

H_p: The evidence is a mixture of S_1, S_2, and V.
H_d: The evidence is a mixture of two unknown individuals and V.

6.2.3 Minimum number of contributors

If H_p is true, then there is drop-out occurring from all three individuals (Fig. 6.14). The level of drop-out appears to be greatest with S_2, where five loci are partial, and locus D21S11 has dropped out completely. There is only one drop-out in V at locus D2S1338. The number of distinct alleles is no greater than four, which would indicate a two-person mixture under H_d. However, under H_p, we must factor in the alleles observed in reference samples that are not observed in crime samples. For example,

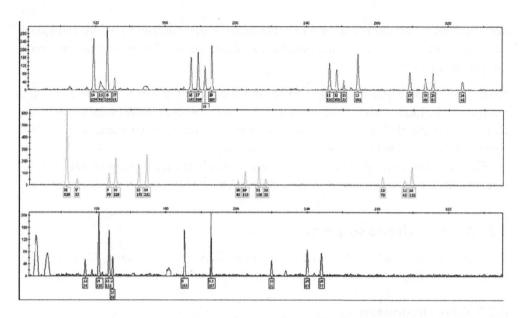

Figure 6.13 Two suspect case EPG. Reproduced from [224] with permission from Elsevier.

for locus D21S11, there are three alleles observed: 29, 31, 32. S_1 is $\boxed{28}$, 32; S_2 is $\boxed{30, 30}$ and the victim is 29, 31. The alleles highlighted by boxes in S_1 and S_2 are *not* observed in the crime sample, making a total of five unique alleles: 28, 29, 30, 31, 32 in the combined set of references and crime sample. Under H_p the extra alleles in the references can only be explained if they have dropped out of the crime-stain sample. Because of the additional alleles in the reference sample, a total of five, this requires a minimum of three contributors, including the victim.

Under H_p, there are also five alleles at D19S433 and FGA loci when the two suspects are added to the set. Strictly, under the defense proposition, we can just invoke two contributors, but we are in an exploratory mode, so we assume three contributors for each of the propositions. The sensitivity analysis is shown in Fig. 6.15. Because there is drop-out observed in the victim's profile, the drop-out tick box is marked. The conservative estimate of drop-out is 0.15 across all contributors and loci, and this value is plugged into the Analysis page (Fig. 6.16). The $LR = 24,000$ which appears to be strong evidence to support the proposition that S_1, S_2, and V are contributors to the crime stain, rather than the victim and two unknown, unrelated individuals.

6.2.4 Non-contributor tests

The next step is to carry out non-contributor tests. With this example, there are two suspects conditioned under H_p. Consequently, there are two different contributor tests that are possible to undertake with S_1 and S_2, respectively (Fig. 6.17).

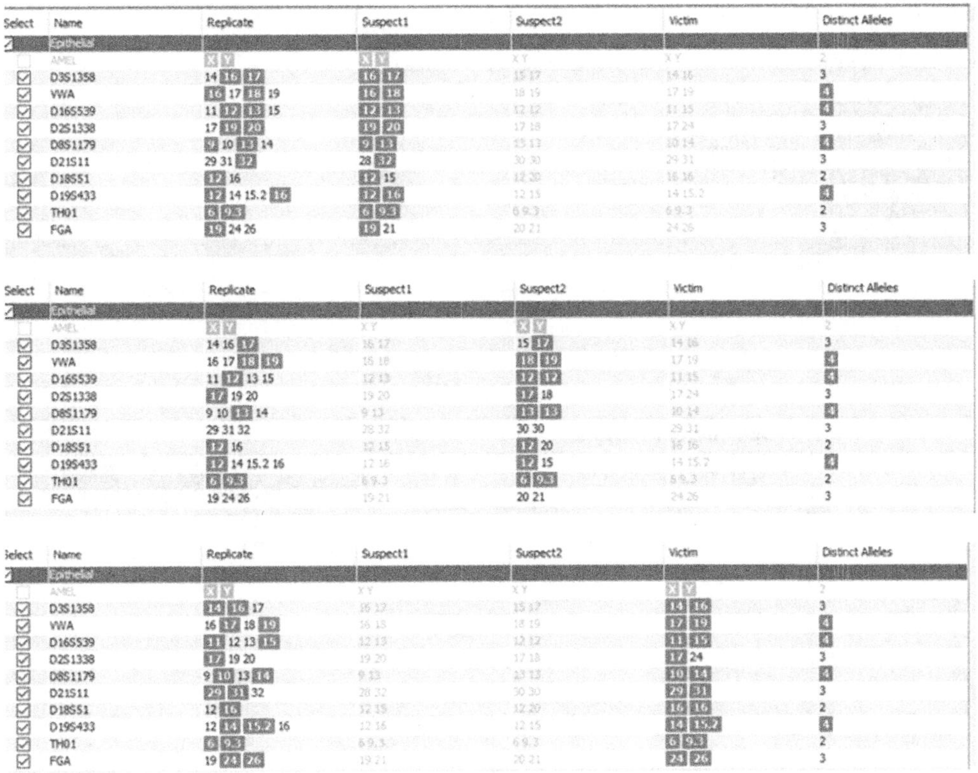

Figure 6.14 A summary of suspect 1, suspect 2, and victim "matching" alleles with the replicate.

The analyses show that 24,000 random persons substituting S_1 give $log_{10}LR_{max} = -4.2$, and the model can therefore be described as robust with respect to S_1. However, with S_2, non-contributors give $log_{10}LR_{max} = 7$ for the 99th percentile. This shows that the model is non-discriminating for S_2, and it would clearly be an error if he was prosecuted on the basis of the combined LR.

6.2.5 Formulation of propositions and exploratory data analysis

This example demonstrates that the formulation of propositions must follow guidelines described by Gill and Haned [224]. The likelihood ratio does exactly what it says on the tin. It compares two alternative propositions. This does not mean to say that either are true. Indeed, in the example, neither are true. But propositions do not need to be true for one to be more likely than the other.

Exploring the data with non-contributor tests leads to the conclusion that the contribution to the likelihood ratio by contributor S_2 is neutral.

Figure 6.15 Sensitivity analysis for the "two suspect" case used to estimate drop-out range and the associated conservative *LR*.

The next step is to carry out exploratory data analysis to determine the effect of analyzing different sets of propositions.

Table 6.1 Results of the non-contributor analysis for different sets of propositions and drop-out parameter d.

Propositions				Non-contributor analysis	Percentiles of $log_{10} LR$			
H_p	H_d	$log_{10} LR$	d	Substitution	50	99	max	No. of simulations
S_1, S_2, V	U, U, V	4.394	0.15	S_1	−17	−9.5	−4.2	24,000
S_1, S_2, V	U, U, V	4.394	0.15	S_2	2.73	7.041	9.5	24,000
S_1, V	U, V	7.129	0.01	S_1	−31	−16	0.392	1,000,000
S_1, V	U, U, V	7.788	0.44	S_1	−16	−8.7	−0.884	500,000
S_2, V, U	U, U, V	−2.9	0.15	S_2	−5.5	−0.56	0.988	1,000

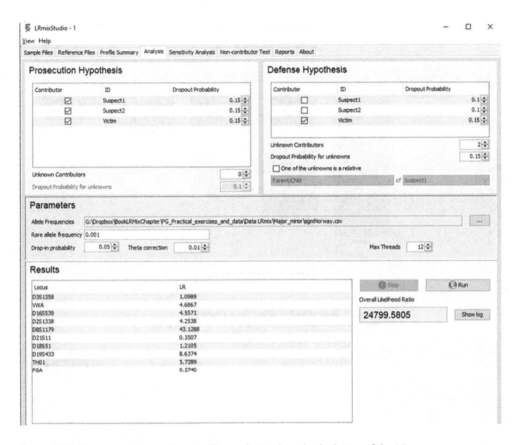

Figure 6.16 Two suspect case showing the analysis tab and calculation of the *LR*

Table 6.1 illustrates *LR*s obtained as a result of testing several sets of propositions, along with percentiles of non-contributor tests. The first set of propositions showed a high $log_{10}LR$ in favor of the prosecution proposition; that was shown by non-contributor tests to be misleading with respect to the suspect S_2. The way forward is to refine the propositions so that only one defendant is considered in the numerator per proposition. This now allows an evaluation of the evidence with respect to specific individuals. For S_1, it is only necessary to condition upon two persons, because the maximum number of alleles is four at any given locus. This provides a $log_{10}LR = 7.1$, which is much greater than that obtained when the two suspects were combined together in the numerator. Furthermore, non-contributor tests on 1 m simulations showed that random individuals give a much lower $log_{10}LR$, which supports the robustness of the model. When S_2 is tested in the absence of S_1, three contributors are required, because locus FGA has a total of five alleles under H_p. This test provides a low $log_{10}LR$ that

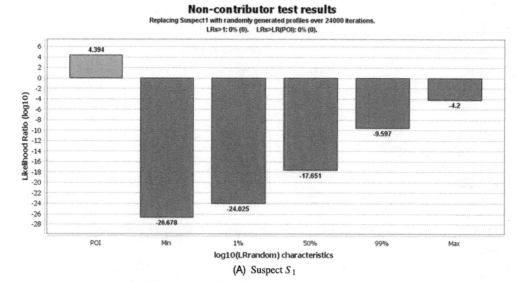

(A) Suspect S_1

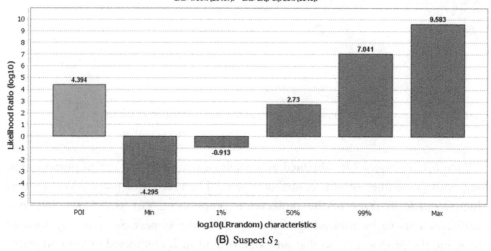

(B) Suspect S_2

Figure 6.17 Non-contributor analysis of S_1 and S_2, respectively. Whereas the model is discriminating with respect to S_1, the LR values achieved with random persons with respect to S_2 shows that the model used is uninformative with respect to this individual.

favors H_d; the non-contributor test shows that the profile behaves no differently from a random person, since the $log_{10}LRs$ from 50th–95th percentiles range between -5.5 to -0.56.

There may sometimes be dispute about the number of contributors to test. This was discussed by the ISFG DNA commission [34], which concluded that restricting the number of contributors based upon the number of alleles (Eq. (1.6)) suffices. So long as the number of contributors is anchored under the prosecution proposition, it does not usually help the defense to declare additional contributors, because the *LR* will generally increase, favoring the prosecution. This is illustrated in Table 6.1, where the alternate propositions $H_p : S_1, V$ vs. either $H_d : U, V$ or $H_d : U, U, V$. Note that as the number of contributors increases under H_d, so does the *LR* increase from $log_{10}LR = 7.1$ to $log_{10}LR = 7.7$. A study by Benschop et al. [228] showed that the premise was generally true (Fig. 6.18). In summary, it is useful to check the model by adding an additional contributor to H_d. If one extra contributor leads to increased *LR*, then subsequent additions will lead to further increases, hence there is no need to carry out extensive testing. A trend can be established with just one additional contributor.

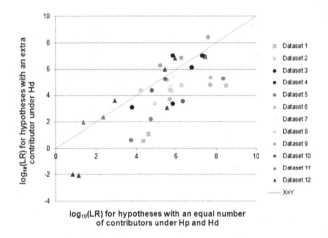

Figure 6.18 Likelihood ratios ($log_{10}LR$) for four-person NGM profiles, with one of the contributors conditioned under H_p and H_d. Under H_d, the same number of contributors (x-axis) were inferred. On the y-axis an additional contributor was added (four unknowns). Data points are grouped per dataset; "extreme heterozygote", "random", and "extreme homozygote" datasets are presented using squares, circles, and triangles, respectively. The 12 datasets have the following lay-out: datasets 1 and 2 are "heterozygote extreme", as they use donors that are heterozygous at every NGM locus with low allele sharing between both donors; datasets 11 and 12 are "homozygote extreme", as they are composed of entries with very similar profiles or a high number of homozygote loci (6 out of 15 NGM loci; these constitute the most frequent alleles). The remaining eight datasets are "random", as they comprise DNA from randomly chosen samples. The allelic diversity is therefore highest for the heterozygote extreme datasets and lowest for the homozygote extreme datasets. Reproduced from [228] with permission from Elsevier.

6.3. Considerations of the ISFG DNA commission

The ISFG DNA commission [34] (Appendix C) summarized:

C.1. The formulation of propositions It is not always easy to specify propositions in complex cases, where multiple perpetrators or victims may be present. The DNA result itself may indicate that different explanations are possible. Furthermore, it is possible that H_p and H_d could be very different from each other. For example, under H_p, we might consider a victim and suspect to be the contributors ($V + S$), whereas under H_d we might examine more complex scenarios, such as three unknowns being the contributors to the stain ($U_0 + U_1 + U_2$). There is a common misconception that the numbers of contributors under H_p and H_d should be the same. There is no requirement for this.

C.2. Formulation of H_p and H_d In principle, H_p is the province of the prosecutor, and H_d is the province of the defense. Both are constrained by what is known about the circumstances of the case. The forensic scientist usually formulates both H_p and H_d. In a typical example, H_p may propose that the DNA is a mixture of the suspect (S) and an unknown (U_1) individual. Under H_d, S is substituted by U_0. However, the defense may alter H_d (but not H_p), for example, if the number of contributors is contested. Consequently, some dialogue between the forensic scientist and defense is desirable to establish H_d. If this cannot be carried out pre-trial, the analyst may acknowledge in the report that the defense may offer alternative propositions, which will require additional calculations.

C.3. Number of contributors The number of contributors under H_p and H_d may be different. The most parsimonious explanations (the smallest number of unknown contributors needed to explain the evidence) are usually the ones that maximize the respective likelihoods [36]. But further research is needed to clarify, hence it may be wise explore options for different numbers of contributors.

6.3.1 Formulation of propositions: summary

1. The formulation of propositions can be complex, but a few simple guidelines help to assist the process.
2. Keep propositions simple. They may be informed by case-related circumstances and the appearance of the EPG. Ideally, propositions should be set before the case is analyzed to prevent bias. In the light of analysis, e.g., analysis of the EPG, it may be necessary to refine propositions.
3. The two-suspect example, described above shows that propositions that attempt to describe multiple contributors in the numerator, and replaced by unknowns in the

denominator,

$$\frac{S_1 + S_2 + V}{U + U + V}$$

are likely to be misleading. If there are two suspects, then it is recommended to analyze each one separately to provide two likelihood ratios, one for each suspect:

$$\frac{S_1 + V + U}{V + U + U} \quad \text{and} \quad \frac{S_2 + V + U}{V + U + U}$$

4. So long as contributors appear in both numerator and denominator, then there is no issue. For example, if the defense agrees that the DNA from S_1 can be conditioned, then the following construct is allowed:

$$\frac{S_1 + S_2 + V}{S_1 + U + V}$$

5. The number of contributors is best constrained by the minimum allele count at a locus; include the conditioned reference samples in the calculation (Eq. (1.6)). The minimum number of contributors for a given proposition tends to maximize the strength of evidence, and is therefore usually favorable to the defense.

6. Propositions may not be clear cut. Multiple pairs of propositions can be analyzed. The effect of different numbers of contributors can be explored.

7. The non-contributor test is a useful tool used to check the robustness of the likelihood ratio and to highlight modeling deficiencies (illustrated if random persons also give high LRs).

6.4. An example of a replicate analysis

Sample 5 consists of three replicates labeled 5.1, 5.2, 5.3. The alleles are listed in Fig. 6.19. Alleles matching the POI are highlighted in red (dark grey in print version). Different alleles have dropped out in each of the replicates: sample 5.1, D12S391 allele 19; sample 5.2, FGA, allele 26; 5.3, D2S441, allele 15, and D3S1358, allele 15. In addition, each replicate shows alleles that are not observed in the POI and can be attributed to an unknown individual. The non-matching alleles differ between the replicates, though the samples are taken from exactly the same extract. This is an illustration of the stochastic effect discussed in Chapter 3.

Select	Name	Replicate	#5_POI	Distinct Alleles
☑	**#5.1**			
☑	D10S1248	12 13 15	12 15	3
☑	VWA	14 16	14 16	2
☑	D16S539	9 10 11	9 10	3
☑	D2S1338	20 22 23	20 23	3
☐	AMEL	X Y		2
☑	D8S1179	12 13	12 13	2
☑	D21S11	28 31	28 31	2
☑	D18S51	12 15 17	12 15	3
☑	D22S1045	11 16	11 16	2
☑	D19S433	14 15	14 15	2
☑	TH01	7 9.3	7 9.3	2
☑	FGA	24 26	24 26	2
☑	D2S441	12 14 15	14 15	3
☑	D3S1358	15 16	15 16	2
☑	D1S1656	13 14 16	13 16	3
☑	D12S391	18	18 19	1
☑	**#5.2**			
☑	D10S1248	12 15	12 15	2
☑	VWA	14 16	14 16	2
☑	D16S539	9 10 11	9 10	3
☑	D2S1338	20 22 23	20 23	3
☐	AMEL	X Y		2
☑	D8S1179	12 13 14	12 13	3
☑	D21S11	28 31	28 31	2
☑	D18S51	12 15 17	12 15	3
☑	D22S1045	11 15 16	11 16	3
☑	D19S433	14 15	14 15	2
☑	TH01	7 9.3	7 9.3	2
☑	FGA	24	24 26	1
☑	D2S441	14 15	14 15	2
☑	D3S1358	15 16	15 16	2
☑	D1S1656	13 14 16	13 16	3
☑	D12S391	18 19	18 19	2
☑	**#5.3**			
☑	D10S1248	12 15	12 15	2
☑	VWA	14 16 19	14 16	3
☑	D16S539	8 9 10	9 10	3
☑	D2S1338	20 22 23	20 23	3
☐	AMEL	X Y		2
☑	D8S1179	12 13	12 13	2
☑	D21S11	28 31	28 31	2
☑	D18S51	12 15	12 15	2
☑	D22S1045	11 16 18	11 16	3
☑	D19S433	14 14.2 15	14 15	3
☑	TH01	7 9.3	7 9.3	2
☑	FGA	24 26	24 26	2
☑	D2S441	14	14 15	1
☑	D3S1358	16	15 16	1
☑	D1S1656	13 14 16	13 16	3
☑	D12S391	18 19	18 19	2

Figure 6.19 Replicate overview in *LRmix Studio*.

The joint probability estimation of replicate samples increases the likelihood ratio, because more information is incorporated into the calculation, provided that the ground truth is the prosecution proposition (Table 6.2).

Replicate probability theory is discussed in Chapter 5.4. From a practical aspect, Steele et al. [80] show that as replicates are added into the analysis (Fig. 6.20), *LR*s tend to increase towards the inverse match probability (IMP) of the known individual (Q). The IMP is a limitation that cannot be exceeded by any likelihood ratio model. If Q is minor, then more replicates are required, because the information per replicate is less, due to more drop-out per replicate.

Table 6.2 Comparison of likelihood ratios for sample 5 replicates.

Sample	$log_{10}LR$
5.1	11.45
5.2	11.04
5.3	10.7
5.1 and 5.2	12.98
5.1, 5.2, and 5.3	13.167

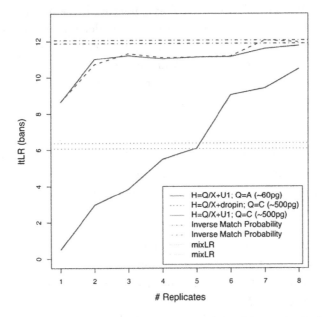

Figure 6.20 Low-template likelihood ratios from two-contributor lab-prepared crime stains profiled at up to eight replicates. Solid lines indicate a two-contributor analysis, with one unknown individual (U1). The blue line is conditioned with the known (Q = individual A) as a minor contributor, and the red line is conditioned with individual C as the as the major contributor. Dashed lines indicate a one-contributor analysis that also allows for drop-in (only for the known individual (Q) who is the major contributor). The inverse match probability $1/(2p_ap_b)$ is shown with dot-dash lines, colored according to the known individual (Q). The mixLR is the likelihood ratio that would be obtained using the standard model as described in Chapter 1.7, without peak height, is shown with dotted lines, colored according to Q. In the legend boxes, H indicates the propositions with X, an unknown alternative to Q. Reproduced from Steele et al. [80], with permission from Elsevier.

6.5. Relatedness

The formulae described in Chapter 5.5.4 have been adopted by *LRmix Studio* and *EuroForMix* to enable relatedness calculations. Worked examples using *EuroForMix* are provided in Chapter 8.8.

6.6. Summary

Earlier chapters explained that the theory was too complex to carry out hand calculations, hence the availability of software solutions was paramount.

This chapter describes the implementation of the methodology described in Chapter 5, to create the software known as *LRmix Studio*. This software was built and is maintained by the Netherlands Forensic Institute (NFI). This chapter also describes the importance of using the case circumstances to formulate the alternative propositions that are required to run the calculations. An example court-going statement is provided. To test the robustness of a model, non-contributor tests are introduced. The idea of these tests is to replace the profile of a person of interest under the prosecution proposition with a randomly produced profiles to determine the effect upon the likelihood ratio. These are known as "H_d = true" tests. A distribution of likelihood ratios is obtained from a thousand or more such tests, each is carried out against a different reference random profile. A robust model will provide non-contributor LRs that are much smaller than that achieved with the original test.

A complex case is discussed, where there are two suspects accused in a case. It is shown that it is problematic to derive a likelihood ratio, where there are two known individuals in the numerator, and none in denominator. The LR that results may be misleading. The way forward is to split the calculations so that each one considers a POI separately. We advocate exploratory data analysis to determine the effect of analyzing different sets of propositions. Non-contributor analysis is useful to test the propositions to ensure that the results are meaningful. Exploratory data analysis is also used to optimize the number of contributors that are posited.

Replicates are samples that are taken from the same extract. Analysis of multiple replicates will increase the LR, provided "H_p = true", but the value cannot exceed the inverse match probability of the POI. However, whether replicates can be analyzed is dependent upon the amount of sample that is available.

It is not necessary for propositions to be tested against "random unknown" individuals under H_d. Instead, relatedness calculations may be carried out using propositions such as "the donor is a sibling of the POI".

Calculations based on the qualitative model are typically fast, even if a high number, such as five unknown contributors are conditioned. The quantitative model, however, requires more computational effort, since it takes stutter and peak heights into account. The qualitative model is very useful in large scale comparisons of many DNA profiles, such as a national DNA database. Consequently, software as *CaseSolver* and *dnamatch2* (Chapter 11) incorporate it using the open source R-package forensim [209]. Though the model does not perform as well as a quantitative model (Chapter 9), it is useful as a preliminary step to reduce the number of comparisons required (since analysis with the quantitative model is much more demanding).

Notes

1. This generation uses the allele frequencies and does not assume any sub-population structure correction.
2. This caveat is important to include because the scientist has conditioned the statement according to his understanding of the circumstances of the case and the evidence. The defense may wish to offer a different proposition. The calculations are complex and the scientist wants to avoid having to make new calculations when the case is at trial. Pre-trial discussions are always preferable to resolve any issues.

CHAPTER 7

The quantitative (continuous) model theory

7.1. Introduction

The development of *quantitative* continuous models depends upon the incorporation of the allele peak height information. Early protocols to take account of peak height followed the Clayton guidelines [94], described in Chapter 2.3. The guidelines described how to "extract" contributors from mixtures, particularly major/minor mixtures, where the major contributor can be identified based on heterozygote balance $H_b > 0.6$. However, these guidelines are quite crude, as they are binary. Consider a mixture genotype combination from two contributors, where the first contributor is the POI under H_p and has alleles A and B at a locus, and the second is an unknown contributor with C and D alleles, giving a genotype combination AB, CD. If contributor 1 is present as the clear major and the POI under H_p, then the strength of evidence is $LR = 1/(2p_A p_B)$, where p_A and p_B are the probabilities of the respective alleles. If $p_A, p_B, p_C, p_D = 0.1$, then the $LR = 50$. If the two contributors are evenly balanced, i.e., the heterozygote balance guideline $H_b > 0.6$ identifies more than one pair of potential alleles from a single contributor, then the strength of evidence calculation must incorporate all possible pairs of alleles (Chapter 1.7), and the likelihood ratio is consequently much lower: $LR = 1/(12p_A p_B) = 8.3$. The problem with all threshold guidelines is that they are binary; the calculated $LR = 50$ or 8.3 are bounds reflecting the two extremes of separation or no separation of genotypes, with nothing in between them. Intuitively, we expect that the strength of evidence should decline gradually as the differences in peak heights between the two contributors become similar, reflecting the increased uncertainty that the two genotypes can be separated. Our binary model cannot accommodate this, hence there is something missing in our understanding.

The purpose of this chapter is to describe the historical development of the quantitative model, working through the prototype stages. The theory is accompanied by Excel spreadsheets, published on the book's website https://sites.google.com/view/dnabook/, which the reader can use in conjunction with the text to achieve an understanding of how the various models work.

7.2. Towards a quantitative model

The first step towards understanding a quantitative model begins with determining the relative contribution of each individual, which we call the mixture proportion M_x.

Forensic Practitioner's Guide to the Interpretation of Complex DNA Profiles
https://doi.org/10.1016/B978-0-12-820562-4.00015-8

Copyright © 2020 Elsevier Inc.
All rights reserved.

Consider an evidence profile from one locus, where there are four allele peaks A, B, C, D of heights $\gamma_A, \gamma_B, \gamma_C,$ and γ_D (in ascending order of molecular weight), where the first individual is genotype AB and the second individual is genotype CD, then the proportion of the mixture from the first contributor (conditioned on the combination of genotypes) is straightforward:

$$M_x = \frac{(\gamma_A + \gamma_B)}{(\gamma_A + \gamma_B + \gamma_C + \gamma_D)} \tag{7.1}$$

It is easiest to work out M_x from individuals that are heterozygote, showing four different alleles. If another locus has four alleles, then a second estimate of M_x can be obtained.

However, some loci will consist of just two or three alleles, which means that an allele(s) will be shared between individuals, also known as "masking" (Chapter 1.8). Gill et al. [229] showed that the mixture proportion is similar across all loci in a sample, but there is stochastic variation. Given an estimate of M_x, the expected allelic proportions (denoted as $E[Y'_A]$ for the proportion of allele A) can be calculated for mixtures, including 2, 3, or 4 alleles, using Tables 7.1, 7.2, 7.3.

The formulae are derived as follows:

1. M_x is the proportion of the genotype of contributor 1 (C1), and $1 - M_x$ is the proportion of the genotype of contributor 2 (C2)[1];
2. Each genotype consists of two alleles, hence the expected proportion of each allele is $M_x/2$ and $(1 - M_x)/2$ for C1 and C2, respectively;
3. Given observed peak heights $\gamma = (\gamma_A, \gamma_B, ...)$, we normalize the peak heights such that $\gamma' = \gamma/\Sigma_\gamma$, where Σ_γ is the sum of all the peak heights. Furthermore, we let $n_{A,k}$ be the sum of alleles type A for contributors $k = 1$ and $k = 2$, respectively (could be zero, one or two). From this, the expected peak height proportion for allele A is

$$E[Y'_A|g] = \left(M_x \times n_{A,1} + (1 - M_x) \times n_{A,2}\right)/2 \tag{7.2}$$

where g is an assumed genotype combination for the contributors, deciding $n_{A,1}$ and $n_{A,2}$.

See Appendix B for an extension of formulae to multiple contributors.

As a simple two-contributor example, consider the combined genotype $g = AB, CC$:

1. For allele A, there is one copy in C1 and zero in C2, hence $E[Y'_A|g] = (M_x \times 1) \times 1/2$.
2. For allele B, there is similarly one copy in C1 and zero in C2, hence $E[Y'_B|g] = (M_x \times 1) \times 1/2$.
3. For allele C, there are zero copies in C1 and two in C2, hence $E[Y'_C|g] = ((1 - M_x) \times 2) \times 1/2$.

Where alleles are shared, such as genotype AB, AC, then $E[Y'_A|g] = (M_x \times 1 + (1 - M_x) \times 1) \times 1/2$.

The calculations are easily programmed into spreadsheets. If the interpretation is correct, then the observed and expected peak heights should be similar. This can be tested by measurement of the *residual sum of squares (RSS)*, which is the sum of the squared residuals of each alleles; for any given combination of genotypes, the residual of mixtures in each row of Tables 7.1, 7.2, 7.3 can be calculated by reference to observed proportions of the peak heights. This is formally defined as a "loss function", which is a measure of how well a model performs in terms of being able to predict the expected outcome. The further away the expected peak heights are from the observed peak heights, the higher the error (which is squared), and the worse the prediction is:

$$RSS(g) = \sum_{\text{all alleles}} (observed - expected)^2 = \sum_{\text{allele } a} (y'_a - E[Y'_a|g])^2 \tag{7.3}$$

Table 7.1 Calculation of expected peak heights from M_x: four alleles. Reproduced from [229] with permission from Elsevier.

Genotype	Expected proportions			
	A	B	C	D
AB, CD	$M_x/2$	$M_x/2$	$(1-M_x)/2$	$(1-M_x)/2$
AC, BD	$M_x/2$	$(1-M_x)/2$	$M_x/2$	$(1-M_x)/2$
AD, BC	$M_x/2$	$(1-M_x)/2$	$(1-M_x)/2$	$M_x/2$
BC, AD	$(1-M_x)/2$	$M_x/2$	$M_x/2$	$(1-M_x)/2$
BD, AC	$(1-M_x)/2$	$M_x/2$	$(1-M_x)/2$	$M_x/2$
CD, AB	$(1-M_x)/2$	$(1-M_x)/2$	$M_x/2$	$M_x/2$

Example: Assume a locus has three alleles, A, B, C, and let $M_x = 0.4$ be an estimate of the mixture proportion parameter. The observed peak heights are $y_A = 1000$; $y_B = 1900$; $y_C = 1100$. Hence, the observed proportions are $y'_A = 0.25$, $y'_B = 0.475$, $y'_C = 0.275$, respectively. The expected proportions $E[Y'|g]$, if the genotype is $g = AB, BC$ (from Table 7.2), are

$$E[Y'_A|g] = M_x/2 = 0.2$$

$$E[Y'_B|g] = 0.5$$

$$E[Y'_C|g] = (1 - M_x)/2 = 0.3$$

The sum of the squared residuals (RSS) are calculated based on the allele peak height proportions using Eq. (7.3):

$$RSS(g) = (0.25 - 0.2)^2 + (0.475 - 0.5)^2 + (0.275 - 0.3)^2 = 0.004$$

The process can be repeated for each genotype combination, each leading to a different residual value shown in the last column of Table 7.4.

Table 7.2 Calculation of expected peak heights from M_X: three alleles. Reproduced from [229] with permission from Elsevier.

| Genotype | Expected proportions | | |
	A	B	C
AA, BC	M_x	$(1 - M_x)/2$	$(1 - M_x)/2$
BB, AC	$(1 - M_x)/2$	M_x	$(1 - M_x)/2$
CC, AB	$(1 - M_x)/2$	$(1 - M_x)/2$	M_x
AB, AC	0.5	$M_x/2$	$(1 - M_x)/2$
BC, AC	$(1 - M_x)/2$	$M_x/2$	0.5
AB, BC	$M_x/2$	0.5	$(1 - M_x)/2$
BC, AA	$(1 - M_x)$	$M_x/2$	$M_x/2$
AC, BB	$M_x/2$	$1 - M_x$	$M_x/2$
AB, CC	$M_x/2$	$M_x/2$	$1 - M_x$
AC, AB	0.5	$(1 - M_x)/2$	$M_x/2$
AC, BC	$M_x/2$	$(1 - M_x)/2$	0.5
BC, AB	$(1 - M_x)/2$	0.5	$M_x/2$

Table 7.3 Calculation of expected peak heights from M_X: two alleles. Reproduced from [229] with permission from Elsevier.

| Genotype | Expected proportions | |
	A	B
AA, AB	$(M_x/2) + 0.5$	$(1 - M_x)/2$
AB, AB	0.5	0.5
AA, BB	M_x	$1 - M_x$
AB, AA	$1 - (M_x/2)$	$M_x/2$
BB, AA	$1 - M_x$	M_x
AB, BB	$M_x/2$	$(1 - M_x)/2$
BB, AB	$(1 - M_x)/2$	$(M_x/2) + 0.5$

It follows that the evidence supports genotype combinations that have the *lowest* RSS, rather than the listed alternatives, because the expected and observed data are closest.

Computer programs carry out a similar analysis, except that the principle is simultaneously extended across all loci, and the residuals are converted into *weightings* that can be used in probabilistic calculations. To do this, in the simplest format, it is necessary to assume that the residuals follow a *normal distribution*[2] conditional on the genotype information of the contributors. Then M_x is simultaneously varied across the entire range of loci in a multiplex, and selected, such that RSS is minimized.[3]

Table 7.4 Analysis of a three-allele mixture, showing calculation of residual sum squares (RSS) for each possible genotype combinations.

Genotype combinations	Expected proportions			Observed proportions			RSS
	A	B	C	A	B	C	
AA, BC	0.4	0.3	0.3	0.250	0.475	0.275	0.054
BB, AC	0.3	0.4	0.3	0.250	0.475	0.275	0.009
CC, AB	0.3	0.3	0.4	0.250	0.475	0.275	0.049
AB, AC	0.5	0.2	0.3	0.250	0.475	0.275	0.139
BC, AC	0.3	0.2	0.5	0.250	0.475	0.275	0.129
AB, BC	0.2	0.5	0.3	0.250	0.475	0.275	0.004
BC, AA	0.6	0.2	0.2	0.250	0.475	0.275	0.204
AC, BB	0.2	0.6	0.2	0.250	0.475	0.275	0.024
AB, CC	0.2	0.2	0.6	0.250	0.475	0.275	0.184
AC, AB	0.5	0.3	0.2	0.250	0.475	0.275	0.099
AC, BC	0.2	0.3	0.5	0.250	0.475	0.275	0.084
BC, AB	0.3	0.5	0.2	0.250	0.475	0.275	0.009

Furthermore, in this context the genotypes for the unknown contributors can be considered as unknown parameters, which need to be estimated. This is illustrated later in Section 7.3.1. To find the genotype combination which best explains the observations (i.e., the highest likelihood), every possible profile genotype is considered in turn for different values of M_x. The genotype combination and mixture proportion M_x providing the highest likelihood is the one which simultaneously minimizes the RSS of all loci. This is called *maximum likelihood estimation* (MLE). The advantage of using this approach to calculate the minimum RSS is that the analysis can support the original inference of the expert by considering all of the possible mixture combinations, without any prior conditioning on a genotype combination. Then, depending upon the circumstances of the case and the observed ranking of the mixture genotypes, a statement could ensue: *"The evidence supports the proposition that combination AB, CD is the best supported genotype"*. The important point is that no genotype is specifically excluded, but they can be ranked in order. In Table 7.4, using the lowest RSS,[4] genotype AB, BC ranks first, followed by BB, AC, and BC, AB, and so on (in a real case we would be considering complete profile genotypes rather than a single locus).

For further details, the reader is referred to Gill et al. [229].

7.2.1 An example using the "MasterMix" Excel spreadsheet program

The principles described above in Section 7.2 are encoded into Excel spreadsheets. The workbook is called "MasterMix" and is available from the book's website https://sites.google.com/view/dnabook/.

7.2.1.1 Step 1

Using the "2-allele simulation" spreadsheet as an example, input the peak heights and a desired M_x. In the example, $y_A = 2183$, and $y_B = 899$ (Table 7.5). The allele peak height proportions and mixture proportions, M_x and $1\text{-}M_x$, are automatically calculated.

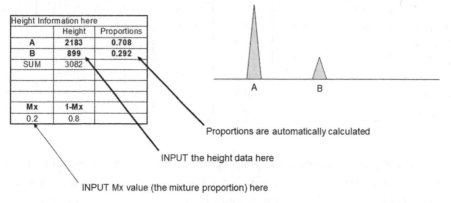

Table 7.5 Mastermix, two allele spreadsheet. Input the two peak heights, the proportions are automatically calculated. A desired M_x is input (it can be arbitrary at this stage); use $M_x = 0.2$, and $1 - M_x = 0.8$ is automatically calculated.

7.2.1.2 Step 2

The expected allele peak height proportions (for a given value of M_x) are automatically calculated, using the general formulae from Eq. (7.2) to obtain the specific formulae that are listed in Table 7.3. When iterated over a grid of M_x values, we obtain Table 7.6. For example, for genotype AA, AB:

1. The contribution per allele in C1 is $M_x/2$.
2. The contribution per allele in C2 is $(1 - M_x)/2$.
3. Consequently, the expected C1 proportion of allele A is $2M_x/2 = M_x$.
4. The expected C2 proportion for allele A is $(1 - M_x)/2$.
5. So the total proportion for allele A from C1 and C2 is a summation: $(2M_x + (1 - M_x))/2 = M_x/2 + 0.5$ (Eq. (7.2)),
   giving $E[Y'_A|g] = 0.6$ when $M_x = 0.2$, which is the value shown in the spreadsheet (Table 7.6).
6. All of the other expected mixture proportions conditioned on genotype are similarly calculated. The formula are the same as shown in Table 7.3.
7. The RSS is calculated from summing the square of the *observed − expected* for all allele peak height proportions.

The "M_x conditioned columns" calculate M_x (contributor C1) and $1 - M_x$ (contributor C2), conditioned on the genotype with observed peak heights (proportions) of

The quantitative (continuous) model theory   187

alleles A and B, which are 0.71 and 0.29, respectively. Following the example shown in Table 7.6:

1. The same genotype combination is under consideration: $g = AA, AB$.
2. There are two copies of A in C1 and one copy in C2. By rearranging the formula in (Eq. (7.2)), we obtain the estimate of the mixture proportion as

$$M_x|g = 2y'_A - 1$$

3. The observed proportion of allele $A = 0.71$, hence

$$M_x|g = 2 \times 0.71 - 1 = 0.42$$

which is calculated in Table 7.6.

4. The same procedures are encoded into the remainder of the table, and a range of different M_x values are provided depending on the genotype considered.
5. An estimate of M_x cannot be made for genotype $g = AB, AB$, because the expected proportions of alleles $E[Y'_A|g] = E[Y'_B|g] = 0.5$ are the same regardless of M_x.

Table 7.6 MasterMix program showing calculation of residuals, M_x conditioned on the observed peak height proportion, and the expected heterozygote balance, if relevant. Here "difference (residuals)" is RSS.

Genotypes	Expected proportions		observed proportions		difference	Mx (conditioned)		Heterozygote balance	
	A	B	A	B	(residuals)	Mx	1-Mx	PHR1	PHR2
AA,AB	0.6	0.4	0.708	0.292	0.023	0.42	0.583	NA	0.00
AB,AB	0.5	0.5	0.708	0.292	0.087	NA	NA	0.41	NA
AA,BB	0.2	0.8	0.708	0.292	0.517	0.71	0.292	NA	0.41
AB,AA	0.9	0.1	0.708	0.292	0.073	0.58	0.417	NA	NA
BB,AA	0.8	0.2	0.708	0.292	0.017	0.29	0.708	NA	NA
AB,BB	0.1	0.9	0.708	0.292	0.740	1.42	-0.417	NA	NA
BB,AB	0.4	0.6	0.708	0.292	0.190	-0.42	1.417	NA	NA

All possible combinations

Expected proportions conditional on the Mx.

Observed from epg

Sum of squares dif.

Conditioned on the Observed allele proportions

7.2.1.3 Step 3

Press the simulation button (Table 7.7). This generates a new table in rows 22–27 and automates calculations of RSS against values of M_x ranging between 0.1–0.9 (in steps of 0.05):

188 Forensic Practitioner's Guide to the Interpretation of Complex DNA Profiles

Table 7.7 MasterMix program showing calculation of the RSS for each genotype across all $M - x$ values between 0.1–0.9.

Height Information here				combination	Expected proportions		observed pro
	Height	Proportions			A	B	A
A	2183	0.708		AA,AB	0.6	0.4	0.708
B	899	0.292		AB,AB	0.5	0.5	0.708
SUM	3082			AA,BB	0.2	0.8	0.708
				AB,AA	0.9	0.1	0.708
				BB,AA	0.8	0.2	0.708
				AB,BB	0.1	0.9	0.708
Mx	1-Mx			BB,AB	0.4	0.6	0.708
0.2	0.8						
	CLICK FOR TWO-ALLELE SIMULATION						

PRESS THIS BUTTON AFTER FILLING IN DETAILS ABOUT PEAK HEIGHT

The program simulates residuals (in cells J3:J9) between Mx= 0.1 – 0.9

Mx

Genotype	0.1	0.15	0.2	0.25	0.3	0.35	0.4	0.45	0.5	0.55	
AA,AB	0.05012177	0.03554114	0.02346051	0.01387968	0.00679925	0.00221862	0.00013799	0.00055736	0.00347673	0.0088961	0.01
AB,AB	0.08678302	0.08678302	0.08678302	0.08678302	0.08678302	0.08678302	0.08678302	0.08678302	0.08678302	0.08678302	0.08
AA,BB	0.7400731	0.62341184	0.51675058	0.42000932	0.33342806	0.2567668	0.19010554	0.13344428	0.08678302	0.05012177	0.02
AB,AA	0.11683169	0.09391232	0.07349295	0.05557358	0.04015421	0.02723484	0.01681547	0.0088961	0.00347673	0.00055736	0.00
BB,AA	0.07349295	0.04015421	0.01681547	0.00347673	0.00013799	0.00679925	0.02346051	0.05012177	0.08678302	0.13344428	0.19
AB,BB	0.86673436	0.80215373	0.7400731	0.68049247	0.62341184	0.56883121	0.51675058	0.46716995	0.42008932	0.37550869	0.33
BB,AB	0.13344428	0.16052491	0.19010554	0.22218617	0.2567668	0.29384743	0.33342806	0.37550869	0.42008932	0.46716995	0.51

- The calculation cycles through stepwise increments of $M_x = 0.1, 0.15, 0.2, 0.25$ ...0.90. The results are plotted graphically (Fig. 7.1).
- If a value is manually input, e.g., $M_x = 0.9$ in cell A10 of the Excel spreadsheet, then the associated expected allele peak height proportions, and RSS can be visualized in Table 7.6.

Fig. 7.1 shows that the RSS minimizes at $M_x = 0.3$ for genotypes BB, AA and the converse $M_x = 0.7$ for genotypes AA, BB (at this stage we do not know which genotype corresponds to which contributor). RSS is also minimized at $M_x = 0.4$ and 0.6 for genotypes AA, AB, and the converse genotypes AB, AA. If we condition *contributor 1* as minor, and *contributor 2* as major, then we can state that the evidence best supports genotypes BB, AA. The remaining possible genotype combinations (e.g., AB, BB) appear less well-supported as their residuals do not minimize.

A four-allele example: Using spreadsheet "4–allele simulation", now consider a locus, where there are four alleles A, B, C, D present; the peak heights are 1255, 1200, 533, 642, respectively (Table 7.8).

The quantitative (continuous) model theory

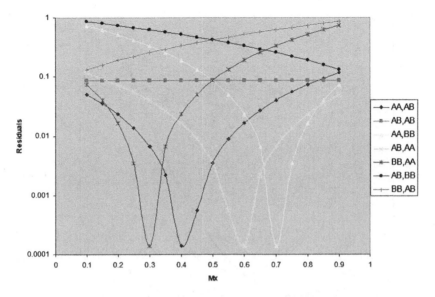

Figure 7.1 Plot of M_x vs. RSS shown on a log scale.

Table 7.8 Mastermix, four-allele spreadsheet showing observed vs. expected proportions of alleles A, B, C, D for $M_x = 0.3$.

Height Information here			combination	Expected proportions				observed proportions			
	Height	Proportions		A	B	C	D	A	B	C	D
A	1255	0.346	AB,CD	0.150	0.150	0.350	0.350	0.346	0.331	0.147	0.177
B	1200	0.331	AC,BD	0.150	0.350	0.150	0.350	0.346	0.331	0.147	0.177
C	533	0.147	AD,BC	0.150	0.350	0.350	0.150	0.346	0.331	0.147	0.177
D	642	0.177	BC,AD	0.350	0.150	0.150	0.350	0.346	0.331	0.147	0.177
SUM	3630		BD,AC	0.350	0.150	0.350	0.150	0.346	0.331	0.147	0.177
			CD,AB	0.350	0.350	0.150	0.150	0.346	0.331	0.147	0.177
Mx	1-Mx										
0.3	0.7										

Run the simulation to show that the genotypes CD, AB minimize at $M_x = 0.3$, and the converse AB, CD minimizes at $M_x = 0.7$ (Fig. 7.2), i.e., the major, minor contributors are CD, AB, respectively.

The four-allele analysis is complemented by an analysis of heterozygote balance (Fig. 7.3) that are conditioned upon the putative genotypes

The evidence supports the two genotype combinations AB, CD or CD, AB as the preferred options:

1. M_x is optimized (the most likely) for these genotypes.
2. The heterozygote balance (PHR) > 0.6 guideline passes AB and CD.
3. The heterozygote balance for remaining genotypes < 0.6.
4. The M_x values conditioned on the first contributor genotype are 0.676 and 0.324 for genotypes AB, CD and CD, AB, respectively (i.e., close to the 0.7 and 0.3 estimates from minimum residuals). Conditioning on contributor 1 as minor, the best supported option is CD, AB.

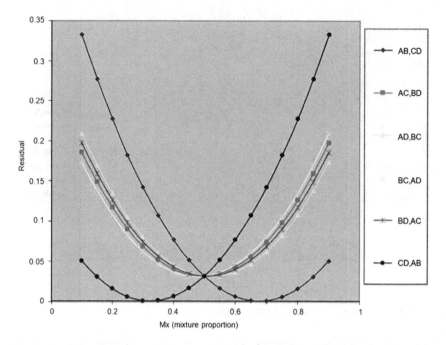

Figure 7.2 Four-allele mixture plot of M_x vs. RSS.

7.2.2 Using the information across loci

In a typical multiplex test of 15 or more loci, there are many more opportunities to measure M_x per locus. A residual analysis (using RSS) can be extended across all of these loci, so instead of measuring a local M_x per locus, we now measure a global value to be applied across all loci (hence more data are used to estimate M_x). This has clear advantages to better estimate the unknown combined genotypes.

So far the discussion has been based upon the use of threshold tests for heterozygote balance, and the use of M_x. This kind of knowledge is used in expert assessments, where major contributors may be selected from a simple major/minor mixture of two contributors for evidential interpretation as a single contributor, a method known as subtraction. Of course there are serious limitations to such a method:

1. It is dependent upon clear major/minor profiles. It cannot be used to inform even mixtures (where contributions are equivalent).
2. The extracted profile needs to be well represented (we do not consider the effects of drop-out or drop-in here).
3. A threshold test is used (typically the $H_b > 0.6$ test is required to pair alleles as heterozygotes from a single contributor).

Threshold tests are unsatisfactory, because they are "all or nothing"; this leads to the falling-of-the-cliff effect (Fig. 3.6). The predicament arises from the notion that the

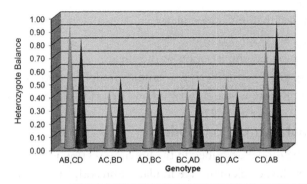

Figure 7.3 Four-allele mixture showing heterozygote balance conditioned on the various genotype combinations. M_x values conditioned on observed allele peak height proportions are given along with heterozygote balances in the accompanying table, where PHR is peak height ratio for the first and second genotypes, respectively. The residual analysis is calculated from $M_x = 0.3$ and shows that CD, AB is the best-supported option (bottom row) if contributor 1 is minor. Note that the conditioned M_x value is 0.324, and heterozygote balance is good at 0.83 and 0.96, respectively.

$H_b \geq 0.6$ threshold test passes, but imagine a result that gives $H_b = 0.5999$. This fails the threshold test, though it is just 0.0001 lower than the threshold. This illustrates the dilemma. In nature, nothing is an absolute yes or no. Uncertainty is continuous. In probabilistic terms, this means that a measurement of certainty will gradually change from absolute yes ($Pr \approx 1$) to absolute no ($Pr \approx 0$) on a gradual sliding scale, rather than a flip of states from $Pr = 0$ to 1, based upon some arbitrary setting. The previous exercise showed how evidence, i.e., the residuals, can be used to rank genotypes in order of their best support. The next step is to turn residuals into probabilistic weights that can be used to apply a probability of the genotype, given allele peak heights and M_x, so that measurement is no longer binary, rather it is continuous on a scale of 0 to 1. Then we can start to think in terms of "likelihood".

7.3. Likelihood ratio estimation using probabilistic models

The main attributes of a mixture that need to be considered by a continuous model are as follows:
1. The number of contributors.
2. The mixture proportions.

3. The observed peak heights of the alleles.
4. The expected peak heights of the alleles.
5. The degree of peak height variation of the alleles.

To illustrate, we begin by considering a simple model of two contributors, but the extension to three or more is straightforward and described in Appendix B.3.7.

7.3.1 The normal distribution model

The limitation of the model described in the previous section is that it could not be used probabilistically, yet the key elements are in place. Spreadsheet "MasterMix" shows how to calculate M_x by minimizing the residuals. This is accomplished by using an optimization algorithm that evaluates all possible residuals relative to all values of M_x between 0 and 1. It is a small step to convert the residuals into probabilistic "weights"; the procedure to do this is best illustrated by assuming a normal distribution for the residuals. This follows a prototype model that was originally proposed by Evett et al. [230]. The calculations are shown in the Excel workbook "NORMAL_DISTR_ANALYSIS" found in the "Normal_Distribution_Model" folder on the book's website https://sites.google.com/view/dnabook/.

7.3.2 Step 1: calculation of expected peak heights

Instead of using the formulae in Tables 7.1, 7.2, 7.3, originally introduced in Eq. (7.2) to calculate the expected peak height proportions, we now work with the absolute peak heights, as they are simpler to work with when the model is extended (for instance, in order to model allele drop-out). In the following, *proportions* of the total peak height are no longer used in our calculations.

Given observed peak heights $y = (y_A, y_B, ...)$, and assumed genotype $g = (g_1, g_2)$ for two contributors with mixture proportion M_x for contributor 1 and $1-M_x$ for contributor 2, $n_{A,k}$ is the sum of alleles of type A for contributors $k = 1$ and $k = 2$, respectively. The expected peak height for allele $E[Y_A|g]$ is

$$E[Y_A|g] = \left(M_x \times n_{A,1} + (1 - M_x) \times n_{A,2} \right) \Sigma_y/2 \qquad (7.4)$$

where Σ_y is the sum of the peak heights. Notice that Eq. (7.4) is almost the same as formula in Eq. (7.2), which considered the expected peak height proportions, only differing by multiplying the peak height sum Σ_y.

Example: The four-allele example discussed in Section 7.2.1 is shown in Table 7.9. The expected peak heights are calculated using the formulae shown above in spreadsheet "4-allele simulation" from workbook "NORMAL_DISTR_ANALYSIS".

The quantitative (continuous) model theory **193**

Table 7.9 Expected peak heights calculated using formulae (7.4).

Height Information here				Expected peak height			
Allele	Height	Proportions		Genotype	A	B	C	D
A	**1255**	0.346		AB,CD	544.500	544.500	1270.500	1270.500
B	**1200**	0.331		AC,BD	544.500	1270.500	544.500	1270.500
C	**533**	0.147		AD,BC	544.500	1270.500	1270.500	544.500
D	**642**	0.177		BC,AD	1270.500	544.500	544.500	1270.500
SUM	3630			BD,AC	1270.500	544.500	1270.500	544.500
				CD,AB	1270.500	1270.500	544.500	544.500
Mx	**1-Mx**							
0.3	0.7							

7.3.3 Step 2: calculate the weighting

Calculations of the strength of evidence require two components: the weighting and the probability of the genotype given the proposition H_p or H_d:

$$Pr(E|H) = \sum_g \underbrace{Pr(E|G, H)}_{\text{weighting}} \times \underbrace{Pr(g|H)}_{\text{genotype|proposition}} \qquad (7.5)$$

The weighting is the probability of the evidence given the genotype and the proposition. It only takes account of the expected and observed peak heights, i.e., the residuals described in Section 7.2. But to allow residuals to become probabilistic requires an assumption that they follow some distribution. Since the peak height information (the evidence E) is continuous, we need to consider a continuous distribution for it; the simplest is the normal distribution. This is easily programmed into Excel spreadsheets using the NORM.DIST function. There are three arguments required:

1. y: the observed peak height.
2. μ: the expected peak height.
3. σ: the standard deviation of the peak heights.

The formula for the probability density function of the normal distribution is

$$f(y|\mu, \sigma) = \frac{1}{\sigma\sqrt{2\pi}} \exp\left\{-0.5\left(\frac{y-\mu}{\sigma}\right)^2\right\} \qquad (7.6)$$

Note that the exponent of Eq. (7.6) contains the expression $(y - \mu)^2$, which is the squared residual calculation $(observed - expected)^2$. Here the expected peak height parameter μ is equivalent to $E[Y|g]$, defined in Eq. (7.4), which depends on the specified genotype g and the mixture proportion parameter M_x.

The weightings are calculated by evaluating the probability density function for every allele using the observed and expected peak heights listed in Table 7.9; the results are shown in Table 7.10. The combined weights for each genotype combination is calculated by multiplying the allele weightings together.

Continued example: Consider the combined genotype CD, AB from Table 7.9; $M_x = 0.3$; assume $\sigma = 40$,[5] then the weights for the four alleles are

$$f(\gamma_A|\mu = 1270.5, \sigma = 40) = 9.25 \times 10^{-3}$$

$$f(\gamma_B|\mu = 1270.5, \sigma = 40) = 2.11 \times 10^{-3}$$

$$f(\gamma_C|\mu = 1270.5, \sigma = 40) = 9.57 \times 10^{-3}$$

$$f(\gamma_D|\mu = 544.5, \sigma = 40) = 5.11 \times 10^{-4}$$

The combined weighting for genotype $CD, AB = 9.55 \times 10^{-11}$ is the product of the individual allele weightings calculated above.

The spreadsheet workings for all genotype combinations are shown in Table 7.10.

Table 7.10 Weightings calculated using the normal distribution formula. Combined weightings shown in yellow, per genotype are the product of the individual rows. The CD, AB genotype is shown in green background. $M_x = 0.3$ and $\sigma = 40$. Frequencies of alleles A, B, C, D are 0.1, 0.2, 0.3, and 0.1, respectively.

Genotype	weightings per allele				combined weights
	A	B	C	D	
AB,CD	3.07E-71	4.83E-61	1.52E-76	2.45E-56	5.520E-263
AC,BD	3.07E-71	2.11E-03	9.57E-03	2.45E-56	1.519E-131
AD,BC	3.07E-71	2.11E-03	1.52E-76	5.11E-04	5.035E-153
BC,AD	9.25E-03	4.83E-61	9.57E-03	2.45E-56	1.047E-120
BD,AC	9.25E-03	4.83E-61	1.52E-76	5.11E-04	3.470E-142
CD,AB	9.25E-03	2.11E-03	9.57E-03	5.11E-04	9.553E-11

7.3.4 Step 3: combine weightings with probability of genotype given the proposition

Finally, the weightings are multiplied by the probability of the genotype, given the proposition, $Pr(g|H)$, where H is either H_p or H_d, from Eq. (7.5). The calculation incorporates the allele probabilities based on population frequency data, outlined earlier in Chapter 1.8.1 (Table 7.11).

In the example, the propositions are as follows:

H_p: The DNA came from the suspect and one unknown individual.
H_d: The DNA came from two unknown individuals.

Calculation under the prosecution proposition

The reference sample from the suspect is genotype CD. Under the prosecution proposition, the unknown individual must be AB. The $Pr(g|H_p) = 2p_Ap_B$ is derived in the same manner, as described in Chapter 1.7.8, Eq. (1.7). If alleles A, B, C, D are given probabilities of 0.1, 0.2, 0.3, 0.1, respectively, $(M_x = 0.3, \sigma = 40)$, then $Pr(g|H_p) = 2 \times 0.1 \times 0.2 =$

The quantitative (continuous) model theory   **195**

Table 7.11 The "combined weights" are multiplied by $Pr(g|H)$ to give the products under H_d and H_p propositions for each genotype pair specified. The likelihood ratios are calculated for each genotype, where H_p conditions upon the first contributor in the "Genotype" column. In row one, for example, H_p is conditioned upon genotype AB shown in Table 7.10. Under H_d, the alternative calculation is the sum of the products in the column "Product Hd". The "LR with peak heights" column is formulated by dividing individual components of the "Product Hp" column by the sum of the "Product Hd" column. This is compared with the LR calculated if no weighting was employed in the "LR without weighting" column, i.e., without peak heights. The "LR max" is the maximum possible LR calculated from the inverse of the match probability of the conditioned individual under H_p, e.g., $1/(2p_Ap_B)$ in the first row. Alleles A, B, C, D are given probabilities of 0.1, 0.2, 0.3, 0.1, respectively, $M_x = 0.3$. The highlighted bottom row are calculations for the CD, AB genotype. Refer to Table 7.10 for the row order of genotypes.

combined weights	Pr(g|Hd)	Product Hd	Pr(g|Hp)	Product Hp	LR with peak heights	LR without weighting	LR max
5.520E-263	0.0024	1.3247E-265	0.06	3.3117E-264	1.4445E-251	4.166666667	25
1.519E-131	0.0024	3.6465E-134	0.04	6.0776E-133	2.6508E-120	2.777777778	16.6666667
5.035E-153	0.0024	1.2084E-155	0.12	6.0421E-154	2.6354E-141	8.333333333	50
1.047E-120	0.0024	2.5133E-123	0.02	2.0944E-122	9.1351E-110	1.388888889	8.33333333
3.470E-142	0.0024	8.3288E-145	0.06	2.0822E-143	9.0818E-131	4.166666667	25
9.553E-11	0.0024	2.29271E-13	0.04	3.82119E-12	16.66666667	2.777777778	16.6666667
	sum	2.29271E-13					

0.04, which is shown in Table 7.11, bottom row. All of the other genotype probabilities in the column are calculated by following the same methodology, where the second listed contributor genotype is always the unknown individual.

Calculation under the defense proposition

The probability of genotype combinations given the defense proposition $Pr(g|H_d)$, listed in second column of Table 7.11 are calculated; each genotype probability is $4p_Ap_Bp_Cp_D$, as described in Chapter 1.7.8, Eq. (1.7). The genotype probabilities are multiplied by the weightings to form the products, "Product Hd" in Table 7.11. Then the products are summed together in accordance with Eq. (7.5) and $Pr(E|H_d) = 2.29 \times 10^{-13}$.

The likelihood ratio

Continuing the CD, AB example: dividing $Pr(E|H_p)$ by $Pr(E|H_d)$ gives the likelihood ratio $LR = 16.67$ (Column "LR with peak heights", bottom row in Table 7.11). In the adjacent column, "LR without weighting", i.e., the standard calculation without peak height described in Chapter 1.7.8, gives a much lower $LR : 2.78$. The observed peak height weighted LR is the same as LR_{max} in the final column, which is calculated as the inverse of match probability of the suspect's genotype CD, i.e., $LR_{max} = 1/(2p_Cp_D)$. With this example, the major and minor contributors are in substantially different proportions, which allows an easy separation of the AB and CD alleles using subtraction, as described in Chapter 2.3.4. Of course, the advantage of using probabilistic genotyping is that we do not need to make a decision about whether a genotype can be subtracted in this way, using arbitrary heterozygote balance thresholds. The software automatically takes care of this. Now, if we use the example shown in Table 7.9 and changed the conditions so that all of the alleles show equal peak heights, then the model will give

196   Forensic Practitioner's Guide to the Interpretation of Complex DNA Profiles

the same answer as the LR calculated without weighting, because now there is no useful information in the peak heights. The LR calculated for many profiles will often be somewhere between the two extremes offered by LR_{max}, which is the inverse of the match probability of the suspect and LR_{min}, the calculation without considering peak height.

To conclude, we have solved the problem of the binary model by utilizing the residual calculations of the expected vs. observed peak heights in a probabilistic model.

7.3.5 Estimating the parameters of the normal distribution: maximum likelihood estimation (MLE)

In the workbook "NORMAL_DISTR_ANALYSIS", the spreadsheet labeled "ENFSI 1 case" is used as an example, using the first 11 loci only. Full instructions are provided with the spreadsheet.

The alternate propositions used to formulate the LR are $H_p : S + U$ and $H_d : U + U$, where $S =$ suspect and $U =$ unknown.

There are two unknown parameters in the normal distribution formula (Eq. (7.6)), namely M_x (the mixture proportion), which is defined by the μ parameter, and σ, the standard deviation of the peak heights. To optimize the parameters, the ISFG DNA commission recommendations [34] state:

"The aim of the defence is to maximise the probability of the evidence under H_d. Similarly, the prosecution aim is to maximise the probability of the evidence under H_p, consistent with their theory of the case."

This requires two separate calculations, one for H_d and one for H_p (Table 7.12). For example, at locus VWA, the genotype BC, AB is highlighted in green (medium grey in print version), where the conditioned suspect is BC, and the unknown (second) contributor is either AB, or AC or CC—the latter two are not specifically listed in the highlighted row, but they appear in two upper rows as BC, AC and BC, CC, and are taken into account in the calculations made in the "Product Hp" column. The same formulae from Table 1.7 are used. The only difference is that the individual genotype probabilities are multiplied by their weightings, as explained in Section 7.3.4 and illustrated in (Table 7.13).

The same process is carried out to calculate $Pr(E|H_d)$, and the worked results are shown in the "Pr(g|Hd)" and "Product Hd" columns. The sum of H_d products is also shown.

In the Excel spreadsheet, "Solver", found under tab: "Data">"Solver", can be used to optimize the M_x and standard deviation parameters[6] —there is just one value for each parameter per DNA profile. Solver is set up as shown in Table 7.14. The two parameters (M_x and "St Dev" in cells \$B\$187–\$B\$188 are automatically copied/linked to every locus in the spreadsheet, e.g., cells \$A\$175–\$B\$175 for VWA, so that the

Table 7.12 Analysis of "ENFSI exercise 1" using an Excel spreadsheet "ENFSI 1 case", showing the VWA locus. The row highlighted in green (medium grey in print version) is the H_p proposition, where the first contributor BC is the suspect, and the second (unknown) contributor is either AB, or AC or CC (all are included in the calculation). The M_x and St. Dev. parameters are optimized using Excel "Solver". H_p and H_d are maximized separately to produce the log likelihoods and the likelihood ratio.

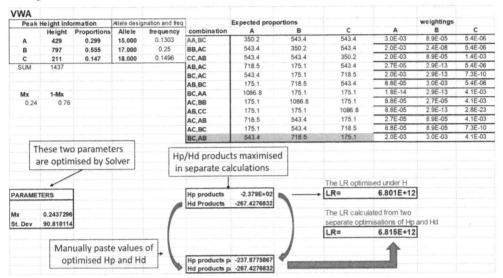

Table 7.13 Derivation of $Pr(E|H_p)$, where the suspect is type BC and the crime stain is ABC. The worked results are shown in spreadsheet ENFSI 1 case in the "weighting", "Pr(g|Hp)" and "Product Hp" columns.

Genotype	$Pr(E = BC\|H_p)$	Weighting	Products
BC, AB	$2p_A p_B$	w_1	$2p_A p_B . w_1$
BC, AC	$2p_A p_C$	w_2	$2p_A p_C . w_2$
BC, CC	p_C^2	w_3	$p_C^2 . w_3$
Products are summed to give $Pr(E\|H_p)$			

optimization is carried out concurrently across all of the loci in the DNA profile. The H_p or H_d products in cells $G$186–$G$187 are maximized by continually altering the M_x, and the same is done to standard deviation values in cells $B$187–$B$188, until no further improvement can be achieved. It is important to note that the Solver iterations of M_x and standard deviation parameters are reflected in every locus simultaneously. Steps 1–3 (Section 7.3.1) described results for a single locus. The extension to multiple loci is to multiply the H_p and H_d products (summing natural logs is numerically, the most robust method) and is achieved in cells $G$186–$G$187.

In the simple "Mastermix" example, described in Section 7.2.1, we discovered the lowest residual using a hand calculation, where all M_x possibilities were evaluated across the entire range $M_x = 0.1 - 0.9$ (Table 7.7). We could have accomplished the same

Table 7.14 "Solver" is set up as shown. The objective or target cell is $G$186, which refers to the H_d products. The tick box is set to "Max", which means that we seek the maximum value. M_x is constrained to be between 0 and 1, and the standard deviation is constrained between 10 and 2000. Choose the evolutionary solving method. Rather than multiplying individual H_d products for each locus, it is computationally more efficient to take the sum of natural logs instead. There are two calculations required. The first maximizes the H_p products in cell $G$186, and the second maximizes the H_d products in cell $G$187. The results have to be physically pasted into cells $G$192:193, and the likelihood ratio is calculated from their exponents in cell $J$189 (Table 7.12).

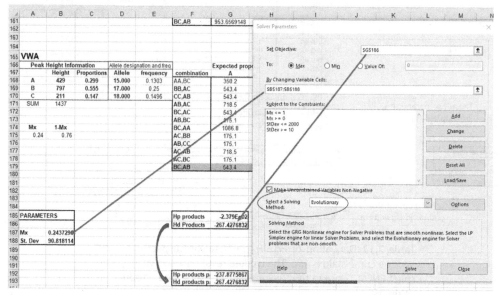

calculation with Solver. As soon as there is more than one parameter to include, the hand method of calculation is no longer practical. The log likelihoods of the H_p and H_d propositions are separately maximized using Solver. Then the exponentials of the log likelihoods are divided to produce the likelihood ratio (Table 7.14).

7.4. Recap

1. In this section, we showed the importance of calculating the mixture proportion from allele peak heights and an early illustration of optimizing M_x carried out by analysis of residuals. Calculations were carried out in an Excel spreadsheet called "MasterMix". Calculations of expected peak heights conditioned upon M_x were also illustrated.

2. Although the "MasterMix" calculations illustrated the basic principles to be followed in probabilistic software, none of the calculations were themselves probabilistic, neither could they be combined with the genotype probability information based on allele frequencies.

3. If the residuals of the peak heights (given a genotype), *observed − expected*, are assumed to follow a normal distribution, then this enables a probabilistic assessment of peak heights, known as "weightings", to be calculated conditioned upon the genotype and the prosecution and defense propositions respectively.

4. The additional assumption that the peak heights followed a normal distribution (probabilistic) required the extra parameter σ (the standard deviation), describing the variance of the peak heights.

5. Using the normal distribution assumption, the peak height weightings are calculated using M_x and σ. The weightings are multiplied by the genotype probabilities, as described in Section 7.3.5, conditioned upon the genotype combinations specified under H_p and H_d, respectively. The sum of probabilities ("Product Hp" and "Product Hd", respectively) are used to calculate likelihood ratios per locus.

6. The unknown parameters (σ and M_x) are estimated simultaneously by maximizing the log likelihoods of the propositions under H_p and H_d, respectively. The process of optimization is known as maximum likelihood estimation. It is carried out by iteration, and is illustrated in spreadsheet "ENFSI 1 case" using the Excel "Solver" add-in function. This optimization is carried out simultaneously across all of the loci so there is just one value of M_x and σ per profile.

7.5. The Gamma model

The first quantitative continuous model described in the literature used the normal distribution (Evett et al. [230]). Although a useful demonstration, it was recognized that peak heights do not follow a convenient bell–shaped curve. The actual distribution is notably skewed. A new model was suggested by Cowell et al. [231] to take account of the skewness. The model proposed adopted the Gamma distribution, which we use in *EuroForMix*.

7.5.1 Gamma distribution

Unlike the normal distribution, the gamma distribution is more complex; it requires specification of two parameters known as shape α and scale β; the gamma distribution takes these as arguments. Example distributions are shown in (Fig. 7.4).

The probability density function of the gamma distribution is given as

$$f(\gamma|\alpha, \beta) = \frac{1}{\beta^{\alpha}\Gamma(\alpha)}\gamma^{\alpha-1}\exp\{-\frac{\gamma}{\beta}\} = gamma(\gamma|\alpha, \beta) \tag{7.7}$$

where $\Gamma(x)$ is called the gamma function. The density function given in Eq. (7.7) provides the "weightings" in *EuroForMix*.

The scale parameter has the effect of stretching or compressing the distribution. Together, the shape and scale parameters define the gamma distribution.

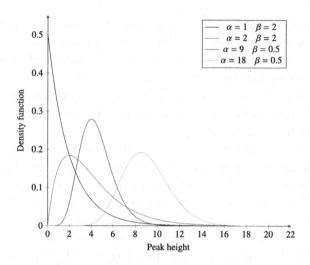

Figure 7.4 The shape α and scale β parameters define the gamma distributions presented as density functions, as shown. The x-axis is the outcome of the peak heights, whereas the y-axis gives the density function values (i.e., the "weightings").

In Excel, the function GAMMA.DIST(y, alpha, beta, cumulative) is used to calculate the weightings, where $y =$ the observed peak height, alpha and beta are the shape, and scale parameters and cumulative is set to FALSE to consider the probability density function of gamma (and not the cumulative one).

7.5.2 Model for one contributor

For the model in *EuroForMix*, the scale parameter will be constant for all markers, but the shape parameter will depend on the expected contribution over all contributors. An example of this follows.

If we consider only one contributor with genotype AB, the weightings for alleles A and B would be $f(y_A|\alpha, \beta) \times f(y_B|\alpha, \beta) = gamma(y_A|\alpha, \beta) \times gamma(y_B|\alpha, \beta)$. However, if the genotype was AA, the weighting for allele A would be $f(y_A|\alpha, \beta) = gamma(y_A|\alpha \times 2, \beta)$.

The multiplication of two is an additive property of the gamma distribution, meaning that if we add two or more stochastic variables together, the shape parameters are simply added. This only holds if the scale parameters are the same. Because the shape parameter is scaled before it is put into gamma density function, it is useful to define the input to this function as the "shape argument" and "scale argument". Hence, for our application, the shape argument is proportional to the contribution of the specific alleles.

7.5.3 Reparameterization

For the gamma model, the expectation of peak heights (consider a peak height Y) is defined as the product of the shape and scale parameters, giving $E[Y] = \alpha \times \beta$. Furthermore, the variance of the peak heights is given as $Var[Y] = \alpha \times \beta^2$. Another measure for variation is called the coefficient-of-variance, which is the standard deviation divided by the peak height expectation. This is given by $CV[Y] = \frac{\sqrt{Var[Y]}}{E[Y]} = \alpha^{-\frac{1}{2}}$. A useful property of this measure is that it is invariant to the size of the peak height values. For instance, if peak height values vary in the range of 10000–20000 RFU, the variance of the peak heights would also typically be very large. However, if we scale with peak height expectation, we obtain a much smaller number, which would be more comparable across different data (which could have smaller RFU output). Hence CV is a standardized measure of variation.

In *EuroForMix*, we have carried out the following reparameterization for easier interpretation of the parameters[7]:

$$\mu = E[Y] = \alpha \times \beta \tag{7.8}$$

$$\omega = CV[Y] = \alpha^{-\frac{1}{2}} \tag{7.9}$$

Hence, converting back to shape and scale parameters we get

$$\alpha = \frac{1}{\omega^2} \qquad\qquad \beta = \mu\omega^2 \tag{7.10}$$

and so we have an alternative representation of Eq. (7.7):

$$f(\gamma|\mu, \omega) = \frac{1}{(\mu\omega^2)^{\omega^{-2}}\Gamma(\omega^{-2})}\gamma^{(\omega^{-2}-1)}\exp\{-\frac{\gamma}{\mu\omega^2}\} = gamma(\gamma|\omega^{-2}, \mu\omega^2) \tag{7.11}$$

where ω^{-2} is inserted for shape argument, and $\mu\omega^2$ is inserted for the scale argument.

The parameter μ can be estimated with the mean of the summed peak heights (divided by 2) measured across the DNA profile if the analytical threshold $AT = 0$ RFU, otherwise another estimate is obtained, because of possible peak height truncation.

For the one contributor example in the previous section, the weighting is $gamma(\gamma_A|\omega^{-2}, \mu\omega^2) \times gamma(\gamma_B|\omega^{-2}, \mu\omega^2)$, if the genotype is AB, and $gamma(\gamma_A|\omega^{-2} \times 2, \mu\omega^2)$ if the genotype is AA.

For multiple contributors the mixture proportion parameters are also included for each individual, so that the shape argument will be a sum of the relative contributions of all the contributors for a specific allele. It is easiest to illustrate this with an example.

7.5.4 An example

This example is taken from "ENFSI exercise 1" example and is found encoded in the Excel workbook "Gamma". Readers who wish to follow the example using *Eu-*

202 Forensic Practitioner's Guide to the Interpretation of Complex DNA Profiles

roForMix, described in Chapter 8, must place all the settings to zero, except for the limit of detection threshold, which is set to 50 RFU. The example described here is on the book's website https://sites.google.com/view/dnabook/ in Chapter 7 of "Gamma_Model" folder. The spreadsheet "Gamma">"ENFSIcase with Q" is basic in that it does not incorporate drop-in or F_{ST}. Neither stutter nor degradation is attempted at this stage, hence these options must also be switched off in *EuroForMix*. The example locus is D2S1338. This is a four-allele locus, where the suspect is genotype AD, and the unknown contributor is BC, denoted by the green (medium grey in print version) row (Table 7.15).

Maximum likelihood estimation is used to optimize the unknown parameters. This is the same procedure as described for the normal distribution example in Section 7.3.1, except here we have to optimize more parameters. The parameters optimized by Solver are M_x (mixture proportion), mu, symbol μ (the peak height expectation), omega, symbol ω (the peak height coefficient-of-variation). As with the previous example, the optimization is carried out simultaneously across all loci; the aim is to maximize the respective probabilities (as a function of the parameters) under H_p and H_d in two separate calculations to formulate the LR. The layout is shown in Table 7.15; the procedure is explained in the spreadsheet "ENFSIcase with Q".

Table 7.15 Locus D2S1338 from the "ENFSI exercise 1" example ("Gamma">"ENFSIcase with Q" spreadsheet optimized under H_d). The M_x, mu, and omega parameters have been optimized using the Solver function to maximize the log likelihoods under H_p and H_d across all loci. Here the corresponding shape and scale parameters, which provide the best fit to the observed peak heights, are returned by using Eq. (7.10). The weightings are calculated from =GAMMA.DIST(y,shape,scale,cumulative=FALSE), where y is the observed peak height, with the shape and scale arguments.

D2S1338														combined
Height Information here					Expected peak height (shape*scale)				weightings					weights
	Height	peak height			Genotype	A	B	C	D	A	B	C	D	
A	300	0.190	17.000	0.2447	AB,CD	285.473	285.473	722.419	722.419	2.35E-03	9.17E-04	1.43E-03	3.24E-04	1.001E-12
B	471	0.298	18.000	0.0634	AC,BD	285.473	722.419	285.473	722.419	2.35E-03	1.24E-03	6.91E-04	3.24E-04	6.555E-13
C	512	0.323	19.000	0.1109	AD,BC	285.473	722.419	722.419	285.473	2.35E-03	1.24E-03	1.43E-03	2.35E-03	9.847E-12
D	300	0.190	20.000	0.1761	BC,AD	722.419	285.473	285.473	722.419	3.24E-04	9.17E-04	6.91E-04	3.24E-04	6.661E-14
SUM	1583				BD,AC	722.419	285.473	722.419	285.473	3.24E-04	9.17E-04	1.43E-03	2.35E-03	1.001E-12
					CD,AB	722.419	722.419	285.473	285.473	3.24E-04	1.24E-03	6.91E-04	2.35E-03	6.555E-13
Mx	1.Mx													
0.2832379	0.7167621											Omega	0.292	
												mu	1007.893	

Parameters (global)
shape 11.692592 (alpha) ←── | The shape and scale parameters are calculated from Omega and mu ↙
scale 86.199263 (beta)

Parameters per contributor
shape A= 3.3117855 in contributor 1 ←── | Relative proportions of shape parameters calculated using Mx | These parameters
shape A= 8.3808066 in contributor 2   Optimised with Solver
scale= 86.199263 universal
mu= 285.47347 in contributor 1
mu= 722.41936 in contributor 2

Given the mixture proportions M_x for contributor 1 and $1 - M_x$ for contributor 2, $n_{A,k}$ is the number of A alleles for contributor $k = 1$ or $k = 2$; the shape argument for allele A becomes

$$\alpha_A = \frac{M_x \times n_{A,1} + (1 - M_x) \times n_{A,2}}{\omega^2} \tag{7.12}$$

and so on for allele B, C, D, etc. Notice the origin of the numerator of this formula in relation to the "MasterMix" spreadsheet analysis described in Section 7.2.

This formula is easily expanded to accommodate three or more contributors by adding ($M_k \times n_{A,k}$) terms into the numerator, one for each contributor k, where M_k is the mixture proportion for contributor k (see Appendix B). For two contributors, we simply have $M_1 = M_x$ and $M_2 = 1 - M_x$.

To give an example from Table 7.15, the weighting for allele A from the conditioned genotype AB, CD, requires the shape argument Eq. (7.12), calculated as: $\alpha_A = \frac{M_x \times 1}{\omega^2}$.

For a genotype with copies of allele A in both contributors: AA, AB the calculation of the shape argument for this allele is $\alpha_A = \frac{M_x \times 2 + (1 - M_x) \times 1}{\omega^2}$.

In the example shown in Table 7.15, the distributions of observed peak heights are defined by two shape arguments (α_1 and α_2, one per contributor) and a global scale parameter (β). These result in the two probability density distributions shown in Fig. 7.5. The model gives the peak height expectations μ_1 and μ_2. Note the skewed nature of the lower-level contributor, which is typical, and illustrates why the gamma distribution is preferable to the normal distribution to describe the data.

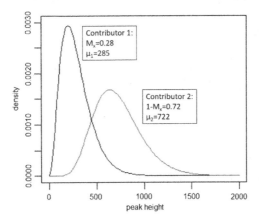

Figure 7.5 Gamma distributions for the peak heights of the two contributors in the ENFSI exercise 1 example. See Box 7.1 for R-code used to generate plots.

Box 7.1 R-code used to generate Fig. 7.5

```
k <- c(3.312, 8.381)# the shape parameters for contributors 1 and 2
theta <- c(86.2,86.2)#scale parameters for contributors 1 and 2
plot(0,0, xlim = c(0, 2000), ylim = c(0,0.003), type = "n",
xlab="peak height", ylab="density")
for(i in seq_along(k)) curve(dgamma(x, shape = k[i],
scale = theta[i]), from = 0, to = 2000, col = i, add = TRUE,
xlab="peak height", ylab="density")
```

204 Forensic Practitioner's Guide to the Interpretation of Complex DNA Profiles

As already described, the scale parameter (and hence the argument) is globally defined as $\beta = \mu \times \omega^2$, meaning that these parameters are assumed to be constant across all markers.

What remains to produce the weight $Pr(E|g)$ for the specific genotype combinations g is to multiply the weights of each of the alleles together:

$$Pr(E|g) = gamma(\gamma_A|\alpha_A, \beta) \times gamma(\gamma_B|\alpha_B, \beta) \times ... \qquad (7.13)$$

7.5.4.1 A summary of parameter calculations

The parameters are illustrated in the spreadsheet (Table 7.15).

1. M_x is the mixture proportion for contributor 1, and $1 - M_x$ is the mixture proportion for contributor 2; ω is the coefficient of variation; μ is the peak height expectation. To carry out the analysis in *EuroForMix*, these three parameters are regarded as unknown, and they are estimated by optimization to provide the best fit to the model. All other parameters are derived from these three.
2. The global parameters are calculated as
   - $shape(\alpha) = 1/\omega^2$
   - $scale(\beta) = \mu \times \omega^2$
3. The per contributor parameters are calculated as follows:
   - contributor 1: $\alpha_1 = M_x/\omega^2$
   - contributor 2: $\alpha_2 = (1 - M_x)/\omega^2$
   - $\beta = \mu \times \omega^2$
   - $\mu_1 = \alpha_1 \times \beta$
   - $\mu_2 = \alpha_2 \times \beta$

   To recover the global parameters, add the two contributor parameters as follows:
   - $\mu = \mu_1 + \mu_2$
   - $\alpha = \alpha_1 + \alpha_2$
4. The expected allele peak heights are calculated by multiplying the per contributor shape and scale parameters, as shown in Table 7.16.
5. The weightings are calculated from the Excel function:
   =GAMMA.DIST(γ,shape,scale,cumulative=FALSE), where γ is the *observed* peak height, with the shape and scale arguments.
   - The shape parameter is calculated as described in point (3) above, multiplied by the number of alleles per contributor and divided by ω^2. For example, for genotype combination AA, AB, the shape parameter for allele A is

$$\alpha = \frac{2 \times M_x + (1 - M_x) \times 1}{\omega^2} \qquad (7.14)$$

and for allele B,

$$\alpha = \frac{0 \times M_x + (1 - M_x) \times 1}{\omega^2} \qquad (7.15)$$

The quantitative (continuous) model theory   205

Table 7.16 Calculation of expected peak heights for an allele that is conditioned on the number of observed instances in the conditioned genotype, either 0, 1, 2. α_1 is the shape parameter for contributor 1, and α_2 is the shape parameter for contributor 2. The totals give the expected peak heights for a given allele (i.e., the contribution from both individuals). The total contributions can also be expressed in terms of M_x and μ, as shown by substituting formulae in point (3) above.

No. of alleles per contributor	Contributor 1	Contributor 2	Total contribution
0,2	$\alpha_1 \times \beta \times 0$	$\alpha_2 \times \beta \times 2$	$2\alpha_2\beta = 2(1 - M_x)\mu$
1,1	$\alpha_1 \times \beta \times 1$	$\alpha_2 \times \beta \times 1$	$(\alpha_1 + \alpha_2)\beta = \mu$
2,0	$\alpha_1 \times \beta \times 2$	$\alpha_2 \times \beta \times 0$	$2\alpha_1\beta = 2M_x\mu$
1,2	$\alpha_1 \times \beta \times 1$	$\alpha_2 \times \beta \times 2$	$(\alpha_1 + 2\alpha_2)\beta = (2 - M_x)\mu$
2,1	$\alpha_1 \times \beta \times 2$	$\alpha_2 \times \beta \times 1$	$(2\alpha_1 + \alpha_2)\beta = (1 + M_x)\mu$
2,2	$\alpha_1 \times \beta \times 2$	$\alpha_2 \times \beta \times 2$	$(2\alpha_1 + 2\alpha_2)\beta = 2\mu$

- The scale parameter is the same as previously described, $\beta = \mu \times \omega^2$.
- The overall weighting for the genotype combination being considered is calculated by multiplying together the individual weightings.

6. Finally, the H_d and H_p products are calculated in exactly the same way as described for the normal distribution model in Section 7.3.4. Comparisons with LRs calculated without peak height consideration and LR_{max} are also carried out as described in that section.

The relationship of the parameters is illustrated in Fig. 7.6. There are three parameters that are optimized to find the best fit to the model: M_x, ω, and μ. They calculate the shape α and scale β parameters of the gamma distribution. This in turn calculates the weights that are multiplied by $Pr(g|H)$ without peak height (frequency databases and the conditioned genotype combinations are required for this). Each proposition $Pr(E|H_p)$ and $Pr(E|H_d)$ is optimized separately—the aim is to maximize the log likelihoods under each proposition, by varying the M_x, ω, and μ parameters until this is achieved. The likelihood ratio $LR = \frac{Pr(E|H_p)}{Pr(E|H_d)}$.

7.6. Drop-out for the gamma model explained

Using *LRmix Studio*, drop-out of an allele was accommodated by considering a drop-out parameter d (common for all contributors), and when conditioning on the a genotype, the drop-out probability for an allele a, D_a (from Eq. (5.7)), could be calculated. A single global value of d was estimated and applied across the entire DNA profile in question. The procedure is different with the quantitative model. Recall that in Chapter 3.1 it was explained that allele drop-out was an extreme form of heterozygote imbalance. To predict allele drop-out, we simply need to model the peak heights. An allele that is estimated to be below the analytical threshold (AT), has dropped out. For quantitative models, the probability of drop-out is not required as a parameter. Instead, it is estimated

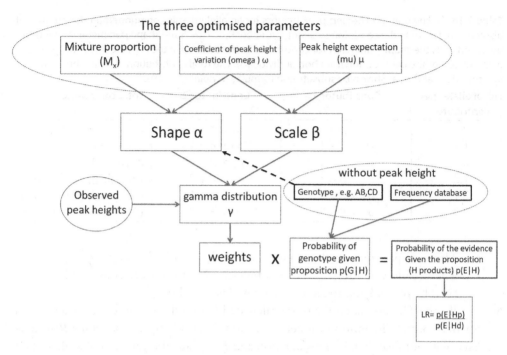

Figure 7.6 A flow chart showing how the parameters of the gamma model are formed to produce the likelihood ratio.

using the continuous peak height model, given as the area under the gamma density function curve from zero RFU to AT RFU. Hence the drop-out probability is provided as an integral from zero to AT. This integral can be calculated directly by the gamma cumulative function (an integrated variant of the density function).

7.6.1 The Q allele

It is best to illustrate with an example. Suppose we have a single contributor crime stain typed as A, and the suspect is genotype AB. If the prosecution proposition is correct, allele B must have dropped out. As part of the defense alternative, it can be proposed that no drop-out has occurred—the alternative explanation is that the donor is an AA homozygote (Chapter 3.7).

Under the prosecution proposition then, provided A is at low level in the crime stain, it may be reasonable to postulate that the B allele has dropped out, hence it is not visible. In Chapter 3.7, the virtual Q allele was introduced. This is defined as any allele, *except* for those observed in the crime stain. In this example, the probability of the Q allele is $1 - p_A$. A worked example showing the use of the Q allele in *LRmix Studio* was described in Chapter 4.4.1.

In the "ENFSI exercise 1" example, the crime-stain shows a single allele for TPOX type 8. The suspect is type 8, 12, hence under the prosecution proposition, allele 12 has dropped out. To analyze this case, it is necessary to consider all the genotype alternatives ($AA, AQ; AQ, AQ$....) listed in Table 7.17.

Table 7.17 Calculation of weightings for a single allele crime stain, type 8, where the suspect is heterozygote 8, 12. Spreadsheet "Gamma">"ENFSIcase with Q".

TPOX

Height Information here						Expected peak height		weightings			combined
	Height	peak height	Allele	Frequency	Genotypes	A	Q	A	Q		weights
A	1258	1.000	8.000	0.4859	AA,AQ	1293.366301	722.419355	1.21E-03	6.76E-08		8.214E-11
					AQ,AQ	1007.892828	1007.89283	7.90E-04	4.55E-12		3.593E-15
SUM	1258				AA,QQ	570.9469457	1444.83871	5.21E-05	3.49E-19		1.818E-23
					AQ,AA	1730.312183	285.473473	5.64E-04	1.18E-02		6.652E-06
					QQ,AA	1444.83871	570.946946	1.11E-03	6.89E-06		7.637E-09
					AQ,QQ	285.4734728	1730.31218	9.63E-07	3.39E-24		3.261E-30
Mx	1-Mx				QQ,AQ	722.4193552	1293.3663	1.90E-04	1.24E-16		2.357E-20
0.2832379	0.7167621				AA,AA	2015.785656		1.64E-04			1.635E-04
											sum
Parameters (global)								Omega			0.292
shape	11.692592	(alpha)						mu			1007.892828
scale	86.199263	(beta)									
Parameters per contributor											
shape A=	3.3117855	in contributor 1									
shape A=	8.3808066	in contributor 2									
scale=	86.199263	universal									
mu=	285.47347	in contributor 1									
mu=	722.41936	in contributor 2									

All of the defense alternative genotype combinations are listed. There is only a single allele present; the presence of three or more alleles at other loci in the profile preclude the possibility of the profile being from a single contributor. The absence of allele 12 must reduce the strength of the evidence in favor of the prosecution proposition, because the crime-stain profile has a missing allele (under H_p), and consequently does not "match" the reference profile.

To be exhaustive, there are eight alternative possible variants of genotype combinations. These are listed in Table 7.17. They include zero to three doses of allele Q (at least one allele A must be present in each genotype combination). In addition, under the defense proposition, there is no *a priori* reason to condition that drop-out *has* occurred, which means that an option is for both contributors to be AA, AA homozygotes.

The weightings for allele A are calculated in exactly the same way as previously described in Section 7.5.4. First, the number of contributors from each contributor for allele A is counted; second, the shape argument is constructed as presented in Eq. (7.12); third, the gamma density function is constructed by inserting the shape and scale arguments, and the weight is obtained by evaluating the density function on the corresponding observed peak height; GAMMA.DIST function(γ,shape,scale,cumulative=FALSE). If more alleles had been observed, the weights are calculated for each and are then multiplied together.

The Q allele is calculated differently, however. In the "weightings" column (Table 7.17), γ is set to the drop-out threshold (AT) in the GAMMA.DIST function(AT,shape,scale,cumulative=TRUE), $AT = 50$ RFU in this example, and the cumulative option is set to "TRUE". This is carried out to calculate the drop-out probability, which we define to be the probability that the peak height is in the interval between 0 and 50 RFU.

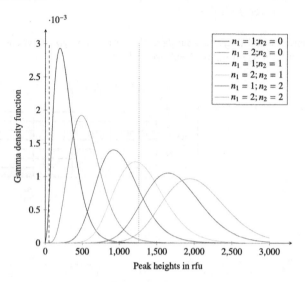

Figure 7.7 The figure shows the shape of the gamma density function of the peak height RFU values for different number of allele contributions 0, 1, or 2 for contributor 1, n_1, and contributor 2, n_2. The vertical dashed line indicates the $AT = 50$ RFU threshold, whereas the dotted dashed line indicates the observed peak height (1258 RFU) of allele A.

Fig. 7.7 shows the gamma density function over the peak height outcome for different numbers of allele contributions for each of the contributors, which is specified via the genotype combination assumptions. For example, the peak height distribution for allele A in the genotype combination AQ, AA, has one A allele from contributor 1, and from contributor 2, there are two A alleles. Distributions are defined by the gamma function as *gamma*(shape,scale) where the shape parameter is calculated per contributor and the scale parameter is universal as shown in Table 7.17. Using these data, the distribution for allele A for this genotype combination is *gamma*(20.17, 86.2), shown in Fig. 7.7 as a purple line. The shape parameter is calculated from Eq. (7.14), and the scale parameter is $\beta = \mu \times \omega^2$.

Scale parameter calculation (same for all alleles):

$$\beta = \mu \times \omega^2 = 1007.89 \times 0.2925^2 = \beta = 86.2 \qquad (7.16)$$

Shape parameter calculation for allele A:

$$\alpha_A = \frac{1 \times M_x + (1 - M_x) \times 2}{\omega^2} = \frac{1 \times 0.28 + (1 - 0.28) \times 2}{0.2925^2} = 20.1 \qquad (7.17)$$

If we consider allele Q (the potentially dropped out allele), for this genotype combination, it is only present in contributor 1, and has a much smaller shape argument, *gamma*$(3.31, 86.2)$, which gives a slight possibility for drop-out (black line in Fig. 7.7).

Shape parameter calculation for allele Q:

$$\alpha_Q = \frac{1 \times M_x + (1 - M_x) \times 0}{\omega^2} = \frac{1 \times 0.28 + (1 - 0.28) \times 0}{0.2925^2} = 3.3 \qquad (7.18)$$

The scale parameter is the same as previously calculated. The reader can follow the same calculations in the spreadsheet associated with Table 7.17.

The suspect is TPOX 8, 12, hence the prosecution proposition is that the crime-stain evidence is type 8, Q (Allele TPOX $8 = A$ in the example; the 12 allele is not visible, but it is subsumed into the Q allele). Consequently, there are several possible genotype products that must be summed under H_p. By assuming that the suspect is contributor 1, these are AQ, AA; AQ, AQ, and AQ, QQ.

Table 7.18 Calculation of *LR*s for the TPOX example, "ENFSI exercise 1". The suspect is AQ, and the genotype products that are summed under the prosecution proposition are AQ, AQ: AQ, AA, and AQ, QQ. This is divided by the sum of H_d products to calculate the likelihood ratio.

Genotypes	combined weights	Pr(g|Hd)	Product Hd	Pr g|Hp	product Hp	LR with peak height	LR without weighting	LRmax
AA,AQ	8.214E-11	0.117955527	9.68858E-12	0.499602	3.861E-05	3.900E+00	1.075099877	4.235514783
AQ,AQ	3.593E-15	0.249602538	8.96849E-16	0.499602	1.571E-06	1.586E-01	1.075099877	2.001591746
AA,QQ	1.818E-23	0.062400635	1.13437E-24	0.264299	3.861E-05	3.900E+00	1.075099877	4.235514783
AQ,AA	6.652E-06	0.117955527	7.84663E-07	0.236099	1.571E-06	1.586E-01	1.075099877	2.001591746
QQ,AA	7.637E-09	0.062400635	4.76528E-10	0.236099	1.803E-09	1.821E-04	0.790952259	3.783596301
AQ,QQ	3.261E-30	0.132044315	4.30632E-31	0.264299	1.571E-06	1.586E-01	1.075099877	2.001591746
QQ,AQ	2.357E-20	0.132044315	3.11227E-21	0.499602	1.803E-09	1.821E-04	0.790952259	3.783596301
AA,AA	1.635E-04	0.055742648	9.11645E-06	0.236099	3.861E-05	3.900E+00		
sum		0.930146139	9.9016E-06					

Recall that two different calculations are needed to optimize the unknown parameters under H_p and H_d separately, using Solver in Excel so that the *LR* with peak height column would be based on the optimization under each of these propositions (Section 7.3.5). The purpose of the spreadsheet is to enable the reader to explore the formulae in the cells. The H_d calculation is shown in Tables 7.17, 7.18. The likelihood ratio is calculated as 0.1268, which favors the defense proposition, and this number is identical to that achieved with *EuroForMix* to four decimal places. If the calculation had been carried out without considering peak heights (*LR* without weighting column), then the *LR* would be higher, $LR = 1.08$: this slightly favors the H_p proposition. In the table, $LR_{max} = 2.0$ is based upon a modified $2p$ rule ($LR = p_A \times (1 - p_A)$) described in Chapter 3.6; it is distinctly anti-conservative. This simple example shows that taking a neutral stance by leaving out the TPOX locus in a formal calculation is the same as designating $LR = 1$ to the locus, which—in this case—it is not justified and would result in over-estimation of the overall *LR*.

The rules described above are applied to all other possible genotype combinations. The Q allele is used whenever masking alleles could explain a suspect's genotype, since the defense proposition always includes the possibility that an unknown contributor has dropped one or more alleles. Consequently, the Q allele is not required for two contributors, where there are four alleles present, but it is always used when there is one, or there are two or three alleles present. The calculations are quite lengthy compared to the simple examples (without drop–out) that are described in Chapter 1.7. Table 7.19 shows all H_d genotype combinations for 1–3 alleles in a two-person mixture. It is easy to see that the computing requirement increases exponentially with increased numbers of contributors, so that a simple spreadsheet calculation cannot be used to illustrate three or more.

Table 7.19 Exhaustive list of genotype combinations under the defense proposition if there are two contributors with drop-out—illustration for one, two, three, or four alleles in the crime-stain evidence. The Q allele is shown in the unshaded areas, the yellow (light grey in print version) areas are genotypes, where there is no drop-out. This assumes that drop-in is not a possibility.

Number of alleles			
one	two	three	four
AA,AQ	AA,BQ	AB,CQ	AB,CD
AQ,AQ	BB,AQ	AC,BQ	AC,BD
AA,QQ	QQ,AB	AQ,BC	AD,BC
AQ,AA	AB,AQ	BC,AQ	BC,AD
QQ,AA	BQ,AQ	BQ,AC	BD,AC
AQ,QQ	AB,BQ	CQ,AB	CD,AB
QQ,AQ	BQ,AA	AA,BC	
AA,AA	AQ,BB	BB,AC	
	AB,QQ	CC,AB	
	AQ,AB	AB,AC	
	AQ,BQ	BC,AC	
	BQ,AB	AB,BC	
	AA,AB	BC,AA	
	AB,AB	AC,BB	
	AA,BB	AB,CC	
	AB,AA	AC,AB	
	BB,AA	AC,BC	
	AB,BB	BC,AB	
	BB,AB		

7.6.2 Comparison of the Excel spreadsheet with *EuroForMix*: a summary

The complete crime-stain profile using "ENFSI exercise 1", is analyzed in the Excel spreadsheet "Gamma">"ENFSIcase with Q" using the gamma model. The purpose

The quantitative (continuous) model theory **211**

of the exercise is to make clear the calculations that are needed. It also illustrates the principle of performing the maximum likelihood estimation.

To carry out the maximum likelihood estimation, Solver is used as shown in Table 7.20:

Step 1: Maximize the logged likelihood value given as a product of the likelihood value for each loci (the sum of natural logarithms) by optimizing the three parameters in cells B379:B381, i.e., M_x, ω, and μ under H_p. When the calculation has finished, copy/paste the value, without formula from cell B385 to cell F385.

Step 2: Use Solver to maximize the Log Likelihood in cell B386. Copy/paste this value into cell F386. This gives the likelihood ratio in cell F387.

Step 3: Referring to the spreadsheet itself, the individual LRs of each locus can be discovered by copy/pasting the H_p product (shown in the green rows) and dividing by the H_d product highlighted in yellow, remembering to carry out two separate optimizations, one for H_p and one for H_d to carry out the calculation.

Table 7.20 Excel Solver set-up to carry out the maximum likelihood estimation. Two separate analyses are carried out to optimize parameters under the alternative H_p and H_d propositions.

212   Forensic Practitioner's Guide to the Interpretation of Complex DNA Profiles

Step 4: A comparison with the results of analysis in *EuroForMix* reveals the same answers (Table 7.21) to approximately three decimal places (differences due to rounding errors).

Table 7.21 Results of *EuroForMix* analysis (Fst = 0, drop-in = 0, no stutter or degradation) comparing log likelihoods and *LR* from the spreadsheet analysis—they are the same.

7.7. Deconvolution

Deconvolution is the method used to estimate the genotypes that are best supported. A demonstration spreadsheet is available in the "Gamma" workbook, spreadsheet "Deconvolution". This spreadsheet replicates the four–allele (including allele Q) example, as described for "ENFSI exercise 1". The method used to calculate the weights and $Pr(g|H)$ is the same as described in Section 7.5.4. Because two separate parameter optimizations are required, there are two parts to the spreadsheet that carry out the respective calculations under H_p and H_d. Part of the H_d spreadsheet is shown in Table 7.22. The CSF1PO locus from the "Gamma">"ENFSIcase with Q" spreadsheet is used as an example. The allele frequencies, peak heights, and parameters are copy/pasted as indicated. The necessary calculations are automated.

Table 7.22 "Deconvolution" spreadsheet showing parameter, peak height, and allele frequency inputs using CSF1PO as an example, from the "ENFSI exercise 1".

Spreadsheet used to calculate the weights under Hd

Peak Height Information here

	Height	Proportions
A	282	0.185
B	455	0.299
C	786	0.516
SUM	1523	

Hd parameters

Mx	1-Mx	
0.283	0.716759813	

Parameters (global)

shape	11.69266043	(alpha)
scale	8.620E+01	(beta)

Parameters per contributor

shape A=	3.311831329	in contributor 1
shape A=	8.380829105	in contributor 2
scale=	86.19875983	universal
mu=	285.4757533	in contributor 1
mu=	722.4170751	in contributor 2

Insert the peak heights here

Genotype	Expected peak height (shape*scale)				weightings	
	A	B	C	Q	A	B
AB,CQ	285.476	285.476	722.417	722.417	2.51E-03	1.02E-03
AC,BQ	285.476	545.813	285.476	722.417	2.51E-03	1.16E-03
AQ,BC	285.476	545.813	545.813	285.476	2.51E-03	1.16E-03
BC,AQ	722.417	285.476	285.476	722.417	2.53E-04	1.02E-03
BQ,AC	722.417	285.476	722.417	285.476	2.53E-04	1.02E-03
CQ,AB	722.417	722.417	215.687	215.687	2.53E-04	1.16E-03
AA,BC	570.9515066	722.4170751	722.4170751		9.60E-04	1.16E-03
BB,AC	722.4170751	570.9515066	722.4170751		2.53E-04	1.90E-03
CC,AB	722.4170751	722.4170751	570.9515066		2.53E-04	1.16E-03
AB,AC	1007.892828	285.4757533	722.4170751		7.43E-06	1.02E-03
BC,AC	722.4170751	285.4757533	1007.892828		2.53E-04	1.02E-03
AB,BC	285.4757533	1007.892828	722.4170751		2.51E-03	1.66E-04
BC,AA	1444.83415	285.4757533	285.4757533		5.32E-09	1.02E-03
AC,BB	285.4757533	1444.83415	285.4757533		2.51E-03	1.35E-06
AB,CC	285.4757533	285.4757533	1444.83415		2.51E-03	1.02E-03
AC,AB	1007.892828	722.4170751	285.4757533		7.43E-06	1.16E-03
AC,BC	285.4757533	722.4170751	1007.892828		2.51E-03	1.16E-03
BC,AB	722.4170751	1007.892826	285.4757533		2.53E-04	1.66E-04

CSF1PO example

	Allele Frequencies
Allele A	0.2623
Allele B	0.3011
Allele C	0.3151

Insert the allele frequencies and parameters for Hp and Hd here - the calculations are automatic

INPUT PARAMETERS	Hp param	Hd param
Mx	0.261	0.283
omega	0.270	0.292
mu	1008.901	1007.893

As previously described for the normal distribution model (Table 7.11), "Product Hd" column = weight $\times Pr(g|H_d)$ (Table 7.23). The proposition pairs that are tested are H_p: $S + U$ and H_d: $U + U$.

The first contributor in the list of genotypes is C1 = suspect, and the second is C2 = unknown under H_p. Under H_d, both C1 and C2 are unknown. The joint probabilities of individual C1, C2 genotypes can be calculated from the corresponding values in the "Product Hd" column, divided by the sum of "Product Hd" (Table 7.24). The sum of joint probabilities = 1. It can be seen that the "top genotype" is the AC, BC option, giving probability 0.618, and the same answer is provided if *EuroForMix* is used to analyze the same data.

7.7.0.1 Calculation of marginal probabilities

The *marginal* probabilities describe per contributor C1, C2 genotypes (i.e., two per "joint genotype") and are calculated as follows:

1. A complete list of possible genotypes $CQ, BQ, BC...$ is provided separately for contributors C2 and C1, respectively (Table 7.23).

Table 7.23 Calculation of marginalized probabilities from the "ENFSI exercise 1".

Q	weights	Pr(G|Hd)	Product Hd	C2 Genotype Tested	sum of products | G	probability C2
6.76E-08	**2.441E-16**	0.012094662	2.9529E-18	CQ	2.953E-18	1.6E-08
1.06E-08	**2.404E-18**	0.012094662	2.90794E-20	BQ	2.908E-20	1.6E-10
1.18E-02	**4.849E-11**	0.012094662	5.86486E-13	BC	1.51655E-10	8.3E-01
6.76E-08	**1.352E-18**	0.012094662	1.63555E-20	AQ	1.63555E-20	8.9E-11
1.18E-02	**4.291E-12**	0.012094662	5.18933E-14	AC	2.0491E-11	1.1E-01
1.18E-02	**2.686E-13**	0.012094662	3.24844E-15	AB	4.192E-12	2.3E-02
	1.57E-09	0.013055266	2.05385E-11	AA	5.48947E-18	3.0E-08
	6.79E-10	0.01498643	1.0172E-11	BB	3.92473E-15	2.1E-05
	2.60E-10	0.015683242	4.07356E-12	CC	6.40747E-12	3.5E-02
	1.07E-11	0.0261	2.78931E-13		**SUM**	**1.0E+00**
	3.18E-10	0.031366484	9.98819E-12			
	5.89E-10	0.029972861	1.76453E-11	**C1 Genotype Tested**	**sum of products | G**	**probability C1**
	4.20E-16	0.013055266	5.48947E-18	CQ	3.24844E-15	1.8E-05
	2.62E-13	0.01498643	3.92473E-15	BQ	5.18933E-14	2.8E-04
	4.09E-10	0.015683242	6.40747E-12	BC	1.00859E-11	5.5E-02
	6.69E-13	0.026110533	1.74607E-14	AQ	5.86486E-13	3.2E-03
	3.60E-09	0.031366484	1.12884E-10	AC	1.12906E-10	6.2E-01
	3.26E-12	0.029972861	9.77343E-14	AB	2.43318E-11	1.3E-01
		SUM	**1.82749E-10**	AA	2.05385E-11	1.1E-01
Omega	**0.292**			BB	1.0172E-11	5.6E-02
mu	1.008E+03			CC	4.07356E-12	2.2E-02
					SUM	**1.000E+00**

2. For the C2 genotype, the "sum of products $|G$" is the sum of Product Hd values taken whenever a given C2 genotype appears. For example, genotype *CQ*, the only possible option for C1 = genotype *AB*, hence the sum of products given $G = CQ$ is the "Product Hd" for genotype combination *AB*, *CQ*.
3. Now consider the *BC* genotype for C2. There are four different possibilities for C1, where the "Product Hd" values are summed together into the "sum of products $|G$" column: *AQ*, *BC*; *AA*, *BC*; *AB*, *BC*; *AC*, *BC*. The principle is the same as described in Chapter 1.8.1 for the numerator.
4. This process is repeated for all remaining genotypes in the list (Table 7.23).
5. The entire column of "Product Hd" values is summed following Section 1.8.1 for the denominator.
6. The "Probability C2" is calculated by dividing the sum of products $|G$ by the sum of "Product Hd".
7. The "top genotype" is the genotype with the greatest probability. With this example, the probability $Pr(g = BC|H_d) = 0.83$ for contributor C2 ($1 - M_x = 0.72$) (Table 7.23), shown in the "Probability C2" column. Collectively, the results are referred to as "marginal probabilities" in the *EuroForMix* software.
8. The "Ratio to next genotype" is calculated by dividing the top C2 genotype (*BC*) by the second ranking C2 genotype (*AC*): $0.83/0.11 = 7.4$.
9. The process is repeated for all remaining genotypes to calculate their respective probabilities.
10. The sum of the probabilities in the "Probability C2" column is one.
11. The same process is repeated to deconvolve contributor C1.
12. The same process is followed to deconvolve contributor C2 under the H_p proposition (since we condition on the suspect as C1, this genotype is not deconvolved).

Table 7.24 Joint probabilities of C1,C2 genotypes using CSF1PO as an example, from the "ENFSI exercise 1". The best supported genotype combination is highlighted.

C1,C2	Joint Probabilities
AB,CQ	1.616E-08
AC,BQ	1.591E-10
AQ,BC	3.209E-03
BC,AQ	8.950E-11
BQ,AC	2.840E-04
CQ,AB	1.778E-05
AA,BC	1.124E-01
BB,AC	5.566E-02
CC,AB	2.229E-02
AB,AC	1.526E-03
BC,AC	5.466E-02
AB,BC	9.656E-02
BC,AA	3.004E-08
AC,BB	2.148E-05
AB,CC	3.506E-02
AC,AB	9.554E-05
AC,BC	6.177E-01
BC,AB	5.348E-04
Sum=	1

The probabilities of each genotype conditioned under H_p and H_d are separately listed for contributors in Table 7.23. The data can conveniently be represented in expanded pie charts (Fig. 7.8). The highest genotype probability for unknown contributor C2 corresponds to BC under H_p (0.91) and H_d (0.83). The probabilities differ under the two alternative propositions, because the parameters are different, and C1 is not conditioned in the latter. For C1, under H_d, the highest probability (0.62) corresponds to genotype AC.

The results shown in spreadsheet Deconvolution are also achieved using the *EuroForMix* software that is described in detail in the next chapter.

7.8. Degradation

Crime stains consist of body fluids that are nutritional to bacteria, which will grow in humid/damp conditions at room temperature. Bacteria have DNA-ase activity that will

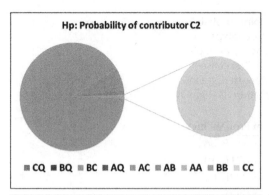
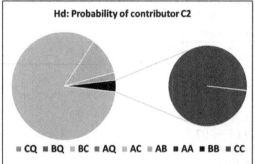
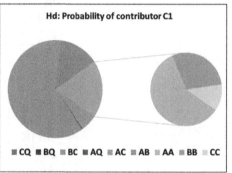

Figure 7.8 A visual representation of contributor probabilities of deconvolved genotypes $Pr(g|H)$ using extended pie charts under H_p and H_d, utilizing CSF1PO as an example from the "ENFSI exercise 1". Data from Table 7.23 were used.

cut the DNA molecule into smaller lengths. If the DNA strand is cut in between two primer binding sites, then it is no longer available for PCR amplification. It follows that the larger the DNA fragment, the greater the chance that degradation will occur. The causality of degradation is described in Chapter 4.5. The effect is the observation that a given DNA profile shows marked decrease in the allele peak heights relative to increasing fragment size, which can be modeled by a regression coefficient.

An example follows using "ENFSI exercise 1". The regression analysis can be followed in the associated "RegressionAnalysis" spreadsheet found in the "Degradation" Excel workbook on the book's website https://sites.google.com/view/dnabook/.

Step 1: The regression coefficient is determined from the sum of peak heights observed vs. average peak heights at the observed locus.

For example: Locus D8S1179 has three alleles; their sizes (bp) are: 132; 148; 152 bp, and the mean is 144 bp. Peak heights are 288; 1525; 1129 RFU, respectively, hence the sum = 2942 RFU. The first x, y coordinates are 144, 2942. Table 7.25 shows a matrix of data used for regression analysis.

The quantitative (continuous) model theory   **217**

Step 2: To carry out the regression, the peak heights are converted into natural logarithms, as this best describes a linear relationship. The regression is $LN(y) = a + bx$, where $y =$ peak height, $x =$ fragment length, $a =$ the intercept coefficient, and $b =$ the regression (gradient) coefficient. These are calculated as $a = 8.15$ and $b = -0.00268$, respectively.

Step 3: The expected peak heights are converted from natural logarithms $y = exp(LN(y))$, and these are listed in Table 7.25 and plotted in Fig. 7.9.

Table 7.25 Data used in regression analysis of "ENFSI exercise 1" data. The locus sizes (bp) are averages and the peak heights are summed. The expected peak heights are calculated from regression analysis using natural logarithms of the allele peak height. The scaled bp sizes $(x - 125)/100$, where $x =$ size(bp), are used to calculate the regression parameter used in *EuroForMix*.

Locus	Size (bp)	Scaled size (bp)	Height (RFU)	Expected peak height
D8S1179	144.00	0.19	2942.00	2371.49
D21S11	210.00	0.85	1820.00	1987.27
D7S820	274.00	1.49	1555.00	1674.24
CSF1PO	326.63	2.02	1523.00	1454.13
D3S1358	131.00	0.06	2988.00	2455.50
THO1	179.33	0.54	2627.00	2157.37
D13S317	225.65	1.01	2693.00	1905.70
D16S539	275.30	1.50	2182.00	1668.42
D2S1338	323.31	1.98	1583.00	1467.12
D19S433	126.00	0.01	2522.00	2488.61
VWA	179.67	0.55	1437.00	2155.44
TPOX	232.99	1.08	1258.00	1868.60
D18S51	293.00	1.68	1286.00	1591.18
D5S818	153.00	0.28	1729.00	2315.01
FGA	233.00	1.08	2084.00	1868.55

A similar regression analysis is automatically generated in *EuroForMix* (Fig. 7.9) when visualizing the evidence profile data. Here a gamma distribution to the summed peak heights is fitted, and a 99% "coverage" interval is provided to quantify the summed peak height variability.

Step 4: In *EuroForMix*, a degradation slope parameter τ is built in as part of the shape argument by scaling it with $\tau^{(x-125)/100}$, without including the intercept coefficient. A decreasing slope requires that τ is between zero and one, where one gives a constant slope. The scaling makes the other model parameters interpretable at base pair $bp = 125$, and it makes the estimation of τ more robust.

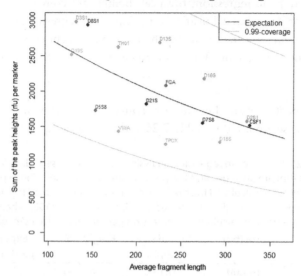

Figure 7.9 "ENFSI exercise 1" data. Regression analysis of average fragment lengths vs summed allele peak heights generated from *EuroForMix*; tab:"import data">"View evidence".

Step 5: In the example we estimated $b = -0.267$ using our simple linear regression. This value is transformed by taking the exponent $\exp(b) = \tau = 0.765$, which is very close to the τ parameter estimated by *EuroForMix* (0.756). The figures are slightly different, because τ is optimized simultaneously with the other parameters (μ, ω, M_x) in *EuroForMix*.

Step 6: Calculation of the weighting for the Q allele: The identity of the Q allele is not known. The regression weighting for the Q allele uses x as the allele that has the maximum molecular weight in the multiplex kit-specific data.

Step 7: In all cases, the regression weighting is multiplied by the shape parameter such that the gamma density function becomes $gamma(y_A | \alpha_A \tau^{(x_A - 125)/100}, \mu \omega^2)$, where the original shape argument α_A was defined in Eq. (7.12).

For example, for genotype BC, AC the shape parameter for the alleles A, B, and C are

$$\alpha_A = \frac{(1 - M_x)\tau^{(x_A - 125)/100}}{\omega^2} \tag{7.19}$$

$$\alpha_B = \frac{M_x \tau^{(x_B - 125)/100}}{\omega^2} \tag{7.20}$$

$$\alpha_C = \frac{((1 - M_x) + M_x)\tau^{(x_C - 125)/100}}{\omega^2} \tag{7.21}$$

7.8.1 Demonstration with a spreadsheet

The gamma model spreadsheet demonstration described in Section 7.5.4 is expanded to a new workbook entitled "Degradation". The spreadsheet is the same as that previously described, except that the regression parameter τ has been added to the list of unknown parameters. As described in Step 6 of the previous section, the GAMMA.DIST function shape parameter found in the "weightings" columns of the Excel spreadsheet, is multiplied by $\tau^{(x-125)/100}$, where x is the observed fragment size of a given allele. The fragment size for each allele is provided in the spreadsheet (Table 7.26).

Table 7.26 Input data used for locus FGA in "Degradation" spreadsheet. The sizes of alleles FGA 21 and 22 are included along with a hypothetical size of allele Q, which corresponds to the allele with the maximum observed molecular weight in the multiplex kit-specific data.

FGA

Insert Peak Height Information here

	Height	peak height	Allele	Frequency	Size bp
A	1288	0.618	21.000	0.1602	231.000
B	796	0.382	22.000	0.1919	235.000
SUM	2084		Q Allele	0.6479	349.000

Solver can be used to find the maximum likelihood estimation, in the same way as described in Section 7.6.2, except that more parameters are optimized (Table 7.27), hence the process takes a little longer to complete.

The spreadsheet results were compared to those of *EuroForMix* (Table 7.28). The parameters optimized by *EuroForMix* and Solver are in very good agreement, as are the log likelihoods and the $log_{10}LRs$. There is a small difference in the likelihood ratio: 7.681E+16 for *EuroForMix* vs. 7.656E+16 for the spreadsheet analysis, that is attributed to rounding errors.

7.8.2 Recap

A regression model is used in *EuroForMix* to provide the regression slope (Fig. 7.9). The slope coefficient τ is optimized by *EuroForMix* as part of the shape parameter of the Gamma function. This optimization is carried out simultaneously with other parameters previously described (M_x, μ, ω), using maximum likelihood estimation. There are two separate optimizations under H_p and H_d, and the estimated parameters will differ as a result. The spreadsheet analysis shown in Table 7.27 illustrates the complete calculation, including degradation, for ENFSI exercise 1 example.

Table 7.27 Excel Solver set-up to carry out the maximum likelihood estimation. The degradation parameter *tau* is included. Two separate analyses are carried out to optimize parameters under the alternative H_p and H_d propositions.

	Height	peak height	Allele
350 FGA			
351 Insert Peak Height Information here			
352	Height	peak height	Allele
353 A	1288	0.618	21.000
354 B	796	0.382	22.000
355 SUM	2084		Q Allele
356			
357			
358			
359 Mx	1-Mx		
360 0.265664849	0.734335151		
361			
362 Parameters (global)			
363 shape	23.281	(alpha)	
364 scale	55.734	(beta)	
365			
366 Parameters per contributor			
367 shape A=	6.185	in contributor 1	
368 shape A=	17.096	in contributor 2	
369 scale=	55.734	universal	
370 mu=	344.714	in contributor 1	
371 mu=	952.837	in contributor 2	
372 tau=	0.755728216		
373			
374			
375			
376 INPUT			
377 PARAMETERS		Parameters from EFM	
378		Hp param	Hd param
379 Mx	0.266	0.254	0.266
380 omega	0.207	0.198	0.207
381 mu	1297.551	1300.000	1298.000
382 tau	0.755728216	0.7553	0.7556
383			

Solver Parameters window:

Set Objective: $B$386
To: ● Max ○ Min ○ Value Of: 0
By Changing Variable Cells: $B$379:$B$382
Subject to the Constraints:
Mx <= 1
Mx >= 0
Omega <= 1
Omega >= 0
mux <= 20000
mux >= 0
tau <= 1
tau >= 0

[Add] [Change] [Delete] [Reset All] [Load/Save]

☑ Make Unconstrained Variables Non-Negative
Select a Solving Method: Evolutionary [Options]

Solving Method
Select the GRG Nonlinear engine for Solver Problems that are smooth nonlinear. Select the LP Simplex engine for linear Solver Problems, and select the Evolutionary engine for Solver problems that are non-smooth.

[Help] [Solve] [Close]

			from EFM parameters	optimised by solver
384 **Maximum likelihood calculations**				
385 Hp products	-3.396E+02	LogLik Hp products	-3.394E+02	-3.394E+02
386 Hd products	-3.783E+02	LogLik Hd products	-3.783E+02	-3.783E+02
387	Copy/paste	**LR**	7.656E+16	7.6563E+16

Gamma | Regression Results | RegressionAnalysis | Scaled Regression Analysis | raw data

7.9. Stutter

In *EuroForMix*, a model to explain "backward-stutter" is included by adding an additional parameter, epsilon (ϵ), given as the expected proportion of a non-stuttered peak height at a parent allele, molecular size n four-base pair repeats, which is added to the peak height at allele $n - 1$ repeats. A separate stutter parameter could be used per locus, but this greatly increases the model complexity, the computation time, and convergence issues, hence the software currently assumes a single parameter across all loci.

Other/alternative probabilistic genotyping software based on a quantitative model typically pre-calibrate the stutter model based on validation studies, avoiding the need to optimize the stutter parameter (as carried out in *EuroForMix*).

To illustrate how stutter is accommodated, the parent allele is assumed to lose a proportion of its peak height (ϵ) to an allele that is $n - 1$ repeats less than the progenitor or parent. If there is already an allele present at the $n - 1$ repeat position, then the stutter

Table 7.28 Comparison of spreadsheet parameter results using Solver to those optimized by *EuroForMix*, along with likelihood ratio results.

	Parameters from EFM		From Solver	
	Hp param	Hd param	Hp param	Hd param
Mx	0.254	0.266	0.254	0.266
omega	0.198	0.207	0.198	0.207
mu	1300.000	1298.000	1299.683	1297.551
tau	0.7553	0.7556	0.755477055	0.75572822

Estimates under Hd

Parameter estimates:

param	MLE	Std.Err.
Mix-prop. C1	2.656e-01	2.417e-02
Mix-prop. C2	7.344e-01	2.417e-02
P.H.expectation	1.298e+03	9.356e+01
P.H.variability	2.071e-01	2.619e-02
Degrad. slope	7.556e-01	5.161e-02

Maximum Likelihood value

logLik= -378.3
Lik= 5.335e-165

Further Action

Estimates under Hp

Parameter estimates:

param	MLE	Std.Err.
Mix-prop. C1	2.536e-01	2.028e-02
Mix-prop. C2	7.464e-01	2.028e-02
P.H.expectation	1.300e+03	8.853e+01
P.H.variability	1.979e-01	2.158e-02
Degrad. slope	7.553e-01	4.853e-02

Maximum Likelihood value

logLik= -339.4
Lik= 4.098e-148

Further Action

Weight-of-evidence (MLE based)

Joint LR

LR= 7.681e+16
log10LR= 16.89

LR for each locus

D8S1179 109.1
D21S11 9.112
D7S820 12.7
CSF1PO 3.945
D3S1358 26.49
TH01 6.182
D13S317 35.78
D16S539 8.936
D2S1338 8.644

	Using EFM parameters	Optimised by solver
LogLik Hp products	-3.394E+02	-3.394E+02
LogLik Hd products	-3.783E+02	-3.783E+02
LR	7.656E+16	7.6563E+16
log10LR	16.88403	16.88402

Further evaluation

Optimize model more

LR sensitivity

Save results to file

Create report

Only LR results

Select reference to replace with non-contributor:

SUSPECT_1

Sample maximum based

is added to this existing allele so that it now consists of a stutter/allele mixture. If there is no allele at the $n-1$ repeat position, then the "allele" is pure stutter.

Fig. 7.10 illustrates three alleles A, B, C; a pure stutter product derived from allele A is labeled Z. If we also assume that there is a dropped out allele Q (which cannot be observed), the expected allele quantities (peak heights) from the contributors are given as E_A, E_B, E_C, E_Z, and E_Q. For the *EuroForMix* model, these will be proportional to the shape arguments $\alpha_A, \alpha_B, \alpha_C$, and α_Q, but we present these in terms of peak height expectation for clarification. Assume that these three alleles are separated by 4 bp each, from $A=$ low molecular weight to $C=$ high molecular weight; stutter/allele Z is also 4 bp less than A and the Q allele is unknown (the *EuroForMix* implementation assumes that it has a high molecular weight as described in Section 7.8). See B.3.11 for precise mathematical definitions on how to calculate the likelihood function when the stutter model is adopted.

To illustrate, consider a two-person mixture, where the genotype under consideration is AB, CQ, i.e., there are no shared alleles in this example. Refer to Fig. 7.10.

1. Starting with allele C, the expected proportion of stutter contributing to allele B is: $\epsilon \times E_C$.
2. Therefore the amount of expected peak height remaining to allele C is $(1 - \epsilon) \times E_C$.
3. Allele B also loses a proportion of its expected peak height to the position occupied by allele A, and this stutter proportion is defined as $\epsilon \times E_B$. Because of this, the expected peak height at allele B is reduced by $(1 - \epsilon) \times E_B$.
4. Consequently, the peak height expectation for allele B comprises two components: a) stutter from allele C: $\epsilon \times E_C$ and b) the remainder of allele B after loosing its portion to stutter: $(1 - \epsilon) \times E_B$.
5. Therefore the expected peak height of allele B is $(1 - \epsilon) \times E_B + \epsilon \times E_C$.
6. By the same reasoning, the expected peak height of allele A becomes $(1 - \epsilon) \times E_A + \epsilon \times E_B$.
7. A proportion of allele A generates an expected stutter peak height, which is simply $\epsilon \times E_A$ to allele Z found at the position 4 bp less than for position A.
8. Allele Q is not observed, a potential peak height being below the threshold value for drop-out. Therefore any stutter provided by Q is also below the threshold and will not be observed and has negligible affect on any other allele. In addition, we cannot apportion any stutter, because the identity of Q is unknown. In the calculations, only the expected peak height proportions M_x and $(1 - M_x)$ are taken into account.

7.9.1 Recap: taking account of peak height expectations using mixture proportions M_x

Recall from Section 7.5.4, the peak height expectations are given by the mixture proportion of two contributors C1 and C2 as M_x and $1 - M_x$, respectively, and the shape argument for allele A used in the gamma model is

$$\alpha_A = \frac{M_x \times n_{A,1} + (1 - M_x) \times n_{A,2}}{\omega^2} \tag{7.22}$$

For a genotype $g = AB, CC$, the shape argument for the alleles A, B and C are

$$\alpha_A = \frac{M_x \times 1 + (1 - M_x) \times 0}{\omega^2} \tag{7.23}$$

$$\alpha_B = \frac{M_x \times 1 + (1 - M_x) \times 0}{\omega^2} \tag{7.24}$$

$$\alpha_C = \frac{M_x \times 0 + (1 - M_x) \times 2}{\omega^2} \tag{7.25}$$

If instead genotype AB, AC is considered, then there are contributions from both C1 and C2 on allele A, hence

$$\alpha_A = \frac{M_x \times 1 + (1 - M_x) \times 1}{\omega^2} \qquad (7.26)$$

7.9.2 The full stutter model

The peak height expectations, given stutter, are obtained by multiplying together the mixture proportion argument in the previous section, by the expected stutter proportion ϵ argument, also described above. To illustrate, all the derived shape numerators for a three-allele example, with drop-out, are shown in Table 7.29.

The values shown are divided by ω^2 to form the shape parameter, which is plugged directly into the gamma model.

An Excel spreadsheet "StutterAndDegradation">"Stutter" is provided to show all the detailed calculations for a locus to illustrate how this feature is modeled. Parameter ϵ is optimized along with other parameters (μ, ω, M_x, and τ), as previously described in Section 7.8. Fig. 7.10B shows how the expected peak heights are changed when taking account of stutter.

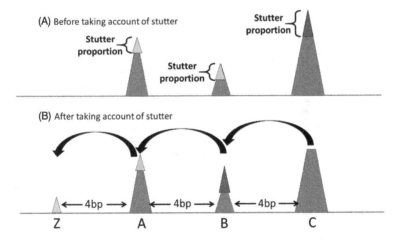

Figure 7.10 (A) Expected peak heights before taking account of stutters. When alleles are PCR amplified, a proportion of each one produces stutter. This proportion is defined by ϵ, and the amount of allele peak height remaining is $1 - \epsilon$. (B) The expectation of the peak heights are adjusted by removing the stutter proportion of allele C and moving it $n - 1$ repeats or -4 bp, adding it to allele B; the stutter proportions or alleles B and A are also moved -4 bp as illustrated. Allele Z is pure stutter.

7.9.3 A worked example showing the impact of stutter in *EuroForMix*

To demonstrate the stutter model, the filtered .csv file: E02_RD14-0003-42_43-1; 9-M2S10-0.15IP-Q1.0_001.20sec.fsa was downloaded from the PROVEDIt database

Table 7.29 Formulae used to describe the peak height adjustment of alleles when stutter is taken into account. The example relates to the three allele EPG shown in Fig. 7.10 and allows for drop-out with allele Q. The formulae shown form the numerator of the shape parameter used in the gamma model, the denominator is ω^2.

Genotype	Z	A	B	C	Q
AB, CQ	$M_X\epsilon$	$(M_X(1-\epsilon))+(M_X\epsilon)$	$(M_X(1-\epsilon))+((1-M_X)\epsilon)$	$(1-M_X)(1-\epsilon)$	$(1-M_X)$
AC, BQ	$M_X\epsilon$	$(M_X(1-\epsilon))+((1-M_X)\epsilon)$	$((1-M_X)(1-\epsilon))+(M_X\epsilon)$	$M_X(1-\epsilon)$	$(1-M_X)$
AQ, BC	$M_X\epsilon$	$(M_X(1-\epsilon))+((1-M_X)\epsilon)$	$((1-M_X)(1-\epsilon))+((1-M_X)\epsilon)$	$(1-M_X)(1-\epsilon)$	M_X
BC, AQ	$(1-M_X)\epsilon$	$((1-M_X)(1-\epsilon))+(M_X\epsilon)$	$(M_X(1-\epsilon))+(M_X\epsilon)$	$M_X(1-\epsilon)$	$(1-M_X)$
BQ, AC	$(1-M_X)\epsilon$	$((1-M_X)(1-\epsilon))+(M_X\epsilon)$	$(M_X(1-\epsilon))+((1-M_X)\epsilon)$	$(1-M_X)(1-\epsilon)$	M_X
CQ, AB	$(1-M_X)\epsilon$	$((1-M_X)(1-\epsilon))+((1-M_X)\epsilon)$	$((1-M_X)(1-\epsilon))+(M_X\epsilon)$	$M_X(1-\epsilon)$	M_X
AA, BC	$2M_X\epsilon$	$(2M_X(1-\epsilon))+((1-M_X)\epsilon)$	$((1-M_X)(1-\epsilon))+((1-M_X)\epsilon)$	$(1-M_X)(1-\epsilon)$	
BB, AC	$(1-M_X)\epsilon$	$((1-M_X)(1-\epsilon))+(2M_X\epsilon)$	$(2M_X(1-\epsilon))+((1-M_X)\epsilon)$	$(1-M_X)(1-\epsilon)$	
CC, AB	$(1-M_X)\epsilon$	$((1-M_X)(1-\epsilon))+((1-M_X)\epsilon)$	$((1-M_X)(1-\epsilon))+(2M_X\epsilon)$	$2M_X(1-\epsilon)$	
AB, AC	$(M_X\epsilon)+((1-M_X)\epsilon)$	$(M_X(1-\epsilon))+((1-M_X)(1-\epsilon))+(M_X\epsilon)$	$(M_X(1-\epsilon))+((1-M_X)\epsilon)$	$(1-M_X)(1-\epsilon)$	
BC, AC	$(1-M_X)\epsilon$	$((1-M_X)(1-\epsilon))+(M_X\epsilon)$	$(M_X(1-\epsilon))+(M_X\epsilon)+((1-M_X)\epsilon)$	$(M_X(1-\epsilon))+((1-M_X)(1-\epsilon))$	
AB, BC	$M_X\epsilon$	$(M_X(1-\epsilon))+(M_X\epsilon)+((1-M_X)\epsilon)$	$(M_X(1-\epsilon))+((1-M_X)(1-\epsilon))+((1-M_X)\epsilon)$	$(1-M_X)(1-\epsilon)$	
BC, AA	$2(1-M_X)\epsilon$	$(2(1-M_X)(1-\epsilon))+(M_X\epsilon)$	$(M_X(1-\epsilon))+((M_X)\epsilon)$	$M_X(1-\epsilon)$	
AC, BB	$M_X\epsilon$	$(M_X(1-\epsilon))+(2(1-M_X)\epsilon)$	$(2(1-M_X)(1-\epsilon))+(M_X\epsilon)$	$M_X(1-\epsilon)$	
AB, CC	$M_X\epsilon$	$(M_X(1-\epsilon))+(M_X\epsilon)$	$(M_X(1-\epsilon))+(2(1-M_X)\epsilon)$	$2(1-M_X)(1-\epsilon)$	
AC, AB	$(M_X\epsilon)+((1-M_X)\epsilon)$	$(M_X(1-\epsilon))+((1-M_X)(1-\epsilon))+((1-M_X)\epsilon)$	$((1-M_X)(1-\epsilon))+(M_X\epsilon)$	$M_X(1-\epsilon)$	
AC, BC	$M_X\epsilon$	$(M_X(1-\epsilon))+((1-M_X))$	$((1-M_X)(1-\epsilon))+(M_X\epsilon)+((1-M_X))$	$(M_X(1-\epsilon))+((1-M_X)(1-\epsilon))$	
BC, AB	$(1-M_X)\epsilon$	$((1-M_X)(1-\epsilon))+(M_X\epsilon)+((1-M_X)\epsilon)$	$(M_X(1-\epsilon))+((1-M_X)(1-\epsilon))+(M_X\epsilon)$	$M_X(1-\epsilon)$	

[232]: https://lftdi.camden.rutgers.edu/provedit/files/. This two-person mixture was run with Identifiler Plus, using the AB3130 platform, injected for 20 seconds. Two contributors (IDs 42 and 43) were combined in a 1:9 mixture; a total of 0.15 ng; the sample was sonicated for 10 seconds to degrade it. The data were reorganized into *EuroForMix* Excel spreadsheet files folder "Stutter Sample", where there are three files: "ProvedIt-SampleForStutter" and the references "Suspect42" and "Victim43", where the suspect is the minor contributor, chosen because this is a low level mixture, where alleles and stutter are similar in peak height. To compare, a stutter filtered file was prepared in file "ProveditSampleStuttersRemoved", where all peaks < 0.15, the size of a putative parent peak, were removed from the data. The "Identifiler_Caucasian" frequency database file was used for all analyses; the file is found in the "Stutter Sample" folder. To load the project into *EuroForMix*, load project file "with stutter". The "Settings" tab must be switched to "Default detection threshold" = 50; default F_{ST} and drop-in probabilities are both set to zero (Fig. 7.11).

The model specification was H_p: $S + U$; H_d: $U + U$, where $S =$ Suspect43, $U =$ Unknown (Fig. 7.11).

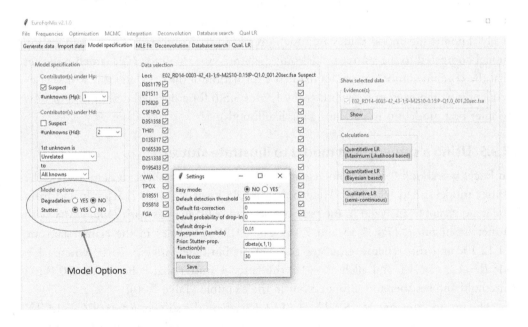

Figure 7.11 Model specification to demonstrate stutter.

If the model options buttons for "Stutter" and "Degradation" are both switched off, then *EuroForMix* fails to run, giving the following error message: *"The specified model could not explain the data. Please re-specify the model"*. The error message occurs, because there are too many alleles present to explain a two-person mixture (Fig. 7.12).

226 Forensic Practitioner's Guide to the Interpretation of Complex DNA Profiles

For example, there are five allele designations at locus D8S1179, and six at D21S11. A minimum of three contributors would be required if stutter was not taken into account. However, inspection shows that for D8S1179, alleles 10 and 12 might be explained by stutter, and for D21S11, alleles 26 and 28 could be similarly ascribed; if taken into account this reduces the model to two contributors.

Accordingly, switching the Stutter option on, as shown in Fig. 7.11, allows the model to run successfully; the model parameters and likelihood ratios are shown in Fig. 7.13.

The $log10LR = 5.395$. The model parameters are listed under H_d and H_p, respectively, noting that the "Stutter-prop" (stutter proportion) is ϵ in our notation; it differs under $H_d = 0.14$ and $H_p = 0.08$.

7.9.4 Combining stutter and degradation in the same model

This sample is highly degraded (Fig. 7.14), therefore it would be useful to combine both stutter and degradation models together. This is achieved by switching the two "Model options" buttons to "Yes" for both stutter and degradation (Fig. 7.11).

When rerun, the model gives a much higher $log10LR = 7.92$ (Fig. 7.15) and the modeled stutter proportions are much lower at 0.067 and 0.049 for H_d and H_p, respectively. The log likelihood values are much greater in the combined stutter/degradation model compared to the stutter model only (-343.7 vs -367.9 for H_d), which indicates that the combined model provides the best explanation of the data, and this would consequently be reported in casework (see Chapter 8.5.6 for a detailed description of how to infer best model fits to data using log likelihoods).

7.9.5 Using a spreadsheet model to illustrate stutter

In Excel workbook "StutterAndDegradation", there is spreadsheet to demonstrate the stutter model called "Stutter". Here only a single locus (D13S317) is evaluated from the same example analyzed in the previous section. The analysis with *EuroForMix* with stutter is shown in Figs. 7.13 and 7.15. The D13S317 alleles in the crime stain are 11,12,13, and this scheme emulates the pattern illustrated in Fig. 7.10, where $A = 11$; $B = 12$; $C = 13$, and allele $Z = 10$; the latter is stutter that is below the 50 RFU threshold and has therefore dropped out in the example (Table 7.30).

The propositions are H_p: $S + U$; H_d: $U + U$, where the suspect is type $BC = 12, 13$.

The spreadsheet model is essentially the same as previously described for the basic gamma model described in Section 7.6, except that an additional allele Z is added to account for stutter from allele A, and the peak height expectations are adjusted according to the stutter proportion ϵ and M_x, as shown in Table 7.29. As allele/stutter Z is below the limit of detection, it has dropped out, hence the weightings are calculated in the same way as for the Q allele (Table 7.31).

The quantitative (continuous) model theory 227

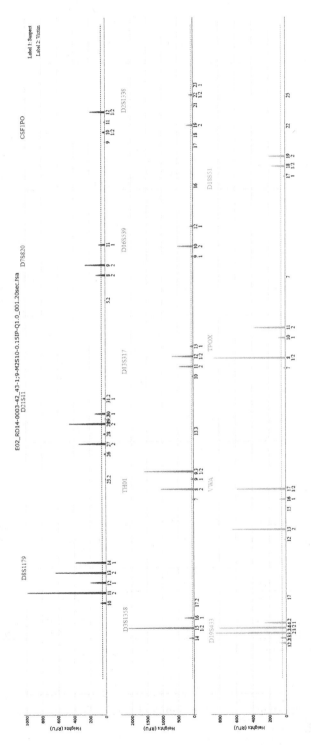

Figure 7.12 EPG for Stutter profile. For clarity, only three dye-panels are shown.

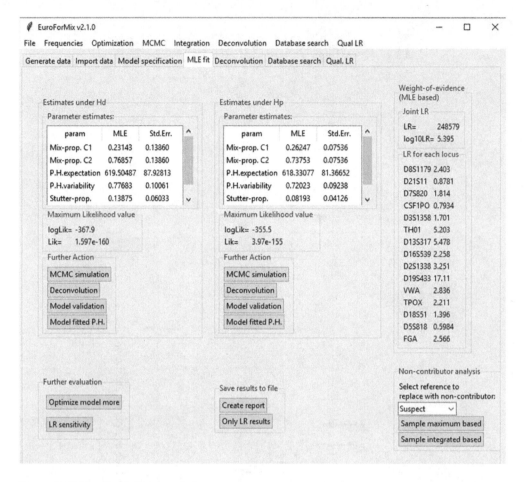

Figure 7.13 Results of stutter analysis.

Table 7.30 Spreadsheet details of locus D13S317 showing allele designations, peak heights, proportions, frequencies, and sizes in base pairs. Allele Z is pure stutter that has dropped out.

Allele Designation	Height	proportion peak height	allele	frequency	Size bp
A	448	0.368	11.000	0.29904219	229.650
B	674	0.553	12.000	0.28467507	233.650
C	97	0.080	13.000	0.10741998	237.650
z	0	0.000	Q	0.30886276	249.65
sum	1219				

To calculate the effect of stutter and degradation together, the ϵ and τ parameters are both included in the shape parameter, hence Table 7.29 is modified accordingly, as shown in Table 7.32.

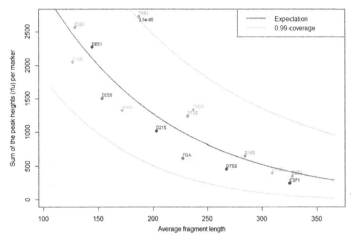

Figure 7.14 Regression analysis of Stutter profile, showing degradation of high molecular weight alleles.

Taking genotype AB, CQ as an example. Alleles Z, A, B, C are separated by 4 base pairs each (Fig. 7.10):
1. For stutter/allele Z
   a. The stutter portion of allele A contributing to allele Z is $M_x \epsilon$.
   b. The peak height of allele A is affected by degradation, which reduces the amount available to stutter. The degradation term used to define the peak height expectation is the same as described in step 7 in Section 7.8. $\tau^{(x_A-125)/100}$, where x_A is the fragment length for allele A.
   c. Each stutter term is multiplied by the degradation term so that the shape formula for allele/stutter Z is

$$\frac{M_x \epsilon \times \tau^{(x_A-125)/100}}{\omega^2}$$

2. For allele A
   a. The stutter portion of allele A that is lost, reducing its peak height, is $M_x(1-\epsilon)$.
   b. The peak height of allele A is affected by degradation. The term used to define the peak height expectation is $\tau^{(x_A-125)/100}$, where x_A is the fragment length in bp of allele A.
   c. In addition, allele A receives a portion from allele B, and this is defined by the term $M_x \epsilon$;
   d. Allele B is affected by degradation so the expected peak height is adjusted: $\tau^{(x_B-125)/100}$.

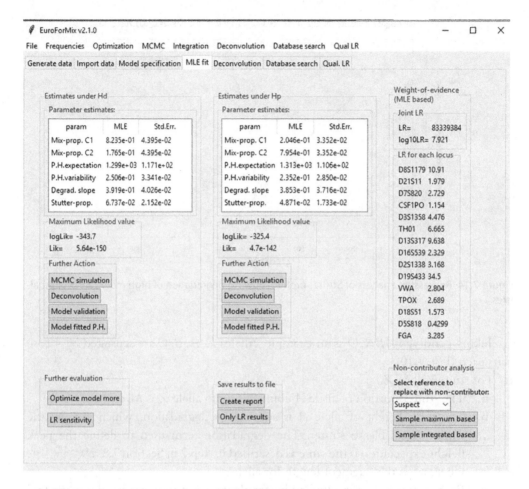

Figure 7.15 Running the model with stutter and degradation modules switched on.

e. Each stutter term is multiplied by a degradation term so that the shape formula for allele A is

$$\frac{\overbrace{M_x(1-\epsilon)}^{\text{Stutter reduction of }A} \times \overbrace{\tau^{(x_A-125)/100}}^{\text{Degradation of }A} + \overbrace{\widetilde{M_x\epsilon}}^{\text{Stutter gain from }B} \times \overbrace{\tau^{(x_B-125)/100}}^{\text{Degradation of }B}}{\omega^2}$$

3. For allele C
   a. Allele C does not receive a stutter contribution from any allele, hence it can only lose peak height.
   b. The amount lost by stutter is $(1 - M_x)\epsilon$.
   c. The peak height expectation, because of degradation is $\tau^{(x_C-125)/100}$.

Table 7.31 The gamma model weightings showing incorporation of the stutter model. The lower table shows the numerators for the shape parameters under H_d, and the formulae are shown in Table 7.29. The suspect genotype is BC; the four possible genotype combinations, including the unknown, are outlined in green (medium grey in print version).

Genotype	z	weightings A	B	C	Q	combined weights	Pr(g|Hd)	Product Hd
AB,CQ	9.18E-01	3.116335E-04	1.885757E-04	1.900794E-03	6.234838E-02	6.396E-12	0.011297764	7.226E-14
AC,BQ	9.18E-01	4.221562E-04	5.162517E-04	1.883216E-03	6.234838E-02	2.350E-11	0.011297764	2.655E-13
AQ,BC	9.18E-01	4.221562E-04	5.744121E-04	1.900794E-03	5.018677E-01	2.124E-10	0.011297764	2.400E-12
BC,AQ	7.43E-01	8.887438E-04	1.323582E-04	1.883216E-03	6.234838E-02	1.027E-11	0.011297764	1.160E-13
BQ,AC	7.43E-01	8.887438E-04	1.885757E-04	1.900794E-03	5.018677E-01	1.188E-10	0.011297764	1.342E-12
CQ,AB	7.43E-01	9.402272E-04	5.162517E-04	1.883216E-03	5.018677E-01	3.410E-10	0.011297764	3.852E-12
AA,BC	8.40E-01	6.966230E-04	5.744121E-04	1.900794E-03		6.39E-10	0.005206506	3.50E-12
BB,AC	7.43E-01	9.127110E-04	3.561219E-04	1.900794E-03		4.59E-10	0.005206506	2.39E-12
CC,AB	7.43E-01	9.402272E-04	5.418221E-04	2.389611E-03		9.05E-10	0.001964636	1.78E-12
AB,AC	6.75E-01	9.938131E-04	1.885757E-04	1.900794E-03		2.40E-10	0.0109	2.63E-12
BC,AC	7.43E-01	8.887438E-04	2.142356E-04	1.308678E-03		1.85E-10	0.003929271	7.28E-13
AB,BC	9.18E-01	4.692893E-04	7.040171E-04	1.900794E-03		5.77E-10	0.010413013	6.01E-12
BC,AA	5.33E-01	8.940783E-04	1.323582E-04	1.883216E-03		1.19E-10	0.005469271	6.49E-13
AC,BB	9.18E-01	5.753388E-04	8.128809E-04	1.883216E-03		8.09E-10	0.005206506	4.21E-12
AB,CC	9.18E-01	3.116335E-04	2.762362E-04	3.754288E-04		2.97E-11	0.001964636	5.83E-14
AC,AB	6.75E-01	1.006941E-03	5.162517E-04	1.883216E-03		6.61E-10	0.010938542	7.22E-12
AC,BC	9.18E-01	4.221562E-04	5.980690E-04	1.308678E-03		3.03E-10	0.003929271	1.19E-12
BC,AB	7.43E-01	9.579041E-04	6.606599E-04	1.883216E-03		8.86E-10	0.010413013	9.22E-12
						Sum	0.143629062	4.763E-11

omega	0.777
mu	6.195E+02

Numerator of scale parameter when stutter is incorporated into gamma model

Genotype	z	A	B	C	Q
AB,CQ	0.032	0.231	0.306	0.662	0.769
AC,BQ	0.032	0.306	0.694	0.199	0.769
AQ,BC	0.032	0.306	0.769	0.662	0.231
BC,AQ	0.107	0.694	0.231	0.199	0.769
BQ,AC	0.107	0.694	0.306	0.662	0.231
CQ,AB	0.107	0.769	0.694	0.199	0.231
AA,BC	0.064	0.505	0.769	0.662	
BB,AC	0.107	0.726	0.505	0.662	
CC,AB	0.107	0.769	0.726	0.399	
AB,AC	0.139	0.893	0.306	0.662	
BC,AC	0.107	0.694	0.338	0.861	
AB,BC	0.032	0.338	0.968	0.662	
BC,AA	0.213	1.356	0.231	0.199	
AC,BB	0.032	0.413	1.356	0.199	
AB,CC	0.032	0.231	0.413	1.324	
AC,AB	0.139	0.968	0.694	0.199	
AC,BC	0.032	0.306	0.801	0.861	
BC,AB	0.107	0.801	0.893	0.199	

0.035

d. The shape parameter for allele C is

$$\frac{(1 - M_x)\epsilon \times \tau^{(x_C - 125)/100}}{\omega^2}$$

4. Stutter is not considered in allele Q, because it is inconsequential. Consequently, the shape argument is only adjusted for degradation, as previously described in Section 7.8:

$$\frac{(1 - M_x) \times \tau^{(x_C - 125)/100}}{\omega^2}$$

All shape formulae can be elucidated following the rules outlined above. An abbreviated tabulated derivation is shown in Table 7.32. A complete example is provided in spreadsheet "Stutter" in the "StutterAndDegradation" folder, where the reader can

Table 7.32 A portion of the formulae used to calculate the numerator of the shape parameter for the stutter allele Z and alleles A and C only, when both stutter and degradation are taken into account together. Each stutter term $M_x\epsilon$ is multiplied by a degradation term $\tau^{\frac{x_A-125}{100}}$, where x_A is the peak height for allele A. These formulae are reproduced in the Excel spreadsheet "StutterAndDegradation">"Stutter" in the Weightings columns.

Genotype	Z	A	C
AB, CQ	$M_x\epsilon\tau^{\frac{x_A-125}{100}}$	$M_x(1-\epsilon)\tau^{\frac{x_A-125}{100}}+M_x\epsilon\tau^{\frac{x_B-125}{100}}$	$(1-M_x)(1-\epsilon)\tau^{\frac{x_C-125}{100}}$
AC, BQ	$M_x\epsilon\tau^{\frac{x_A-125}{100}}$	$M_x(1-\epsilon)\tau^{\frac{x_A-125}{100}}+(1-M_x)\epsilon\tau^{\frac{x_B-125}{100}}$	$M_x(1-\epsilon)\tau^{\frac{x_C-125}{100}}$
AQ, BC	$M_x\epsilon\tau^{\frac{x_A-125}{100}}$	$M_x(1-\epsilon)\tau^{\frac{x_A-125}{100}}+(1-M_x)\epsilon\tau^{\frac{x_B-125}{100}}$	$(1-M_x)(1-\epsilon)\tau^{\frac{x_C-125}{100}}$
BC, AQ	$(1-M_x)\epsilon\tau^{\frac{x_A-125}{100}}$	$(1-M_x)(1-\epsilon)\tau^{\frac{x_A-125}{100}}+M_x\epsilon\tau^{\frac{x_B-125}{100}}$	$M_x(1-\epsilon)\tau^{\frac{x_C-125}{100}}$
BQ, AC	$(1-M_x)\epsilon\tau^{\frac{x_A-125}{100}}$	$(1-M_x)(1-\epsilon)\tau^{\frac{x_A-125}{100}}+M_x\epsilon\tau^{\frac{x_B-125}{100}}$	$(1-M_x)(1-\epsilon)\tau^{\frac{x_C-125}{100}}$
CQ, AB	$(1-M_x)\epsilon\tau^{\frac{x_A-125}{100}}$	$(1-M_x)(1-\epsilon)\tau^{\frac{x_A-125}{100}}+(1-M_x)\epsilon\tau^{\frac{x_B-125}{100}}$	$M_x(1-\epsilon)\tau^{\frac{x_C-125}{100}}$

follow the gamma model, incorporating stutter and degradation for all genotype combinations.

The combined weightings are calculated in exactly the same way as described for the gamma model—by multiplying together the individual weightings; then the "Product Hd" values are calculated by multiplying the "combined weights" with $Pr(g|H_d)$. The sum of the "Product Hd" values form the maximum likelihood estimation values, shown in Table 7.33. The H_p products are similarly generated using the same protocol previously described (Section 7.6.1). The user can copy/paste parameters calculated using *EuroForMix* into the "Input Parameter" field in the spreadsheet to generate likelihood ratios for the "Regression and stutter" model and the "Stutter" model only. Note that the spreadsheet accommodates both models. To "switch off" the degradation model, the *tau* parameter is set to one, so that the model only evaluates stutter if this is done.

There are large differences between the two models. The "Stutter only" model optimizes the stutter parameter (epsilon) as 0.08 under H_p and 0.14 under H_d, compared with 0.05 and 0.068 for the "Stutter and degradation" model. Likelihood ratios are different: 5.51 for the "Stutter only" model and 9.73 for the "Stutter and degradation" model. The sample is highly degraded (Fig. 7.14), so there is an expectation that degradation would provide a better model.

The "best" model is indicated by the log likelihood values, from the *EuroForMix* model, where all the loci are analyzed. Under H_d, the values are −343.7 and −367.9 for the "Stutter and degradation" and "Stutter only" models, respectively (Figs. 7.13 and 7.15). The largest value indicates that the former is preferred. Model selection is covered in detail in the next chapter, Chapter 8.5.6.

The spreadsheet model evaluates a single locus D13S317. The "Hd products"= 9.95e-11 and 4.76e-11, respectively, for the "Stutter and degradation" model vs. the

Table 7.33 Spreadsheet "StutterAndDegradation" > "Stutter", showing the input parameters, which are used to calculate the weights of locus D13S317 shown in Table 7.31. The complete model with all loci is run in *EuroForMix*, and the parameters have been stored in the spreadsheet for the "Stutter and degradation" model, along with the "Stutter" model only. The user copy/pastes the relevant data into the input parameter field and this produces the maximum likelihood calculation. In the table, the H_p parameters for the "Stutter only" model are shown as an example. But this must be repeated with the H_d parameters to produce the "Hd products". Copy/paste the relevant values into the "Hp/Hd products" fields to calculate the likelihood ratio, which is compared to that achieved by *EuroForMix*.

These parameters are copied and pasted from the EuroForMix results

INPUT		Degradation and stutter		Stutter only	
PARAMETERS		Hp	Hd	Hp	Hd
Mx	0.2625	0.2046	0.1765	0.2625	0.2314
omega	0.7375	0.2352	0.2506	0.7375	0.7768
mu	618.3311	1313.0000	1299.0810	618.3311	619.5048
tau	1.0000	0.3853	0.3919	1.0000	1.0000
epsilon	0.0819	0.0487	0.0674	0.0819	0.1388

Copy and paste the value

Maximum likelihood calculations				St + deg	St no deg
Hp products	2.626E-10		**Hp products**	9.68E-10	2.63E-10
Hd products	6.0004E-11		**Hd products**	9.95E-11	4.76E-11
			LR	9.73E+00	5.51E+00
			EFM LR	9.64E+00	5.48E+00

"Stutter only" model. If these values are compared with those of the *EuroForMix* model for D13S317 only, the values are 1.01e-10 and 5.75e-11, respectively. There are small differences in *LR* values between the spreadsheet and EFM models (Table 7.33). These differences in the calculations are explained by the list of genotypes analyzed. In the spreadsheet, there are 18 alternatives given in Table 7.31. Each alternative genotype combination contains one or more of each allele A, B, C. However, *EuroForMix* also considers other options, because it is possible under the defense proposition that allele A is a pure stutter of allele B, or allele B is a pure stutter of allele C. These options are very unlikely, because the peak heights of D13S317 are too great to be stutter. Nevertheless, within the context of the probabilistic model, there is a finite, albeit small probability, that for an option such as $A, A; A, C$ if B is pure stutter, or $B, C; C, C$ if A is pure stutter. Each alternative genotype combination must have allele C present, because it cannot be explained by stutter.

Consequently, there are 38 extra alternative genotype combinations that are not considered by the spreadsheet model. Summation of the weights shows that the impact is small (sum of weights = 1.22e-12 and 9.86e-12 for the "Stutter and degradation" and

"Stutter" only models), but is sufficient to explain the small differences in likelihood ratios that were observed in Table 7.33.

7.9.6 Dealing with forward and complex stutters

Exactly the same rationale can be applied to forward $n+1$ and "complex" stutters defined here as any stutter other than forward or backward stutters, e.g., $n-2$ (double backward-stutter). Version 3.0.0 onwards of EuroForMix has the capability to deal with forward stutter. Each kind of stutter will require a different ϵ value, which could in turn be subdivided per locus. However, this would require very extensive parameterization of the model, which has some disadvantages that are pointed out by You and Balding [233], who compared two computer programs: *LikeLTD* with *EuroForMix*. The former is able to include backward-stutter, forward-stutter, and $n-2$ (double backward-stutter). Although this has an advantage when the person of interest contribution is very small, the computation speed becomes greatly compromized. Any advantage is therefore restricted to very low level profiles, with a lot of drop-out. There are inevitable questions concerning whether such profiles should be interpreted in the first place (ISFG DNA commission recommendation 8 [34][8]). Our opinion is to always keep the model simple: do not overparameterize, but at the same time, ensure that the model is adequate and fit for purpose; remember that the model is not a replacement for expert opinion and common sense. Neither does it negate the need to optimize the biochemistry (reextraction and reanalysis) to ensure that signals are sufficient to interpret.

7.9.6.1 An example calculation using backward and forward stutter

This final example follows on from the previous one explained in Section 7.9.5. The allelic arrangement follows Fig. 7.10, except that an additional allele $+4$ bp $>$ allele C would be required to explain forward stutter. As before, we evaluate genotype AB, CQ, and only the derivation of allele B stutters are described. Note that two epsilon (stutter) parameters are now required, one to describe backward-stutter ϵ and one for forward-stutter ϵ'.

1. The backward-stutter portion of allele B that is lost, reducing its peak height is $M_x(1-\epsilon)$.
2. The forward-stutter portion of allele B that is lost, reducing its peak height is $M_x(1-\epsilon')$.
3. In addition, allele B receives a portion of backward-stutter from allele C, and this is defined by the term $(1-M_x)\epsilon$.
4. Allele B also receives a proportion of forward-stutter from allele A, and this is $M_x\epsilon$.
5. Allele B is affected by degradation, so the expected peak height is adjusted: $\tau^{(x_B-125)/100}$, where x_B is the fragment length in bp of allele B.
6. Each stutter term is multiplied by a degradation term so that the shape argument for allele B is derived:

The quantitative (continuous) model theory   235

Backward-stutter numerator terms:

$$\underbrace{M_x(1-\epsilon)}_{\text{Stutter reduction of } B} \times \underbrace{\tau^{(x_B-125)/100}}_{\text{Degradation of } B} + \underbrace{M_x\epsilon}_{\text{Stutter gain from } C} \times \underbrace{\tau^{(x_C-125)/100}}_{\text{Degradation of } C}$$

Forward-stutter numerator terms:

$$\underbrace{M_x(1-\epsilon')}_{\text{Stutter reduction of } B} \times \underbrace{\tau^{(x_B-125)/100}}_{\text{Degradation of } B} + \underbrace{M_x\epsilon'}_{\text{Stutter gain from } A} \times \underbrace{\tau^{(x_A-125)/100}}_{\text{Degradation of } A}$$

so the shape argument numerator is a summation of the above terms, divided by the peak height variability parameter ω^2:

$$\text{Shape argument} = \frac{\text{Backward-stutter terms} + \text{Forward-Stutter terms}}{\omega^2}$$

7. Expansion to other complex stutters such as $n-2$ can be accomplished within the framework described above, but each new stutter moiety requires a different stutter ϵ parameter to optimize.

7.10. The drop-in model

Drop-in theory was described in Chapter 4.2. For *LRmix Studio*, only the absolute number of drop-in events were used to inform the model. The formula is

$$p_C = \frac{n}{N \times L} \tag{7.27}$$

where p_C is probability of drop-in; n is number of observed drop-in events; L is number of loci, N is number of negative control samples, each consisting of L loci.

An exponential distribution is assumed, starting from AT RFU, as a model for all allele drop-in peak heights (similar to Taylor et al. [60]):

$$f(y|\lambda, AT) = \lambda \times \exp^{-\lambda(y-AT)} \tag{7.28}$$

The λ parameter measures the steepness of the curve, and this was used as a plug-in value to model the drop-in peak height:

$$\lambda = \frac{n}{\sum_i(y_i - AT)} \tag{7.29}$$

where AT is the analytical threshold; y_i is the peak height of the ith drop-in event, being above AT; n is number of peak heights above AT (the number of drop-in events).

7.10.1 Estimating lambda using *EuroForMix*

The lambda parameter can be estimated directly from *EuroForMix* from the "Import Data" > "Fit drop-in data" button. The peak height data are presented in a .csv file, and the output shown in Fig. 7.16 is produced.

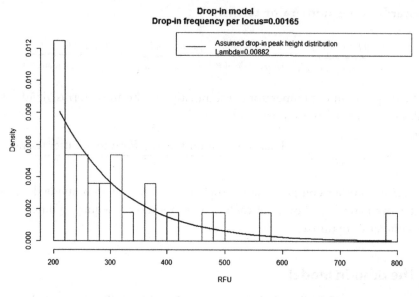

Figure 7.16 Drop model for ESX17 data showing calculation of λ. Peak height data in the .csv file are 208, 252, 330, 200, 379, 202, 240, 488, 226, 312, 318, 271, 577, 208, 795, 220, 250, 413, 245, 286, 238, 273, 367, 306, 291, 217, 202, 461. The data were collected using the Promega ESX17 multiplex analyzed with the AB 3500 instrument.

7.10.2 Characterization of drop-in

The majority of drop-in events are low in peak height. This means that it is much more likely that large peaks are drop-in events (therefore more likely to be alleles from an actual contributor). Hence, a drop-in event at 600 RFU will be very heavily penalized compared to a drop-in event at 200 RFU.

Drop-in only makes a difference to a calculation if the conditioning demands that it is used. Typically, this will happen if the number of contributors is under-estimated. For example, consider a single locus in a DNA profile: under H_p, there is a known genotype AB and suspect CD; the crime stain is A, B, C, D. Two contributors are modeled. There is no need to postulate drop-in, because all alleles in the crime stain are accommodated by the conditioned individuals comprising two contributors. Now, keeping the conditioned references the same, consider crime-stain genotype A, B, C, E. It is no longer possible to explain the crime stain with the two contributors using the same H_p conditioning: the suspect D allele is missing and has dropped-out; allele E in the crime stain must be a drop-in event therefore, and H_p is penalized accordingly. Note that the need to invoke drop-in is circumvented if an additional contributor is included (three instead of two). If this is carried out, the H_p conditioning is based on the suspect, known, unknown individuals, respectively. It is never a good idea to invoke too many drop-in events per DNA profile. The limitation can be assessed with fitted Poisson distributions of drop-in/ contamination events [121], as discussed in Chapter 4.2.1.

The model for explaining allele a (with peak height y_a and allele frequency p_a) as a drop-in is incorporated by the formula

$$Pr(\text{Drop-in of allele } a) = p_C \times p_a \times \lambda \times e^{-\lambda(y_a - AT)}, \tag{7.30}$$

or $(1 - p_C)$ if there were no drop-in.

7.11. Summary

The quantitative (continuous) model incorporates allele peak height information. This chapter describes the early development of the theory, beginning with the "Clayton" guidelines [94] which were empirical, taking into account heterozygote balance to distinguish major/minor contributors of mixtures. The mixture proportion (M_x) is an important concept that is used to estimate the expected allele peak heights strictly conditioned upon a genotype, thereby enabling a ranking of the "best fit" of the evidence conditioned upon given genotypes. This method is encoded into a spreadsheet "MasterMix" [229], but is limited to two individuals; furthermore there is no probabilistic model associated with the calculations, hence it too is empirically based.

Nevertheless, the key elements were in place to develop the first probabilistic model using the assumption that the M_x residuals (i.e., the square of observed - expected allele peak heights) were normally distributed [230]. The residuals are converted into probabilistic "weights" that are then applied to each conditioned genotype from a fully inclusive list of possible options. Drop-out is modeled by the allele peak heights (there is no longer a drop-out parameter associated with the qualitative model). These calculations are shown in the Excel workbook "NORMAL_DISTR_ ANALYSIS". The method is easily extended to multiple contributors.

However, the distribution of peak heights do not follow a convenient normal distribution curve, the data are notably skewed. To take account of this, a new model was proposed by Cowell et al. [234] based upon the Gamma distribution, which we use in *EuroForMix*. The model has been adapted to deal with degradation, where the peak heights are affected by their molecular weights; stutters and drop-in are modeled; mixtures can be deconvolved into candidate contributor genotypes ranked in order of their likelihood. The formulae to carry out the calculations are encoded into Excel spreadsheets in workbook "Gamma".

Notes

1. Here only two contributors are assumed and hence this notation of mixture proportion works. In Appendix B we introduce generalized formulae for multiple number of contributors.
2. The RSS values then becomes part of the weightings (see Section 7.3.1).
3. This is equivalent with the maximum likelihood estimation for the normal distribution assumption.
4. Here M_x is fixed to 0.4.
5. We show how to calculate sigma in the next section.
6. 'Solver' is used to find an optimal (maximum or minimum) value for a formula in one cell — called the objective cell — subject to constraints, or limits, on the values of other formula cells on a worksheet.
7. The reparameterization also improves the likelihood optimization.
8. "If the alleles of certain loci in the DNA profile are at a level that is dominated by background noise, then a biostatistical interpretation for these alleles should not be attempted."

CHAPTER 8

EuroForMix

EuroForMix [76] is a continuous (quantitative) model programmed by Øyvind Bleka. It is implemented as the R-package *euroformix* (using the R-language [218]), which is freely available and open-source at www.euroformix.com (compiled windows version) and https://github.com/oyvble/euroformix (source-code). The *EuroForMix* software itself is programmed as a user-friendly interface using the *gWidgets* R-package. The *euroformix* R-package contains several separate R-functions to perform certain kinds of calculations, such as likelihood ratios (both maximum likelihood-based and Bayesian-based), deconvolution and model validation. The R-functions run a C++ script for fast computation of the likelihood function. More information about how to install and teach material is available at the site www.euroformix.com.

8.1. *EuroForMix* theory

EuroForMix implements an extended version of the model proposed by Cowell et al. [235,234], which assumes the peak heights to be gamma distributed with mixture proportions, stutter proportion, peak height mean, and variation as unknown parameters. The extension presented here includes models for allele drop-in, degradation, and sub- population structure. Similar to the method used by *DNAmixtures* [74], *EuroForMix* employs a maximum likelihood approach to handle unknown parameters. In addition, *EuroForMix* also includes a Bayesian framework, where the unknown parameters are "integrated out" (this is called marginalization). The methods of *EuroForMix* differ from *STRmix* [60] and *TrueAllele* [59] in that we compute the "total sum" expression (see Eq. (5.4)) using exact methods without any need for MCMC [71] sampling. However, as an additional optional tool available within *EuroForMix*, the posterior distributions of the unknown parameters can be efficiently explored using MCMC sampling over the parameter space. Appendix B contains a formal description of the statistics used in *EuroForMix*.

8.2. Interpretation using *EuroForMix*

Trace samples are short tandem repeat (STR) allele data with corresponding peak height intensities measured in relative fluorescence units (RFU). The allelic peak heights are proportionate to the quantities that originate from the contributing individuals. An individual has either a homozygous genotype (two identical alleles) or a heterozygous genotype (two different alleles). In an ideal PCR-amplification, the peak heights belonging to a heterozygote genotype are expected to be equal in size, whereas the peak

Forensic Practitioner's Guide to the Interpretation of Complex DNA Profiles
https://doi.org/10.1016/B978-0-12-820562-4.00016-X

height of a homozygote genotype is expected to be twice as large. In reality, these peak heights are stochastic and will vary between PCR-amplifications, as described in Chapter 2. A detection threshold is usually introduced to remove as much background "noise" as possible, without removing alleles that truly originate from contributors. If the amount of DNA is small or influenced by degradation, then an allele may fall below the detection threshold. This event is expressed as allele drop-out (Chapter 3). A backward stutter occurs when an allele sequence of n repeats loses one tandem repeat in the PCR-amplification process, which is then added to the peak height at the $n - 1$ allele position (Fig. 7.10). There are other kinds of stutters that are described in Chapter 2.2, e.g., $n + 1$ (forward stutter) and complex stutters, such as $n - 2$. Not all types of stutter are modeled in *EuroForMix*. There are a number of reasons for this:

- Each additional parameter has a significant effect on computation time.
- Stutters other than $n - 1$ are low-level; alleles from a POI, where the allele peak heights are similar to those of stutters from a major contributor are low level, usually with drop-out—many such profiles will not be reported, being close to baseline noise.
- Forward and complex stutters can be removed by employing a stutter filter, as described in Chapter 2.2, but caution is required if the POI is at the same level in terms of peak height, since both probative and non-probative alleles will be removed, which may adversely affect the interpretation.

Note that version 3 of *EuroForMix* now has the capability to model $n + 1$ forward stutter.

8.3. Theoretical considerations

Our aim is to quantify the weight-of-evidence if a POI is a contributor to a crime-scene DNA profile E. As described in Chapter 1.6, two alternative propositions are specified, where H_p is the prosecution proposition, and H_d is the defense proposition. A probabilistic model is specified, which gives the probability of observing evidence E, given that proposition H is true, $Pr(E|H)$. The two alternate propositions defined by H_p and H_d are compared via the likelihood ratio (LR):

$$LR = \frac{Pr(E|H_p)}{Pr(E|H_d)} \tag{8.1}$$

The LR evaluates how many times more likely it is to observe the evidence, given that H_p is true, compared to the alternative that H_d is true.

8.4. Model features

The model supports the following:

- Multiple contributors
  - Can condition on any number of reference profiles
  - Can specify any number of unknown individuals (practical limit is 4)
- Extensions
  - Allele drop-out (Chapter 7.6)
  - Allele drop-in (Chapter 7.10)
  - $n - 1$ stutter (Chapter 7.9)
  - Degradation (Chapter 7.8)
  - Sub-population structure (F_{st}/θ-correction) (Chapter 5.5.2)
  - $n + 1$ stutter (new from version 3.0.0)
- Replicated samples
  - Replicates can be analyzed—there is no need to produce a consensus sample
  - The model assumes same contributors and the same peak height properties for each replicate

8.5. An example

An example follows in detail. Before analysis proceeds, it is necessary to consider the case circumstances in detail to construct the alternate propositions that represent the prosecution and defense cases, respectively. The following example was supplied by Lourdes Prieto (University of Santiago de Compostela), and it was used in a laboratory exercise organized by the European Network of Forensic Science Institutes (ENFSI). We choose a relatively simple example here, because the program will run quickly, and this enables new users to rapidly familiarize themselves. More complex examples, e.g., four or more contributors will take much longer to run, but the principles employed are the same throughout.

The examples are provided in increasing order of complexity so that the reader can get used to the various features of the program in a structured way. For the first two exercises, the data have been stutter-filtered, as described in Chapter 2.2. The last exercise includes all data, including stutters, in the DNA profile.

8.5.1 ENFSI exercise 1: a major/minor profile, where the minor component is evidential

8.5.1.1 Circumstances of the case

A man was stabbed in Madrid. An eye witness identified a suspect, and he was apprehended by the police. The suspect denies the offence, and states that he was not in the area at the time. Biological material underneath the nails of the victim was collected during the autopsy. The judge asks the scientist if there is evidence to suggest that the suspect was a contributor to this material.

As a suspect has been found, the scientist acts to *evaluate* the evidence, as outlined in Chapter 12. To do this, he/she must gather as much information as possible about the case so that the alternative propositions can be formulated *before* the results of the test are known (this is to prevent bias; see Chapter 12 for a discussion). Here we consider the evidence at the *sub-source* level—the probative value of the DNA itself. This must not be confused with the evidence at the *activity* level—the assault itself—this is a separate consideration.

The scientist proceeds by putting forward two alternate propositions which are the following:

H_p: DNA from the suspect and victim are present in the crime-sample.
H_d: DNA from an unknown person and the victim are present in the crime-sample.[1]

The next step is to process the sample and analyze the EPG information with *Euro-ForMix*.

Step 1a: Load the data from the book's website https://sites.google.com/view/dnabook/, and launch the settings window from "File>Settings" tab. Input the detection threshold AT, F_{ST}, probability of drop-in in the corresponding boxes (Fig. 8.1). The default drop-in hyperparameter[2] (lambda) accommodates the shape of the drop-in distribution (Chapter 7.10). If lambda is not known, then we generally default to 0.05. However, it is preferable to carry out experiments as described in Chapter 4.2, as the value is often much smaller than this. However, the overall effect on the LR is small (see Appendix E in [236]). If there is no allele that needs to be explained by drop-in, there is very little effect. Leave the "Prior stutter-prop." button alone (For a description of this function see Appendix B.3.12.2). The "Max locus" button is defaulted to 30, and this can also be left alone (unless your kit has more than 30 loci). If the "Easy mode" button is selected, then in subsequent steps the scientist is guided to carry out the MLE method.

Step 1b: Click the "View evidence" button. This prints the allelic data (designations and peak height) in both the R Console (Fig. 8.2) and, provided the "plotly" R-package is installed (see user manual for instructions), it will provide a high resolution graphical representation of the EPG in the browser window. Allele designations and their relative peak heights (Fig. 8.3) are displayed. Underneath the allele designations, alleles that match the contributors 1 and 2 are also shown.

Secondly, a degradation curve is generated (Fig. 8.4), as described in Chapter 7.8. The points in the plot show the sum of the observed peak heights versus the mean fragment lengths of the alleles (per marker). The black line shows the expected peak heights, with the grey lines indicating the 99% coverage intervals of the summed peak heights (i.e., 99% of the summed peak heights are expected to be within the intervals). The purpose is to show if there is evidence of degradation in the crime-stain profile. There is a downward slope showing higher fragment lengths to be smaller, which is characteristic of degradation, hence it is reasonable to take account of this in subsequent LR calculations which follow.

Figure 8.1 Step 1 showing the "Import data" tab and "Settings" option.

8.5.2 Reference samples

Pressing the View references button produces the print-out in the R-console, shown in Fig. 8.5. The alleles of the suspect and victim are shown, along with a list of alleles that match the evidence sample. Homozygotes are scored twice if there is a corresponding allele in the evidence. The "matching allele count" (MAC) is the sum of matching alleles and "nLocs" is the number of loci.

8.5.3 Preliminary assessment of the evidence

All of the victim's alleles are well represented in the evidence profile. All but one of the alleles of the suspect "TPOX 12" are found in the evidence. If the suspect is a contributor, then he would be minor; see alleles "D7S820 11" and "THO1 6" as

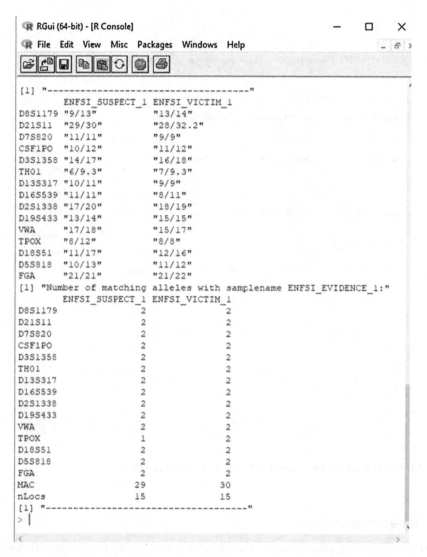

Figure 8.2 Evidence print-out generated in the browser, showing allele designations and peak heights and "matches" with known individuals.

examples. There are no more than four unique alleles at any locus, and this suggests a minimum two-person mixture.

8.5.4 Model specification

Still on the "Import Data" tab, press the "Weight-of-Evidence" button. This reveals the "Model Specification" tab (Fig. 8.6). There is an option to deselect loci using

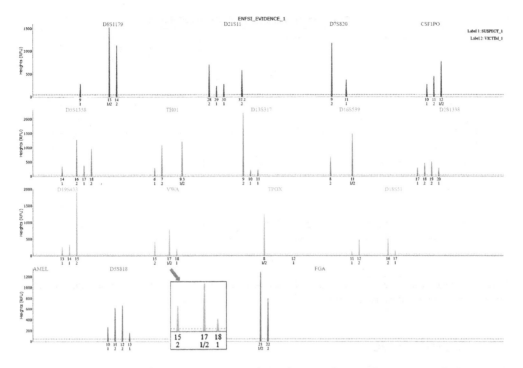

Figure 8.3 EPG generated from step 1: "View evidence" button. The VWA locus is magnified.

tick boxes. The model specification is straightforward. Select the known individuals that are to be conditioned under each proposition. This is achieved using tick boxes. Because the DNA was obtained from underneath the victim's fingernails, he can be conditioned under both H_p and H_d. The inspection of the data suggested a minimum of two contributors, hence there are zero unknown individuals under H_p, and one unknown under H_d (since the suspect cannot appear here). The "Model options" allow the operator to include degradation and/or stutter using a button. In the calculations section, two buttons are "greyed-out", but these are both available for advanced users if the Easy mode is disabled. Press the "Continuous LR" ("Maximum Likelihood based") button to show the "MLE fit" page.

Because the model is a simple two-person mixture, it will only take a few seconds to run. More complex models with more contributors will take longer to run. It will cycle through four optimizations to ensure that the results are reproducible, as described in Appendix B.3.12.

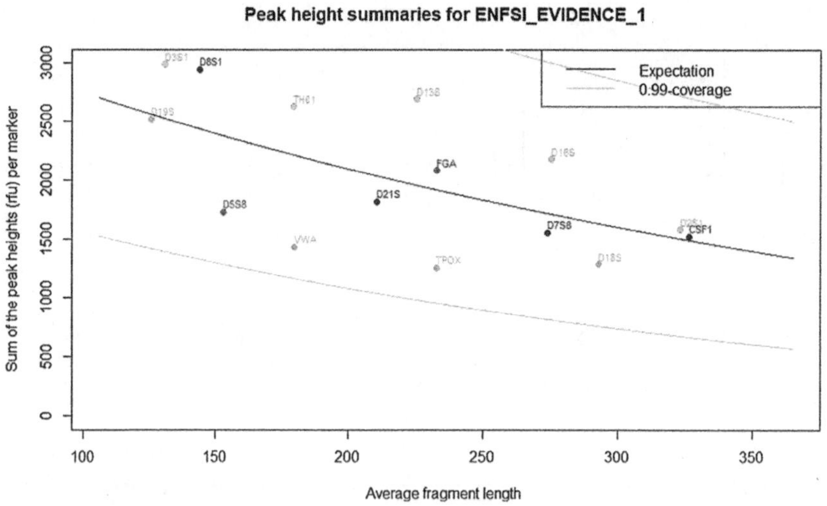

Peak height summaries for ENFSI_EVIDENCE_1

Figure 8.4 Degradation pattern from step 1: View evidence button showing summed peak heights per marker relative to fragment length.

8.5.5 The MLE fit tab

The MLE fit tab (Fig. 8.7) contains all of the results required to interpret the evidence.

Starting with the "Estimates under Hp" section, the boxes show the MLE parameters calculated by the program:

- "Mix-prop. C1": the mixture proportion of the first contributor C1, (parameter M_x)
- "Mix-prop. C2": the mixture proportion of the second contributor C2 (1−parameter M_x)
- "P.H. expectation": the peak height expectation (parameter μ)
- "P.H. variability": the peak height variability (parameter ω)

C1 and C2 are ordered, as described in the "Import data" tab, i.e., C1 = suspect and C2 = victim. The mixture proportions (M_x) are given as 0.26 and 0.74, respectively, confirming that if H_p is true, then the suspect's contribution is minor; the victim's contribution is major.

Under H_d, notice that the only known individual is the victim, hence he is designated as C1 and C2 is unknown. The M_x proportions for the victim and unknown are similar to those described under H_p as 0.73 and 0.27, respectively.

Before we report the results, it is necessary to check that the model is chosen as optimal. Recall that we have not taken account of stutter or degradation yet. Make a note of the maximum likelihood value under H_d (LogLik) = −338.5, and the likelihood ratio $log_{10}LR = 15.38$.

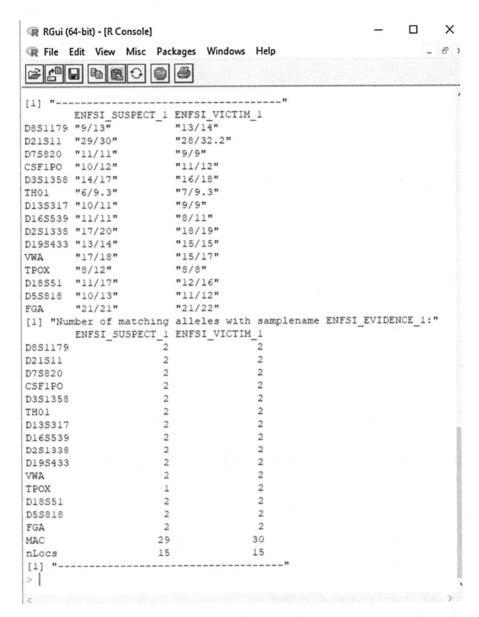

Figure 8.5 Print-out showing the allele designations of the reference samples, along with alleles that match the evidence. MAC = matching allele count, and nLocs = number of loci.

The aim is to determine the model that provides the best fit to the data. We return to the model specification tab and include the "Degradation" option by clicking on the button (Fig. 8.8), and record the results obtained on the MLE fit page (do not forget to press the "Quantitative LR" button to fit a new model). We try out different

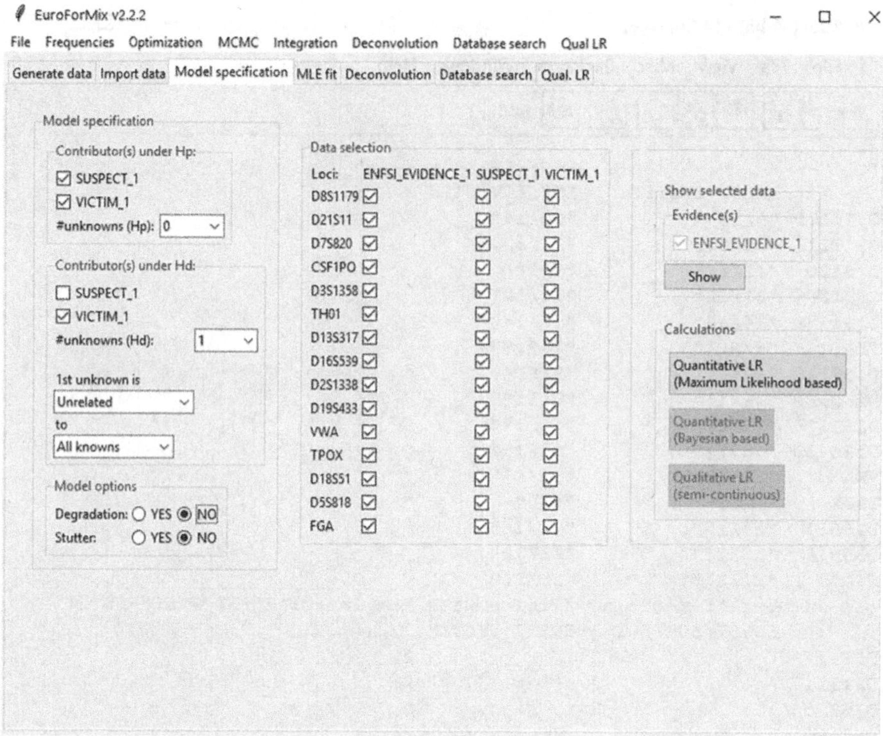

248 Forensic Practitioner's Guide to the Interpretation of Complex DNA Profiles

Figure 8.6 Model specification tab.

models, with and without the degradation/stutter options, record the data generated, and proceed as described in the next section.

8.5.6 Model selection

There are a number of possible models that can be used:
- No stutter versus stutter
- No degradation versus degradation
- No allele drop-in versus allele drop-in
- Changing the number of contributing individuals

We consider a model search strategy, starting with the simplest model. The complexity is increased by adding more parameters to the model. The search for the "best" model stops when it is unlikely that a more complicated model performs better than the one already found.

To choose the final model, we use the "Akaike information criterion" (AIC) [237]. This method favors the simplest model that fits the data best; there is a penalty ap-

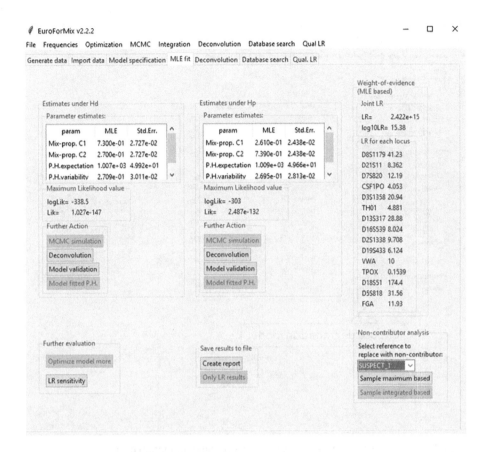

Figure 8.7 Maximum likelihood estimation tab.

plied to avoid "over-parameterization": the simplest model is chosen under H_d—in this case no degradation, no stutter, and two persons. There is a zero penalty for this model. The next model, still with two persons, included degradation without stutter, so a penalty of -1 is applied; the degradation and stutter model requires two penalty points (-2), and so on. If an extra contributor is proposed, then an additional penalty is needed for this. A table is built up and the "Adjusted logLik values" compared (Table 8.1).

In this example, the simplest model to fit the data is found with the selection of two-persons, degradation, and no stutter. Notice that regardless of the model chosen, the $log_{10}LR$s are almost the same. The addition of a new contributor in the three person model has virtually no effect. This is because the third contributor only fits the model if it is at very low level, $M_x = 10^{-10}$ under H_d, and 10^{-8} under H_p. These levels are far too low to detect with any conventional system, hence their contribution to the LR is negligible (Fig. 8.9).

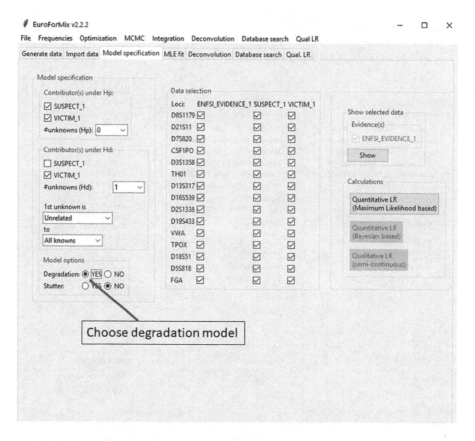

Figure 8.8 Model specification tab showing model selection degradation button.

Table 8.1 The model selection procedure. The simplest model, highlighted in yellow (light grey in print version), is chosen that provides the lowest adjusted LogLik value under H_d. Notice that regardless of the model used, the effect on the likelihood ratio is minimal.

Model with degradation	Model with stutter	LogLik with penalty in brackets	Adjusted LogLik value	$log_{10} LR$
Two persons				
no	no	−338.5	−338.5	15.38
yes	no	−330.8 (−1)	−331.8	15.61
no	yes	−338.5 (−1)	−339.5	15.41
yes	yes	−330.9 (−2)	−332.9	15.63
Three persons				
yes	no	−330.9 (−2)	−332.9	15.63

This also illustrates the point that it is not necessary to know a definitive "number of contributors". Rather, the question is: "What number of contributors optimizes the

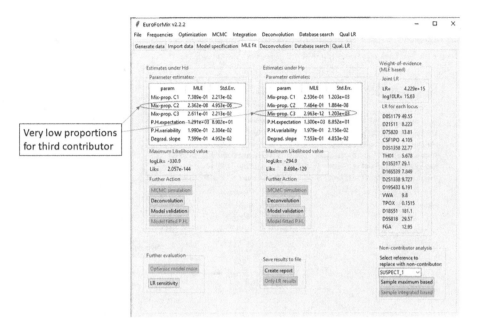

Figure 8.9 Model run under suspect, victim, and unknown under H_p, and victim and two unknown individuals under H_d. Notice the low allele proportions for the minor contributor C2 and C3, respectively, under both propositions.

model". From the ISFG DNA commission recommendations [34], Appendix C, it is not necessary for the number of contributors to be the same under H_p and H_d. The minimum number of contributors is based on the maximum number of alleles at a locus, including those in the conditioned known reference samples, divided by two (Eq. 2.5), as described in Chapters 2.3.2 and 6.2.3.

8.5.7 Model validation

To carry out the next step, ensure that the correct model is defined in the model specification tab and press the "Continuous LR" button. On the MLE fit tab, the "Model validation" buttons are found under "Further Action" sections for both H_p and H_d. Pressing the buttons creates a dialogue box (Fig. 8.10). Set the significance level to 0.01 in the Model validation (Chapter 8.5.8). This generates a plot for H_p, which can be repeated for H_d (Fig. 8.11).

8.5.8 Probability-probability, PP-plots

The PP-plot compares two empirical cumulative distributions of the observed peak heights compared with the theoretical underlying model. If the model is reasonable, then there should be a 45° straight-line relationship. This will never be perfect, because

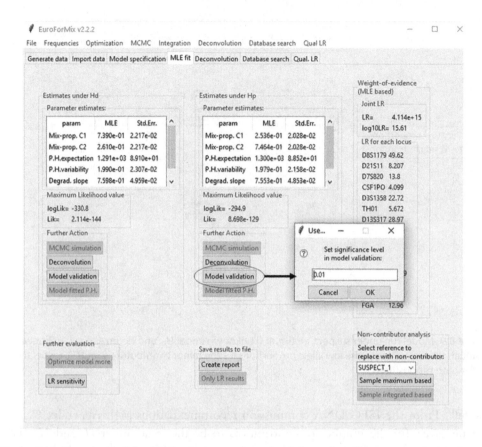

Figure 8.10 Press the Model validation button to show the dialogue box. This generated a PP-plot.

of stochastic variation. To infer whether the underlying peak height model (i.e., the gamma distribution) is adequate for the peak height observations, the observed probability points can be compared with an envelope reflecting some significance level. The quantiles of the distribution are shown as envelopes in Fig. 8.11. The black dashed lines are the 0.005 and 0.095 quantiles (for significance level 0.01), whereas the red dashed lines are the equivalent "Bonferroni-adjusted" quantiles. The Bonferroni-adjusted significance level becomes 0.01 divided by the number of PH observations. Use the red-dashed line as the reference. We do not specify a threshold probability for "acceptance" of a model, however. If significance level 0.05 is used, then this means that one in 20 examples is expected to wrongly "fail" the test. Levels at 0.01 and 0.001 will specify a failed test at one in 100 and 1000, respectively, and these levels may be more appropriate if it is desired to set a practical threshold. If the model validation has values outside the envelope, then check the sample again: perhaps replicates deviate too much in peak height; maybe a large artefact peak is responsible; there may be a high

EuroForMix 253

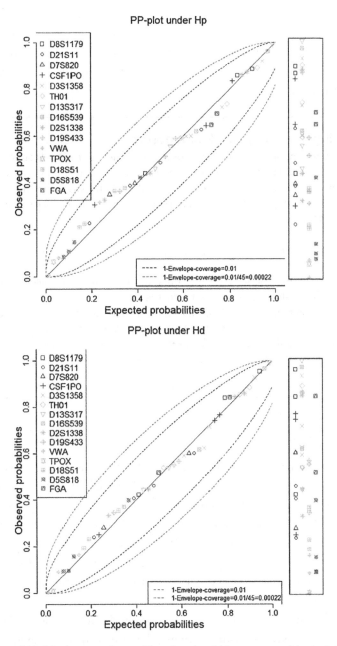

Figure 8.11 H_p and H_d PP-plots are shown. The plot should be a reasonable straight-line fit that is encompassed by the envelope coverage.

allele sharing because of relatives contributing to the mixture. The solution may be to omit replicates in one analysis, or to leave out a locus, which appears to be problematic. If the deviation from the straight line is great (i.e., there are many points outside the envelope), then it may be best not to report the mixture, or alternatively analyze the profile with another model. See Chapter 10.3.5 for further discussions on the role of PP-plots, and their use for decision-making.

Box 8.1 Validation using the PP-plot (formal)

The last step in the model inference procedure is to check whether the fitted continuous model is reasonable for the peak heights above the detection threshold AT (Fig. 8.11). We perform model evaluation under a setting H including both propositions. With $\hat{\beta}$ as the maximized argument under H from Eq. (8.2), the conditional observed cumulative probability for each allele is defined by Cowell et al. [231]:

$$Pr_{m,a}(y_{m,a}) = Pr(Y_{m,a} \leq y_{m,a}|H, \hat{\beta}, \boldsymbol{y}_{(m,-a)}, Y_{m,a} \geq AT) \tag{8.2}$$

Y is a stochastic variable. Here $y_{m,a}$ is the observed peak height for allele a at marker m, and $\boldsymbol{y}_{(m,-a)}$ are the other observed alleles in the same marker, which exceed AT. EuroForMix provides a probability-probability (PP) plot between all the cumulative probabilities $\{Pr_{m,a}(y_{m,a})\}_{y_{m,a} \in \boldsymbol{y}_m}^{m=1,...,M}$ and the standard uniform distribution to check whether the fitted continuous model is a reasonable assumption for the observed peak heights $\boldsymbol{y}_1, ... \boldsymbol{y}_M$. Deviation against this assumption indicates whether the continuous model should be changed or improved.

8.5.9 *LR* sensitivity

The final part of the procedure is to carry out the *LR* sensitivity test as described by Bleka et al. [76]. This button is found on the "MLE fit" tab. It prepares a distribution of *LR*s based upon the errors of the parameters that were estimated to produce the MLE. The method uses Markov chain Monte Carlo (MCMC) simulation, hence two different runs will not yield identical results. The 5% quantile is chosen as a conservative value to report. In this example, the $log_{10}LR = 14.1$, compared to the MLE expectation of 15.76. Results are rounded down to the nearest order of magnitude, hence $log_{10}LR = 14$ is the reported value (Fig. 8.12).

MCMC can be time-consuming. We recommend setting at least 1000 sample iterations from the MCMC drop-down menu, but this can be lowered by the user if necessary for more complex cases. The speed to process a certain number of iterations will be proportional to the number of CPUs in the computer (which are run in parallel).[3]

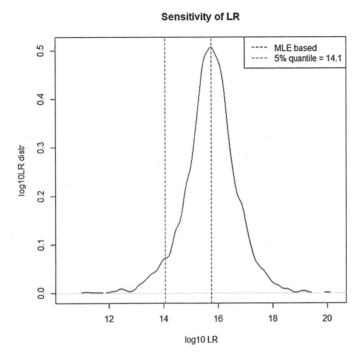

Figure 8.12 Sensitivity analysis using the uncertainty in the parameters to show the distribution of *LR*s. The MLE and 5% quantile are shown.

8.5.10 Model fitted peak height tab

To select the "Model fitted P.H." in the "Further Action" section of the "MLE fit" tab, the user must disable "Easy mode" in the settings dialogue box. This function plots the calculated expected peak heights for contributors and unknown individuals, estimated as the most likely genotype by deconvolution (Section 8.5.12), and superimposes these on top of the EPG as stacked histograms (Fig. 8.13). In the example, the H_p results are illustrated: the suspect contributes $M_x = 0.25$ to the profile and the victim contributes the remainder $(1 - M_x = 0.75)$. A similar plot is provided for the Model fitted P.H. under H_d, where the respective M_x proportions are calculated for an unknown individual rather than for the suspect. If replicates are analyzed, then histograms are plotted side-by-side per replicate. This plot is a useful check of the model to make sure that the individual allele "fits" are reasonable.

8.5.11 Non-contributor analysis

Details of non-contributor analysis are given in Chapter 6.1.6 for *LRmix Studio*. The non-contributor analysis dialogue box is found on the MLE fit tab. There is a drop-down box to select the reference to replace with non-contributors. It is necessary to

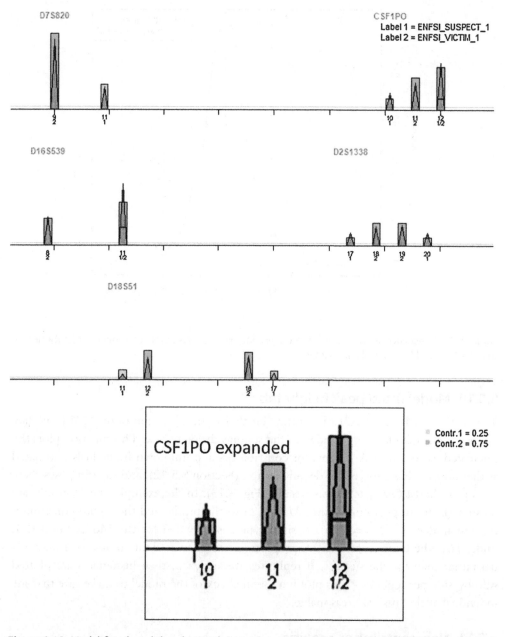

Figure 8.13 Model-fitted peak heights under H_p, showing part of the EPG. CS1PO is expanded to make clear. Allele 12 shows that it is shared by the two conditioned contributors, where the minor is the suspect.

set the number of non-contributors tested by entering a number into the dialogue box under "Database search" > "Set number of non-contributors". Input 10 here to begin, to work out how long it will take to run. Afterwards, adjust the number to something suitable—try to do at least 1000 tests. To carry out the calculation, the "Sample maximum based" button is pressed (if the continuous Bayesian had been earlier specified then the "sample integrated based" method would be chosen). The speed of analysis is faster if F_{ST} is set to zero, otherwise it can be very time-consuming for more complex analyses.

The analysis prints the 0.5, 0.95, 0.99 percentiles, and maximum observations (Fig. 8.14). All values are very low (99 percentile is $log_{10}LR = -15$), which indicates that the model is robust.

```
[1] "100% finished..."
[1] "0.5-quantile=-25"
[1] "0.95-quantile=-19"
[1] "0.99-quantile=-16"
[1] "Max=-13"
[1] "rate(LR>0)=1.0e+00"
[1] "rate(LR>1)=0.0e+00"
[1] "Mean LR=2.8e-16"
[1] "Std LR=6.7e-15"
      0.5    0.95     0.99      Max
-25.14881 -18.84314 -15.74159 -12.68856
>
```

Figure 8.14 Non-contributor analysis showing the results of 1000 simulations, listing 5, 95, 99 percentiles and maximum observations; mean and standard errors of the *LR*, and proportion of *LR* > 0 and 1 are also provided.

8.5.12 Deconvolution

Deconvolution is used to predict the genotype of an "unknown" individual. The theory is described in Chapter 7.7, and the current example is described in Chapter 7.7 using an Excel spreadsheet to explain the statistics. Here we explain how to deconvolve the unknown individual under the defense proposition; the victim is "known". The Deconvolution button is located under "Further Action" on the "MLE fit" tab. This creates the "Deconvolution tab" (Fig. 8.2). There are a number of different ways to visualize the results. The most convenient, illustrated in Fig. 8.2 is the "Top Marginal". There is only one option for the "victim" (C1), because it is conditioned, which is why the probabilities (C1) are all equal to one. The unknown (C2) top genotypes are listed with probabilities < 1. The "ratio to next genotype" is the ratio of the top probability divided by the second highest probability. The larger the number, the greater the certainty. For example, D21S11 genotype 28/32.2 has a ratio of 1291, whereas D7S820 genotype 11/11 is less certain, since the ratio is 4.9.

Selecting the "All Joint" button on the "Deconvolution" tab lists the ranked C1,C2 genotypes (Table 8.3). For example, with D7S820, the second best alternative genotype for C2 is 9/11 ($Pr = 0.1651$). The "All Marginal (G)" button also gives a list of probabilities, per individual contributor, *per genotype*. The "All marginal (A)" button gives a list of probabilities per contributor *per allele* (so the C2 DS7S820 allele 11 has a marginal probability of 0.99, whereas allele 9 has a marginal probability of 0.1652).

In this example, the top genotypes for C2 are correctly deduced. It will not be as clear-cut with more complex examples, however.

8.6. ENFSI exercise 2: illustration of the advantage of using the quantitative model

8.6.1 Case circumstances

A policewoman was raped in a city of Europe and a suspect was detained after a few hours. The pathologist took a sample from the suspect (a penile swab) and sent it to the laboratory for analysis. The judge wants to know if there is evidence to support the proposition that the suspect has raped the policewoman. The defense deny the allegation, countering that he was not in the vicinity at the time of the attack—an unknown perpetrator was responsible.

If the prosecution proposition is correct, then there is an expectation that cells from the policewoman would be recovered from the penile swab (along with those of the suspect). The suspect was detained within the timeframe, where persistence would be expected. He had not bathed or washed in the interim. Reference samples from victim and suspect are available. In this case, we are interested in DNA transfer from victim to suspect, hence the victim is conditioned only under H_p.

The following alternative propositions can be formulated before analysis:

H_p: The victim has contributed to the penile swab.
H_d: The victim has not contributed to the penile swab.

To evaluate the evidence, load the data from the ENFSI exercise 2 folder (Fig. 8.15).

It is clear from the EPG and the recovered genotypes that we are dealing with a minimum two-person mixture, and the alternative propositions to be considered by *EuroForMix* are the following:

H_p: The DNA evidence is a mixture of the suspect and victim.
H_d: The DNA evidence is a mixture of the suspect and an unknown person.

Table 8.2 Deconvolution of the victim (C1) and unknown (C2) contributors under H_d, showing the top marginal results, i.e., the most likely genotypes, given the fitted model. Probabilities of C1 = 1, because we condition on this contributor.

Locus	TopGenotype_C1	probability_C1	ratioToNextGenotype_C1	TopGenotype_C2	probability_C2	ratioToNextGenotype_C2
D8S1179	13/14	1	NA	9/13	0.8768	7.438
D21S11	28/32.2	1	NA	29/30	0.9971	1291
D7S820	9/9	1	NA	11/11	0.8127	4.923
CSF1PO	11/12	1	NA	10/12	0.7404	4.344
D3S1358	16/18	1	NA	14/17	0.9863	162.4
TH01	7/9.3	1	NA	6/9.3	0.7528	3.301
D13S317	9/9	1	NA	10/11	0.9853	134.2
D16S539	8/11	1	NA	11/11	0.9807	81.8
D2S1338	18/19	1	NA	17/20	0.9861	186.8
D19S433	15/15	1	NA	13/14	0.997	616.4
VWA	15/17	1	NA	17/18	0.954	38.62
TPOX	8/8	1	NA	8/8	0.9322	13.75
D18S51	12/16	1	NA	11/17	0.9943	570.4
D5S818	11/12	1	NA	10/13	0.9954	410
FGA	21/22	1	NA	21/21	0.5726	1.534

Table 8.3 Deconvolution of the victim (C1) and unknown (C2) contributors under H_d, showing the "All joint" results, i.e., the most likely genotypes, given the model.

EuroForMix v2.2.2

File Frequencies Optimization MCMC Integration Deconv

Generate data Import data Model specification MLE fit **Deconvo**

Select layout: ○ Top Marginal ⦿ All Joint ○ All Marginal (G

Locus	Rank	C1	C2	
D8S1179	1	13/14	9/13	0.8768
D8S1179	2	13/14	9/14	0.1179
D21S11	1	28/32.2	29/30	0.9971
D7S820	1	9/9	11/11	0.8127
D7S820	2	9/9	9/11	0.1651
D7S820	3	9/9	11/99	0.02217
CSF1PO	1	11/12	10/12	0.7404
CSF1PO	2	11/12	10/10	0.1704
CSF1PO	3	11/12	10/11	0.08103
D3S1358	1	16/18	14/17	0.9863
D3S1358	2	16/18	16/17	0.006073
TH01	1	7/9.3	6/9.3	0.7528
TH01	2	7/9.3	6/7	0.228
TH01	3	7/9.3	6/6	0.01294

Save table

Running through the various analyses discussed in Section 8.5.1, the best model includes degradation without stutter (Fig. 8.16 and Table 8.4). The $log_{10}LR = 11.3$. Once again the model chosen has little effect on the LR; the mixture proportion (M_x) ascertained under H_p is suspect (C1) $M_x = 0.79$ and victim (C2) $M_x = 0.21$ (Fig. 8.16). The victim is a minor contributor to the DNA profile.

Using the conservative method (Section 8.5.9) to calculate the LR, by pressing the LR sensitivity button on the MLE fit tab: $log_{10}LR = 9.9$. If we compare this result with that achieved by *LRmix Studio*, a lower one order of magnitude $log_{10}LR = 8.98$ is obtained.

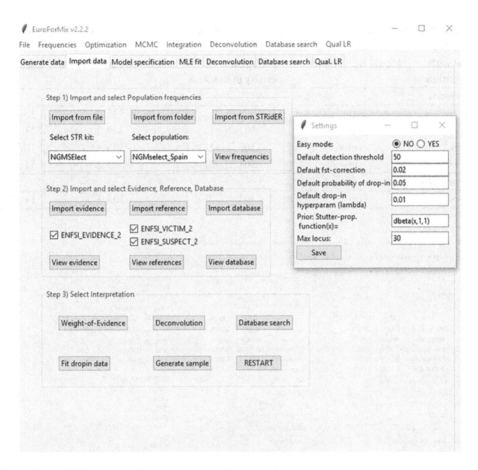

Figure 8.15 "ENFSI exercise 2" samples and settings.

8.6.2 Effect of removing the conditioned suspect from the analysis

We now consider an alternative analysis, where the same data are used, but we now use different propositions to see the effect on the LR:

H_p: The crime stain is a mixture of the victim and an unknown individual.
H_d: The crime stain is a mixture of two unknown individuals.

The suspect is no longer conditioned in the propositions. The *EuroForMix* analysis is carried out as described previously. The MLE $log_{10}LR = 11.06$ and the adjusted conservative $log_{10}LR = 9.61$, which means that the strength of evidence is hardly altered. Compare this with the *LRmix Studio* analysis, using the lowest LR within the most plausible range of drop-out, and the difference is quite marked, as the $log_{10}LR = 0.79$ ($LR = 6.1$), which can be regarded as "weak evidence" using the verbal scale (Table 12.2 in Chapter 12).

Table 8.4 "ENFSI exercise 2" *LR* and LogLik results for different models compared. The best fit model is highlighted.

Model with degradation	Model with stutter	LogLik with penalty in brackets	Adjusted LogLik value	$Log_{10}LR$
Two persons				
no	no	−305.9	−305.9	10.87
yes	no	−301.2(−1)	−302.2	11.28
no	yes	−305.7(−1)	−306.7	10.77
yes	yes	−301.2(−2)	−303.2	11.28
Three persons				
yes	no	−301.3(−2)	−303.3	11.32

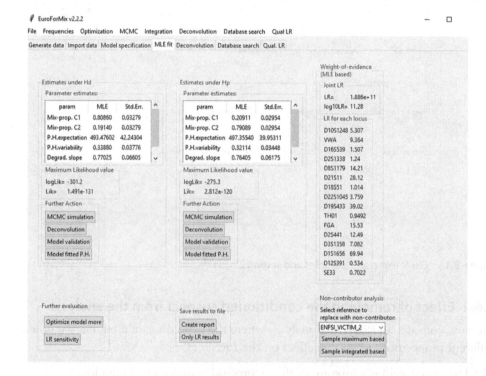

Figure 8.16 "ENFSI exercise 2" *LR* results using the degradation model.

To conclude, conditioning with $H_p : V + S$ vs. $H_d : U + S$ makes little difference whether *EuroForMix* or *LRmix Studio* are used, since the conservative methods give $log_{10}LR > 9$ for both, but there is a marked difference when the conditioning is altered to $H_p : V + U$ vs. $H_d : U + U$. Whereas the *EuroForMix LR* is virtually unaltered, the *LRmix Studio LR* is greatly reduced. We can generalize that minor evidential DNA profiles in major/minor mixtures, where there are unknown contributors in the prosecution (H_p) proposition are best evaluated with a quantitative model (*EuroForMix*) rather than the qualitative *LRmix Studio*.

8.7. A complex case: robbery

8.7.1 Case circumstances

A robbery was committed by two individuals, one of them wore a balaclava during the crime, whereas the accomplice waited outside the premises in a car. An individual R was apprehended, and a balaclava was found in his car. He admits the offence and he provides a reference sample. He implicates individual S, who he says wore the balaclava at the crime scene, although R had also purportedly worn the balaclava at a different crime scene.

Person S is questioned. He denies wearing a balaclava, or being part of the robbery. He provides a reference sample.

The balaclava is a key piece of evidence, which the scientist has been asked to analyze. He has sufficient information to formulate the following alternate propositions:

H_p: Individuals R and S both contributed to the balaclava E.
H_d: Individual R contributed to the balaclava, but suspect S did not.

8.7.2 Analysis

The data are loaded from the "Robber Case Example" folder (from book's website https://sites.google.com/view/dnabook/) and settings applied (Fig. 8.17).

The settings are different to those shown for the previous examples. The kit used was Promega ESX17 and the CE equipment is the AB 3500. This instrument is much more sensitive than its predecessors, and the laboratory applies a detection threshold of 200 RFU. The drop-in parameters are based on actual observations, and the levels are very much lower than those used in the previous exercises: $p_C = 0.00165$ and $\lambda = 0.0082$. This has the effect of severely penalizing likelihood ratios that incorporate drop-in events.

From the EPG (Fig. 8.18), it can be seen that the profile is complex—a minimum of three individuals.

It is useful to get an overview of the allele matches using the *LRmix Studio* gui. All of the known individual (R) alleles match alleles found in the evidence. Around 90% of the suspect's (S) alleles also "match" (Fig. 8.19).

Alleles "D21S11 32.2"; "D16S539 9"; "SE33 20" are dropped out under H_p. The evidence shows a maximum of six distinct alleles in the evidence. Note that taking into account the suspect reference genotype, allele "SE33 20" must be added to the total count, making seven unique alleles. This implies four or more contributors *before* stutter is taken into account. If allele "SE33 24.2" is a stutter product of allele "SE33 25.2", this will imply a minimum of three contributors.

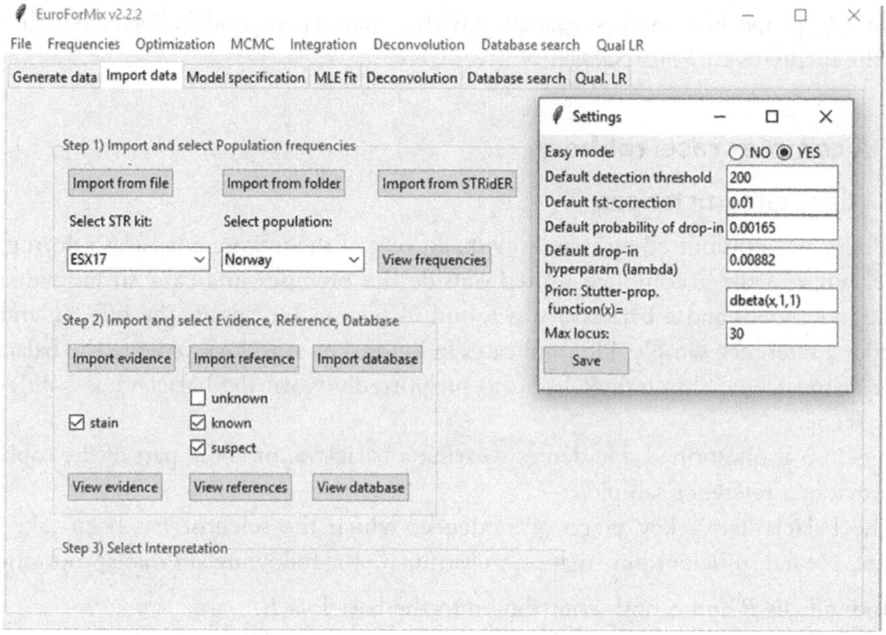

264 Forensic Practitioner's Guide to the Interpretation of Complex DNA Profiles

Figure 8.17 Settings for robber case example.

It is interesting to compare the results with those achieved with *LRmix Studio*. This program does not consider stutter or peak heights. SE33 has six unique alleles in the crime stain. The conditioned propositions H_p include the "known" individual and "suspect", whereas H_d includes only the known. In addition, it is apparent that if H_p is true, that allele "SE33 20" (in red (medium grey in print version) type) in Table 8.5 is missing in the crime stain—so it must have dropped out under this proposition.

If H_d is true, the list of unique alleles is shorter by one, because under this proposition the suspect is replaced by an unknown person, and this individual does not have the SE33 20 allele. The effect is to reduce the minimum number of contributors to three. To summarize, the minimum number of contributors differs between the propositions $H_p = 4$ and $H_d = 3$. Next, the peak heights of the alleles can be examined. Alleles 23.2, 24.2 are in stutter positions. The former is less likely, because its peak height is bigger than allele 24.2, which is in turn smaller than allele 25.2, so allele 24.2 may be attributed to stutter. The peak height proportion is quite high, however, at $229/779 = 0.29$. As the sample is low template, there is an expectation that high-level stutters may occur (stutters are usually < 0.15, the size of the parent allele, but this can be exceeded with low template; Chapter 2.2.4). Alternatively, it may be a combination of allele and stutter. The *EuroForMix* model is run with degradation and stutter options and under $H_d = 3$ contributors (see next section). When the mixture is deconvolved using the All Joint

Table 8.5 Robbery case: list of SE33 alleles and inference under two alternative propositions using *LRmix Studio*.

Conditioning proposition	Alleles in the crime-stain						Alleles in reference profiles		List of unique alleles	Minimum no. of contributors
	1	2	3	4	5	6	Known	Suspect		
H_p	14	18	23.2	24.2	25.2	29	14, 25.2	23.2, 20	14,18,20,23.2,24.2,25.2,29	4
H_d	14	18	23.2	24.2	25.2	29	14, 25.2		14,18,23.2,24.2,25.2,29	3
Peak heights	1312	373	318	229	779	279				

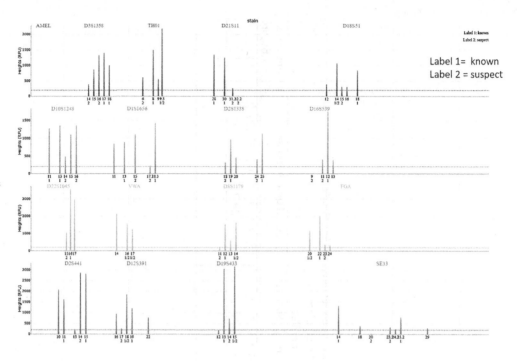

Figure 8.18 Robbery case EPG.

option Table 8.6, then the top ranking genotype for unknown (C2) is 29/99 ("99" is used to signify a drop-out event). The suspect's genotype 23.2/99 is recovered in the second rank. Inspection of the top 20 ranks shows a selection of possible genotypes. Allele 24.2 tends to be classed as a pure stutter in C2 and C3 (in all but four genotypes each).

8.7.3 *EuroForMix* analysis

As described in earlier exercises, a range of models with/without stutter and degradation were run to explore the data. The results for the current exercise are provided in Table 8.7. The "best fit" model was three-persons with stutter and degradation ($log_{10}LR = 7.1$) and the mixture proportions (H_p) were "known" (C1) = 0.52; "suspect" (C2) = 0.015; "unknown" (C3) = 0.33. Hence the suspect, if H_p is true, is a minor contributor to the DNA profile.

Notice that the assumption of four individuals has no effect on the MLE *LR* model with stutter and degradation, with an identical LogLik value, and is not optimum when the AIC correction is made; it also takes a lot longer to run. In addition, the mixture proportion of the second unknown individual "C3" under H_p is extremely low, $M_x = 10^{-8}$; under H_d, $M_x = 10^{-12}$ (Fig. 8.20), hence the mixture proportions of known

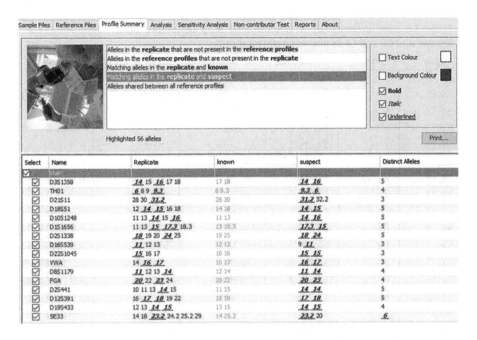

Figure 8.19 Robbery case, showing comparison of suspect with the evidence ("Replicate") alleles.

"C1", suspect "C2" and "C3" are effectively unaltered. There might be four or more contributors to the crime stain, but their levels are so low that they could not realistically be detected in an EPG, hence there is no effect on the *LR* (Fig. 8.20). It would take a long time to run five contributors with this case, but it would make no difference to the *LR*, because we know that additional contributors would be similarly assigned minute mixture proportions.

When stutter is not included in the model, the only way to analyze three contributors is to condition the alleles in stutter positions as drop-in. This penalizes the *LR*, which explains why the LogLik value is higher in the four-contributor test, where stutters are treated as originating from an additional individual. This is reflected in the LogLik values, showing that the four-contributor (without stutter) models perform better than the equivalent three contributor models.

A general guideline follows from this kind of analysis:
- The number of contributors cannot be definitively ascertained: a good model will assign excess contributors with very low M_x values and will minimize the number of drop-in events. It is useful to think in terms of the "effective" number of contributors, which is the smallest number that achieves a stable *LR* calculation. The use of exploratory data analysis shows that it is possible to estimate the optimum number of contributors that provides a "best fit" model measured by the log likelihood value. Adding an additional contributor to the model has very little effect on

268 Forensic Practitioner's Guide to the Interpretation of Complex DNA Profiles

Table 8.6 Joint probabilities of deconvolved SE33 genotypes under H_d showing C1 known, and C2 and C3 as unknown contributors.

Locus	Rank	C1 (known)	C2 (unknown)	C3 (unknown)	Probability
SE33	1	14/25.2	29/99	18/23.2	0.1122
SE33	2	14/25.2	23.2/99	18/29	0.1076
SE33	3	14/25.2	18/99	23.2/29	0.09878
SE33	4	14/25.2	23.2/29	18/99	0.048
SE33	5	14/25.2	23.2/24.2	18/29	0.04729
SE33	6	14/25.2	24.2/29	18/23.2	0.0462
SE33	7	14/25.2	18/29	23.2/99	0.04406
SE33	8	14/25.2	18/23.2	29/99	0.04227
SE33	9	14/25.2	18/24.2	23.2/29	0.04068
SE33	10	14/25.2	23.2/29	18/24.2	0.03187
SE33	11	14/25.2	18/23.2	24.2/29	0.02807
SE33	12	14/25.2	18/29	23.2/24.2	0.02641
SE33	13	14/25.2	29/99	18/24.2	0.0192
SE33	14	14/25.2	24.2/99	18/29	0.01699
SE33	15	14/25.2	18/99	24.2/29	0.01691
SE33	16	14/25.2	14/29	18/23.2	0.01539
SE33	17	14/25.2	25.2/29	18/23.2	0.0152
SE33	18	14/25.2	14/23.2	18/29	0.01476
SE33	19	14/25.2	23.2/25.2	18/29	0.01458
SE33	20	14/25.2	23.2/29	14/18	0.01425

the LR once the optimum is found, because the mixture proportion that is assigned is negligible. Adding other contributors has no effect for the same reason.

Finally the model is tested with the PP-plots (Fig. 8.21) and the conservative 5 percentile LR calculated from the sensitivity analysis as described in Sections 8.5.8 and 8.5.9.

8.8. Relatedness calculations

So far we have only considered likelihood ratio calculations that are conditioned upon individuals being unrelated under H_p and H_d. In Chapter 1.16, it was pointed out that an alternative defense explanation of the evidence may entail a contribution to the crime stain by a sibling (or some other close relative), so instead of the following propositions:

H_p: The DNA is from Mr. S.
H_d: The DNA is from an individual unrelated to Mr. S.

we can consider

H_p: The DNA is from Mr. S.
H_d: The DNA is from a sibling of Mr. S.

Table 8.7 Exploratory data analysis of the robbery case example. K = number of contributors; penalty = the penalty parameter that is added to the *LogLik* to provide the penalty adjusted value. The *log₁₀LR* is the calculated value and the reported *LR* is the "conservative" estimate calculated from the *LR* sensitivity analysis ("MLE fit" tab). The "best-fit" model is highlighted.

| | EuroForMix analysis | | | | | | Conservative $log10LR$ | |
| | | | | | | | | |
K	Stutter	Degradation	Penalty	LogLik	Adjusted LogLik	MLE log10LR	EuroForMix	LRmix Studio
3	no	no	0	−577.7	−577.7	2.62	1.1	−2.85
3	no	yes	−1	−567.3	−568.3	4.45		
3	yes	no	−1	−572.6	−573.6	4.6		
3	yes	yes	−2	−560.7	−562.7	7.1	5.1	
4	no	no	−1	−574.9	−575.9	4.05	2.58	1.62
4	no	yes	−2	−564.3	−566.3	6.52		
4	yes	no	−2	−572.6	−574.6	4.6		
4	yes	yes	−3	−560.7	−563.2	7.1	5.61	
$H_p = 4, H_d = 3$	yes	yes	−2.5	−560.7	−563.2	7.1	5.76	−0.22

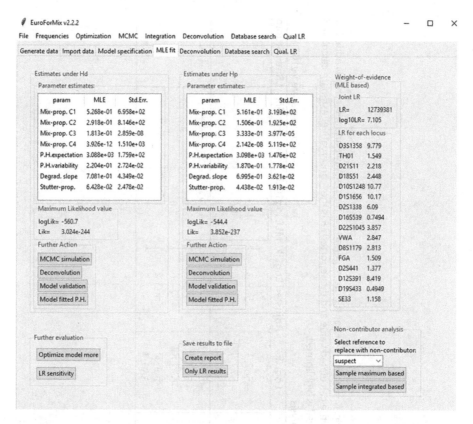

Figure 8.20 Four-person model with stutter and degradation. The unknown individual "C4" peak height proportion $M_x = 10^{-8}$ is at very low level under H_p and for H_d, the $M_x = 10^{-12}$, which is why the impact on the *LR* is negligible.

The likelihood ratio of the latter propositions follows the detailed formulae described in Chapter 5.5.4 for this and all other common kinds of relationships.

To demonstrate use of *EuroForMix* to carry out relatedness calculations, load the files from the "Relatedness" folder from the book's website https://sites.google.com/view/dnabook/. This file contains a laboratory derived sample that is a three-person mixture "6B3.3" using the "PowerPlex Fusion 6C" kit and Dutch database frequencies. This was from a study by Benschop et al. [238] that is discussed further in Chapter 9.10.2. The sample is a mixture of three individuals: "Z", "AA", "AB" (true donors), and there are two simulated brothers of sample AA, namely "B-AA007" and "B-AA038". These samples were deliberately chosen from 100 simulations, because they exhibited high overlap of alleles with the mixture profile, and are therefore more likely to match. The settings used are shown in Fig. 8.22.

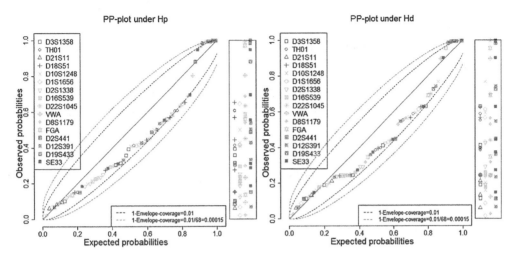

Figure 8.21 PP-plot validation showing 0.01 envelope. A single point falls outside the red-dashed line under H_p (D22S1045 allele 17). This is not sufficient for the model to fail.

The propositions to calculate likelihood ratios covered the whole range of relationships:

H_p: The DNA is from Mr. S and two unknown, unrelated individuals.
H_d: The DNA is from a sibling of Mr. S and two unknown unrelated individuals.

Where
- The unrelated individuals are unrelated to each other and to Mr. S.
- Multiple relationships using the same proposition formulation above were tested (substituting "sibling" under H_d for another relationship listed in Table 8.8).

8.8.1 Results and discussion

Neither of the simulated brothers (AA038 and AA007) were present in the evidence profile, but both were assigned high $log_{10}LR \approx 6$ (Table 8.8) under the H_d "unrelated" proposition. To reiterate, it is unusual for simulated siblings to provide such high likelihood ratios (out of 100 simulations, six examples gave $LR > 100$). This pair was chosen for demonstration purposes. When the samples were tested against parent/child or sibling, the $LR < 1$, which indicated support for the defense proposition of the given level of relatedness; neither the uncle/nephew nor cousin propositions were supported, however. Turning attention to the true contributors, all gave very high *LR*s for the unrelated category, with reduced *LR*s for all levels of relationships tested, i.e., there was no support for the alternative proposition of relatedness with the "true" contributors.

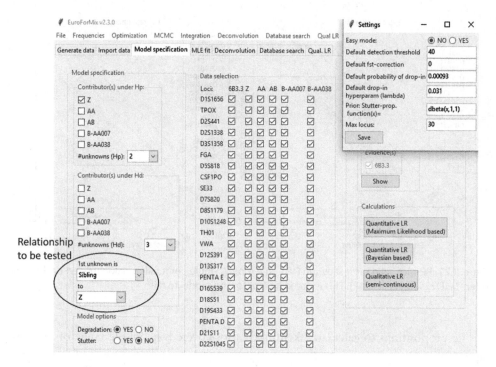

Figure 8.22 Model specification for the relatedness exercise. Data are stutter filtered, hence only the degradation module is utilized.

Table 8.8 Likelihood ratios ($log_{10}LR$) generated for various levels of relationships. Z, AA and AB are true contributors. Mixture proportions (M_x) are shown for H_p. The LRs are calculated by conditioning upon each in turn, using the specified relationship under the defense proposition. There are two samples, AA038 and AA007, which are simulated brothers of sample AA. The Uncle/nephew category includes half-siblings, grandparent/grandchild relationships.

	\multicolumn{3}{c}{Individual tested}		
	\multicolumn{3}{c}{True contributors}	\multicolumn{2}{c}{Simulated siblings}
Sample	Z	AA	AB	AA038	AA007
M_x	0.8	0.09	0.09	0.07	0.061
	\multicolumn{5}{c}{$log_{10}LR$}
Unrelated	32.79	14.07	12.84	6	5.96
Parent/child	17.85	4.86	4.66	−2.77	−0.88
Sibling	10.34	2.84	3.448	−3.48	−1.73
Uncle/nephew	22.53	7.58	7.4	0.95	1.22
Cousin	26.21	9.75	9.31	2.04	2.86

8.9. Important updates to *EuroForMix*

EuroForMix will continue to evolve over time, and important updates will be released in response to users feedback and requirements. The examples discussed in this chapter were processed with version 2.3.1. Version 3.0.0 (and further) will have important added functionalities:

- Faster calculations due to the way that the C++ code utilizes parallelization; causes speed to scale with the number of CPU cores (Table 8.9).

Table 8.9 Results of time trials using a high-spec. computer with Intel Core i7-8700CPU@3.20GHz; 6 cores; 12 logical processors. The example used is the "robber sample" described in Section 8.7.2, where S = suspect; K = known; U = unknowns. The model includes degradation, drop-in, F_{ST} and backward stutter. The propositions are shown in the table. All times are for one optimization and with "set.seed(1)" for direct comparisons to be made with other computer systems. *='set.seed(2)'. The seed value can make a big difference to the times taken to run.

Proposition		Time
H_p	H_d	
$S+K$	$K+U$	1.5 sec
$S+K+U$	$K+2U$	3 sec
$S+K+2U$	$K+3U$	21 sec
$S+K+3U$	$K+4U$	37 min*
$S+3U$	$4U$	142 sec

- Progress bar for all types of calculations; time estimates given for the MLE method.
- Model extensions: Optional Forward stutter model (Chapter 7.9.6) and optional specific settings for Marker/Dye, analytical thresholds (Chapter 3.1), drop-in model (Chapter 7.10) and F_{ST} (Chapter 5.5.2).
- The procedure shown in Table 8.1 to decide the best MLE model based upon the highest adjusted LogLik value, using the Akaike information criteria under H_d, is automated. The user can compare LogLik, LR, and M_x values for different numbers of contributors, degradation (ON/OFF), $n-1$ backward-stutter (ON/OFF), $n+1$ forward-stutter (ON/OFF).
- Validation PP–plots created (almost) instantly (Section 8.5.8).
- Seed settings: If the seed is set to a given value, then the MCMC and conservative LR values (Section 8.5.9) will be reproducible between different runs.

- The sub-source *LR* is now provided along with the sub-sub-source *LR* (discussed in Chapter 12.5).

All updates to *EuroForMix* will be fully described in addenda to the book, which will be published on the website.

8.10. A summary of the interpretation process

The interpretation process can be summarized in a series of steps (Fig. 8.23):

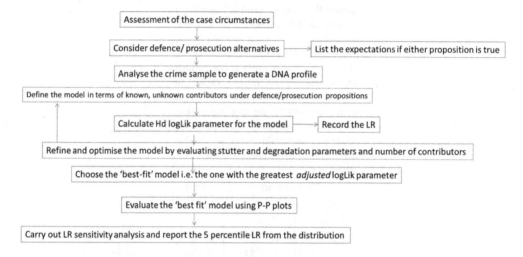

Figure 8.23 Flowchart showing the detailed workflow required to interpret a case.

1. The interpretation starts with an assessment of the case circumstances. To build the case, the scientist may be asked to analyze samples retrieved from a crime scene. The first step is to gather all the relevant information to formulate preliminary propositions given the case circumstances. What are the expectations if the prosecution proposition is true? What are the expectations if the defense proposition is true? Is there a suspect available? What other known individuals may have contributed to the evidence? For example, if the evidential item is article of clothing that was forcibly handled by a perpetrator during an assault then the expectation is that a) the victim's DNA will be present b) the perpetrator's DNA profile will be present. Is it possible that a relative of the suspect is the perpetrator?
2. Once the propositions are formulated, the next step is to analyze the crime stain to generate a DNA profile:
    a. Examine the profile to estimate the minimum number of contributors from the locus that displays the highest number of unique alleles—this includes alleles from any conditioned known contributors. The minimum number may differ

between H_p and H_d, because the conditionings are different (Section 8.7.2). Do not allow too many drop-in alleles when determining the number of contributors; see Chapter 4.2.1 for details.

b. Combine this information to define H_p and H_d in terms of "known" individuals (e.g., victim, suspect) and "unknown" individuals, so that there are sufficient to account for the minimum number of individuals required.

c. Is there evidence of degradation? If so, then use this parameter in the model at the beginning.

d. Carry out the analysis, and record the log likelihood for H_d along with the *LR*. The log likelihood is used to give an indication of the "best fit" model (e.g., Section 8.7.3).

e. The next step is to refine the model: include stutter to see if it makes a difference to the log likelihood value recorded previously. Add an additional unknown contributor under H_p and H_d to see if there is an improvement to the model. An excess of unknown contributors have very little effect on the *LR*, because their relative contributions are extremely small.

f. Choose the best fit model with optimized stutter/degradation parameters and number of contributors from the tested models adjusted (using Akaike Information Criterion) maximum log likelihood value.

g. Check the best fit model using PP plots to ensure that the fitted continuous model is a reasonable assumption for the observed peak heights.

h. Carry out an optional non-contributor test to check the effect of substituting the person of interest with a random person.

i. Carry out an optional *LR* sensitivity test, and report the 5 percentile *LR* from the distribution (it is a laboratory decision to determine which method is preferred).

3. The *LR* is used to test the strength of evidence to support either H_p or H_d at sub-level 1 in the hierarchy of propositions (Chapter 12), and will be used as the basis to write the statement (Chapters 6.1.7 and 12.11).

Notes

1. In Chapter 7.5.4, the case is worked using Excel spreadsheets. The propositions only included a single known contributor so that they are: DNA from the suspect and an unknown person is present in the crime-sample vs. DNA from two unknown persons is present in the crime-sample.
2. A hyperparameter is typically fixed based on other data and is used as a prior; it is not part of the set of unknown parameters to be optimized.
3. A computer with 8 cpu's will be 4 times faster than a computer with 2 cpu's to produce 8000 iterations in total (if they have the same processing speed): The computer with 8 cpu's must process "1000" iterations per cpu, whereas the computer with 2 cpu's must process "4000" iterations per cpu (hence it is 4 times slower).

CHAPTER 9

Validation

9.1. Context

There are a number of publications that review the question of "validation" in the literature, notably from SWGDAM [239], ISFG [240], and the UK Forensic Regulator [241]. Some laboratories have published validation studies, e.g., [242,243,77,67]. See Coble and Bright [62] for a full review. The U.S. president's council of advisors on science and technology (PCAST) published a report that discussed forensic evidence in general, including DNA mixtures [244,245]. The report urged for tests to be carried out across a broad range of profile types, and supported transparency and sharing within the forensic community via publications and validation studies. It was proposed that researchers investigated under certain (what) circumstances and why different methods produced different results.

The basic question that is being asked is: "How can we be sure that a complex computer program is providing the "right answer"?"

Unfortunately, there is no right answer. In a famous quote of George Box [246], he says:

"Since all models are wrong the scientist cannot obtain a 'correct' one by excessive elaboration. On the contrary following William of Occam he should seek an economical description of natural phenomena. Just as the ability to devise simple but evocative models is the signature of the great scientist so over-elaboration and over-parameterization is often the mark of mediocrity".

William of Occam (1287–1347) was a medieval English monk, whose views had great influence; he is credited for a principle known as "Occam's razor" [247]: *"when presented with competing hypothetical answers to a problem, one should select the one that makes the fewest assumptions"*. The "razor" term is used to distinguish between two hypotheses by shaving away unnecessary assumptions:

"the simplest explanation tends to be the right one".

"Entities should not be multiplied beyond necessity".

We see an application of this principle in the previous chapter, where we simultaneously seek to maximize the log likelihood of a proposition, whilst minimizing the number of parameters in the model. The optimum model is found by applying the "Akaike information criterion", which favors the simplest explanation by penalizing the log likelihood score as the number of parameters increases.

Essentially, the model should be as simple as possible, but not so simple that important parameters are left out—for example, virtually all models benefit from application

---

Forensic Practitioner's Guide to the Interpretation of Complex DNA Profiles
https://doi.org/10.1016/B978-0-12-820562-4.00017-1

Copyright © 2020 Elsevier Inc.
All rights reserved.

of the degradation parameter, but there may be no benefit in positing more contributors than necessary (i.e., the minimum number of contributors, as described in Chapter 2.3.2).

To summarize, we seek a "Goldilocks" solution: the model should be neither over- nor under-parameterized. But from this discourse, it follows that there can be no "correct" likelihood ratio either. Some authors refer to the likelihood ratio as a "personal belief" [248].

This is because the likelihood ratio itself is entirely dependant upon the assumptions that it is conditioned upon. It does not question *if* the assumptions are correct. The analysis is presented under the premise: "if the propositions are true". This is not the same as testing *whether* the propositions are true, since this would fall foul of the "prosecutor's fallacy". The scientist does not evaluate the propositions, the scientist evaluates the results *if* the propositions are true. This is implicit in the formal expression $Pr(E|H, I)$—the probability of the evidence, given the proposition (H) and the background information (I), where H is provided by the respective positions of the prosecution and the defense, respectively.

9.2. Avoiding the black-box

Software is used, because the formulae are too complex to allow hand calculations. It is not intended as a black-box solution, where the results are fed into one end, and the answer comes out the other end. This is why we advocate an "exploratory approach", where the output is investigated using reasonable assumptions, and the model that provides the highest log likelihood is the one that is usually reported.

Haned et al. [249] provide guidance to validation. Model validation is a process that results in an explicit statement about the behavior of the model (and subsequently the software). In the case of an interpretation model, such a statement would be:

> "The implementation of model X in software Y is valid for application in forensic casework subject to limitations described in the operational validation document".

Model and software validation are inherently entangled, as software implementation is always needed to implement and use a model. However, the two concepts can be related in a simple way; the software is merely a vector for the model. As illustrated in Fig. 9.1, validated software can actually rely on an invalid model, for example, if the underlying theory or mathematics are shown to be flawed. The goal is to implement a valid model, but it is important to realize that correct implementation of the mathematics of a model by a piece of software provides no information about the validity of the model itself; conversely, demonstration of correct implementation is a critical part of validation.

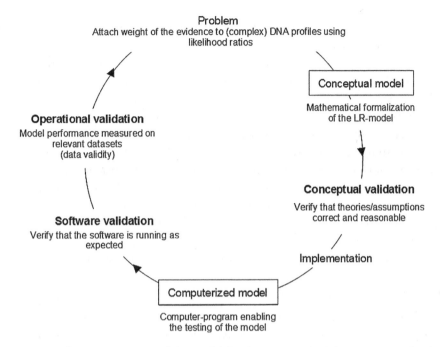

Figure 9.1 Simplified representation of the model development and validation process. The diagram shows the different stages of conceptual, operational, and software validation. Reproduced from [249] with permission from Elsevier.

9.3. Model validation

Model validation ensures that the model has been extensively checked to be sound and fit for purpose. This can be achieved through two steps: conceptual validation and operational validation [250].

9.3.1 Conceptual validation

Conceptual validation verifies that the mathematical formalization of the model, and its underlying assumptions, is fundamentally correct. Publication of the theory of the model in peer-reviewed scientific journals allows an opportunity for the underlying theory to be independently assessed, articulates the underlying assumptions, and, most importantly, documents the scientific support for the model structure. For this step to be successful, the model theory must be thoroughly explained. Publication, while necessary, is not sufficient; an editorial decision to publish a paper does not constitute fundamental proof of the scientific validity or usefulness of the contents.

The advent of electronic publication removes space restrictions, and allows for the possibility of publishing online supplementary material; it also gives modelers the opportunity to expand on their methods. The underlying data on which the conclusions are based can and should be published as supplementary material, so that independent researchers can inspect it and use it to independently verify the results obtained. For open-source software, the computer code can also be published as supplementary material, or as a link provided to the location of the code [251]. The code can then be studied by independent researchers, facilitating an understanding of the model, an important component of conceptual validation. The implementation of the model can also then be independently assessed by interested parties.

The most straightforward way to demonstrate conceptual validity is for the model developer to embrace a transparent approach, which allows for true independent review and verification. A transparent approach requires all of the model assumptions to be described, and accessible to anyone who wishes to independently reimplement the model, as demonstrated by [70,252]. This is diametrically opposed to a black-box approach, in which only partial explanations are provided, denying an independent researcher the ability to scrutinize the details and reimplement the model if desired [63,253].

9.3.2 Operational validation

We follow [254] and define operational validation as the procedure that determines whether *"the model's output behavior has the accuracy required for the model's intended purpose over the domain of the model's intended applicability"*. Operational validation is usually verified using a "computerized model". In other words, unless a computer implementation of the model is available that can run a profile and yield an output, the operational validity of the model cannot be tested (Fig. 9.1). Operational validity is tested via user-defined criteria that can be either accepted or rejected. These can be determined for LR-based models. For example, the following properties can readily be tested:

- Comparison to a standard basic model that operates with minimal assumptions so that the effectiveness of models that take into account additional parameters may be measured objectively. Gill and Haned [224] defined the requirements for such model, which allows the evaluation of complex DNA profiles without using all available information.
- The LR of a set of propositions for any profile is lower or equal to the inverse match probability of the profile questioned under the numerator proposition [255].
- The LR obtained for a given profile decreases with increasing ambiguity and decreasing information content [255]. Specifically, any deviation from a one-to-one correspondence of the suspected contributor profile and the evidence profile, and any loss of information from the evidence profile itself, should reduce the LR.
- The LR can be compared to a benchmark LR value. A benchmark LR can be calculated when most parameters of the model can be estimated from known profiles (see below). The reasons for any differences between the observed and expected output can be investigated and the model can be subsequently modified to yield the expected output.

9.4. Defining benchmarks for *LR*-based models

Benchmark likelihood ratios can be calculated for certain models, where parameters can be estimated directly from samples with known input. The *LR*s obtained with parameters estimated from such samples and the *LR*s calculated for another test dataset with the estimates should converge [85].

The quality and range of the data used for operational validation are critical [250, 254]. We follow Sargent [254] and define data validity as:

> *"ensuring that the data necessary for model building, model evaluation and testing, and conducting the model experiments to solve the problem are adequate and correct".*

Typically, experimental data sets are used, where the true composition of the samples is known (see, for example, [252,67]). Test samples chosen should represent the spectrum of situations encountered in real-world casework. Profiles representing extreme situations should be included, even if these profiles ultimately might not be interpreted in casework. The idea is to determine not only when the system works as expected, but also when it may fail. Specifically, it is important to investigate the boundaries of the model within its domain of application. Common characteristics of forensic casework samples that can increase their complexity include multiple contributors, low quantity (provoking possible drop-out), and low quality (e.g., degradation, inhibition, contamination). All of these factors increase ambiguity and reduce information content. Both the limitation of the model and the limitations of the evidence must be tested. For example, validation may determine that, past a certain number of contributors, the information content of the profile is simply too limited to reliably distinguish a true contributor from a non-contributor, who shares some of the detected alleles by chance. Therefore based on an operational validation of the model, as implemented by software, it might be relevant to impose a limitation on attempting to interpret casework samples that exceed some defined number of contributors to a mixture.

Simulated data can prove helpful in exploring model limitations; however, they cannot substitute for experimental data [253]. Any parameters modeled using simulated data must always be tested on profiles generated from physical samples, and the model refined based on the outcome. The most robust models are those tested with the widest range of data [254]. This is well illustrated by Nordstrom:

> *"The greatest weaknesses of any model computation are the quality of the input data and the adequacy of the assumptions (implicit and explicit); remember GIGO ('garbage in, garbage out')."*

9.4.1 Software validation

Model and software validation usually are carried out simultaneously, as it is the computerized version of the model that enables the model validation exercise (Fig. 9.1).

We define software validation as ensuring that the programmed algorithms follow the mathematical concepts defined in the model. We suggest the following main steps for software validation:

1. Define the statistical specifications of the software: This is an outline of the theory behind the model to be implemented in the computerized version of the model. This document compiles the information that is typically available in peer-reviewed papers describing the model and software implementation.

2. Carry out analytical verification: For example, analytical calculations of likelihood ratios using simple cases (e.g., single-source and two-person mixtures) can be derived and compared to the software output. Depending on the complexity of the model, analytical verification may or may not be possible. This has been termed the "complexity paradox" by [253]; the more complex a model is, the more difficult it is to verify the different blocks of the model. In such a case, the software output can be compared to output from alternative software that implements a similar model.

3. Compare to parallel implementations: Comparisons to alternative software, either relying on a similar or a different probabilistic model, can be useful to verify software behavior. Such comparisons rely on the "convergence principle" described by Gill and Haned [224], as well as Steele and Balding [61]. Modeling differences between software, corresponding to one unit on the log_{10} scale are negligible [61].

4. Verification of the code itself through visual inspection and recoding. Open-source software allows unrestricted access to software.

9.5. Validation study of *LRmix Studio* and *EuroForMix*

LRmix Studio is the "basic standard model". The assumptions in the model are minimal. It uses drop-out, drop-in, and allele frequencies described in Chapter 5. Its limitations are that it does not model stutter or peak height. Stutter can be modeled as extra contributor(s), however. *EuroForMix* is a quantitative continuous model. It takes account of peak height, and drop-out is modeled as a peak that falls below the detection threshold (AT). It models drop-in as an exponential function that takes account of peak height (Chapter 7.10), so that allelic peaks of high RFU incur a higher penalty than those that are low. *EuroForMix* also models $n-1$ backward stutter (where $n =$ no. of tandem repeats), however, it does not currently model forward $n+1$ stutter (rectified with v.3 of *EuroForMix*) or complex variants like $n-2$; this can be regarded as a limitation of the model. If necessary, alleles in stutter positions can be either filtered, or can be modeled as additional contributors.

Our first validation study was published by Bleka et al. [236], performed using the AmpFlSTR NGM kit. An additional validation study was carried out with Promega PowerPlex Fusion 6C (abbreviated to PPF6C) profiles, and described by Benschop et al. [238]. Experimental details can be obtained by referring to these studies. The results are compared and summarized below.

9.5.1 NGM DNA profiles

A total of four two-person mixtures and 55 three-person mixtures were generated using known reference profiles of 33 individuals (subset described by Benschop et al. [81] and Haned et al. [252]).[1] Two siblings were included in the study, references 9A and 10B. Table 9.1 gives a summary of all the 59 samples.

Table 9.1 The table gives a summary over all samples considered, with corresponding amounts of DNA (quantified in picograms (pg)) for the contributors. '#contr.' is the number of contributors, and "DNA (pg)" denotes the amount of DNA for each contributor (separated by ":"). The bracketed information in the "Sample(s)" column denotes the replicate number, e.g., (2–4) means that "2", "3" and "4" replicates were analyzed by the software. The first eight samples include components that are low-template (i.e., less than 50 pg). The next two samples, "8.7d", and "9.6d" have components with more than 50 pg but are greatly degraded. The rest of the samples consist of one replicate, but with different amounts of DNA. "Degraded" indicates whether the samples are degraded or not. Reproduced from [236], with permission from Elsevier.

Sample(s)	#contr.	DNA (pg)	Degraded
0.5.(1–4), 0.24.(1–4)	2	150:30	No
0.9.(1–4), 0.28.(1–4)	2	300:30	No
0.6.(1–4)	3	150:30:6	No
0.7.(1–4)	3	150:30:30	No
0.10.(1–4)	3	300:30:6	No
0.11.(1–4)	3	300:30:30	No
8.7d.(2–4)	3	500:250:250	Yes
9.6d.(2–4)	3	500:250:50	Yes
1.1, 2.1, 3.1, 6.1, 8.1, 9.1, 10.1, 11.1, 12.1, 14.1	3	100:50:50	Yes
1.2, 2.2, 3.2, 6.2, 8.2, 9.2, 10.2, 11.2, 12.2, 14.2	3	250:50:50	Yes
2.3, 3.3, 6.3, 8.3, 9.3, 10.3, 11.3, 12.3, 14.3	3	250:250:50	Yes
1.5, 2.5, 3.5, 6.5, 8.5, 9.5, 10.5, 11.5, 12.5, 14.5	3	500:50:50	Yes
1.6, 2.6, 3.6, 6.6, 8.6, 9.6, 10.6, 11.6, 12.6, 14.6	3	500:250:50	Yes

9.5.2 PPF6C DNA profiles

A total of 120 mixed DNA extracts (six datasets, each consisting of 20 mixtures) were amplified in triplicate using the PPF6C kit. These mixtures varied for the number of contributors, amount of DNA, level of allele sharing, and level of drop-out (Tables 9.2 and 9.3). Sample nomenclature was as follows: In a mixture denoted, for example, 1A2.1, the first number represents the dataset (1–6), the letter corresponds to the mixture type (A–E), the second number denotes the number of contributors (2–5), and the number after the dot represents each PCR replicate number (.1, .2, or .3). During analysis, a total of six samples (1E4.1, 1E5.1, 3E5.1, 4E3.1, 5E3.2, 6E5.1) that did not meet the required quality criteria (i.e., poor/broadened peak shapes) were removed from the sample set leaving 354 mixed profiles.

284 Forensic Practitioner's Guide to the Interpretation of Complex DNA Profiles

Table 9.2 Overview of the six donor combinations used for mixture preparation and PPF6C profiling. Reproduced from [238], with permission from Elsevier.

		Number of contributors			
Dataset number	Type of dataset	2	3	4	5
		Donor combinations per dataset			
1	High allele sharing	a:b	a:b:c	a:b:c:d	a:b:c:d:e
2	Low allele sharing	f:g	f:g:h	f:g:h:i	f:g:h:i:j
3	Random	k:l	k:l:k	k:l:k:n	k:l:m:n:o
4	Random	p:q	p:q:r	p:q:r:s	p:q:r:s:t
5	Random	u:v	u:v:w	u:v:w:x	u:v:w:x:y
6	Random	z:aa	z:aa:ab	z:aa:ab:ac	z:aa:ab:ac:ad

Table 9.3 Mixture proportions and amounts of DNA used per donor to create a total of 20 different mixtures per dataset. These mixtures were used for PPF6C profiling. Reproduced from [238], with permission from Elsevier.

	Number of contributors			
Mixture type	2	3	4	5
	Picograms DNA per contributor			
A: major 2x more than any minor	300:150	300:150:150	300:150:150:150	300:150:150:150:150
B: major 10x more than any minor	300:30	300:30:30	300:30:30:30	300:30:30:30:30
C: 2 majors with equal amount	150:150	150:150:60	150:150:60:60	150:150:60:60:60
D: major 5 to 2.5x more than minors	150:30	150:30:60	150:30:60:30	150:30:60:30:30
E: major 20 to 10x more than minors	600:30	600:30:60	600:30:60:30	600:30:60:30:30
Number of mixtures	5	5	5	5

9.5.3 Replicates

Replicates are defined as DNA profiles obtained from independent PCR amplifications from the same DNA extract (Chapter 4.4). All replicates within a sample were amplified simultaneously using the same PCR plate and PCR machine. For low template replicates, stochastic effects cause much variation in peak height, heterozygote balance, and drop-out [142] (Chapter 3).

9.5.4 Stutter filter

Stutter filters were applied as described in Chapter 2.2.3. Application of the stutter model has the effect of slowing the speed of calculation, which may be problematic if there are a large number of contributors. If a major contributor is the POI, then pre-treatment with the genotyping software stutter filter is an acceptable way forward. If minor contributors are evidential, and their alleles are at the same peak height as backward or forward stutter, then we naturally approach the limits of interpretation. However, results from Section 9.14 show that a stutter filter is sometimes useful for evidential minors as well.

9.5.5 Allele frequency database

A total of 2085 Dutch male donors were typed with six different STR kits to create a representative population database for the allele frequencies [256]. These include a total of 23 different autosomal markers: 16 of these are present in the NGM kit, and all 23 are present in the PPF6C kit.

9.6. Design of experiments

9.6.1 Experiments using NGM profiles

For weight-of-evidence calculations, a person of interest (POI) was compared with a given mixture sample (see Table 9.1).

1. Propositions tested were:

    H_p: The POI and k unknown individuals contributed to the crime stain.
    H_d: $k + 1$ individuals contributed to the crime stain.

    so that the POI under H_p is always replaced by an unknown individual under H_d.

2. For a given mixture sample (out of the 59 samples), the POI is considered as each of the 33 reference samples in turn, giving 33 comparisons per mixture sample. Only two or three are true contributors, the rest are non-contributors.

3. For 29 of the mixture samples, one of the contributors was conditioned as *a priori* "known" beforehand so that the propositions tested were:

    H_p: The POI, a known individual V and k unknown individuals contributed to the crime stain.
    H_d: A known individual V and $k + 1$ individuals contributed to the crime-stain.

    This gave an additional 32 comparisons for each of the 29 mixture samples.

4. By repeating 2) for all 59 mixture samples and 3) for the 29 "conditioning" mixture samples, we end up with 228 comparisons, where the POI is a true contributor, and 2646 comparisons, where the POI was a non-contributor. The latter reduces to 2634 when comparisons involving siblings were omitted.

9.6.2 Experiments using PPF6C profiles

Propositions tested were the same as described for NGM profiles. *EuroForMix* weight-of-evidence calculations with PPF6C profiles were performed using one of the true contributors as the POI under H_p (i.e. H_p = true tests, $n = 427$) or using a non-contributor as POI under H_p (i.e., H_d = true tests, $n = 408$). In these H_d = true tests, non-contributors were selected deliberately to a have large overlap with the alleles within the mixture and worst-case scenarios were examined, in which a simulated relative of one of the true contributors was considered as the POI under H_p. In addition, 330 LR results from $EuroForMix$ were compared to $LRmix$ $Studio$ LRs.

9.7. Method

The qualitative (semi-continuous) model $LRmix$ $Studio$ and quantitative (continuous) model $EuroForMix$ were compared for weight-of-evidence LR tests. In addition, using NGM profiles, performances of $EuroForMix$ and $LoCIM$-$tool$ (Chapter 10.2) were compared in their estimation of the most likely profile of the unknown major component. Note that the statistical models assumed in $LRmix$ and $EuroForMix$ require that the number of contributors is specified, whereas this is not the case for $LoCIM$-$tool$.

Both $LRmix$ $Studio$ and $EuroForMix$ include a model to adjust for sub-population relatedness using the coancestry coefficient F_{st} [42]. For all analyses, we followed Haned et al. [252] by applying $F_{st} = 0.01$ to accommodate the possibility that contributors belong to a sub-population of the population database.

Drop-in was modeled in either package, as described in Chapters 4.3 and 7.10.

9.7.1 Defining characteristics of the models

The aim of the validation was to define the performance of the model. There is no "true" or "correct" likelihood ratio that can be calculated. But we are interested in how many times a model may report an error and finding out the circumstances that this will happen. There are two kinds of errors. If an $LR > 1$, then it provides evidence in support of the prosecution proposition of inclusion, whereas if the $LR < 1$, then it provides evidence in support of the defense proposition of exclusion. It follows that errors can be defined as follows:

- False positive error: where a non-contributor provides a $LR > 1$.
- False negative error: where a true contributor provides a $LR < 1$.

A false positive error might result in a wrongful conviction, whereas a false negative error may result in a wrongful exoneration of a suspect. There is a guideline followed in that it is usually good practice to be "conservative" [34]. Consequently, systems are often designed to deliberately under-estimate the strength of the evidence that favors the prosecution proposition.

To discover false positive and false negative error rates, mixtures composed of known individuals (as described in Tables 9.1, 9.3 and 9.3) were analyzed using the software tested. LRs can be calculated under two different conditions:

- The *LR* was calculated using a known non-contributor as the POI (H_d = true test); we expect the *LR* to be less than one, otherwise it is a false positive error.
- The *LR* was calculated using a known true contributor as the POI (H_p = true test); we expect the *LR* to be greater than one, otherwise it is a false negative error.

Maximum likelihood estimation (Chapter 7.5) was used for *EuroForMix*, and was extended to *LRmix Studio* (for NGM profiles) to enable direct comparison of the results, in addition to the standard conservative methods described in Chapters 6.1.5 and 8.5.9.

H_p = true and non-contributor analyses provide the basic tests to carry out performance studies and to compare different methods.

9.8. Comparison of *LRmix Studio* and *EuroForMix* when the POI was the true contributor

When the POI was the true contributor, the *LR* values from *EuroForMix* (quantitative model) were nearly always greater than those from *LRmix Studio* (qualitative model). For these comparisons using the MLE method and the NGM data, there were 28 cases with *LRmix Studio* and five cases with *EuroForMix* (out of a total of 228), where the POI was below *LR* = 1. With the conservative method, these numbers increased to 67 and 11, respectively. These were false negative results (Fig. 9.2).

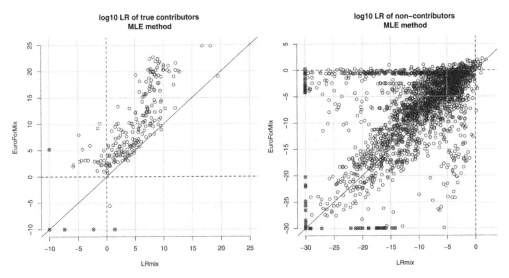

Figure 9.2 $Log_{10}LRs$ comparison using *LRmix Studio* (x-axis) and *EuroForMix* (y-axis). The left plot describes the MLE method, and the right plot describes the conservative method. Reproduced from [236] with permission from Elsevier.

With PPF6C data, 93% (253/272) yielded a larger *LR* using *EuroForMix* compared to *LRmix Studio* (Fig. 9.3). A total of 88% were more than one ban[2] higher, and 3%

were more than one ban lower. Many laboratories use an upper reporting threshold for casework, e.g., a million or a billion. For example, whether $log_{10}LR = 10$ or 25 does not make a difference, because they are both larger than the threshold, and therefore considered to be equivalent for reporting purposes. When the POI is a *major* contributor without allelic drop-out, large *LRs* are always obtained with both *LRmix Studio* and *EuroForMix*. It is apparent, therefore, that the primary benefit derived from using the peak height information is for mixtures, where a *minor* contributor is the POI under H_p.

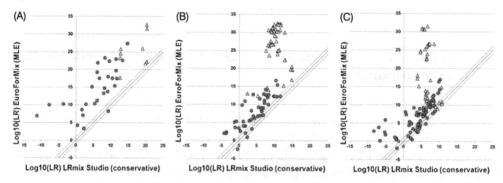

Figure 9.3 *Log*10*LRs* from H_p-true tests obtained using *EuroForMix* (y-axes) plotted against the corresponding *LRs* obtained using *LRmix Studio* (x-axes) for two-person (A), three-person (B), and four-person mixtures (C). Grey circles and white triangles represent analyses using a true donor as POI that contributed 30/60 pg and 150/300/600 pg, respectively. Figure reproduced from [238] with permission from Elsevier.

9.9. Comparison of *LRmix* and *EuroForMix* when the POI was not a true contributor

When peak height information was used in the *LR* calculations, there was a variable effect on H_d = true tests. With the PPF6C data used in [238], a lower number of false positive errors was obtained with *LRmix Studio* compared to *EuroForMix* (Fig. 9.4).

Where the POI was a non-contributor, it was shown that most $LR < 1$ for both *EuroForMix* and *LRmix Studio*, conservative, and MLE methods. However, for the MLE method for NGM profiles, there were a number of small false positive errors (*LR* values just above one), 17 with *LRmix* and 121 with *EuroForMix* (out of a total of 2634). When the conservative method was used, these numbers were reduced downwards to four and five, respectively. Results are summarized in Table 9.4.

The H_d = true tests using PPF6C profiles were more challenging than those using NGM profiles, as the non-contributors were selected to have a low number of "unseen" alleles, defined as alleles in the reference sample that were not observed in the crime stain. Therefore these profiles showed a large overlap of alleles with the mixture profiles. PPF6C profiles include 23 instead of 16 NGM autosomal markers. Hence, it is expected

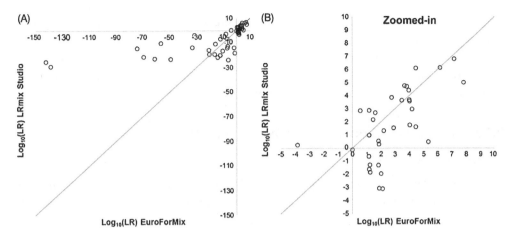

Figure 9.4 Log10 *LRs* obtained using *EuroForMix* (x-axis) and *LRmix Studio* (y-axis) with a non-contributor related (triangles) or unrelated (circles) as the POI under H_p. (A) Shows the data of 58 comparisons, (B) Figure A zoomed-in on the largest LR values. Figure reproduced from [238] with permission from Elsevier.

Table 9.4 NGM counts of number of observations, where *LR* is smaller or greater than one for *LRmix Studio* (given by LR_{LRmix}) and *EuroForMix* (given by LR_{EFM}). The table shows the number of observations when either H_p is true (i.e., considering true contributors), or H_d is true (i.e., considering non-contributors) for the maximum likelihood LR-based method (MLE), or the conservative *LR*-based method (CONS). Table reproduced from [236] with permission from Elsevier.

Method	Truth		$LR_{LRmix} < 1$	$LR_{LRmix} \geq 1$	Total
MLE	H_p	$LR_{EFM} < 1$	3	2	5
		$LR_{EFM} \geq 1$	25	198	223
		Total	28	200	228
	H_d	$LR_{EFM} < 1$	2509	4	2513
		$LR_{EFM} \geq 1$	108	13	121
		Total	2617	17	2634
CONS	H_p	$LR_{EFM} < 1$	11	0	11
		$LR_{EFM} \geq 1$	56	161	217
		Total	67	161	228
	H_d	$LR_{EFM} < 1$	2625	4	2629
		$LR_{EFM} \geq 1$	5	0	5
		Total	2630	4	2634

to obtain larger *LRs* with true contributors, and lower *LRs* with non-contributors for these two multiplexes. Out of 180 H_d = true tests, 173 (92.8 %) yielded a true negative, i.e., *LR* < 1 result with the MLE function of *EuroForMix*. Results that yielded an *LR* larger than 10 using *EuroForMix* were reanalyzed using *LRmix Studio*. This concerned three analyses using three- or four-person mixtures; all three yielded a true negative result with *LRmix Studio*.

False-positive rates were much larger when the POI was a simulated relative of one of the true contributors, showing a large overlap with the mixture profile (Fig. 9.4). These results are discussed in the next section.

9.10. Characterization of false positive results

9.10.1 NGM results

Table 9.5 describes the false positives observed with *EuroForMix* and *LRmix Studio* (using NGM profiles and the conservative method). Notice that reference 9A was a true

Table 9.5 Tables (A) and (B) list *LR*s for all false positive errors with threshold $LR = 1$. Table (A) shows the false positive results, where the POI is sibling to one of the true contributors in the sample, whereas Table (B) shows the false positive results, where the POI is not related to the contributors in the sample. "POI|cond" is the compared POI with possible conditional reference. #d is the number of drop-outs for the POI (average if replicates where available). K and $\hat{K}$ are the true and the predicted number of contributors, respectively. "Cons sibling LR" indicates the conservative *LR*, computed using *LRmix Studio*, where under H_d: "A sibling of the POI is a contributor". Reproduced from [236] with permission from Elsevier.

Sample	POI|cond	#d	Model	K	$\hat{K}$	MLE LR	Cons LR	Cons sibling LR
9.3	10B	3	*LRmix*	3	3	959356	70	3
9.2	10B	8	*LRmix*	3	3	236768	161385	1e-5
9.5	10B	5	*LRmix*	3	4	165044	138318	12
10.6	9A|10A	6	*LRmix*	3	4	55972	3193	1
10.6	9A	6	*LRmix*	3	4	1327	9	0.02
10.5	9A	15	*EuroForMix*	3	3	288	8	na
10.2	9A	13	*EuroForMix*	3	3	72	2	na
9.3	10B	3	*EuroForMix*	3	3	23	1	na
10.3	9A	7	*EuroForMix*	3	3	20	1	na

(A): False positives, siblings

Sample	POI|cond	#d	Model	K	$\hat{K}$	MLE LR	Cons LR	Cons sibling LR
8.7d	3C	17.7	*EuroForMix*	3	3	162	6	na
8.7d	6B	19.3	*EuroForMix*	3	3	92	1	na
8.5	10B|8A	10	*LRmix*	3	4	85	2	0.7
8.5	9A|8A	9	*EuroForMix*	3	4	41	1	na
3.3	14C|3B	11	*EuroForMix*	3	3	35	3	na
2.1	1A	7	*EuroForMix*	3	3	30	2	na
3.2	11B	8	*LRmix*	3	3	14	8	0.8
8.5	1B|8A	8	*LRmix*	3	4	9	2	0.2
11.2	8C	7	*LRmix*	3	4	6	4	0.7

(B): False positives, non-related

contributor in the samples "9.x", whereas reference "10B" was a true contributor in samples "10.x". Recall that samples 9A and 10B were siblings, sharing 19 out of 30 alleles. *LRmix Studio* does not take into account peak heights, hence high *LR* values were recorded when a sibling of the true contributor was compared. There was a single high ($LR > 200$) *EuroForMix* result for sample "10.5", where the POI 9A was low level with 15 allele drop-outs, making the comparison very unreliable. The conservative method reduced most of the *LR* values considerably, at the cost of introducing additional six false negatives for *EuroForMix*, and 39 for *LRmix Studio*. When the propositions were changed to test for relatedness, e.g., for sample "9.2" H_p: "*10B is contributor*" versus H_d: "*A sibling of 10B is contributor*", the *LR* values using *LRmix Studio* were close to 1, which means that the evidence could be explained by either the POI, or a sibling (see Chapter 8.8 for further details and examples of relatedness tests).

In summary, for cases where the POI was not a sibling to one of the true contributors, false positive matches for *EuroForMix* were limited: $LR < 200$, for *LRmix Studio* $LR < 100$ when the MLE method was used, and $LR < 10$ for both when the conservative method was used.

9.10.2 PPF6C results

False positive results for non-contributors that showed a large overlap with the PPF6C mixtures profiles occurred infrequently: 13/180 yielded an *LR* larger than 1, of which three had an *LR* larger than 10. These *LRs* were 14, 64, and 129, and were obtained with three- or four-person mixtures using the MLE function of *EuroForMix*. When the conservative method was used with *EuroForMix*, the largest *LR* for a non-contributor was 2.3.

In casework it is generally unknown whether a relative of the POI is a possible alternative contributor to the mixture. Therefore we examined the effect on the *LR* when simulated brothers or father/sons of a true contributor were compared. Worst-case scenarios were examined using only those simulated relatives that showed a large overlap with the mixture profiles (0–14 unseen alleles). False positives were obtained for 0/36 two-person mixtures, 11/36 three-person mixtures, and 23/36 four-person mixtures. These false positives occurred more often with a simulated brother ($n = 21$) than with a simulated father/son ($n = 13$) (Table 9.6). Nineteen analyses yielded an $LR > 100$, and these are shown in more detail in Fig. 9.5. This figure shows that the false positive errors were obtained with a varying number of unseen alleles (0–11). Furthermore, these errors were obtained at least once for each of the datasets (donor combinations), and for each of the mixture types that was used in this study.

Single replicate $H_d =$ true tests that yielded an $LR > 10$ (a total of $n = 3$ observations) were subsequently reanalyzed with *EuroForMix* using three replicates, if available ($n = 2$ tests). These represent one three-person and one four-person mixture. Also, the analyses using a relative as POI that yielded an $LR > 100$ ($n = 20$) with one replicate (Fig. 9.6)

Table 9.6 *EuroForMix* MLE *LR* results for analyses using a simulated relative of a true contributor as POI under H_p in PPF6C profiles. NOC = no. of contributors. Reproduced from [238] with permission from Elsevier.

NOC	Brother				Father/son			
	LR <1	LR 1–100	LR >100	Max. LR observed (rounded values)	LR <1	LR 1–100	LR >100	Max. LR observed (rounded values)
2	18	0	0	0.04	18	0	0	0.0007
3	10	2	6	2,800	15	3	0	8
4	5	3	10	64,000,000	8	7	3	220,000

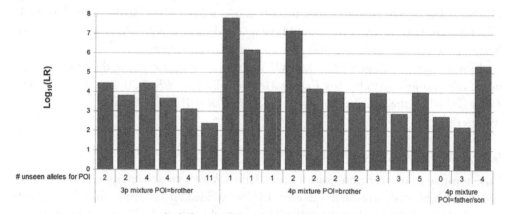

Figure 9.5 Overview of the *EuroForMix* analyses that yielded an *LR* > 100 with a simulated relative of a true donor as POI under H_p. Results for PPF6C profiles. Reproduced from [238] with permission from Elsevier.

were re-examined using three replicates, if available ($n = 19$). In all but one case, the *LRs* using three replicates were lower than those with one replicate (Fig. 9.6). This trend was anticipated and has previously been reported using other probabilistic genotyping software [257]. More true negatives were obtained with three replicates, although four of the 19 false positives remained when using a brother or father/son of a true contributor as POI under H_p in a four-person mixture.

Replicates can be used to reduce the number of false positive errors, although a few were still observed with a simulated relative of the true contributor (shown as triangles above the zero line in Fig. 9.6).

To conclude, the likelihood ratio is an expression of the value of the evidence. For well-represented profiles with two contributors, there is low expectation of false positive matches with non-contributor analysis if H_p = true, but for partial DNA profiles with multiple (three or more) contributors, the expectation of chance matches is much higher. In addition, siblings of donors can provide high *LRs* as false positive results,

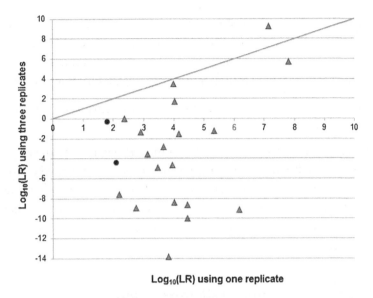

Figure 9.6 $Log_{10}LRs$ obtained in H_d = true tests using either a single replicate (x-axis) or three replicates of the same DNA extract (y-axis). Black circles indicate unrelated individuals that yielded an $LR > 1$ with a single replicate, whereas grey triangles are from simulated relatives of a true contributor that produced an $LR > 100$ with a single replicate. The diagonal line represents $x = y$. Reproduced from [238] with permission from Elsevier.

especially with *LRmix Studio* (since there is no quantitative account). To obviate, it is important for statements to contain caveats when *LRs* are reported—the H_d proposition qualifies the contributor to be an "unknown" individual who is unrelated to the suspect. These conditions are not written in stone; it will be entirely appropriate for the defense to ask for a calculation that includes the possibility that the perpetrator is a brother of the suspect. It is also appropriate to alert a court to the implications of the effect of relatedness upon the *LR*. The easiest way forward, if there is a serious contention that an individual related to the suspect is the perpetrator of the crime, is always to collect samples from relatives, and carry out parallel analysis.

9.11. Characterization of false negative results

The number of NGM false negatives is lowest when the MLE method is utilized (28 for *LRmix Studio* and five for *EuroForMix*), and increased when the conservative method is used (67 for *LRmix Studio* and 11 for *EuroForMix*) (Table 9.4). However, all the false negatives encountered can be characterized as originating from a particular category of mixtures. Minor components with less than or equal 50 pg contributions, except for the very degraded sample 9.6d, accounted for all situations of the false negatives. Considering the MLE method, the smallest observed number of drop-outs for the POI was four (in average across replicates) for *LRmix Studio* and 12 for *EuroForMix*; for the conservative method, there were two and eight observations, respectively.

To conclude, this information could be used to derive a complexity threshold, as described in Chapter 7 of Butler [160]. For example, a guideline may state the following:

"if less than x alleles match the POI, the sample is regarded too complex for further statistical analysis using the conservative method of LRmix Studio".

The more partial the DNA profile, the lower the *LR* will be, and the more likely it is that a false negative result will occur. Imagine an extreme example, where the contributor provides an amount that is less than 1% of the total. If this is below the detection level, it will not provide enough information to give a *LR* > 1, and will therefore be a false negative result. The principle of defining guidelines to use in casework decision-making is expanded in Section 9.17.

9.12. LR values as a function of allele drop-out

9.12.1 NGM results

For low-template, complex DNA profiles, mixture interpretation is often considered to be borderline for a minor contributor when proportions of 10:1 are encountered; the peak heights of the minor contributor are close to the detection threshold, and stutters from the major contributor are similar in peak height. Fig. 9.7 shows how the *LR* values based on the MLE method using *LRmix Studio* and *EuroForMix* are related to the number of drop-outs, where the POI was a true contributor to an NGM profile, and the number of "apparent" drop-outs (i.e., number of unseen alleles), where the POI was not a true contributor to an NGM profile. As the POI is not a contributor, alleles in the crime stain will either match by chance, or there will be no match. With real case-work, under H_p, if the POI is present, then drop-out is the reason for missing alleles, and this is the conditioning used in Fig. 9.7.

For $H_p =$ true, we also indicated whether the POI was the minor or major contribution. When the POI was major, $log_{10}LR > 10$ was high and the drop-out rate was 0–2 alleles (one outlier with 6 drop-out alleles). The more the drop-out events, the lower the *LR* becomes. Turning to results where the POI was absent, from the plot we observed (for both *LRmix Studio* and *EuroForMix* with NGM profiles) that false positives were occasionally observed with six or more drop-out events, but the corresponding *LR* was always low (< 200). When H_p was true, the limit for observing *LR* > 1 with *LRmix Studio* was up to three allele drop-outs before false negatives *LR* < 1 were recorded; for *EuroForMix* up to 11 allele drop-outs, before false negatives *LR* < 1 were recorded.

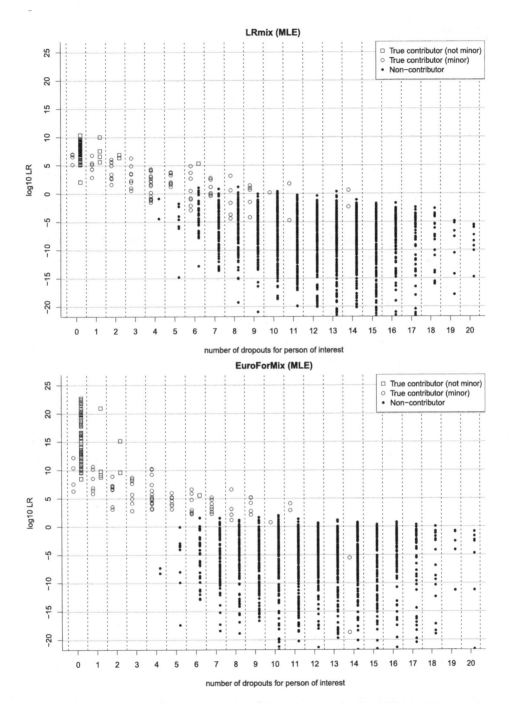

Figure 9.7 NGM plots show how the LR values using the MLE method for different POIs are related to the number of drop-outs for the corresponding POI, where no conditional reference was assumed; replicated samples and the sibling comparisons were omitted. "Major" is a contributor having 100 pg, 250 pg or 500 pg amounts of DNA. "Minor" is a contributor with only 50 pg DNA.

9.12.2 PPF6C results

Similar trends were observed with PPF6C three- and four-person mixtures (see Fig. 9.8 [238]). As the PPPF6C kit includes more autosomal markers than NGM (23 instead of 16), the limit for observing $LR > 1$ is higher. With *EuroForMix*, no false negatives or false positives were recorded with two-person mixtures. With three- and four-person mixtures, false negatives were obtained with at least five and 11 drop-outs, respectively; false positives occurred with at least 12 and five unseen alleles in three- and four-person mixtures, respectively (Fig. 9.8). As with NGM profiles, the LRs for false positives were always low (< 200).

9.13. Comparing the performance of two or more different models using ROC plots

A good model simultaneously minimizes the proportion of false positive: $LR > 1$ if H_d is true and false negative $LR < 1$ if H_p is true. When these errors do occur, we also want the strength of evidence for the false positive LR to be as low as possible. An alternative way to represent the information is to create receiver operating characteristic (ROC) plots [258], as shown in Fig. 9.9 (NGM data, comparisons between siblings, 9A and 10B omitted). This was created by plotting the true positive rate versus the false positive rate at various threshold settings relative to $LR = t$. This corresponds to a decision rule, where H_d is rejected if $LR > t$. For instance, if $t = 1$, and H_p is true while giving $LR < 1$, this is defined as a false negative. Conversely, a true positive occurs if $LR > 1$. A false positive is defined if H_p is false and $LR > 1$. Fig. 9.9 shows the proportion of false positives along the x-axis, and the proportion of true positives along the y-axis relative to values of t, ranging from $t = 0 - Infinity$.

In Fig. 9.9, threshold $LR = 1$ is denoted as a cross on each curve with the precise number of instances counted in Table 9.4. For the MLE method (with $t = 1$), the false positive rate is 0.006 and 0.046 for *LRmix Studio* and *EuroForMix*, respectively. The corresponding true positive rates are 0.88 for *LRmix Studio* and 0.98 for *EuroForMix*. For the conservative method, the false positive rate is 0.002 for both models, with a true positive rate of 0.71 for *LRmix Studio* and 0.95 for *EuroForMix*. An ideal model gives a ROC plot, which simultaneously shows a false positive rate equal to zero and a true positive rate equal to one for some values of t (yielding a point in the upper left corner in the ROC curve). In Fig. 9.9, this condition is approached more effectively with *EuroForMix* than with *LRmix Studio*. Furthermore, MLE performed better than the conservative method. In casework, we would always prefer to minimize the number of false positives, hence the conservative method may be preferred, though the incidence of false negatives is increased.

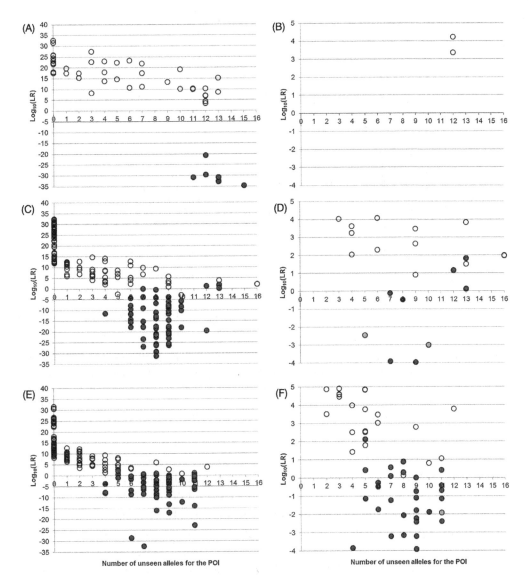

Figure 9.8 PPF6C, Log10 *LRs* for two-person (panels A&B), three-person (panels C&D), and four-person mixtures (panels E&F) computed using H_p-true tests (open circles), or H_d-true tests (grey circles) plotted against the number of allelic drop-outs or unseen alleles for the POI. Plots B, D, and F are zoomed on the Y-axis to allow inspection of false negative and false positive errors (denoted by blue and red circles, respectively). Reproduced from [238] with permission from Elsevier.

9.14. Comparison of the stutter model in *EuroForMix* versus GeneMapper stutter filter

Stutters from an allele *a* occur due to strand slippage during PCR ([259]), typically resulting in "backward stutter" of $n-1$ STR repeat unit (−4 bp for a tetrameric repeat).

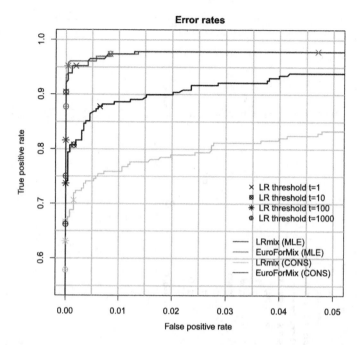

Figure 9.9 Receiver operating characteristic (ROC) plot, where the rate of false positives (FP) (along horizontal axis) and true positives (TP) (along vertical axis) are plotted as a function of LR thresholds. The plot shows the results for the maximum likelihood estimation method (MLE) and the conservative method (CONS) for both *LRmix Studio* and *EuroForMix*. The points on the curves show the FP and TP rates for different *LR* thresholds. Reproduced from [236] with permission from Elsevier.

Other stutter artefacts can also be observed at allele $n-2$ repeat units (i.e., double backward stutter) and $n+1$ repeat units (i.e., forward stutter [110]), however, these occur less often, and are usually much smaller in peak height[3] (Chapter 2.2). More complex stutters are possible, and these may be present in over-amplified samples. A filter can be optionally applied in GeneMapper to remove alleles that are coincident with stutters in both $n-1$ and $n+1$ positions [111]. In practice, stutter filters are often calibrated based on the average stutter peak height +3 standard deviations (SD) per marker. It does not consider stutter peak variation on an allelic basis, hence the risk that a stutter is not removed increases with the number of repeats of the parent allele. Conversely, the risk of a minor allele being removed as a stutter decreases with the number of repeats of the "parent" allele. A problematic situation occurs when contributors with large amounts of DNA (major contributors) produce stutters that are similar in peak height to the alleles from minor contributors. Therefore there is no guarantee that alleles from true contributors will not be removed as well. Application of the stutter model has the effect of slowing the speed of calculation of *EuroForMix*, which may be problematic if there are a large number of unknown contributors. If a major contributor is assumed to be the POI, then pre-treatment with the GeneMapper stutter filter is an acceptable way forward. On the other hand, if minor contributors are evidential and their alleles are at similar peak heights to backward or forward stutter, then we naturally approach the limits of interpretation.

MLE is used to determine the distribution of the backward-stutter $(n-1)$ proportion in *EuroForMix* (this is assumed to be the same for all markers), and the distribution is used in the *LR* calculation (as described in Chapter 7.5). Version 3 of *EuroForMix* is able to evaluate forward $(n+1)$ stutter.

We used the model selection framework, described in Chapter 8.5.6, to predict whether a stutter-model should be utilized after applying the stutter filter. For the purposes of this investigation, the correct number of contributors were applied in all comparisons.

Fig. 9.10 shows that the method using the GeneMapper stutter-filter improves the performance when all data (except siblings) were included in the analysis. It was observed that for the samples "1.6", "3.6", "8.6", "8.3", "3.3", and "3.5", where minor contributors were the POI under H_p, showed substantially increased *LR*s when the GeneMapper filter was used. This occurred because a forward-stutter at allele 17 in D22S1045 was removed in each case. This improved the fit of the model to the data. This had the effect of increasing the *LR* using the GeneMapper stutter filter (compared to the stutter model in *EuroForMix*), even if some low-level minor alleles of the minor POI contributor were removed. Conversely, for samples "3.2", "2.3", "2.6", "10.6", and "3.5", there were no forward-stutters in the original data. Therefore, for these samples, the *LR*s decreased significantly, since one or two alleles were removed for each. Details about how the *LR* changed for each sample when the stutter filter was applied is shown in Fig. 9.11.

9.15. Calibration of the likelihood ratio

In 1983 Ramos and Gonzalez-Rodriguez [260] introduced the concept of calibration of the likelihood ratio. Their motivation was to provide a method that complements existing methods previously discussed, e.g., non-contributor tests in Section 9.9 and ROC plots (Section 9.13).

They define calibration as *"a property of a set of LR values which can be measured"*.

"The methodology measures the performance and the calibration of a set of LR values, no matter how they were computed."

The ideas of Ramos and Gonzalez-Rodriguez have been adapted to probabilistic genotyping models, using *STRmix* by Buckleton et al. [261]. The purpose of calibration is to measure whether the *LR*s from a large dataset provided from a probabilistic system behave according to expectations when comparing two alternative propositions: H_p:

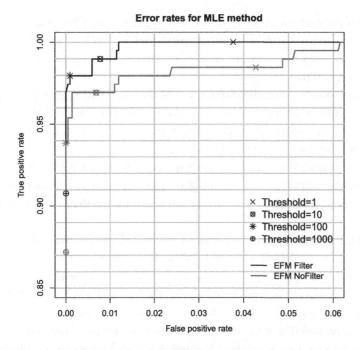

Figure 9.10 Receiver operating characteristic (ROC) plot, where the number of false positives (along horizontal axis) and true positives (along vertical axis) are plotted as a function of *LR* thresholds. Results shown for *EuroForMix* using the maximum likelihood estimation method based on either stutter-filtered data (EFM Filter) or non-filtered data (EFM NoFilter), where the samples with replicates are omitted.

"POI is a contributor" vs. H_d: "POI is not a contributor". A set of data, where the POI is the true donor, and a set of data (where the POI are from non-contributors are prepared). The latter may be simulated to easily generate large numbers. From a dataset of *LRs*, where the contributors are of known provenance, the next step is to apply a method that can determine the expected number of true donors relative to a given *LR*; this is accomplished as follows:

Turing's rule is discussed in detail in Chapter 12.17. For simple proposition pairs, under Turing's expectation, the probability that a non-contributor $LR_{nc} = x$ or more is accommodated by $Pr(LR_{nc} > x|H_d) \leq 1/x$, so we expect less than N/x matches, where there are N comparisons [227], and the LR_{avg} is expected to be one [262].

In other words, if the crime-stain $LR_x = 24,000$, and we simulate $N = 24,000$ non-contributor tests, then there is an expectation that there will be up to one example ($N/x = 24,000/24,000 = 1$), where the LR_{nc} is the same as or greater than that of LR_x.

This rule is tested with a large dataset of non-contributors and true contributors. We expect that a "good" model will conform to the Turing expectations, and is therefore deemed to be "reliable".

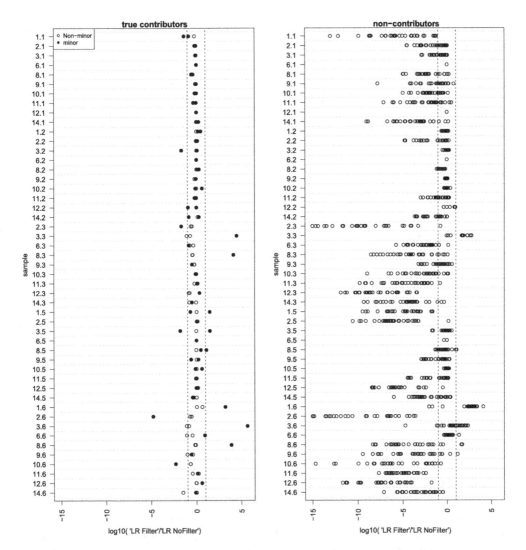

Figure 9.11 The plots show the difference of $\log_{10} LR$ values between applying the GeneMapper stutter-filter and the stutter model within *EuroForMix* (left plot shows true contributors, right plot shows non-contributors). Replicate samples were not considered. The dashed vertical line indicates $LR = 10^{\pm 1}$.

But to carry out the calibration testing, it is first necessary to use probabilities instead of likelihood ratios. We can convert the *LR* into posterior odds by multiplying it by the prior odds, as described in Chapter 12.8:

$$\text{Posterior odds} = \text{Prior odds} \times LR \qquad (9.1)$$

Next we need to calculate the priors: If we have a set of data that consists of y ($H_p = true$) contributors and z ($H_d = true$) non-contributors), then the prior odds that any given POI is a true contributor is given by prior odds $= z/y$.

To illustrate, the example provided by Buckleton et al. [261] is followed, where a dataset of $y = 28,250,000$ false donors and $z = 10,297$ true donors were compared and provided a prior odds calculation of $\frac{z}{y} = 0.000364$. The data came from a previous extensive multi-laboratory study [263].

The posterior odds must be converted into a posterior probability. This is easily calculated by the following equation:

$$Pr = \frac{odds}{odds + 1} \qquad (9.2)$$

Using Eq. (9.1) to inform the posterior odds in Eq. (9.2) enables the posterior probability of $Hp = true$ of each LR to be determined:

$$\text{Posterior prob. } (H_p = true) = \frac{1}{1 + (LR \times prior\ odds)^{-1}} \qquad (9.3)$$

The posterior probability ranges between zero and one. With the example cited, a small $LR = 100$ converts to a posterior $Pr = .035$, whereas a very high $LR = 10^9$ gives a posterior $Pr = .9999997$ (close to one), but very few, if any, false positives are expected at such a level with a dataset of 28 m. The probability of observing false positives with a high LR are dependent upon very large sets of data, since there is a direct relationship between the magnitude of the LR and the probability of detecting a false positive (assuming a reliable model). Hence the sample size of 28 m used by Buckleton et al. [261] enables a calibration test to be extended to LRs of corresponding magnitude.

Once a posterior probability of $Hp = true$ has been assigned to every one of the true donors and non-contributors, the data are arranged as shown in Table 4 of Buckleton et al. [261]. Posterior probabilities are divided into a number of categories. For example, in the "posterior probabilities of $H_p = true$" range of 0.398–0.813 (corresponding to $LR = 110 - 150,000$, approximately), there were 60 false donors and 314 true donors observed in the dataset. This converts into an *observed* posterior probability of $\frac{314}{314+60} = 0.6055$. This is higher than the expectation, taken as the mean of the category. Consequently, there are more true donors than expected, which indicates that the model is well-calibrated, and that the LR is conservative. The exercise was repeated for all categories assigned to the entire posterior probability range from zero to one, as shown in Table 4 of Buckleton et al. [261].

9.16. Further comparative studies between different software

The PCAST report [244,245] asked a pertinent question:

"Under what circumstances - and why - does the method produce results (random inclusion probabilities) that differ substantially from those produced by other methods?"

In earlier sections, we have compared performance of *EuroForMix* and *LRmix Studio*, introducing methods that both characterize and compare the performance of different software under a range of different conditions. Of course, these are not the only software solutions that are utilized by the community, so the question arises whether different programs based on different criteria provide similar results. There are very few such studies, in part this is because commercial programs have restricted access to researchers. You and Balding [233] carried out a comparison of *EuroForMix* and *LikeLtd*. Both are gamma distribution models, but there are differences in the way that drop-in and stutter are treated. Unlike *EuroForMix*, which models $n-1$ backward stutters, *LikeLtd* also models forward $n+1$ and complex $n-2$ stutters. Both use MLE, but there are differences in implementation between the two models. The study compared one to three contributors at varying DNA masses. They used ROC analysis to help form their conclusions:

"Overall results from likeLTD and EFM were similar, despite being based on different modeling assumptions. LikeLTD often reported better results for low-level contributors in DNA mixtures, leading to a slightly better AUC[4] for likeLTD based on all the mixture profile analyses in our study."

The authors noted that there was an advantage to modeling forward and complex stutters with *LikeLtd*, if the POI was a low-level contributor, but the downside was the increased computational time that resulted.

Manabe et al. [78] compared *EuroForMix* with *Kongoh*. The latter is also based on a gamma distribution model, but there are differences in implementation. These authors compared 2–4 person mixtures and found that the resulting *LR*s "tended to be similar".

Alladio et al. [264] compared several software with two- to three-person mixtures: *LRmix Studio*, *Lab Retriever DNA-View*, *EuroForMix*, and *STRmix*. They noted that the "semi-continuous" (qualitative models), *LRmix Studio* and *Lab Retriever*, tended to give lower *LR*s compared to the continuous models (as expected). In general, results based upon continuous methods gave consistently similar answers, as did the two semi-continuous methods, but there was divergence between the two methodologies, especially when the mixture was high-template and the POI was a minor contributor. These authors proposed a method that employed a "statistic consensus approach", originally suggested by Garafano et al. [265], where several statistical methods are compared, and only the most conservative approach is reported, provided that the *LR* results were convergent:

"our statistic consensus approach consists in comparing likelihood ratio values provided by different software and, only if results turn out to be convergent, the most conservative likeli-

hood ratio value is finally reported. On the contrary, if likelihood ratio results are not convergent, DNA interpretation is considered inconclusive."

If adopted, the approach would lead to some inconclusive results, especially with major/minor mixtures, where the minor was the POI, since continuous methods take full account of allele peak heights, they are clearly superior with this kind of test. The rationale of the "statistical consensus" approach was challenged by Taylor et al. [266]:

"If a model has been demonstrated to out-perform another one, then why should we rely upon the less efficient version for decisions about reporting, particularly if it has a recognized limitation to evaluate certain types of evidence?"

9.17. Defining guidelines for using probabilistic genotyping software in forensic casework

The PCAST report [244,245] encouraged forensic scientists to share results from internal validation of probabilistic interpretation software. Internal laboratory guidelines that address issues about when or how to apply probabilistic genotyping software, or when to report the LR results are shared less often. Such guidelines are based on outcomes of internal validation studies, and as such are informed by the expertise derived during casework. However, it is important to standardize methods so that they may be replicated by different users. In a study carried out by NIST [267], where mixtures were analyzed by 69 different laboratories, it was shown that the majority used RMNE or CPE to report conclusions. However, these laboratories typically had divergent practices, hence the results that were generated were also divergent. In contrast, the adoption of probabilistic genotyping (LR) methods removes much of the need to depend upon strict rule sets, since features like drop-out and drop-in are accommodated within a statistical framework and the probabilities are continuous. This leads to much closer inter-laboratory standardization, as shown by [268,269].

In summary, we wish to perform LR calculations when it is useful to the case, but to do this effectively, a process is needed to decide whether/or not to carry out calculations. To ensure standardization, there also needs to be uniformity among reporting officers within the laboratory in the application of software programs and the interpretation process itself.

A stepwise approach is used by the Netherlands Forensic Institute (NFI): first the profiles are analyzed technically and independently. Next, the quality of the profiles is assessed after which they can be compared to reference profiles. Finally, and only when certain criteria are met, one proceeds to carry out an LR calculation [94]. These criteria are different between laboratories, exemplified by several inter-laboratory studies, such as [268], [270], [271], [267], and [269]. For example, reporting criteria can be based on the following: the number of assumed contributors; the expected level of drop-out and/or the number of unseen alleles (i.e., "mismatches" between a reference sample and the evidence). In addition, case circumstances and the availability of other stains and/or DNA profiles are also part of the decision-making process. After LR calculations are performed, the results can be examined. In *EuroForMix* and *DNAStatistX* (Chapter 10), calculated LRs are validated by examination of the PP-plots, described in Chapter 8.5.8. If the cumulative probability of the model's observed and expected peak heights vary; possible causes can be considered. Known causes of failing model validations are also listed in Chapter 8.5.8. If model validation failed under H_p, because H_p is false, LRs will be low (< 1), and no further action is required. If validation fails, because the parameters or model do not explain the data very well, other options can be assessed, e.g., a different number of contributors or applying the degradation model. If case model validation fails as a result of deviating peak heights between replicates, it is advisable to perform LR calculations with the individual replicates, rather than jointly. The optimizer searches for the best explaining parameters for the combination (average) of the replicates, which may not fit each of the individual replicates when peak heights differ between them. Other aspects of the results that can be examined are the differences in expected mixture proportions under H_p and H_d and the variation in LRs per locus. If, for instance, just one locus shows a very low $LR < 1$, whereas all other loci are inclusionary, this one locus can be examined to see whether the result is expected based on the (number of) alleles and peak heights. A possible cause could be an elevated stutter, caused by a somatic mutation. By performing LR calculations on samples with known content and by examining the results, one will gain knowledge of expectations regarding the outcome.

When model validation passes, LR results can be reported, though this reporting also differs among laboratories. Some report the actual value, whereas others prefer reporting the range or a verbal scale. Furthermore, a lower and/or upper reporting threshold is sometimes applied. Laboratories, e.g., in the UK, may use an upper threshold of $log_{10}LR = 9$, i.e., LRs greater than this are rounded down. A lower reporting threshold, where the sample may be deemed as "inconclusive", e.g., $LR = 200$, can be based on validation data and examination of false positives/Type I errors ($LR > 1$ with a non-contributor as POI under H_p).

As an example, the guidelines used at the NFI, with the implementation of the first version of *DNAStatistX*, are shown in 9.12. These guidelines are based on validation study outcomes using PowerPlex Fusion 6C profiles described earlier; the usefulness to a forensic case is informed by the expertise derived in casework. LRs are reported when they exceed a threshold of $log_{10}LR = 4$, since calculations resulting in lower LRs can be more sensitive to the model and parameters used.

Replicate analyses are performed in cases where the result based on one sample is between $log_{10}LR = 4 - 6$. Replicate analyses tended to increase LRs for true contributors, and decrease LRs for non-contributors, such as relatives of a true contributor, described by Benschop et al. [238] and Section 9.10.2. In the comparison preceding the *LR* calculation, "mismatches"/unseen alleles of the reference profile may occur, because of drop-out in the trace profile, or because the reference profile is from a non-contributor. Following these guidelines one proceeds to an *LR* calculation, provided that there are no more than 15 mismatches (the maximum allowed; i.e., unseen alleles of the POI) with two-person, ten mismatches with three-person, and five mismatches with four-person PPF6C profiles. Most mismatches led to *LRs* in the uninformative zone, i.e., $log_{10}LR < 4$ [238]. *LRs* that are below the threshold are not reported. Sometimes a true positive *LR* for a true contributor may be missed, because of these restricted guidelines, which is a risk that is accepted by the laboratory, although deviation from the guidelines is possible if a proper argument is put forward. When one replicate yields an *LR* in the range $log_{10}LR = 6 - 10$, replicate analyses are performed in a case-dependent manner, i.e., when more information on the POI or number of contributors is needed. Clearly, the case circumstances, availability of other stains and profiles within the case are factors considered in the process. The summarized guidelines, as presented in Fig. 9.12, were not intended as strict rules, but to be used as helpful tool in the decision-making process.

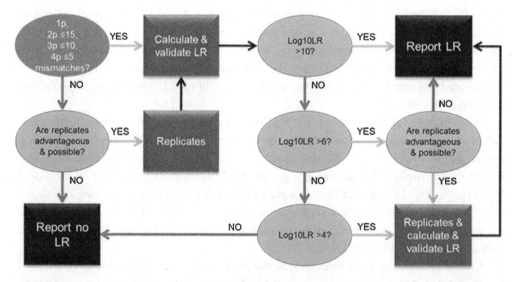

Figure 9.12 Summarized example of guidelines for the application of *DNAStatistX* or *EuroForMix* to PPF6C profiles in casework.

9.18. Summary

1. This chapter is about validation. The purpose of validation is to define the scope and limitations of a software. There are three parts to a validation exercise (Section 9.3):

a. Conceptual validation, where the mathematical formulae that underpin a software are verified as correct.

b. Software validation, to ensure that the software is running as expected; verification of the code, e.g., by independent coding of the software.

c. Operational validation, where output behavior of the model is tested against a wide range of different evidence types that represent "typical" casework and extreme examples.

2. Two validation studies are described, using the AmpFlSTR NGM kit and the Promega PowerPlex Fusion 6C. A series of mixtures were prepared that contained one to five contributors, where each of the contributors was a known individual, and a comparative study of *EuroForMix* and *LRmix Studio* was undertaken.

3. Two kinds of tests were carried out. Likelihood ratios were calculated using propositions:

H_p: The POI and $k-1$ unknown individuals contributed to the mixture;
H_d: k unknown individuals contributed to the mixture.

In real casework, we do not know the identity of the contributors, and we cannot make any assumptions. Since the experimental set of mixtures are contrived, we do know the identity of each individual contributor. This enables us to carry out two different kinds of comparisons:

$H_p =$ True, where we know that the POI is a contributor, and we know that the prosecution proposition is true;
$H_d =$ True, where we know that the POI is not a contributor, and the proposition is false.

4. When $H_p =$ True, then we expect the $LR > 1$, whereas if $H_d =$ True, the converse is expected, i.e., $LR < 1$. A set of samples, was used to test the LR expectations, and to record deviance from expectations. Therefore if $H_p =$ True and $LR < 1$, then this is false negative error, whereas if $H_d =$ True and $LR > 1$, then this is a false positive error (Section 9.7). The false positive error is of concern, because it may result in a false inclusion of an individual. However, we expect false positive and false negative errors will naturally occur. The purpose of the validation exercise is to quantify their occurrence, and to record the corresponding magnitude of LRs that may be observed. The implications on the interpretation strategy are discussed in Chapter 12.17.

5. False positive results were increased when the non-contributor POI was a close relative of the true donor (Section 9.10.2). The effect was particularly prevalent with *LRmix Studio*. Since *EuroForMix* is a quantitative model, the effect was mitigated, but was still observed. Higher orders of mixtures (e.g., four contributors) were more prone to providing high LRs when the POI was a sibling of the true donor.

6. To compare the performances of two or more different models, "receiver operator characteristic" (ROC) plots were produced (Section 9.13). These are created by plotting the true positive rate versus the false positive rate at various threshold settings relative to $LR = t$, where values of t are varied from the minimum observed to the maximum observed LR. These plots provide a measure of the comparative performances of two or more different methods, where the best system simultaneously minimizes the number of false positive and negative errors for low values of $LR = t$.

7. The calibration method of Ramos and Gonzalez-Rodriguez is described. The purpose is to measure whether the LRs from a large dataset provided from a probabilistic system behave according to expectations when comparing two alternative propositions. The observed vs. expected numbers of true donors and non-contributors can be derived relative to a given likelihood ratio.

8. Finally, there is a description of how validation results are used to design an internal laboratory process to decide how and when to report cases using probabilistic genotyping. This is facilitated by a flow chart (Section 9.17).

Notes

1. All data can be found in the zip-file "NFIdata" at www.euroformix.com/data.
2. Ban is a measurement used to compare difference between two specified propositions: $log_{10} LR = x$ bans [61].
3. Typically falling below the detection threshold (AT).
4. AUC is area under the curve, and is used as a measurement to compare different models.

CHAPTER 10

Development and implementation of *DNAxs*

The DNAxs Team

EuroForMix implements and extends the model proposed by Cowell and coworkers [234] and Graversen and Lauritzen [272], and was first released in 2015. Since *Euro-ForMix* is open-source and freely available, anyone can use the software or the code and implement it in another software. For example, the eDNA consortium [http://ednalims.com/probabilistic-genotyping/] has used *EuroForMix* as the basis for their software named *BulletProof*. Furthermore, the Netherlands Forensic Institute (NFI) created *DNAStatistX*, a Java implementation of some of the functionalities as available in *EuroForMix*. *DNAStatistX* is a statistical library, which is a module in the DNA expert system denoted *DNAxs*.

10.1. DNA expert system

Over the last two decades, the proportion of complex profiles (e.g., three or more contributors and/or low-template amounts of DNA) obtained in forensic casework has clearly increased. This is partly the result of the increased sensitivity and the availability of a larger number of markers analyzed in the global STR typing systems. Moreover, there has been a change in the type of evidence being submitted for analysis by forensic DNA laboratories; from high- to low-quality and quantity stains. As a single case may have multiple complex profiles, possibly with multiple replicates, comparisons to (sometimes many) reference profiles can be complex, time-consuming and error-prone if performed manually. This has increased the demand for a software that enables fast and automated comparison of sets of profiles assisting the DNA experts in routine DNA casework. *eDNA* was one such application, where development was supported by the European Union 2014–2016. [https://www.berlin.de/polizei/allgemeine-seiten/artikel.255413.en.php, [273]]. Although its functionalities can be very useful, the *eDNA* application may not be easily implemented in every forensic laboratory. This prompted the development of other expert systems, such as *CaseSolver* [274] at the Oslo University Hospital and *DNAxs* at the NFI. This chapter focuses on *DNAxs*, which is maintained at https://www.forensicinstitute.nl/research-and-innovation/european-projects/DNAxs. The software system is server-based; it was written using structured programming (so that multiple software engineers

Forensic Practitioner's Guide to the Interpretation of Complex DNA Profiles
https://doi.org/10.1016/B978-0-12-820562-4.00018-3

Copyright © 2020 Elsevier Inc.
All rights reserved. **309**

can integrate their work), and uses a modular approach, which means that novel features can be easily incorporated. The *DNAxs* software system has been in use in routine forensic casework at the NFI since December 2017. It is constantly being improved in response to feedback from a group of users, which has proven crucial. Besides having a match matrix tool, as implemented in *eDNA*, the software has many functionalities and covers most, if not all, steps from profile interpretation to reporting.

10.1.1 Functionalities of *DNAxs*

The first version of *DNAxs* (v1.0.0) was released for internal use at NFI and contained features to import, view, infer, match, and export autosomal STR profiles. Table 10.1 presents an overview of the features, and Fig. 10.1 shows a screenshot of one part of *DNAxs*, in which a mixed DNA profile is presented as bar graphs and compared to two reference profiles. An example of a match matrix comparing a large set of DNA profiles is presented in Fig. 10.2. For further detailed information and more screenshots, we refer the reader to the manual that is presented within the *DNAxs* software. Since its release in December 2017, new features were implemented, bugs were fixed, and user-friendliness was improved based upon feedback from a large group of users. In 2018 a grant was awarded by the EU (ISFP-2017-AG-FORENSIC, Grant Agreement Number 820838 — DNAxs2.0), which enabled the following:

1. The implementation of a statistical library that contains the algorithm to calculate the MLE as published in Cowell et al. [234] and Bleka et al. [76],
2. The implementation of a tool to estimate the number of contributors,
3. The development and implementation of integration tests.

The statistical library supports parallel computing, which can be delegated to a computer cluster, and enables automated queuing of *LR* calculation requests. The library is programmed in Java and is accessible separately or via *DNAxs*. A modular approach is used in building *DNAxs*, which means that new features can be easily incorporated; also existing features can be replaced if others are preferred, or show improved performance. A documented web-API was built, which contains methods to import and export profiles. This web-API allows connection to various systems, e.g., LIMS, to *DNAxs*. Within this EU project, partner laboratories test the software's performance under varying environments and provide input for broadened use. By the end of the project (2020), the software DNAxs v2.0 was made available to the forensic community. DNAxs itself is not open-source, but many of its features are (e.g., LoCIM, DNAStatistX, SmartRank).

10.2. *LoCIM-tool*

LoCIM-tool is the abbreviation of locus classification and inference of the major. It was developed in 2013 [81] and was first written as an Excel spreadsheet. To make investigative inferences about genotypes, it uses allele peak heights, and stochastic and

Table 10.1 Main functionalities of DNAxs version 1.1.0. Reproduced from [75] with permission from Elsevier.

Functionality	Details
Login	• Login with a user name and password • The login screen contains release notes and version changes as well as instruction videos
Import profiles	• Various file formats are accepted • Supports CE and MPS data
View profiles	• Electropherograms • Bar graphs visualizing the alleles and peaks heights/read counts − In case of replicates: Different colors representing whether or not an allele is reproduced in at least half of the replicates. − Different colors representing whether an allele is part of the major component or not (according to LoCIM)
View summary statistics	• Total allele count (TAC) • Maximum allele count (MAC) • Numbers of Type I, II and III loci (according to LoCIM)
Match profiles	• Matching of alleles in the bar graphs
Derive profiles	• Inference of a major contributor (according to LoCIM)
Match matrix	• Match matrix enabling comparisons of (many) stains to (many) reference profiles • Color coding for the number of non-matching alleles and a slider to set this number • The match matrix can be exported to PDF
Export profiles	• To LIMS/CODIS/SmartRank/Bonaparte etc. • Options to choose which alleles are exported (manual/replicate/consensus/composite/LoCIM inference)
Audit trail	• Keeps track of which actions are performed when and by who

heterozygote balance thresholds (Chapters 2 and 3), and the ratio between the heights of the largest allele peak, and all other peaks. The detailed criteria are presented in Table 10.2, and these are used to define a locus as *Type I*, *Type II*, or *Type III*. These categories represent classes of increasing complexity to infer a major contributor's genotype. A *Type I* locus fulfills the most stringent criteria and will most likely be correctly inferred. *Type II* loci may have lower peak heights or a smaller difference in peak heights compared to minor donors. *Type III* loci do not meet one or more of the *Type II* criteria, and are the most complex to infer a major contributor's genotype. Once the loci are classified, the largest peak at a locus is inferred, plus all alleles within 50% of the largest peak for *Type I* and *Type II* loci, or within 33% of the largest peak for *Type III* loci. These percentages were chosen to include only one or two alleles at *Type I* and *Type II* loci, and to include at least the genotype of the major contributor, but possibly more

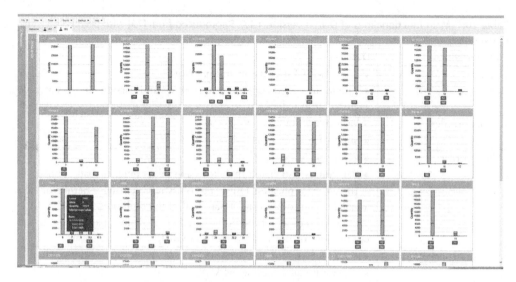

Figure 10.1 Screenshot of *DNAxs* bar graphs of a mixed autosomal profile that is compared to two reference profiles, shown in colored squares underneath the bars.

alleles for *Type III* loci. Searches of DNA databases using moderate search stringency settings are more likely to yield the true donor when more alleles are included. For example, if the donor was genotype 10,11, it would be highlighted with a moderate stringency search with alleles 10,11,12, but would be missed with a high stringency search (e.g., if the donor had genotype 10,11 searched with 11,12).

Table 10.2 Criteria for defining loci as *Type I*, *Type II*, or *Type III*, which corresponds to increasing complexity of inferring a major contributor's genotype.

Locus type	Peak height of alleles of the major contributor	Heterozygous balance of alleles of the major contributor	Mixture ratio of major to minor(s) in case major is heterozygous	Mixture ratio of major to minor(s) in case major is homozygous
Type I	All above stochastic threshold (ST) (in case of replicates: all above ST multiplied by number of replicates)	at least 0.60	at least 4:1	at least 8:1
Type II	–	at least 0.60	at least 2:1	at least 4:1
Type III	–	–	–	–

The *LoCIM-tool* can handle replicates with peak heights within the stochastic range. With replicates, the sum of the peak heights per allele are used. The peak height thresh-

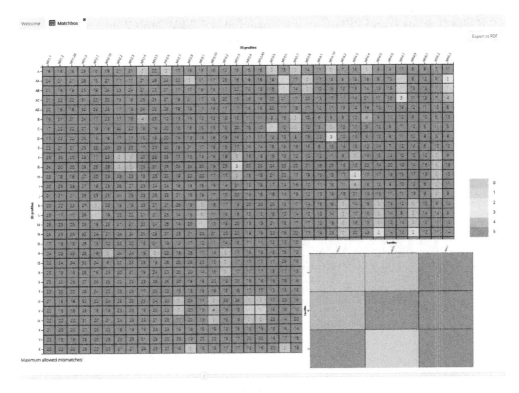

Figure 10.2 Example of a large match matrix generated using *DNAxs*. The user can choose which stain or reference profiles are shown horizontally or vertically. In this example, the 30 references "A" to "AD" are presented vertically and the stain profiles are shown horizontally. The numbers represent the number of alleles that are not-matching. Green, orange, and red represent "low", "medium", and "high" numbers of alleles that are not matching. These numbers can be set manually, using the slider on the bottom. The lower right shows a zoomed-in part of a smaller match matrix.

old that is required for a *Type I* locus is then the stochastic threshold multiplied by the number of replicates.

LoCIM-tool results are presented per locus, although a consideration of the results of the whole profile will help to determine whether the *Type I*, *Type II*, and/or *Type III* loci are correctly inferred. For instance, if a profile yields predominantly *Type I* loci, some *Type II* loci, and only one or few *Type III* loci, the whole profile, including the *Type III* loci, will likely be inferred correctly. The opposite could also occur: for example, if a profile yields predominantly *Type III*, a few *Type II*, and just one *Type I* locus, it is possible that the *Type I* locus is incorrectly inferred. Fig. 10.3 shows examples of whether or not a major contributor's genotype can be correctly inferred from the locus *Type*. These same trends were observed when *LoCIM-tool* was validated for NGM profiles analyzed using 9 kV 10 s CE injection settings with a stochastic threshold of

600 RFUs (Fig. 10.4) and PPF6C profiles analyzed at 1.2 kV 24 s CE injection settings with a stochastic threshold of 800 RFUs (Fig. 10.5).

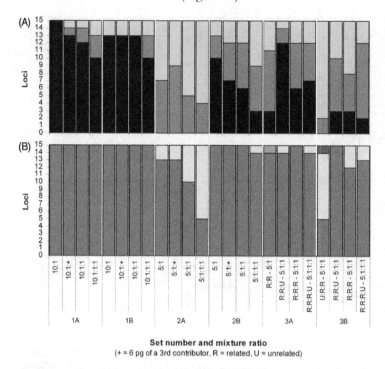

Figure 10.3 *LoCIM-tool* results for 24 NGM consensus profiles in the training set that were generated using four replicates and 3 kV 5 s CE injection settings. (A) Numbers of *Type I, II,* and *III* loci, shown as black, dark grey, and light grey bars, respectively. (B) Inference results: green, correctly deduced; yellow, extra alleles; orange, alleles of the major are missing; red, both an extra allele deduced and an allele of the major is missing.

Although *LoCIM-tool* is not a probabilistic method, it was shown that it performed almost as well as the Top Marginal option in the *EuroForMix* Deconvolution tab (Chapter 8.5.12) [236], and performance was greatly improved compared to manual inference of the major contributor's genotype (Fig. 10.6).

The *LoCIM-tool* in Excel was originally developed for autosomal DNA-profiles with up to 15 markers. Now it is implemented in *DNAxs* and can accommodate more markers: validated for PPF6C profiles consisting of 23 autosomal markers. The *LoCIM-tool* results are visually presented, and the user can export the inferred profile to, e.g., CODIS or *SmartRank* for searching a national DNA database. In the future, this method might be replaced by a method that can deconvolve all donors of mixed profiles. Currently, probabilistically deconvolving a (complex) mixed profile is very time consuming, whereas the *LoCIM* inference is completed in seconds, and has proven to be a very useful and practical investigative alternative in forensic casework.

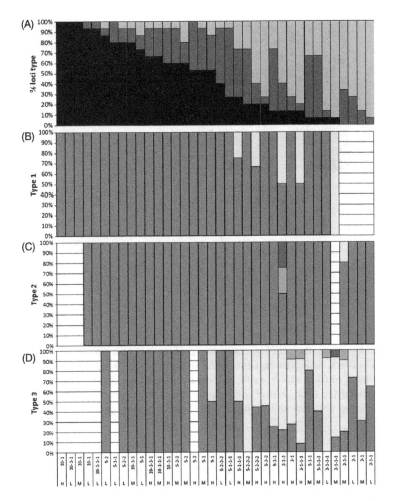

Figure 10.4 *LoCIM-tool* results for 36 NGM consensus profiles analyzed at 9 kV 10 s CE injection settings. (A) Locus classification results (loci *Type* 1, 2, and 3 shown as black, dark grey, and light grey, respectively). (B) Results of inference of the major *Type I* loci, (C) *Type II*, and (D) *Type III* loci. Correct, extra alleles, missing alleles, extra, and missing alleles are shown as green, yellow, orange, and red bars, respectively. Where no color is shown, a locus type was not observed. Each vertical line represents one mixture sample, the ratio on the X-axis represents the amount of DNA in pg per contributor and H, L, and M denote, high, low, and moderate allele sharing between contributors, respectively. Reproduced from [81] with permission from Elsevier.

10.3. DNAStatistX

Since 2019 *DNAxs* has implemented *DNAStatistX* (*DNAxs* v1.3.2 and *DNAStatistX* v1.0.0), a statistical library that contains the algorithm used to calculate the maximum likelihood estimate (MLE), which is based on the model published by Cowell

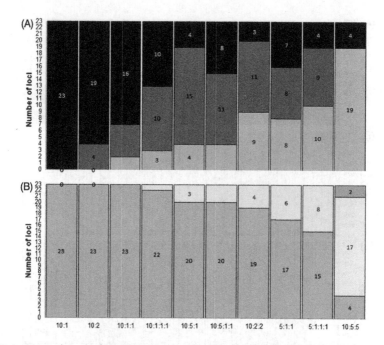

Figure 10.5 *LoCIM-tool* results for PPF6C consensus profiles. (A) Locus classification results (loci *Type I*, *II*, and *III* shown as black, dark grey, and light grey, respectively). (B) Results of inference of the major. Correct, extra alleles, missing alleles, extra, and missing alleles are shown as green, yellow, orange, and red bars, respectively. Each vertical line represents one mixture sample, the ratio represents the amount of DNA in pg per contributor. Numbers in the bar graphs show the number of loci in the particular category.

et al. [234] and Bleka et al. [76]. The statistical library supports parallel computing, which can be delegated to a computer cluster, and enables queuing of requested *LR* calculations. The library (*DNAStatistX*) is written in Java and is accessible separately or via *DNAxs*.

10.3.1 Similarities and differences between *EuroForMix* and *DNAStatistX*

EuroForMix has three different methods to calculate the *LR*: a) the MLE approach (incl. a "conservative" method), b) the full Bayesian approach, and c) the qualitative (semi-continuous) approach from *LRmix*. *DNAStatistX* includes an algorithm to calculate the MLE. As with *EuroForMix*, it includes theta correction, a degradation model, model validation using PP-plots, and accommodates replicates. Since *EuroForMix* is written in R and C++, not all of the functions that *EuroForMix* uses are available for *DNAStatistX*, which is written in Java. An overview of the differences regarding the MLE implementation is presented in Table 10.3. For the optimizer and the model validation function, alternatives were explored and selected. In addition, *DNAStatistX* allows the use of

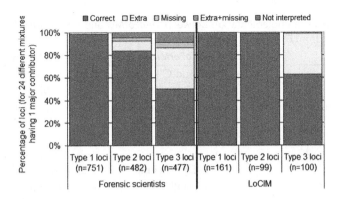

Figure 10.6 Manual versus automated *LoCIM-tool* inference of the major contributor's genotype. Manual inference was performed by a total of 19 forensic scientists. Reproduced from [81] with permission from Elsevier.

dye-specific, or even locus-specific detection thresholds (instead of an overall detection threshold), which improves the distinction between alleles and noise.

Whereas *EuroForMix* includes both a degradation and stutter model, in the first version of *DNAStatistX* (v1.0.0), only the degradation model was implemented. The stutter model was not realized for the following reasons: At the NFI, DNA profiles are analyzed using locus specific stutter filters at the $n-2$, -1, -0.5, $+0.5$, and $n+1$ repeat unit positions, whereas *EuroForMix* only considers $n-1$ repeat unit stutter positions (version 3.0.0 onwards incorporates $n+1$ stutter).

In *EuroForMix* the likelihoods are maximized using the parameters that best explain the data for each proposition. *EuroForMix* has an option that models the parameter errors by performing sensitivity analysis that considers the *LR* as a function of the parameters involved [236]. As a so-called "conservative" value (in favor of the defense proposition), one can use the lower 5% percentile of this sensitivity analysis (this is the value termed as "the conservative *LR*" when using *EuroForMix*). This results in somewhat lower *LRs* when compared to the MLE. Since the lowering effect was very small with PowerPlex Fusion 6C profiles with a minimal effect on the number of false positives [238], and because sensitivity analyses are very time-consuming, this option was not implemented in *DNAStatistX* v1.0.0.

The effects of the differences between *DNAStatistX* and *EuroForMix* are elucidated in the sections that follow.

10.3.2 Optimizer to estimate parameters

The first version of *DNAStatistX* used the same calculation of the MLE function as provided in *EuroForMix*. In *EuroForMix* the "nlm" optimizer is used to search for best

Table 10.3 Differences in implementation between *EuroForMix* and *DNAStatistX*. Reproduced from [75] with permission from Elsevier.

	EuroForMix	*DNAStatistX*
Code	R and C++	Java
Optimizer	nlm	CMA-ES
Number of optimizer start points	User defined, default = 4	Programmed dynamically to have 3 times the same largest likelihood out of 3 up to 10 iterations
Model validation	AdaptIntegrate	TrapezoidIntegrator
Detection threshold	Overall	Dye (locus) specific
Drop-in parameters	Overall	Dye (locus) specific
Stutter model	Yes	No
Sensitivity analysis	Yes	No
Support kinship model	Yes	No
Automated queuing of LR calculation	No	Yes (within *DNAxs*)

explaining parameters for mixture proportions, peak height expectation, peak height variance, degradation slope, and stutter proportion. As nlm is not available in Java, an alternative was implemented, namely "CMA-ES". A different optimizer may invoke slight differences between the results for the two software programs. These differences were examined by comparing the results from 160 sets of propositions that did not include rare alleles, analyzed using an overall detection threshold to be comparable with *EuroForMix*. These 160 analyses included samples that varied the number of contributors between 1 and 4, degradation slope, mixture proportion, peak height, level of drop-out, level of allele sharing, and STR typing kit (NGM or PowerPlex Fusion 6C). Either a true or a known non-contributor was the POI under H_p; models were tested with either a true or an incorrect number of contributors, with or without conditioning on a known contributor. *LR* comparisons between the two software programs were performed per and over all markers, compared up to two significant digits. Estimated parameters were compared up to four significant decimals, i.e., the first four digits of the mantissa in scientific notation. For the expected peak height a minimum difference of 1.0 was used; differences that were smaller than the level up to which the comparisons were performed were regarded as equal results.

Results from the 160 analyses revealed small differences between the two software programs, shown in Table 10.4.

When the parameter values obtained by the *EuroForMix* were plugged into *DNAStatistX* no differences were obtained between the two software programs. This confirmed that the implementation of the code to calculate the *LR*s was correct, and that differences were the result of using different optimizers [75].

Table 10.4 Overview of the largest differences observed between *EuroForMix* and *DNAStatistX* resulting from the implementation of a different optimizer. Reproduced from [75] with permission from Elsevier.

Difference in	Number of analyses	Range of differences (*DNAStatistX* minus *EuroForMix*)
None of the parameters, LR or likelihoods	38/160	Not applicable
Log10 LR	12/160	−0.59 to +0.63
Log likelihood Hp	5/160	−1.3 to +7.6
Log likelihood Hd	2/160	+1.6 to +7.2
LR per locus	97/3520	−72 to +5.2
Expected peak height (RFU /percentage)	5/160	−135 to +32 RFU /0.6 to 2.1 percent
Expected peak height (percentage)	5/160	0.6 to 2.1 percent
Peak height variation	27/160	−0.1 to +0.4
Mixture proportion	220/470	−0.4 to +0.3
Degradation slope	26/160	−0.01 to +0.02

10.3.3 Number of optimizer iterations

For a two-person mixture with four alleles at a locus and two unknowns under H_d, there are 15 possible genotypes per contributor (including drop-out and/or drop-in events), which gives a total of 225 different genotype combinations for the two contributors (15×15). These calculations require about 5,000 optimizer steps, and for a profile with 23 autosomal markers, this yields a total of about 25,875,000 calculation terms under H_d ($225 \times 23 \times 5000$). With a four-person mixture, this number increases to hundreds of billions of calculations. To improve the processing-time efficiency of *DNAStatistX*, the number of optimizer start points, or iterations, was examined in more detail. The optimizer runs multiple times (denoted as the number of iterations) to reach the global optimum. By default, the number of optimizer iterations is four in *EuroForMix*. *DNAStatistX* uses a different optimizer and showed robust results with four iterations. To minimize processing time, it was explored whether fewer iterations would suffice. In 96.1% (23,233/24,184) of the repeated optimizer runs, the same largest log likelihood was obtained (Fig. 10.7, log likelihood differences of zero on the x-axis). For the 3.9% of the optimizer runs, where there were differences, it was apparent that the lower the log likelihood, the greater the variation between optimizer iterations (Fig. 10.7). However, with three iterations, the probability of missing the optimum likelihood was 1 in 16,445 (Table 10.5), which can be regarded as an acceptable risk. Although this probability is rather low, for 3% of the H_p/H_d calculations, the optimum was missed in more than 30% of the repeated analyses (data not shown). Therefore the number of optimizer iterations in *DNAStatistX* was programmed dynamically to have a minimum of three iterations: if with three iterations the likelihoods were not identical (with a maximum difference of two decimal places on log_{10} scale), the number of iterations was increased by one, until three times the same largest likelihood is obtained. The maximum number of iterations was set to ten. This flexibility saves computing time and enables efficient use of the calculation capacity, as more than three iterations are only applied when needed. Furthermore, using the "rule of three" approach, the probability of missing the optimum is almost negligible; the probability of missing the optimum after ten iterations was calculated as $Pr = 10^{-12}$.

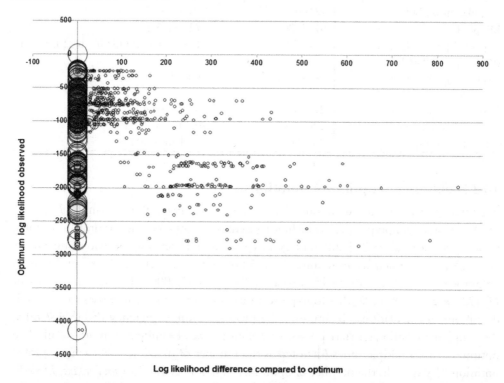

Figure 10.7 Variation in log likelihoods between iterations of the optimizer in *DNAStatistX*. The sizes of the circles are proportional to the number of analyses that yielded this optimum. The large circles at $x = 0$ are the iterations yielding the global optimum. The smaller circles on the right show the iterations that did not yield the global optimum. The further to the right, the larger the difference compared to the global optimum. Reproduced from [75] with permission from Elsevier.

10.3.4 Overall versus dye-specific detection threshold

In *EuroForMix* (up to version 2.3.1), an overall detection threshold is applied across all loci. In *DNAStatistX* a dye- (or even locus-) specific detection threshold can be utilized. A study to compare overall vs. dye-specific detection thresholds was undertaken using

Table 10.5 Overview of the numbers/percentages of H_p and H_d analyses that yielded the optimal likelihood ("succeeded"), and the probabilities of missing the optimum when one, two, three, or four iterations were used for the optimizer in *DNAStatistX*.

	Total	H_p	H_d
Number of analyses	24,184	12,092	12,092
Number of succeeded analyses	23,233	11,594	11,639
p(missed) (%)	3.9	4.1	3.7
1 iteration: Missed: 1 in	25	24	27
2 iterations: Missed: 1 in	647	590	713
3 iterations: Missed: 1 in	16,445	14,315	19,020
4 iterations: Missed: 1 in	418,206	347,596	507,691

profiles analyzed with GeneMarker ($n = 20$ analyses for two different sets of dye-specific detection thresholds). As expected, results showed larger likelihoods with dye-specific rather than the overall threshold, the former therefore provides a better explanation for the data. However, effects on $log_{10}LR$ were minimal as the increase in likelihoods was approximately equivalent under H_p and H_d.

However, if dye-specific detection thresholds are used, there is a need to collect dye-specific drop-in data, which requires the analysis of large numbers of casework blanks. At the NFI, PowerPlex Fusion 6C was used at 29 cycles PCR and 1.2 kV 24 s CE injection settings on an 3500xL apparatus. This kit was validated using "low" and "high" dye-specific detection thresholds, varying per dye from 40 to 80 RFUs and from 85 to 140 RFUs, respectively. Drop-in parameters were obtained from 1119 casework DNA extraction blanks analyzed at both the low (see Table 10.6) and high dye-specific detection thresholds. This resulted in 240 and 48 drop-in events, for low- and high-detection thresholds, respectively. The relative frequency of drop-in per marker varied between 0.0004 and 0.0133. Lambda for these data varied between 0.024 and 0.045. In a previous study using NGM data (29 cycles 3 kV 5 s CE settings on an ABI 3130xL and using an overall detection threshold of 50 RFUs in GeneMapper) a total of 14,757 casework blanks were analyzed. These included 80 false positive alleles, yielding a drop-in frequency per marker of 0.00036, and lambda of 0.018 [236].

10.3.5 Model validation

The second difference between *EuroForMix* and the Java implementation of *DNAxs* concerns the model "Validation" option, where the cumulative probability of the expected peak height for each allele is plotted against the cumulative probability of the observed peak height, yielding a PP (probability-probability) plot (Chapter 8.5.8). During model validation, a Bonferroni-corrected "goodness of fit test" is performed, for which the significance level is set to 0.01 by default. When the observed peak heights

Table 10.6 Drop-in probabilities and lambda computed using the autosomal markers in PowerPlex Fusion 6C casework blanks. Reproduced from [75] with permission from Elsevier.

Dye	Number of loci	Detection threshold	Number of drop-ins	Sum of the drop-in peak heights shifted by the detection threshold	Drop-in probability (C)	Lambda (λ)
Blue	6	45	89	3569	0.0133	0.025
Green	5	50	54	1574	0.0097	0.034
Yellow	6	45	67	1652	0.0100	0.041
Red	5	80	16	439	0.0029	0.036
Purple	1	40	14	574	0.0125	0.024
Total	23		240		0.0093	0.031

deviate from the expected peak heights, alleles will plot outside this "0.01-line". The model validation can be used as a quality check, which is recommended for every analysis performed. If a specified number of, for example, five or more data points reside out of the 0.01-line, one may consider the model validation as "failed", as the expected and observed peak heights deviate. In *EuroForMix* the "AdaptIntegrate" function was used, and in *DNAStatistX* the "TrapezoidIntegrator", was used for model validation. When an *LR* calculation in *DNAStatistX* is carried out, the model validation is automatically performed, whereas in *EuroForMix* model validation is optional. Comparisons between the *EuroForMix* and *DNAStatistX* model validation showed the same data points (with a maximum difference of 0.01) for the two software programs. As a result, the analyses that fail model validation in *EuroForMix* (v1.11.4) will also fail in *DNAStatistX* (v1.0.0).

When a large and variable set of H_p and H_d analyses ($n = 180$ each) was examined, model validations with at least two data points outside the 0.01-line were observed in three types of analyses. The first related to H_p analyses with a non-contributor as POI. Failing model validations can be expected for analyses with a non-contributor, as peak heights are more difficult to explain, since H_p is false. Generally, these analyses will yield low (exclusionary) *LRs*. The second type were analyses, where the degradation model was not applied, whereas the data showed a degradation pattern (descending peak heights with increasing fragment lengths). The peak heights expected by the model will not fit the data. The third type were analyses with three replicates that had extraordinary variation for the peak heights between the replicates. As the optimizer searches for parameters that best explain the combined data, not all individual data points followed the expected peak heights.

Furthermore, failing model validations can be expected in other cases, e.g., if the data cannot be explained by the number of contributors put forward by the proposition.

Failing model validations were observed from replicates data that were obtained using a larger cycle number than the default for the PowerPlex Fusion 6C STR typing kit (32 instead of 29). These profiles exhibited greater stochastic variation. The stochastic threshold for the 29 cycles profiles was 800 RFUs, with 32 cycles the stochastic threshold was around 3700 RFUs. This demonstrated that the gamma distribution model appeared to be unsuitable for the category of profiles that showed large stochastic variation.

10.3.6 *DNAxs* software testing

Testing of software during development, prior to release and during validation is important to ensure that the software is robust and behaves as designed. With a growing number of features, software testing becomes a very time-consuming task if performed manually. To save time, to improve the test coverage, to increase *ad-hoc* and exploratory testing, and to reduce cost and maintenance, dedicated test engineers designed and built automated tests for *DNAxs*.

To carry out this software testing, four levels were defined:

1. Unit testing (a level of software testing, where individual units/components of a software are tested).
2. Integration testing (in which individual units are combined and tested as a group).
3. System testing (a level of software testing, where a complete and integrated software is tested).
4. Acceptance testing (a type of testing done by users and/or stakeholders, to test if the software meets the requirements and works as intended). In this section, integration testing will be further elucidated.

The purpose of integration testing is to expose faults in the interaction between integrated units. This is important as separately features may perform well, whereas they can fail when used simultaneously. Since integration testing is a key component of the development process, bugs are found at an early stage. The code coverage is high and easy to track, and test reports are generated automatically. With regard to software development, this saves much time and effort, and furthermore it delivers insight into the quality of the software.

In the test process, the test engineers perform six consecutive steps (Box 10.1).

Box 10.1 Steps in software integration testing

1. Perform a product risk analysis (PRA).
2. Create process flow per functionality.
3. Create test scenarios.
4. Create automated test steps.
5. Run the automated tests on a build server.
6. Check the automatically generated test report.

At first, a PRA is performed to define which parts of the software have the highest risk of damage and failure, identifying areas where it is most important to build test scripts. The product risk is defined as "Damage × Chance of failure" and results in an A, B, or C notation, which is defined as high, moderate, or low risk, respectively (Fig. 10.7). A PRA may consider a system under test from a variety of viewpoints, e.g., a) from a business viewpoint: How does the system fit in the business processes? Which features are most important?; b) also from a technical/IT viewpoint: Is proven technology used? How stable is an installed source code base? etc. PRA analyses ensure that the various stakeholders, expert users, software- and test-engineers achieve a joint view of the risks that are inherent in the various parts of the system. For *DNAxs*, for instance, the user might not mention the login/logout functionality as the most important feature to build tests for. However, from a technical point of view, this is the functionality with the highest product risk: i.e., if the login functionality fails, the software is useless (Fig. 10.7).

Once the functionalities are labeled A, B, or C by the PRA, the test engineers start by creating process flows for the category A functionalities. A process flow consists of creating an overview of all possible paths, decision points (decisions made either by the software or the user), and actions that relate to the specific functionality. An example of a process flow is presented in Fig. 10.8.

Next, test scenarios are created for each of the process flows and using "Gherkin" language (https://cucumber.io/docs/gherkin/reference/). Gherkin language is a readable, human language, which describes software behavior from a user perspective. All parts of the process flow are translated to text using a principle of "given", "when", "then" in a certain scenario (Fig. 10.9). An example is presented in Fig. 10.10.

For each scenario, test steps are created (Fig. 10.11). These steps translate the user readable syntax into code that can interact with the software.

With every change made to the code, all the tests are run on a build server. The build process includes unit tests and integration tests. When the build is completed, the automatically generated test reports are examined. In case of failing tests, the test report indicates which particular part failed, and the software developers will modify the code to fix the bug(s). All tests scripts are run after every change in the software, and once every night as scheduled. Only when all tests succeed the build will be accepted and can be sent through to release.

10.4. An exemplar case analyzed with *DNAxs-DNAStatistX* and *EuroForMix*

10.4.1 Analysis using *DNAxs-DNAStatistX*

As with previous sections, an exemplar case is analyzed, this time using *DNAxs* that implements *DNAStatistX*. *DNAStatistX* is based on the same *LR* model, as described for *EuroForMix*, and results are therefore very similar [238]. *DNAxs* and *DNAStatistX* are described at the start of this chapter.

Table 10.7 Example of a product risk analysis for functionalities within *DNAxs*. The product risk = damage × chance of failure and results in an A (high risk), B (moderate-risk), or C (low-risk) notation.

	Number	Test goal	Damage	Chance of failure	User frequency	Chance of faults	Product risk
Functionality	1	Login/logout	H	H	H	M	A
Functionality	2	Case management	H	M	H	M	B
Functionality	3	Settings – User: display settings, user preferences – Bonaparte settings	M	L	L	L	C
Functionality	4	Help function	L	L	L	L	C
Functionality	5	View button	L	L	L	L	C
Functionality	6	Match matrix (+ compare EPG)	H	H	M	M	B
Functionality	7	Export to file	H	L	L	L	B

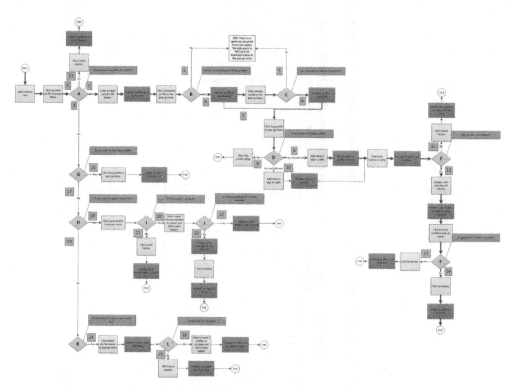

Figure 10.8 Example of a process flow for the functionality of all the actions that can be performed on a profile in *DNAxs* from a specific menu. Light green (light grey in print version) boxes indicate actions performed by the user, orange diamonds show decision points, dark green (medium grey in print version) boxes present questions regarding the goal of the end-user, and blue (dark grey in print version) boxes show validation actions performed within the software.

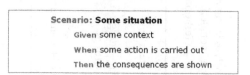

Figure 10.9 Principle of a "given", "when", "then" scenario, which is used to translate all parts of the process flow into Gherkin language.

The exemplar case consists of a mixed PowerPlex Fusion 6C profile of one major and two minor contributors (denoted "4E3_2.csv"); a reference profile of a person of interest (POI) (e.g., the suspect) (denoted "RefR.csv") and major conditioned individual "4E3_U1.csv". The data files are made available on the book's website https://sites.google.com/view/dnabook/. Below, we go through the steps within *DNAxs/DNAStatistX*; further detailed information and screen shots can be found in the user manual that is provided within the software.

```
   Scenario: 0200 Empty fields warning Login
13 Given I am on the login page
14 When I click the login button
15 Then a warning message on the username field is shown: Please fill out this field
16
17 When I enter user1 in the username textfield
18 And I click the login button
19 Then a warning message on the password field is shown: Please fill out this field
20
21 When I clear the username textfield
22 And I enter password1 in the password textfield
23 And I click the login button
24 Then a warning message on the username field is shown: Please fill out this field
25
26
```

Figure 10.10 Example of a test scenario for the *DNAxs* login functionality.

```
@When("I click the login button")
public void loginButtonClick() {
    _loginPage.clickLoginButton();
}

@When("I enter $username in the username textfield")
public void enterUsername(final String username) {
    _loginPage.enterTextInUsernameTextfield(username);
}

@When("I enter $password in the password textfield")
public void enterPassword(final String password) {
    _loginPage.enterTextInPasswordTextfield(password);
}

@When("I enter $username as username and $password as password")
public void enterCredentials(final String username, final String password) {
    _loginPage.enterTextInUsernameTextfield(username);
    _loginPage.enterTextInPasswordTextfield(password);
}
```

Figure 10.11 Example of test steps created for the *DNAxs* login scenario.

The first step is to login to the *DNAxs* software with a user name and password. After login, a welcome screen is shown, and one can navigate to the version changes, user manual with screen shots, and tutorial videos.

In the second step a case can be opened or generated by pressing "File" > "Open Case", after which the case folder with data can be selected.

The third step is to add trace profile data under the heading "Traces".

Once the trace profile is loaded, the DNA profile is visually presented as bar graphs similar to the original electropherogram. Details on the profile and summary statistics are presented for the kit settings, maximum allele count (MAC), total allele count (TAC), and *LoCIM* information (Figs. 10.12 and 10.13). The output includes the numbers of

Type I, II, and *III* loci (defined in Section 10.2), classification per locus, and colors representing whether an allele would be regarded as belonging to the major component of the DNA profile. For further details on *LoCIM* see Section 10.2.

This exemplar profile shows a clear major contributor, which is indicated by the blue (medium grey in print version) colored peaks. Because all loci are classified as *Type I*, in *DNAxs*, this major contributor can be inferred using the button "Create unknown", after which alleles can be selected to be included in the inferred profile. In this case, all loci are of *Type I*, and we accept all alleles as inferred by *LoCIM* (Fig. 10.14). After pressing "Create", a file with the genotype is created and stored as "4E3 U1". "U1" stands for Unknown 1 and this profile is automatically added to the tab "Persons". By selecting this reference profile, the alleles are shown underneath the alleles of the trace profile. If desired, one can change the color of the alleles of the reference profile by double clicking on color.

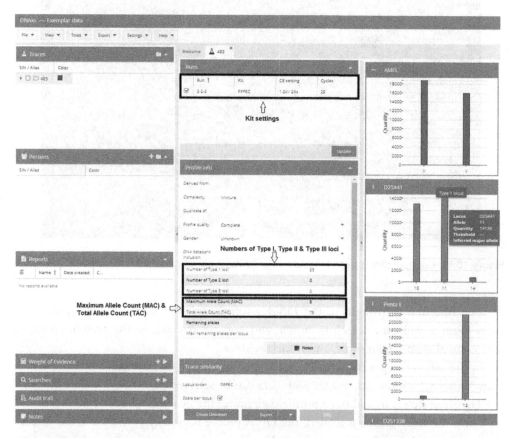

Figure 10.12 Overview of profile details that are presented after loading a trace PowerPlex Fusion 6C profile into *DNAxs*.

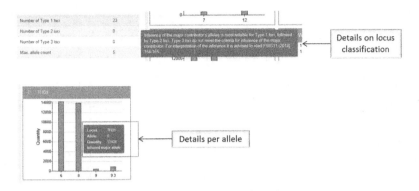

Figure 10.13 Further details presented in *DNAxs* with tool tip function.

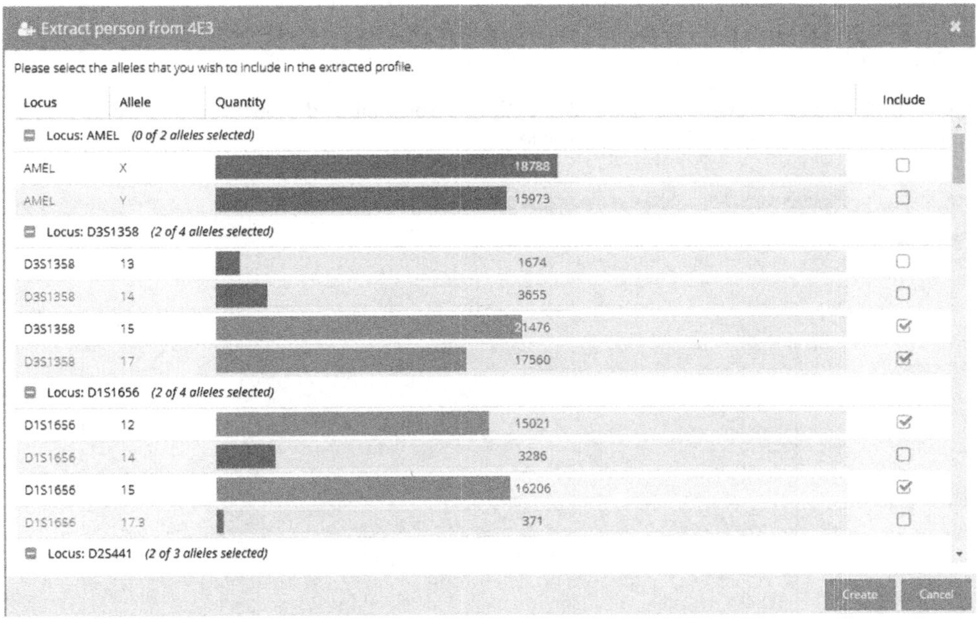

Figure 10.14 Inferring the major contributor (alleles marked by the blue (medium grey in print version) bars) in *DNAxs*. This genotype will be denoted the sample name, plus U1, for Unknown 1. In this case example the inferred genotype is "4E3 U1".

The fourth step is similar to the third, although now we can add the reference profile of the POI, i.e., "RefR.csv" (Fig. 10.15). Comparison between the reference and trace profile reveals that there are four alleles of the reference profile that are not observed in the trace profile. Another way of examining differences between profiles can be done using the Match box, or Match matrix, option, which is particularly useful when comparing many profiles (Fig. 10.16).

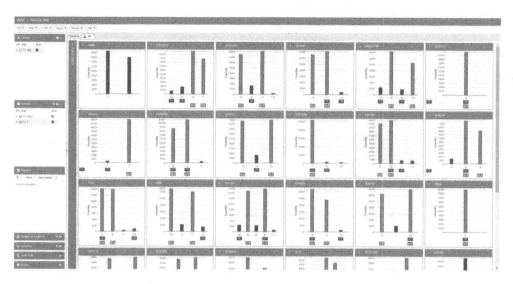

Figure 10.15 Reference "RefR.csv" was added to the "Persons" tab and shown as red (medium grey in print version) labels underneath the trace profile.

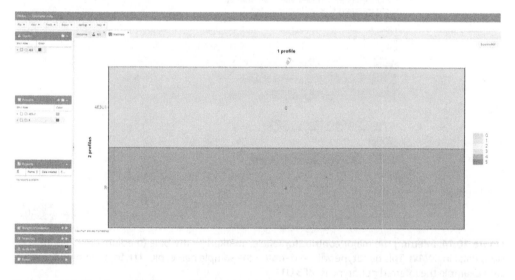

Figure 10.16 Match matrix of trace 4E3 2 against the inferred major (4E3 U1) and RefR. The color represents the number of non-matching alleles, which is 0 for the inferred major and four for RefR.

The fifth step is to compute the *LR* using *DNAStatistX*, which can be found under the button Weight of Evidence (from version 1.4.0 and up). After selecting the trace profile and kit settings, we can define our propositions (Fig. 10.17). Furthermore, in the advanced settings tab, it is possible to select the population's frequency file, set the value

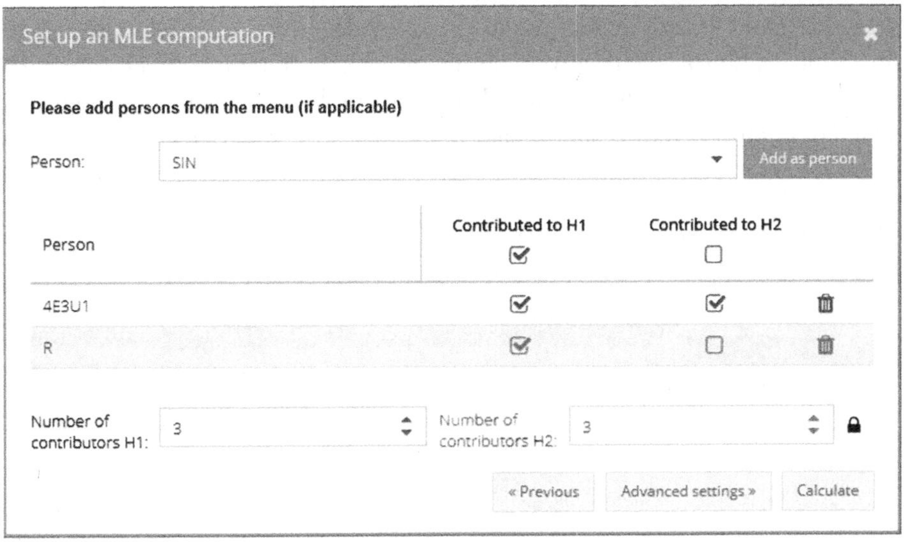

Figure 10.17 Defining propositions for the LR calculation.

for theta correction and the rare allele frequency. In this exemplar, we used the "Fusion 6C holland2" frequencies file, a rare allele frequency of 0.0003 and theta = 0.01. Dye-specific detection thresholds and drop-in parameters were applied as presented in Table 10.6. By pressing Calculate, the MLE job will be submitted. Next, in the weight of evidence tab it is shown whether the job is submitted (and queued), calculating, finished or failed. Once the calculation is finished, the results can be viewed. Fig. 10.18 shows the results table that includes the information on the calculation, the estimated parameters under H_p and H_d, the LRs per locus, and the overall LR. The estimated mixture proportions are shown as pie charts under H_p and H_d. This screen also shows whether the model validation passed (green (light grey in print version)), failed for up to four data points (orange (medium grey in print version)), or failed with four or more data points (red (dark grey in print version)). In addition, the number of iterations required to reach three times the same optimum is presented. For further information on the number of iterations programmed in *DNAStatistX*, see Section 10.3.3. Further details that can be viewed are the model validations under H_p and H_d (Fig. 10.19), and the optimizer results (Fig. 10.20). In this exemplar case, the model validations passed and a global optimum was found. The propositions were:

H_p: R+4E_3_U1+U;
H_d: 4E_3_U1+U+U.
R = POI and 4E_3_U1 is the conditioned major reference.

The $log_{10}LR = 10.05$.

Note that *DNAStatistX* makes use of the same degradation model as *EuroForMix*, but does not apply a $n-1$ backward-stutter model. In addition, in *DNAStatistX* it is possible to make use of dye-specific detection thresholds, which were used in this example. For comparison, this same example was analyzed with *EuroForMix* in the next section.

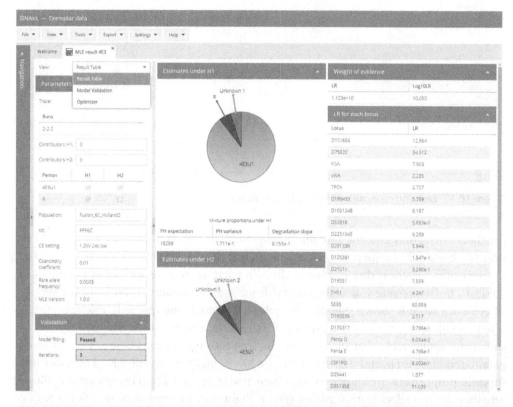

Figure 10.18 Overview of the MLE results table showing the overall *LR*, *LRs* per locus and parameters estimated for H_p (H1) and H_d (H2). The left panel presents the parameters and propositions, and shows that the model fitting (model validation) passed and that out of three iterations, three times the same optimum was obtained by the optimizer.

10.4.2 Comparison of the exemplar using *EuroForMix*

A comparative study of mock crime sample "4E3.2_2_2.hid" (filename "4E3_2.csv"), analyzed by *DNAxs*, was carried out with *EuroForMix*. The procedures previously described in Chapter 8 were used. The same thresholds and propositions described for *DNAxs* in the previous section were applied, with the exception that a universal limit of detection threshold RFU = 40 and drop-in parameter $p_C = 0.0093$, $\lambda = 0.031$ was adopted by *EuroForMix* in lieu of the dye-specific thresholds used by *DNAxs*.

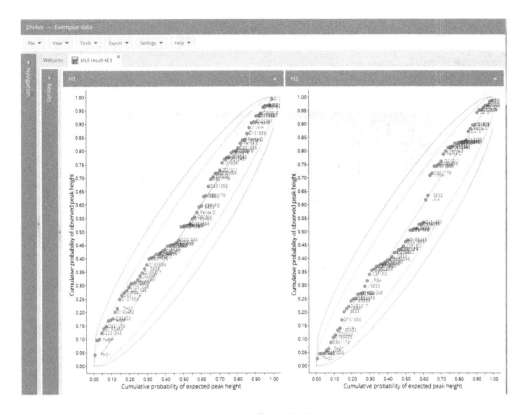

Figure 10.19 Model validation showing results of the PP-plots.

To recap, the "suspect" under H_p is sample "R" loaded from file "RefR.csv"; conditioned; contributor "4E3_U1" is from file 4E3_U1.csv. R is present as a minor contributor ($M_x \approx 0.06$), and 4E3_U1 is a major conditioned (under both H_p and H_d) contributor, where $M_x \approx 0.9$. A three-contributor LR was calculated using propositions:

H_p: R+4E_3_U1+U;
H_d: 4E_3_U1+U+U.

The same *DNAxs* file, to which locus specific stutter filters were applied, was analyzed with *EuroForMix*. There are two peaks that do not belong to any of the true contributors, one is on a $n + 1$ stutter position (allele 14 at D8S1179), the other is not on a stutter position (allele 27 at D12S391). The degradation module was utilized throughout, and this resulted in a $log_{10}LR = 9.4$. The corresponding result from *DNAxs* was $log_{10}LR = 10.05$. The difference can be attributed to the different dye-specific detection thresholds used in *DNAxs*, and the different MLE optimizer algorithms that are used by the two models.

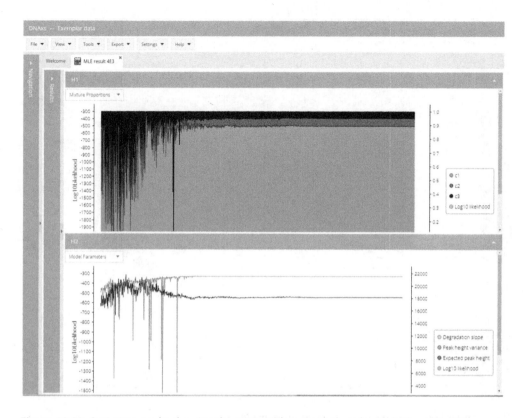

Figure 10.20 Optimizer results showing the estimated parameters under H_p (H1) and H_d (H2).

DNAxs does not incorporate a stutter module, so the next step was to determine the effect upon the *LR*. A raw data file "4E3_2 0% DTH low" contains this data. Loaded into *EuroForMix*, using the same settings described previously, this time using the stutter and degradation modules, resulted in a reduced $log_{10}LR = 6.5$. This reduction in *LR* was quite dramatic; e.g., in locus D8S1179, the *LR* was reduced from 3.018 to 0.007.

On closer inspection (Table 10.8), the unfiltered dataset for this locus consisted of eight alleles, ranging from type 10 to type 17. Before version 3 of *EuroForMix* only $n-1$ backward-stutter was taken into account; only alleles 11 and 15 can be fully accounted for in this way, leaving an additional six alleles to consider. Under H_p, individual R is homozygote 13, and 4E3_U1 is heterozygote 12,13. Versions prior to *EuroForMix* v3 do not take account of forward $n+1$ stutter, hence this leaves three unknown alleles (10, 14, 17), which would require a total of two unknown contributors to explain, i.e., a total of two known and two unknown contributors. Under H_d, R is unknown, hence only three contributors would be required.

Table 10.8 D8S1179 alleles in the filtered vs non-filtered data. Alleles 11 and 15 are removed as $n - 1$ back-stutters and the 17 allele is removed as a forward $n + 1$ stutter.

Allele	Known (Hp)	Peak height
10		1225
11		**1499**
12	4E3	15355
13	R	2398
14		321
15		**1620**
16	4E3	15846
17		**204**

When there are too many alleles to explain the number of contributors posited, they are treated as drop-in events. Given that the drop-in rate is very low ($p_C = 0.0093$), all such events are strongly penalized, and this accounts for the low LR compared to the stutter-filtered data. Consequently, with such a case, it is recommended that either the data are stutter-filtered, or that the number of contributors is increased to negate the effect of the low drop-in parameter. It is important to take account of the H_d maximum likelihood values to determine the optimal model for reporting purposes, as explained in Chapter 8.5.6, using the Akaike information criterion (AIC). The compiled results for various models are shown in Table 10.9. This table compares fully stutter-filtered, no stutter-filter, and other stutter-filters (i.e., forward stutters and $n - 2$ backward stutters), leaving for analysis $n - 1$ backward-stutters only. The optimal model for the fully filtered data is achieved with three contributors, whereas with the unfiltered data, the optimum is four or five contributors. Here there is a small reduction in the LR when five contributors are analyzed, but the model is shown to be essentially stable at four contributors, since both models provide a similar $log_{10}LR = 14$. This LR is noticeably larger than that achieved with the fully filtered model, and this is because it provides an overall better fit to the data if stutter is included. The $n - 1$ backward-stutter proportion returned by the four-contributor model is $\epsilon = 0.07$. This is within the same range of the estimated proportion of individual R, where $M_x = 0.06$ (Table 10.10). It can be argued for low-level contributors that $n - 1$ stutter should be retained to reduce potential bias, since their peak heights are equivalent. Forward and complex stutters are much smaller, for example, the $n + 1$ forward stutter in D8S1179 is 204 RFU = 0.013, the size of the parent 16 allele (Table 10.8). This is less likely to have an impact on the interpretation, so long as it is accounted for as an extra contributor rather than drop-in.

Further examination of the M_x results in Table 10.10 shows that excess unknown contributors are given equal proportions to each other, e.g., for the five-contributor,

336 Forensic Practitioner's Guide to the Interpretation of Complex DNA Profiles

Table 10.9 Comparison of models analyzed using stutter filtered data vs unfiltered data across 3–5 contributors, showing the sensitivity of the *LR* relative to model optimization measured by the loglik parameter. Note that this parameter can only be compared for models using the same data. The unfiltered data are in bold type, and these can be directly compared, as can the complex stutter (leaving $n - 1$ back-stutter alleles in the data) filtered and fully stutter filtered datasets.

Stutter filtered data?	No. of Contributors	Loglik with penalty in brackets	Adjusted LogLik value	Log10LR	Comment
Yes	3	$-763.3(-1)$	-764.3	9.39	
Yes	4	$-763.3(-2)$	-765.3	9.39	Stable at 3 contributors
No	**3**	**$-1331(-2)$**	**-1333**	**6.46**	
No	**4**	**$-1298(-3)$**	**-1301**	**14.02**	
No	**5**	**$-1290(-4)$**	**-1294**	**13.95**	**Stable at 4 contributors**
Complex stutters removed	3	$-1063(-1)$	-1064	15.65	
Complex stutters removed	4	$-1063(-2)$	-1065	15.65	Stable at 3 contributors
DNAxs	3			10.05	

Table 10.10 M_x proportions for known and unknown contributors (U1–U3) for the various datasets analyzed: fully stutter filtered; not filtered, and complex stutter filtered data leaving $n - 1$ back-stutter alleles in the data.

Data	Sample	No. of contributors		
		3	4	5
Filtered	4E3_U1	0.89	0.89	
Filtered	R	0.055	0.059	
Filtered	U1	0.052	0.026	
Filtered	U2		0.026	
Not filtered	4E3_U1	0.9	0.88	0.88
Not filtered	R	0.066	0.06	0.055
Not filtered	U1	0.32	0.026	0.021
Not filtered	U2		0.026	0.021
Not filtered	U3			0.021
Complex stutters filtered	4E3_U1	0.9	0.9	
Complex stutters filtered	R	0.06	0.06	
Complex stutters filtered	U1	0.039	0.039	
Complex stutters filtered	U2		10^{-10}	

not-filtered example, each unknown $M_x = 0.021$. This happens, because the peak heights of the minor contributors are very low, and peak height information cannot distinguish between possible genotypes. The exception is with the complex stutter filtered sample, where there is an unknown contributor present at $M_x = 0.039$ and another at vanishingly low level, $M_x = 10^{-10}$, which is highly stable in terms of modeling additional contributors, and the LR is also the greatest achieved in the set of experimental results.

The conclusion of this particular comparison would indicate that the results of *DNAxs* and *EuroForMix* are comparable, provided that the data are filtered of stutters. When the person of interest is within stutter size, then it may be advantageous to use *EuroForMix* to utilize the stutter model. With our example it actually results in a much higher LR, but this may not always be the case. Filtering out the complex stutters seems to be a reasonable compromise. It increased the LR by a smaller amount compared to the fully filtered data; the minor contributor R was at a higher peak height compared to the range occupied by these artefacts, and their removal was less likely to cause bias. However, if the POI alleles were within range of complex stutters, then it would be preferable to leave them in the data and posit an extra contributor to take account of the extra alleles. However, *EuroForMix* version 3 is able to model forward stutter.

Balding et al. [233] compared results from *EuroForMix* with *LikeLTD*, where the latter software models complex stutters. The authors noted that there was an advantage with *LikeLtd* if the POI was a low-level contributor, but the downside was the increased computational time that resulted.

10.5. Summary

The Netherlands Forensic Institute has created a DNA expert system *DNAxs*. A module known as *DNAStatistX* is a Java implementation of the gamma model provided in *EuroForMix*.

1. The *LoCIM-tool* was developed as an empirical method to make inferences about genotypes, using allele peak heights, and stochastic and heterozygote balance thresholds. Loci are divided into three categories, which represent the classes of increasing complexity of a mixture, which affect the ability to predict a major contributor to deconvolve. Replicates can also be accommodated by this software.

2. *DNAStatistX* is compared with *EuroForMix*. *DNAStatistX* allows dye-specific or locus-specific detection thresholds to improve the distinction between alleles and noise, whereas *EuroForMix* only has a single universal threshold (version 3.0.0 onward will allow dye-specific thresholds). Whereas *EuroForMix* includes both a degradation and stutter model, in the first version of *DNAStatistX* (v1.0.0), only the degradation model was implemented. The programs use different optimizers to estimate the parameters, and this results in some small differences in the results when compared. In *EuroForMix* the default number of optimizer iterations is four, whereas in *DNAStatistX*, a dynamic facility is implemented that initially restricts

the number of optimizations to three. Provided that there are three results the same, the program terminates, but if they are different, then additional optimizations are initiated, until three results are the same, at which point the program finishes. This reduces the processing time required for completion.

3. The software testing of *DNAxs* is described. There are six consecutive steps that are followed by test engineers. Product risk analysis identifies which parts of the software are at highest risk of damage and failure. Functionalities of the software are defined by process flows, which are encoded into scripts that are used to test *DNAxs*. The scripts are run once a night, and every time software changes are made to highlight potential bugs. Only when all the tests succeed will the build be accepted and released.

4. An exemplar case is analyzed with *DNAxs* and *EuroForMix*. Model validation using PP-plots is described. Results were comparable, provided that stutter–filtered data were analyzed. If the person of interest is within stutter size, then it may be beneficial to use *EuroForMix* with the stutter module.

CHAPTER 11

Investigative forensic genetics: *SmartRank, CaseSolver* and *DNAmatch2*

11.1. National DNA databases

The forensic DNA scientist has a dual role, *investigative* vs. *evaluative* that is summarized by the ISFG DNA commission [275] as follows:

Typically, DNA may be recovered from items at a crime scene, but there are no suspects that are available to compare—then the scientist is said to be operating in an *investigative* mode. With such a case, a national DNA database may be searched to discover potential candidates for further investigation.

In a database of N individuals, before the comparison is carried out, all individuals may be considered to be possible candidates. Consequently, each candidate R_i, where $i = 1..N$, is compared with the crime stain in turn.

Where there is a single-contributor crime stain, and there is no known person of interest, sub-source-level propositions would be:

H_p: Candidate R_i is a contributor to the evidence profile E;
H_d: An unknown person is a contributor to the evidence profile E.

And the likelihood ratio is calculated: $LR = \frac{Pr(E|H_p)}{Pr(E|H_d)}$.

To begin, we consider a well-represented DNA profile from a single individual. Either candidate R_i gives a high $LR \gg 1$ so that he/she will be forwarded for further investigation, else a low $LR < 1$ is achieved, in which case he/she may be eliminated from the investigation, and is no longer considered a possible candidate. If the LR is very high (e.g., $log_{10}LR > 10$, and there is a large database of several million), typically, either one person remains after the search and comparison, or none is discovered. Alternatively, in the case of partial DNA profiles, which give intermediate $LRs > 1$, there may be several candidates found; clearly the crime stain could not have originated from all, hence we have to contend with the possibility of false positive matches.

If a likelihood ratio $LR = x$ is obtained (for a true contributor), then the probability of finding a random matching DNA profile in a national DNA database is roughly proportional to the size of the database N. The number of random matches (false positives) expected is N/x per database search. With a database size 5 m, and a $LR = 1$ m, approximately 5 random matches are expected. Even if the LR is much greater, for example, an $LR = 1$ bn would normally be considered sufficient for reporting purpose, but there is still a possibility that false positive matches can occur.

Forensic Practitioner's Guide to the Interpretation of Complex DNA Profiles
https://doi.org/10.1016/B978-0-12-820562-4.00019-5

Copyright © 2020 Elsevier Inc.
All rights reserved. **339**

340 Forensic Practitioner's Guide to the Interpretation of Complex DNA Profiles

The probability of obtaining exactly one chance match from a database of a given size can be determined by applying the binomial distribution function. This can be calculated in Excel as BINOM.DIST(number_s=1,trials,probability_s,cumulative=FALSE), where the following apply:

- number_s is the number of random matching profiles in the database k. If we were interested in the probability of a single match from the database we would set this to one.
- trials is the number of independent trials, i.e., the size of the database N.
- probability_s is the probability of a random match.
- cumulative is set to "FALSE" to determine the probability of k random matches or "TRUE" to determine the cumulative probability of k random matches in the database (Note that the cumulative function will include the probability of zero matches, hence this value would need to be subtracted if we were interested in the cumulative probability between 1 and 5 chance matches, for example).

The formula for the binomial distribution function[1] is

$$b(k; N = trials, p = probability\_s) = \binom{N}{k} \cdot p^k (1 - p)^{N-k} \tag{11.1}$$

However, we are interested in the probability of one *or more* matches (without a limit). This is calculated by setting $k = 0$ to calculate the expectation of the number of non-random matches per database search, and subtracting this probability from one. This conveniently simplifies the binomial expression to

$$1 - b(0; N, p) = 1 - (1 - p)^N \tag{11.2}$$

This is easily programmed into Excel (Table 11.1). The probability of at least one random match, where the $LR = N = 5$ m is 0.63 (which is less than the rough N/x formula given above). Where the database size is 5 m (similar to some of the larger national DNA databases), given a $LR = 1$ bn, there is a probability of 0.005 of one or more random matches. This probability appears to be low, but we must consider the cumulative effect of multiple searches in databases. Using the same rationale, with $LR = 1$ bn and probability $p = 0.005$ for a random match per database search of $N = 5m$, if 1,000 independent searches are undertaken, then from the binomial expression, there is a probability of 0.99 that one or more random false-positive matches from at least one of the database searches will be detected.

The explanation above is simplified, since we only consider complete matches of two complete DNA profiles of unrelated individuals. Weir [276] provides a much more detailed investigation, where he considered incomplete or partial matches. He showed that the observed and expected numbers of pairs of individuals with various numbers of matching or partially matching loci in FBI and Australian databases were in good

Table 11.1 The probability of at least one random match for a given database size, and likelihood ratio of a questioned sample.

Database size	Likelihood ratio		
	1.00E+05	5.00E+06	1.00E+09
1.00E+06	1.000	0.181	0.001
5.00E+06	1.000	0.632	0.005
1.00E+07	1.000	0.865	0.010
1.00E+08	1.000	1.000	0.095
1.00E+09	1.000	1.000	0.632

agreement, provided that F_{ST} (θ) was small. Therefore the prevalence of partial/ incomplete matches in database searches can be predicted. This is relevant, because low stringency database searches are allowed according the Prüm matching rules described in Section 11.4.2.

The above discussion shows why it is important to use database searches for *investigative* purposes. Even if the *LR* is substantial, it does not mean that the candidate donated the crime-stain material. The probability of a random false positive match can be calculated using the binomial expression as illustrated. However, this does not take account of close relatives. The probability of false positive matches with close relatives is greatly increased compared to random person calculations [276–278] (Chapter 8.8). Partial matches with crime-stain profiles are also more likely to occur with relatives of a perpetrator that is held on a database; this has led to the use of familial searches to find perpetrators of crimes via their relatives held on a reference database [279,280]. More recently, direct-to-consumer (DTC) genetic testing vendors have allowed police to search their databases of many millions of customers to be searched for high-profile perpetrators; see Phillips [281] for a discussion on the nascent field of "forensic genealogy". Using massive parallel sequencing of high-density > 500 K SNP datasets enables the detection of 2nd to 9th cousinships [282].

To reiterate, regardless of the method used, at this stage, there is no defendant, and the scientist is working as an *investigator*. The prosecuting authorities will be notified about the potential candidates, and they decide if he/she subsequently becomes a person of interest (POI).

11.2. When is evaluative reporting appropriate?

Once the POI has been identified, further investigation will follow (interviews, witness information, searches of premises, etc.), where non-DNA evidence will be gathered, and where the POI's account of the facts will be asked. Once a suspect is identified, the scientist switches to evaluative mode. If there is sufficient combined evidence, then it may be decided to prosecute him/her, and the person consequently becomes a defendant.

The scientist then operates in an "evaluative" mode, and the principles of interpretation apply [283]. As a model, we refer the reader to the ENFSI guidelines for evaluative reporting [284], where the conditions under which evaluative reporting must take place are described as follows:

"Evaluative reports for use in court should be produced when two conditions are met:

- The forensic practitioner has been asked by a mandating authority or party to examine and/or compare material (typically recovered trace material with reference material from known potential sources).
- The forensic practitioner seeks to evaluate results with respect to particular competing propositions set by the specific case circumstances or as indicated by the mandating authority."

11.3. A cautionary tale

In 1999 Raymond Easton, a 49-year-old man from Swindon, UK, was arrested and charged with a burglary in Bolton, UK (175 miles away), after a DNA sample from the crime scene matched his DNA profile in the UK national DNA database. Mr. Easton was in the advanced stages of Parkinson's disease, and was unable to walk more than ten meters without help. His DNA profile had been loaded onto the database four years earlier following a domestic dispute. The crime scene sample matched Mr. Easton's DNA profile at six loci, which was considered enough to secure an identification at that time — although the total number of STRs required has since been extended to 16 plus a sex marker. The chances of a match was reported as 37-million-to-one. Mr. Easton spent several months in custody before his solicitor persuaded police to run further DNA tests, which eliminated him [285]. This case illustrated the importance of clearly distinguishing between the investigative vs. evaluative aspects of forensic genetics, and the need to ensure that prosecutions only proceeded after all the non-evidence has been considered in a case.

11.4. Current methods used to compare crime stains with national DNA databases

In Europe, DNA hits are reported if a profile with at least six loci matches another profile [286]. The comparison of DNA profiles across European borders is governed by the Prüm treaty. The member States retain approximately 6,120,000 DNA profiles of known individuals, and 1,139,000 traces from unsolved crimes for cross-border comparison in the period 2016 to 2017. With such large amounts of data being compared, six and seven loci hits become problematic, as many false-positive matches will be identified [287,288], (see Section 11.1). The largest national DNA databases are those of England and Wales (5,491,000); USA (16,200,000) and China (40,000,000).[2] Of course, to be able to compare DNA profiles across borders, it was necessary to standardize the loci used. The international development of standardization and harmonization that led to the European Set of Standard (ESS) loci is described in Chapter 1.2. The original seven were extended to twelve core European loci [26,289], expanded to an effective sixteen loci (the expanded ESS), since there are four additional loci that are in common to European multiplexes (D16S539, D19S433, D2S1338, SE33).

11.4.1 Prüm inclusion rules

Under the 2009 Prüm inclusion rules [286], DNA profiles have to meet certain criteria to be included in international comparisons [287]:

1. Must include at least 6 of the 7 old ESS loci for known persons.
2. Must include at least 6 ESS loci for crime scene stains.
3. One allele of a locus can be a wildcard.
4. No mixed profiles (a maximum of two values per locus) are allowed.
5. No profiles that have already matched a person are allowed.
6. No profiles that a country does not want to make available (e.g., DNA profiles of laboratory personnel kept for contamination detection purpose).
7. The European Standard Set (ESS) were extended by five additional loci in 2009, officially adopted by the EU Commission [28].

11.4.2 Prüm matching rules

The Prüm software was developed jointly by DNA and IT experts from the Bundeskriminalamt (BKA) in Germany, the Ministry of the Interior of Austria, and the Netherlands Forensic Institute in the Netherlands. It produces a match when there are at least six fully matching loci between two DNA profiles. In addition, one deviation (wildcard or mismatch) is allowed, and this is called a near match. Any type of profile sent for a comparison will be compared to any type of DNA profile available for comparison, so the following types of matches can occur: stain-stain, stain-person, or person-person. Matches can be of different qualities:

- Quality 1: All alleles of all loci that can match are identical.
- Quality 2: One of the two matching profiles contains a wildcard.
- Quality 3: One of the alleles of one locus contains a mismatch of one base pair (e.g., $9.2 \rightarrow 9.3$).
- Quality 4: One of the alleles of one locus contains a mismatch of more than one base pair (e.g., $22 \rightarrow 26$).

344 Forensic Practitioner's Guide to the Interpretation of Complex DNA Profiles

11.4.3 CODIS inclusion and matching rules

In North America, an FBI-sponsored CODIS core loci working group recommended an expanded set of loci from the thirteen in use in 2011 [18,19]. There followed an extensive validation study, which resulted in the recommendation that seven new loci were to be adopted [20], resulting in 20 CODIS core loci that were implemented by 2017. The additional seven loci included the five new European ESS markers, plus D2S1338 and D19S433. This resulted in fifteen CODIS core and expanded ESS loci in common with each other [21].

The following apply to submit a profile to a CODIS database (from 2017):
1. "All core loci must be attempted but at least 8 of the original CODIS core loci combined with a match rarity of at least one in ten million are required."[3]
2. Searches are carried out at high stringency, which means that all alleles in the questioned sample must match the reference, except that a single mismatch is allowed.
3. If the profile is partial (some alleles missing), then a moderate stringency search is carried out, which requires all alleles present in the crime sample to match with the reference DNA profile, which may contain a different number of alleles.
4. Finally, a low stringency search can be carried out to discover partial matches with a crime sample, e.g., parent/offspring.

11.5. Limitations of traditional national DNA databases: introducing "SmartRank"

Searching a national DNA database with complex and incomplete profiles usually yields very large numbers of possible matches that can present many candidate suspects to be further investigated by the forensic scientist and/or police. Current practice in most forensic laboratories consists of ordering these "hits" based on the number of matching alleles with the searched profile. Thus candidate profiles that share the same number of matching alleles are not differentiated, and due to the lack of other ranking criteria for the candidate list, it may be difficult to discern a true match from the false positives or notice that all candidates are in fact false positives. *SmartRank* was developed to put forward only relevant candidates, and rank them accordingly. The *SmartRank* software computes an *LR* for the searched profile against each reference profile in the DNA database, so a database of one million will result in one million *LRs*. These values are ranked from high to low; the highest values that are above a pre-defined *LR* threshold are highlighted for further investigation [290,291].

SmartRank is based upon *LRmix* [292,290]. The model was modified to enable searching of very large DNA databases of reference samples. A number of enhancements were made to *SmartRank* to speed the operation without compromising the effectiveness.

Investigative forensic genetics: *SmartRank, CaseSolver* and *DNAmatch2*   345

1. The "Q" designation described in Chapter 3.7 is not used under H_p, regardless of whether the evidence shows signs of drop-out. This reduces the number of possible genotype combinations for unknown contributors, which is expected to yield a higher *LR* if a candidate is a true contributor to the DNA mixture, and is not subject to drop-out. If drop-out is needed to explain the profile under H_p, then a lower *LR* is expected.

2. The defense proposition is calculated once only, instead of for each candidate in the database, and subsequently applied in the *LR* calculation for every candidate profile.

To test the system, a total of 15 samples of two- to three-contributor-mixed DNA profiles were generated, and each of these was tested against 44 known reference profiles. Each reference was treated as a POI under H_p, and this resulted in a total of $15 \times 44 = 660$ *LR* comparisons. The *LRs* were ranked to determine whether the known contributors were ranked highly by *SmartRank*. Nearly all POIs appeared in the top five list of ranked candidates (there was one sample with drop-out, where $LR < 1$). However, for the most complex sample in this study (three persons with 30% drop-out), two of the three true contributors resulted in *LR* below 1 (false exclusion). This was attributed to the Q designation shutdown under H_p, which was used as a speed optimization measure.

The total time required to search a DNA database is dependent upon the computer that is used, the size of the DNA database, and the complexity of the searched profile (i.e., number of contributors, number of alleles, drop-out: yes or no). Applying the speed optimization enabled a search of 220,000 references against 44 three-contributor mixtures to be accomplished in 3 h 44 min.

11.6. Experimental details to test efficiency of *SmartRank*

A total of 44 reference profiles were used consisting of 15 STR loci (D3S1358, vWA, D16S539, D2S1338, D8S1179, D21S11, D18S51, D19S433, TH01, FGA, D10S1248, D22S1045, D2S441, D1S1656, D12S391). First, 23 profiles were selected from a reference set of 2085 Dutch males [256,293], and a single locus genotype for locus SE33 was added to ten of these, while taking care that these SE33 alleles were observed more than once in the 2,085 reference set [256]. Next, 21 virtual genotypes were derived from these 23 genotypes to generate a set denoted "resembling donors": for five resembling genotypes one randomly chosen allele was replaced by a rare allele (having a frequency of 0.00024 from Westen et al. [256]). For 12 resembling genotypes, alleles from two or three of the selected 23 genotypes were combined in such a manner that the resembling genotype had 100% ($n = 4$), 75% ($n = 4$), or 50% ($n = 4$) allelic overlap with a two- or three-person mixture. Existing genotypes were adapted to represent a father ($n = 2$; at least one allele per locus in common) or a brother ($n = 2$; sharing half of the overall profile) of one of the 23 donors. This set of 44 reference genotypes formed the basis of the *SmartRank* performance study—they were added to anonymized copies of reference DNA databases, and used to derive mixed DNA profiles to search them.

346 Forensic Practitioner's Guide to the Interpretation of Complex DNA Profiles

A total of 343 mixed DNA profiles that had two to five contributors with variable levels of allele-sharing were generated from the 44 reference genotypes. To test the system, anonymized copies of parts of the national DNA databases of Belgium (37,595), the Netherlands (206,535), Italy (69985) "large" France (1,552,754), "small" France (43,861), and Spain (189,867) were used. In addition, a simulated DNA database (220,044), with 23 different loci, was used to examine the effects of drop-out estimation on the *LR*s. To each of these DNA databases, the 44 reference profiles were added to examine retrieval of true donors for the simulated DNA mixtures achieved by *SmartRank* or CODIS searches.

11.6.1 *SmartRank* performance

First, the performance of *SmartRank* on five different DNA databases was examined with 20 profiles comprising two-, three-, and four-person mixtures without drop-out. These *SmartRank* searches resulted in the retrieval ($LR > 1$) of all true donors to these mixtures (Fig. 11.1, green diamonds); i.e., the two donors to the two-person mixtures, the three donors to the three-person mixtures, etc. Known donors were not searched for, thus only two donors could be retrieved for three-person mixtures if one known donor was anchored under both propositions. Results were irrespective of the DNA database or population statistic that was used. Besides these true donors, resembling donors were retrieved, especially those that were simulated to have 100% overlap with alleles present in the mixed profile (Fig. 11.1, blue squares). The retrieval of non-donors (a.k.a. false positives or adventitious matches) was dependent on the size and composition of the DNA database. The effect of database size is implied from the observation that the smallest two DNA databases, Belgium and "small France" having sizes of 37,595 and 43,861, respectively, did not yield false positives, whereas the larger databases from the Netherlands, Spain, Italy, and "large France" with sizes of 206,535, 189,867, 69,985, and 1,552,754, respectively, did yield false positives (Fig. 11.1, red triangles). An effect of database composition is implied from the observation that more false positives were obtained with the Italian DNA database than with the Spanish database, though it is substantially smaller in size. An (additional) effect of a different population statistic used by each country, however, cannot be ruled out.

The more complex the profile, i.e., the more contributors there are, if there is more drop-out leading to fewer informative loci or common alleles leading to a high degree of allele sharing, then these combined effects will reduce the *LR* for true donors. It also tends to increase the *LR* for non-donors, resulting in smaller differences between true and non-donors. The combined effect means that for these compromised profiles, it becomes less likely that they will rank highly compared to non-contributors. Fig. 11.2 shows the effect relative to comparisons of 5 to 8 loci against the 2015 Dutch DNA database. The more loci, the higher the ranking achieved. Drop-out also has a notable effect on ranking efficiency. Generally, we consider that lists of more than 10–20 possible

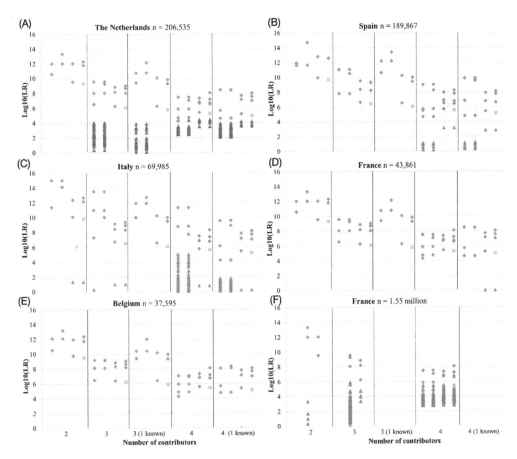

Figure 11.1 Retrieval of true (green diamonds), false positives (blue squares), and non-donors (red triangles) for two-, three-, or four-person mixtures without drop-out. Results obtained when using the Dutch (A) Spanish (B), Italian (C), small France (D), Belgian (E), or large France (F) DNA database. Each vertical line represents the analysis of one mixed profile. Note that only part of the samples were analyzed using the large France DNA database, and known contributors were not searched for. Reproduced from Benschop et al. [290] with permission from Elsevier.

candidates are difficult to manage, and this criterion can be used as an indication of efficiency.

11.7. *SmartRank* versus CODIS

Both *SmartRank* and CODIS are user friendly software that enable DNA database searches. However, their potential and purpose is different. CODIS is a powerful software designed to search large numbers of crime scene profiles against a large number of offender profiles on a daily basis. CODIS was originally designed to search single

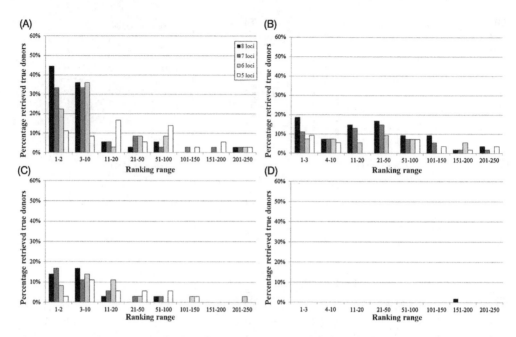

Figure 11.2 Ranking position for true donors in two-person (A&B) and three-person mixtures (C&D) with 10% (A&C) or 40% drop-out (B&D). The black, dark gray, light gray, and white bars represent profiles with eight, seven, six, and five loci, respectively. Analyses were performed using the Dutch 2015 DNA database, and using nine different loci combinations. Reproduced from Benschop et al. [290] with permission from Elsevier.

donor profiles and up to two-person mixtures without drop-out. CODIS does not rank potential candidates; multiple matches are considered to be equivalent.

SmartRank is designed to be used for DNA database searches using more complex mixed DNA profiles. To discover profile-types, using *SmartRank*, which can complement CODIS, 30 DNA profiles with various characteristics (both with and without drop-out) were selected from the full list of 343 mixed profiles. Each of these mixed profiles was used for one *SmartRank* analysis, and two CODIS searches with moderate search stringency: one with no mismatches, and the second allowing one mismatch. Recall that a list of up to 20 candidates is regarded as manageable for further evaluation by investigators. Therefore to carry out the comparison, two criteria were assessed:

1. Did the true donor rank within the top ten (or top 20) of the candidate list for *SmartRank*-based searches?
2. Was the total number of matches less than ten (or 20) candidates when CODIS was used?

Both *SmartRank* and CODIS successfully retrieved true contributors for the two-, three-, and four-person mixtures without drop-out (Table 11.2). Using *SmartRank*, all true donors were ranked within the top ten ranks. CODIS searches retrieved more than ten candidates when one mismatch was allowed, or when there were more contributors. The candidate list can be truly unmanageable; for example, a total of 4302 adventitious matches occurred in one test of a four-person mixture searched against the Dutch DNA database (Table 11.2).

The occurrence of drop-out and availability of fewer loci clearly complicated the retrieval of true donors, especially in CODIS searches, which do not allow a mismatch. Although *SmartRank* did not always retrieve all of the true donors in these searches, true donors that ranked within the top ten (or twenty) list of candidates, were retrieved more often compared with CODIS. Searches with CODIS resulted in large lists of candidate matches that occurred primarily when there were few loci or large drop-out levels in the mixtures. *SmartRank*'s potential to complement CODIS is clearest for the 16-loci mixed profiles with low or moderate drop-out (Table 11.2).

Table 11.2 Performance of SmartRank and CODIS for two-, three-, and four-person mixtures that (A) lack drop-out or (B) have 5% to 50% overall drop-out. Results for searches using the DNA databases of Belgium, Spain, and the Netherlands are combined. Reproduced from [290] with permission from Elsevier.

A	Number of contributors	Number of loci	Drop-out	Number of samples per DNA database	Total number of searches	SmartRank			CODIS – 0 mismatches		CODIS – 1 mismatch	
						Donors retrieved	Ranking position of retrieved donors		Donors retrieved	Number of adventitious matches	Donors retrieved	Number of adventitious matches
							1–10	1–20				
	2	15	0%	2	6	100%	100%	100%	100%	2–7	100%	3–25
	3	15	0%	2	6	100%	100%	100%	100%	3–38	100%	5–369
	4	15	0%	4	12	100%	100%	100%	100%	4–418	100%	7–4302
B	2	16	5%	1	3	100%	100%	100%	0%	–	100%	2–4
			15%[a]	1	3	100%	83%	100%	33%	1–2	33%	2–3
			50%	1	3	0%	–	–	0%	–	0%	0–3
		8	10%	2	6	100%	100%	100%	0%	0–968	75%	2–985
			40%	2	6	100%	100%	100%	0%	0–968	83%	1–985
		6	10%	2	6	100%	58%	75%	0%	1–9	92%	13–396
			40%	2	6	100%	25%	100%	0%	1–9	100%	13–396
	3	16	5%	1	3	100%	100%	100%	22%	0–3	44%	4–68
			20%[a]	1	3	33%	100%	100%	33%	1–2	33%	2–4
			50%	1	3	0%	–	–	0%	–	0%	–
		8	10%	2	6	89%	0%	0%	0%	0–2359	89%	10–2461
			40%	2	6	0%	–	–	0%	0–317	0%	2–326
		6	10%	2	6	67%	0%	0%	0%	0–141	56%	64–2399
			40%	2	6	0%	–	–	0%	0–10	0%	0–154

[a] Major 0% drop-out, minor(s) 30% drop-out.

11.7.1 Specifying a likelihood ratio threshold and a top ranked candidate list

The most optimal balance between true and false positives was obtained when an *LR* threshold of 1000 or 10,000 was applied (Table 11.3), although resembling donors may still be retrieved (data not shown). When *LR* thresholds of 1000 and 10,000 were applied to the top ten and top twenty lists of candidates, significantly fewer non-donors were retrieved with little effect on the retrieval of the true donors, especially when the $LR > 1000$ threshold was used (results not shown). Therefore an *LR* threshold of 1000 is used as the default value. Since the number of true positives hardly increased when

350 Forensic Practitioner's Guide to the Interpretation of Complex DNA Profiles

the top twenty were examined instead of the top ten ranking candidates, ten candidates were chosen for the default value. However, the values for the *LR* threshold and top list of candidates are configurable in *SmartRank*; specifically for five-person mixtures with one or two known contributors, it may be useful to examine the top twenty ranking candidates to increase the true-positive rate. Furthermore, an *LR* threshold of 10,000 may be chosen if the major component is of interest for less complex mixtures (those without drop-out or two-person mixtures with up to 15% drop-out), as fewer false positives are expected, whereas the true positives are still retrieved.

Table 11.3 Effect of applying an *LR* threshold on the effectiveness of retrieving the true donors amongst non-donors for profiles carrying 15 or 16 loci. The candidate lists of the indicated *LR* threshold and the *LR* > 1 boundary (top 250 ranking candidates only) are compared regarding percentage of true donors missed, and percentage of non-donors lost (designed resembling donors excluded). The color scaling presents preferable results in green (light grey in print version), and less preferable results in orange (medium grey in print version) or red (dark grey in print version). Reproduced from [290] with permission from Elsevier.

Number of contributors	Percentage of drop-out		Number true donors missed [a]	Percentage true donors missed				Percentage non-donors lost			
		LR threshold:	1	100	1,000	10,000	100,000	100	1,000	10,000	100,000
2	0%	(n=20)	0/40	0%	0%	0%	0%	100%	100%	100%	100%
	5%	(n=6)	0/12	0%	0%	0%	0%	97%	98%	99%	100%
	15%	(n=5)	0/10	0%	0%	0%	0%	98%	99.5%	100%	100%
	15% [b]	(n=5)	0/10	50%	50%	50%	50%	97%	100%	100%	100%
	30%	(n=5)	0/10	0%	0%	40%	100%	100%	100%	100%	100%
3	0%	(n=20)	0/60	0%	0%	0%	0%	49%	78%	98%	100%
	5%	(n=6)	0/18	0%	0%	0%	20%	72%	90%	98%	100%
	15%	(n=5)	0/15	0%	20%	33%	67%	78%	97%	99%	100%
	20% [b]	(n=5)	10/15	0%	0%	0%	0%	100%	100%	100%	100%
	30%	(n=5)	9/15	100%	100%	100%	100%	89%	100%	100%	100%
4	0%	(n=20)	0/80	0%	0%	0%	18%	23%	72%	93%	99%
	5%	(n=6)	1/18	10%	20%	30%	75%	82%	96%	100%	100%
4 (1 known) [c]	0%	(n=20)	0/60	0%	0%	0%	17%	34%	80%	98%	100%
5 (1 known) [c]	5%	(n=6)	7/24	7%	13%	53%	87%	60%	95%	99%	100%
5 (2 knowns) [c]	5%	(n=6)	4/18	7%	21%	36%	71%	57%	94%	100%	100%

[a] The total number of true donors is the number of (unknown) contributors times the number of SmartRank searches (presented as (n = xx)).

[b] Major 0% drop-out, minor(s) 30% drop-out.

[c] Known contributors do not have drop-out and were not searched for.

11.7.2 Limitations

SmartRank was developed to put forward only relevant candidates from a DNA database search, and to rank them accordingly. To achieve this aim, the *SmartRank* software computes an *LR* for the searched profile and each profile in the DNA database, and ranks database entries above a defined *LR* threshold. *SmartRank* was validated against many mixed DNA profiles and databases of various compositions. To assist users of the *SmartRank* software, guidelines were provided for best practice that followed from the data described in the validation study. These are not to be confused with standards. Note that to enable flexibility, several options in *SmartRank* are made configurable by the user. For instance, it was decided to set the default value for the top list of candidates to 10, and the *LR* threshold to 1000, as this has been shown to minimize false negatives and false positives with the data searched against the DNA databases used in this study. However, these values can be changed by the users. A guide to decide whether there is an expectation of success for a *SmartRank* DNA database search is presented in Table 11.4. This guide is based upon the combination of the number of contributors using STR profiles containing 15 or 16 loci, and a DNA database of size 37,000–1.55 million. Database searches with profiles containing less than 15 loci are likely to negatively influence the retrieval of true donors. The presence of a rare allele, on the other hand, can have a positive effect on the retrieval of true donors. Searching with profiles containing larger numbers of loci (e.g., 23 loci) is expected to extend the applicable domain of the software; more complex DNA profiles may be suitable for a *SmartRank* search. Using a DNA database that is larger in size than tested in this study can result in larger numbers of false positives, and smaller DNA databases are expected to yield fewer false positives.

Table 11.4 Guide for deciding whether a *SmartRank* DNA-database search can be successful for the type of DNA profile at hand. This guide follows from the data described in this study. Expectations are for STR profiles containing 15 or 16 loci, using a DNA database of size 37,000–1.55 million. Reproduced from [290] with permission from Elsevier.

Percentage of drop-out	Number of contributors				
	2	3	4	5 (1 known)	5 (2 knowns)
0% [a]	Successful SmartRank search expected				
5% [b]			The loss of true donors is expected		
15%		Successfulness dependent on complexity; further considerations advised			
30%		Some or (all) donors may be missed			
50%	SmartRank searches did not yield informative results and are therefore not advised				

[a] For two-person mixtures without drop-out, a CODIS search may be successful too.
[b] For five-person mixtures with 5% drop-out and known contributors, extending the maximum list of candidates to 20 is expected to yield more true positives.

Depending on the type of case and keeping in mind the expected trends, the scientist can decide to perform a *SmartRank* search for DNA mixtures with characteristics described in the orange boxes in Table 11.4. The user may wish to extend the list of candidates to 20, for example, as this may result in more true positives for some of the mixtures, although the number of false positives may also increase. In Section 11.10, we show how the *SmartRank* list of candidates can be further refined by application of the quantitative model (using allele peak heights) in *CaseSolver*.

Overall, whether or not a *SmartRank* DNA database search is successful depends on the combinations of the size and composition of the DNA database and the various mixtures characteristics, and, of course, whether or not the true contributors to the DNA mixtures are present in the DNA database.

352 Forensic Practitioner's Guide to the Interpretation of Complex DNA Profiles

11.8. *SmartRank* exercise

SmartRank can be downloaded from https://github.com/smartrank/smartrank, and the user guides examples and data are available at the book's web-site: https://sites.google.com/view/dnabook/ folder "SmartRank_Exercises". The reader should turn to the methods guide for the full details on how to run *SmartRank*, summarized here:

Step 1: Open *SmartRank* and load the CODIS database file labeled: "database_codis_generated_220044". This file consists of an Excel spreadsheet of a simulated database of 220,044 samples, which was described in detail earlier in Section 11.6. Summarized here, the data are 220,000 randomly generated reference profiles with 23 known individuals added. There are 15 reference loci. A further 23 profiles were generated by adding the SE33 locus to ten of them; other virtual profiles were generated so that they would have many alleles in common, or represented father or sibling genotypes; a further five genotypes had a random rare allele replacement. These genotypes are "resembling genotypes", because there would be a higher expectation of a false positive match with the original 23 progenitor known individuals on account of the high allele-sharing. On loading the data, the user will notice an error message: "Specimen excluded as it has 94 fields, but 93 were expected!". A corrupt dataset has been intentionally included (to show that the software can recognize such data). We continue with a dataset of 220,043 samples.

Step 2: Once data are loaded, a visual representation of the number of loci and the identity of the loci expressed as percentages of the total number of samples is available (Fig. 11.3).

Step 3: Load a sample. In the demonstration, sample "SMAR9999NL#2", found in folder "exercise 2" is loaded (Fig. 11.4). Inspection of the profile suggests that it is at least a four-person mixture; there are seven alleles present at D1S1656.

Step 4: Next go to the "Search" tab and fill in the parameter fields (Fig. 11.5)
1. Fill in number of unknown contributors under the prosecution and defense propositions. There is always an additional unknown contributor under the latter.
2. Click the "Estimate Drop-out Probabilities" button. This estimates drop-out probabilities, following the method described in Chapter 6.1.5. Drop-out probabilities are automatically inserted in all fields, hence there is no need for the user to do anything additional.
3. Load the allele frequencies database file "NFI_frequencies.csv" from the "SmartRank Exercises" folder.
4. Set the "LR threshold" to a desired level (1,000 in the example). This level can be changed after the program has been run.
5. Set "Report top" to 250 or some other desired level.
6. Set "Theta correction" and "Rare Allele Frequency".

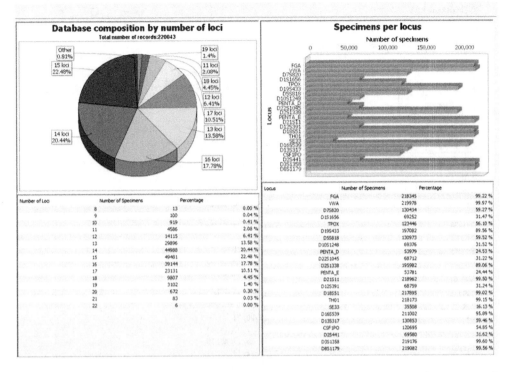

Figure 11.3 Breakdown of data in the database. Left panel summarizes the number of loci per sample expressed as a percentage of the total. The right panel provides the number of specimens per locus, also expressed as a percentage of the total.

7. Press the "Search" button.

The filled-in fields and the resulting output is shown in Fig. 11.5. The output shows that there are 512 samples, where the $LR > 1$. Of these, there are five ranked "hits", where $LR > 1000$.

Double clicking a ranked candidate produces an output to compare the crime-stain profile with the reference profiles (Fig. 11.6).

Step 5: Once a ranked list is generated, this is provided to investigators. Remember that the process is currently investigative, which means that the police search for additional evidence to build a case before evaluation can occur. Suppose the police interview suspect Z, there is substantial other non-DNA evidence in the case, and he confesses. Since Z has confessed, he can be conditioned in the evidence (Fig. 11.7). This results in a new reordered ranked list of candidates. Individual AB now ranks first, followed by X,Y and JCFD177BE#77. The latter candidate did not appear in the first list (without conditioning), ranking 8th with $LR = 495$. This shows that a flexible approach may be employed in investigations. Once the evidence has been collected and the propositions properly formulated, then the reporting officer enters evaluative mode. It will be neces-

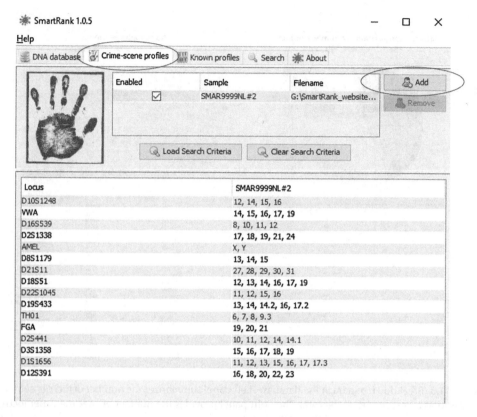

Figure 11.4 Sample is loaded. Click "Crime-scene profile" tab and "Add", then browse to the sample in folder "exercise 1". The loci and allele designations of the mixture are shown.

sary to rerun samples using *LRmix Studio*, as described in Chapter 6, using appropriate frequency databases and other parameters, depending upon the case circumstances.

11.9. Using *EuroForMix* for database searching

As an alternative to *SmartRank*, *EuroForMix* also contains a highly advanced module for database searching. This module is tailored around searching one or several reference databases, which may include thousands or even millions of references, against one evidence profile at the time (or possibly replicates). Here the user can do different kinds of searches: simple matching allele comparison (MAC[4]), which is very fast, or *LR*-based search using either the qualitative or quantitative model.

When *LR* calculations are based on the qualitative model only, the drop-out probability parameter is estimated as the median of the posterior drop-out probability, given the total number of alleles in the profile under H_d.

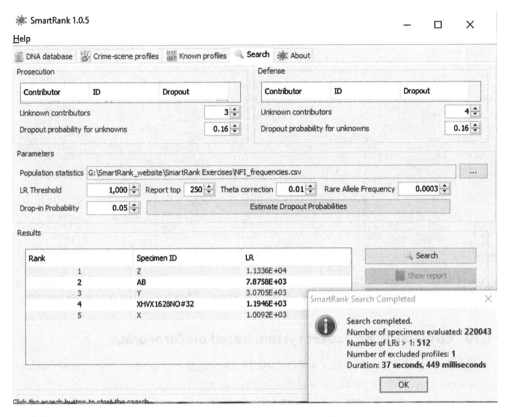

Figure 11.5 The search fields shown completed and run. The resultant matches are shown in the lower part of the output field.

LR calculations can also be based on the quantitative model, where the user must select whether the *LR* should be calculated based on ML or the Bayesian approach. The ML approach is always considerably faster than the Bayesian approach. In addition, together with the MAC score, the qualitative-based *LR* is calculated with a default drop-out parameter of 0.1 (for comparison). It is worth mentioning here that the qualitative *LR* is much faster to calculate than the quantitative *LR*, because it is a much simpler model.

After the calculations have been carried out, the software provides a full list of comparisons, where the list can be ranked with respect to MAC, qualitative *LR* (if calculated), or quantitative *LR* (if calculated).

Finally, it is worth noting that the search can be executed with a theta-correction, however, this reduces the speed, because of additional computations required for all the references to be considered under H_d.

SmartRank 1.0.5 Profile details for AB

Detail for profile: AB   [Export Profile]
Number of loci: 15

Locus	SMAR9999NL#2	AB	LR
D10S1248	12 14 15 16	14 15	1.0949E+00
VWA	14 15 16 17 19	14 17	1.4780E+00
D16S539	8 10 11 12	11 11	7.8027E-01
D2S1338	17 18 19 21 24	17 24	1.4193E+00
AMEL	X Y		
D8S1179	13 14 15	13 15	1.9469E+00
D21S11	27 28 29 30 31	30 31	1.6055E+00
D18S51	12 13 14 16 17	16 17	1.9086E+00
D22S1045	11 12 15 16	16 16	6.6632E-01
D19S433	13 14 14.2 16	14 15	7.5310E-02
TH01	6 7 8 9.3	7 9.3	1.1076E+00
FGA	19 20 21	19 21	2.2430E+00
D2S441	10 11 12 14 14	12 14.1	1.7022E+03
D3S1358	15 16 17 18 19	16 17	9.1776E-01
D1S1656	11 12 13 15 1	13 17.3	2.5403E+00
D12S391	16 18 20 22 23	18 20	1.4891E+00
Overall			*7.8758E+03*

SmartRank 1.0.5 Profile details for Z

Detail for profile: Z   [Export Profile]
Number of loci: 15

Locus	SMAR9999NL#2	Z	LR
D10S1248	12 14 15 16	15 15	1.0153E+00
VWA	14 15 16 17 19	16 19	1.6276E+00
D16S539	8 10 11 12	11 12	9.3222E-01
D2S1338	17 18 19 21 24	17 18	1.8575E+00
AMEL	X Y		
D8S1179	13 14 15	10 15	2.7496E-01
D21S11	27 28 29 30 31	27 30	3.0393E+00
D18S51	12 13 14 16 1	14 19	3.9370E+00
D22S1045	11 12 15 16	12 16	9.1843E+00
D19S433	13 14 14.2 16	14 16	2.0996E+00
TH01	6 7 8 9.3	6 7	1.3731E+00
FGA	19 20 21	20 21	1.5124E+00
D2S441	10 11 12 14 1	14 14	5.0593E-01
D3S1358	15 16 17 18 19	15 19	1.3525E+01
D1S1656	11 12 13 16	11 15	1.2221E+00
D12S391	16 18 20 22 23	20 22	2.0705E+00
Overall			*1.1336E+04*

Figure 11.6 Double clicking candidates AB and Z produces the output shown. Alleles that are missing in the crime stain and reference sample, respectively, are highlighted in red (dark grey in print version).

11.10. *CaseSolver*: an expert system based on *EuroForMix*

CaseSolver (CS) is a novel expert system used to manage comprehensive casework data (open-source and freely available at http://www.euroformix.com/casesolver). CS provides a graphical user interface in the statistical software R, where it can perform rapid comparisons of reference DNA profiles from single-source profiles and mixtures. Additionally, CS also contains useful options for *LR* and deconvolution recalculations with different propositions, and may also give expected peak height graphs under evaluated propositions. CS follows the method presented by Bleka et al. [294], where a stepwise sequential analysis is performed: First a simple allele comparison is undertaken, followed by analysis with a qualitative model *LRmix*, using *forensim* [219] (Chapter 5), and finally the quantitative model *EuroForMix* [76] (Chapter 8), is used to provide the ultimate list of candidate matches. These steps require that the user has defined the thresholds required in the sequential analysis, which may differ for different usages of the software.

The large number of loci in modern multiplexes produce a lot of data to manage. The interpretation and comparison of DNA profiles becomes a time-consuming bottleneck. This can be a challenge in routine casework, especially if multiple stains produce different DNA mixtures of different complexity. Also, when there is little information available about the case circumstances, the list of potential suspects may be vast, as it could comprise individuals held on a national DNA database. The police will expect the scientist to provide investigative leads to identify potential suspects. This means that numerous cross-comparisons of complex crime-stain profiles with reference samples may be needed.

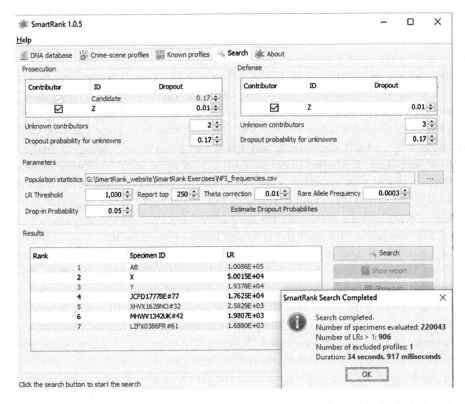

Figure 11.7 Individual Z is conditioned. This results in a new ranking list with individual AB at the top with $LR = 10^5$.

To demonstrate the potential of the CS software, we analyzed a real case based on the Promega "GlobalFiler" kit, involving 119 evidence profiles and three reference profiles. To provide a demonstration of the power of the system, we also added the three references to a fictive large database of 1 million individuals to test subsequent recovery of the presumed true contributors [274]. *CaseSolver* was used on a Promega Powerplex Fusion 6C validation study, involving 25 two- to four-person mixture profiles based on 14 reference profiles. The sequential use of simple allele comparison, the qualitative model (*LRmix*), and the quantitative model (*EuroForMix*) makes the analysis very fast and accurate, and finally, the software generates a list of potential match candidates, which can be exported as a report. From these two studies, we found that the resolution of match candidates from *CaseSolver* was the same as that reported by a scientist who worked manually through the samples, except that *CaseSolver* highlighted two manual errors. For the validation study, we found low-template DNA samples giving negative results, which demonstrate the limitations of the tool, but overall our assessment shows that *CaseSolver* will benefit all analyses, involving mixture interpretation and screening.

Importantly, *CaseSolver* removes the very time-consuming aspect of manual comparison, and gives improved quality by preventing manual errors. There are also useful functions to visualize the results as a graphical match network or a match matrix.

A precursor software named eDNA was developed to assist with this task by Haldemann et al. [273] (see Chapter 10); it automatically provides an overview of all data in casework in a structured manner based on categorization and simple allele comparison. However, the software is not suitable for analyzing very large cases or database searches, and it does not incorporate any possibility to carry out statistical analysis for mixtures. *SmartRank*, described in Section 11.5, is an open-source software for searching DNA databases with complex STR profiles. The software implements the *LRmix* model [219,68], which was adapted to enable fast and efficient searching of voluminous databases [290,292]. *SmartRank* presents the top ranking candidate(s) that exceed a predefined *LR* threshold. Although the software has proven to be useful and efficient in forensic casework, it does not take peak heights into account, and it does not provide a structured overview of evidence and reference profiles. Consequently, there is still a need for advanced data management tools that can provide an automated overview of all the evidence profiles (both mixtures and non-mixtures), where the peak height information is taken into consideration. The purpose is to discover potential matches when a large number of references are provided. Additionally, there is also a need for reporting scientists to extract as much information from the data as possible in an exploratory fashion, for instance by being able to deduce the DNA profile of unknown components in mixtures (deconvolution), or by investigating possible propositions.

To demonstrate how the software can be used as an efficient tool to resolve candidate matches for reporting scientists, we applied CS to a real case (based on GlobalFiler) containing over 100 evidence profiles. To test CS more extensively, we generated a large database containing 1 million references and analyzed these together with the real case data [274].

11.10.1 Method

11.10.1.1 Estimation of the number of contributors

When CS imports the data (both alleles and peak heights), the software first estimates the minimum number of contributors using the simple rule $K = \lceil$('maximum allele count for any markers'/2) [224], where $\lceil$ means rounding up to closest integer, as described in Chapter 2.3.2. Based on this rule, it is possible to assign whether an evidence profile is most likely to be a single-source profile ($K = 1$) or a mixture ($K > 1$). A consequence is that artefacts creating additional alleles, such as stutters or drop-in, may over-estimate the number of contributors. After carrying out "the number of contributors" classification, CS compares all the imported references against all evidence profiles, which were classified as single-source profiles (i.e., evidence profiles with $K = 1$). If the alleles of the reference (non-empty loci) match with all the alleles of the single-source profile, then CS tags the reference name under the "Match-Status" column of the evidence profile. To take into account partial profiles, the user can set a threshold to determine the number of non-empty loci in the single-source profile to designate "a match" (seven is set as a default). If no reference matched the single-source profile, CS creates an "unknown" reference profile with a specific ID. If several of these unknown single-source profiles are identical, they will have the same unknown ID. The "MatchStatus" for mixtures is always given as "mixture".

If $K > 1$, then estimating the number of contributors is very challenging if the amount of allele drop-out is unknown. There are several methods proposed for the qualitative model, where the likelihood function is used [295,296]. However, these methods do not consider partial profiles, where some of the components have dropped out.

One method which performs well and is fast, is using the maximum likelihood value L_{max} (of the qualitative model) across the proposed number of contributors (i.e., $\arg \max_K L_{max}(K)$). The method sometimes over-estimates the number of contributors. An *ad hoc* way to correct for this is to penalize the maximum log-likelihood value, $l_{max} = \log L_{max}$, with the number of assumed contributors (we used $\arg \max_K \{l_{max}(K) - K\}$. This method compensates for over-estimation, but is more likely to under-estimate three or four true contributors (Fig. 11.8).

11.10.2 Mixture comparison

The total number of comparisons in a case is "the number of references" multiplied by "the number of mixtures", and the time taken to perform such a number of comparisons relies heavily upon on the methods used. "Matching Allele Count" (MAC[5]), Chapter 8.5.2 [291], is extremely rapid to perform (seconds), whereas inference of the qualitative model would be slower (minutes), and the inference of the quantitative model slower still (hours). Hence, to save computing time, the mixture comparison in CS is based on a three-step approach, as described by Bleka et al. [294]. Each step produces a selected list of candidates from the previous step, which are based on user specified thresholds.

The procedure is divided into three steps. The first step performs MAC, followed by *LR* calculations based on the qualitative model (*LRmix* [219], Chapter 5). Finally, *LR* calculations based on the quantitative model (*EuroForMix*, Chapter 8) were used to filter the list of candidates. To recap how the *LR* is calculated for both the qualitative and quantitative models, consider the two investigative propositions, assuming K number of contributors:

Hp: "Person of interest (POI) and $K - 1$ unknowns (unrelated) are contributors to evidence profile E".

Hd: "K unknowns (unrelated) are contributors to evidence profile E".

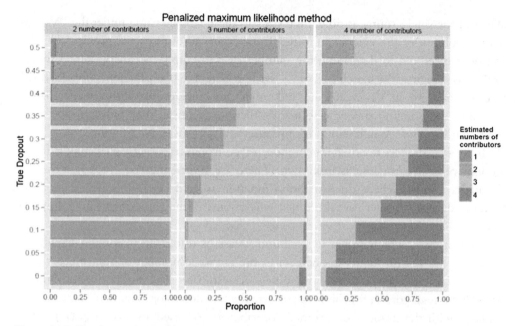

Figure 11.8 The figure shows the proportion of the predicted number of contributors for different true values of number of contributors and drop-out probability (based on 1000 randomly simulated evidence samples). The figure shows the predicted number of contributors using maximum likelihood estimation penalized with number of contributors in the model (i.e., arg max$_K L_{max}(K)$). All the generated samples were based on the 15 NGM markers using the Dutch allele frequencies database. Reproduced from [236] with permission from Elsevier.

The LR is given by the expression $LR = \frac{Pr(E|H_p)}{Pr(E|H_d)}$. A statistical model $Pr(E|\beta, H)$ ($H = H_p$ or $H = H_d$) is substituted for $Pr(E|H)$, which contains unknown parameters β that must be inferred. For this, the maximum likelihood approach is used to infer the unknown parameters [76,234] (Appendix B.3.12) for both the qualitative and the quantitative models, and the LR is given as

$$LR = \frac{max_\beta Pr(E|\beta, H_p)}{max_\beta Pr(E|\beta, H_d)} \quad (11.3)$$

For the qualitative model (*LRmix*), β is the drop-out parameter, giving the probability of drop-out (per contributor) (considered as the "basic model") [224,68]. Here the evidence profile data (E) are the presence/absence of the alleles. For the quantitative model (*EuroForMix*), the peak heights (P.H.) of each allele are also considered as part of E, with the set of following parameters described in Chapter 8: "Mixture proportions", "P.H. expectation", "P.H. variability", "Degradation slope" (if turned on), "Stutter prop." (if turned on). The ML approach means that the parameters are selected such that they maximize the probability of observing the evidence profile E. The number of contributors is optimized using the maximum likelihood method described in Section 11.10.1.1. For both the qualitative and the quantitative models, allele frequency data were used to inform the genotype probabilities. Unobserved alleles were assigned with the minimum observed allele frequency. For our data, this was 0.0018 for GlobalFiler and 5.2×10^{-5} for Fusion 6C frequencies.

11.10.2.1 Step 1: matching allele count

The first step to compare references against mixture profiles is carried out by applying the matching allele count (MAC). In CS, the MAC is given as a proportion of the alleles of the reference that are included in the evidence profile (given as a decimal format). Empty loci are ignored. This method does not use the allele frequencies, the information of the peak heights, or the detection threshold indicated in the model. The results for all comparisons are present in the output. A user-specified "MAC threshold" is utilized to select the candidates for the next comparison step, which is based on LR. The default threshold in CS is 0.8 (this corresponds to a 20% mismatch with the evidence profile), making it potentially possible to detect contributors with a lot of drop-out in low-template evidence profiles. Depending on the application, it is for the user to decide the value of the threshold.

11.10.2.2 Step 2: qualitative *LR* approach

In the second step (which is based on applying the *LRmix* qualitative model[6]), the *LR* is calculated for each candidate generated from the first step: Here, the number of contributors (K) is estimated for each evidence profile (see Section 11.10.1.1), and then the corresponding candidate reference profiles are specified in turn as the POI (as defined by the H_p proposition). The *LR* results are then listed under "Match list (Qual LR)". The Qualitative *LR* threshold is specified by the user to select the candidates for the next comparison step (step 3), which is based on the quantitative model (EuroForMix).

11.10.2.3 Step 3: quantitative *LR* approach

In the third step, the *LR* for each candidate passing the threshold defined from the second step is recalculated based on the quantitative model (*EuroForMix*); the number of contributors is defined as described for the second step. A user-specified quantitative *LR* threshold is utilized to indicate the final list of candidates, which is provided. It is also possible for the user to either skip the step, which is based on the qualitative model (step 2), or the step which is based on the quantitative model (step 3). Also, the user can, at any time after running step 2, calculate the quantitative-based *LR* for a specific comparison with a user-specified proposition set; he/she can condition on a reference (under both H_p and H_d), which is given as a match candidate.

11.10.3 Model parameters

The models used to calculate the LR require the user to specify some parameters, which are not optimized by the software. For both the qualitative and quantitative models he/she must specify the drop-in probability. For all analyses, we used drop-in probability equal to 0.05 (this is the default value). For the quantitative model, we used the drop-in peak height parameter equal to 0.01 (this is the default value), and the detection threshold (AT) and kit, as specified for the particular dataset. CS also allows the possibility to set several model configurations: whether to apply degradation or/and stutter model. In our analysis, we always used the degradation model, but not the stutter model, since this increases computation time, and instead, a stutter filter was applied (see Appendix of Bleka et al. [236] for performance comparison). The "Advanced options" (under "Advanced") makes it possible to specify the maximum number of contributors (K_{max}) for the qualitative/quantitative models. The reason for this setting is that the user may want to avoid the very time-consuming calculations that are executed if the number of contributors is estimated to be large. This is typically not an issue for the qualitative model, which is fast for more than four contributors, however, for the quantitative model, it is challenging. In our analysis, we used $K_{max} = 4$ for the qualitative model (default), and either three or four contributors for the quantitative model, and the results were compared to determine the effects on the LR. Also, the number of optimizations used for the quantitative model is configurable (we recommend four optimizations). As opposed to the interpretation software, $LRmix$ and $EuroForMix$, the user of the current CS version (1.5.0) cannot specify the F_{ST} correction to take sub-population structure into account [42]: this is fixed to zero to reduce computation time. However, the value is typically low and has little effect on the LR. Once candidate matches have been found, evaluation of the evidence will proceed according to laboratory protocols, and the value of the evidence will be provided with the desired value (for instance by using $EuroForMix$). CS also has the possibility to open $EuroForMix$ automatically with selected profiles ready for analysis.

11.11. Demonstration using a real case example

The folder containing the data "CaseSolver_Data" can be downloaded from the book's website https://sites.google.com/view/dnabook/.

11.11.1 Case circumstances

Following a report from a concerned relative, whose sister (REF1) had been missing for several days, the police forcibly entered her residence to find her deceased, along with her son (REF2). There had clearly been a violent struggle, where the victims had been stabbed multiple times. As the investigators had no indication of a suspect or suspects, it was decided to carry out comprehensive sampling of the crime scene to discover potential suspects from DNA analysis (a representation of the crime scene is presented in Fig. 11.9). A reference sample was taken from a suspect (REF3), who was later apprehended by the police.

11.11.1.1 Crime stains and DNA profiles

A total of 119 crime stains were collected from 46 different items. The majority were blood stains, but contact traces were also recovered from cigarette butts, swabs of mobile telephones, and handles of drawers and knife handles and blades that may have been used as weapons by one or more perpetrators and victims. The DNA profiles were generated using GlobalFiler (ThermoFisher Scientific) and the analytical threshold (AT) was set to 70 RFU. All the DNA profiles (alleles and peak heights) are provided at http://www.euroformix.com/datasets. Also provided is a file of allele frequencies used to calculate the LRs [297], based on 284 individuals analyzed with GlobalFiler.

Figure 11.9 A representation of the crime scene, showing location of the victims and the crime-stain evidence collected. Reproduced from [274] with permission from Elsevier.

Online learning material is published at http://www.euroformix.com/casesolver to show how to install and set up CS and to import data. The following description should be read in conjunction with the learning material (the latter is more extensive and provides step-by-step instructions).

11.11.2 Importing data to CS

1. Open CS.
2. Select "Setup">"Set case directory" and choose the directory containing the case folder "RealCase1" (Fig. 11.10). It is important that the directory does not refer to the case folders themselves, rather the folder containing folders with case names.
3. Select "Setup". Select "Set importData function" and choose the file "importDataFile.R". This file contains an R-script that tells CS how to load data from the evidence and reference files.
4. The two previous steps are important for being able to load data into CS. Now, select "RealCase1" from the drop-down menu[7] and click the "Import" button, and CS will then load the data such that they appear on the screen. The remaining steps will be model and search configurations.
5. Select "Setup: Population frequencies" and the frequency file "freqs.csv". This contains Spanish data from the GlobalFiler kit.
6. Select "Setup: Kit Selection". Choose "GlobalFiler". This selection is necessary for CS to show EPG plots and to adapt the degradation model.
7. Other settings can be selected under "Setup: Model settings", "Setup: Threshold settings" (Fig. 11.11), and "Advanced: Advanced options" (use default values).

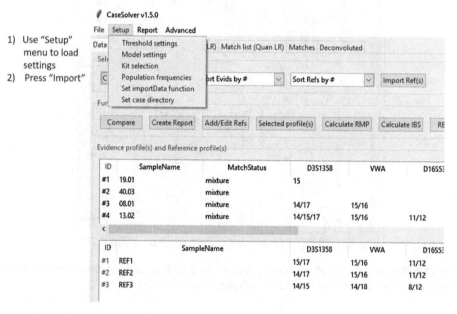

Figure 11.10 CaseSolver GUI showing "Setup" menu accessed via the "Data" tab. Panes show a list of case samples and reference samples after pressing the "Import" button.

The crime samples along with their matches are listed in the top pane of Fig. 11.10, and the three reference samples are listed in the lower pane. If there is a match with a

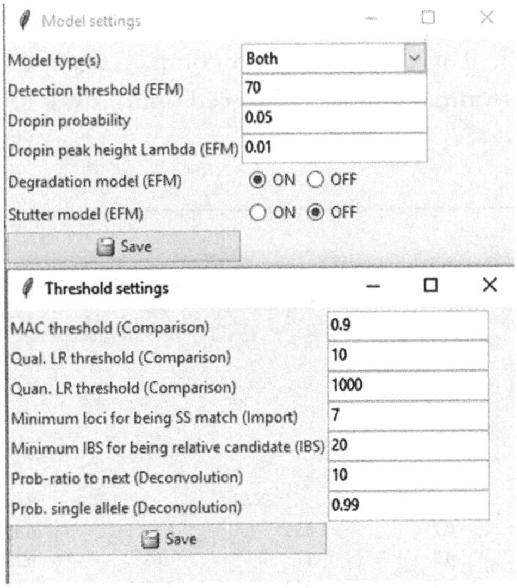

Investigative forensic genetics: *SmartRank, CaseSolver* and *DNAmatch2*   365

Figure 11.11 From the "Setup" menu, "Model" (upper pane), and "Threshold" (lower pane) settings are shown.

crime sample and the reference sample, then this information is provided in the Match-Status column, for example, scrolling down the list shows that there is a single profile match between sample "02.01" and reference "REF3". If a single-source profile does not match any of the reference samples, then its status is marked "Unknown 1", and the corresponding profile is added to the reference list. This enables the possibility for unknown single-contributor profiles to be compared against crime sample mixtures in the "Compare" step. Notice that different single-source profiles (not matching any references) are assigned with a consecutive number identifier. If the MatchStatus is described as "mixture", this means that the sample, e.g., "19.01", has at least three alleles for any of the markers—further analysis is described in the next step. If the user double clicks on a sample, then an EPG will be generated. To display multiple profiles on the same EPG, hold "CTRL" on the computer keyboard to select them, and press "ENTER". Additional functionalities for the selected profiles can be found by selecting "Selected profile(s)".

11.11.3 Comparing references to mixtures

The next step is to compare all reference samples to the mixtures. Press the Compare button in the "Data" tab. To carry out the matching process, the three-step process described in Section 11.10.2 is followed.

Step 1: All reference profiles are compared against all mixtures to provide a score that is based on the proportion of alleles in the reference sample that is included in the mixture (based on the matching allele count, MAC). These data are shown under the "Match matrix" tab (Fig. 11.12). It is also possible to compare against all evidence profiles as well if "Compare single-sources" under Advanced options was checked when data were imported.

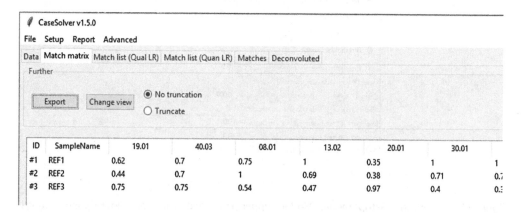

Figure 11.12 "Match matrix" results showing proportions of alleles that match the crime sample, for example, 0.62 of REF1, 0.44 of REF2, and 0.75 of REF3 match sample 19.01.

Step 2: The MAC method is a first filter. The MAC threshold settings (Fig. 11.11) were set to 0.9 (the user can change this parameter), hence only those samples with one or more references with ≥ 0.9 in matching allele count (proportion) will be passed to the next stage of the analysis, i.e., the qualitative model to calculate LR. From the "Qual. LR threshold settings", only those results showing $LR \geq 10$ are displayed. A ranked list of $log_{10}LR$s is shown under the "Match list (Qual LR)" tab (Fig. 11.13).

Step 3: The list of comparisons in Fig. 11.13 surviving the qualitative LR threshold is then subject to the analysis using the quantitative model, which provides the list shown in Fig. 11.14. There is a threshold of $log_{10}LR = 3$, which is provided in the "Threshold settings" "Quan. LR threshold (Comparison)" box. Note that the ranking is altered compared to the previous qualitative step.

11.11.4 Viewing the results

The "Matches" tab (Fig. 11.15) provides an alternative view of the sample matches with the references (the comparisons satisfying the quantitative threshold $LR \geq 10^3$ from Fig. 11.14). The data can be exported; a match network can be generated and all mixtures can be deconvolved by pressing the buttons shown in this tab. Also, separate match networks for the mixtures and single-source profiles can be provided.

A very informative method to combine all of the results into a graphical network is shown by pressing the "Show match network" button (Fig. 11.16). Many of the

Investigative forensic genetics: *SmartRank, CaseSolver* and *DNAmatch2*   367

.	Evidence	Reference	MAC	log10LR	numCont
#1	30.01	REF1	1	27.3	1
#2	37.01	REF1	1	27	1
#3	39.06	REF2	1	26.44	1
#4	38.15	REF1	1	19.24	2
#5	40.02	REF2	1	18.9	2
#6	40.04	REF2	1	18.85	2
#7	03.01	REF1	1	18.84	2
#8	39.07	REF1	1	18.84	2
#9	37.03	REF1	1	18.69	2
#10	45.01	REF1	1	18.69	2
#11	16.12	REF1	1	18.68	2

Figure 11.13 "Match list (Qual LR)" results, showing a ranked list of samples compared to a named reference. The MAC proportion is provided along with the ranked $log_{10}LR$ results using the qualitative model; finally, the estimated number of contributors to the mixture is provided.

orange and red nodes only match to a single reference. This indicates that the second contributor is either "unknown", or fails to achieve an LR greater than the threshold value ($log_{10}LR = 3$ in the example) relative to the reference sample. There is an option to change the thresholds if required, which will change appearance of the network.

11.11.5 Deconvolution

Deconvolution results are displayed under the "Deconvoluted" tab. These results are based on the same probabilistic calculations as performed by *EuroForMix*, and details about how the calculations are carried out is described in Chapter 7.7, with more details presented in the supplementary material of [274]. Here the deconvolution is based on the top ranked genotype (giving highest probability), and if this probability is above a threshold, the genotype is said to be a deconvolved solution. The deconvolution threshold can be changed under "Setup">"Threshold settings">"Prob-ratio to next (Deconvolution)" (10 is default). This is the ratio of the probabilities of the first-ranking genotype vs. the second-ranking genotype, i.e., the higher the number, the more "certain" the evidence supports the higher ranking genotype. If the highest probability is below this threshold, there is still a possibility that only one of the alleles is certain, hence single allele probabilities are also calculated. If one allele has a probability of at least a specified threshold, called "Prob. single allele (Deconvolution)" (default 0.99), CS says that this allele is certain, and it is added to the deconvolution result. In CS (and *EuroForMix*), dropped out alleles are designated as allele "99" (representing any

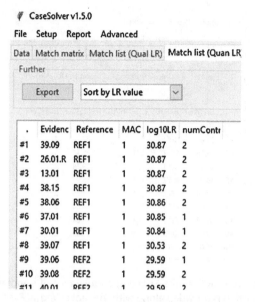

Figure 11.14 "Match list (Quan LR)" results, showing a ranked list of samples compared to a named reference. The MAC proportion is provided along with the ranked $log_{10}LR$ results using the quantitative model; finally, the number of contributors to the mixture is provided.

of the alleles not being observed). In our data, sample 01.01-C1 is of interest, because the whole profile of an unknown component has been deconvolved. If this profile is "double-clicked" with the left mouse button, then a message appears (Fig. 11.17) asking if the user wishes to add the profile to the reference list in Fig. 11.10. This gives the opportunity to search the data with deconvolved "unknown" profiles, which may highlight new investigative leads (a new search is required following details in Section 11.11.3). CS also has the possibility to export the selected deconvolved profile(s) in Genemapper format by the "Export selected" button.

11.11.6 Relatedness searches

CS has a button called "Calculate IBS" under the Data tab, which simply calculates the number of shared alleles between all references (IBS stands for "Identical by state"). This is a useful feature to find out if any of the reference samples are potential relatives, or to discover mistyping in single-source profiles. An IBS threshold can be selected under "Setup"> "Threshold Settings">"Minimum IBS for being relative candidate". If the relationship under consideration is father/son or two siblings, then about 50% of their alleles will match. There are 21 autosomal loci in GlobalFiler, hence we expect about 20 alleles to match for this level of relationship (the default is threshold is $IBS = 20$). Press the "Calculate IBS" button (Fig. 11.18), and this shows that REF2-REF1 are potentially related with $IBS = 27$ shared alleles (we know that these references are

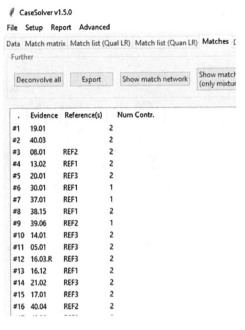

Figure 11.15 "Matches" tab results, showing a list of samples compared, matched named references, and number of contributors.

from mother/son), but it also appears that the deconvoluted unknown sample 01.01-C1 shares a close relationship with the suspect REF3 with 24 alleles matching. CS includes a method to estimate the probability of observing IBS $\geq x$, for $x = 0, 1, 2..., 2 \times L$ (L is the number of loci) under the assumption that two reference samples are unrelated. These probabilities can be calculated exactly by selecting "Advanced">"Random IBS"—a small probability (p-value) for an observed IBS indicates relationship. If required, further formal probabilistic calculations should be made to assess the likelihood of any given relationship; this is not implemented in CS, but can be carried out in the open-source *Familias* https://familias.no/ [298,299]. For mixtures, the open-source software *RelMix* [57] https://cran.r-project.org/web/packages/relMix/index.html can be utilized.

11.11.7 Advanced options

The Advanced options tab provides additional, but minor, settings for the model estimations and search strategies. Here the user has the option to define the maximum number of contributors in the qualitative and quantitative steps, thereby limiting the automated contributor estimator outlined in Section 11.10.1.1. This will typically drastically reduce the computational time for the quantitative model if a high number of contributors is estimated. The option "Use SNP module" will assume that all evidence

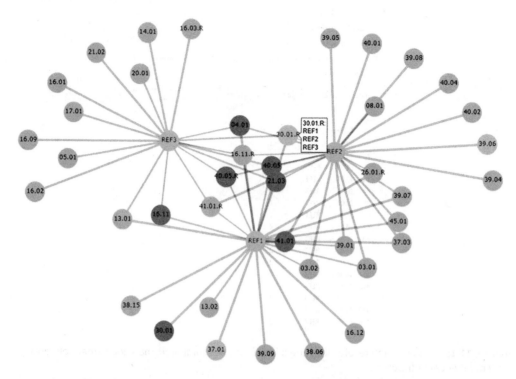

Figure 11.16 "Show match network" from the Matches tab generates the network. The references are the green nodes. Single-contributor evidence are in cyan; two contributors are in orange, and three or more contributors are in red. If the "plotly" function in R is used, then the mouse can be hovered over a node, and this displays a list of the matches, as shown for sample 30.01. The thickness of the edges and the distance between the nodes is inversely proportional to the size of the LR on a log_{10} scale.

profiles are 3-person mixtures in the compare analysis (the rationale for defaulting to three contributors is described by Bleka et al. [300] and Chapter 13.7).

11.11.8 More detailed summary of results
11.11.8.1 Comparison against single-source profiles

It was observed that 68 of the total 112 evidence samples imported were classified as single-source profiles ($K = 1$). In this case, two (related) reference profiles, which were the victims, REF1 and REF2, had been sampled (sharing 27 alleles), and many of the single-source profiles matched these as well (29 samples matched REF1 and 17 samples matched REF2). CS was also able to assign 22 of the single-source profiles as an unknown male profile (Unknown 1), which subsequently matched a known individual who had previously inhabited the flat (REF3). The remaining 44 evidence samples were categorized as mixtures (K was at least 2).

Investigative forensic genetics: *SmartRank, CaseSolver* and *DNAmatch2*   371

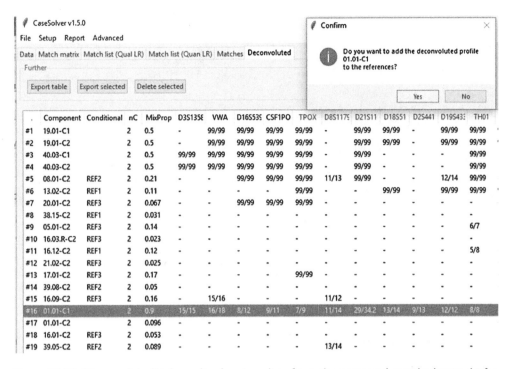

Figure 11.17 "Deconvoluted" tab results, showing a list of samples compared, matched named references, and number of contributors.

11.11.8.2 Comparisons against mixtures

As a starting point for the analysis, MAC = 0.8 and $LR = 1000$ were used as LR thresholds (for both model types). From this analysis, profiles 40.03, 19.01 and 01.01 did not give any candidate matches. We were able to extract a full major profile, MAJ, from sample 01.01 using the deconvolution function (assuming $K = 2$). This profile was again compared to all of the other mixtures using the same thresholds. The first step provided a list of 76 comparisons with a MAC above 0.8 (176 comparisons completed within 1 s), whereas 73 of these had a qualitative LR above 1000 (completed in 21 s). Out of these, 70 comparisons had a quantitative LR above 1000 (completed in 2.8 h, but restricting the maximum number of contributors to three reduced time of analysis to only 10 min). The corresponding match tree graph is shown in Fig. 11.16.

11.11.8.3 Relatedness

In the real case example, we calculated IBS between four references (six pairwise comparisons). "Settings">"Threshold settings">"Minimum IBS for being a relative candidate" was set to 20 (Fig. 11.11) as the minimum number of matching alleles between any two references, that must be present to be flagged as a potential relative.

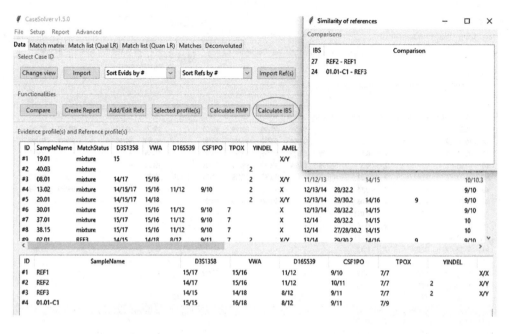

Figure 11.18 Searching for potential relatives amongst reference samples.

From activating Calculate IBS button on the Data tab, there were two reference pairs highlighted:

a) REF2 with REF1, where 27 alleles match;
b) 01.01-C1 with REF3, where 24 alleles match (01.01-C1 is renamed MAJ).

Next we ran "Advanced">"Random IBS"; this created a table of p-values for random matches between pairs of unrelated individuals for 0–42 alleles. We selected two p-values for the observed matches, i.e., for 27 allele match, $p = 1.2\text{e-}07$, and for the 24 allele match, $p = 2.0\text{e-}05$. These p-values need to be Bonferroni-corrected to take into account the number of comparisons conducted (n_{com}):

$$n_{com} = \frac{n_{ref} \times (n_{ref} - 1)}{2} = 6. \qquad (11.4)$$

The Bonferroni-corrected p-value = p-value $\times\ n_{com}$. Hence, the corrected p-values were

a) REF1 with REF2 = $1.22\text{e-}07 \times 6 = 7.3\text{e-}07$;
b) MAJ with REF3 = $1.98\text{e-}05 \times 6 = 1.2\text{e-}04$.

These corrected p-values give the probability that a random pair of individuals will match at $x = 27$ and 24 alleles respectively (when conducting $n_{com} = 6$ comparisons). It does not give an indication of the kind of relationship that may be present (e.g., siblings, parent/child). To evaluate, further tests are needed, as described in Appendix A.2. Software such as *Familias* [298,299] can be used to provide this information.

When there is limited information in a case, information on potential relatedness may be useful to investigations.

11.11.8.4 Potential false positives and negatives

In addition to the standard search strategy, we considered a more thorough analysis to discover potential false negatives or positives. Here we lowered the MAC threshold to 0.7, and the qualitative-based *LR* threshold to 1, and then applied the quantitative model, where we conditioned on presumed matching profiles. This work was carried out interactively on the Matches (Qual LR) panel. Consequentially, we obtained the following (updated) results in about 1 h of work using CS.

Potential false positives:

- 30.01.R–REF2 (MAC $= 0.9$):
  - Conditioning on REF1 with $K = 3$ contributors, reduced $log_{10}LR$ from 6.4 to -0.2
  - Conditioning on REF1/REF3 with $K = 3$ contributors, reduced $log_{10}LR$ further to -1.7
- 38.06–REF2 (MAC $= 0.86$):
  - Conditioning on REF1 with $K = 2$ contributors, reduced $log_{10}LR$ from 4.6 to -4.1
  - Conditioning on REF1 with $K = 3$ contributors, reduced $log_{10}LR$ from 4.6 to 1.7

Potential false negatives:

- 39.04–REF3 (MAC $= 0.76$): Conditioning on REF2 with $K = 2$ contributors, returned $log_{10}LR = 9.4$
- 41.01–REF3 (MAC $= 0.79$): Conditioning on REF2 with $K = 2$ contributors, returned $log_{10}LR = 8.7$
- 40.03–REF3 (MAC $= 0.75$): Conditioning on none with $K = 2$ contributors, returned $log_{10}LR = 4.0$

REF3 has allele 9 in marker DYS391, which was also obtained for all the three mixtures, increasing the support for the proposition that REF3 could be a contributor (however this was not taken into account in the *LR* calculation).

11.11.9 Searching a large fictive national DNA database

Often, the candidate list of suspects may extend to national DNA databases. A portion of a database may be selected based on the geographical location of the offence and known offenders within a given area. To test the efficiency of CS, the three profiles of known persons of interest in the real case described above, i.e., the two victims and the suspect, were added to 1 million randomly generated reference profiles, and these were compared to the evidence profiles (based on the crime stains in the case) using CS. Here the GlobalFiler allele frequencies were used, but in addition, we inserted a minimum frequency of 0.0018 for allele 5.3 and allele 28 at the SE33 locus (and afterwards all frequencies were normalized). Importantly, the generation of such a database enables us to count (and estimate) the number of false positives obtained. The generation of 1 million random individuals can be carried out automatically by the "importDataFile" by placing a copy of the "freqs.csv" file into the "Real1" case folder, and pressing the Import button on the Data tab.

The time taken to simulate, import, and visualize the data was about 14 min, with a high internal memory requirement of 13.4 GB. Storing the project required a file of 25 MB, which could be imported in about 10 min. The time taken to compare all 1 million references (including case references) against the 44 classified mixtures with the MAC method (44 million comparisons in total), and generating the results in a huge table, was 34 min and required 12.5 GB. Of these, 56,521 comparisons satisfied the threshold of MAC = 0.8. We next calculated the qualitative LR for all candidates (completed in almost 8 h). A total of 302 of the comparisons satisfied a qualitative LR of at least 1000. Calculating the quantitative LR for these remaining candidates took 16 min/4 h ($K_{max} = 3/4$), and resulted in 210/190 match candidates with LR above 1000 ($K_{max} = 3/4$), and 68 with LR above 10^6. Table 2 gives an overview of the number of generated references found after applying the "threshold test" in each of the comparison steps in CS. The presumed four-person mixture profile 04.01 yielded the most false positives, using the MAC method, due to the high number of observed alleles, whereas the qualitative LR method removed most of these with a threshold $LR = 1000$. In the next step, the quantitative model reduced the number of candidates further; however, many candidates still had a LR above 1000. For the presumed four-person mixture profile 04.01, the number of false positives was increased from 7 to 27 when conditioning changed from three to four contributors in the quantitative model; here the LR of the top-ranked generated reference was increased. The largest false positive quantitative-based LR for a randomly generated reference was $log_{10}LR = 6.1$ (MAC = 0.94), obtained for the low-quality sample, 19.01. This was the only comparison with a LR above 1 million. Hence, all the comparison results for the known references in the previous section (Fig. 11.5) obtained the highest rankings when a LR threshold of 1 million was used.

11.12. The need for new digital tools in forensic genetics: improving efficiency of searching large DNA databases

The rapid change and use of DNA technology requires new analytical software to be developed to deal with vast amount of information generated. Traditional DNA analyses are often based on manual comparisons of alleles, together with peak heights, using pen

Table 11.5 The table gives an overview of the observed number of generated references (out of 1 million total) found after applying the filter in each of the comparison steps in CS, for each evidence profile. "Expected" is the expected number of references, which are expected to satisfy the MAC = 0.8 threshold. Here, only evidences with at least one generated reference candidate, are presented. For sample 04.01, we evaluated both for $K = 3$ and $K = 4$ number of contributors for the quantitative model. The last column represents the maximum observed LR for the generated reference profile with the observed MAC, shown in parentheses. Reproduced from [274] with permission from Elsevier.

Sample Name	Expected	MAC = 0.8	Qual. LR = 1000	Max Qual. LR (log10) w/MAC	Quan. LR = 1000	Quan. LR = 1e6	Max Quan.LR (log10) w/MAC
04.01 (maxK = 3/4)	44567	44397	41	5.3 (0.95)	7/27	0/0	4.8 (0.95)/5.9 (0.95)
16.11.R	2691	2665	12	4.6 (0.90)	2	0	4.8 (0.88)
41.01.R	2456	2466	10	5.9 (0.93)	6	0	5.0 (0.86)
30.01.R	1616	1639	24	4.8 (0.88)	23	0	4.5 (0.86)
21.03	1183	1200	21	5.3 (0.90)	13	0	4.7 (0.86)
19.01	1170	1190	35	4.5 (0.94)	32	1	6.1 (0.94)
40.05	1120	1182	17	5.3 (0.90)	8	0	4.6 (0.86)
40.05.R	1073	1100	17	5.3 (0.90)	6	0	3.9 (0.90)
16.11	226	251	0	−0.4 (0.81)	−	−	−
40.03	114	94	24	4.7 (0.85)	22	0	5.5 (0.85)
13.01	83	82	0	2.4 (0.81)	0	0	5.3 (0.83)
16.02	72	65	0	2.8 (0.81)	−	−	−
08.01	43	57	26	4.6 (0.82)	21	0	4.7 (0.82)
41.01	35	41	1	3.6 (0.81)	0	−	−4.2 (0.81)
39.04	11	13	1	3.4 (0.81)	0	−	−2.0 (0.81)
38.06/16.09/39.05	1.4/0.6/0.4	1/1/1	0/0/0	2.0 /1.0/2.5 (0.81/0.81/0.81)	−	−	−

and paper. As the number of markers increases, such work requires a lot of resources and transcription errors are a particular concern. The increased sensitivity of DNA typing has also led to the generation of more mixture profiles, and analyzing these together with a large number of other profiles in complex cases is required by routine caseworkers. CS is an exploratory investigative tool used to filter large sets of data to discover candidate matches (potential matches between reference profiles and evidence profiles), either single-source profiles or mixtures. We provided a demonstration of a challenging case, and we also showed the benefits of being able to perform more thorough analyses (LR calculation, deconvolution, or simple relatedness testing), where propositions can be specified more carefully, without exporting to other software.

With complex investigations, there are often no suspect(s). Under these circumstances, investigators will usually resort to a search of the national DNA database to discover potential candidates. Whereas this is quite a straightforward process for single, well-represented DNA profiles, when the evidence profiles are mixtures, a different approach is needed. Most national DNA databases are geared to work with single-source profiles. If a mixture is obtained, then deconvolution may be carried out to extract a candidate reference to search with, but this procedure is problematic, because it is realistically restricted to clear major contributors; if the person of interest is a minor contributor, the approach does not work, because masking and drop-out means that there can be no definitive reference sample to search with. As a result, reliance upon deconvolution is inefficient as many crime stains cannot be analyzed. Consequently, many cases remain unsolved.

The likelihood ratio approach employed by probabilistic models is a preferable way forward, because there is no restriction on profiles that can be searched (no deconvolution), so that minor contributors can be investigated—there is no need for a clear major contributor to be the person of interest. Such an approach is employed by *SmartRank* (Section 11.6). This is a rapid search engine that employs the qualitative model of Haned et al. [68]. However, quantitative models are more informative, because they take account of the peak height information in the evidence profile. But the downside is that the computational requirements are much greater. Consequently, this may act as a limitation on the number of reference samples that may be searched. To solve this problem, we have devised a three-step test. Clearly, there is no point in carrying out extensive computations on samples, where only a few alleles match. Therefore, these can be quickly filtered by carrying out simple allele matching, and eliminating those references that fall below a threshold. The remainder can be searched by the qualitative model, and the final list refined by the quantitative model. The investigative procedure is outlined in Fig. 11.19. A list of reference profiles to search may arise from staff elimination databases (contamination search); mass screens of local populations; national DNA databases, or persons of interest highlighted as a result of other investigations.

The purpose of the laboratory is to compare the reference profiles against the relevant evidence profile(s) to provide a ranked list of candidates. This list is forwarded to the police who carry out further investigations. The list of candidates may be restricted according to criteria, such as age or geographic location [193]. If phenotyping information is available, e.g., geographic ancestry or hair/eye color, then this can also be used to reduce the size of candidate lists [285], noting that no test is 100% definitive, hence there is a risk of false negatives. Either all candidates are eliminated, or one is identified as a suspect, who is carried forward to the prosecuting authorities for evaluation based on additional evidence in the case. If all are eliminated, the police contact the lab and request an extension to the candidate list, either including references with lower ranking, or by considering a new set of references based upon new criteria. When there is sufficient non-DNA evidence in the case to proceed with the prosecution, then the scientist switches to evaluative mode as reviewed by Gill et al. [275]. Once in the evaluative mode, the strength of evidence is considered using refined propositions that are posited by the relevant authorities [284], and with a suitable "F_{ST}-correction" (the current version of CS does not consider F_{ST}-correction). Importantly, CS can export the selected DNA profiles directly to *EuroForMix*, or to text files for other software users, so that there is no method restriction for the evaluative phase to take place. The idea of investigative searches is to prioritize police resources, where there is limited information in the case. If the DNA evidence profile is non-complex and well-represented at 16+ loci, then there is usually no issue with searching very large reference databases of several million individuals. The risks of missing someone are low. However, when the profile is a complex mixture of three or more persons, then it is inevitable that there are

Investigative forensic genetics: *SmartRank, CaseSolver* and *DNAmatch2* 377

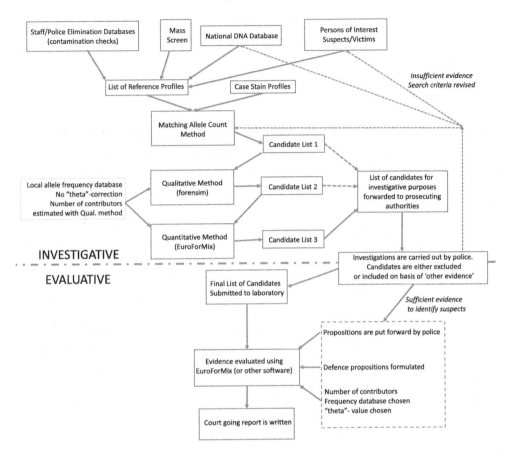

Figure 11.19 Reference profiles are collected (part of case circumstances or databases) and compared to evidence profiles. A three-step procedure identifies matches, which are forwarded to prosecuting authorities for further investigation. Either the candidates are all eliminated, in which case a more relaxed or focused search may be requested, or one or more candidates become suspects and the lab moves from investigative to evaluative mode, in considering the evidence in relation to propositions put forward by the authorities and the case circumstances. Dotted arrow lines are optional. Reproduced from [274] with permission from Elsevier.

many false positive matches in the candidate list. To carry out an investigation, this list is ranked according to the likelihood ratio, and the police will investigate the individuals in this ranked order. To forward a person to the evaluative stage, it is necessary to have additional evidence, e.g., eye witness, fibers. It is therefore a time-consuming process. For example, if no candidate is found after the first one hundred comparisons, then there is an option to extend the list to the next one hundred, and so-on. This process is dictated entirely by the police investigator, and it is ultimately dependent upon the resources and time available to investigate a particular crime. There will be more resources for a serial killing than for a petty burglary. In addition, rather than search entire databases, subsets of databases may be prioritized based on, for example, geographical location, age, and sex of proposed offender; previous convictions of offenders with a known *modus operandi*, etc. These are examples of criteria that may be used to prioritize investigations without the need to search entire databases.

11.12.1 Why use a stepwise strategy to extract candidate matches?

The *LR* method is preferred to the MAC when mixtures are compared to large DNA reference databases [291]. Studies show that a quantitative model, such as *EuroForMix*, outperforms the qualitative model [236,301]. However, the time taken to perform analyses with *EuroForMix* is a limitation, hence the stepwise approach was introduced. An argument for using MAC as a first step is consistent with many labs that have introduced an upper threshold on the number of mismatches allowed before a result can be reported. For example, if the analytical procedure accepts a maximum of 4 drop-outs, such a rule would be easy to apply in CS, with the added benefit of speeding up comparisons (as opposed to not using this threshold). CS makes use of the qualitative model, since it is very fast and performs well (also used by *SmartRank*). We have implemented the ML approach for improved performance [236]. From the Fusion 6C validation study, presented in [274], we found that this approach performed well by giving a high *LR* for contributors and a low *LR* for non-contributors (except for samples with high levels of drop-out, where the numbers of contributors were under-estimated). However, as illustrated for the real case example, this model can sometimes give misleading *LR* values, since it does not use the peak height model—this would typically happen when large DNA databases are searched or relatives considered. Consequently, we recommend that the three-step strategy is normally applied (Fig. 11.19). This approach is accomplished within a reasonable time period.

11.12.2 The flexibility of CS

An important aspect of CS is that it is very easy to customize: The user can provide different model settings and search strategy thresholds, and even tailor the type of data that can be imported into the software. CS also has the possibility to create simple HTML reports, with the limitation that it does not directly produce reports in pdf format. Here, the user can select which part of the data or results that should be exported to the report. CS makes it possible to define a lab-specific "ImportData" function. This means that there are no rules to describe the format of DNA profiles used as input, so long as the function returns a valid format, which is recognizable by CS. This enables a general framework to import data into CS, limited by the R language [218] and its supporting R-packages. This flexibility of approach means that it can be integrated into laboratory systems that have different data formats to that used by us. Another possibility, which is currently implemented, would be to use CS to analyze next-generation sequencing-based data, where one may want to consider the "longest uninterrupted sequence (LUS)" using Verogen's ForenSeq DNA Signature Prep Kit, for instance [302] (see Chapter 13.9). The performance of software in terms of false positives and negatives is an important part of validation and provides a benchmark statement of the performance to compare future improvements, i.e., validation is a continuous process. There will be limitations, particularly when the person of interest is a contributor with very low level DNA template. Alleles will be below the analytical threshold and the corresponding LRs will be small (Chapter 3.2). The system is designed to be exploratory, and there is flexibility for the user. After matches have been found, the scientist enters the evaluative phase of the analysis, which forms the basis of the court report—this means that the LR can be recalculated with *EuroForMix* or any other probabilistic software using specific frequency databases, F_{ST}-correction, number of contributors, etc., as shown in Fig. 11.19; this is covered by separate validation studies reported elsewhere (e.g., [236,252,264]).

Appendix Section D of [274] describes numerical/program checking carried out using R scripts that are available at the webpage www.euroformix/evaluations in a file named "NumEval_2.1.0" (also available for newer versions). Since November 2017, CS has been actively used in casework at the Department of Forensic Sciences (Oslo University Hospital) in Norway. There, CS has been integrated into the data system and work flow to allow seamless transfer of data. CS is an important tool to support the findings of the reporting scientists, and to discover manual typing errors or artefacts from an earlier stage in the analysis process. There is a lot of flexibility in the software so that it can be utilized for specific purposes. Consequently, it is necessary for labs to carry out in-house validation, but this is true for any software.

11.12.3 Searching large national DNA databases

To test the limitations of CS, we tried different sizes of reference databases, which were based on 24 loci (also included non-autosomal markers). For one million generated references, in addition to the profiles in the real-case example, the memory required was 13 GB. It was not possible to carry out computations with an 8 GB platform. Once all the data were imported into CS, the total time taken for CS to compare and visualize the results of comparing more than 1 million references against 44 mixtures was 35 min + "additional". Here, "additional" refers to the strategy used after the MAC comparison. As a result, we found that the qualitative/quantitative based methods were important to apply to reduce the very high number of false positives: The MAC = 0.8 threshold returned 56,445 (generated) candidates, where the higher-order mixture sample 04.01 constituted 44,397. Sequentially using the qualitative method with threshold $LR = 1000$ recovered 229 (generated) candidates. Last, when the quantitative model was applied, an LR threshold of 1000 was suitable to obtain a manageable list of 140/160 (generated) candidates ($K_{max} = 3/4$). However, increasing the threshold to 1 million removed

380 Forensic Practitioner's Guide to the Interpretation of Complex DNA Profiles

almost all (generated) references from the match list, except of one instance, which had $log_{10} LR = 6.1$. This observation is entirely in keeping with theory by Gill et al. [227] who stated:

> "How often a $LR = x$ or more occurs is accommodated by $Pr(LR > x|Hd) < 1/x$, so we never expect more than N/x chance matches, where N is the size of the database. The number of non-contributors with a greater LR than x, in a database of size N, is $N \times Pr(LR > x|H_d)$ and it is crucially dependant on N."

Searching against a large number of reference samples with low LRs as thresholds (LR_t) causes an investigative limitation, because of the increase of false-positive results. Still, the number of false positives observed in our demonstration were much less than the expected upper boundary from such a search, i.e., expected number of samples $n_{exp} = \frac{N}{LR_t}$ [85,227]. This would be 44,000 with a threshold of $LR_t = 1000$, and 44 with $LR_t = 1m$. Regarding large DNA databases, CS is very memory demanding. The bottleneck comes down to the visualization of large matrices in the graphical user interface. We recommend using the non-graphical software *dnamatch2* [294] as a memory–efficient alternative (it is based on the same methods used in CS). Another alternative is to use *EuroForMix* or *SmartRank* for searching one evidence profile (also replicates) at a time for a specified set of propositions.

11.12.4 Using *DNAmatch2* to search large databases and as a contamination search engine

CaseSolver is designed to carry out complex investigative searches. *DNAmatch2* [294] has the same three-step search functionality as *CaseSolver*, but is more efficient to carry out large database searches in terms of memory (i.e., the profiles are not shown in a graphical user interface). It is also the recommended platform to carry out contamination searches during routine casework. A new version of *DNAmatch2* (v2.0.0) now contains a GUI, which makes it easy to set up and execute (managing) the contamination searches. The software is available at http://www.euroformix.com/dnamatch2 along with a user manual.

There are two kinds of contamination:

1. Contamination from an investigator at the crime scene, or from a scientist working in the laboratory (type 1 contamination).
2. Contamination within the laboratory, where DNA from case (a) has been accidentally transferred to an unrelated case (b), for example, see the case of "wrongful arrest of Adams" [193], where a used microtitre plate was accidentally reused (type 2 contamination).

Detection of type 1 contamination relies upon maintaining an "elimination database" comprised of police officers, scientists, and anyone who may be handling crime-scene evidence, since these individuals are the most probable to accidentally con-

Investigative forensic genetics: *SmartRank, CaseSolver* and *DNAmatch2*   381

taminate crime-scene evidence. Failure to identify these individuals wastes countless hours of resources investigating "unknown" (irrelevant) DNA profiles. Since contaminants are often in admixture and usually minor contributors, they cannot be detected by deconvolution. However, the likelihood ratio approaches described in this chapter are the most efficient ways to detect contamination, either by reference to elimination databases, or by cross comparisons of casework over a designated time period.

To demonstrate [294], we used the ESX17 kit (16 markers) with the Norwegian population frequency database to simulate $N = 100$ random reference profiles. The "genDataset" function in *EuroForMix* was used to create $M = 1000$ random stain profiles (with gamma distributed peak heights) comprising one-, two-, or three-person mixtures. First, a type 1 contamination search (reference vs crime stain) was carried out. This took about 1 min for $M \times N = 100,000$ comparisons. A total of 35 out of 50 true positives were discovered, whereas one false positive was recorded out of the remaining 99,950 comparisons. The 15 false negatives occurred, because of the high levels of allele drop-out (typically around 10 drop-outs per profile), whereas some of the true positives had up to 6 drop-outs.

Secondly, we performed a type 2 contamination search (crime stain vs crime stain) of $M \times (N + M - 1) = 1,094,000$ comparisons. The first step, utilizing the MAC procedure took 5 seconds, whereas the second and third steps (estimating the number of contributors and calculating the qualitative *LR*), based on 4218 combinations, took 140 seconds. The last step (quantitative *LR*), based on 848 combinations, took 3.3 hours. In addition to the results for the type 1 database search, this procedure found extra matches. There were 88 out of 225 true positives when "crime-stain-against-crime-stain" comparisons were considered. However, a total of 37 false positives out of the remaining 499,275 were discovered.

In Norway, *dnamatch2* has been used as a valuable tool to find potential contamination events, since 2015. References in an elimination database of employees and technicians are compared to routine case work profiles (reference to evidence comparisons). Routine profiles are also compared to each other (across different cases only). This exercise is carried out every week, and any resulting candidate hits are manually investigated. In the period from year 2016 to 2019 (November), a total of 22 contamination events were discovered.

In addition to this search, "wipe-tests" of laboratory surfaces are routinely conducted on a monthly basis to check for "hot spot DNA contamination"; the results are compared against the elimination database.

Early versions of *dnamatch2* contained only an R-function to run the search. However, the new update (version 2.0 or newer) also contains a GUI, so that the user can set up all configurations for the search. Importantly, *dnamatch2* automatically produces session logs for all executions.

11.12.5 Future improvements for estimating the number of contributors

The estimation of the number of contributors was conducted using the maximum likelihood estimation of the qualitative model with a penalty term, introduced by Bleka et al. [236]. Sometimes the number of contributors was under-estimated, leading to false negatives. We hope to further improve the method in a future update. The method for relatedness testing in CS was only based on simple allele sharing (IBS). In a future update, the *LR* for hypothesized relationships could also be calculated to further improve the test. More sophisticated theory can be developed to identify whether contributors in two separate mixtures are the same (mix-mix searches). By generalizing the traditional methodology, it is possible to calculate an *LR* score for the comparison of proposition "Two mixtures share a common contributor" versus "Two mixtures do not share any contributors" [303]. Hence, this method could be applied to infer investigative leads about common unknown contributors of complex mixtures that are otherwise difficult to resolve.

11.13. Summary

The forensic scientist has a dual role of *investigative* vs. *evaluative*. The scientist is said to be in the investigative mode when there is no suspect in a case. This will usually lead to a search for potential suspects on a national DNA database. In addition, some cases may be complex, with numerous case stains and suspects to investigate. A number of different solutions that employ different software have evolved to cope with the challenges raised.

National DNA databases comprise large numbers of reference samples. To interrogate a database, it is necessary to infer a single contributor from a crime sample to carry out the search. Whereas this is straightforward, where the crime stain is one contributor, it is problematic when a mixture is analyzed. It may be possible to deconvolve a contributor from a mixture; this is easiest if the POI is major.

The alternative strategy to interrogate a database is to use probabilistic genotyping software to calculate likelihood ratios substituting a reference sample for the POI in the numerator proposition. This will result in a large list of *LR*s that can be ranked, the highest may identify potential POIs that can be taken forward for further investigation.

In regards to carrying out *LR* interrogation of a database, *SmartRank* is a qualitative software that is based upon *LRmix*; *DNAmatch2* is a quantitative software based upon *EuroForMix* that takes account of allele peak heights. *DNAmatch2* can also be used to discover contamination events if crime samples are routinely screened against staff elimination databases. These software offer improved solutions compared to traditional database interrogation.

CaseSolver is also based upon *EuroForMix*. This software is designed to assist reporting scientists to investigate cases that have numerous case stains and reference samples. The software will highlight potential crime stain to crime stain, as well as reference sample to crime stain "matches". The results can be illustrated as a graphical "match network".

Notes

1. The binomial coefficient $\binom{N}{k}$ is the number of ways of picking k unordered outcomes from N possibilities, also known as a combinatorial number.
2. Sources: https://www.gov.uk/government/statistics/national-dna-database-statistics; https://www.fbi.gov/services/laboratory/biometric-analysis/codis/ndis-statistics; https://www.hrw.org/news/2017/05/15/china-police-dna-database-threatens-privacy (accessed June 20, 2019).
3. Frequently Asked Questions on CODIS and NDIS: https://www.fbi.gov/services/laboratory/biometric-analysis/codis/codis-and-ndis-fact-sheet#Expert-Systems.
4. Here, MAC must not be confused with the 'maximum allele count' method.
5. Here, MAC must not be confused with 'maximum allele count'.
6. However we use the ML approach instead of the drop-out simulation approach.
7. This list shows the name of each of the folder in the selected "case directory", if not, the directory has been misspecified.

CHAPTER 12

Interpretation, reporting, and communication

Guidance to reporting cases has been provided by the "ENFSI Guideline for Evaluative Reporting" [284], and for mixtures there are two ISFG DNA Commission publications [34,63]. The most recent publications [275,304] are also the most up-to-date and comprehensive exposition that examines the formulation of propositions. Rather than providing a highly detailed account, which is already available in the cited literature, this chapter is a summary of the major points. In particular, many of the recommendations made by the ISFG DNA Commission [275] are repeated here. Parallel discussions are continually taking place in the United States under auspices of the Scientific Working Group on DNA Analysis Methods (SWGDAM), where deliberations are published at https://www.swgdam.org/publications.

12.1. Early methods used to express the value of the evidence and their limitations

Early ISFG DNA Commissions [34,63] recommended the likelihood ratio in preference to the then widely used random man not excluded (RMNE) calculation, the probability that a random person *would not* be excluded as a contributor to a mixture. The converse calculation is the probability of exclusion, which is the probability that a random person *would* be excluded as a contributor to the observed DNA mixture. With respect to alleles that have "dropped out", the practice has been to simply omit these loci from the calculation.

The formula for the RMNE, otherwise known as the probability of inclusion $Pr(I)$ is calculated as follows:

$$Pr(I) = (\sum_{i=1}^{n} Pr(A_i))^2 \tag{12.1}$$

where, at a given locus, there are n alleles $A_{i..n}$ (this is the outcome of all possible alleles), the probabilities of each allele are summed together, the total squared.

The combined probability of inclusion (CPI) is the product of the locus $Pr(I)$ results across k loci:

$$CPI = \prod_{l=1}^{k} Pr(I_l) \tag{12.2}$$

Forensic Practitioner's Guide to the Interpretation of Complex DNA Profiles
https://doi.org/10.1016/B978-0-12-820562-4.00020-1

To calculate the probability of exclusion the corresponding formula is

$$Pr(E) = 1 - Pr(I) \tag{12.3}$$

and for the combined probability of exclusion (CPE),

$$CPE = 1 - \prod_{l=1}^{k} Pr(I_l) \tag{12.4}$$

These calculations found favor and were widely used, because they were very easy to implement and assumptions about the numbers of contributors were not needed. There are two drawbacks however:

1. There is an implicit assumption that all of the contributors have all alleles fully represented in the EPG. There is no allele drop-out present, i.e., the calculation is not valid for minor contributors with drop-out that is or may be present.
2. The calculation exists by itself and is unchanged by the suspect's profile, i.e., the calculation is unmodified by the presence of a suspect who matches or does not match.

Contrast the RMNE calculation with the likelihood ratio,

$$LR = \frac{Pr(E|H_p, I)}{Pr(E|H_d, I)} \tag{12.5}$$

The likelihood ratio is represented by two distinct propositions, the numerator calculates the value of the evidence if the prosecution (H_p) proposition is true and the denominator calculates the value of the evidence if the defense (H_d) proposition is true; I is the background information. The likelihood ratio cannot exist without a probabilistic assessment of the suspect's contribution to the numerator.

When an RMNE is reported, then it is necessary to make a binary decision about whether a suspect could have contributed to a crime stain. Either he has (probability = 1) or he has not (probability = 0). No calculation is possible with the latter, since the numerator is zero. Once again, we meet the falling-off-the-cliff-effect, as described in Chapter 3.5 and the problems associated with it—there is nothing in between. This inevitably leads to the problem: "What is a match?"; "Does the suspect match if all but one of his alleles are found in the evidence trace?" In a study carried out by NIST [267], where mixtures were analyzed by 69 different laboratories, it was shown that the majority used RMNE or CPE to report conclusions. However, these laboratories typically had divergent practices, hence the results that were generated were also divergent. In contrast, the adoption of probabilistic genotyping (LR) methods removes much of the need to depend upon strict rule-sets, since features like drop-out and drop-in are accommodated within a statistical framework and the probabilities are continuous. This leads to much closer inter-laboratory standardization [268,269].

12.2. An outline of the important principles to interpret scientific evidence

The likelihood ratio framework forms the foundation of reporting evidence to courts (Chapter 1.6). Consequently, recommendation 1 of the ISFG DNA Commission "Assessing the value of forensic biological evidence" [275] states (Box 12.1):

Box 12.1

"The value of DNA and biological results is given by assigning a likelihood ratio. This implies the formulation of at least two mutually exclusive propositions. Assumptions regarding the model and the background information (i.e., case information and data) used should be disclosed."

Following Jackson et al. [305], there are two requirements:

1. A prosecution and alternative defense proposition must be proposed;
2. "These should be formulated from the framework of circumstances of the case and through dialogue between parties in the criminal justice system".

In this regard, the "framework of circumstances" is a detailed consideration of all the relevant aspects of the case, that includes the alternative views of the prosecution and defense.

The value of the evidence depends critically upon the propositions that are put forward by the mandating authorities. If the propositions are altered, then the value of the evidence is also altered.

The likelihood ratio is the ratio of two conditional probabilities (Eq. (12.5)). In other words, it is the probability of the evidence *if* the prosecution proposition is true and *given* the conditioning information, divided by the probability of the evidence *if* the defense proposition is true and *given* the conditioning information.

1. If the probability of the evidence, given the prosecution proposition, is greater than the probability of the evidence given the defense proposition, then the *LR* is greater than one, and the evidence provides support for the prosecution proposition.
2. If the probability of the evidence, given the prosecution proposition, is less than the probability of the evidence given the defense proposition, then the *LR* is less than one, and the evidence provides support for the defense proposition.
3. If the probability of the evidence, given the prosecution proposition, is the same as probability of the evidence given the defense proposition, then the *LR* equals one, and the evidence is neutral, it does not provide support for either of the propositions.

Provided that the model used to calculate the likelihood ratio is robust, then the value of the evidence is objective within the strict context of the propositions that are conditioned. The magnitude of the likelihood ratio is a measure of the value or strength of the evidence. However, it is important to understand that there are no true (or correct) likelihood ratios.

388 Forensic Practitioner's Guide to the Interpretation of Complex DNA Profiles

Consideration 2 of the ISFG DNA Commission [275] provides the following summary (Box 12.2):

Box 12.2

"As described by Evett et al. [306], there are no true likelihood ratios, just like there are no true models [246]. Depending on our assumptions, our knowledge and the results we want to assess, different models will be adopted, hence different values for the LR will be obtained. It is therefore important to outline in our statements what factors impact evaluation (propositions, information, assumptions, data, and choice of model)."

12.3. Propositions

There are a number of guidelines that are associated with the formulation of propositions:

1. The propositions must be reasonable. They are dictated by the circumstances of the case:

    There is a proposition put forward by the prosecution and an alternative one from the defense. The propositions should be formed to highlight the differences of opinion between the prosecution and defense. The scientist's role is to advise on the formulation of propositions. In this role he/she is *investigative* (Chapter 11 and Section 12.4), and this phase is normally carried out prior to court proceedings. Once the case goes to court, the scientist enters the *evaluative* phase: the propositions have been fixed and agreed by the mandating authorities. The scientist acts as the neutral arbiter between the two parties.

2. It follows that the scientist does not decide the propositions to be tested. The role of the scientist is to evaluate the value of the evidence, given the alternative propositions.

3. The scientist does not evaluate propositions, i.e., a scientist cannot tell a court *if* a proposition is true or not. The scientist can only evaluate the value of the evidence if a particular proposition is true (this will later lead to a discussion of the pitfall known as the prosecutor's fallacy in Section 12.8).

4. To construct propositions, it is important to avoid bias. In particular, confirmation bias [193] may infect the propositions that are tested. Confirmation bias is *"the tendency to interpret new evidence as confirmation of one's existing beliefs or theories, whilst ignoring evidence that may point in the opposite direction"*. To mitigate risks of confirmation bias, it is important to set propositions independent of any results. Before an analysis is carried out, the scientist must form a view on the expectations of the results if a particular proposition is true.

12.4. Scope of the forensic scientist as an investigator or evaluator

The scientist has two different roles: a) as an investigator and b) as an evaluator. Likelihood ratios can be used in both roles, but it is important to distinguish between the two. In the investigative phase (described in Chapter 11), a crime has been committed, but there is no suspect that is apparent. Consequently, there is usually a request to search a National DNA database. The purpose is to provide *investigative leads* that can be followed. In a database with N individuals, each individual $X_i = 1..N$ is compared with the crime stain in turn. Before the comparison is carried out, all individuals in the database may be considered to be possible candidates, and a likelihood ratio would be formed for each candidate in turn.

Typically, if the crime-stain profile is well represented, either one or more candidates may be found with a high LR, otherwise, if the profile is partial, then the top-ranking candidates may have a low LR, and there are many possibilities for further investigation. However, there is always a limitation of how many candidates may be investigated, and this is dictated by the resources available to the investigating authorities.

Consideration 1 of the ISFG DNA commission states (Box 12.3):

Box 12.3

"The scientist works in an investigative mode if there is no person of interest in the case. If a suspect is identified, then generally the scientist switches to evaluative mode with respect to this suspect and needs to assign the value of their results in the context of the case. If there is new information (in particular from the POI), the scientist will need to re-evaluate the results. It is thus important that reports contain a caveat relating to this aspect."

Once the POI has been identified, then the scientist operates in an evaluative mode. A framework is provided by the "ENFSI guidelines for evaluative reporting" [284].

In the evaluative role, the forensic practitioner has been asked to evaluate the results in the case with respect to two alternative propositions that are "set by the specific case circumstances, or as indicated by the mandating authority", where the mandating authorities are typically a judge, prosecution lawyers, and defense lawyers.

Finally, when formulating propositions, ideally there should be a dialogue between the prosecution and defense so that the respective propositions can be agreed and tested.

The evaluation framework provides a structure that can be used by both prosecution and defense experts to properly evaluate the results to decide the value of the evidence. This presupposes that the case has scientists from both sides of the "debate" who are working within the framework. This may not be the case, however. It is problematic if a scientist only has access to the prosecution-based argument, as there may be insufficient understanding of the defense case. This position may lead to potential confirmation bias. It is avoided by ensuring that scientists representing both sides of the argument have "equality of arms", and are educated to similar levels regarding the preferred methods of interpretation of evidence [307]. In the absence of defense propositions, it is beholden to the expert, called by the prosecution, to formulate the alternative propositions in the case. Under these circumstances, the "ENFSI guideline" [284] recommends the following:

- Adopt alternative propositions that are most likely and reasonably reflect the party's position and prepare an evaluative report. Only this option can lead to the production of an evaluative report. The report should specify that any change to the propositions (for example any new propositions proposed by the parties or mandating authority) may impact on the assessment of the strength of the forensic findings, and so will necessitate further evaluation and possibly the provision of a new report.
- Explore a range of explanations for the findings and prepare, if needed, an investigative report. Provision of such a range of explanations is not an evaluation of the probative force of the findings.
- State the findings, if needed, in a technical report. The report should stress that in the absence of an alternative proposition, it is impossible to evaluate the findings.

12.5. Hierarchy of propositions

The concept of the hierarchy of propositions, described by Cook et al. [308], is described in detail by the "ENFSI guideline to Evaluative Reporting" [284], and is widely used to help the court understand the meaning and limitations of the evidence within the context of a case. Each level of the hierarchy is associated with a particular structure that defines the alternative propositions that are used to evaluate the evidence. Each of the levels is discrete in that the LR calculation at one level cannot be carried over to the next level, which would be misleading. Therefore an appreciation of the hierarchy of propositions is an important foundation to prevent miscarriages of justice occurring.

There are four main levels:

- **The sub-source level**

  This refers solely to the information provided by the DNA profile only. Examples of sub-source level propositions are

  H_p: The DNA is from Mr. S.
  H_d: The DNA is from an unknown person, unrelated to Mr. S.

  If a mixture:

  H_p: The DNA is from Mr. S and an unknown person.
  H_d: The DNA is from two unknown persons unrelated to each other and to Mr. S.

  Note that it is standard practice to include the "unrelated" caveat, but likelihood ratios can be formulated using calculations that specify particular relatives. See Section 3.5.3 of [309] and Chapter 8.8 for a worked example using *EuroForMix*.

- **The source level**

  The source level considers information about the body fluid or cell type that the DNA came from. If a large pool of blood is found at the crime scene, then it would not be problematic to use the word "blood" in both propositions. An example could be:

  H_p: Mr. S is the origin of the blood.
  H_d: An unknown person is the origin of the blood.

  The source of the biological fluid/cell type may be disputed. This may occur if the sample is low-level DNA or a presumptive test is negative, or if the profile is a mixture and the contributions may themselves come from different cell types and it is not possible to determine which cell type came from which contributor. Where there is uncertainty, then it may not be appropriate to report given source level propositions.

- **The activity level**

  Activity level considers the "activity" associated with the offence. Often in court cases, the question of the origin of the DNA profile is not an issue, rather it is "how", "why", "when" did the DNA become evidential? For example, the victim may allege a sexual assault, whereas the suspect denies the assault, but explains that he had social contact instead, e.g., shaking hands. The alternative propositions may be:

  Hp: Mr. S sexually assaulted Ms. Y.
  Hd: Mr. S only had social contact with Ms. Y.

  A DNA profile may be recovered that is evaluated at the sub-source level. To evaluate evidence at the activity level, it is necessary to apply a caveat to the statement to make clear that this is valid, only if it is accepted by the court that a DNA sub-source contribution had come from the suspect (either the LR has a high value so that the court accepts the prosecution sub-source proposition, else both defense and prosecution agree the source of the DNA is from the suspect). The value of the evidence at sub-source does not affect the value at activity level; a new calculation is required for the latter. It follows, that if it is not accepted by the court that a DNA profile has originated from a suspect, then activity-level evaluation cannot proceed under this assumption. These options will be made clear by the expert in his/her statement.

- **The offence level**

  The offence level addresses the ultimate issue of innocence or guilt. This is entirely a matter for the court, and the scientist would not take any part in the decision. The decision is made after a consideration of all of the evidence (DNA and non-DNA).

- **The sub-sub-source level**

  Described by Taylor et al. [310], which expands an idea by Evett [311], the sub-sub-source refers to part of a mixture that can be extracted. Earlier in Chapter 7.2.2, it was shown that, provided a mixture was easily separated into major and minor contributors, it was possible to subtract the minor contributor, treating the major profile as a single contributor. Therefore the propositions considered for a two person mixture would be as follows:

  H_p: The POI is the origin of the DNA from the major component.
  H_d: An unknown person, unrelated to the POI is the origin of the DNA from the major component.

  The separation of major/minor contributors is carried out *before* any comparison is made. If the POI genotype (g_S) subsequently matches the major component of the crime-stain evidence (g_{major}), then the LR is reported at sub-sub-source level:

  $$LR = \frac{1}{Pr(g_{major})} \tag{12.6}$$

  However, the separation of a major contributor is often not unambiguous. The ISFG DNA Commission [275], Section 4.4, summarizes:
  "Sub-sub-source level propositions are not appropriate if any of the following circumstances are fulfilled:

  1. If both minor and major components have been compared to the POI.
  2. The components cannot be clearly classified into major/minor.
  3. The probabilistic genotyping method takes into account peak height, or assigns different rates of drop-out to different contributors.

     Then the whole mixture should be considered using standard sub-source propositions."

  To convert sub-sub-source into a sub-source LR, for a two-person mixture, where a major contributor cannot be selected, the propositions are as follows:

  H_p: The POI and an unknown person are the origin of the DNA mixture.
  H_d: Two unknown persons are the origin of the DNA mixture.

  A factor of two is introduced into the denominator:

  $$LR' = \frac{1}{2Pr(g_{major})} \tag{12.7}$$

  Taylor et al. [310] show a formal calculation to calculate the precise adjustment required, but they describe an approximation that can be used for multiple contributors. The simplest form is to adjust the LR by dividing it by the factorized number of contributors $N!$ An alternative method described by Taylor et al. is as follows:

"If U1 is the number of unknown individuals in H1 and U2 is the number of unknowns in H2 then the LR at the sub–sub-source level can be multiplied by U1! = U2! to obtain the LR' at the sub-source level."

This method is more complex than dividing by $N!$, but it takes more information into account and is therefore preferred (Duncan Taylor, pers. comm.). This method will be provided by *EuroForMix* in a future release. However the effect is small, e.g., for two unknown contributors under H_p and three unknown contributors under H_d, the adjustment required is $2!/3! = 1/3$, i.e., the effect is most pronounced with a low *LR*.

For comprehensive information on the hierarchy of propositions, the reader is referred to [275,284].

12.6. Formulation of propositions to avoid bias

Ideally, propositions should be formulated without the knowledge of the results. Suppose we have an example, where a defendant, Mr. S, is suspected of a crime, where an iron-bar was used to break into a premises, and left at the crime scene.

The iron-bar is received at the laboratory, and the police have asked that the implement is examined to see if there is any DNA that can be recovered. The sub-source propositions put forward are therefore:

H_p: The DNA came from Mr. S.
H_d: The DNA came from an unknown person.

Now suppose that the evidence is analyzed and the likelihood ratio supports the first proposition. It is not allowed to alter these propositions to:

H_p: The matching DNA came from Mr. S.
H_d: The matching DNA came from an unknown person.

This is because the results or observations (i.e., the "match") should not be interwoven with propositions. Such propositions can only be formulated after the analysis of the data.

A DNA profile is said to "match" if for all shared markers, the allele designations in the crime-stain profile are the same as the alleles with which it is being compared to. This should not be confused with the "identity" of the donor. DNA does not give a yes/no answer. The value of the evidence is always expressed as a probability within the likelihood ratio framework. For a discussion on "match" versus "identity", see [285].

The problem is exemplified by a case that is described in [285], where a 49 year old man, Raymond Easton, from Swindon, UK, was arrested and charged with a burglary in Bolton, UK ($\approx$175 miles away), after a DNA sample from the crime scene matched his DNA profile in the UK national DNA database. Mr Easton was in the advanced stages of Parkinson's disease, and was unable to walk more than ten meters without help. His DNA profile had been loaded onto the database four years earlier following a domestic dispute. The crime scene sample "matched" Mr Easton's DNA profile at six loci, which was considered enough to secure an identification at that time— although the total number of STRs required has since been extended to 16 plus a sex marker. The chances of a match was reported as 37–million-to-one. Mr Easton spent several months in custody before his solicitor persuaded police to run further DNA tests, which eliminated him (i.e., the DNA profile that "matched" Mr. Easton came from someone else).

The word "match" should be avoided in statements. Recommendations 2 and 3 of [275] state (Box 12.4):

Box 12.4

"Results should clearly be distinguished from propositions [312], as DNA specialists assess the former and decision makers the latter. Avoid terms like: 'The matching DNA comes from X'."

"Propositions should be formulated in order to help answer the issue at hand and be based on the case information (not on the results of the comparison). They should be formulated without knowledge of the results of the comparison made between the trace and the person whose DNA presence is contested (e.g., the suspect's)."

12.7. Activity level propositions

Consider a hypothetical case: A murder has been committed, where the victim is beaten to death. A suspect has been identified. The murder weapon is not found, but the police investigators find a small stain, which may be blood, but a presumptive test is negative, on a carpet of the basement of the suspect's property. The investigators have a prior expectation of finding DNA profiles that had been transferred, persisted and recovered as a direct result of the activity of moving a weapon used in the crime to the basement. The expectation is that body fluids from the victim would be detected. The defense contend that there is a prior expectation to find DNA profiles from the item as a result of social activity from individuals who had access to the basement. These propositions may be formulated without knowledge of the results of testing.

Once tested, it was shown that the item was a complex mixture of two or more individuals. The information can be used to make assessments of the minimum number of contributors, as described in Chapters 2.3.2 and 6.2.3. The value of the evidence can be calculated in relation to known individuals, given the alternative propositions. However, the information cannot be used to make a direct statement about the identity of individuals that may be present in the crime stain, because this invites the prosecutor's fallacy described later in Section 12.8.

It may well be that the identity of contributors to the DNA profile may be of secondary interest to the court, especially if the victim had access to the suspect's basement, and there was opportunity for the transfer of DNA by "innocent" means, e.g., social contact. Here the questions will relate to transfer, persistence, and recovery of DNA. To evaluate the "activity" that led to the evidence, a different set of propositions are required, which are formulated completely separately to the sub-source propositions, e.g.,

H_p: Mr. X moved the murder weapon to the basement.
H_d: Mr. X did not move the murder weapon to the basement.

Background information: The victim was known to the suspect and had visited the premises one week previous to his murder.

Readers interested in activity level propositions, are referred to the ISFG DNA Commission deliberations [304] and the "ENFSI Guideline for Evaluative Reporting" [284] for further information. It will suffice to say here that the evaluation of evidence at the DNA level (known as the sub-source level) has nothing to do with the evaluation of the evidence at the activity level. The likelihood ratio at the sub-source level cannot be carried over to activity. If there are sufficient information and data, it is possible to formulate opinion on the likelihood ratio at activity level based on the alternative propositions put forward by defense and prosecution. But this is a completely different consideration, along with different likelihood ratios that we do not explain further here.

12.8. The prosecutor's fallacy and prior probabilities

The prosecutor's fallacy was described by Thompson [313]. It is an error that is commonly encountered. Suppose that a crime is committed; a DNA profile has been analyzed and the match probability of the profile is 1/100,000. A prosecutor may make a statement: "A random person from the population will match the evidence with a probability of one in 100,000" and "furthermore this number represents the probability of the DNA found at the crime scene randomly matching Mr X, if it had come from some other unknown person", or "only one in 100,000 would have the same DNA profile as the offender, hence there was only a 0.00001% chance that Mr. X was innocent".

The problem with these statements is that they evaluate the probability of the DNA (E) if ($|$) it had come from a random person (H_d), i.e., $Pr(H_d|E)$, which is the probability of *innocence given* the evidence instead of the converse $Pr(E|H_d)$, which is probability of the evidence *given innocence*.

It is an error, because to calculate $Pr(H_d|E)$ application of Bayes rule is required, so a different calculation is required:

$$Pr(H_d|E) = Pr(E|H_d) \times \frac{Pr(H_d)}{Pr(E)} \tag{12.8}$$

where $Pr(H_d)$ is known as a *prior*, because it is based upon information that is independent of the DNA evidence. As an example, consider if the perpetrator of the crime is believed to be someone from a discrete population of 3m people. *Before* the DNA evidence (and in the absence of any other information), *a priori*, initially, each person is equally likely to have committed the offence. Therefore for each individual $Pr(H_p) = 1/3m$, and $Pr(H_d) = 1 - (1/3m)$. It is relatively straightforward to fill in the individual parts of Eq. (12.8):

$$Pr(E|H_d) = 1/100,000$$

$$Pr(E|H_p) = 1$$

$$Pr(H_p) = 1/3m$$

$$Pr(H_d) = 1 - 1/3m$$

$$Pr(E) = Pr(E|H_p) \times Pr(H_p) + Pr(E|H_d) \times Pr(H_d)$$

$$Pr(H_d|E) = \frac{(1/100,000) \times (1 - 1/3m)}{(1 \times 1/3m) + (1/100,000) \times (1 - 1/3m)}$$

$$Pr(H_d|E) = 0.967$$

$$Pr(H_p|E) + Pr(H_d|E) = 1$$

$$Pr(H_p|E) = 0.033$$

The probability of $(H_d|E)$, *innocence given the evidence*, is 96.8% with this example and not 0.00001% as claimed by the prosecutor. This is quite a difference and it illustrates the reason why the prosecutor's fallacy is a misleading error.

Since $Pr(H_p|E) + Pr(H_d|E) = 1$, and $Pr(H_p) + Pr(H_d) = 1$, an alternative derivation is known as the *odds* form of Bayes Theorem. We can write the *ratio* of posterior probabilities using Eq. (12.8). By dividing $H_p|E$ by $H_d|E$, $Pr(E)$ cancels, and the familiar likelihood ratio is recovered in the context of the posterior and prior odds:

$$\underbrace{\frac{H_p|E}{H_d|E}}_{\text{posterior odds}} = \underbrace{\frac{Pr(E|H_p)}{Pr(E|H_d)}}_{\text{likelihood ratio}} \times \underbrace{\frac{Pr(H_p)}{Pr(H_d)}}_{\text{prior odds}} \tag{12.9}$$

posterior odds = likelihood ratio × prior odds.

Using the same example described above, posterior odds in favor of H_p (guilt) are:

$$\frac{Pr(H_p|E)}{Pr(H_d|E)} = \frac{1}{1/100,000} \times \frac{1/3m}{1 - (1/3m)} = 0.033 : 1$$

Posterior odds in favor of H_d (innocence) are the inverse $30 : 1$.

Only if $Pr(H_p) = Pr(H_d) = 0.5$, i.e., where the prior odds are evens, does $\frac{Pr(H_p|E)}{Pr(H_d|E)} = LR$, however, it is rarely the case that such initial prior odds are justified. Consequently, the prosecutor's fallacy is a real concern, because if the prior odds in favor of guilt are low, then the posteriors are also less than the value provided by the LR. Nevertheless, for a court to decide a verdict in a case, it is necessary to combine the prior odds in favor of guilt/innocence, with the LR. The scientist provides a likelihood ratio that is based upon "objective" reasoning. The difficulty is that the decision of the prior odds is subjective[1] and regarded as the province of the court and not the scientist. In principle, it is possible for the scientist to assist the court by explaining the impact of the prior odds on the posterior odds, as explained in the next section.

12.8.1 Prior odds can be updated

Deciding what the prior odds $\frac{Pr(H_p)}{Pr(H_d)}$ should be is not straightforward. In the previous section, a calculation was provided based upon the sole evidence of a population size of 3m people, one of whom is the perpetrator. But there may be other information in the case that is relevant, for example, if there is eye-witness evidence, or some other non-DNA evidence, such as glass or fibers, then the combination of this information will change the priors. This evidence may be probative, and could be used to decrease the prior probability of innocence, hence the posterior odds of guilt are increased. In the absence of any other information, it seems reasonable to base the prior on the number of people in the population that could have committed the crime. Populations can be filtered according to specific geographic locations, sex, age, etc. A way to provide guidance to a court, is to provide a chart showing the effect of a range of priors on the posterior odds (Table 12.1), as proposed by Meester and Sjerps [314]. Although it has to be said that we are not aware of this approach actually being used in practice, it is nevertheless valid.

12.9. Avoidance of the prosecutor's fallacy

The first example of the prosecutor's fallacy leading to a successful appeal was the case of Regina v. Andrew Deen (1993).[2] The scientist agreed with the statement:

> "the likelihood of the [source of the semen] being any other man but Andrew Deen is 1 in 3 million".

A second successful appeal in a UK case was provided by Regina v. Doheny and Adams [315].

The dialogue between lawyer and scientist in this case illustrated how the trap was set by the former and concurred with by the latter.

Table 12.1 The relationship between prior and posterior odds of "Mr. X left the stain" versus "someone else left the stain", where the *LR* is 100,000 in support of the first proposition.

Prior odds	Posterior odds
3.33E–07	0.03
0.00001	1.0
0.0001	10.0
0.001	100.1
0.01	1010.1
0.1	11111.1
0.5	100000.0

Q. "What is the combination [i.e., the statistical combination of tests carried out], taking all those into account?

A. Taking them all into account, I calculated the chance of finding all of those bands and the conventional blood groups to be about 1 in 40 million.

Q. The likelihood of it being anybody other than Alan Doheny?

A. Is about 1 in 40 million.

Q. You deal habitually with these things, the jury have to say, of course, on the evidence, whether they are satisfied beyond doubt that it is he. You have done the analysis, are you sure that it is he?

A. Yes."

Examples of the prosecutor's fallacy are demonstrable throughout the dialogue. The second leading question provides the first example to which the scientist agreed. If the lawyer commits the fallacy, it is for the scientist to correct the statement. The second and third questions compound the fallacy. The statements were not challenged by the scientist.

In his summing up, the judge reinforced the fallacy by stating: "... in the end his opinion was that his tests were reliable and they did show that the chance of Mr. Doheny not being the person responsible was so remote as to be possible to discount entirely for all practical purposes".

From Chapter 7.1 of [275]: "There are a couple of ways to avoid the prosecutor's fallacy [316]: for example in the scientist's statement there should always be an 'if' or a 'given', and the statement ought to be on the results not on the propositions. An example of a correct statement of the value of DNA profiles would be:

*"(...) using the Caucasian population sample data the DNA results are a billion times more probable **if** the sample originated from the accused than **if** it originated from an unknown person taken at random."*

When the statement contains the word 'that', then this should raise a red flag." Recommendation 9 of the ISFG DNA commission [275] summarizes (Box 12.5):

Box 12.5

"It is crucial to outline that scientists do not give their opinion on who is the source of the DNA. There is a difference between the probability of the results given that the DNA is from an unknown person and the probability that the DNA is from an unknown person given the result. To equate one with the other is known as the transposed conditional, the prosecutor's fallacy, or the source probability error. It is thus important to explain what a likelihood ratio is and what it is not. This can be done by training or by providing a table with different odds, the LR and resulting posterior odds [314]. Because of the dangers of misrepresentation, it is essential to convey that scientists do not give opinions on the probability of propositions [285] and this is reinforced here."

12.10. Database searches

In Chapter 11.1, it was shown that adventitious matches (i.e., false positive matches) may occur when profiles are compared against a large national DNA database. The probability of a false positive match depends upon the probability of the questioned genotype and the size of the national DNA database. The larger the database, the greater the opportunity that a false positive result will occur. A real example is provided by the "Easton case" discussed in Section 12.6 that illustrates the dangers of reporting evidence, based solely upon DNA.

When databases are searched for potential suspects, this is regarded as *investigative* as discussed in Section 12.4. In the Easton case, described in the previous section, there was no other evidence apart from a match on the national DNA database of $n = 5m$ males. Furthermore, assume that every male in the UK, a total of $N = 30m$ candidate suspects, has an equal prior probability of guilt. Before the database search, the prior probability of guilt for each candidate is $1/N$ (Section 12.8). However, the national DNA database search has eliminated all but one individual $n = 5m$ of the total UK database population, so that the prior odds of guilt can be updated to $1/(N - n - 1) = 1/25m$.

Recall that the posterior odds = prior odds $\times LR$, hence

$$\text{posterior odds} = \frac{1}{N - n - 1} \times LR \tag{12.10}$$

$$\text{posterior odds} = \frac{1}{25 \times 10^6} \times 37 \times 10^6$$

$$\text{posterior odds} = \frac{37}{25} = 1.48 : 1 \text{ in favor of guilt.}$$

Although the strength of the evidence of the likelihood ratio provides extremely strong support in favor of the prosecution proposition, it can be shown that in the absence of other evidence, an (investigative) posterior odds is only weakly in favor. This should serve as a red-flag to a potential miscarriage of justice should a prosecution proceed. If such an approach was carried out beforehand, it would highlight the need for further investigation so that new information could be collated to update the prior odds.

Consideration 6 of the ISFG DNA Commission [275] states (Box 12.6):

Box 12.6

"If DNA is the sole evidence in a case, then a suspect may be identified from a database search. If the investigation does not yield any other evidence, then investigators should be all the more aware of the fallacy of the transposed conditional. To assign the probability of a proposition, they should take into account prior odds and the DNA results, in order to establish if there is sufficient evidence to prosecute a case. In court, it is not the remit of the scientist to assign prior odds. However, the scientist should explain to the court that they do not give an opinion on propositions."

Note that there has been much debate on the question of evaluation of evidence in relation to national DNA database hits. The interested reader is referred to Section 7.2 of [275] for further details and references [53,314,317]. The allocation of prior odds for evaluative purposes remains a contentious issue, not from the point of view of the theory, but from the difficulty in communication with courts. A previous attempt in a UK court (case of R. v. Adams [318] failed, because of the difficulties associated in explaining the evidence [319]. However, use of prior odds for *investigative* purposes do not have the same restrictions, although there is a requirement for investigators to be properly trained. Investigative priors can be used to highlight deficiencies in a case before it is forwarded for prosecution in the courts, where the forensic scientist enters the evaluative mode.

12.11. Statement writing

An example statement follows:

Statement of findings:
STR profiles have been obtained from the swabbed area of the garage floor (Item I). Upon analysis this revealed a complex profile of at least three individuals, and I have progressed my evaluation based upon this assumption.

State the alternative propositions:

To assess the significance of the above findings, I have considered two alternative propositions:

a) The DNA came from Mr. X and two unknown persons, unrelated to him.
b) The DNA came from three unknown persons unrelated to Mr. X.

Consider the alternatives:

The probability of the evidence is more than 1 billion times more likely if the first proposition (a) is true, compared to the alternative described by (b). This analysis provides extremely strong support for the proposition that Mr. X is a contributor to the DNA obtained from Item I.

Writing the statement in this way is transparent; both the prosecution and defense alternatives are stated clearly; it states precisely what the conditioning is based on and most important of all, it avoids the prosecutor's fallacy by using the conditional statement (the if word): *"The probability of the evidence **if** the DNA did not come from Mr. X"* not the transposition: *"the probability **that** the DNA evidence did not come from Mr. X"*. The use of a verbal qualifier is optional; this is discussed further in the next section.

12.12. The use of the verbal scale and the "weak evidence effect"

Verbal equivalents to express the value of evidence are often included in statements [284,320–323]. However, it must be emphasized that the scientist must first evaluate the numeric strength of the evidence; if applied, the verbal equivalent is secondary. The declared purpose of verbal qualifiers is to improve understanding by the court. An example taken from the ENFSI guideline for evaluative reporting [284] is shown in Table 12.2. The verbal scale ends at a likelihood ratio of greater than 1 million, which is specified as "extremely strong support". The verbal scale is universally applied across all evidence types, where the range of reported evidential numeric values (e.g., for glass or fibers) are typically much lower than for DNA. In discussions, it has been proposed to use a verbal scale that is specific to DNA profiling (to accommodate terms to describe very large LRs like 1 bn). But this idea has not found traction. It would be unwieldy and confusing to propose a different scale per evidence type. All verbal scales are arbitrary, and we simply run out of language to verbally explain the meaning of very large numbers.

The purpose of the verbal scale is to improve communication between the scientist and the decision-maker, so that the understanding of the meaning of the value of the evidence is imparted as intended by the scientist. However, there has been relatively little research into the impact of likelihood ratios and verbal equivalents to facilitate court understanding. Most verbal scales, and recommendations for their use, have originated from forensic scientists working in the area of interpretation, who influence policy-makers [324,325]. It is becoming increasingly recognized that the expertise of cognitive psychologists is required to assess whether the information is understood by the courts.

Martire et al. [322] devised an experiment, where a sample of 404 participants, who were representative of individuals, who would qualify for jury duty, were provided with the facts of a mock criminal case. They were then provided with a statement of an expert witness, where the value of the evidence was presented as: a) the likelihood ratio, without a verbal qualifier; b) a verbal qualifier, without the likelihood ratio; c) a likelihood ratio concurrent with a verbal qualifier, as shown in Table 12.2. The responses were measured in terms of "belief-change" in terms of "subtracting the stated prior-belief from the posterior-belief".

The "weak evidence effect" was highlighted by the experiments: when participants were presented with evidence that weakly supported (using the verbal scale only) the prosecution's claim, most participants elected to decrease their belief in the guilt of accused, i.e., the value of the evidence was understated to the extent that evidence supporting a proposition H_p may be wrongly interpreted as supporting H_d. The effect was not observed when the evidence was presented numerically. Surprisingly, the "numeric only" method also performed better than the "joint verbal/numeric" method. These findings cast doubt upon the use of verbal qualifiers in any form, although undoubtedly more research is needed.

The conclusion of the Martire experiment was:

"Our results suggest that numerical expressions, as opposed to verbal, dual verbal–numerical (table) expression and visual (scale) methods, produce belief-change and implicit likelihood ratios most commensurate with the intentions of the expert. This method of presentation was also the most resistant to weak evidence effects."

ISFG DNA Commission [275] recommendation 11 states (Box 12.7):

Box 12.7

"The verbal scale is optional but cannot be used by itself. If it is used, then the numeric equivalents must also be available/provided. In practice, one would provide first one's likelihood ratio, then the verbal equivalent is applied afterwards. An example would be: "My LR is in the order of 60. This means that - in my opinion - the results are much more probable (in the order of 60 times) if the proposition that 'X' is true than if the alternative 'Y' is true. According to the verbal scale used in our laboratory, these results provide moderate support for the first proposition rather than the alternative." These 'verbal equivalents' are by nature subjective and a number of verbal equivalence tables have been published. So, it is above all a convention."

The "Recommendations of the SWGDAM ad hoc working group on genotyping results reported as likelihood ratios" [326] suggests a verbal scale that is broadly in line to that described in Table 12.2, except that there are just five categories, and there are

Table 12.2 Verbal scale based on ENFSI guideline [284]. "The forensic findings provide [***] support for the first proposition relative to the alternative."

Values of the LR	Verbal equivalent
1	no support
2–10	weak support
10–100	moderate support
100–1,000	moderately strong support
1,000–10,000	strong support
10,000–1,000,000	very strong support
1,000,000 and above	extremely strong support

differences in the language used to describe the level of support: When $LR = 1$ this is described as "uninformative", and when $LR = 2 - 99$, this is described as "limited support"; $LR > 1m$ is "very strong support".

12.13. Using terms like "inconclusive" and "excluded" as expressions in statements

When the likelihood ratio is below some arbitrary level (typically in the region of a few hundred), many laboratories prefer to report the value of the evidence as "inconclusive", or the POI is "excluded", so an "inclusion" is reserved for those LRs that are greater than some threshold (T) value. The question then arises: "How to decide what the "inconclusive" threshold (T) should be"?

Some laboratories define the "inconclusive" category as the upper limit of the LR range, where false-positive results have been observed during validation exercises. This aspect of validation is discussed in Chapter 9.9: out of 2634 non-contributors, a total of 121 *EuroForMix* LRs were greater than one using the ML method, and the maximum value observed was $LR = 200$. Based on this information, an "inconclusive" zone could be designated between $LR = 1$ and $T = 200$. This zone is also sometimes referred to as the "uninformative LR zone" [257], [75]; see Chapter 9.17 for an example. Although this strategy is based upon real observations, the problem is that it cannot capture all potential false positive results. Turing's expectation, discussed in Section 12.17, shows that since the average non-contributor $LR_{avg} = 1$, we expect that some non-contributor samples will be observed with very high LRs. The limitation of the inconclusive definition is that it is restricted by the number of samples that are tested, i.e., the greater the sample size, the more likely it is that higher false positive LRs will be detected. Since these high LRs will be outliers, a way forward would be to report a 99th percentile, which would be much more stable, and less dependant upon sample size, but of course a threshold based on such a criterion cannot act as a guarantee that all false positives are captured.

The SWGDAM guidance (recommendation 3.1) [326] states:

"likelihood ratios should not be deemed inconclusive to mitigate a potential risk of adventitious support".

Consider a low $LR = 10$ for a single contributor ($H_p = true$) profile. Out of 100 people randomly sampled, there is an expectation that approximately ten of these will provide false-positive matches ($T = 10$). This information is encapsulated in the value of the likelihood ratio itself, and should be sufficient, without any need to qualify the result as inconclusive. A verbal descriptor (weak support) may be applied to a statement, but in light of the "weak evidence effect", described in Section 12.12, where the decision-maker may understate the strength of evidence in favor of H_p, it is questionable whether a verbal qualifier should be applied.

Recommendation 3.1 of the SWGDAM paper [326] continues:

"A likelihood ratio appropriately conveys the weight of the evidence and should not be reported as inconclusive based on its magnitude",

i.e., the report discourages the use of the "inconclusive" category.

A similar argument can follow around the definition of "exclusion". False negative results will occur, especially when a contribution is low-level, so that there are few alleles observed. However, this does not mean that an individual is excluded. Probabilistic genotyping methods calculate $LR < 1$, hence there is no reason why the value should not be used directly in a report to provide an opinion on the strength of evidence in favor of H_d.

To provide statements, such as "X is excluded as a contributor", or "X is included as a contributor", invites the prosecutor's fallacy. Instead, it is better to use phrases like "The evidence supports the defense proposition of exclusion", or "The evidence supports the prosecution proposition of inclusion", although the use of categories, such as "inconclusive", is a decision for the laboratory. Some caution is required to ensure that its use does not result in misinterpretation by the receiver of the information. This is best avoided by providing the likelihood ratio in the report.

12.14. Conditioning and the application to DNA mixtures

All likelihood ratios follow the basic principles described above, but they can be complex.

Reproduced from Section 4.1.2 of the ISFG DNA Commission [275]: For mixtures, the main considerations are the number of contributors, and whether there is conditioning on a known person (e.g., a victim, or the owner of the item). Under a typical set of propositions, the prosecution's view would be that the person of interest contributed to the DNA mixture. The defense's proposition would be that an unknown person is the source.

Depending on the situation and the object analyzed, the presence of DNA from one of the known persons may not be contested. For example, it may also be appropriate to include the victim as a contributor in both propositions. A typical case would be, where a vaginal swab is analyzed that contains semen. Indeed, there would generally be no dispute that the item came from the victim, thus there is a prior expectation of the presence of this person's DNA under both propositions. Let us suppose that the issue here is whether the DNA is from Mr. S or some other person(s), and that there is no assumed known contributor (such as the person to whom the objects belongs). From the case information and from the observation of the crime-stain profile, we can infer that the DNA mixture is from two persons. For this case, where the issue regards whether the DNA is from Mr. S or not, the competing propositions could be:

H_p: The DNA mixture is from Mr. S and an unknown person unrelated to Mr. S.
H_d: The DNA mixture is from two unknown persons, unrelated to each other, or to Mr. S.

The complexity of the propositions may be increased. Consider the following example: A three-person mixed crime-scene DNA profile is retrieved in a situation, where an individual's DNA is assumed to be present under both views; competing propositions could be:

H_p: The crime stain contains DNA from Mr. S, the victim, and an unknown person unrelated to Mr. S and the victim.
H_d: The crime stain contains DNA from the victim and two unknown persons, unrelated to Mr. S and the victim.

Here we see the importance of understanding the issue in the case (e.g., whose DNA presence is contested) to formulate useful propositions. Depending on these propositions, the likelihood ratio formulae will differ. They will also differ, depending on the assumptions made; hence these should always be mentioned as indicated above. The likelihood ratio approach is very flexible. It may be expanded, for example, to accommodate multiple contributors. The number of contributors do not need to be equivalent under both propositions.

Although, it is standard to apply the "unrelated" caveat to propositions, it is not compulsory. Of course it should be pointed out that if there is the possibility from case circumstances that a relative, such as a brother was a contributor to the evidence, then the propositions ought to reflect this. It is possible to carry out a single calculation that includes grouping potential relatives, e.g., brothers, cousins (see Section 3.5.3 in [309]; discussion in Section 6.1 of [275] and Chapter 8.8 for a worked example with *EuroForMix*).

12.15. The effect of relatedness on the likelihood ratio

The value of the evidence is critically dependent upon the propositions that are put forward by the defense and the prosecution. If these arguments are altered in any way, then the likelihood ratio is also altered, and recalculation is needed.

This issue of relatedness was first discussed by Ian Evett [54]; an example was introduced in Chapter 1.16. Starting with the following competing propositions:

H_p: The DNA is from Mr. S.
H_d: The DNA is from an individual who is unrelated to Mr S.

it may be suggested that the alternative proposition is that a sibling (or some other close relative) could have left the stain material. The propositions that form the likelihood ratio have now changed to:

H_p: The DNA is from Mr. S.
H_d: The DNA is from a sibling of Mr. S.

The worked example in Chapter 1.16 shows a dramatic decrease in the LR.

Fung and Hu [55] have derived kinship coefficients for cases with pairwise relationships, as described above. For further examples, e.g., parent/child/cousin relationships, see Section 5.5.4 in Chapter 5 for comprehensive details and Appendix A.2 for relatedness (kinship) formulae.

Probabilistic genotyping software, such as *EuroForMix*, *LRmix Studio* and *STRmix*, have the capability to evaluate evidence when relatedness is an issue with complex mixtures; described in detail in Chapter 8.8, along with a worked example that can be downloaded from the book's website. However, analyses are currently restricted to quite simple propositions, such as

H_p: The DNA is a mixture of Mr. S, and 2 unknown individuals, who are unrelated to Mr. S and each-other.
H_d: The DNA is a mixture of a sibling of Mr. S and 2 unknown individuals, who are unrelated to him and each other.

It is more difficult to model increasingly complex relationships such as

H_p: The evidence is a mixture of a typed individual and two unknown unrelated individuals.
H_d: The evidence is a mixture of three untyped (unknown) siblings.

To carry out these kinds of analyses, the approach described by Egeland et al. [56] is needed. To facilitate the calculations, open-source software *Familias* is available [298, 299]; for mixtures *relmix* [57] can be used.

12.16. Assigning the number of contributors

From the ISFG DNA Commission, Section 4.3.2. The number of contributors may impact the value of the results (i.e., LR) significantly. A commonly used method to assign the number of contributors, called the maximum allele count (MAC), is based upon summing the maximum number of unique alleles (L_{max}) observed at a locus in a crime stain, including the set of known contributors in a proposition and dividing by two [224]. The number of contributors is portrayed as equal or greater than $L_{max}/2$ (Chapter 2.3.2). The assessment of the number of contributors may be corroborated by using the total allele count (TAC), as described by [236] and [141]. However, this scheme does not take into account peak height, which can be an important factor, and is often used by analysts in the determination of the number of contributors to a DNA profile. Utilization of peak heights requires a basic understanding of DNA profile behavior (i.e., stutter, peak height variability, and additivity of masked peaks), and there has been ample literature on these behaviors (Chapter 2).

The higher the number of contributors, the more likely it is that the number is under-estimated, because of "allele masking", where alleles are shared between different individuals [137].[3] If this is a concern, one can add a contributor to the propositions. Quantitative models are usually insensitive to an excess number of contributors being postulated (i.e., the LR is changed very little), especially if there is little drop-out of the alleles shared between the trace and the POI. This is because quantitative models assign very low mixture proportions to excess contributors [234], hence their contribution to the LR is minimal. A worked example is described in Chapter 8.7.3. Recommendation 4 of the ISFG DNA Commission states (Box 12.8):

Box 12.8

"The scientist should assign a value (or several) to the number of contributors to the trace. This will be based on case information, the observation of the DNA profiles of the trace and of the persons whose DNA presence is not contested (e.g. a victim in an intimate swab). The reasoning to support this decision should be indicated."

12.17. Non-contributor tests

Non-contributor tests are discussed in Chapter 6.1.6, and examples are provided therein. A discussion on the background of non-contributor testing ensues here, with greater emphasis upon the theory.

Gill and Haned [224] proposed using non-contributor tests to investigate the robustness of a case specific LR. These tests are based on the "Tippett test" [226] pp. 213–215, later introduced for DNA profiling on a specific *per case* basis by Gill et al. [221]. The test can be used to indicate

"How often will there be misleading evidence that favors the prosecution hypothesis if an innocent individual is profiled" [327].

The idea is to replace the profile of the questioned contributor (POI), e.g., the suspect, by a number of random profiles, and for each random profile, the likelihood ratio is recomputed. These tests are often called "$H_d = true$" tests, since this was the condition simulated (i.e., individual genotypes were randomly simulated, using the population frequency database, under the $H_d = true$ proposition). Consider a simple LR calculation with two contributors, where S is the questioned contributor (e.g., suspect), V is the victim in the numerator and denominator, and U is an unknown unrelated person in the denominator; E is the DNA evidence:

$$LR = \frac{Pr(E|S + V)}{Pr(E|U + V)} \tag{12.11}$$

In non-contributor testing, S is substituted by N random profiles $R_{1..N}$, where N is usually a large number ≥ 1000, and this gives a distribution of random man LRs if the defense proposition is true:

$$LR_n = \frac{Pr(E|R_n + V)}{Pr(E|U + V)} \tag{12.12}$$

Once a distribution of non-contributors has been propagated, some useful statistics can be provided:

- Quantile measurements, e.g., median and 99 percentile.
- p-values.

If N non-contributor substitutions (under the $H_d = true$ condition) are used to calculate a likelihood ratio, the majority of LR values will be less than one. Turing's expectation, discussed in detail by Taylor et al. [262,328] states that if the average LR is calculated across a distribution of all possible non-contributor genotypes, then there is an expectation $LR_{avg} = 1$, and this measurement has been suggested as a way to "validate" a probabilistic model [262].

To explain why the Turing expectation works, Taylor et al. [262] provide a simple but elegant demonstration as follows:

"Consider a single source stain giving a full profile, G_s. The probability of G_s is 1 in a billion. The LR for a POI containing the same alleles as G_s is 1 billion for the propositions

H_p: POI is the donor
H_d: an unknown person is the donor

It follows that if people were chosen at random (or simulated) we would expect that 1 in every billion people would have the same reference profile as the POI and yield an LR of 1 billion when compared to the evidence. We would also expect that 999,999,999 out of 1

Interpretation, reporting, and communication **409**

billion randomly chosen people would have a different reference to the POI and yield an LR of 0 when compared to the evidence. The average LR of these 1 billion comparisons is then 1."

Assume a single locus with just two alleles, a and b, that are found in the population. There is a crime stain, which is from a single individual and is heterozygote a, b. A non-contributor test of $R_{1..N}$ samples will therefore select all three genotypes aa, ab, and bb; their proportions will conform to Hardy–Weinberg expectations: p_a^2, $2p_a p_b$, p_b^2, respectively.

To illustrate, the qualitative model described in Chapter 6 is used, where d is the drop-out probability parameter being the probability of an allele drop-out from a heterozygote genotype (for a particular contributor). If the genotype is homozygote, the probability d^2 is used. We also let p_C be the probability of drop-in.

For each non-contributor genotype (R_n) selected, the LRs are as follows:

$$LR_n = \frac{Pr(E|R_n)}{Pr(E|U)} \tag{12.13}$$

$$R_n = aa: \quad LR_{aa} = \frac{(1-d^2)p_C p_b}{(1-d^2)p_C p_b p_a^2 + (1-d^2)(1-p_C)2p_a p_b + (1-d^2)p_C p_a p_b^2}$$

$$R_n = ab: \quad LR_{ab} = \frac{(1-d^2)(1-p_C)}{(1-d^2)p_C p_b p_a^2 + (1-d^2)(1-p_C)2p_a p_b + (1-d^2)p_C p_a p_b^2}$$

$$R_n = bb: \quad LR_{bb} = \frac{(1-d^2)p_C p_a}{(1-d^2)p_C p_b p_a^2 + (1-d^2)(1-p_C)2p_a p_b + (1-d^2)p_C p_a p_b^2}$$

The expectation of the LR under $H_d = true$ is given as

$$Exp[LR|H_d] = LR_{aa} \times p_a^2 + LR_{ab} \times 2p_a p_b + LR_{bb} \times p_b^2.$$

Notice that the denominators are the same for each genotype, hence

$$Exp[LR|H_d] = \frac{(1-d^2)p_C p_b p_a^2 + (1-d^2)(1-p_C)2p_a p_b + (1-d^2)p_C p_a p_b^2}{(1-d^2)p_C p_b p_a^2 + (1-d^2)(1-p_C)2p_a p_b + (1-d^2)p_C p_a p_b^2} = 1$$

Because the terms are identical in the numerator and denominator, they cancel, and so the expectation becomes one.

In practice, we estimate the expectation by taking the average LR of a finite number of non-contributors. Consider a sample of randomly selected non-contributor genotypes $R_{1..N}$ (under $H_d = true$). The (finite) average LR for the entire sample is given as the sum of the LRs divided by the total number of samples N, i.e., $LR_{avg} = \frac{1}{N} \sum_{n=1..N} LR_n$.

Since we expect to observe a total of Np_a^2 of the R_ns to have genotype aa, $2Np_a p_b$ to have genotype ab and Np_b^2 to have genotype bb, the expectation of the average (under

H_d) becomes

$$Exp[LR_{avg}|H_d] = \frac{1}{N}(Np_a^2 \times LR_{aa} + 2Np_ap_b \times LR_{ab} + Np_b^2 \times LR_{bb})$$

which is equal to one. Importantly, the convergence of the average LR to the expectation $LR_{avg} = 1$ will depend on the number of non-contributor samples, and the probability space of the genotypes.

The principle can be extended to multiple loci and complex mixture models with multiple parameters and contributors.

Following from Turing's expectation, a useful criterion can be defined [227,262]:

nc = non-contributor;
LR_x = the value of the LR achieved in the case, e.g., using Eq. (12.11).

How often $LR_{nc} > LR_x$ is observed using $H_d = true$ tests, as shown in Eq. (12.12), is accommodated by $Pr(LR_{nc} > LR_x|H_d) \leq \frac{1}{LR_x}$, so we expect less than N/LR_x matches, where there are N comparisons.

The following example is a simple case, typed with the SGM plus kit, using data described in the next section. There were two propositions: $H_p : S_1 + U$; $H_d : U + U$. An $LR_x = 100,000$ was recorded.

Non-contributor analysis was carried out as follows:

A sample of $R_{n=1..100,000}$ non-contributors were simulated and substituted for S_1 (Eq. (12.13)); the likelihood ratios were recorded and plotted in Fig. 12.1. The majority of LRs are $\ll 1$, so that the *median* of the distribution is $LR_{median} \approx 10^{-15}$. In comparison, $LR_{avg} \approx 10^{-2}$ for the standard Monte-Carlo simulation (Fig. 12.2). The reason that we do not recover the Turing expectation $LR_{avg} = 1$ is that the sample size is too small. For very high LRs, the sample size would be too large to simulate. To solve this problem Taylor et al. [328] introduced "importance sampling", which is a mathematical method to reduce the sample size when we want to measure the probability of a rare event. As shown in Fig. 12.2, importance sampling returns the Turing expectation $LR_{avg} = 1$. Out of 100,000 non-contributors, the $LR_{max} = 1000$, which is less than the LR_x (Fig. 12.1), thereby fulfilling the expectation of a reasonable model for this number of non-contributors.

The $LR_{median} \approx 10^{-15}$ is very much less than the importance sampling $LR_{avg} = 1$. In addition, the observed LR_{avg} depends upon the sample size of non-contributors (Fig. 12.2). To demonstrate the Turing expectation ($LR_{avg} = 1$), it is also necessary to carry out sequential tests with increasing sample sizes to demonstrate convergence (i.e., where two consecutive tests show very little change). As expected, this convergence is achieved much earlier with importance sampling (a sample size of about 100,000 with the test example). Convergence requires much larger samples using classic Monte-Carlo sampling; even 10^8 samples were insufficient with this example.

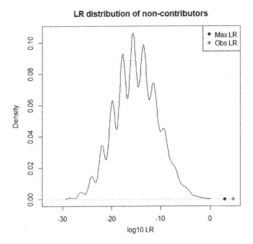

Figure 12.1 Non-contributor probability density plot using a sample size of 100,000, showing a wide distribution of results that predominantly range between $log_{10}LR = 0$ to -30 with $log_{10}LR_{median} \approx -15$. $LR_{max} \approx 1000$ and $LR_x \approx 100,000$.

12.17.1 The "two suspect" problem

In a case where there are multiple POIs, it may be of interest to the police investigation to know if it is possible that the mixture originated from multiple named persons.

Taking the example from Chapter 6.2: Two different suspects were both accused by the police as collaborators in a crime. The defense asserted that neither suspect was present, hence the propositions initially appear as

H_p: The DNA mixture originates from Mr. Smith (S_1), Mr. Doe (S_2), and the victim (V).
H_d: The DNA mixture originates from the victim (V) and two unknown (U, U) individuals.

The likelihood ratio was calculated with *LRmix Studio*. A probative $LR = 24,000$ was obtained.

The prosecution regarded this as evidence to infer support for the proposition that *both* individuals were contributors to the DNA evidence recovered from the crime scene.

The victim appears under both alternatives, and this is not problematic. However, the formulation of the propositions does not differentiate between S_1 and S_2. A single LR cannot indicate the relative contributions of the two individuals to the value of the evidence.

Non-contributor analysis can be used to show if either of the contributors under H_p is probative or not. A worked example is described in Chapter 6.2.4, reproduced here in Table 12.3.

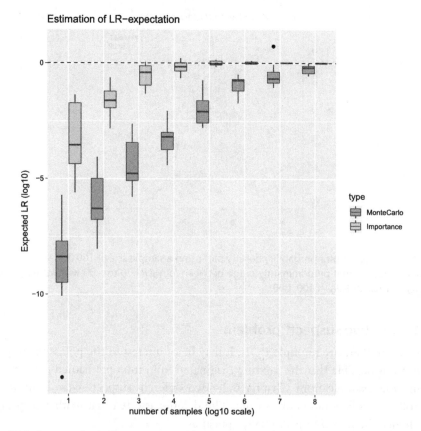

Figure 12.2 A comparison of importance vs. classic Monte-Carlo testing to demonstrate convergence with the Turing's expectation $LR_{avg} = 1$. Sample sizes (x-axis) ranged from $N = 10 \rightarrow 10^8$. The box whisker plots were created from ten sample sets, size N that were randomly simulated from the Norwegian SGM plus database.

For the propositions described above, a likelihood ratio ($LR = 24,000$) was obtained. Non-contributor testing was carried out to determine if the model was reasonable as described in Section 12.17. To do this, a total of $N = 24,000$ random profiles ($R_{i=1..N}$) were simulated to form the population of the non-contributors. Non-contributor (nc) tests were carried out by replacing each suspect (S_1 and S_2) in turn with random ($R_{i=1..N}$) profiles to generate a new LR_{nc} per random profile, which tested the following propositions:

H_{p1}: The DNA originates from the victim, Mr. Smith (S_1), and an unknown person (R_i).
H_{p2}: The DNA originates from the victim, Mr. Doe (S_2), and an unknown person (R_i).
H_d: The DNA originates from the victim and two unknown persons.

Interpretation, reporting, and communication   413

Table 12.3 Exploratory data analysis showing different sets of propositions and the results of non-contributor analysis. For the complex propositions in the first two rows, both S_1 and S_2 are tested separately (substituted by R) in non-contributor analysis, noting that S_2 performs poorly as the $LR_{max} > LR_x$; d was the drop-out probability parameter. There was an attempt to keep the number of simulation (N) the same size as the LR_x to test the expectation $N/LR_x \leq 1$, however, this aspiration is limited by the computing time required—restricted to approximately 10^6 simulations.

Propositions				Non-contributor analysis	Percentiles (log_{10})LR			
H_p	H_d	(log_{10})LR_x	d	Substitution	50	99	max	No. of simulations
S_1, S_2, V	U, U, V	4.394	0.15	S_1	-17	-9.5	-4.2	24,000
S_1, S_2, V	U, U, V	4.394	0.15	S_2	2.73	7.041	9.5	24,000
S_1, V	U, V	7.129	0.01	S_1	-31	-16	0.392	1,000,000
S_1, V	U, U, V	7.788	0.44	S_1	-16	-8.7	-0.884	500,000
S_2, V, U	U, U, V	-2.9	0.15	S_2	-5.5	-0.56	0.988	1,000

For simple proposition pairs (Tables 12.4), under Turing's expectation (Section 12.17), the probability that a $LR_{nc} = x$ or more is accommodated by $Pr(LR_{nc} > x|H_d) \leq 1/x$, so we expect less than N/x matches, where there are N comparisons [227] and the LR_{avg}, is expected to be one [262].

In other words, if the crime-stain $LR_x = 24,000$, and we simulate $N = 24,000$ non-contributor tests, then there is an expectation that there will be up to one example ($N/x = 24,000/24,000 = 1$), where the LR_{nc} is the same as or greater than that of LR_x. Importance sampling is not used for this particular test, since unbiased selection is required.

Table 12.4 Non-contributor (nc) and Turing's expectations for simple propositions (e.g., $H_p : S + U$; $H_d : U + U$), where suspect S_a (S_1 = Mr. Smith; S_2 = Mr. Doe) is replaced by random profiles ($R_{1..N}$) in nc tests to generate a series of $LR_{nc} = x$ profiles (V = victim; U = unknown). For complex propositions (e.g., $H_p : V + S_1 + S_2$; $H_d : V + U + U$), either S_1 or S_2 are replaced in turn with $R_{1..N}$ profiles to carry out non-contributor tests. Reproduced from [275] with permission from Elsevier.

Proposition type	Hp	H_p (nc test)	H_d	Expectation (nc)	LR_{avg} (Turing's expectation)
Simple proposition pairs	$S + U$	$R + U$	U+U	$Pr(LR_{nc} > x|H_d) \leq 1/x$	$LR_{avg} = 1$
	$S + V$	$V + R$	$V + U$	$Pr(LR_{nc} > x|H_d) \leq 1/x$	$LR_{avg} = 1$
Complex proposition pairs	$V+S_1 + S_2$	$V+S_1+R$	V+U+U	$Pr(LR_{nc} > x|H_d) \leq LR_{S_1}/x$	LR_{avg} scaled to LR_{S_1}
	$V + S_1 + S_2$	$V + R + S_2$	$V + U + U$	$Pr(LR_{nc} > x|H_d) \leq LR_{S_2}/x$	LR_{avg} scaled to LR_{S_2}

414 Forensic Practitioner's Guide to the Interpretation of Complex DNA Profiles

For complex proposition pairs shown in Tables 12.3 and 12.4, how often $LR_{nc} > x$ occurs is accommodated by $Pr(LR_{nc} > x | H_d) \leq LR_{S_a}/x$, where LR_{S_a} is the LR produced using propositions, where the known contributor in the numerator is S_a. For example, in the top row of Table 12.3, $S_a = S_2$, since S_1 is substituted by R in non-contributor tests, and the corresponding distribution of LRs is shown in the table for comparison.

For the complex propositions pairs in the first two rows of Table 12.3, there is an expectation that the distribution of 24,000 non-contributor random persons ($R_{1..24000}$) will be less than or equal to the observed likelihood ratio of the crime stain (Table 12.4). Non-contributor analysis ($S_a = S_2$), where S_1 is substituted by $R_{1..24000}$ "$H_d = true$" profiles gives a maximum observed $log_{10}LR = -4.2$. This is within expectations. However, the Turing $log_{10}LR_{avg} = -2.5$, which suggests that the model is insufficient. In addition, when S_2 is substituted by $R_{1..24000}$ "$H_d = true$" profiles ($S_a = S_1$), the $log_{10}LR_{max} = 9.5$; the $log_{10}LR$ 50 percentile $= 2.73$, and the Turing $log_{10}LR_{avg} \approx 7$. This clearly demonstrates that the evidence of S_2 inclusion in the mixture is unsupported by the non-contributor analysis. Since a series of randomly generated profiles gave LRs that were of the same order of magnitude or greater than that achieved in the case, then we can conclude that the model is not discriminating with regard to that particular individual, i.e., the results of this test are not informative.

The way forward to evaluate the evidence is to reformulate the propositions so that S_1 and S_2 are considered separately, as shown in Tables 12.3 and 12.4:

H_{p1}: The DNA originates from the victim, Mr. Smith (S_1) and an unknown person.
H_{p2}: The DNA originates from the victim, Mr. Doe (S_2) and an unknown person.
H_d: The DNA originates from the victim and two unknown persons.

When S_1 is conditioned under H_p, the analysis can be justified as two instead of three contributors (since no locus has more than four alleles; see Chapter 6.2.5); the $log_{10}LR = 7.1$, and the Turing $LR_{avg} = 1$. If H_d insists on three contributors, and H_p is anchored as two (Chapter 6.2.5), then the LR increases and does not therefore assist the defense position. On the other hand, S_2 must be evaluated with a three-contributor model, otherwise there are too few alleles to support the model, and the $log_{10}LR = -2.9$, which supports the defense proposition of exclusion. The Turing $LR = 1$, which indicates a reasonable model, though the observed $LR_x < 1$, i.e., the test does not depend upon ground truth $H_p = true$ for its application.

The ISFG DNA Commission [275], Section 4.3.1.2., states that (reasonable) non-contributor tests may be reported in investigative mode. An example statement is shown in Box 12.9.

Interpretation, reporting, and communication   415

Box 12.9

"This figure can be qualified with an investigative test known as a 'non-contributor test'. To do this we replace Mr Smith with a random unrelated individual and we repeat the measurement of the likelihood ratio. We do this a total of 24,000 times, with a different random individual each time. When this was carried out with Mr. Smith, the maximum likelihood ratio observed was of the order of 0.0001. However, when Mr Doe was substituted with 24,000 random samples, the maximum LR observed was 1 billion. This shows that although the trace can be explained as a mixture of the three persons, the possible contribution of Mr Doe needs to be viewed with great caution and one should assess the value of the profiles (from Mr Doe and Mr Smith) separately. Indeed, the likelihood ratio given the proposition where both POIs are contributors may be large, but the information provided by the minor contributor (Mr Doe) is too small to help discriminate him from a random person."

To summarize, we show that when multiple contributors are considered under H_p, but not H_d, it is necessary to consider each POI in a separate calculation. If a known individual is conditioned under H_p and H_d, then this is non-problematic. A combined $H_p : V + S_1 + S_2$ calculation does not discriminate between the relative contributions to the LR by each POI. Consequently, when S_1 and S_2 are evaluated separately, the latter is shown to provide an exclusionary LR less than one, whereas the contribution by S_1 is supported by a high LR. Therefore the evidence could be used to support prosecution of S_1, but not S_2. The ISFG DNA Commission Recommendation 3 [275] summarizes (Box 12.10):

Box 12.10

"When the issue regards the possible presence of DNA from several persons of interest, effort should be made to evaluate the profiles separately, and not as a whole. This is especially important if the information available from one part of the profile (e.g. major) is different from the other (minor, partial). For evaluation, this can be achieved by considering the result of the comparison between the given person and the trace and calculating individual LRs for each person. The report should be fully transparent on what propositions have been considered and on what basis.

For investigative purpose, it might be useful to explore whether the results support the proposition that the two persons together are (or not) the source of the DNA. In such a case, one can assign one LR. A non-contributor test can be helpful, also for investigative purposes."

For further details see Section 4.3 of the ISFG DNA Commission [275] and the included discussion on the "two suspect" problem.

12.18. Summary

1. The likelihood ratio is the only framework that can be properly utilized to interpret complex DNA profiles.

2. The likelihood ratio is formulated from two mutually exclusive propositions, usually from a prosecution and alternative defense proposition. The model assumptions and the background (case) information should be disclosed.

3. Although a model used to calculate a likelihood ratio may be robust, there are no true likelihood ratios or true models. The magnitude of the likelihood ratio is a measure of the value or the strength of the evidence.

4. The likelihood ratio may be less than one (favors the defense proposition) or greater than one (favors the prosecution proposition), else it may equal one, in which case neither proposition is supported over the other.

5. There are a number of important criteria required to set propositions in a case:

    a. It is the role of the mandating authorities to formulate the propositions to be tested. To prevent any possibility of bias, the role of the scientist is to take a neutral position. The scientist may advise the mandating authorities relating to the propositions that should be tested. However, this is part of the *"investigative"* phase of reporting. When a statement is written for court, the scientist is now in the *"evaluative"* phase of reporting. The scientist's role is to advise the prosecution and defense in equal measure.

    b. Propositions must be reasonable. They are dictated by the circumstances of the case.

    c. The propositions should highlight the differences of opinion between the prosecution and the defense.

    d. It is necessary to distinguish between the evaluative and investigative roles of the scientist.

    e. The scientist does not evaluate propositions. A scientist cannot tell a court if a proposition is true or not.

    f. The scientist can only evaluate the value of the evidence *if* a particular proposition is true.

    g. To avoid confirmation bias, propositions should be set before the results of tests are known.

    h. An appreciation of the hierarchy of propositions is a prerequisite to ensure that the evidence is correctly interpreted within context. Most interpretation of DNA profiles is at the sub-source level. The likelihood ratio cannot be carried over to higher levels in the hierarchy, in particular to the activity level.

6. Avoid the prosecutor's fallacy by ensuring that statements prefix the conditional word "if" before stating the proposition under consideration.

7. The value of the evidence is represented by the likelihood ratio itself. An optional verbal equivalent can also be provided, but verbal equivalents must not be provided without the numeric value.
8. Avoid terms such as "inconclusive", since the value of the evidence is provided by the *LR* itself.
9. A model will require information on the number of contributors. Usually a caveat will be applied to highlight the assumption that the contributors are unrelated to the POI and each other. If relatedness is claimed, then a different calculation will be required that takes the level of relationships into account.
10. Non-contributor tests are useful to show that models are performing in a robust way.

Notes

1. The meaning of subjectivity vs. objectivity is contentious. For a discussion see [307].
2. The Times, January 10, 1994.
3. When close relatives are considered, the amount of DNA marker sharing and masking is expected to increase further.

CHAPTER 13

Interpretation of complex DNA profiles generated by massively parallel sequencing

Peter Gill, Rebecca Just[a,b], Walther Parson, Chris Phillips, Øyvind Bleka

13.1. Introduction

Massively parallel sequencing (MPS), otherwise known as next-generation sequencing (NGS) is becoming increasingly utilized within the forensic community. For a review see Bruijns et al. [329]. Whereas conventional DNA profiling produces results in terms of sequence length, MPS returns the complete sequence of the locus of interest. Because sequence differences between loci are not reflected in length variants, for STRs, this greatly increases the amount of variation per locus, i.e., the number of alleles that can be detected in a population. It is also standard to analyze many more loci than is possible with conventional analysis, which further drives discriminating powers to unimaginable levels. Shorter amplicon lengths means that, theoretically, it should be possible to detect DNA fragments that are more highly degraded than can be detected using conventional CE analysis. By the same token, however, the increased sensitivity also increases the potential to detect contamination events, and will detect more

---

[a] This work was funded under Agreement No. HSHQDC-15-C-00064 awarded to Battelle National Biodefense Institute by the Department of Homeland Security Science and Technology Directorate (DHS S&T) for the management and operation of the National Biodefense Analysis and Countermeasures Center a Federally Funded Research and Development Center. The views and conclusions contained in this document are those of the authors and should not be interpreted as necessarily representing the official policies, either expressed or implied, of the U.S. Department of Homeland Security or the U.S. Government. The Department of Homeland Security does not endorse any products or commercial services mentioned in this presentation. In no event shall the DHS, BNBI or NBACC have any responsibility or liability for any use, misuse, inability to use, or reliance upon the information contained herein. In addition, no warranty of fitness for a particular purpose, merchantability, accuracy or adequacy is provided regarding the contents of this document.

[b] This research was supported in part through the FBI's Visiting Scientist Program, an educational opportunity administered by the Oak Ridge Institute for Science and Education (ORISE). Names of commercial manufacturers are provided for identification purposes only, and inclusion does not imply endorsement of the manufacturer, or its products or services by the FBI. The views expressed are those of the authors and do not necessarily reflect the official policy or position of the FBI or the U.S. Government. This is FBI Publication #20-52.

Forensic Practitioner's Guide to the Interpretation of Complex DNA Profiles
https://doi.org/10.1016/B978-0-12-820562-4.00021-3

Copyright © 2020 Elsevier Inc.
All rights reserved.

low-level contributors. To date, there have only been a very few publications that apply probabilistic genotyping methods to massively parallel sequencing, specifically for mixture analysis [300,330,302]. Fortunately, the essential principles of mixture analysis, described in earlier chapters, are equally applicable to MPS data. SNPs are simple two-allele loci. Calculations are simplified, because there are no stutters to consider, hence they are much faster. The analysis of MPS-STRs also follows the same rationale previously described for conventional STRs, except that stutters have to be taken into account, and to identify these, a specialized nomenclature is required.

13.2. SNP analysis

To carry out SNP testing, a series of two- and three-person mixtures of varying dilutions were prepared and analyzed with Life Technologies' HID-Ion AmpliSeq Identity Panel v2.2 using the Ion PGM massively parallel sequencing (MPS) system. From this panel, 134 autosomal SNPs were analyzed against a series of mixtures prepared from three known individuals labeled P1, P2, and P3. Two-person mixtures from individuals P1 and P2 were prepared, in ratios of "P1:P2". These ranged from 1:1, 1:3, 1:9, and included the reverse ratios 3:1, 9:1. For three-person mixtures, the mixture ratios of P1:P3:P2 were prepared as 1:1:1, 1:1:5, 1:5:1, 1:5:5, 5:1:1, 5:1:5, and 5:5:1. All mixtures were analyzed in replicate, e.g., 1:1a/1:1b.

For each mixture analysis, two competing propositions were compared:

H_p: The person of interest (POI) and $K - 1$ unrelated unknown individuals are contributors to the evidence.
H_d: K unknown unrelated individuals are contributors to the evidence.

From this, we constructed the likelihood ratio $LR = Pr(E|H_p)/Pr(E|H_d)$, where K is the number of contributors to the evidence, and E is the evidence of the observed replicates. The person of interest is either P1, P2, or P3. For two-person mixtures, there are ten possible combinations to calculate the LR, whereas there are 21 combinations with three-person mixtures. Likelihood ratios were calculated for both replicates combined and for individual replicates.

The likelihood ratios were calculated from either a qualitative model ($LRmix$), or a quantitative model ($EuroForMix$). The component SNP allele frequencies used were compiled by the 1000 Genomes Project Consortium [331] for five European populations; see Figure 2 in [332] (Allele frequency estimates were made from the five combined population genotypes, and all data are listed in the population frequency file "EUR/SNP_Freqs" provided on the book's website) with a theta correction, $F_{ST} = 0.01$. The detection threshold was set to 10 "sequence reads". This implies that alleles from contributors registered with less than 10 sequence reads are considered as drop-out events, or very low level non-specific nucleotide incorporation.

Interpretation of complex DNA profiles generated by massively parallel sequencing   421

A worked example is available on the book's website.

Bleka et al. [300] applied both the qualitative model as implemented in *LRmix* and the quantitative model (*EuroForMix*). For the qualitative model, the drop-out parameter *d* (see Chapter 5 and Appendix B.3.2) was assumed to be equal across all contributors, markers, and replicates. Homozygote drop-out was calculated as d^2. Drop-in was modeled as $p_C = 0.05$. The quantitative model used was *EuroForMix*, without applying the degradation model (Chapter 8). The drop-in parameters were set to $p_C = 0.05$, $\lambda = 0.01$. Both conservative and MLE methods were compared. Non-contributor tests were carried out as described in Chapter, Section 6.1.6 and Chapter, Section 12.17. Full details are provided in Bleka et al. [300].

13.3. Number of contributors

A potential drawback to the interpretation of SNP mixtures is the necessity to define the number of contributors. In Chapter 2.3.2, a simple rule, known as the maximum allele count (MAC), used to determine the minimum number of contributors (nC_{min}) in STRs is as follows:

$$nC_{min} = ceiling\frac{L_{max}}{2} \tag{13.1}$$

where "*ceiling x*" is the least integer that is greater than or equal to *x*, and L_{max} is the maximum number of observed alleles in any of the observed loci. However, the operation of this rule is dependent upon the potential number of alleles that may be detected at a locus, which acts as a restriction upon the upper limit of nC_{min}. The difficulty with di-allelic SNPs is that there can be no more than two alleles at any locus; consequently, $nC_{min} = 1$ for all loci, regardless of the number of actual contributors, so this strategy does not work.

For two or more contributors, the level of apparent heterozygosity will increase and high levels of "masking" will restrict the usefulness of qualitative models, particularly for mixtures of three or more contributors. However, coverage (analogous to peak height) is expected to be proportional to quantity of allelic DNA present in the mixture. Consequently, coverage is amenable to analysis using *EuroForMix*.

13.4. Effect of choosing the wrong number of contributors

Because it is impossible to determine the minimum number of contributors using conventional methods using simple allele counts, an alternative strategy is required. In Chapter 8.5.6, a method of model selection using an exploratory analysis that varied the number of contributors to determine the effect upon the likelihood ratio is presented. It was demonstrated that models became stable once a critical number of contributors was reached, i.e., the addition of excess, or too many, contributors had very little effect on the likelihood ratio. This was because excess contributors were assigned to have very low (undetectable) mixture proportions, hence they had very little influence upon the final LR. To discover the minimum number of contributors that results in a stable LR, it is not necessary to know the *actual* number of contributors.

13.5. Comparison of quantitative and qualitative methods

Table 13.1 shows that all true contributors gave $LR > 10^8$ for all mixtures. However, much higher probative values were obtained with the quantitative model. This indicates that there is a lot of useful information that can be utilized in the form of "sequence reads" from forensic SNP genotype data generated by MPS tests.

For two-person mixtures, both the qualitative and quantitative models performed well: true contributors, conditioned under H_p, produced high LRs, whereas non-contributors, conditioned under H_p, produced low LRs. Whereas a quantitative model can give an extremely high $log_{10}LR > 20$ (Table 13.1) compared to qualitative results where $log_{10}LR \approx 10$, this arguably has no impact on a jury outcome, i.e., there is an effective redundancy of information embodied in high LRs above a certain value.

With respect to three-person mixtures, there was an obvious benefit to utilizing a quantitative model, particularly when a major contributor was the POI (Table 13.2). This was exemplified by mixtures, such as 5:1:1, where the strength of evidence of a major contributor was usually greatly in excess, $log_{10}LR \gg 10$. Qualitative models take no account of the "read" number, and the LRs are consequently considerably lower at $LR \approx 100$, even when mixtures were evenly proportioned (1:1:1). However, for mixtures, where the POI was low level, e.g., 1:5:5, both the qualitative and quantitative models gave similar LR results, i.e., the effect of sequence read information does not have much impact on this type of mixture. LRs are usually very much lower for three-persons rather than two-persons mixtures. Note that for qualitative methods, the LR results were observed to be the same for several mixtures, e.g., samples 1:1, 1:9, and 3.1 (Table 13.1); samples 1:1:1, 5:1:5, and 5:1:1 (Table 13.2); this occurred, because the samples shared the same genotypes. The "sequence reads" differed considerably between these samples, but this information was only incorporated by the quantitative method.

13.6. Limitations

The LR was greatest when the mixture proportion (M_x) of the POI was also high. From observation of data in Table 13.2 for three-person mixtures, samples 5:1:1, 1:5:1, and 1:1:5, where the major component coincides with the POI and $M_x > 0.5$, the strength of evidence was typically $log_{10}LR > 20$, whereas low-level POI contributors, $M_x < 0.25$, were in the region of LR 10–1000. We surmised that there was a clearly discernible limit

Interpretation of complex DNA profiles generated by massively parallel sequencing **423**

Table 13.1 Likelihood ratio analysis of all two-person mixtures. The mixture ratios e.g., 3:1a/3:1b are two replicates combined to form a single likelihood ratio (given in log_{10} scale). They are given in order of the contributing individuals P1:P2. The three adjacent columns contain the *LR* calculations conditioned on P1, P2, and non-contributor P3, respectively, as the POI. Calculations were carried out using qualitative (Qual) and quantitative (Quan) models. MLE denotes the maximum likelihood–based approach, whereas CONS denotes the conservative simulated–based approach. The results of total of 100 non-contributor tests are given at the 50, 90, 95, 99 percentiles along with the maximum observation. Reproduced from [300] with permission from Elsevier.

Sample	Method	PI	P2	P3	Max	99%	95%	90%	50%
1:1a/1:1b	Qual (MLE)	11.1	12.4	−28.6	−8.9	−17.7	−19.2	−21	−27.5
1:1a/1:1b	Qual (CONS)	8.4	9.6	−75.8	−25.6	−43.7	−49	−53.7	−71.4
1:1a/1:1b	Quan (MLE)	32	16.3	−33.8	−16.3	−20.4	−23	−24	−30.4
1:1a/1:1b	Quan (CONS)	30.8	15.2	−35	−17.4	−21.5	−24.2	−25.1	−31.6
1:3a/1:3b	Qual (MLE)	10.5	11.9	−23.7	−5.5	−13.5	−16.5	−17.6	−24.1
1:3a/1:3b	Qual (CONS)	7.6	8.9	−67.9	−19.6	−35.5	−44.7	−48.6	−67.5
1:3a/1:3b	Quan (MLE)	23.9	27.7	−42.3	−26	−27.9	−32.6	−34.4	−42.2
1:3a/1:3b	Quan (CONS)	22.7	26.7	−43.5	−27.1	−29	−33.8	−35.6	−43.5
1:9a/1:9b	Qual (MLE)	11.1	12.4	−28.6	−8.9	−17.7	−19.2	−21	−27.5
1:9a/1:9b	Qual (CONS)	8.4	9.6	−75.8	−25.6	−43.7	−49	−53.7	−71.4
1:9a/1:9b	Quan (MLE)	27.2	53.5	−33.5	−19	−20.3	−23.3	−25.7	−33.8
1:9a/1:9b	Quan (CONS)	26	52.3	−34.6	−20.1	−21.4	−24.4	−26.8	−34.9
3:1a/3:1b	Qual (MLE)	11.1	12.4	−28.6	−8.9	−17.7	−19.2	−21	−27.5
3:1a/3:1b	Qual (CONS)	8.4	9.6	−75.8	−25.6	−43.7	−49	−53.7	−71.4
3:1a/3:1b	Quan (MLE)	56.3	22.6	−26.4	−9.6	−15.2	−16.4	−18.6	−24.6
3:1a/3:1b	Quan (CONS)	55.2	21.4	−27.6	−10.8	−16.4	−17.5	−19.7	−25.7
9:1a/9:1b	Qual (MLE)	11.1	12.1	−25.2	−5.1	−15	−16.3	−17.6	−23.7
9:1a/9:1b	Qual (CONS)	8.1	8.8	−70.2	−21.2	−42.1	−45.7	−49.4	−66.3
9:1a/9:1b	Quan (MLE)	58.2	19.4	−46.7	−23.3	−28.1	−33.2	−35.6	−47.3
9:1a/9:1b	Quan (CONS)	57.1	18.2	−47.9	−24.4	−29.3	−34.4	−36.8	−48.5

to interpretation that was dependent on the M_x value. Therefore, it was of interest to properly characterize the effect.

To do this, we simulated one hundred mixtures with two persons, three persons, etc., up to a maximum six persons. Likelihood ratios were calculated with varying mixture proportions (M_x) assigned to the POI. Propositions used to form the *LR* are as described in Section 13.2.

In support of our initial findings, it was clear from the simulations that two-person mixtures gave much higher *LR*s for low M_x proportions compared to three or more persons. Interestingly, the relationship of a given M_x and its corresponding *LR* was largely unaffected by the number of contributors greater than two. For example, an $M_x \approx 0.4$ (measured between 0.35–0.45) for three-contributor simulations approximated to a range of $log_{10} LR \approx 9.6 - 15.2$ in all examples. A practical lower limit to interpretation

424 Forensic Practitioner's Guide to the Interpretation of Complex DNA Profiles

Table 13.2 The mixture ratios, e.g., 5:5:1a/5:5:1b, are two replicates combined to form a single likelihood ratio (given in log_{10} scale). They are given in order of the contributing individuals P1:P3:P2. The three adjacent columns contain the *LR* calculations conditioned on P1, P3, and P2, respectively, as the POI. Calculations were carried out using qualitative (Qual) and quantitative (Quan) models. MLE denotes the maximum likelihood–based approach, whereas CONS denotes the conservative simulated-based approach. The results of a total of 100 non-contributor tests are given at the 50, 90, 95, 99 percentiles along with the maximum observation. Mixture ratios of the quantitative MLE method, for asterisked samples labeled 5:1:1, were observed to be 4.6:2.9:20.8 (approximately 1:1:5), whereas samples labeled 1:1:5 were 54:8.3:3.8 (approximately 5:1:1), suggesting that the labels for these samples had been inadvertently transposed. Reproduced from [300] with permission from Elsevier.

Sample	Method	PI	P3	P2	Max	99%	95%	90%	50%
1:1:1a/1:1: lb	Qual (MLE)	5.1	5	5.6	1	0.9	−1.2	−2	−6.2
1:1: la/1:1: lb	Qual (CONS)	1.8	1.6	2.1	−3.3	−3.5	−7.7	−8.6	−18.1
l:l:la/l:l:lb	Quan (MLE)	15.6	12.1	2.1	−0.5	−1.5	−2.4	−2.8	−4.1
l:l:la/l:l:lb	Quan (CONS)	14.1	10.6	0.5	−2	−3	−3.8	−4.3	−5.2
5:5:la/5:5:lb	Qual (MLE)	6.1	6	0.7	0.3	−0.4	−3.7	−4.2	−8.1
5:5:la/5:5:lb	Qual (CONS)	2.6	2.4	−7.5	−7.3	−8.5	−16.9	−17.5	−27.6
5:5:la/5:5:lb	Quan (MLE)	20.8	16.2	3.8	0.6	0.1	−0.6	−0.9	−2.9
5:5:la/5:5:lb	Quan (CONS)	19.5	14.8	2.4	−0.8	−1.2	−2	−2.2	−4.2
5:l:5a/5:l:5b	Qual (MLE)	5.1	5	5.6	1	0.9	−1.2	−2	−6.2
5:l:5a/5:l:5b	Qual (CONS)	1.8	1.6	2.1	−3.3	−3.5	−7.7	−8.6	−18.1
5:l:5a/5:l:5b	Quan (MLE)	34.7	1.7	5.3	−0.6	−0.9	−1.6	−2.5	−4
5:l:5a/5:l:5b	Quan (CONS)	33.1	0.3	3.5	−2	−2.4	−2.9	−3.8	−5.3
l:5:5a/l:5:5b	Qual (MLE)	5.1	5	5.6	1	0.9	−1.2	−2	−6.2
l:5:5a/l:5:5b	Qual (CONS)	1.8	1.6	2.1	−3.3	−3.5	−7.7	−8.6	−18.1
l:5:5a/l:5:5b	Quan (MLE)	1.9	28.3	4.3	0.4	−1.5	−2.3	−2.8	−4.1
l:5:5a/l:5:5b	Quan (CONS)	0.3	26.9	2.8	−1.1	−3.1	−3.8	−4.2	−5.4
5:l:la/5:l:lb★	Qual (MLE)	5.1	5	5.6	1	0.9	−1.2	−2	−6.2
5:l:la/5:l:lb★	Qual (CONS)	1.8	1.6	2.1	−3.3	−3.5	−7.7	−8.6	−18.1
5:l:la/5:l:lb★	Quan (MLE)	4.6	2.9	20.8	0.2	−1.6	−2.6	−3	−4.5
5:l:la/5:l:lb★	Quan (CONS)	3.1	1.4	19.3	−1.2	−3.1	−4	−4.4	−5.7
l:l:5a/l:l:5b★	Qual (MLE)	5.1	5	2.1	1.2	−1.4	−2.6	−3.7	−8
l:l:5a/l:l:5b★	Qual (CONS)	1.8	1.6	−2.6	−3.4	−8.1	−9.2	−13.1	−23.4
l:l:5a/l:l:5b★	Quan (MLE)	54	8.3	3.8	0.4	0.1	−0.3	−0.7	−2.1
l:l:5a/l:l:5b★	Quan (CONS)	52.6	6.9	2.4	−1.1	−1.3	−1.8	−2.2	−3.6
l:5:la/l:5:lb	Qual (MLE)	5.8	5.7	2.8	1.8	0	−2.1	−2.7	−6.6
l:5:la/l:5:lb	Qual (CONS)	2.2	2.1	−3.3	−4	−7.6	−12.3	−13.1	−22.9
l:5:la/l:5:lb	Quan (MLE)	8.6	49.8	3.9	0.3	0	−0.4	−0.8	−2.1
l:5:la/l:5:lb	Quan (CONS)	7.1	48.3	2.5	−1.2	−1.4	−1.8	−2.3	−3.6

of three or more contributors is $M_x \approx 0.2$, which gave a range of $log_{10} LR \approx 1.6 - 11.4$, although it is difficult to generalize, because even at this level some gave highly probative results.

13.7. The effect of uncertainty of the number of contributors on the likelihood ratio

Because SNPs are di-allelic, it is much more difficult to estimate the minimum number of contributors to mixtures compared to multi-allelic STRs, hence this might be conceived as a difficult drawback to the use of SNPs in the analysis of casework samples, since many mixtures are encountered.

To resolve this issue, we carried out further simulations to determine the effect of over- and under-estimation of the number of contributors. To begin with, we simulated two contributors as the ground-truth and calculated the likelihood ratio conditioned upon three, four, and five contributors, respectively. The plots all follow the 45-degree line (Fig. 13.1), showing that there was little effect on the LR.

Next, we simulated three-contributor mixtures, and calculated the LR conditioned on an under-estimated two-contributor mixture and mixtures over-estimated as four, five, and six contributors. When the ground-truth three-contributor mixtures that gave $log_{10}LR > 6$ (approximately) were interpreted as two-person mixtures, there was concordance. Conversely, when ground-truth three-person contributors gave $log_{10}LR < 6$ (approximately) were conditioned on two-persons, the calculated LR could be greatly under-estimated. On the other hand, when the number of contributors was over-estimated (> 3), the LRs showed full concordance.

The experiment was repeated with simulations of four, five, and six contributors that were interpreted, conditional upon under-estimates and over-estimates of the true number, as described in the previous paragraph. The patterns were the same—under-estimation to two contributors also resulted in LR under-estimation, as described for three contributors.

These findings were consistent with those experienced with conventional STR analysis, showing that LRs of quantitative models changed little when excess contributors were postulated (Chapter 8.7.3). Consequently, exploratory analysis, where additional contributors are added can be utilized to determine when a stable LR is reached. Because there are only two alleles per locus, the calculation rates are fast, though there are many more loci (134) compared to standard STR tests, e.g., six seconds for three contributors, and 1015 seconds for six-contributor analyses.

13.8. Summary

In summary, mixture analysis of SNPs is best carried out using quantitative models, especially if there are more than two contributors. Because there are no more than two alleles per locus, this estimation is difficult to achieve, hence some exploratory data analysis is required to determine when the LR becomes stable relative to this parameter, i.e., it is very unlikely to overstate the value of the evidence, because too many contributors are posited. With the current SNP panel tested, there is a generalized limitation, where

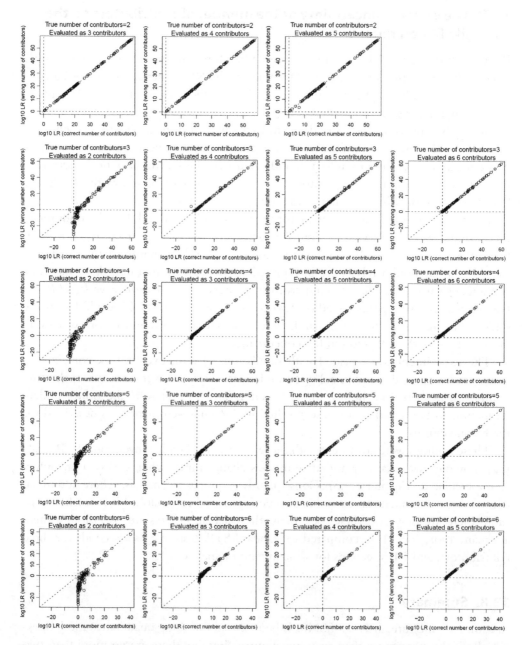

Figure 13.1 Plots of the ML-based (*EuroForMix*) likelihood ratio (log_{10} scale) of the person of interest vs M_x for 100 simulated mixtures samples. The true number of contributors (between 2–6) is evaluated against wrongly assumed numbers of contributors (also between 2–6). Reproduced from [300] with permission from Elsevier.

Interpretation of complex DNA profiles generated by massively parallel sequencing **427**

the M_x of the POI must exceed 0.2 to achieve a $LR > 100$ (although this is sample dependent). However, this limitation would be removed with larger SNP panels.

13.9. Short tandem repeats

There is considerable interest in STR–MPS, as there are realistic prospects of this method eventually replacing conventional CE. In particular, the MPS platform allows for a much larger number of loci to be analyzed. Because the analysis is sequence-based, this reveals more variant alleles per locus. More loci, and more polymorphism per locus combine to greatly increase existing discriminating powers of systems. In common with SNPs, an advantage is that it can potentially increase the sensitivity of analysis, because shorter, therefore more degradation resistant amplicons can be utilized. Mixture analysis may also be facilitated, because the phenomenon of masking will be reduced by the presence of more allele variants.

However, several challenges need to be addressed before MPS-STRs can be fully adopted. Fortunately, there are considerable on-going community discussions that are working towards solutions. The field is rapidly changing, and doubtless new methods will be implemented over coming months and years. A snapshot is presented here to highlight the important issues that are specific to the interpretation of MPS-STR evidence.

Central to the widespread adoption of MPS-STRs is a need for common standards of quality control to ensure that frequency databases are reliable. The second requirement is for agreed standards of nomenclature, so that data can be incorporated into national DNA databases, and shared by users. The platform STRidER, a publicly available, centrally curated online allele frequency database and quality control platform for autosomal STRs now accepts sequence data for MPS-STRs [32]; see Chapter 1.3.2 for further details. There is a need to increase sample sizes to capture the much increased levels of sequence variation in some STRs (e.g., D12S391), hence combined data (facilitated by STRidER QC and standardization) is increasingly going to be a necessary contingency.

13.9.1 Nomenclature

The conventional nomenclature of simple STRs is based upon the number of repeats per allele (Chapter 1.7). Partial repeats are signified by a decimal point: TH01 9.3 means that there are 9 complete repeats and a partial repeat of 3 bases. An early ISFG/ISFH DNA Commission [4] laid the ground rules for nomenclature, and standard sets of loci (Chapter 1.2.1). Both were adopted and became universal practice. Standardization was needed, because different laboratories need to share and upload data to national DNA databases. A nomenclature based upon a simple set of digits allows for easy search algorithms to be implemented. On the NIST website, "STRBase" https://strbase.nist.

428 Forensic Practitioner's Guide to the Interpretation of Complex DNA Profiles

gov/index.htm, commercial kits are listed, and there are links to individual STR loci that provide a complete list of alleles sequences. Where available, the primer sequences for different kits are published, the amplicon sizes are provided, along with the repeat sequence. There are two basic classes of repeat sequences: simple and compound repeats.

Simple STR sequences include TH01 as an example. This locus has a series of 15 alleles ranging between n = 3–14 repeats, where the sequence is $[AATG]_n$. Allele 9.3 contains a partial repeat and is sequenced as $[AATG]_6ATG[AATG]_3$, i.e., a series of six [AATG] repeats, followed by a partial [ATG] repeat, concluded with a further three [AATG] repeats.

Complex STR sequences have many more variant alleles compared to simple repeat sequences, and are therefore more discriminating. An example is D21S11. There are two kinds of basic repeats [TCTA] and [TCTG], interspersed with a number of partial repeats and a solitary [TCCA] repeat. For D21S11, there are many different variants; some polymorphisms have the same repeat length, but have different structures. For example, there are three different allelic variants for allele 27 listed in the STRBase website:

$[TCTA]_4$ $[TCTG]_6$ $[TCTA]_3$ TA $[TCTA]_3$ TCA $[TCTA]_2$ TCCA TA $[TCTA]_9$
$[TCTA]_6$ $[TCTG]_5$ $[TCTA]_3$ TA $[TCTA]_3$ TCA $[TCTA]_2$ TCCA TA $[TCTA]_8$
$[TCTA]_5$ $[TCTG]_5$ $[TCTA]_3$ TA $[TCTA]_3$ TCA $[TCTA]_2$ TCCA TA $[TCTA]_9$

For each of the three variants, the lengths of the fragments are all exactly the same size. The sum of nomenclature repeats = 27 (these are highlighted in bold type). Sequences TA, TCA, TCCA are not included in the repeat count. The system of nomenclature per locus can be traced back to historical foundation papers, e.g., in the case of D21S11, see the 1994 paper of Möller et al. [333]. Since not all alleles were observed by early workers, the discovery of new variants have to "fit" within the scheme that was first widely adopted. The allelic designation, does not therefore take account of the internal sequence variation, which is of course always unknown (unless sequenced) in conventional CE-based STR analysis. Analysis with MPS is able to unlock this hidden variation, thereby increasing the discriminating power of existing markers.

Therefore, existing designation systems that are universally applied to national DNA databases are based upon the repeating structure of "typical" reference alleles that were discovered and characterized in the early to mid 1990s. All new allelic variant designations must fit within the scheme, regardless of sequence, and are strictly based upon the number of bases that are counted in the fragment length. Comparisons are made against an allelic ladder. This means that the length of the STR repeat, and its correspondence to the reference sequenced repeat does not necessarily hold. Let us suppose that there is a deletion of a single base in the flanking region of an amplicon in an allele 27 variant listed above; though the repeating structure is identical to that listed, the allelic designation must change to 26.3. Consequently, this allele designation no longer reflects the repeat structure of the reference sequence.[1]

Interpretation of complex DNA profiles generated by massively parallel sequencing **429**

The above discussion has no impact upon the population genetics and interpretation of conventional STRs. This is because statistical analysis is not compromised by the existence of multiple variants of an allelic fragment of a given size; the fragment will be consistently designated and will always "match" the alleles the same size on a national DNA database, along with a multiplicity of alleles that share the same size, but have different sequences.

Nevertheless, the move to MPS is not without challenge. An ISFG DNA commission [1] that was convened to consider the minimal nomenclature requirements made some important recommendations:

- Data should be exported and stored as sequence strings.
- A unified nomenclature system of MPS-STR sequences is required to ensure compatibility between laboratories and databases.
- Forward strand (5'→ 3') direction to be adopted, since this is consistent with all human genome studies since 2001 (some historical sequences are based upon the reverse strand).
- There must be back-compatibility with conventional STR designations that are stored on national DNA databases.

A collaborative initiative led by the STR Sequence Working Group (STRAND) [334] was convened to harmonize related efforts across laboratories: STRidER (Chapter 1.3.2); STRSeq catalog of sequences [335]; STRait Razor bioinformatic freeware [336]. For an up-to-date review of all of the efforts underway, the reader is referred to the deliberations of the STRAND group [334] for further information. Here we consider the issues of nomenclature strictly within the requirements of probabilistic genotyping software.

13.10. Historical perspective: lessons of the past

In relation to the evolution of DNA databases, driven by the adoption of new loci and/or methods, in 2006, a European position paper was published [26] that reflected the views of the ENFSI/EDNAP group. As national DNA databases were starting to become very large, there was a recognition that existing multiplexes used at the time needed to be upgraded to improve discriminating powers, to avoid the impact of having to deal with high numbers of adventitious matches. At the same time, there was a concern that national DNA databases had a potential to lock us into old technology that would in time become inefficient and outdated. There needed to be a mechanism that would encourage progression and adoption of new technology as it became available. Consequently, this is highly relevant to MPS.

In 2006 the challenge was to introduce new core loci to increase discriminating power. But there was also recognition that different kinds of loci were required to increase success rates, particularly for highly degraded samples. At the time, there

430 Forensic Practitioner's Guide to the Interpretation of Complex DNA Profiles

was considerable interest in "mini-STRs" [24,337], because the small fragment size showed increased utility to analyze degraded material [338]. Three new loci exhibiting these characteristics were recommended for adoption (D10S1248, D14S1434, and D22S1045). The D14S1434 locus was dropped in favor of D2S441, as the latter had a much better discriminating power [289]. This increased the number of core European Standard Interpol loci from 7 to 10. After subsequent discussions [289], manufacturers were encouraged to increase the number of loci in their multiplexes to 15 or more, and also to reduce the amplicon sizes of existing loci to improve the capability to detect degraded material. There was a parallel initiative in the United States [20], where the original 13 core STR loci were expanded to 20. The seven new loci incorporated those ESS loci, which were absent in the old CODIS, thereby providing a standardized system across both North America and Europe. New multiplexes were subsequently released with 15 European core STR loci, including AmpFlSTR Identifiler, from Applied Biosystems and PowerPlex 16 from Promega Corporation. With new advances in biochemistry, such as 6-dye chemistry, multiplexes have culminated in providing a large number of loci per reaction. For example, the PowerPlex Fusion 6C kit encompasses 23 autosomal STRs, 3 Y-STRs and Amelogenin; the Applied Biosystems GlobalFiler kit comprises 24 autosomal STRs, Y-Indel, and Amelogenin. These advanced kits are becoming widely adopted. The advantage is that they are truly universal in that they encompass both the CODIS and the ESS standard set of loci. The probabilities of random matches are extremely low, at $< 10^{-25}$ [339,117].

For further details on the historical development and harmonization of multiplexes, see Chapters 1.1.1, 1.2, and 1.2.1.

The adoption of new multiplex kits comprising 24 autosomal loci is not without challenge. The field is progressing rapidly towards adopting new multiplex kits based on MPS technology. For example, the Illumina ForenSeq Signature Prep kit, primer mix A, contains primer pairs for 58 STRs, including 27 autosomal STRs, 7 X and 24 Y haplotype markers, and 94 identity-informative SNPs. Primer mix B has additional primer pairs for 56 ancestry-informative SNPs and 22 phenotypic-informative SNPs.

The main potential for MPS is its ability to increase the number of loci that can be analyzed per reaction test that is far beyond the capability of traditional CE instrumentation to emulate. In addition, there are many more allelic variants that can be accessed. Gettings et al. [340] provide a detailed study of D1S1656, D2S1338, D8S1179, D12S391, and D21S11, showing a substantial increase in the number of allelic variants observed. Sequences can be accessed, along with Genbank accession numbers from the STRSeq BioProject (https://www.ncbi.nlm.nih.gov/bioproject/380127).

However, the main challenge with the new technology is information processing. With so much information, manual processing, inspection of individual loci for characteristics is no longer feasible, and furthermore, introduces risks of human error. For example, *FDSTools* [341] employs automatic threshold-based allele calling with noise

Interpretation of complex DNA profiles generated by massively parallel sequencing **431**

correction and automated identification of stutter. *CaseSolver* (Chapter 11) has been extended to MPS [330]. These (and other) software were introduced to streamline the interpretation process, and to help to remove the information bottleneck. Quality was improved by removing human error.

13.11. STR-MPS stutters

Stutters are defined and characterized, in relation to CE, in Chapters 2.2 and 2.2.1. In Chapter 2.2.2, stutters were characterized as increasing in size relative to the increasing number of repeats for the parent allele. Many STRs have microvariants, e.g., 9.3 and 10.3 in TH01, and sequence variants, such as those described for D21S11, in Section 13.9.1. When repeating blocks are interrupted, this results in stutters that are smaller in size than would be predicted on the basis of entire STR repeat length. Instead, the longest uninterrupted repeat stretch (LUS) is a better predictor than the total number of repeats.

The analysis of stutter takes on a new dimension with MPS. This is because the sequence of $n - 1$ repeats can be identified. In the same way that new allelic variants are recognized, so are new stutter variants similarly identified. Just and Irwin [302], Figure 3, shows how potential stutters can be generated from a given sequence, incorporating the LUS notation. The concept is illustrated in Fig. 13.2. The repeat unit (RU) is provided first—this is the same as the conventional STR nomenclature utilized in CE—the second part defines the number of repeats found in the LUS block. Stutter prediction follows from the LUS nomenclature. For example, D12S391 has a structure of two blocks of repeats $[AGAT]_{n1}[AGAC]_{n2}$ (with $n1$ and $n2$ as the block/motif repetition number). For the 23_14 allele, an $n - 1$ stutter would either be 22_13 or 22_14. The repeat block position of the stutter is defined by the nomenclature. In this example, 22_13 refers to a stutter in the [AGAT] repeat block, whereas, by default, 22_14 would refer to a stutter in the [AGAC] repeat block. Since the length of the $[AGAC]_{n2}$ repeat block is typically less than that of the $[AGAT]_{n1}$ block, the probability of stutter is also lower. It is also important to emphasize that both blocks could simultaneously stutter—such events would combine within CE and would only be visualized as a single stutter, but both would be explicit within MPS. Prediction of $n + 1/n - 2$ stutters naturally follow from the same nomenclature, e.g., for the 23_14 parent allele, the $n + 1$ stutter is either 24_15 or 24_14, and the affected repeat block follows from the LUS nomenclature.

The LUS notation provides a means to identify potential stutters, which is an important requirement when utilizing the stutter model in *EuroForMix*.

Note that the LUS notation is dynamic. This is because the position of the LUS block of repeats may differ according to the allele, and locus (Table 13.3). For example, CSF1PO alleles are most commonly present as a single LUS block of repeats, e.g.,

Table 13.3 Table showing the principle of the LUS+ nomenclature. Reference alleles are displayed using the UAS data range, but in accordance with ISFG recommendations as to strand. Core repeat regions used to determine repeat unit alleles are in upper case text. LUS length reference regions are underlined and are identical to those described in Table 1 of Just et al. [302]. See the "look-up" Table S5 in Just et al. [342] for LUS sequences for other alleles. The LUS nomenclature repeat sequences, for the examples specified above, are shown in red text. Secondary reference regions are indicated by blue text. Tertiary reference regions are indicated by green text. This is part of Table 1, reproduced from Just et al. [342] with permission from Elsevier.

Locus	Example Alleles Showing Reference Regions	Allele Designations		
		Repeat Unit	LUS	LUS+
CSF1PO	$(ATCT)_7 ACCT (ATCT)_3$	11	11_7	11_7_1
D10S1248	$(GGAA)_6$ GTAA $(GGAA)_7$	14	14_7	
D12S391	$AGGT(AGAT)_{11}(AGAC)_6 AGAT$	19	19_11	19_11_6_1
D13S317	$(TATC)_9$ $(aatc)_2$ $(atct)_3$ ttct gtct gtc	9	9_9	9_9_3_1
D16S539	$(GATA)_5$ GACA $(GATA)_4$	10	10_5	10_5_1
D17S1301	$(AGAT)_{10}$ AGGT AGAT	12	12_10	
D18S51	$(AGAA)_4$ AGGA $(AGAA)_{10}$ aaag agag ag	15	15_10	15_10_1
D19S433	ct ctct ttct tcct ctct $(CCTT)_{11}$ cctg CCTT cttt CCTT	13	13_11	13_11_1_1
D1S1656	ca $(caca)_2$ CCTA $(TCTA)_{12}$ TCA TCTG $(TCTA)_3$	17.3	17.3_12	17.3_12_1_1
D20S482	$(AGAT)_{11}$	11	11_11	
D21S11	$(TCTA)_4$ $(TCTG)_6$ $(TCTA)_3$ TA $(TCTA)_3$ TCA $(TCTA)_2$ TCCA TA $(TCTA)_{10}$	28	28_10	28_10_4_6

Interpretation of complex DNA profiles generated by massively parallel sequencing   **433**

Sample	Locus	Repeat Unit	LUS Concept Designation	Allele Coverage	Sequence
136	D12S391	19	19_12	57	(AGAT)12 (AGAC)6 AGAT
136	D12S391	20	20_13	395	(AGAT)13 (AGAC)6 AGAT
136	D12S391	22	22_14	25	(AGAT)14 (AGAC)7 AGAT
136	D12S391	22	22_13	74	(AGAT)13 (AGAC)8 AGAT
136	D12S391	23	23_14	330	(AGAT)14 (AGAC)8 AGAT

Parent Allele   20_13   23_14

	Stutter from the LUS	Stutter NOT from the LUS	Stutter from the LUS	Stutter NOT from the LUS
-1 Repeat Stutter	19_12	19_13	22_13	22_14
(% of allele signal)	(14.4%)	(0%)	(22.4%)	(7.6%)

Figure 13.2 Illustration of LUS concept product designations for stutter isoforms. Actual D12S391 ForenSeq typing results for a single-source sample were used to depict how multiple $n - 1$ repeat stutter products would be designated using the LUS concept. Stutter occurring from the LUS reference region would be represented as -1_-1, as compared to the parent allele, whereas stutter that occurs from any other region of the STR would be represented as -1_0, as compared to the parent allele. Reproduced from [302] with permission from Elsevier.

[ATCT]$_{12}$. This is designated 12_12. When sequence variation occurs with one of the ATCT repeats, the LUS block of ATCT repeats may occur before or after the interrupting sequence variant. For example, [ATCT]$_4$ GTCT [ATCT]$_7$ will be notated 12_7, whereas [ATCT]$_8$ ACCT [ATCT]$_3$ will be notated 12_8.

13.11.1 Extension to LUS+ nomenclature

The LUS nomenclature has a dual purpose: a) it can be used to identify variants that are indistinguishable using the RU nomenclature; b) the block repeats defined by the LUS sequence readily predict the sequences that are most likely to be generated by the $n - 1$, $n + 1$ and $n - 2$ stutters.

In an examination of a dataset of 1059 sequenced alleles for 27 aSTR loci [342], the defined LUS reference region was the longest uninterrupted stretch in > 99% of these allele sequences. The LUS nomenclature captured greater than 80% of the sequence variation observed amongst four population datasets of 777 individuals. Whereas the LUS nomenclature captures nearly all sequence variants for simple repeats such as TPOX, THO1, and D20S482, for more complex STRs with multiple block repeats, such as D21S11, D12S391, and FGA, the LUS nomenclature is insufficient (Fig. 13.3).

Just et al. [342] extended the LUS nomenclature to LUS+ to identify as many sequence variants as possible within the context of a notation that was easy to implement within probabilistic genotyping programs. Much of the variation is found in the LUS block repeats. With simple repeats, e.g., [AGAT]$_n$ found in D20S433, nothing beyond the original LUS nomenclature is required since variants, such as [AGAT]$_{12}$AGCT, are

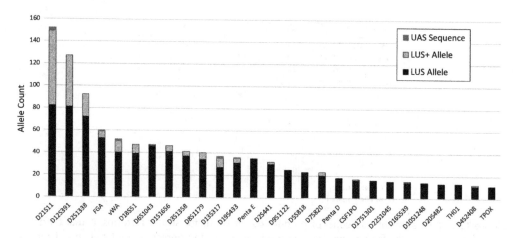

Figure 13.3 The histogram displays the number of unique sequence alleles by locus (n = 1059 in total) examined in this study. The solid blue bars represent the number of sequence alleles per locus differentiated by LUS allele designations, whereas the striped blue bars denote the additional number of alleles per locus differentiated by LUS+ designations. The red bars (at top) indicate the number of sequence alleles that are not resolved using the LUS+ allele designations. This figure is reproduced from [342] with permission from Elsevier.

rarely observed. CSF1PO is also a simple variant repeat [ATCT]$_n$, sometimes interspersed with a single CTCT, GTCT, or ACCT repeat. These variants are quite rare. There are two 11_7 variants observed, but one has an ATAT repeat, whereas the other has an ACCT repeat. The latter sequence is used as an LUS+ secondary identifier, giving the designation 11_7_1; 11_7_0 is reserved for the former. Each allele designation is tied to a specific sequence in the look-up table, so this prevents ambiguity.

In the D12S391 example cited in Fig. 13.2, the LUS sequence is [AGAT]$_{n1}$; the secondary sequence is [AGAC]$_{n2}$, and the tertiary sequence is AGGT (which is sometimes observed at the 5' end of the sequence). The secondary sequence signifies the second longest uninterrupted sequence and can be used to signify stutters in their respective repeat blocks, so that with the LUS+ notation, $n - 1$ stutters of 23_14_8_0 allele become 22_13_8_0 and 22_14_7_0, respectively. Since the tertiary sequence refers to a singleton repeat, this plays no part in stutter prediction, instead, it is used to identify rare variants.

Extension to LUS+ identified 1050 out of 1059 sequenced alleles, or more than 99.15% of the dataset.

The greatest information gain with the LUS+ notation is with complex loci, such as D21S11. This locus is a compound repeating sequence (Table 13.3). The LUS block of repeats is the terminal 3' [TCTA]$_{n1}$ sequence. The secondary block is provided by the first 5' [TCTA]$_{n2}$ sequence. A third (tertiary) repeat block is required to capture the majority of polymorphisms for this locus, the second block of repeats [TCTG]$_{n3}$.

Here there are three different possibilities, where stutters may arise. Theoretically, a single allele could give rise to nine different stutter types. In addition, it may be possible that stutters could arise simultaneously in two or more different blocks, which increases the number of possibilities. This has been observed by Li et al. [343], who identified additional complex stutter[2] products, such as $n-4$, $n-3$, $n-2$, and $n0$ repeats. However, these accounted for just 11% of the total number of stutter products. The $n0$ variants are the same molecular size as the parent allele, but simultaneously have a backward $n-1$ and forward $n+1$ stutter at different repeats. These "compound" stutters tend to be low-level, and a stutter filter of 3% is sufficient to remove most of them from data-sets (see supplementary Tables 2, 3 of Li et al. for a list of stutter ratios for specific loci).

Regardless, the LUS+ format does provide a basis to assist with stutter prediction that can be easily utilized by probabilistic genotyping models (and can be expanded as necessary). As further information becomes available it may be necessary to adjust the LUS+ nomenclature. Whether it is worthwhile extending models, such as *EuroForMix*, to specifically model all kinds of stutter is a moot point. Following the principle of Occam's razor,[3] it is preferable to keep programs as simple as possible, focusing upon the important information, rather than that which has little overall impact. It will never be possible to model all potential effects that may be encountered. However, rare events (such as complex stutters) can be accommodated by the drop-in model, which takes account by penalizing the likelihood ratio calculation. In Section 13.16, we show how to measure the information gain relative to a specific attribute of a model, using nomenclature and stutter as examples, to justify increasing its complexity.

13.12. Characterization of stutters with MPS

There is a detailed review of stutter characterization in Chapter 2.2. CE and MPS stutter based characteristics are comparable [344]. By far, the biggest influence is with $n-1$ stutter, but $n-2/n+1$ "complex" stutters are also observed.

MPS allows a much more detailed appraisal of stutter characteristics, because both the stutter proportion and its sequence are divulged. Vilsen et al. [345] compare the LUS method with the "block length of the missing motif". Using D12S391 as an example (Fig. 13.2), there are two blocks of repeats: [AGAT] and [AGAC]. When a stutter occurs, it originates from one block or the other. The longest block tends to produce the largest stutters, and there is a clear relationship illustrated by regression analysis of block length vs stutter ratio. The smaller block also stutters, but the stutter ratio is smaller, so that the regressions of the two types of block are not overlapping. In characterizing stutter ratio, each locus/allele block needs separate evaluation. For example, in D2S441,

Vilsen et al. [345] note that PCR process does not appear to differentiate between [TCTG] and [TCTA] repeats (i.e., the blocks should be combined to define the LUS). Woerner et al. [346] made similar observations, showing that flanking regions outside the block-repeating sequence has an influence on the block structure by introducing "quasi-repeats" that influence stutter characteristics.

Whereas, the characterization of stutters is complex, and dependant upon locus and allele sequence, the use of the LUS+ nomenclature [302,342] identifies allele blocks of varying lengths and is similar to the Vilsen et al. [345] method. Once an allele is identified, the challenge is to predict stutter sequences that need to be inserted into a "look-up" table. To facilitate this process, software packages such as *FDSTools* [341] incorporate a package *Stuttermark* [344], which automatically identifies potential $n-1$, $n-2$, and $n+1$ stutters based upon sequence (see Section 13.15 for further details). Stutters can be selectively filtered, using thresholds that are compared against the coverage of the parent allele. From the same package, *Stuttermodel* fits polynomial functions to the repeat length and stutter ratio to refine the expectations of stutter noise relative to the repeat length.

FDSTools can be used to predict the noise from stutter and other PCR artefacts, and this information can be used to devise specific thresholds based upon the artefact in question, and its allele specificity.

The alternative to filtering stutters, and other noise artefacts, is to model the variation within a probabilistic genotyping system. With *EuroForMix*, this is achieved on a per sample basis, across loci. Currently, only $n-1$ stutters are modeled. Filtering has the effect of limiting the threshold, where low-level profiles can be interpreted. Because $n-1$ stutters can reach levels $> 10\%$, the coverage of the parent allele, it may be preferable to leave these alleles unfiltered, especially if the mixture proportion $M_x < 10\%$ POI. Complex stutters, $n-2$ and $n+1$ repeats, tend to have much lower coverage, so that a filter of approximately 3% suffices to remove them [112]. Alternatively, they can be left and treated as drop-in, so long as the number of drop-in events does not violate independence assumptions predicted by the Poisson model, described in Chapter 4.2.1.

An improved understanding of stutter can lead to improved models following the methods described in Chapter 7.9. However, this comes at the expense of increased computation time. Whether such improvements also translate into significant *information gain* is dependent upon the level of contribution from the POI [233], i.e., very low level POI $Mx < 0.05$ may benefit from a consideration of complex stutters, but because of other unmodeled noise that may be present, we may be close to the limitations of the technique to carry out reliable analysis. The advantages of filtering vs not filtering are investigated further in Section 13.16.

13.13. MPS programming using *EuroForMix*

13.13.1 Automated conversion of sequence into RU/LUS/LUS+ nomenclature

To incorporate sequence information into *EuroForMix*, it is necessary to convert sequences into a simple nomenclature that can be based upon the conventional RU (repeat unit), or the LUS/LUS+ system devised by Just et al. [302,342]. To illustrate, file "seq2lusData/evids2.txt" contains a text file of raw sequence data derived from the ForenSeq Verogen universal analysis software (UAS). The nomenclature conversion is carried out using the R-program *seq2lus*. An online tutorial is provided at http://euroformix.com/seq2lus. Once loaded, the software provides the gui shown in Fig. 13.4.

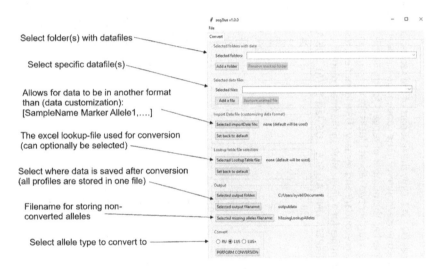

Figure 13.4 *seq2lus* gui showing file settings and conversion buttons.

To carry out the conversion, a look-up table file "LookupTable.xlsx" is used (Table S5 in Just et al. [342]). This file contains the sequences for all loci and their respective alleles, so far identified in the STRseq database, that are found in the ForenSeq kit. Note that as new alleles are discovered, the look-up table will require continual up-dates. An abbreviated example showing D21S11 sequences is provided in Table 13.4.

The table shows that multiple allelic variants are observed. For example for the D21S11 27 allele, there are three LUS variants: 27_10; 27_9; 27_8. These can be subdivided further using the LUS+ notation into 27_10_4_5; 27_10_4_6, etc., so that the original 27 allele has a total of six separated LUS+ variants; similarly, the 28 allele has eight variant LUS+ alleles.

Table 13.4 A portion of the look-up table for locus D21S11. Only the first part of the sequence is shown in column 1, to save space. Similarly, only the first two block repeats are shown in the STR sequence (column 2). The conventional repeat unit (RU) designation is provided. This is compatible with all CE-based nomenclature. The LUS is defined as the number of repeats for the last TCTA repeat (not shown), and this appears in the LUS allele nomenclature. For the LUS+ nomenclature, a further two repeat blocks are chosen, namely the first TCTA block and the adjacent TCTG block (shown in the STRseq column). These are used as secondary and tertiary LUS+ identifiers, respectively. Combining these two identifiers with the LUS designation in column 5 gives the LUS+ identifier for a given allele in the final column.

UAS SEQUENCE	STRseq	REPEAT UNIT ALLELE	LUS (last TCTA)	LUS ALLELE	SEC (first TCTA)	TER (TCTG)	LUS+ ALLELE
TCTATCTATCTAT	[TCTA]5 [TCTG]6	24.2	9	24.2_9	5	6	24.2_9_5_6
TCTATCTATCTAT	[TCTA]6 [TCTG]6	25.2	9	25.2_9	6	6	25.2_9_6_6
TCTATCTATCTAT	[TCTA]4 [TCTG]6	26	8	26_8	4	6	26_8_4_6
TCTATCTATCTAT	[TCTA]6 [TCTG]6	26.2	10	26.2_10	6	6	26.2_10_6_6
TCTATCTATCTAT	[TCTA]4 [TCTG]5	27	10	27_10	4	5	27_10_4_5
TCTATCTATCTAT	[TCTA]4 [TCTG]6	27	10	27_10	4	6	27_10_4_6
TCTATCTATCTAT	[TCTA]4 [TCTG]6	27	9	27_9	4	6	27_9_4_6
TCTATCTATCTAT	[TCTA]4 [TCTG]7	27	8	27_8	4	7	27_8_4_7
TCTATCTATCTAT	[TCTA]5 [TCTG]5	27	9	27_9	5	5	27_9_5_5
TCTATCTATCTAT	[TCTA]6 [TCTG]5	27	8	27_8	6	5	27_8_6_5
TCTATCTATCTAT	[TCTA]4 [TCTG]6	28	10	28_10	4	6	28_10_4_6
TCTATCTATCTAT	[TCTA]4 [TCTG]7	28	9	28_9	4	7	28_9_4_7
TCTATCTATCTAT	[TCTA]5 [TCTG]5	28	10	28_10	5	5	28_10_5_5
TCTATCTATCTAT	[TCTA]5 [TCTG]6	28	10	28_10	5	6	28_10_5_6
TCTATCTATCTAT	[TCTA]5 [TCTG]6	28	10	28_10	5	6	28_10_5_6
TCTATCTATCTAT	[TCTA]5 [TCTG]6	28	9	28_9	5	6	28_9_5_6
TCTATCTATCTAT	[TCTA]6 [TCTG]5	28	9	28_9	6	5	28_9_6_5
TCTATCTATCTAT	[TCTA]7 [TCTG]5	28	8	28_8	7	5	28_8_7_5

Interpretation of complex DNA profiles generated by massively parallel sequencing   **439**

Using *seq2lus*, in conjunction with the look-up table, three different conversions can be carried out: RU, LUS, or LUS+. A comparison is shown in Table 13.5. This output can be directly loaded into *EuroForMix*.

Table 13.5 Tables of *seq2lus* partial output comparing RU, LUS, and LUS+ allele notations, along with their respective peak heights. These tables can be input directly into EuroForMix.

RU notation

SampleName	Marker	Allele 1	Allele 2	Allele 3	Height 1	Height 2	Height 3
E2_01	CSF1PO	12	NA	NA	1221	NA	NA
E2_01	D10S1248	12	13	14	61	1346	731
E2_01	D12S391	21	22	NA	357	1661	NA
E2_01	D13S317	10	11	8	1072	866	33
E2_01	D16S539	10	13	9	524	1295	383
E2_01	D17S1301	11.3	14	7	76	1527	820
E2_01	D18S51	10	23	NA	530	547	NA
E2_01	D19S433	10	17.2	NA	1041	686	NA
E2_01	D1S1656	15	15.3	NA	688	1259	NA

LUS notation

SampleName	Marker	Allele 1	Allele 2	Allele 3	Height 1	Height 2	Height 3
E2_01	CSF1PO	12_8	NA	NA	1221	NA	NA
E2_01	D10S1248	12_12	13_13	14_14	61	1346	731
E2_01	D12S391	21_11	22_13	NA	357	1661	NA
E2_01	D13S317	10_12	11_13	8_8	1072	866	33
E2_01	D16S539	10_5	13_13	9_8	524	1295	383
E2_01	D17S1301	11.3_8	14_14	7_7	76	1527	820
E2_01	D18S51	10_10	23_23	NA	530	547	NA
E2_01	D19S433	10_8	17.2_15	NA	1041	686	NA
E2_01	D1S1656	15.3_11	15_14	NA	1259	688	NA

LUS+ notation

SampleName	Marker	Allele 1	Allele 2	Allele 3	Height 1	Height 2	Height 3
E2_01	CSF1PO	12_8_1	NA	NA	1221	NA	NA
E2_01	D10S1248	12_12	13_13	14_14	61	1346	731
E2_01	D12S391	21_11_9_0	22_13_7_1	NA	357	1661	NA
E2_01	D13S317	10_12_3_0	11_13_3_0	8_8_3_1	1072	866	33
E2_01	D16S539	10_5_0	13_13_0	9_8_0	524	1295	383
E2_01	D17S1301	11.3_8	14_14	7_7	76	1527	820
E2_01	D18S51	10_10_1	23_23_1	NA	530	547	NA
E2_01	D19S433	10_8_1_0	17.2_15_0_0	NA	1041	686	NA
E2_01	D1S1656	15.3_11_1_0	15_14_1_0	NA	1259	688	NA

440   Forensic Practitioner's Guide to the Interpretation of Complex DNA Profiles

13.14. Demonstration of likelihood ratio calculations using *EuroForMix*

To illustrate, data were taken from two examples that can be downloaded from the book's website, along with the reference samples:

1. "2P_0.75ng10-1": This is a mixture composed of two contributors, who are denoted as JTO (major) and JUD (minor) in approximate 10:1 ratio, and a total of 0.75 ng of DNA.
2. "2P_0.375ng20-1": This is a mixture composed of two contributors JTO (major) and JUD (minor) in approximate 20:1 ratio, and a total of 0.375 ng of DNA.

The samples were analyzed using ForenSeq: 27 autosomal STR loci.

The propositions tested to calculate the likelihood ratios, with the person of interest (POI = JUD) were:

Conditioned
H_p: JUD + JTO
H_d: JTO + Unknown

Unconditioned
H_p: JUD + Unknown
H_d: Unknown + Unknown

Allele frequency tables were from the following files (African American):

RU: "NIST1036Freqs-AfAm-RU.csv"
LUS: "NIST1036Freqs-AfAm-LUS.csv"
LUS+:"NIST1036Freqs-AfAm-LUS+.csv"

Because the POI = JUD is the minor contributor in both samples, there is an expectation that alleles will be within the range of stutters; consequently, it was of interest to compare the effect applying the *EuroForMix* model with and without the $n-1$ stutter modeling option included. Because the evidence data showed classic degradation, this was also modeled in all analyses.

13.14.1 Analytical threshold (AT)

A global analytical (static) threshold $AT = 30$ reads was applied to all samples, regardless of whether stutter filters were applied.

13.14.2 Rules for stutter filtering

Stutter filter threshold (T_s) settings were determined empirically by Moreno et al. [347]; they are listed in Table 13.6. Stutters were identified as $n-1$, $n-2$, or $n+1$, relative to the parent allele n. However, we never know for certain if an allele in a stutter position is pure stutter, pure allele, or a mixture of the two. Consequently, stutter filters may sometimes remove allelic products, and the risks of this happening are increased when the POI is a minor contributor. If stutter filtering was employed, alleles in stutter positions were removed if the coverage of $n-1$ was less than $T_{s=n-1} \times A_n$, where A_n is the coverage of the parent n allele. The UAS stutter filter thresholds for $n-2$ and $n+1$ were both calculated as $T^2_{s=n-1}$. Therefore $n-2$ stutters were removed if they were less than $T_{s=n-2} \times A_n$; alleles in $n+1$ stutter positions were removed if they were less than $T_{s=n+1} \times A_n$.

Table 13.6 Stutter filter thresholds reported by Moreno et al. [347] for ForenSeq UAS data analysis, used for the experiments.

Locus	$n-1$ **stutter**	$n+1/-2$ **stutter**
Amelogenin	0%	0%
D1S1656	30%	9%
TPOX	10%	1%
D2S441	17%	2.89%
D2S1338	25%	6.25%
D3S1358	20%	4%
D4S2408	28%	7.84%
FGA	30%	9%
D5S818	20%	4%
CSF1PO	30%	9%
D6S1043	20%	4%
D7S820	15%	2.25%
D8S1179	25%	6.25%
D9S1122	20%	4%
D10S1248	20%	4%
TH01	15%	2.25%
vWA	22%	4.84%
D12S391	33%	10.89%
D13S317	25%	6.25%
PentaE	15%	2.25%
D16S539	20%	4%
D17S1301	25%	6.25%
D18S51	30%	9%
D19S433	15%	2.25%
D20S482	20%	4%
D21S11	30%	9%
PentaD	7.5%	0.5625%
D22S1045	40%	16%

442 Forensic Practitioner's Guide to the Interpretation of Complex DNA Profiles

13.14.3 Noise

Moreno et al. [347] also describe the identification and removal of noise, based upon sequences that did not match alleles, or their stutter products from known individuals. These products were shown to be low-level (less than 50 reads), and were not commonly observed above the analytical threshold of 30 reads (in fact, for the two mixture examples, none were observed). Within the context of probabilistic genotyping, we treat noise as "drop-in" (Chapter 7.10). Consequently, there is no need to remove such alleles within our framework.

13.14.4 Experimental summary

To summarize: two different sets of experiments were carried out. The data came from the 1:10 and 1:20 mixtures. These mixtures were composed of two contributors, and the minor contributor (JUD) was chosen as the POI, to provide challenging data. Using *EuroForMix*, for each of the samples, the following analyses were carried out:

1. Analytical threshold ($AT = 30$ reads) in all cases.
2. Degradation model utilized in all cases.
3. Conditioned vs unconditioned models tested.
4. For each model, stutter filter vs. no stutter filter tested.
5. All analyses were repeated three times using the RU, LUS, and LUS+ nomenclature, where *LR*s were calculated using the corresponding frequency data.
6. Possible noise alleles were kept in all analyses and evaluated as drop-in.
7. An outline of the protocol is shown in Fig. 13.5,

i.e., a total of four different analyses per sample × three nomenclature comparisons for each, making a total of 12.

13.15. Automating the interpretation strategy

Much of the process that is outlined in simple terms in Fig. 13.5 can already be automated. Thanks to Jerry Hoogenboom (NFI) for the following explanation:

FDSTools [341] incorporates an initial data processing tool "TSSV" [348] that is used to identify repeat sequence blocks from raw sequence data. Each sequence read is scanned for user-input flanking sequences that are used for alignment. *STRnaming* identifies the repeating sequence blocks, and the best repeating structure is determined by calculating a score. The highest scores maximize the number of repeats, and minimize the number of interruptions in the sequence. This is important when it comes to stutters, since their prediction will be improved if based upon sequences that are optimized in this way. *STRnaming* provides a simple notation that can be converted back into sequence (including flanking region mutations). Furthermore, provided that marker specific rules are defined in the configuration file of *FDSTools*, there is full compatibility with CE-based nomenclature.

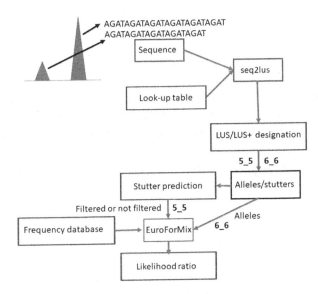

Figure 13.5 A schematic diagram showing the workflow from sequence to likelihood ratio. An allele and stutter are defined by their sequences. The *seq2lus* program converts the data into the LUS nomenclature, 6_6 and 5_5, respectively. The stutter model in *EuroForMix* identifies potential stutters; frequency databases are interrogated to produce the likelihood ratio.

FDSTools has two tools that are built specifically to identify stutters: *Stuttermark* and *Stuttermodel*. *Stuttermark* is the more primitive of the two, as it relies completely upon the user's input to adequately recognize stutter, and to tell it exactly how much stutter is to be expected. *Stuttermodel* is more sophisticated, as it is capable of detecting repetition in sequences all by itself, and it models the amount of expected stutter as a function of the length of the repeat. With *Stuttermark*, that is not the case—all stutters are equal.

Stuttermark first converts the raw sequences to a shortened "tssv-style" notation, e.g., [AGATAGTA]$_1$ [AGAT]$_{14}$ [CAGA]$_8$ [TAGATG]$_1$, where red (medium grey in print version) type indicates flanking sequence. To do this, the user is required to describe the STR structure of each locus so that *Stuttermark* is able to recognize the repeated sections. In the next version of *FDSTools*, the *STRNaming* algorithm [349] will be used to do this instead, which will improve usability.

With all the sequences converted to tssv-style notation, one more input from the user is required: the maximum amount of stutter that is expected to occur. The default value for this is 15% of $n-1$ stutter and 4% of $n+1$ stutter, but user-defined values can be used instead; any other whole number of repeats gained/lost can be defined as well. Normally that is not needed, because *Stuttermark* will apply the values of $n-1$ and $n+1$ stutter to *all* sequences in the file, regardless of whether they are allelic or stutter. Consequently, with default settings, it will already recognize $n-2$ stutter as a stutter

444 Forensic Practitioner's Guide to the Interpretation of Complex DNA Profiles

product of the $n-1$ stutter (provided the $n-2$ stutter product has less than 4% of the reads of the $n-1$ stutter product).

The software recognizes stutter in non–LUS positions, i.e., those repeats that may be identified as secondary or tertiary in the LUS+ nomenclature. User-supplied stutter thresholds are applied to all repeats in the sequence. In the example provided above, it will expect the same amount of $[AGAT]_{13}[CAGA]_8$ as $[AGAT]_{14}[CAGA]_7$. *Stuttermark* also tries different combinations of stutter, so that $[AGAT]_{13}[CAGA]_7$ is also detected as a "two times $n-1$ stutter" provided that it is below the maximum of $15\% \times 15\% = 2.25\%$. Sequences such as $[AGAT]_{15}[CAGA]_7$ are detected in a similar fashion. With default settings, any block that is repeated three or more times is treated as something that can produce stutter.

To summarize, *FDSTools* can automate the process that is illustrated in Fig. 13.5 up to the point, where the data are input into *EuroForMix*: it converts a sequence into recognized repeat blocks; applies a nomenclature; predicts all possible stutters; builds databases. The software has suites of filters for stutter, noise, and other artefacts.

The alternative to using filters is to deal with stutter and noise within the probabilistic genotyping environments offered by *EuroForMix*, described in the next section.

13.15.1 *EuroForMix* analysis

The settings used for all models are shown in Fig. 13.6.

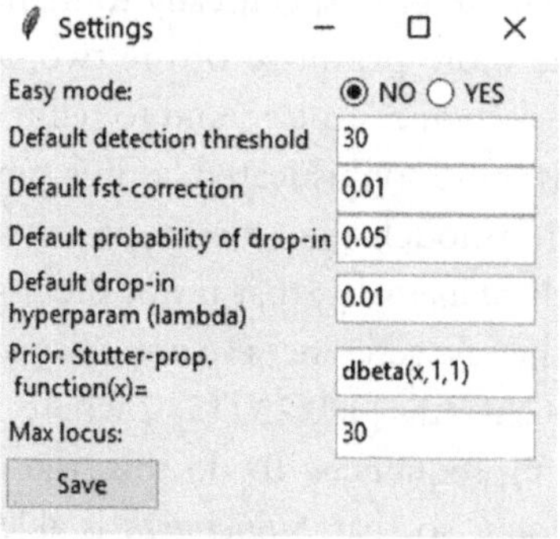

Figure 13.6 *EuroForMix* settings used in analyses.

The data were imported as shown in Fig. 13.7.

10:1 mixture (0.75 ng)

A number of loci were observed, where two or more allele sequences were present in the sample that could not be differentiated by the RU nomenclature. They benefited from the LUS/LUS+ nomenclature, as this system was able to separate and to identify the variants, thereby assigning reduced match probabilities to each, resulting in an increased

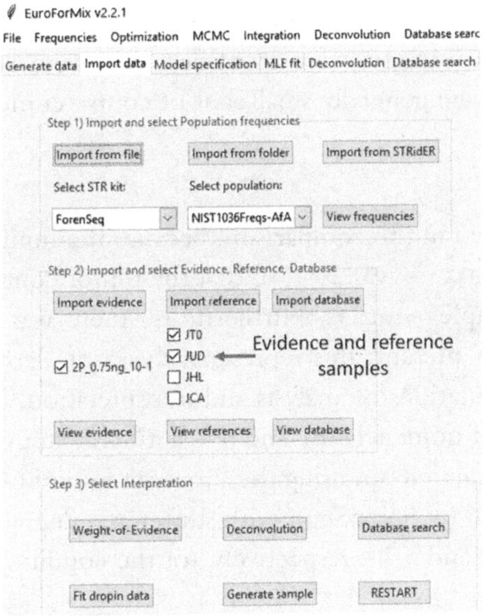

Interpretation of complex DNA profiles generated by massively parallel sequencing **445**

Figure 13.7 EuroForMix Import Data settings used in analyses.

likelihood ratio (Table 13.7). More details are provided below (conditioned model was used):

1. There were four loci, where allele variants were unresolved by the RU nomenclature: D3S1358 (allele 17); D8S1179 (alleles 14 and 15); D13S317 (allele 11); D21S11 (allele 29, three variants). For any given RU notation, the reads of the corresponding allelic variants were added together.

2. There were three variants at locus D21S11 (allele 29_10) that were unresolved by the RU nomenclature; two variants were identified by the LUS nomenclature (29_10 and 29_11). The 29_10 allele was further separated into two variants, namely 29_10_4_7 and 29_10_6_5. In terms of the observed LR relative to different nomenclature, the biggest effect was at the D21S11 locus. Using the RU nomenclature for this marker, the $LR = 1.29$; LUS nomenclature, $LR = 2.71$; LUS+ nomenclature, $LR = 26.99$. For the latter, the rare variant 29_10_6_5 allele had a frequency of 0.0088, compared to the LUS 29_10 frequency of 0.094.

3. Both of the alleles at the D8S1179 locus were separated into two variants each when the LUS/LUS+ notation was applied. However, the increase in LR for this marker was marginal ($LR = 1.84 \rightarrow 1.9$), because there was relatively small decrease in allele frequencies for the POI = JUD using LUS compared to RU notation.

4. The LUS notation returned higher LRs for both D13S317 and D3S1358.

446 Forensic Practitioner's Guide to the Interpretation of Complex DNA Profiles

5. Multiple loci, other than those listed in Table 13.7, also benefited from the LUS nomenclature, where variants were identified that were rarer in the population. The increased LRs were generally small, but of course cumulative over all loci.

20:1 mixture (0.375 ng)

This mixture was included in the comparison, because the limitations of interpretation were approached. The mixture was 20:1, so that the minor contributor was well within range of $n-1$ and complex stutters. Furthermore, there was an estimated 18 pg of minor contributor DNA present; this represents the equivalent of three diploid cells, which is close to the limitations of analysis and interpretation, hence it was interesting to ascertain the impact of nomenclature and $n-1$ stutter filter on these results.

1) If the analysis was carried out using the Promega Fusion 6C loci (excluding SE33, as this locus is not utilized by ForenSeq), with stutter and degradation model, the result would be $log_{10}LR = 3.89$ and 3.79, respectively, for the conditioned and unconditioned models.

2) The incorporation of seven extra loci with the ForenSeq kit increased the $log_{10}LR$ by less than an order of magnitude to 4.31 and 4.39, respectively.

13.15.2 Stutter filter effect

The stutter filter removed alleles that did not match either of the contributors. Because we know the ground-truth of these samples, it was possible to count the number of stutter alleles and determine those which coincided with contributor genotypes. Matching allele counts, i.e., the number of alleles that matched those found in the ground-truth genotypes were calculated for 10:1, 20:1 samples, with and without stutter filter using the LUS+ nomenclature (Table 13.8). For the 10:1 mixture, the stutter filter increased the effective drop-out from $0.2 \rightarrow 0.35$ by removing alleles that matched JUD. This was even more pronounced with the 20:1 mixture, the stutter filter resulted in an increased drop-out level from $0.39 \rightarrow 0.54$.

These estimates can only be made if we know the ground-truth. With casework samples, we never know the ground-truth, hence we cannot assume that "stutters" removed that happen to match a POI are true stutters (they could be allelic or a combination of allele and stutter).

13.16. Information gain: measuring the effect of the stutter filter and different nomenclatures

Increases in LR were reflected in the overall values relative to the various nomenclatures utilized (Table 13.9), also relative to stutter. To quantify the various effects of nomen-

Interpretation of complex DNA profiles generated by massively parallel sequencing **447**

Table 13.7 Table showing the change in *LR* relative to the nomenclature notation for 10:1 mixture (0.75 ng); utilizing the RU, LUS, LUS+ schemes, respectively, for the conditioned model. For example, with D21S11, there are three different sequences identified. The RU nomenclature defaults to allele 11 for all three sequences. However, the LUS nomenclature identifies two sequences as 29_10, and one sequence as 29_11. The latter is resolved by the LUS+ nomenclature that splits it into 29_10_4_7 and 29_10_6_5. The consequent improved resolution is reflected in the increased *LR*, shown in blue (medium grey in print version) type. The conditioned model, H_p: JTO + JUD; H_d: JTO + U, with no stutter filter was used. The $n - 1$ stutter predicted from the LUS+ nomenclature is shown in the right hand column.

Locus		RU	LUS	LUS+	Predicted Stutter
D13S317	*LR*	12.4	21.17	20.37	
	Alleles	11	11_11	11_11_3_1	10_10_3_1
			11_12	11_12_3_1	10_11_3_1
D21S11	*LR*	1.29	2.71	26.99	
	Alleles	29	29_10	29_10_4_7	28_9_4_7
				29_10_6_5	28_9_6_5
			29_11	29_11_4_6	28_10_4_6
D3S1358	*LR*	1.87	2.71	2.83	
	Alleles	17	17_13	17_13_3	16_12_3
			17_14	17_14_2	16_13_2
D8S1179	*LR*	1.84	1.9	1.94	
		14	14_11	14_11_1_0	13_10_1_0
	Alleles		14_12	14_12_1_0	13_11_1_0
		15	15_12	15_12_1_0	14_11_1_0
			15_13	15_13_1_0	14_12_1_0

Table 13.8 Matching allele counts (MAC) recorded for the two mixtures JTO:JUD, comparing the effect of the stutter filter, using the LUS+ nomenclature. The effective drop-out level for JUD is calculated as $1 - (MAC/54)$.

Mixture	Stutter	JTO	JUD	Drop-out
10:1	Stutter included	54	43	0.20
	Stutter filtered	54	35	0.35
20:1	Stutter included	54	33	0.39
	Stutter filtered	54	25	0.54

clature and stutter, we utilized the information gain value (*IG*), a modified idea from [84,233][4]:

$$IG_{RU \to LUS} = log_{10}LR_{LUS} - log_{10}LR_{RU} \tag{13.2}$$

$$IG_{RU \to LUS+} = log_{10}LR_{LUS+} - log_{10}LR_{RU} \tag{13.3}$$

448 Forensic Practitioner's Guide to the Interpretation of Complex DNA Profiles

The IG measures the relative increase (or decrease) of the $log_{10}LR$ when LUS is used instead of RU notation (Eq. (13.2)). A similar measurement was made to describe the information gain when comparing RU with LUS+ (Eq. (13.3)). Finally, the measurements were repeated to evaluate the effect of using a stutter filter in the model, compared to analysis of the data, where no alleles were omitted, $AT = 30$ reads. The results of the IG tests are shown in Table 13.9. The greatest effect in information gain of around two or more orders of magnitude are highlighted. The $log_{10}LR$s for the 10:1 mixture are similar, regardless of whether the conditioned or unconditioned models were analyzed. In all cases, there was information gain when a higher-order nomenclature was used, at least two orders of magnitude for RU→LUS+ comparisons. Use of the stutter filter always reduced the LR. Nevertheless, for this sample $log10LR > 9$, hence for reporting purposes, the probative impact would not be compromised.

The same cannot be said to be true for the 1:20 sample, where the drop-out of alleles is significantly greater, leading to much lower $log_{10}LR \approx 4$ that could potentially be described as borderline for reporting purposes. However, utilization of LUS/LUS+ nomenclature increases the $log_{10}LR > 6$, provided that the unfiltered data was analyzed. The effect was much lower with stutter filtered data (since many probative alleles had been removed); the unconditioned data were hardly affected by the use of higher-order nomenclature.

Table 13.9 $Log_{10}LR$ comparisons across different nomenclatures and with/without stutter filter applied. Two different mixture ratios and DNA quantities are compared: JTO:JUD, 1:10 (0.75 ng) and 1:20 (0.375 ng). The propositions tested for JTO conditioned are H_p: JTO + JUD; H_d: JTO + U, and for unconditioned, the propositions were H_p:JUD + U; H_d:U + U. In all cases, degradation was modeled. Stutter was modeled for unfiltered profiles, whereas for stutter-filtered profiles, the stutter option was not modeled. Information gain (IG) is calculated as $IG = log_{10}LR_a - log_{10}LR_b$, where $a = LR_{RU}$ and $b = LR_{LUS}$ for the RU→ LUS column, and $a = LR_{LUS}$ and $b = LR_{LUS+}$ for the RU→ LUS+ column. The largest increases in likelihood ratio are denoted by the blue (grey in print version) cells.

		Nomenclature			Information gain	
1: 10 (0.75 ng) mixture	Conditioning	RU	LUS	LUS+	RU→ LUS	RU→ LUS+
Stutter included	JTO conditioned	11.69	12.52	13.61	0.83	1.92
	Unconditioned	11.47	12.36	13.47	0.89	2.00
Stutter filtered	JTO conditioned	9.92	12.06	12.3	2.14	2.38
	Unconditioned	9.5	11.51	11.75	2.01	2.25
1:20 (0.375 ng) mixture						
Stutter included	JTO conditioned	4.39	6.62	6.64	2.23	2.25
	Unconditioned	4.31	6.45	6.47	2.14	2.16
Stutter filtered	JTO conditioned	4.48	5.19	5.2	0.71	0.72
	Unconditioned	4.08	4.28	4.29	0.20	0.21

13.16.1 Information gain: comparing stutter filter vs no stutter filter

The data in Table 13.9 were used to compare the IG between stutter-filtered and unfiltered data. All except the 1:20 JTO conditioned set, interpreted using RU nomenclature, benefited if the stutter filter was not used, however, the differences were marginal. To summarize the effect of stutter filter and nomenclature together, comparing RU (stutter filtered)→LUS+(unfiltered), showed $IG > 3.6$ for the 1:10 mixtures, and > 2.1 for the 1:20 mixture. The effect is more important for low-level samples, because the increase in LR is significant; on the ENFSI verbal scale, the evidence would be described as showing very strong support for the first instance (RU, filtered) rising to extremely strong support (LUS+, unfiltered).

Table 13.10 Information gain relative to application of the stutter filter using the three different nomenclatures. Refer to Table 13.9 legend for explanation. In the final column, the information gain using the LUS+ nomenclature *without* the stutter is recorded relative to the RU nomenclature *with* the stutter filter.

		Information gain (stutter filter→no stutter filter)			
1: 10 (0.75 ng) mixture		RU	LUS	LUS+	RU → LUS+
	JTO conditioned	1.77	0.46	1.31	3.69
	Unconditioned	1.97	0.85	1.72	3.97
1:20 (0.375 ng) mixture					
	JTO conditioned	−0.09	1.43	1.44	2.16
	Unconditioned	0.23	2.17	2.18	2.39

The IG can be averaged with respect to entire datasets, comparing the different methods of analysis, and applying linear regression. An example is shown in Fig. 13.8, where a sample of data was taken from a variety of different two- to four-person mixtures using a variety of different DNA quantities, selecting only those data, where the RU $LR > 1$. The data shown are from a preliminary study that is currently underway. The purpose is to illustrate how the IG can be used to monitor improvements to models by making changes to the method used to analyze data (e.g., filtering vs. not filtering; RU vs. LUS+ nomenclature).

The regression analysis confirmed the trend for the LUS+ method to provide larger LRs. To summarize data trends, the IG is defined by two linear regression constants (b and c) defined by $y = c + bx$, using $IG_{x\to y} = y - x$:

$$IG_{x\to y} + x = c + bx$$

$$IG_{x\to y} = bx + c - x$$

$$IG_{x\to y} = x(b - 1) + c$$

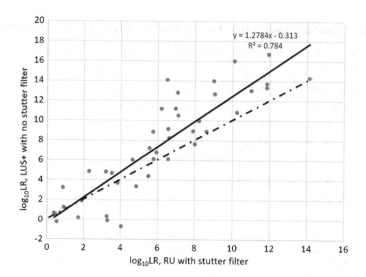

Figure 13.8 Regression analysis of a set of data, where *LR*s are analyzed using the basic RU method without filtering stutters, noise, and artefacts, compared with the LUS+ method where no stutters, noise, or artefacts are filtered. The solid line is the regression. The dashed line is the 45-degree line that shows the expectation if $x = y$.

In this example we estimated the trend:

$$IG_{x \to y} = x(1.28 - 1) - 0.313,$$

where $x = log10LR$ of the RU calculation (stutter filtered), and $y = log10LR$ of the LUS+ calculation (with stutter). The data show a general trend for the unfiltered LUS+ data to provide higher *LR*s compared to the RU data, and the effect is proportionate to the size of the LR. For example, if the RU $log10LR = 4$, then the expectation of the LUS+ $log10LR = 4.8$, whereas for higher RU $log10LR = 10$, then the expectation for LUS+ $log10LR = 12.5$. This is broadly in line with the observations shown in Table 13.10, but here we do not go further to analyze the finer details. From Fig. 13.8, there is clearly a lot of scatter in the data, so that some individual points do not appear to benefit from LUS+ (unfiltered) nomenclature. This research is still at an early stage. Consequently, issues relating to data preparation, filtering noise, stutter, and other artefacts, combined with the development of probabilistic genotyping to automatically take account of these phenomena, will provide a strong focus for future investigation.

13.17. Summary

1. The use of probabilistic genotyping software simplifies the analysis of complex DNA profiles. Apart from applying an analytical threshold, programming can take care of

$n-1$ stutters. It is also possible to deal with rarer $n-2/n+1$ stutters using algorithms, but there is a disadvantage of increased processing time.

2. Current software utilized by *EuroForMix* only incorporates $n-1$ stutter for the reasons that are outlined in Chapter 7.9. However, the LUS+ notation does provide a basis for predicting complex stutters. Most complex stutters will be based upon the LUS repeats, and are easily predicted. *FDSTools* also incorporates stutter prediction modeling.

3. Whereas it is important to model $n-1$ stutter for low-level POIs $Mx < 0.1$, the sequence reads of $n+1/n-2$ stutters are much lower, and are much less frequent. Either stutters can be filtered, or along with "noise" alleles, they can be treated as drop-in.

4. The increase in discriminating power that is offered by sequence-based nomenclature is important for low-level DNA profiles to provide probative *LRs*. There is considerable interest in building tools to process data (e.g., *FDSTools*) and to integrate with probabilistic genotyping software. This research is facilitated, because the programs mentioned are open-source and freely available.

5. To measure benefits of different strategies, it is important to be able to objectively measure the various effects. The information gain (IG) value was used as a simple means to do this. The method was applied to regression analyses to establish general trends with datasets.

Notes

1. STRBase https://strbase.nist.gov/STRseq.htm reports such an example with TPOX where a deletion in the flanking region converted an 11 allele to a 10.3 allele. The visualization depended on the multiplex kit used. Whereas PowerPlex 1.1 and Identifiler were unaffected, PowerPlex 2.1 and PowerPlex 16 products were affected because the primer binding sites were further away from the repeat structure.
2. Defined as any stutter that is not forward $n+1$ or backward $n-1$ in Chapter 7.9.6.
3. The principle states "Entities should not be multiplied without necessity." Attributed to English Franciscan friar William of Ockham (c. 1287–1347), a scholastic philosopher and theologian. It is sometimes paraphrased by a statement like "The simplest solution is most likely the right one." Occam's razor says that when presented with competing hypotheses that make the same predictions, one should select the solution with the fewest assumptions.
4. These authors used the information gain ratio $IG = log_{10}LR/log_{10}IMP$ where IMP is the inverse match probability of the POI.

APPENDIX A

Formal descriptions of the genotype probabilities

A.1. Extending the F_{ST}-formula to mixtures

Here we expand the formulae from Chapter 1.12.6 to calculate the genotype probability, $Pr(u|H)$, for multiple unknown contributors in set u and a specified proposition H, where sub-population structuring is accounted for (i.e., when $\theta > 0$). To take into account of sub-population structuring for multiple contributors in the calculation of $Pr(u|H)$, we repeat the formula already presented in Eq. (5.15). For a "newly observed" allele a, the "adjusted" conditional allele probability becomes

$$Pr(a|m_a, m_+) = \frac{m_a\theta + (1-\theta)p_a}{1 + (m_+ - 1)\theta} \tag{A.1}$$

where m_a is the previous number of times that allele a has been observed (these will be alleles from genotypes of both known contributors and known non-contributors under the specified proposition H), and $m_+ = \sum_a m_a$ is the total.

To calculate $Pr(u|H)$, for some proposition H, where u is the genotype set of unknown contributors, part of the full genotype set g (i.e., $u \subseteq g$), Eq. (A.1) is applied sequentially for each allele in u, to take into account the dependency, which will modify the probability of observed alleles compared to estimates without the correction:

$$Pr(u|H) = 2^h \prod_{a \in u} Pr(a|m_a, m_+) \tag{A.2}$$

where m_a, m_+ are added by one for each multiplication, and h is the number of heterozygote genotypes in the set u.

It is easiest to demonstrate with some examples. We will consider the H_d case, where none of the contributors are given as known; the suspect defined under H_p is a known non-contributor, meaning that the alleles of the suspect are already typed under H_d.

Example 1 (One unknown contributor). $g = (a, b)$, where a, b are already typed, giving $m_a = 1$ and $m_b = 1$, initially. This is the typical the case under H_d, where a suspect with genotype a, b is treated as a known non-contributor. The following sequential calculations are carried out:

453

1. $Pr(a|m_a = 1, m_+ = 2) = \frac{1\times\theta+(1-\theta)p_a}{1+(2-1)\theta} = \frac{\theta+(1-\theta)p_a}{1+\theta}$

2. $Pr(b|m_b = 1, m_+ = 3) = \frac{1\times\theta+(1-\theta)p_b}{1+(3-1)\theta} = \frac{\theta+(1-\theta)p_b}{1+2\theta}$

Last step: multiplication of the probabilities gives $Pr(g) = 2Pr(a|m_a = 1, m_+ = 2)Pr(b|m_b = 1, m_+ = 3)$, which is identical to the expression in (1.30). Again, we multiply by two, because the contributor is heterozygote, as also required in (A.2).

Example 2 (Two unknown contributors). $g = (a, b; a, a)$, where a, b are already typed once giving $m_a = 1$ and $m_b = 1$. The first two steps are the same as in example 1, but we will have two additional steps here (one for each allele):

1. $Pr(a|m_a = 1, m_+ = 2) = \frac{1\times\theta+(1-\theta)p_a}{1+(2-1)\theta} = \frac{\theta+(1-\theta)p_a}{1+\theta}$

2. $Pr(b|m_b = 1, m_+ = 3) = \frac{1\times\theta+(1-\theta)p_b}{1+(3-1)\theta} = \frac{\theta+(1-\theta)p_b}{1+2\theta}$

3. $Pr(a|m_a = 2, m_+ = 4) = \frac{2\times\theta+(1-\theta)p_a}{1+(4-1)\theta} = \frac{2\theta+(1-\theta)p_a}{1+3\theta}$

4. $Pr(a|m_a = 3, m_+ = 5) = \frac{3\times\theta+(1-\theta)p_b}{1+(5-1)\theta} = \frac{3\theta+(1-\theta)p_a}{1+4\theta}$

The last step is a multiplication of the probabilities calculated in steps 1–4, and multiplied by two, because contributor 1 is heterozygote.

Example 3 (Three unknown contributors). $g = (a, a; b, c; a, c)$, where a, b are already typed, giving $m_a = 1$ and $m_b = 1$ initially as in example 1. Additionally we also have $m_c = 0$.

1. $Pr(a|m_a = 1, m_+ = 2) = \frac{1\times\theta+(1-\theta)p_a}{1+(2-1)\theta} = \frac{\theta+(1-\theta)p_a}{1+\theta}$

2. $Pr(a|m_a = 2, m_+ = 3) = \frac{2\times\theta+(1-\theta)p_a}{1+(3-1)\theta} = \frac{2\theta+(1-\theta)p_a}{1+2\theta}$

3. $Pr(b|m_b = 1, m_+ = 4) = \frac{1\times\theta+(1-\theta)p_b}{1+(4-1)\theta} = \frac{\theta+(1-\theta)p_b}{1+3\theta}$

4. $Pr(c|m_c = 0, m_+ = 5) = \frac{0\times\theta+(1-\theta)p_c}{1+(5-1)\theta} = \frac{(1-\theta)p_c}{1+4\theta}$

5. $Pr(a|m_a = 3, m_+ = 6) = \frac{3\times\theta+(1-\theta)p_a}{1+(6-1)\theta} = \frac{3\theta+(1-\theta)p_a}{1+5\theta}$

6. $Pr(c|m_c = 1, m_+ = 7) = \frac{1\times\theta+(1-\theta)p_c}{1+(7-1)\theta} = \frac{\theta+(1-\theta)p_c}{1+6\theta}$

The last step is a multiplication of the probabilities calculated in steps 1–6, and multiplied by four, because of the two heterozygote variants, contributors 2 and 3.

A.2. Relatedness

A.2.1 Formulae for relatedness

The relationship between two individuals can be specified in terms of the "relatedness" parameter $\kappa_k = Pr$ (the two individuals shares k alleles by descent). The outcome is the set $\kappa = (\kappa_0, \kappa_1, \kappa_2)$, where $\sum_k \kappa_k = 1$. Table A.1 shows the corresponding relationship for different values of κ.

In our application, we are interested in the probability of observing the genotype of z (the unknown individual), given the related individual t_{rel} and the specified relatedness

Table A.1 The corresponding relationship for different values of κ.

κ_0	κ_1	κ_2	Corresponding relatedness
1	0	0	Unrelated
0	1	0	Parent/Child
1/4	1/2	1/4	Sibling
1/2	1/2	0	Uncle/Nephew/Grandparent/Grandchild/Half-sibling
3/4	1/4	0	Cousin
0	0	1	Twin (ident.)

between the two individuals (κ), $Pr(z|t_{rel}, \kappa)$. The probabilities in Table A.2 shows the conditional probabilities $Pr(z|t_{rel}, \kappa) = \frac{Pr(z, t_{rel}|\kappa)}{Pr(t_{rel})}$, where the formula for $Pr(z, t_{rel}|\kappa)$ can be found in [55]. The exact formulae for each different genotype outcome of profile z and t_{rel} for different specified relationships when $\theta = 0$ can be found in Table 5.7 in Chapter 5.5.

Table A.2 Probability of observing the profile of z, given the profile t_{rel} and the specified relatedness between the two individuals κ, assuming $\theta = 0$.

Allele sharing	Profile z	Profile t_{rel}	Probability $Pr(z|t_{rel}, \kappa)$
2	a,b	a,b	$2p_a p_b \kappa_0 + \frac{p_a + p_b}{2}\kappa_1 + \kappa_2$
2	a,a	a,a	$p_a^2 \kappa_0 + p_A \kappa_1 + \kappa_2$
1	a,b	a,c	$2p_a p_b \kappa_0 + \frac{p_b}{2}\kappa_1$
1	a,a	a,b	$p_a^2 \kappa_0 + \frac{p_a}{2}\kappa_1$
1	a,b	a,a	$2p_a p_b \kappa_0 + p_b \kappa_1$
0	a,b	c,d	$2p_a p_b \kappa_0$
0	a,a	c,d	$p_a^2 \kappa_0$

A.2.2 Extension with the F_{ST}-formula

Inclusion of θ corrections make the formulae in Section A.2.1 more complicated. However the principle is same as before. A correction of the allele probability as presented in Eq. (A.1) is carried out by taking into account the number of previously typed alleles.

We assume that before the probability of the genotypes are calculated, there are m_a, m_b, m_c, m_d number of previously typed alleles of the allele types a, b, c, d, being conditional references or known non-contributors under a considered proposition (this will be H_d for the *LRmix* and *EuroForMix* applications). We also define the sum $m_+ = \sum_a m_a$. Here we use the probability $Pr(a|m_a, m_+)$, as defined in Eq. (A.1), where m_+ and $\theta > 0$ are given as implicit. Table A.3 shows the probabilities $Pr(z|t_{rel}, \kappa)$ when $\theta > 0$ for different genotype outcomes of profile z and t_{rel}. When $\theta = 0$, the probabilities collapse to

456 Formal descriptions of the genotype probabilities

the formula, as defined in Table 5.7, Chapter 5.5. See also the tables in Section A.2.3 for explicit formulae when no known contributors are conditioned in the proposition.

Table A.3 Probability of observing the genotype of the unknown individual z, given the genotype of the related individual t_{rel} for a specified relatedness between the two individuals κ when θ/Fst correction is considered (i.e., in the case of $\theta > 0$). Here we have defined $p_0 = Pr(a|m_a, m_+)Pr(a|m_a + 1, m_+ + 1)\kappa_0$ if $z = a, a$ and $p_0 = 2 * Pr(a|m_a, m_+)Pr(b|m_b, m_+ + 1)\kappa_0$ if $z = a, b$.

Allele sharing	Unknown z	Related t_{rel}	Probability $Pr(z|t_{rel}, \kappa)$
2	a,b	a,b	$p_0 + \frac{Pr(a|m_a, m_+) + Pr(b|m_b, m_+)}{2}\kappa_1 + \kappa_2$
2	a,a	a,a	$p_0 + Pr(a|m_a, m_+)\kappa_1 + \kappa_2$
1	a,b	a,c	$p_0 + \frac{Pr(b|m_b, m_+)}{2}\kappa_1$
1	a,a	a,b	$p_0 + \frac{Pr(a|m_a, m_+)}{2}\kappa_1$
1	a,b	a,a	$p_0 + Pr(b|m_b, m_+)\kappa_1$
0	a,b	c,d	p_0
0	a,a	c,d	p_0

From here it is possible to extend the formulae to multiple contributors, where additional unrelated unknowns are involved. This is carried out in a similar way to that described earlier by applying the formula in Eq. (A.2). A simple example is provided in Chapter 5.5.5.

A.2.3 Specific relatedness formulae F_{ST}-correction

We now derive some specific examples from the formula in Section A.2.2, which are also used in *LRmix Studio*. Here we assumed that there are no conditional references under the H_d proposition, where the 1st unknown individual is considered as related to the POI considered under the H_p proposition. Hence we use the term t_{POI} as the profile of POI. The following tables show the probability of observing the unknown genotype of the related individual, given that it is related to the typed individual t_{POI} (for a given relationship).

The formulae for parent/child and siblings relatedness are given in Table A.4, the formulae for cousins relatedness; Table A.5 provides the probabilities for cousins, and Table A.6 for uncle/nephew, half-siblings, and grandparent/grandchild relationships.

Formal descriptions of the genotype probabilities   457

Table A.4 Conditional probabilities ($\theta \neq 0$) for the genotype z of an unprofiled person, given the genotype t_{POI} of her profiled sibling, or parent/child.

t_{POI}	z	Parent/child	Siblings
12,12	12,12	$\dfrac{2\theta + (1-\theta)p_{12}}{1+\theta}$	$\dfrac{1}{4}\left(1 + \dfrac{2(2\theta + (1-\theta)p_{12})}{1+\theta} + \dfrac{(2\theta + (1-\theta)p_{12})(3\theta + (1-\theta)p_{12})}{(1+\theta)(1+2\theta)}\right)$
	13,13	0	$\dfrac{(1-\theta)p_{13}(\theta + (1-\theta)p_{13})}{4(1+\theta)(1+2\theta)}$
	12,13	$\dfrac{(1-\theta)p_{13}}{1+\theta}$	$\dfrac{(1-\theta)p_{13}}{2(1+\theta)}\left(1 + \dfrac{2\theta + (1-\theta)p_{12}}{1+2\theta}\right)$
	13,14	0	$\dfrac{(1-\theta)^2 p_{13}p_{14}}{2(1+\theta)(1+2\theta)}$
12,13	12,12	$\dfrac{\theta + (1-\theta)p_{12}}{2(1+\theta)}$	$\dfrac{\theta + (1-\theta)p_{12}}{4(1+\theta)}\left(1 + \dfrac{2\theta + (1-\theta)p_{12}}{1+2\theta}\right)$
	12,13	$\dfrac{2\theta + (1-\theta)(p_{12}+p_{13})}{2(1+\theta)}$	$\dfrac{1}{4}\left(1 + \dfrac{2\theta + (1-\theta)(p_{12}+p_{13})}{(1+\theta)} + \dfrac{2(\theta + (1-\theta)p_{12})(\theta + (1-\theta)p_{13})}{(1+\theta)(1+2\theta)}\right)$
	12,14	$\dfrac{(1-\theta)p_{14}}{2(1+\theta)}$	$\dfrac{(1-\theta)p_{14}}{4(1+\theta)}\left(1 + \dfrac{2(\theta + (1-\theta)p_{12})}{1+2\theta}\right)$
	14,14	0	$\dfrac{(\theta + (1-\theta)p_{14})(1-\theta)p_{14}}{4(1+\theta)(1+2\theta)}$
	14,15	0	$\dfrac{(1-\theta)^2 p_{14}p_{15}}{2(1+\theta)(1+2\theta)}$

Table A.5 Conditional probabilities ($\theta \neq 0$) for the genotype z of an unprofiled person, given the genotype t_{POI} of her profiled cousin.

t_{POI}	z	Cousins
12,12	12,12	$\dfrac{2\theta + (1-\theta)p_{12}}{4(1+\theta)}\left(1 + \dfrac{3(3\theta + (1-\theta)p_{12})}{1+2\theta}\right)$
	13,13	$\dfrac{3}{4}\left(\dfrac{(1-\theta)p_{13}(\theta + (1-\theta)p_{13})}{(1+\theta)(1+2\theta)}\right)$
	12,13	$\dfrac{(1-\theta)p_{13}}{4(1+\theta)}\left(1 + \dfrac{6(2\theta + (1-\theta)p_{12})}{1+2\theta\cdot}\right)$
	13,14	$\dfrac{3(1-\theta)^2 p_{13}p_{14}}{2(1+\theta)(1+2\theta)}$
12,13	12,12	$\dfrac{\theta + (1-\theta)p_{12}}{8(1+\theta)}\left(1 + \dfrac{6(2\theta + (1-\theta)p_{12})}{1+2\theta}\right)$
	12,13	$\dfrac{1}{8(1+\theta)}\left(2\theta + (1-\theta)(p_{12}+p_{13}) + \dfrac{12(\theta + (1-\theta)p_{12})(\theta + (1-\theta)p_{13})}{(1+2\theta)}\right)$
	12,14	$\dfrac{(1-\theta)p_{14}}{8(1+\theta)}\left(1 + \dfrac{12(\theta + (1-\theta)p_{12})}{1+2\theta}\right)$
	14,14	$\dfrac{3}{4}\left(\dfrac{(\theta + (1-\theta)p_{14})(1-\theta)p_{14}}{(1+\theta)(1+2\theta)}\right)$
	14,15	$\dfrac{3(1-\theta)^2 p_{14}p_{15}}{2(1+\theta)(1+2\theta)}$

458 Formal descriptions of the genotype probabilities

Table A.6 Conditional probabilities ($\theta \neq 0$) for the genotype z of an unprofiled person, given the genotype t_{POI} of her profiled half-sibling, or uncle/nephew or grandparent/grandchild.

t_{POI}	z	Half-siblings, Uncle/Nephew, Grandparent/Grandchild
12,12	12,12	$\dfrac{2\theta + (1-\theta)p_{12}}{2(1+\theta)}\left(1 + \dfrac{3\theta + (1-\theta)p_{12}}{1+2\theta}\right)$
	13,13	$\dfrac{(1-\theta)p_{13}(\theta + (1-\theta)p_{13})}{2(1+\theta)(1+2\theta)}$
	12,13	$\dfrac{(1-\theta)p_{13}}{2(1+\theta)}\left(1 + \dfrac{2(2\theta + (1-\theta)p_{12})}{1+2\theta}\right)$
	13,14	$\dfrac{(1-\theta)^2 p_{13}p_{14}}{(1+\theta)(1+2\theta)}$
12,13	12,12	$\dfrac{\theta + (1-\theta)p_{12}}{4(1+\theta)}\left(1 + \dfrac{4\theta + 2(1-\theta)p_{12}}{1+2\theta}\right)$
	12,13	$\dfrac{1}{4(1+\theta)}\left(2\theta + (1-\theta)(p_{12}+p_{13}) + \dfrac{4(\theta + (1-\theta)p_{12})(\theta + (1-\theta)p_{13})}{1+2\theta}\right)$
	12,14	$\dfrac{(1-\theta)p_{14}}{4(1+\theta)}\left(1 + \dfrac{4(\theta + (1-\theta)p_{12})}{1+2\theta}\right)$
	14,14	$\dfrac{(\theta + (1-\theta)p_{14})(1-\theta)p_{14}}{2(1+\theta)(1+2\theta)}$
	14,15	$\dfrac{(1-\theta)^2 p_{14}p_{15}}{(1+\theta)(1+2\theta)}$

APPENDIX B

Formal description of the probabilistic models

B.1. Definitions

The steps provided in Chapter 1.7 to calculate the LR can be generalized by specifying the following proposition:

H: "K individuals are contributors to the evidence E, where $x \geq 0$ of these are unknown, and the remaining $J = K - x$ contributors are known individuals with genotype(s) $(g_1, ..., g_J)$, whereas V is the set of known non-contributors",

where in general we assume that the unknown individuals are unrelated, however in our applications, we may consider the 1st unknown under the defense proposition H_d as related to a typed individual.

We let the combined genotype vector of the K contributors be defined as $g = (g_1, ..., g_K)$. Here we let the last x genotype elements belong to the unknown contributors such that $u = (u_1, ..., u_x) = (g_{J+1}, ..., g_K)$ is the genotype vector for the unknowns.

The peak height of an allele a in the evidence E is given as y_a RFU. An analytical threshold AT is typically used to filter background noise and other artefacts, such that alleles present in the evidence profile have corresponding peak heights above this threshold, i.e., $E = \{a : y_a \geq AT\}$.

Furthermore, we define the allele population set for a given observed evidence E as

$$\mathbb{A} = \{E, Q\} \tag{B.1}$$

where $\mathbb{A}$ is the set of alleles in the evidence and Q is the "Q-allele" presented in Chapter 7.6.1, representing all possible alleles except as those in E. The set of possible genotypes for the unknown contributors, outcome $\mathbb{G}$, is defined through the set $\mathbb{A}$, as introduced in Chapter 1.3.2. Notice that we assign the allele frequency of allele Q as $p_Q = 1 - \sum_{a \in E} p_a$.

The evidence probability for a given proposition is calculated using the law of total probability, where all possible outcomes of the unknown genotypes u are considered:

$$Pr(E|H) = \sum_{u_1 \in \mathbb{G}} ... \sum_{u_x \in \mathbb{G}} Pr(u|H) Pr(E|g) \tag{B.2}$$

where we assume that the genotype information about the known contributors $(g_1, ..., g_J)$ and the non-contributors (V) are part of H.

459

460 Formal description of the probabilistic models

In the Chapters 1.3.1 and 1.12.6, we discussed how population statistics of $Pr(u|H)$ are defined based on allele frequencies using either the Hardy–Weinberg formula, or the sub-population formula.

The other component, $Pr(E|g)$, gives the probability of evidence DNA profile E, given the set of genotypes. Later in this section, we use "weight" instead of "probability" for $Pr(E|g)$, when the evidence outcome is continuous (as for the peak heights).

B.2. Extension to parameterized statistical models

The software *LRmix Studio* and *EuroForMix* define a "parameterized" probabilistic model for the $Pr(E|g)$ component, by extending it as $Pr(E|\beta, g)$, where β is the set of unknown parameters. To calculate $Pr(E|H)$, we need to take β into account.

A DNA-profile consists of M multiple markers such that the evidence is $E = (E_1, ..., E_M)$. When we condition on the model parameters β, the product rule can be used as follows:

$$Pr(E|\beta, H) = \prod_{m=1}^{M} Pr(E_m|H, \beta) \tag{B.3}$$

where we, for a given marker $m = 1, ..., M$, have

$$Pr(E_m|\beta, H) = \sum_{u_1 \in G} \cdots \sum_{u_x \in G} Pr(u|H) Pr(E_m|\beta, g) \tag{B.4}$$

If I independent replicates of the DNA-profile are obtained, the formula in Eq. (B.4) is extended to

$$Pr(E_m|\beta, H) = \sum_{u_1 \in G} \cdots \sum_{u_x \in G} Pr(u|H) \prod_{i=1}^{I} Pr(E_{m,i}|\beta, g) \tag{B.5}$$

where $E_{m,i}$ is the data observation at marker m for replicate i. In general, when considering $Pr(E|\beta, H)$, the evidence E consist of all the markers and all the replicated DNA profile of the evidence.

B.2.1 The likelihood for parameterized statistical models

When the evidence data $E = (E_1, ..., E_M)$ are observed, we can define the **likelihood function** of the defined parameterized model. The likelihood function for a specified proposition H is given as follows (we do not consider replicates here):

$$\mathcal{L}(\beta|H) = Pr(E|\beta, H) = \prod_{m=1}^{M} \left(\sum_{u_1 \in G} \cdots \sum_{u_x \in G} Pr(u|H) Pr(E_m|\beta, g) \right) \tag{B.6}$$

where the likelihood function only varies with the model parameters β, where we have fixated on the observed evidence E. The definition of the likelihood function is important for further inference of β, and is used to calculate the LR.

B.2.2 LR calculations for parameterized statistical models

In general, we consider a separate model parameter set β for each of the propositions: β_p for H_p, and β_d for H_d. By using the definition of the likelihood function from Eq. (B.5), we construct the LR as a function of the model parameter sets:

$$LR(\beta_p, \beta_d) = \frac{\mathcal{L}(\beta_p|H_p)}{\mathcal{L}(\beta_d|H_d)} = \frac{Pr(E|\beta_p, H_p)}{Pr(E|\beta_d, H_d)} \tag{B.7}$$

Both frequentist and Bayesian frameworks are used to make inference about the unknown parameters in a statistical model. The frequentist framework treats parameters as unknown values, and the aim is to make a point estimate. In the Bayesian approach, the parameters are considered as unknown variables, and prior distributions for the parameters are required.

B.2.2.1 The maximum likelihood approach

For the frequentist framework, the maximum likelihood estimation is a very popular choice of estimator, because it has elegant mathematical and statistical properties (i.e., it is well-defined and it has useful large-sample properties), typically requiring numerical optimization of the likelihood function. The maximum likelihood estimate of the unknown parameters β under a considered proposition H becomes

$$\hat{\beta} = \arg\max_{\beta} \mathcal{L}(\beta|H) \tag{B.8}$$

with the corresponding maximum likelihood value given as $\mathcal{L}(\hat{\beta}|H) = \max_{\beta} \mathcal{L}(\beta|H)$, hence an estimate for the probability of the evidence would be $Pr(E|\hat{\beta}, H)$.

Balding (2013) [70] and Cowell et al. (2015) [231] considered maximization under each of the propositions separately to construct the final LR:

$$LR_{ML} = \frac{Pr(E|\hat{\beta}_p, H_p)}{Pr(E|\hat{\beta}_d, H_d)} \tag{B.9}$$

where the underscore label ML indicate that the LR is obtained by maximizing the likelihood of the statistical model under each of the propositions by solving Eq. (B.8) for each of the propositions $H = H_p$, and $H = H_d$.

The *EuroForMix* software calculates the maximum likelihood–based LR (i.e., LR_{ML}) for both the qualitative (defined in Chapter 5) and the quantitative model (defined in Chapter 8) by solving Eq. (B.9).

B.2.2.2 The Bayesian approach

The Bayesian approach treats the parameters as unknown variables, hence it is meaningful to talk about distributions of the parameters. This approach requires a pre-defined *a priori* for the parameters, namely a joint probability density function $p(\beta)$. The definition of the prior makes it possible to perform the following marginalization (law of total probability for continuous situation), which provides the "model evidence" for the observation E for a given parameterized model under proposition H:

$$Pr(E|H) = \int_{\beta} Pr(E|\beta, H)p(\beta|H)d\beta \tag{B.10}$$

which is an integral over the domain of the parameter set.

Integration under both H_p and H_d gives

$$LR_B = \frac{\int_{\beta_p} Pr(E|\beta_p, H_p)p(\beta_p)}{\int_{\beta_d} Pr(E|\beta_d, H_d)p(\beta_d)} \tag{B.11}$$

which is also called the Bayes factor.

The Bayes factor gives an accurate assessment of the LR, although anchored in the choice of the prior of the parameters (in addition to the assumed parameterized statistical model). When the number of parameters increases, the integrals typically become very computationally demanding to calculate.

Furthermore, Bayes theorem provides a formula to update the knowledge about the unknown β parameters under a given proposition H by calculating the posterior distribution:

$$Pr(\beta|E, H) = \frac{Pr(E|\beta, H)p(\beta|H)}{Pr(E|H)} \tag{B.12}$$

Hence, we see that the marginalized expression $Pr(E|H)$ from Eq. (B.10) is a normalization factor of the posterior distribution. Instead of using the maximum likelihood estimate in the frequentistic framework, one could also use chosen statistics (e.g., mean, median, lower or upper quantiles) from the posterior distribution as a point estimate provided in the Bayesian framework. However, the posterior distribution can sometimes be difficult to obtain analytically, because of the model evidence factor in the denominator in Eq. (B.12). To avoid calculating this factor, one typically uses stochastic simulations, such as Markov Chain Monte Carlo methods.

B.3. Mathematical details of the probabilistic models

B.3.1 The contribution from assumed genotypes

The assumed combined genotype vector of K contributors is defined as $g = (g_1, ..., g_K)$. We assume that each contributor has exactly two alleles such that $g_k = (g_k^1, g_k^2)$. We define

$n_{a,k}$ to be the number of alleles of type a, which contributor k with genotype g_k has:

$$n_{a,k} = \mathbb{I}(a = g_k^1) + \mathbb{I}(a = g_k^2) \in \{0, 1, 2\} \qquad (B.13)$$

where $\mathbb{I}(x)$ is one if x is true, and zero if x is false. For instance, if $g_k = (a, a)$, then $n_{a,k} = 2$, and $n_{b,k} = 0$ for $b \neq a$. For $g_k = (a, b)$; $n_{a,k} = 1$, and $n_{b,k} = 1$. In addition, we define the total contribution at allele a as

$$n_a = \sum_{k=1}^{K} n_{a,k} \qquad (B.14)$$

The evidence profile has corresponding peak heights above the analytical threshold ($y_a \geq AT$). Before moving to the formula, we first define three possible different events (mutually exclusive and exhaustive) for an allele a:

1. $A = \{a : y_a \geq AT \cap n_a > 0\}$ is the contribution set. These are alleles, which any of the contributors may have, and where the peak heights are above the analytical threshold.
2. $B = \{a : y_a < AT \cap n_a > 0\}$ is the drop-out set. These are alleles, which any of the contributors may have, and where the peak heights are below the analytical threshold.
3. $C = \{a : y_a \geq AT \cap n_a = 0\}$ is the drop-in set. These are alleles, which none of the contributors have, but where the peak heights are above the analytical threshold.

B.3.2 Mathematical details of the qualitative model

The statistical model behind the *LRmix Studio* software is based on the definition by Curran et al. [220]. Here the model extended the use of the drop-out/drop-in model from Gill et al. [142] by also including the possibility of mixtures and correction for sub-population (F_{ST}-correction). Below we give a mathematical description of the model and further discuss a different framework to take into account the unknown parameters in the model, as introduced in Appendix B.2.2.

The qualitative model only uses the information about whether an allele a is present or absent, i.e., whether the corresponding peak height y_a is above the analytical threshold AT or not. This means that an observed allele has either not dropped out, or is a drop-in event. The ingredients of the qualitative model defined in *LRmix Studio* are as follows:

The probability that contributor k has an allele drop-out from a heterozygote genotype is defined with parameter d_k (one for each of the contributors $k = 1, ..., K$). In the case of homozygote genotype drop-out, the probability is defined as d_k^2.

We first consider the description without assuming any allele drop-in model. The likelihood of the evidence profile E, given the assumed genotype set $g = (g_1, ..., g_K)$ and parameter set $\beta = (d_1, .., d_K)$, is given as

$$Pr(E|\beta, g) = \underbrace{\left[\prod_{a \in A}\left(1 - \prod_{k=1}^{K} d_k^{n_{a,k}}\right)\right]}_{\text{Contribution part}} \underbrace{\left[\prod_{a \in B}\prod_{k=1}^{K} d_k^{n_{a,k}}\right]}_{\text{Drop-out part}} \quad (B.15)$$

In *LRmix Studio*, there is a possibility to fix the drop-out probability parameters for any of the conditional references to certain values, and let the drop-out probability for the remaining unknown contributors to be equal (a common parameter). This reduces the number of unknown parameters to only one. When all contributors share the same drop-out probability parameter d, formula in (B.15) simplifies to

$$Pr(E|\beta, g) = \left[\prod_{a \in A}\left(1 - d^{n_a}\right)\right]\left[\prod_{a \in B} d^{n_a}\right] \quad (B.16)$$

The formula above does not take allele drop-in into account. We introduce the drop-in parameter p_C indicating the probability that an allele peak height is above the threshold when there are no contributors for it. If such an event occurs for allele a (i.e., a is in the drop-in set $C = \{a : \gamma_a \geq AT \cap n_a = 0\}$), then the $Pr(E|\beta, g)$ expression above includes the additional product $p_C * p_a$, where p_a is the allele frequency for allele a. If none of the alleles are explained as a drop-in, then instead the $Pr(E|\beta, g)$ expression includes $(1 - p_C)$ as a product. An alternative way to model drop-in for a qualitative model is given in the appendix of [68]. For *LRmix Studio* and other probabilistic models, the drop-in parameter is estimated (pre-calibrated) based on validation data with the same settings as those used to provide the evidence profile (see Chapter 7.10 for more details).

B.3.3 Inference of the drop-out parameter

In this section, we consider LR as a function of the drop-out probability parameter as defined in Section B.2.2, $LR(\beta_p, \beta_d)$, where β_p and β_d are the unknown drop-out parameters under the H_p and H_d propositions, respectively.

B.3.3.1 A maximum likelihood approach

For this approach, we assume a different set of parameters under each of the alternative propositions. If we consider the drop-out parameter $\beta = d$, used in the *LRmix* implementation, we estimate the LR as follows using Eq. (B.9):

$$LR_{ML} = \frac{Pr(E|\hat{d}_p, H_p)}{Pr(E|\hat{d}_d, H_d)} \quad (B.17)$$

where $\hat{d}_p$ and $\hat{d}_d$ are the maximum likelihood estimation of d using Eq. (B.8), carried out separately under H_p and H_d.

This maximum likelihood approach of LR, based on the qualitative model, has been shown to perform well [236], and is also used in investigative search algorithms as part of the software *CaseSolver* [274] and *dnamatch2* [294].

B.3.3.2 A conservative approach

In the *LRmix Studio* software, it is assumed that the model parameters are shared for the two propositions: $\beta_p = \beta_d = d$, such that LR is a function of the drop-out parameter d:

$$LR(d) = LR(\beta_p = d, \beta_d = d) \tag{B.18}$$

A Monte Carlo method is used to estimate the posterior distribution of the drop-out parameter d using the total number of alleles in the profiles as evidence data (as described in Section 6.1.5). Furthermore, both the 5% and the 95% quantiles of the posterior distribution for the drop-out parameter d are estimated (uniform distribution of the drop-out parameter is considered), separately for each propositions:

$$H_p: \quad \hat{d}_p^{.05}, \hat{d}_p^{.95}$$
$$H_d: \quad \hat{d}_d^{.05}, \hat{d}_d^{.95}$$

The four drop-out estimates of d are further plugged into the LR formula in Eq. (B.18), and a final (conservative) LR is calculated as follows:

$$LR = min\{LR(\hat{d}_p^{.05}), LR(\hat{d}_p^{.95}), LR(\hat{d}_d^{.05}), LR(\hat{d}_d^{.95})\} \tag{B.19}$$

B.3.4 Mathematical details of the quantitative model

An illustration of the gamma model used by *EuroForMix* is already described in Chapter 7.5, using a series of excel spreadsheets to allow the user to directly interact with the details of the model. A more formal description of the model follows here.

In this section, we replace the "probability" $Pr(E|\beta, g)$ as part of the likelihood function in Eq. (B.6) with the "weight expression" $w(E|\beta, g)$, because the evidence will be considered as continuous variables (the peak heights).

We first consider the description without assuming any allele drop-in model (defined later). The likelihood of the evidence profile E, given the assumed genotype set $g = (g_1, ..., g_K)$ and parameter set β, is given as

$$w(E|\beta, g) = \underbrace{\left[\prod_{a \in A} f(\gamma_a|\beta, g)\right]}_{\text{Contribution part}} \underbrace{\left[\prod_{a \in B} F(T|\beta, g)\right]}_{\text{Drop-out part}} \tag{B.20}$$

466 Formal description of the probabilistic models

where f and F are the probability and cumulative density functions of the peak heights, respectively, and A is the contribution set and B is the drop-out set, as defined in Section B.3.1.

B.3.5 The gamma distribution

In *EuroForMix*, we assume that the peak heights Y follow a gamma distribution that is parameterized by the shape and scale parameters:

$$Y \sim gamma(\gamma|shape, scale) = \frac{scale^{-shape}}{\Gamma(shape)} \gamma^{shape-1} \exp^{-\frac{\gamma}{scale}} \tag{B.21}$$

where $\Gamma(z) = \int_0^\infty x^{z-1} e^{-x} dx$ is the gamma function. By definition, the expectation and variance of Y is given as $E[Y] = shape * scale$ and $Var[Y] = shape * scale^2$. Furthermore, the definition of the coefficient-of-variation of Y is given as $CV[Y] = \frac{\sqrt{Var[Y]}}{E[Y]} = shape^{-\frac{1}{2}}$. Cowell et al. [234] originally followed the shape-scale parameterization in their paper, but also considered a parameterization based on the expectation and coefficient-of-variation, which gave an easier interpretation, letting $\mu = shape * scale$ and $\omega = shape^{-\frac{1}{2}}$, so that $\mu = E[Y]$, and $\omega = CV[Y]$. From this, it follows that $shape = \frac{1}{\omega^2}$, and $scale = \mu\omega^2$, and so the density function of peak height Y becomes

$$f_Y(\gamma|\beta) = \frac{\gamma^{(\frac{1}{\omega^2}-1)}}{\Gamma(\frac{1}{\omega^2})(\mu\omega^2)^{\frac{1}{\omega^2}}} \exp^{-\frac{\gamma}{\mu\omega^2}} \tag{B.22}$$

An example of the gamma density function is shown in Fig. B.1, where the distribution is related to the peak height of a single peak height observed with CE. The distribution describes the variability of the peak height if the experiment has been reproduced an infinite number of times.

B.3.6 Model for a single contributor

In this section, we assume a single ($K = 1$) contributor, such that $g = g_1 = (g_1^1, g_1^2)$ is the assumed genotype for the contributor, containing alleles g_1^1 and g_1^2. Hence, for one contributor, each possible allele in a marker can potentially be expressed by either zero, one, or two alleles. Here we let n_a be the contribution at allele a, as defined in Eq. (B.13) (without the k index, because of a single contributor).

EuroForMix assumes that the contributor n_a is scaled with the shape parameter in Eq. (B.22) such that the distribution of the peak height of allele a conditional on a selected genotype g becomes

$$f(\gamma_a|\beta, g) = \frac{\gamma_a^{(\alpha_a-1)}}{\Gamma(\alpha_a)(\mu\omega^2)^{\alpha_a}} \exp^{-\frac{\gamma_a}{\mu\omega^2}} \tag{B.23}$$

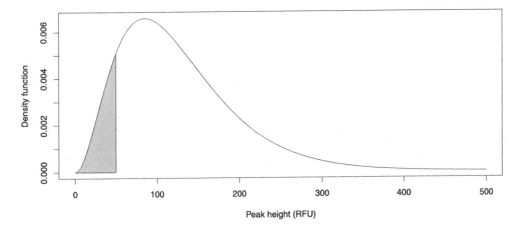

Figure B.1 The probability density function for a gamma distributed allele peak height. The grey shaded area defined from zero to 50 RFU gives the drop-out probability for the allele.

where $\alpha_a = \frac{n_a}{\omega^2}$ is the updated shape argument depending on the assumed g genotype using Eq. (B.13). The corresponding expectation and variance become $E[Y_a|\beta, g] = \mu n_a$, and $Var[Y_a|\beta, g] = (\mu\omega^2) n_a$ respectively.

If $n_a = 1$, one heterozygote allele contribution, we return to the density function in Eq. (B.22). Notice that the coefficient-of-variation (CV) of peak height Y_a is given as $\frac{\sqrt{Var[Y_a|\beta, g]}}{E[Y_a|\beta, g]} = \omega n_a^{-\frac{1}{2}}$. Parameters μ and ω correspond to the expectation, and CV of a heterozygote contributing peak height ($n_a = 1$).

B.3.6.1 Example 1

An evidential sample was observed with alleles $(5, 7)$ with corresponding peak heights y_5 and y_7. The LR is calculated for the alternative propositions H_p: "The POI with genotype $(5, 7)$ is a contributor" vs H_d: "An unknown, unrelated individual is a contributor."

Under H_p, $g = (5, 7)$ is the genotype for the known contributor, hence $Pr(5, 7|H_p) = 1$. Since $G_p = (5, 7)$ is the only genotype outcome under H_p,

$$Pr(E|\beta_p, H_p) = \sum_{g \in G_p} w(E|\beta_p, g) Pr(g|H_p) = f(y_5|n_5 = 1, \beta_p) f(y_7|n_7 = 1, \beta_p) \quad (B.24)$$

In this example, neither drop-out nor drop-in is assumed, so under H_d, the only possible genotype for the unknown unrelated individual is $g = (5, 7)$. The probability of this genotype is estimated with $Pr(5, 7|H_d) = 2p_5 p_7$ with allele frequencies p_5, p_7. Since $G_d = (5, 7)$ is the only genotype outcome under H_d, then

$$Pr(E|\beta_d, H_d) = \sum_{g \in G_d} w(E, g|\beta_d) Pr(g|H_d) = f(y_5|n_5 = 1, \beta_d) f(y_7|n_7 = 1, \beta_d) 2p_5 p_7 \quad (B.25)$$

468 Formal description of the probabilistic models

Hence the LR becomes

$$LR(\beta_p, \beta_d) = \frac{f(\gamma_5|n_5 = 1, \beta_p)f(\gamma_7|n_7 = 1, \beta_p)}{f(\gamma_5|n_5 = 1, \beta_d)f(\gamma_7|n_7 = 1, \beta_d)2p_5p_7} \tag{B.26}$$

which reduces to the conventional $\frac{1}{2p_5p_7}$ when $\beta_p = \beta_d$.

B.3.7 Model for multiple contributors

We now extend the model from one contributor to K number of contributors, where the vector of the K combined genotypes is defined as $g = (g_1, ..., g_K)$. The contribution from individual k with genotype g_k at allele a is given as $n_{a,k}$, as defined in Eq. (B.13).

In *EuroForMix*, the relative contribution from k at allele a is given as $\pi_k n_{a,k}$, where the parameter π_k is called the mixture proportion, which is a value between zero and one, and the sum of all the mixture proportion parameters are equal to one, i.e., $\sum_{k=1}^{K} \pi_k = 1$. For $K = 2$ contributors for instance, $\pi_2 = 1 - \pi_1$, and hence only one parameter is needed to explain the mixture proportions of the contributors.

We extend the formula in Eq. (B.14), which defines the total genotype contribution at allele a, by including the mixture proportion parameter:

$$n_a = n_a(\pi) = \sum_{k=1}^{K} \pi_k n_{a,k} \tag{B.27}$$

Additive assumption: *EuroForMix* assumes that the peak height at allele a is based on the sum of the peak height contribution from the K contributions, given assumed genotype g:

$$Y_a|g = \sum_{k=1}^{K} Y_{a,k}|g \tag{B.28}$$

where $Y_{a,k}|g \sim gamma(shape = \frac{\pi n_{a,k}}{\omega^2}, scale = \mu\omega^2)$, as defined in Section B.3.5.

Notice that the shape parameters are simply added when summing gamma-distributed variables with identical scale argument, such that

$$Y_a|g \sim gamma(shape = \alpha_a, scale = \mu\omega^2) \tag{B.29}$$

where

$$\alpha_a = \frac{\sum_{k=1}^{K} \pi_k n_{a,k}}{\omega^2} = \frac{n_a}{\omega^2} \tag{B.30}$$

is a more general expression for the contribution formula, as defined in Eq. (7.12), where it now depends on the mixture proportions π_k for each of the contributors

$k = 1, ..., K$. Hence, the expected contribution at allele a for given g becomes

$$E[Y_a|g] = \mu \sum_{k=1}^{K} \pi_k n_{a,k} = \mu n_a \qquad (B.31)$$

B.3.7.1 Example 2

A crime stain has been observed with alleles $(5, 7)$ with corresponding peak heights y_5 and y_7. It is assumed that there are $K = 2$ contributors to the evidence. The alternative propositions for the likelihood ratio are H_p: "The POI with genotype $(5, 5)$ and one unrelated unknown individual are contributors" vs H_d: "Two unknown, unrelated individuals are contributors". Drop-in/drop-out are not assumed in this example.

Under H_p, genotype $g = (5, 5)$ for the contributor is known, hence $Pr(5, 5|H_p) = 1$ for contributor 1. Here $G_p = \{(5, 5; 5, 7), (5, 5; 7, 7)\}$ becomes the set of possible genotype outcomes under H_p:

$$Pr(E|\beta_p, H_p) = \sum_{g \in G_p} w(E|\beta_p, g) Pr(g|H_p) \qquad (B.32)$$

$$= f(y_5|n_5 = 2\pi_1 + \pi_2, \beta_p) f(y_7|n_7 = \pi_2, \beta_p) 2p_5 p_7$$
$$+ f(y_5|n_5 = 2\pi_1, \beta_p) f(y_7|n_7 = 2\pi_2, \beta_p) p_7^2$$

Under H_d it is assumed that two unknown contributors could contribute to the evidence in seven possible ways: $G_d = \{(5, 5; 5, 7), (5, 5; 7, 7), (5, 7; 7, 7), (5, 7; 5, 7), ...\}$, where the remaining variants are symmetric to the first three variants in the list. From this, it follows:

$$Pr(E|\beta_d, H_d) = \sum_{g \in G_d} w(E|\beta_d, g) Pr(g|H_d) \qquad (B.33)$$

$$= f(y_5|n_5 = 2\pi_1 + \pi_2, \beta_d) f(y_7|n_7 = \pi_2, \beta_d)(p_5^2)(2p_5 p_7)$$
$$+ f(y_5|n_5 = 2\pi_1, \beta_d) f(y_7|n_7 = 2\pi_2, \beta_d)(p_5^2)(p_7^2)$$
$$+ f(y_5|n_5 = \pi_1, \beta_d) f(y_7|n_7 = \pi_1 + 2\pi_2, \beta_d)(2p_5 p_7)(p_5^2)$$
$$+ f(y_5|n_5 = \pi_1 + \pi_2, \beta_d) f(y_7|n_7 = \pi_1 + \pi_2, \beta_d)(2p_5 p_7)(2p_5 p_7)$$
$$+ f(y_5|n_5 = \pi_2, \beta_d) f(y_7|n_7 = 2\pi_1 + \pi_2, \beta_d)(p_7^2)(2p_5 p_7)$$
$$+ f(y_5|n_5 = 2\pi_2, \beta_d) f(y_7|n_7 = 2\pi_1, \beta_d)(p_7^2)(p_5^2)$$
$$+ f(y_5|n_5 = \pi_2, \beta_d) f(y_7|n_7 = 2\pi_1 + \pi_2, \beta_d)(p_7^2)(2p_5 p_7)$$

Notice that the mixture proportion parameter π belongs to different parameter sets under each of the propositions (i.e., β_p under H_p, and β_d under H_d). The LR is given as $LR(\beta_p, \beta_d) = \frac{Pr(E|\beta_p, H_p)}{Pr(E|\beta_d, H_d)}$, depending on the parameters under each of the propositions.

B.3.8 Model for allele drop-out

EuroForMix defines allele drop-out to be an allele (from any of the contributors), which has a peak height below a detection threshold $AT > 0$. This threshold is referred to as the "analytical threshold" (AT), and it is used to remove background noise, very low allelic contributions and low-level stutters, to aid the interpretation.

Drop-out assumption: *EuroForMix* assumes that the drop-out probability for an unseen allele a is equal to the area under the peak height distribution curve (the density function of the gamma distribution) from zero to AT:

$$Pr(\text{Drop-out allele } a|g, \beta) = \int_0^{AT} f(x|\beta, g)dx = F(AT|\beta, g) \tag{B.34}$$

where F is the cumulative gamma distribution function (an integral over the probability density function f, as presented in Fig. B.1).

Note that this model takes into account the Q-allele, which is a drop-out event (this will be the only allele in set B when $n_Q > 0$ and stutters are not considered).

B.3.8.1 Example 3

In this example the evidence only has allele 7 with corresponding peak height γ_7, where POI has genotype $(5, 7)$, and one contributor is assumed. We let allele 5 be the Q-allele, because it is unobserved. The list of possible genotypes under H_d are $(7, 7); (Q, 7)$. In this example, it is assumed that drop-out is possible, and the alternate propositions are H_p: "The POI with genotype $(Q, 7)$ is a contributor" vs H_d: "An unrelated individual is a contributor".

Under H_p, genotype $g = (Q, 7)$ is known. There is a single contributor, hence it is the only possible outcome. The absence of allele 5 as an allele drop-out requires explanation; γ_5 may be below the defined analytical threshold AT, for instance, $AT = 50$ RFU. Recall discussion in Chapter 3.6 for further details. The likelihood of the observed evidence under the H_p is given as

$$Pr(E|\beta_p, H_p) = \sum_{g \in G_p} w(E|\beta_p, g)Pr(g|H_p) \tag{B.35}$$

$$= F(AT|n_Q = 1, \beta_p)f(\gamma_7|n_7 = 1, \beta_p) \tag{B.36}$$

Under H_d, we now have more possible genotypes for the unknown contributor than in example 1, since it is assumed that drop-out is a possibility. We do not consider the possibility of drop-in, so that the only possible set of genotypes is: $G_d = \{(7, 7); (7, Q)\}$. The likelihood of the observed evidence under the H_d is given as

$$Pr(E|\beta_d, H_d) = \sum_{g \in G_d} w(E|\beta_d, g)Pr(g|H_d) \tag{B.37}$$

$$= F(AT|n_Q = 1, \beta_d)f(\gamma_7|n_7 = 1, \beta_d)2p_Qp_7 + f(\gamma_7|n_7 = 2, \beta_d)p_7^2$$

Hence, the LR becomes

$$LR(\beta_p, \beta_d) = \frac{F(AT|n_Q = 1, \beta_p)f(\gamma_7|n_7 = 1, \beta_p)}{F(AT|n_Q = 1, \beta_d)f(\gamma_7|n_7 = 1, \beta_d)2p_Qp_7 + f(\gamma_7|n_7 = 2, \beta_d)p_7^2} \quad (B.38)$$

B.3.9 Model for allele drop-in

Additional peaks in the evidence that are not to be explained by any of the contributors may be drop-in events (discussed in Chapter 7.10). The following demonstration does not include stutter.

Drop-in assumption: The drop-in model in *EuroForMix* is an exponential distribution with parameter λ, which determines the slope of the density function. If allele a is a drop-in event with corresponding peak heights γ_a, the probability that this is drop-in is given as

$$Pr(\text{Allele } a \text{ is a drop-in}|\lambda) = p_C * p_a * \lambda * \exp^{-\lambda(\gamma_a - AT)} \quad (B.39)$$

where p_C is the probability of drop-in, p_a is the allele frequency of a, and the function $h(\gamma_a) = \lambda * \exp^{-\lambda(\gamma_a - AT)}$ is a shifted exponential density function.

Hence, the weight expression in Eq. (B.20) is scaled with the drop-in probability defined in Eq. (B.39) for all drop-in alleles (i.e., for alleles in the set $C = \{a : \gamma_a \geq AT \cap n_a = 0\}$), or scaled with $(1 - p_C)$ if no allele drop-in, (i.e., if the C set is empty).

B.3.9.1 Example 4

An evidence DNA-profile is observed with alleles $(6, 7)$ with corresponding peak heights γ_6 and γ_7 (both are above AT). The alternative propositions for the LR are H_p: "The POI with genotype $(6, 7)$ is a contributor" vs H_d: "An unrelated individual is a contributor". In this example, it is assumed that drop-in events are possible; drop-out is not considered.

Under H_p, genotype $g = (6, 7)$ is the only genotype outcome, hence

$$Pr(E|\beta_p, H_p) = f(\gamma_6|n_6 = 1, \beta_p)f(\gamma_7|n_7 = 1, \beta_p)(1 - p_C) \quad (B.40)$$

where the term is multiplied by $(1 - p_C)$, since there is no drop-in.

Under H_d, if the possibility of drop-in is included, then it is possible for the unknown contributor to be any of the genotypes in the set: $G_d = (6, 7); (6, 6); (7, 7)$, such that

$$\begin{aligned} Pr(E|\beta_d, H_d) = &f(\gamma_6|n_6 = 1, \beta_d)f(\gamma_7|n_7 = 1, \beta_d)(1 - p_C)(2p_6p_7) \\ &+ f(\gamma_6|n_6 = 2, \beta_d)(p_Cp_7h(\gamma_7))(p_6^2) \\ &+ f(\gamma_7|n_7 = 2, \beta_d)(p_Cp_6h(\gamma_6))(p_7^2) \end{aligned} \quad (B.41)$$

472 Formal description of the probabilistic models

B.3.10 Model for multiple replicates

In the current version of *EuroForMix*, every replicate is restricted to follow the same statistical model (common parameter set β). This implies that each replicated DNA profile must have the same characteristics, i.e., the same level and variation of peak heights. Also the current model assumes the same number of contributors, and the same mixture proportions for each profile. Replicates are taken into account using Eq. (B.5), which is the same as for the qualitative model presented in Eq. (5.5), in Chapter 5.3.

B.3.11 Model for backward-stutters

Illustrations showing how the stutter model is implemented into *EuroForMix* were presented in Chapter 7.9. Here we describe the precise mathematical definition to calculate the likelihood function, as implemented in *EuroForMix* version 2, or newer.

Until now in this section, the only possible drop-out allele is the Q allele. However, when we include the stutter model, pure stutter alleles can drop-out, and this needs to be taken into account.

The stutter model introduces the expected stutter proportion ϵ as one of the model parameters β, which modifies the shape parameter α_a, as defined Eq. (B.30):

$$\alpha'_a = (1 - \epsilon)\alpha_a + \epsilon\alpha_{a+1}\mathbb{I}(a + 1 \in E \cap g) \tag{B.42}$$

this is calculated for all assumed contributing alleles $a \in E \cap g$ (for an assumed combined genotype g). If $a \in E \cap g$, but $a - 1 \notin E$, then $\alpha'_{a-1} = \epsilon\alpha_a$ is an unobserved pure stutter, which must be considered as a drop-out allele. Last, notice that we do not modify α_a for $a = Q$ allele, since we assume that it is unaffected by stutter (i.e., not stuttering from or to).

The likelihood function is calculated by using the weight formula in Eq. (B.20), where the three events from Section B.3.1 are modified to

1. $A' = \{a : \gamma_a \geq AT \cap \alpha'_a > 0\}$ is the contribution set.
2. $B' = \{a : \gamma_a < AT \cap \alpha'_a > 0\}$ is the drop-out set.
3. $C' = \{a : \gamma_a \geq AT \cap \alpha'_a = 0\}$ is the drop-in set.

B.3.11.1 Example 5

We continue with the previous example, where the evidence DNA profile has alleles $(6, 7)$ with corresponding peak heights γ_6 and γ_7 (both are above AT). The alternative propositions for the LR are H_p: "The POI with genotype $(6, 7)$ is a contributor" vs H_d: "An unrelated individual is a contributor". In this example, we assume that backward-stutter and drop-out is possible, but not drop-in. Hence, we must calculate the modified shape parameters, as defined in Eq. (B.42).

Under H_p, the genotype $g = (6, 7)$ is the only genotype outcome, hence

$$Pr(E|\beta_p, H_p) = F(AT|\alpha'_5, \beta_p)f(\gamma_6|\alpha'_6, \beta_p)f(\gamma_7|\alpha'_7, \beta_p) \tag{B.43}$$

where the modified shape parameters become

- $\alpha_5' = \epsilon\alpha_6$
- $\alpha_6' = (1-\epsilon)\alpha_6 + \epsilon\alpha_7$
- $\alpha_7' = (1-\epsilon)\alpha_7$

where $\alpha_6 = \alpha_7 = \frac{1}{\omega^2}$, as defined in Eq. (B.30).

Since we consider that backward-stutter is possible, but not drop-in, the unknown contributor under H_d can have any of the genotypes in the set: $G_d = \{(6,7); (7,7); (7,Q)\}$. We calculate the modified shape parameters for each genotype:

- For $g = (6,7)$, we are back to the modified shape parameters as under H_p.
- For $g = (7,7)$, $\alpha_6' = \epsilon\alpha_7$ and $\alpha_7' = (1-\epsilon)\alpha_7$, where $\alpha_7 = \frac{2}{\omega^2}$.
- For $g = (7,Q)$, $\alpha_6' = \epsilon\alpha_7$ and $\alpha_7' = (1-\epsilon)\alpha_7$, where $\alpha_7 = \frac{1}{\omega^2}$; $\alpha_Q = \frac{1}{\omega^2}$ is not modified (hence $\alpha_Q' = \alpha_Q$).

Therefore under H_d, we have

$$\begin{aligned}
Pr(E|\beta_d, H_d) = {} & F(AT|\alpha_5', \beta_d)f(\gamma_6|\alpha_6', \beta_d)f(\gamma_7|\alpha_7', \beta_d)(2p_6p_7) \\
& + f(\gamma_6|\alpha_6', \beta_d)f(\gamma_7|\alpha_7', \beta_d)(p_7^2) \\
& + f(\gamma_6|\alpha_6', \beta_d)f(\gamma_7|\alpha_7', \beta_d)F(AT|\alpha_Q, \beta_d)(2p_7p_Q)
\end{aligned} \tag{B.44}$$

where $p_Q = 1 - (p_6 + p_7)$.

B.3.12 Estimating the *LR* in *EuroForMix*

In *EuroForMix* there are three different ways to estimate the *LR*, each has different pros/cons. We will follow the outlined theory as provided in Section B.2.2, where *LR* is defined as a function of the unknown parameters in the model, $LR(\beta_p, \beta_d)$, as provided in Eq. (B.7), where β_p is the set of parameters belonging under the consideration of proposition H_p, and β_d is the set of parameters under the consideration of proposition H_d. The following sections will discuss the different frameworks provided by the *EuroForMix* software.

B.3.12.1 A maximum likelihood approach

The *LR* expression depends on the choice of the parameters, which are typically unknown (some may be known based on pre-experimental data).

The approach described in Chapter 7.5 is to maximize the probability of the evidence under each of the alternative propositions. Hence, $LR = LR(\hat{\beta}_p, \hat{\beta}_d)$, as provided by Eq. (B.9), using the optimization in Eq. (B.8). Here the parameters are chosen so that the probabilistic model describes the observations of allele peak heights in the "best way". This is called maximum likelihood estimation (MLE). Technically, this requires maximizing the likelihood function over the parameters space. Hence, we need to solve a "maximization problem", where the algorithm needs to search for the set of values, which returns the highest possible likelihood value. In Chapter 7.5, this was achieved in an Excel demonstration using "Solver". In *EuroForMix* the algorithm called "nlm" is used to give fast convergence for parameter optimization [350,351]. This method gives very fast convergence if reasonable specification of the initial parameters are provided. *EuroForMix* draws new initial parameters from a normal distribution with the mean equal to the estimated parameters from a regression model of the summed peak heights for each of the markers), and then uses the nlm algorithm to obtain a maximum (possibly a local maximum). This is carried out a number of times to ensure that a global maximum has been found (i.e., the maximum likelihood), ensuring that the model has correctly "converged" to an answer.

In *EuroForMix*, the parameters are determined using the maximum likelihood estimation (MLE) for each proposition in turn, as described in Chapter 7.5.4. The data are from the case evidence itself, so there is no need to inform the model with separate data from additional "control" experiments (or replicated experiments).

B.3.12.2 An integration-based approach ("Full Bayesian")

In the Bayesian framework, the parameters are considered as unknown variables, and not only unknown values (as in the frequentist framework). Importantly, *a priori* distributions need to be specified for the model parameters, and the parameters are integrated out (marginalized), as shown in Eq. (B.10). Integration under both H_p and H_d gives

$$LR_B = \frac{\int_{\beta_p} Pr(E|\beta_p, H_p)p(\beta_p)}{\int_{\beta_d} Pr(E|\beta_d, H_d)p(\beta_d)} \tag{B.45}$$

which is also called the Bayes factor. In the *EuroForMix* software, both integrals in the (B.45) formula is calculated using numerical integration based on the "adaptIntegrate" function from the "cubature" R-package. A relative error argument δ can be included to the function to provide a relative error uncertainty interval of the Bayesian-based LR, $\left[LR_B \frac{(1-\delta)}{(1+\delta)}, LR_B \frac{(1+\delta)}{(1-\delta)} \right]$ [236].

The priors in *EuroForMix* are specified as follows:
1. Mixture proportions: Unif(0, 1)
2. P.H. expectation: Unif(0, upper P.H.exp.)
3. P.H. variation: Unif(0, upper P.H.var.)
4. Degradation slope: Unif(0, 1)
5. Stutter proportion: Unif(0, upper Stutt.prop.) by default, can be changed

where Unif is the uniform distribution, and the values of "upper P.H.exp.", "upper P.H.var.", and "upper Stutt.prop." can be specified by the user.

The *EuroForMix* software also provide an alternative method to estimate the integrals based on Markov chain Monte Carlo (MCMC) approach (see next section). The method is based on the "GD-method" [352] using a multi-variate normal distribution. These calculations are executed when the "LR sensitivity" button is pushed. The estimated integrals under each of the propositions are presented as "Estimation of the marginalized likelihood" in the R-console. The ratio formed under each proposition is used to construct an estimate of the Bayes factor; in the R-console this is given as "Estimation of the Bayesian (unrestricted) LR:". The name "unrestricted" means that there are no defined upper limits of the parameters compared to numerical based integrals (see above). A disadvantage of an MCMC approach over the numerical integral approach is that the convergence to the true integral may be very slow [353].

B.3.12.3 A conservative approach

Instead of calculating the integrals in Eq. (B.45), we aim to quantify the posterior distribution of $LR(\beta_p, \beta_d)$ as a function of the posterior distributions of β_p and β_d considered independently. This provides a "sensitivity analysis" of the LR in the domain of those parameter values that are likely to be obtained for the observed evidence E. We define the "conservative LR" as the 5% quantile of the posterior LR distribution.

Samples from the posterior distributions $p(\beta|E)$ under H_p and H_d are drawn based on Metropolis–Hastings Markov chain Monte Carlo methods [72,71]. The proposal function is chosen as a normal distribution with zero mean, and a covariance being proportional to the inverse Hessian matrix (obtained from the "nlm" function under the maximum likelihood optimization). The initial parameter start value is chosen as the maximum likelihood estimates. It is worth mentioning here that the sampler takes a tuning parameter called "Variation of randomizer" under the "MCMC toolbar" list. This parameter effects the MCMC sampling behavior, which can be identified by the "Sampling acceptance rate", which is provided in the R console. A good sampling behavior should be around 0.23 [354].

Inferring the posterior LR distribution has also been discussed in the literature by [355–362]. In an empirical comparison study [236], we found that the conservative LR method does not provide any additional benefit over the maximum likelihood approach, only shrinking the LRs towards zero. If a Bayesian approach is considered, the "integrated approach" in *EuroForMix* would be recommended rather than the Monte Carlo-based approach.

B.4. Deconvolution

In addition to *EuroForMix*, *CaseSolver* (CS) implements the deconvolution formula presented by Bleka et al. [76,236]. For simplicity, we focus on any marker m (hence $E = E_m$). Here, the deconvolution is based on estimating the posterior probability of the combined genotypes $g = (g_1, \ldots, g_K)$:

$$Pr(g|E, \hat{\beta}, H) \propto Pr(E|g, \hat{\beta}, H) Pr(g|H) \tag{B.46}$$

where $\hat{\beta}$ is the maximum likelihood estimate of the parameter estimates under proposition H, and the normalization constant is found by summing out all the possible genotype combinations.

The marginal probability that contributor k has a specific genotype g_0 is given by

$$Pr\left(g_0|E, \hat{\beta}, H\right) = \sum_{g:g_k=g_0} Pr\left(g_1, \dots, g_k, \dots, g_K|E, \hat{\beta}, H\right) \tag{B.47}$$

After calculation, the posterior genotype probabilities of each contributor k is sorted with regard to the probabilities: $g_k^{(1)}, g_k^{(2)}$, ... etc., where $Pr\left(g_k^{(1)}|E, \hat{\beta}, H\right) \geq Pr\left(g_k^{(2)}|E, \hat{\beta}, H\right) \geq \cdots$ etc.

For deconvolution, the user of CS sets the "Prob-ratio to next" threshold α_G to indicate whether the most likely genotype should be considered as "certain": Contributor k is estimated to have genotype $g_k^{(1)}$ if $Pr\left(g_k^{(1)}|E, \hat{\beta}, H\right)/Pr\left(g_k^{(2)}|E, \hat{\beta}, H\right) \geq \alpha_G$. CS uses $\alpha_G = 10$ by default.

If this test fails, it is possible to check whether single alleles are certain or not. The marginal probability that contributor k has a specific allele a_0 is given by

$$Pr\left(a_0|E, \hat{\beta}, H\right) = \sum_{g_k:a_0 \in g_k} Pr\left(g_k|E, \hat{\beta}, H\right) \tag{B.48}$$

After calculation, the posterior allele probabilities of each of the possible alleles of contributor k are sorted with regard to the probabilities: $a_k^{(1)}, a_k^{(2)}, \dots$, where $Pr\left(a_k^{(1)}|E, \hat{\beta}, H\right) \geq P\left(a_k^{(2)}|E, \hat{\beta}, H\right) \geq \cdots$.

The user of CS uses the "Prob. single allele" threshold α_A to indicate whether the most likely allele should be considered as "certain": Contributor k has allele $a_k^{(1)}$ if $Pr\left(a_k^{(1)}|E, \hat{\beta}, H\right) \geq \alpha_A$. CS uses $\alpha_A = 0.99$ by default.

Bibliography

[1] W. Parson, D. Ballard, B. Budowle, J.M. Butler, K.B. Gettings, P. Gill, et al., Massively parallel sequencing of forensic STRs: considerations of the DNA commission of the International Society for Forensic Genetics (ISFG) on minimal nomenclature requirements, Forensic Science International: Genetics 22 (2016) 54–63.

[2] J.M. Butler, C.R. Hill, Biology and genetics of new autosomal STR loci useful for forensic DNA analysis, Forensic Science Review 24 (1) (2012) 15.

[3] A. Urquhart, C. Kimpton, T. Downes, P. Gill, Variation in short tandem repeat sequences—a survey of twelve microsatellite loci for use as forensic identification markers, International Journal of Legal Medicine 107 (1) (1994) 13–20.

[4] W. Bar, B. Brinkmann, B. Budowle, A. Carracedo, P. Gill, P. Lincoln, et al., DNA recommendations. Further report of the DNA Commission of the ISFH regarding the use of short tandem repeat systems. International Society for Forensic Haemogenetics, International Journal of Legal Medicine 110 (4) (1997) 175–176.

[5] C.P. Kimpton, P. Gill, A. Walton, A. Urquhart, E.S. Millican, M. Adams, Automated DNA profiling employing multiplex amplification of short tandem repeat loci, Genome Research 3 (1) (1993) 13–22.

[6] K.M. Sullivan, A. Mannucci, C.P. Kimpton, P. Gill, A rapid and quantitative DNA sex test: fluorescence-based PCR analysis of X-Y homologous gene amelogenin, Biotechniques 15 (4) (1993) 636.

[7] K.A. Mills, D. Even, J.C. Murray, Tetranucleotide repeat polymorphism at the human alpha fibrinogen locus (FGA), Human Molecular Genetics 1 (9) (1992) 779.

[8] D. Werrett, The national DNA database, Forensic Science International 88 (1997) 33–42.

[9] E. Cotton, R. Allsop, J. Guest, R. Frazier, P. Koumi, I. Callow, et al., Validation of the AMPFlSTR®SGM Plus^{tm} system for use in forensic casework, Forensic Science International 112 (2) (2000) 151–161.

[10] C. Kimpton, P. Gill, E. D'Aloja, J.F. Andersen, W. Bar, S. Holgersson, et al., Report on the second EDNAP collaborative STR exercise. European DNA Profiling Group, Forensic Science International 71 (2) (1995) 137–152.

[11] P. Gill, E. d'Aloja, J. Andersen, B. Dupuy, M. Jangblad, V. Johnsson, et al., Report of the European DNA profiling group (EDNAP): an investigation of the complex STR loci D21S11 and HUMFIBRA (FGA), Forensic Science International 86 (1-2) (1997) 25–33.

[12] P.M. Schneider, P.D. Martin, Criminal DNA databases: the European situation, Forensic Science International 119 (2) (2001) 232–238.

[13] L. Welch, P. Gill, C. Phillips, R. Ansell, N. Morling, W. Parson, et al., European Network of Forensic Science Institutes (ENFSI): evaluation of new commercial STR multiplexes that include the European Standard Set (ESS) of markers, Forensic Science International: Genetics 6 (6) (2012) 819–826.

[14] P.D. Martin, National DNA databases - practice and practicability. A forum for discussion, Progress in Forensic Genetics 10 (2004) 1–8.

[15] C.J. Fregeau, National casework and the national DNA database: the Royal Canadian Mounted Police perspective, Progress in Forensic Genetics 7 (1998) 541–543.

[16] J. Walsh, Canada's proposed forensic DNA evidence bank, Canadian Society of Forensic Science Journal 31 (1998) 113–125.

[17] R. Hoyle, Forensics. The FBI's national DNA database, Nature Biotechnology 16 (11) (1998) 987.

[18] D.R. Hares, Expanding the CODIS core loci in the United States, Forensic Science International: Genetics 6 (1) (2012) e52–e54.

[19] D.R. Hares, Addendum to expanding the CODIS core loci in the United States, Forensic Science International: Genetics 6 (5) (2012) e135.

[20] D.R. Hares, Selection and implementation of expanded CODIS core loci in the United States, Forensic Science International: Genetics 17 (2015) 33–34.

[21] J.M. Butler, US initiatives to strengthen forensic science & international standards in forensic DNA, Forensic Science International: Genetics 18 (2015) 4–20.

[22] A. Leriche, Final report of the Interpol Working Party on DNA profiling, in: Proceedings from the 2nd European Symposium on Human Identification, Promega Corporation, 1998, pp. 48–54.

[23] Council of the European Union, Council decision 2008/615/JHA of 23 June 2008 on the stepping up of cross-border cooperation, particularly in combating terrorism and cross-border crime, https://eur-lex.europa.eu/LexUriServ/LexUriServ.do?uri=OJ%3AL%3A2008%3A210%3A0001%3A0011%3AEN%3APDF. (Accessed January 2020).

[24] M.D. Coble, J.M. Butler, Characterization of new miniSTR loci to aid analysis of degraded DNA, Journal of Forensic Sciences 50 (1) (2005) 43–53.

[25] L.A. Dixon, A.E. Dobbins, H.K. Pulker, J.M. Butler, P.M. Vallone, M.D. Coble, et al., Analysis of artificially degraded DNA using STRs and SNPs–results of a collaborative European (EDNAP) exercise, Forensic Science International 164 (1) (2006) 33–44.

[26] P. Gill, L. Fereday, N. Morling, P.M. Schneider, The evolution of DNA databases—recommendations for new European STR loci, Forensic Science International 156 (2–3) (2006) 242–244.

[27] P. Gill, L. Fereday, N. Morling, P.M. Schneider, New multiplexes for Europe-amendments and clarification of strategic development, Forensic Science International 163 (1–2) (2006) 155–157.

[28] Council of the European Union, Council resolution of 30 November 2009 on the exchange of DNA analysis results, http://eur-lex.europa.eu/LexUriServ/LexUriServ.do?uri=OJ:C:2009:296:0001:0003:EN:PDF, 2009.

[29] A. Edwards, GH Hardy (1908) and Hardy–Weinberg equilibrium, Genetics 179 (3) (2008) 1143–1150.

[30] L. Gusmão, J.M. Butler, A. Linacre, W. Parson, L. Roewer, P.M. Schneider, et al., Revised guidelines for the publication of genetic population data, Forensic Science International: Genetics 30 (2017) 160–163.

[31] S. Wahlund, Composition of populations from the perspective of the theory of heredity, Hereditas 11 (1) (1928) 65–105.

[32] M. Bodner, I. Bastisch, J.M. Butler, R. Fimmers, P. Gill, L. Gusmão, et al., Recommendations of the DNA Commission of the International Society for Forensic Genetics (ISFG) on quality control of autosomal Short Tandem Repeat allele frequency databasing (STRidER), Forensic Science International: Genetics 24 (2016) 97–102.

[33] B.S. Weir, Methods for discrete population genetic data, Genetic Data Analysis II (1996).

[34] P. Gill, C. Brenner, J. Buckleton, A. Carracedo, M. Krawczak, W. Mayr, et al., DNA commission of the International Society of Forensic Genetics: recommendations on the interpretation of mixtures, Forensic Science International: Genetics 160 (2006) 90–101.

[35] I.W. Evett, C. Buffery, G. Willott, D. Stoney, A guide to interpreting single locus profiles of dna mixtures in forensic cases, Journal of the Forensic Science Society 31 (1) (1991) 41–47.

[36] B.S. Weir, C. Triggs, L. Starling, L. Stowell, K. Walsh, J. Buckleton, Interpreting DNA mixtures, Journal of Forensic Sciences 42 (2) (1997) 213–222.

[37] X. Zhang, L. Liu, R. Xie, G. Wang, Y. Shi, T. Gu, et al., Population data and mutation rates of 20 autosomal STR loci in a Chinese Han population from Yunnan Province, Southwest China, International Journal of Legal Medicine 132 (4) (2018) 1083–1085.

[38] M.W. Nachman, S.L. Crowell, Estimate of the mutation rate per nucleotide in humans, Genetics 156 (1) (2000) 297–304.

[39] D.L. Hartl, A.G. Clark, A.G. Clark, Principles of Population Genetics, vol. 116, Sinauer associates Sunderland, 1997.

[40] S. Wright, The genetical structure of species, Annual of Eugenics 15 (1951) 323–354.

[41] M. Slatkin, Inbreeding coefficients and coalescence times, Genetics Research 58 (2) (1991) 167–175.

[42] D. Balding, R. Nichols, DNA profile match probability calculation: how to allow for population stratification, relatedness, database selection and single bands, Forensic Science International 64 (1994) 125–140.

[43] T.R. Mertens, Teaching the concept of genetic drift using a simulation, The American Biology Teacher 52 (8) (1990) 497–499.

[44] M. Nei, Analysis of gene diversity in subdivided populations, Proceedings of the National Academy of Sciences 70 (12) (1973) 3321–3323.

[45] M. Jakobsson, M.D. Edge, N.A. Rosenberg, The relationship between FST and the frequency of the most frequent allele, Genetics 193 (2) (2013) 515–528.

[46] J. Buckleton, J. Curran, J. Goudet, D. Taylor, A. Thiery, B. Weir, Population-specific FST values for forensic STR markers: a worldwide survey, Forensic Science International: Genetics 23 (2016) 91–100.

[47] National Research Council, et al., The Evaluation of Forensic DNA Evidence, National Academies Press, 1996.

[48] J.S. Buckleton, J.A. Bright, D. Taylor, Forensic DNA Evidence Interpretation, CRC Press, 2016.

[49] L Excoffier, H.E. Lischer, Arlequin suite ver 3.5: a new series of programs to perform population genetics analyses under Linux and Windows, Molecular Ecology Resources 10 (3) (2010) 564–567.

[50] S.W. Guo, E.A. Thompson, Performing the exact test of Hardy-Weinberg proportion for multiple alleles, Biometrics (1992) 361–372.

[51] B.S. Weir, C. Cockerham, Genetic Data Analysis II: Methods for Discrete Population Genetic Data, Sinauer Assoc. Inc., Sunderland, MA, USA, 1996.

[52] D.J. Balding, Weight-of-Evidence for Forensic DNA Profiles, John Wiley & Sons, 2005.

[53] N.R. Council, et al., The Evaluation of Forensic DNA Evidence, National Academies Press, 1996.

[54] I. Evett, Evaluating DNA profiles in a case where the defence is "it was my brother", Journal of the Forensic Science Society 32 (1) (1992) 5–14.

[55] W.K. Fung, Y.Q. Hu, Statistical DNA Forensics: Theory, Methods and Computation, Wiley, England, 2008.

[56] T. Egeland, G. Dorum, M.D. Vigeland, N.A. Sheehan, Mixtures with relatives: a pedigree perspective, Forensic Science International: Genetics 10 (2014) 49–54.

[57] E. Hernandis, G. Dørum, T. Egeland, relMix: an open source software for DNA mixtures with related contributors, Forensic Science International: Genetics Supplement Series (2019).

[58] D. Balding, M. Krawczak, J. Buckleton, J. Curran, Decision-making in familial database searching: KI alone or not alone? Forensic Science International: Genetics 7 (2013) 52–54.

[59] M. Perlin, M. Legler, C. Spencer, J. Smith, W. Allan, J. Belrose, et al., Validating Trueallele® DNA mixture interpretation, Journal of Forensic Sciences 56 (6) (2011) 1430–1447.

[60] D. Taylor, J.A. Bright, J. Buckleton, The interpretation of single source and mixed DNA profiles, Forensic Science International: Genetics 7 (2013) 516–528.

[61] C.D. Steele, D.J. Balding, Statistical evaluation of forensic DNA profile evidence, Annual Review of Statistics and Its Application 1 (2014) 361–384.

[62] M.D. Coble, J.A. Bright, Probabilistic genotyping software: an overview, Forensic Science International: Genetics (2018).

[63] P. Gill, L. Gusmão, H. Haned, W. Mayr, N. Morling, W. Parson, et al., DNA commission of the International Society of Forensic Genetics: recommendations on the evaluation of STR typing results that may include drop-out and/or drop-in using probabilistic methods, Forensic Science International: Genetics 6 (6) (2012) 679–688.

[64] M. Bill, P. Gill, J. Curran, T. Clayton, R. Pinchin, M. Healy, et al., PENDULUM–a guideline-based approach to the interpretation of STR mixtures, Forensic Science International 148 (2–3) (2005) 181–189.

[65] P. Gill, A. Kirkham, J. Curran, LoComatioN: a software tool for the analysis of low copy number DNA profiles, Forensic Science International: Genetics 166 (2007) 128–138.

[66] M.W. Perlin, B. Szabady, Linear mixture analysis: a mathematical approach to resolving mixed DNA samples, Journal of Forensic Sciences 46 (6) (2001) 1372–1378.

[67] A.A. Mitchell, J. Tamariz, K. O'Connell, N. Ducasse, Z. Budimlija, M. Prinz, et al., Validation of a DNA mixture statistics tool incorporating allelic drop-out and drop-in, Forensic Science International: Genetics 6 (6) (2012) 749–761.

[68] H. Haned, K. Slooten, P. Gill, Exploratory data analysis for the interpretation of low template DNA mixtures, Forensic Science International: Genetics 6 (6) (2012) 762–774.

[69] R. Puch-Solis, T. Clayton, Evidential evaluation of DNA profiles using a discrete statistical model implemented in the DNA LiRa software, Forensic Science International: Genetics 11 (2014) 220–228.

[70] D.J. Balding, Evaluation of mixed-source, low-template DNA profiles in forensic science, Proceedings of the National Academy of Sciences USA 110 (30) (2013) 12241–12246.

[71] W.K. Hastings, Monte Carlo sampling methods using Markov chains and their applications, Biometrika 57 (1) (1970) 97–109.

[72] N. Metropolis, A.W. Rosenbluth, M.N. Rosenbluth, A.H. Teller, E. Teller, Equation of state calculations by fast computing machines, Journal of Chemical Physics 21 (6) (1953) 1087–1092.

[73] H. Swaminathan, A. Garg, C.M. Grgicak, M. Medard, D.S. Lun, CEESIt: a computational tool for the interpretation of STR mixtures, Forensic Science International: Genetics 22 (2016) 149–160.

[74] T. Graversen, S. Lauritzen, Computational aspects of DNA mixture analysis, Statistics and Computing (2014) 1–15.

[75] C.C. Benschop, J. Hoogenboom, P. Hovers, M. Slagter, D. Kruise, R. Parag, et al., DNAxs/DNAS-tatistX: development and validation of a software suite for the data management and probabilistic interpretation of DNA profiles, Forensic Science International: Genetics 42 (2019) 81–89.

[76] O. Bleka, G. Storvik, P. Gill, EuroForMix: an open source software based on a continuous model to evaluate STR DNA profiles from a mixture of contributors with artefacts, Forensic Science International: Genetics 21 (2016) 35–44.

[77] F.M. Götz, H. Schönborn, V. Borsdorf, A.M. Pflugbeil, D. Labudde, GenoProof Mixture 3—new software and process to resolve complex DNA mixtures, Forensic Science International: Genetics Supplement Series 6 (2017) e549–e551.

[78] S. Manabe, C. Morimoto, Y. Hamano, S. Fujimoto, K. Tamaki, Development and validation of open-source software for DNA mixture interpretation based on a quantitative continuous model, PLoS ONE 12 (11) (2017) e0188183.

[79] K. Inman, N. Rudin, K. Cheng, C. Robinson, A. Kirschner, L. Inman-Semerau, et al., Lab Retriever: a software tool for calculating likelihood ratios incorporating a probability of drop-out for forensic DNA profiles, BMC Bioinformatics 16 (1) (2015) 298.

[80] C.D. Steele, M. Greenhalgh, D.J. Balding, Verifying likelihoods for low template DNA profiles using multiple replicates, Forensic Science International: Genetics 13 (2014) 82–89.

[81] C.C. Benschop, T. Sijen, LoCIM-tool: an expert's assistant for inferring the major contributor's alleles in mixed consensus DNA profiles, Forensic Science International: Genetics 11 (2014) 154–165.

[82] M. Adamowicz, J. Clarke, T. Rambo, H. Makam, S. Copeland, D. Erb, et al., Validation of MaSTR^{TM} software: extensive study of fully-continuous probabilistic mixture analysis using Power-Plex® Fusion 2–5 contributor mixtures, Forensic Science International: Genetics Supplement Series 7 (2019) 641–643.

[83] M.W. Perlin, A. Sinelnikov, An information gap in DNA evidence interpretation, PLoS ONE 4 (12) (2009) e8327.

[84] C.D. Steele, M. Greenhalgh, D.J. Balding, Evaluation of low-template DNA profiles using peak heights, Statistical Applications in Genetics and Molecular Biology 15 (5) (2016) 431–445.

[85] P. Gill, H. Haned, Ø. Bleka, O. Hansson, G. Dørum, T. Egeland, Genotyping and interpretation of STR-DNA: low-template, mixtures and database matches - twenty years of research and development, Forensic Science International: Genetics 18 (2015) 100–117.

[86] SWGDAM, Validation guidelines for forensic DNA analysis methods, https://1ecb9588-ea6f-4feb-971a-73265dbf079c.filesusr.com/ugd/4344b0_813b241e8944497e99b9c45b163b76bd.pdf. (Accessed January 2020).

[87] ENFSI recommended minimum criteria for the validation of various aspects of the DNA profiling process, http://enfsi.eu/wp-content/uploads/2016/09/minimum_validation_guidelines_in_dna_profiling_-_v2010_0.pdf. (Accessed January 2020).

[88] H. Kelly, J.A. Bright, J.M. Curran, J. Buckleton, Modelling heterozygote balance in forensic DNA profiles, Forensic Science International: Genetics 6 (6) (2012) 729–734.

[89] T. Tvedebrink, H.S. Mogensen, M.C. Stene, N. Morling, Performance of two 17 locus forensic identification STR kits—applied biosystems's AmpF-STR® NGMSElect^{TM} and Promega's PowerPlex®ESI17 kits, Forensic Science International: Genetics 6 (5) (2012) 523–531.

[90] J.A. Bright, E. Huizing, L. Melia, J. Buckleton, Determination of the variables affecting mixed MiniFiler^{TM} DNA profiles, Forensic Science International: Genetics 5 (5) (2011) 381–385.

[91] J. Whitaker, E. Cotton, P. Gill, A comparison of the characteristics of profiles produced with the AMPFlSTR®SGM Plus^{TM} multiplex system for both standard and low copy number (LCN) STR DNA analysis, Forensic Science International 123 (2) (2001) 215–223.

[92] P. Gill, R. Sparkes, L. Fereday, D.J. Werrett, Report of the European Network of Forensic Science Institutes (ENSFI): formulation and testing of principles to evaluate STR multiplexes, Forensic Science International 108 (1) (2000) 1–29.

[93] M.D. Timken, S.B. Klein, M.R. Buoncristiani, Stochastic sampling effects in STR typing: implications for analysis and interpretation, Forensic Science International: Genetics 11 (2014) 195–204.

[94] T.M. Clayton, J.P. Whitaker, R. Sparkes, P. Gill, Analysis and interpretation of mixed forensic stains using DNA STR profiling, Forensic Science International 91 (1) (1998) 55–70.

[95] A. Kirkham, J. Haley, Y. Haile, A. Grout, C. Kimpton, A. Al-Marzouqi, et al., High-throughput analysis using AmpFlSTR® Identifiler® with the Applied Biosystems 3500xl Genetic Analyser, Forensic Science International: Genetics 7 (1) (2013) 92–97.

[96] S. Petricevic, J. Whitaker, J. Buckleton, S. Vintiner, J. Patel, P. Simon, et al., Validation and development of interpretation guidelines for low copy number (LCN) DNA profiling in New Zealand using the AmpF, in: lSTR®SGM Plus^{TM} multiplex, Forensic Science International: Genetics 4 (5) (2010) 305–310.

[97] C.R. Hill, D.L. Duewer, M.C. Kline, C.J. Sprecher, R.S. McLaren, D.R. Rabbach, et al., Concordance and population studies along with stutter and peak height ratio analysis for the PowerPlex® ESX 17 and ESI 17 systems, Forensic Science International: Genetics 5 (4) (2011) 269–275.

[98] J.A. Bright, J. Turkington, J. Buckleton, Examination of the variability in mixed DNA profile parameters for the Identifiler^{TM} multiplex, Forensic Science International: Genetics 4 (2) (2010) 111–114.

[99] J.R. Gilder, K. Inman, W. Shields, D.E. Krane, Magnitude-dependent variation in peak height balance at heterozygous STR loci, International Journal of Legal Medicine 125 (1) (2011) 87–94.

[100] V.C. Tucker, A.J. Kirkham, A.J. Hopwood, Forensic validation of the PowerPlex® ESI 16 STR multiplex and comparison of performance with AmpFlSTR® SGM plus^{tm}, International Journal of Legal Medicine 126 (3) (2012) 345–356.

[101] A. Debernardi, E. Suzanne, A. Formant, L. Pene, A.B. Dufour, J.R. Lobry, One year variability of peak heights, heterozygous balance and inter-locus balance for the DNA positive control of AmpF-STR® Identifiler^{tm}STR kit, Forensic Science International: Genetics 5 (1) (2011) 43–49.

[102] B. Leclair, C.J. Frégeau, K.L. Bowen, R.M. Fourney, Systematic analysis of stutter percentages and allele peak height and peak area ratios at heterozygous STR loci for forensic casework and database samples, Journal of Forensic Sciences 49 (5) (2004) 968–980.

[103] J.A. Bright, S. Neville, J.M. Curran, J.S. Buckleton, Variability of mixed DNA profiles separated on a 3130 and 3500 capillary electrophoresis instrument, Australian Journal of Forensic Sciences 46 (3) (2014) 304–312.

[104] J.A. Bright, K. McManus, S. Harbison, P. Gill, J. Buckleton, A comparison of stochastic variation in mixed and unmixed casework and synthetic samples, Forensic Science International: Genetics 6 (2) (2012) 180–184.

[105] P. Gill, B. Sparkes, J. Buckleton, Interpretation of simple mixtures of when artefacts such as stutters are present – with special reference to multiplex STRs used by the Forensic Science Service, Forensic Science International 95 (3) (1998) 213–224.

[106] P.S. Walsh, N.J. Fildes, R. Reynolds, Sequence analysis and characterization of stutter products at the tetranucleotide repeat locus vWA, Nucleic Acids Research 24 (14) (1996) 2807–2812.

[107] G. Levinson, G.A. Gutman, Slipped-strand mispairing: a major mechanism for DNA sequence evolution, Molecular Biology and Evolution 4 (3) (1987) 203–221.

[108] P. Gill, R. Sparkes, C. Kimpton, Development of guidelines to designate alleles using an STR multiplex system, Forensic Science International 89 (3) (1997) 185–197.

[109] J.A. Bright, J.M. Curran, J.S. Buckleton, Investigation into the performance of different models for predicting stutter, Forensic Science International: Genetics 7 (4) (2013) 422–427.

[110] A.J. Gibb, A.L. Huell, M.C. Simmons, R.M. Brown, Characterisation of forward stutter in the AmpF/STR® SGM Plus® PCR, Science & Justice 49 (1) (2009) 24–31.

[111] A.A. Westen, L.J. Grol, J. Harteveld, A.S. Matai, P. de Knijff, T. Sijen, Assessment of the stochastic threshold, back- and forward stutter filters and low template techniques for NGM, Forensic Science International: Genetics 6 (6) (2012) 708–715.

[112] J.A. Bright, J.S. Buckleton, D. Taylor, M. Fernando, J.M. Curran, Modeling forward stutter: toward increased objectivity in forensic DNA interpretation, Electrophoresis 35 (21–22) (2014) 3152–3157.

[113] D. Shinde, Y. Lai, F. Sun, N. Arnheim, Taq DNA polymerase slippage mutation rates measured by PCR and quasi-likelihood analysis: (CA/GT)n and (A/T)n microsatellites, Nucleic Acids Research 31 (3) (2003) 974–980.

[114] O. Hansson, Development of computer software to characterise and simulate molecular biology processes used in forensic profiling assays, Ph.D. thesis, University of Oslo, 2018.

[115] J.M. Butler, C.R. Hill, Biology and genetics of new autosoma STR loci useful for forensic DNA analysis, Forensic Science Review 24 (1) (2012) 15–26.

[116] O. Hansson, P. Gill, T. Egeland, STR-validator: an open source platform for validation and process control, Forensic Science International: Genetics 13 (2014) 154–166.

[117] K. Oostdik, K. Lenz, J. Nye, K. Schelling, D. Yet, S. Bruski, et al., Developmental validation of the PowerPlex® fusion system for analysis of casework and reference samples: a 24-locus multiplex for new database standards, Forensic Science International: Genetics 12 (2014) 69–76.

[118] J.A. Bright, D. Taylor, J.M. Curran, J.S. Buckleton, Developing allelic and stutter peak height models for a continuous method of DNA interpretation, Forensic Science International: Genetics 7 (2) (2013) 296–304.

[119] M. Klintschar, P. Wiegand, Polymerase slippage in relation to the uniformity of tetrameric repeat stretches, Forensic Science International 135 (2) (2003) 163–166.

[120] C. Brookes, J.A. Bright, S. Harbison, J. Buckleton, Characterising stutter in forensic STR multiplexes, Forensic Science International: Genetics 6 (1) (2012) 58–63.

[121] D. Taylor, J.A. Bright, C. McGovern, C. Hefford, T. Kalafut, J. Buckleton, Validating multiplexes for use in conjunction with modern interpretation strategies, Forensic Science International: Genetics 20 (2016) 6–19.

[122] S.B. Seo, J. Ge, J.L. King, B. Budowle, Reduction of stutter ratios in short tandem repeat loci typing of low copy number DNA samples, Forensic Science International: Genetics 8 (1) (2014) 213–218.

[123] K.B. Gettings, R.A. Aponte, P.M. Vallone, J.M. Butler, STR allele sequence variation: current knowledge and future issues, Forensic Science International: Genetics 18 (2015) 118–130.

[124] P. Gill, J. Curran, K. Elliot, A graphical simulation model of the entire DNA process associated with the analysis of short tandem repeat loci, Nucleic Acids Research 33 (2) (2005).

[125] J. Weusten, J. Herbergs, A stochastic model of the processes in PCR based amplification of STR DNA in forensic applications, Forensic Science International: Genetics 6 (1) (2012) 17–25.

[126] T.M. Clayton, J.L. Guest, A.J. Urquhart, P.D. Gill, A genetic basis for anomalous band patterns encountered during DNA STR profiling, Journal of Forensic Sciences 49 (6) (2004) 1207–1214.

[127] G. Shutler, T. Roy, Genetic anomalies consistent with gonadal mosaicism encountered in a sexual assault-homicide, Forensic Science International: Genetics 6 (6) (2012) e159–e160.

[128] A.J. Gibb, A.L. Huell, M.C. Simmons, R.M. Brown, Characterisation of forward stutter in the AmpFlSTR®SGM Plus® PCR, Science & Justice 49 (1) (2009) 24–31.

[129] R.L. Green, R.E. Lagacé, N.J. Oldroyd, L.K. Hennessy, J.J. Mulero, Developmental validation of the AmpF-STR®NGM SElect^{TM} PCR amplification kit: a next-generation STR multiplex with the SE33 locus, Forensic Science International: Genetics 7 (1) (2013) 41–51.

[130] T.M. Clayton, J.L. Guest, A.J. Urquhart, P.D. Gill, A basis for anomalous band patterns encountered during DNA STR profiling, Journal of Forensic Sciences 49 (6) (2004), JFS2003145–8.

[131] C.A. Crouse, S. Rogers, E. Amiott, S. Gibson, A. Masibay, Analysis and interpretation of short tandem repeat microvariants and three-banded allele patterns using multiple allele detection systems, Journal of Forensic Sciences 44 (1) (1999) 87–94.

[132] J.M. Butler, Genetics and genomics of core short tandem repeat loci used in human identity testing, Journal of Forensic Sciences 51 (2) (2006) 253–265.

[133] T. Clayton, S. Hill, L. Denton, S. Watson, A. Urquhart, Primer binding site mutations affecting the typing of STR loci contained within the AMPFlSTR®SGM Plus kit, Forensic Science International 139 (2) (2004) 255–259.

[134] C. Leibelt, B. Budowle, P. Collins, Y. Daoudi, T. Moretti, G. Nunn, et al., Identification of a D8S1179 primer binding site mutation and the validation of a primer designed to recover null alleles, Forensic Science International 133 (3) (2003) 220–227.

[135] E. Cotton, R. Allsop, J. Guest, R. Frazier, P. Koumi, I. Callow, et al., Validation of the AMPFlSTR® SGM Plus^{TM} system for use in forensic casework, Forensic Science International 112 (2–3) (2000) 151–161.

[136] D. Loakes, Survey and summary: the applications of universal DNA base analogues, Nucleic Acids Research 29 (12) (2001) 2437–2447.

[137] J.S. Buckleton, J.M. Curran, P. Gill, Towards understanding the effect of uncertainty in the number of contributors to DNA stains, Forensic Science International: Genetics 1 (1) (2007) 20–28.

[138] A. Biedermann, S. Bozza, K. Konis, F. Taroni, Inference about the number of contributors to a DNA mixture: comparative analyses of a Bayesian network approach and the maximum allele count method, Forensic Science International: Genetics 6 (6) (2012) 689–696.

[139] H. Haned, T. Egeland, D. Pontier, L. Pene, P. Gill, Estimating drop-out probabilities in forensic DNA samples: a simulation approach to evaluate different models, Forensic Science International: Genetics 5 (5) (2011) 525–531.

[140] H. Swaminathan, C.M. Grgicak, M. Medard, D.S. Lun, NOCIt: a computational method to infer the number of contributors to DNA samples analyzed by STR genotyping, Forensic Science International: Genetics 16 (2015) 172–180.

[141] C.C. Benschop, J. van der Linden, J. Hoogenboom, R. Ypma, H. Haned, Automated estimation of the number of contributors in autosomal short tandem repeat profiles using a machine learning approach, Forensic Science International: Genetics 43 (2019) 102150.

[142] P. Gill, J. Whitaker, C. Flaxman, N. Brown, J. Buckleton, An investigation of the rigor of interpretation rules for STRs derived from less than 100 pg of DNA, Forensic Science International 112 (1) (2000) 17–40.

[143] P. Gill, R. Puch-Solis, J. Curran, The low-template-DNA (stochastic) threshold - its determination relative to risk analysis for national DNA databases, Forensic Science International: Genetics 3 (2) (2009) 104–111.

[144] P. Gill, L. Gusmao, H. Haned, W.R. Mayr, N. Morling, W. Parson, et al., DNA commission of the International Society of Forensic Genetics: recommendations on the evaluation of STR typing results that may include drop-out and/or drop-in using probabilistic methods, Forensic Science International: Genetics 6 (6) (2012) 679–688.

[145] J. Bregu, D. Conklin, E. Coronado, M. Terrill, R.W. Cotton, C.M. Grgicak, Analytical thresholds and sensitivity: establishing RFU thresholds for forensic DNA analysis, Journal of Forensic Sciences 58 (1) (2013) 120–129.

[146] U.J. Mönich, K. Duffy, M. Medard, V. Cadambe, L.E. Alfonse, C. Grgicak, Probabilistic characterisation of baseline noise in STR profiles, Forensic Science International: Genetics 19 (2015) 107–122.

[147] R. Alaeddini, Forensic implications of PCR inhibition—a review, Forensic Science International: Genetics 6 (3) (2012) 297–305.

[148] O. Hansson, T. Egeland, P. Gill, Characterization of degradation and heterozygote balance by simulation of the forensic DNA analysis process, International Journal of Legal Medicine 131 (2) (2017) 303–317.

[149] J. Buckleton, C. Triggs, Is the 2p rule always conservative? Forensic Science International 159 (2–3) (2006) 206–209.

[150] P. Gill, J. Buckleton, A universal strategy to interpret DNA profiles that does not require a definition of low-copy-number, Forensic Science International: Genetics 4 (4) (2010) 221–227.

[151] B. Budowle, A.J. Eisenberg, Daal Av, Validity of low copy number typing and applications to forensic science, Croatian Medical Journal 50 (3) (2009) 207–217.

[152] J. Buckleton, H. Kelly, J.A. Bright, D. Taylor, T. Tvedebrink, J.M. Curran, Utilising allelic dropout probabilities estimated by logistic regression in casework, Forensic Science International: Genetics 9 (2014) 9–11.

[153] T. Tvedebrink, P.S. Eriksen, M. Asplund, H.S. Mogensen, N. Morling, Allelic drop-out probabilities estimated by logistic regression—further considerations and practical implementation, Forensic Science International: Genetics 6 (2) (2012) 263–267.

[154] T. Tvedebrink, P.S. Eriksen, H.S. Mogensen, N. Morling, Estimating the probability of allelic dropout of STR alleles in forensic genetics, Forensic Science International: Genetics 3 (4) (2009) 222–226.

[155] S. Inokuchi, T. Kitayama, K. Fujii, H. Nakahara, H. Nakanishi, K. Saito, et al., Estimating allele dropout probabilities by logistic regression: assessments using Applied Biosystems 3500xL and 3130xl Genetic Analyzers with various commercially available human identification kits, Legal Medicine 19 (2016) 77–82.

[156] D.W. Hosmer Jr., S. Lemeshow, R.X. Sturdivant, Applied Logistic Regression, vol. 398, John Wiley & Sons, 2013.

[157] R. Puch-Solis, A. Kirkham, P. Gill, J. Read, S. Watson, D. Drew, Practical determination of the low template DNA threshold, Forensic Science International: Genetics 5 (5) (2011) 422–427.

[158] C. Luce, S. Montpetit, D. Gangitano, P. O'Donnell, Validation of the AMPF-STR® MiniFiler™ PCR Amplification Kit for use in forensic casework, Journal of Forensic Sciences 54 (5) (2009) 1046–1054.

[159] L. Albinsson, J. Hedman, R. Ansell, Verification of alleles by using peak height thresholds and quality control of STR profiling kits, Forensic Science International: Genetics Supplement Series 3 (1) (2011) e251–e252.

[160] J.M. Butler, Advanced Topics in Forensic DNA Typing: Interpretation, Academic Press, 2014.

[161] C.A. Rakay, J. Bregu, C.M. Grgicak, Maximizing allele detection: effects of analytical threshold and DNA levels on rates of allele and locus drop-out, Forensic Science International: Genetics 6 (6) (2012) 723–728.

[162] K.E. Lohmueller, N. Rudin, K. Inman, Analysis of allelic drop-out using the Identifiler ® and PowerPlex® 16 forensic STR typing systems, Forensic Science International: Genetics 12 (2014) 1–11.

[163] T. Tvedebrink, P.S. Eriksen, H.S. Mogensen, N. Morling, Evaluating the weight of evidence by using quantitative short tandem repeat data in DNA mixtures, Journal of the Royal Statistical Society: Series C (Applied Statistics) 59 (5) (2010) 855–874.

[164] I. Findlay, A. Taylor, P. Quirke, R. Frazier, A. Urquhart, DNA fingerprinting from single cells, Nature 389 (6651) (1997) 555–556.

[165] P. Wiegand, M. Kleiber, DNA typing of epithelial cells after strangulation, International Journal of Legal Medicine 110 (4) (1997) 181–183.

[166] D. Van Hoofstat, D. Deforce, V. Brochez, I. De Pauw, K. Janssens, M. Mestdagh, et al., DNA typing of fingerprints and skin debris: sensitivity of capillary electrophoresis in forensic applications using multiplex PCR, in: Proceedings of the 2nd European Symposium of Human Identification, 1998, pp. 131–137.

[167] A. Barbaro, G. Falcone, A. Barbaro, DNA typing from hair shaft, Progress in Forensic Genetics 8 (2000) 523–525.

[168] A. Hellmann, U. Rohleder, H. Schmitter, M. Wittig, STR typing of human telogen hairs–a new approach, International Journal of Legal Medicine 114 (4–5) (2001) 269–273.

[169] R. Szibor, I. Plate, H. Schmitter, H. Wittig, D. Krause, Forensic mass screening using mtDNA, International Journal of Legal Medicine 120 (6) (2006) 372–376.

[170] E. Hagelberg, I.C. Gray, A.J. Jeffreys, Identification of the skeletal remains of a murder victim by DNA analysis, Nature 352 (6334) (1991) 427.

[171] E. Hagelberg, B. Sykes, R. Hedges, Ancient bone DNA amplified, Nature 342 (6249) (1989) 485.

[172] A.J. Jeffreys, M.J. Allen, E. Hagelberg, A. Sonnberg, Identification of the skeletal remains of Josef Mengele by DNA analysis, Forensic Science International 56 (1) (1992) 65–76.

[173] P. Gill, P.L. Ivanov, C. Kimpton, R. Piercy, N. Benson, G. Tully, et al., Identification of the remains of the Romanov family by DNA analysis, Nature Genetics 6 (2) (1994) 130–135.

[174] W.M. Schmerer, S. Hummel, B. Herrmann, Optimized DNA extraction to improve reproducibility of short tandem repeat genotyping with highly degraded DNA as target, Electrophoresis 20 (8) (1999) 1712–1716.

[175] W.M. Schmerer, S. Hummel, B. Herrmann, STR-genotyping of archaeological human bone: experimental design to improve reproducibility by optimisation of DNA extraction, Anthropologischer Anzeiger 58 (1) (2000) 29–35.

[176] J. Burger, S. Hummel, B. Hermann, W. Henke, DNA preservation: a microsatellite-DNA study on ancient skeletal remains, Electrophoresis 20 (8) (1999) 1722–1728.

[177] C.M. Strom, S. Rechitsky, Use of nested PCR to identify charred human remains and minute amounts of blood, Journal of Forensic Sciences 43 (3) (1998) 696–700.

[178] R. Van Oorschot, K.N. Ballantyne, R.J. Mitchell, Forensic trace DNA: a review, Investigative Genetics 1 (1) (2010) 14.

[179] P. Taberlet, S. Griffin, B. Goossens, S. Questiau, V. Manceau, N. Escaravage, et al., Reliable genotyping of samples with very low DNA quantities using PCR, Nucleic Acids Research 24 (16) (1996) 3189–3194.

[180] C.C. Benschop, C.P. van der Beek, H.C. Meiland, A.G. van Gorp, A.A. Westen, T. Sijen, Low template STR typing: effect of replicate number and consensus method on genotyping reliability and DNA database search results, Forensic Science International: Genetics 5 (4) (2011) 316–328.

[181] C. Benschop, H. Haned, T. Sijen, Consensus and pool profiles to assist in the analysis and interpretation of complex low template DNA mixtures, International Journal of Legal Medicine 127 (1) (2013) 11–23.

[182] J.A. Bright, P. Gill, J. Buckleton, Composite profiles in DNA analysis, Forensic Science International: Genetics 6 (3) (2012) 317–321.

[183] A.E. Fonneløp, H. Johannessen, T. Egeland, P. Gill, Contamination during criminal investigation: detecting police contamination and secondary DNA transfer from evidence bags, Forensic Science International: Genetics 23 (2016) 121–129.

[184] ENFSI DNA working group, DNA contamination prevention guidelines, European Network of Forensic Science Institutes. Available at: http://enfsi.eu/documents/forensic-guidelines/, 2017. (Accessed 19 November 2019).

[185] Forensic Science Regulator, The control and avoidance of contamination in crime scene examination involving DNA evidence recovery. Available at: https://assets.publishing.service.gov.uk/government/uploads/system/uploads/attachment_data/file/536827/FSR-anti-contamination.pdf, 2016. (Accessed January 2020).

[186] K. Shaw, I. Sesardić, N. Bristol, C. Ames, K. Dagnall, C. Ellis, et al., Comparison of the effects of sterilisation techniques on subsequent DNA profiling, International Journal of Legal Medicine 122 (1) (2008) 29–33.

[187] E. Archer, H. Allen, A. Hopwood, D. Rowlands, Validation of a dual cycle ethylene oxide treatment technique to remove DNA from consumables used in forensic laboratories, Forensic Science International: Genetics 4 (4) (2010) 239–243.

[188] K. Neureuther, E. Rohmann, M. Hilken, M.L. Sonntag, S. Herdt, T. Koennecke, et al., Reduction of PCR-amplifiable DNA by ethylene oxide treatment of forensic consumables, Forensic Science International: Genetics 12 (2014) 185–191.

[189] P. Gill, D. Rowlands, G. Tully, I. Bastisch, T. Staples, P. Scott, Manufacturer contamination of disposable plastic-ware and other reagents—an agreed position statement by ENFSI, SWGDAM and BSAG, Forensic Science International: Genetics 4 (4) (2010) 269–270.

[190] ENFSI DNA working group, DNA database management review and recommendations, European Network of Forensic Science Institutes. Available at: http://enfsi.eu/wp-content/uploads/2017/09/DNA-databasemanagement-review-and-recommendatations-april-2017.pdf, 2017. (Accessed 19 November 2019).

[191] ISO (the International Organization for Standardization), ISO 18385:2016(en) minimizing the risk of human DNA contamination in products used to collect, store and analyze biological material for forensic purposes — requirements. Available at: https://www.iso.org/standard/62341.html, 2016. (Accessed 19 November 2019).

[192] D. Vanek, L. Saskova, J. Votrubova, Does the new ISO 18385: 2016 standard for forensic DNA-grade products need a revision? Forensic Science International: Genetics Supplement Series 6 (2017) e148–e149.

[193] P. Gill, Misleading DNA Evidence: Reasons for Miscarriages of Justice, Elsevier, 2014.

[194] Forensic Science Regulator, DNA Anti-Contamination – Forensic Medical Examination in Sexual Assault Referral Centres and Custodial Facilities. Available at: https://assets.publishing.service.gov.uk/government/uploads/system/uploads/attachment_data/file/540116/207_FSR_anti-_contam_SARC__Custody_Issue1.pdf, 2016. (Accessed January 2020).

[195] O. Hansson, P. Gill, Characterisation of artefacts and drop-in events using STR-validator and single-cell analysis, Forensic Science International: Genetics 30 (2017) 57–65.

[196] M.H. Toothman, K.M. Kester, J. Champagne, T.D. Cruz, W.S. Street IV, B.L. Brown, Characterization of human DNA in environmental samples, Forensic Science International 178 (1) (2008) 7–15.

[197] P. Gill, A. Kirkham, Development of a simulation model to assess the impact of contamination in casework using STRs, Journal of Forensic Sciences 49 (3) (2004) 485–491.

[198] D.J. Balding, J. Buckleton, Interpreting low template DNA profiles, Forensic Science International: Genetics 4 (1) (2009) 1–10.

[199] R. Alaeddini, S.J. Walsh, A. Abbas, Forensic implications of genetic analyses from degraded DNA - a review, Forensic Science International: Genetics 4 (3) (2010) 148–157.

[200] R. Alaeddini, S.J. Walsh, A. Abbas, Forensic implications of genetic analyses from degraded dna—a review, Forensic Science International: Genetics 4 (3) (2010) 148–157.

[201] E.N. Hanssen, R. Lyle, T. Egeland, P. Gill, Degradation in forensic trace DNA samples explored by massively parallel sequencing, Forensic Science International: Genetics 27 (2017) 160–166.

[202] D.T. Chung, J. Drábek, K.L. Opel, J.M. Butler, B.R. McCord, A study on the effects of degradation and template concentration on the amplification efficiency of the STR Miniplex primer sets, Journal of Forensic Sciences 49 (4) (2004) 1–8.

[203] J.A. Bright, D. Taylor, J.M. Curran, J.S. Buckleton, Degradation of forensic DNA profiles, Australian Journal of Forensic Sciences 45 (4) (2013) 445–449.

[204] M.M. Ewing, J.M. Thompson, R.S. McLaren, V.M. Purpero, K.J. Thomas, P.A. Dobrowski, et al., Human dna quantification and sample quality assessment: developmental validation of the powerquant|r system, Forensic Science International: Genetics 23 (2016) 166–177.

[205] A. Holt, S.C. Wootton, J.J. Mulero, P.M. Brzoska, E. Langit, R.L. Green, Developmental validation of the Quantifiler® HP and Trio Kits for human DNA quantification in forensic samples, Forensic Science International: Genetics 21 (2016) 145–157.

[206] M. Vraneš, M. Scherer, K. Elliott, Development and validation of the Investigator® Quantiplex Pro Kit for qPCR-based examination of the quantity and quality of human DNA in forensic samples, Forensic Science International: Genetics Supplement Series 6 (2017) e518–e519.

[207] A. Loftus, G. Murphy, H. Brown, A. Montgomery, J. Tabak, J. Baus, et al., Development and validation of InnoQuant® HY, a system for quantitation and quality assessment of total human and male DNA using high copy targets, Forensic Science International: Genetics 29 (2017) 205–217.

[208] T. Tvedebrink, P.S. Eriksen, H.S. Mogensen, N. Morling, Statistical model for degradated DNA samples and adjusted probabilities for allelic drop-out, Forensic Science International: Genetics Supplement Series 3 (2011) 489–491.

[209] H. Haned, Forensim: an open-source initiative for the evaluation of statistical methods in forensic genetics, Forensic Science International: Genetics 5 (4) (2011) 265–268.

[210] G. Stolovitzky, G. Cecchi, Efficiency of DNA replication in the polymerase chain reaction, Proceedings of the National Academy of Sciences 93 (23) (1996) 12947–12952.

[211] J.Y. Lee, H.W. Lim, S.I. Yoo, B.T. Zhang, T.H. Park, Simulation and real-time monitoring of polymerase chain reaction for its higher efficiency, Biochemical Engineering Journal 29 (1–2) (2006) 109–118.

[212] P. Kainz, The PCR plateau phase–towards an understanding of its limitations, Biochimica et Biophysica Acta (BBA)-Gene Structure and Expression 1494 (1–2) (2000) 23–27.

[213] R. Hedell, C. Dufva, R. Ansell, P. Mostad, J. Hedman, Enhanced low-template DNA analysis conditions and investigation of allele dropout patterns, Forensic Science International: Genetics 14 (2015) 61–75.

[214] D. Shinde, Y. Lai, F. Sun, N. Arnheim, Taq DNA polymerase slippage mutation rates measured by PCR and quasi-likelihood analysis:(CA/GT) n and (A/T) n microsatellites, Nucleic Acids Research 31 (3) (2003) 974–980.

[215] W.R. Hudlow, M.D. Chong, K.L. Swango, M.D. Timken, M.R. Buoncristiani, A quadruplex real-time qPCR assay for the simultaneous assessment of total human DNA, human male DNA, DNA degradation and the presence of PCR inhibitors in forensic samples: a diagnostic tool for STR typing, Forensic Science International: Genetics 2 (2) (2008) 108–125.

[216] M. Meredith, J.A. Bright, S. Cockerton, S. Vintiner, Development of a one-tube extraction and amplification method for DNA analysis of sperm and epithelial cells recovered from forensic samples by laser microdissection, Forensic Science International: Genetics 6 (1) (2012) 91–96.

[217] A. Kloosterman, P. Kersbergen, Efficacy and limits of genotyping low copy number DNA samples by multiplex PCR of STR loci, in: International Congress Series, vol. 1239, Elsevier, 2003, pp. 795–798.

[218] R Core Team, R: A Language and Environment for Statistical Computing, R Foundation for Statistical Computing, Vienna, Austria, 2013, http://www.R-project.org/.

[219] H. Haned, P. Gill, Analysis of complex DNA mixtures using the Forensim package, Forensic Science International: Genetics Supplement Series 3 (1) (2011) e79–e80.

[220] J. Curran, P. Gill, M. Bill, Interpretation of repeat measurement DNA evidence allowing for multiple contributors and population substructure, Forensic Science International 148 (2005) 47–53.

[221] P. Gill, J. Curran, C. Neumann, A. Kirkham, T. Clayton, J. Whitaker, et al., Interpretation of complex DNA profiles using empirical models and a method to measure their robustness, Forensic Science International: Genetics 2 (2008) 91–103.

[222] D.J. Balding, R.A. Nichols, DNA profile match probability calculation: how to allow for population stratification, relatedness, database selection and single bands, Forensic Science International 64 (2–3) (1994) 125–140.

[223] N. Fukshansky, W. Bar, Biostatistical evaluation of mixed stains with contributors of different ethnic origin, International Journal of Legal Medicine 112 (6) (1999) 383–387.

[224] P. Gill, H. Haned, A new methodological framework to interpret complex DNA profiles using likelihood ratios, Forensic Science International: Genetics 7 (2) (2013) 251–263.

[225] C. Tippett, V. Emerson, M. Fereday, F. Lawton, A. Richardson, L. Jones, et al., The evidential value of the comparison of paint flakes from sources other than vehicles, Journal of the Forensic Science Society 8 (2–3) (1968) 61–65.

[226] E.I. Weir, Interpreting DNA Evidence: Statistical Genetics for Forensic Scientists, Sinauer Associates, Sunderland MA, 1998.

[227] P. Gill, Ø. Bleka, T. Egeland, Does an English appeal court ruling increase the risks of miscarriages of justice when complex DNA profiles are searched against the national DNA database? Forensic Science International: Genetics 13 (2014) 167–175.

[228] C.C. Benschop, H. Haned, L. Jeurissen, P.D. Gill, T. Sijen, The effect of varying the number of contributors on likelihood ratios for complex DNA mixtures, Forensic Science International: Genetics 19 (2015) 92–99.

[229] P. Gill, R. Sparkes, R. Pinchin, T. Clayton, J. Whitaker, J. Buckleton, Interpreting simple STR mixtures using allele peak areas, Forensic Science International 91 (1) (1998) 41–53.

[230] I.W. Evett, P.D. Gill, J.A. Lambert, Taking account of peak areas when interpreting mixed DNA profiles, Journal of Forensic Sciences 43 (1) (1998) 62–69.

[231] R.G. Cowell, T. Graversen, S.L. Lauritzen, J. Mortera, Analysis of forensic DNA mixtures with artefacts, Applied Statistics 64 (1) (2015) 1–32.

[232] L.E. Alfonse, A.D. Garrett, D.S. Lun, K.R. Duffy, C.M. Grgicak, A large-scale dataset of single and mixed-source short tandem repeat profiles to inform human identification strategies: Provedit, Forensic Science International: Genetics 32 (2018) 62–70.

[233] Y. You, D. Balding, A comparison of software for the evaluation of complex DNA profiles, Forensic Science International: Genetics 40 (2019) 114–119.

[234] R. Cowell, T. Graversen, S. Lauritzen, J. Mortera, Analysis of forensic DNA mixtures with artefacts, Journal of the Royal Statistical Society: Series C (Applied Statistics) 64 (1) (2015) 1–48.

[235] R.G. Cowell, S.L. Lauritzen, J. Mortera, A gamma model for DNA mixture analysis, Bayesian Analysis 2 (2) (2007) 333–348.

[236] Ø. Bleka, C.C. Benschop, G. Storvik, P. Gill, A comparative study of qualitative and quantitative models used to interpret complex STR DNA profiles, Forensic Science International: Genetics 25 (2016) 85–96.

[237] H. Akaike, A new look at the statistical model identification, in: Selected Papers of Hirotugu Akaike, Springer, 1974, pp. 215–222.

[238] C.C.G. Benschop, A. Nijveld, F.E. Duijs, T. Sijen, An assessment of the performance of the probabilistic genotyping software EuroForMix: trends in likelihood ratios and analysis of type I & II errors, Forensic Science International: Genetics 42 (2019) 31–38.

[239] SWGDAM, Scientific Working Group on DNA Analysis Methods (2015): Guidelines for the Validation of Probabilistic Genotyping Systems, https://1ecb9588-ea6f-4feb-971a-73265dbf079c.filesusr.com/ugd/4344b0_22776006b67c4a32a5ffc04fe3b56515.pdf, 2015. (Accessed January 2020).

[240] M.D. Coble, J. Buckleton, J.M. Butler, T. Egeland, R. Fimmers, P. Gill, et al., DNA Commission of the International Society for Forensic Genetics: recommendations on the validation of software programs performing biostatistical calculations for forensic genetics applications, Forensic Science International: Genetics 25 (2016) 191–197.

[241] Forensic Science Regulator, Software Validation for DNA Mixture Interpretation, FSR-G-223 Issue 1, 2018. Available at: https://assets.publishing.service.gov.uk/government/uploads/system/uploads/attachment_data/file/740877/G223_Mixtures_software_validation_Issue1.pdf, 2016. (Accessed 19 November 2019).

[242] M.W. Perlin, M.M. Legler, C.E. Spencer, J.L. Smith, W.P. Allan, J.L. Belrose, et al., Validating TrueAllele DNA mixture interpretation, Journal of Forensic Sciences 56 (2011) 1430–1447.

[243] J.A. Bright, D. Taylor, C. McGovern, S. Cooper, L. Russell, D. Abarno, et al., Developmental validation of STRmix^{TM}, expert software for the interpretation of forensic DNA profiles, Forensic Science International: Genetics 23 (2016) 226–239.

[244] Forensic Science in Criminal Courts: Ensuring Scientific Validity of Feature-Comparison Methods, President's Council on Advisors on Science and Technology, 2016, https://obamawhitehouse.archives.gov/sites/default/files/microsites/ostp/PCAST/pcast_forensic_science_report_final.pdf.

[245] Forensic Science in Criminal Courts: an addendum to the PCAST report on forensic science in criminal courts, President's Council on Advisors on Science and Technology, 2016, https://obamawhitehouse.archives.gov/sites/default/files/microsites/ostp/PCAST/pcast_forensics_addendum_finalv2.pdf.

[246] G.E. Box, Science and statistics, Journal of the American Statistical Association 71 (356) (1976) 791–799.

[247] P.V. Spade, C. Panaccio, William of Ockham. Available at: https://www.goodreads.com/author/quotes/85818.William_of_Ockham, 2002.

[248] F. Taroni, S. Bozza, A. Biedermann, C. Aitken, Dismissal of the illusion of uncertainty in the assessment of a likelihood ratio, Law, Probability and Risk 15 (1) (2016) 1–16.

[249] H. Haned, P. Gill, K. Lohmueller, K. Inman, N. Rudin, Validation of probabilistic genotyping software for use in forensic DNA casework: definitions and illustrations, Science & Justice 56 (2) (2016) 104–108.

[250] E. Rykiel, Testing ecological models: the meaning of validation, Ecological Modelling 90 (3) (1996) 229–244.

[251] D.C. Ince, L. Hatton, J. Graham-Cumming, The case for open computer programs, Nature 482 (2012) 485–488.

[252] H. Haned, C.C. Benschop, P.D. Gill, T. Sijen, Complex DNA mixture analysis in a forensic context: evaluating the probative value using a likelihood ratio model, Forensic Science International: Genetics 16 (2015) 17–25.

[253] D.K. Nordstrom, Models, validation, and applied geochemistry: issues in science, communication, and philosophy, Applied Geochemistry 27 (10) (2012) 1899–1919.

[254] R.G. Sargent, Verification and validation of simulation models, Journal of Simulation 7 (2013) 12–24.

[255] R.G. Cowell, T. Graversen, S.L. Lauritzen, J. Mortera, Analysis of forensic DNA mixtures with artefacts, Applied Statistics 64 (1) (2015) 1–32.

[256] A.A. Westen, T. Kraaijenbrink, E.A.R. de Medina, J. Harteveld, P. Willemse, S.B. Zuniga, et al., Comparing six commercial autosomal STR kits in a large Dutch population sample, Forensic Science International: Genetics 10 (2014) 55–63.

[257] S. Noël, J. Noël, D. Granger, J.F. Lefebvre, D. Séguin, STRmix^{TM} put to the test: 300 000 non-contributor profiles compared to four-contributor DNA mixtures and the impact of replicates, Forensic Science International: Genetics 41 (2019) 24–31.

[258] M.H. Zweig, G. Campbell, Receiver-operating characteristic (ROC) plots: a fundamental evaluation tool in clinical medicine, Clinical Chemistry 39 (4) (1993) 561–577.

[259] P.S. Walsh, N.J. Fildes, R. Reynolds, Sequence analysis and characterization of stutter products at the tetranucleotide repeat locus vWA, Nucleic Acids Research 24 (14) (1996) 2807–2812.

[260] D. Ramos, J. Gonzalez-Rodriguez, Reliable support: measuring calibration of likelihood ratios, Forensic Science International 230 (1–3) (2013) 156–169.

[261] J.S. Buckleton, J.A. Bright, A. Ciecko, M. Kruijver, B. Mallinder, A. Magee, et al., Response to: Commentary on: Bright et al. (2018) Internal validation of STRmix™–a multi laboratory response to PCAST, Forensic Science International: Genetics, 34: 11–24, Forensic Science International: Genetics 44 (2020).

[262] D. Taylor, J. Buckleton, I. Evett, Testing likelihood ratios produced from complex DNA profiles, Forensic Science International: Genetics 16 (2015) 165–171.

[263] J.A. Bright, R. Richards, M. Kruijver, H. Kelly, C. McGovern, A. Magee, et al., Internal validation of STRmix™–a multi laboratory response to PCAST, Forensic Science International: Genetics 34 (2018) 11–24.

[264] E. Alladio, M. Omedei, S. Cisana, G. D'Amico, D. Caneparo, M. Vincenti, et al., DNA mixtures interpretation–a proof-of-concept multi-software comparison highlighting different probabilistic methods' performances on challenging samples, Forensic Science International: Genetics 37 (2018) 143–150.

[265] P. Garofano, D. Caneparo, G. D'Amico, M. Vincenti, E. Alladio, An alternative application of the consensus method to DNA typing interpretation for Low Template-DNA mixtures, Forensic Science International: Genetics Supplement Series 5 (2015) e422–e424.

[266] D.A. Taylor, J.S. Buckleton, J.A. Bright, Comment on "DNA mixtures interpretation–a proof-of-concept multi-software comparison highlighting different probabilistic methods' performances on challenging samples" by Alladio et al., Forensic Science International: Genetics 40 (2019) e248–e251.

[267] J.M. Butler, M.C. Kline, M.D. Coble, NIST interlaboratory studies involving DNA mixtures (MIX05 and MIX13): variation observed and lessons learned, Forensic Science International: Genetics 37 (2018) 81–94.

[268] L. Prieto, H. Haned, A. Mosquera, M. Crespillo, M. Alemañ, M. Aler, et al., Euroforgen-NoE collaborative exercise on LRmix to demonstrate standardization of the interpretation of complex DNA profiles, Forensic Science International: Genetics 9 (2014) 47–54.

[269] J.A. Bright, K. Cheng, Z. Kerr, C. McGovern, H. Kelly, T.R. Moretti, et al., STRmix™ collaborative exercise on DNA mixture interpretation, Forensic Science International: Genetics 40 (2019) 1–8.

[270] M. Crespillo, P. Barrio, J. Luque, C. Alves, M. Aler, F. Alessandrini, et al., GHEP-ISFG collaborative exercise on mixture profiles of autosomal STRs (GHEP-MIX01, GHEP-MIX02 and GHEP-MIX03): results and evaluation, Forensic Science International: Genetics 10 (2014) 64–72.

[271] C.C. Benschop, E. Connolly, R. Ansell, B. Kokshoorn, Results of an inter and intra laboratory exercise on the assessment of complex autosomal DNA profiles, Science & Justice 57 (1) (2017) 21–27.

[272] T. Graversen, S. Lauritzen, Estimation of parameters in DNA mixture analysis, Journal of Applied Statistics 40 (11) (2013) 2423–2436.

[273] B. Haldemann, S. Dornseifer, T. Heylen, C. Aelbrecht, O. Bleka, H. Larsen, et al., eDNA - an expert software system for comparison and evaluation of DNA profiles in forensic casework, Forensic Science International: Genetics Supplement Series 5 (2015) e400–e402.

[274] Ø. Bleka, L. Prieto, P. Gill, CaseSolver: an investigative open source expert system based on EuroForMix, Forensic Science International: Genetics 41 (2019) 83–92.

[275] P. Gill, T. Hicks, J.M. Butler, E. Connolly, L. Gusmão, B. Kokshoorn, et al., DNA commission of the international society for forensic genetics: assessing the value of forensic biological evidence-guidelines highlighting the importance of propositions: part I: evaluation of DNA profiling comparisons given (sub-) source propositions, Forensic Science International: Genetics 36 (2018) 189–202.

[276] B.S. Weir, Matching and partially-matching DNA profiles, Journal of Forensic Sciences 49 (5) (2004), JFS2003039–6.

[277] D.R. Paoletti, T.E. Doom, M.L. Raymer, D.E. Krane, Assessing the implications for close relatives in the event of similar but nonmatching DNA profiles, Jurimetrics (2006) 161–175.

[278] T. Tvedebrink, P.S. Eriksen, J.M. Curran, H.S. Mogensen, N. Morling, Analysis of matches and partial-matches in a Danish STR data set, Forensic Science International: Genetics 6 (3) (2012) 387–392.

[279] C.N. Maguire, L.A. McCallum, C. Storey, J.P. Whitaker, Familial searching: a specialist forensic DNA profiling service utilising the National DNA Database® to identify unknown offenders via their relatives—the UK experience, Forensic Science International: Genetics 8 (1) (2014) 1–9.

[280] F.R. Bieber, C.H. Brenner, D. Lazer, Finding Criminals Through DNA of Their Relatives, 2006.

[281] C. Phillips, The Golden State Killer investigation and the nascent field of forensic genealogy, Forensic Science International: Genetics 36 (2018) 186–188.

[282] B.M. Henn, L. Hon, J.M. Macpherson, N. Eriksson, S. Saxonov, I. Pe'er, et al., Cryptic distant relatives are common in both isolated and cosmopolitan genetic samples, PLoS ONE 7 (4) (2012) e34267.

[283] I. Evett, G. Jackson, J. Lambert, S. McCrossan, The impact of the principles of evidence interpretation on the structure and content of statements, Science & Justice 40 (4) (2000) 233–239.

[284] ENFSI Guideline for evaluative reporting in forensic science: Strengthening the evaluation of forensic results across Europe (STEOFRAE), http://enfsi.eu/wp-content/uploads/2016/09/m1_guideline.pdf, [Online; posted 8-March 2015].

[285] Making Sense of Forensic Genetics, https://senseaboutscience.org/wp-content/uploads/2017/01/making-sense-of-forensic-genetics.pdf, [Online; published in 2017].

[286] Cross-border Exchange and Comparison of Forensic DNA data in the Context of the Prüm Decision, http://www.europarl.europa.eu/RegData/etudes/STUD/2018/604971/IPOL_STU(2018) 604971_EN.pdf, [Online; posted June 2108].

[287] K. Van der Beek, Forensic DNA profiles crossing borders in Europe (implementation of the Treaty of Prüm), Profiles in DNA (2011), https://www.promega.co.uk/resources/profiles-in-dna/2011/forensic-dna-profiles-crossing-borders-in-europe/.

[288] B. Prainsack, V. Toom, Performing the union: the Prüm Decision and the European dream, Studies in History and Philosophy of Science Part C: Studies in History and Philosophy of Biological and Biomedical Sciences 44 (1) (2013) 71–79.

[289] P. Gill, L. Fereday, N. Morling, P.M. Schneider, New multiplexes for Europe - amendments and clarification of strategic development, Forensic Science International 163 (1–2) (2006) 155–157.

[290] C.C. Benschop, L. van de Merwe, J. de Jong, V. Vanvooren, M. Kempenaers, C.K. van der Beek, et al., Validation of SmartRank: a likelihood ratio software for searching national DNA databases with complex DNA profiles, Forensic Science International: Genetics 29 (2017) 145–153.

[291] O. Bleka, G. Dorum, P. Gill, H. Haned, Database extraction strategies for low-template evidence, Forensic Science International: Genetics 9 (2014) 134–141.

[292] C. Benschop, H. Haned, et al., Adapting a likelihood ratio model to enable searching DNA databases with complex STR DNA profiles, in: 27th International Symposium on Human Identification, 2016, https://promega.media/-/media/files/products-and-services/genetic-identity/ishi-27-oral-abstracts/4-benschop.pdf.

[293] A.A. Westen, H. Haned, L.J. Grol, J. Harteveld, K.J. van der Gaag, P. de Knijff, et al., Combining results of forensic STR kits: HDplex validation including allelic association and linkage testing with NGM and Identifiler loci, International Journal of Legal Medicine 126 (5) (2012) 781–789.

[294] Ø. Bleka, M. Bouzga, A. Fonneløp, P. Gill, dnamatch2: an open source software to carry out large scale database searches of mixtures using qualitative and quantitative models, Forensic Science International: Genetics Supplement Series 6 (2017) e404–e406.

[295] T. Egeland, I. Dalen, P. Mostad, Estimating the number of contributors to a DNA profile, International Journal of Legal Medicine 117 (2003) 271–275.

[296] H. Haned, L. Pène, J. Lobry, A. Dufour, D. Pontier, Estimating the number of contributors to forensic DNA mixtures: does maximum likelihood perform better than maximum allele count? Journal of Forensic Sciences 56 (1) (2011) 3–8.

[297] O. García, J. Alonso, J. Cano, R. García, G. Luque, P. Martín, et al., Population genetic data and concordance study for the kits Identifiler, NGM, PowerPlex ESX 17 System and Investigator ESSplex in Spain, Forensic Science International: Genetics 6 (2) (2012) e78–e79.

[298] T. Egeland, P.F. Mostad, B. Mevåg, M. Stenersen, Beyond traditional paternity and identification cases: selecting the most probable pedigree, Forensic Science International 110 (1) (2000) 47–59.

[299] D. Kling, A.O. Tillmar, T. Egeland, Familias 3–extensions and new functionality, Forensic Science International: Genetics 13 (2014) 121–127.

[300] Ø. Bleka, M. Eduardoff, C. Santos, C. Phillips, W. Parson, P. Gill, Open source software EuroForMix can be used to analyse complex SNP mixtures, Forensic Science International: Genetics 31 (2017) 105–110.

[301] D. Taylor, J. Buckleton, Do low template DNA profiles have useful quantitative data? Forensic Science International: Genetics 16 (2015) 13–16.

[302] R.S. Just, J.A. Irwin, Use of the LUS in sequence allele designations to facilitate probabilistic genotyping of NGS-based STR typing results, Forensic Science International: Genetics 34 (2018) 197–205.

[303] K. Slooten, Identifying common donors in DNA mixtures, with applications to database searches, Forensic Science International: Genetics 26 (2017) 40–47.

[304] P. Gill, T. Hicks, J.M. Butler, E. Connolly, L. Gusmão, B. Kokshoorn, et al., DNA commission of the international society for forensic genetics: assessing the value of forensic biological evidence-guidelines highlighting the importance of propositions. Part II: evaluation of biological traces considering activity level propositions, Forensic Science International: Genetics 44 (2020) 102186.

[305] G. Jackson, S. Jones, G. Booth, C. Champod, I.W. Evett, The nature of forensic science opinion–a possible framework to guide thinking and practice in investigations and in court proceedings, Science & Justice: Journal of the Forensic Science Society 46 (1) (2006) 33–44.

[306] I.W. Evett, C. Berger, J. Buckleton, C. Champod, G. Jackson, Finding the way forward for forensic science in the US—a commentary on the PCAST report, Forensic Science International 278 (2017) 16–23.

[307] P. Gill, Interpretation continues to be the main weakness in criminal justice systems: developing roles of the expert witness and court, Wiley Interdisciplinary Reviews: Forensic Science 1 (2) (2019) e1321.

[308] R. Cook, I.W. Evett, G. Jackson, P. Jones, J. Lambert, A hierarchy of propositions: deciding which level to address in casework, Science & Justice 38 (4) (1998) 231–239.

[309] D.J. Balding, C.D. Steele, Weight-of-Evidence for Forensic DNA Profiles, John Wiley & Sons, 2015.

[310] D. Taylor, J.A. Bright, J. Buckleton, The 'factor of two' issue in mixed DNA profiles, Journal of Theoretical Biology 363 (2014) 300–306.

[311] I. Evett, On meaningful questions: a two-trace transfer problem, Journal of the Forensic Science Society 27 (6) (1987) 375–381.

[312] S. Gittelson, T. Kalafut, S. Myers, D. Taylor, T. Hicks, F. Taroni, et al., A practical guide for the formulation of propositions in the Bayesian approach to DNA evidence interpretation in an adversarial environment, Journal of Forensic Sciences 61 (1) (2016) 186–195.

[313] W.C. Thompson, E.L. Schumann, Interpretation of statistical evidence in criminal trials, Law and Human Behavior 11 (3) (1987) 167–187.

[314] R. Meester, M. Sjerps, The evidential value in the DNA database search controversy and the two-stain problem, Biometrics 59 (3) (2003) 727–732.

[315] R. v Alan James Doheny and Gary Adams [1996] EWCA Crim 728, http://www.bailii.org/ew/cases/EWCA/Crim/1996/728.html, 1996. (Accessed 30 January 2020).

[316] C. Aitken, P. Roberts, G. Jackson, Fundamentals of probability and statistical evidence in criminal proceedings: guidance for judges, lawyers, forensic scientists and expert witnesses, http://www.rss.org.uk/Images/PDF/influencing-change/rss-fundamentals-probability-statistical-evidence.pdf, 2010.

[317] D.J. Balding, P. Donnelly, Evaluating DNA profile evidence when the suspect is identified through a database search, Journal of Forensic Sciences 41 (4) (1996) 603–607.

[318] R v Adams [1996] 2 Cr. App. R. 467, Crim. LR. 898. Retrieved from: http://www.bailii.org/ew/cases/EWCA/Crim/2006/222.html, 1996.

[319] P. Donnelly, Appealing statistics, Significance 2 (1) (2005) 46–48.

[320] SWGDAM, Recommendations of the SWGDAM Ad Hoc Working Group on Genotyping Results Reported as Likelihood Ratios, www.swgdam.org/publications. (Accessed September 2019).

[321] Department of Justice, Department of Justice uniform language for testimony and reports for forensic autosomal DNA examinations using probabilistic genotyping systems, https://www.justice.gov/olp/page/file/1095961/download. (Accessed September 2019).

[322] K.A. Martire, R. Kemp, M. Sayle, B. Newell, On the interpretation of likelihood ratios in forensic science evidence: presentation formats and the weak evidence effect, Forensic Science International 240 (2014) 61–68.

[323] K.A. Martire, I. Watkins, Perception problems of the verbal scale: a reanalysis and application of a membership function approach, Science & Justice 55 (4) (2015) 264–273.

[324] C. Aitken, C.E. Berger, J.S. Buckleton, C. Champod, J. Curran, A. Dawid, et al., Expressing evaluative opinions: a position statement, Science & Justice 51 (1) (2011) 1–2.

[325] A. Providers, Standards for the formulation of evaluative forensic science expert opinion, Science & Justice 49 (2009) 161–164.

[326] SWGDAM ad hoc working group, Recommendations of the SWGDAM ad hoc working group on genotyping results reported as likelihood ratios, https://1ecb9588-ea6f-4feb-971a-73265dbf079c.filesusr.com/ugd/4344b0_dd5221694d1448588dcd0937738c9e46.pdf, 2017.

[327] P. Gill, J. Curran, C. Neumann, Interpretation of complex DNA profiles using Tippett plots, Forensic Science International: Genetics Supplement Series 1 (1) (2008) 646–648.

[328] D. Taylor, J.M. Curran, J. Buckleton, Importance sampling allows Hd true tests of highly discriminating DNA profiles, Forensic Science International: Genetics 27 (2017) 74–81.

[329] B. Bruijns, R. Tiggelaar, H. Gardeniers, Massively parallel sequencing techniques for forensics: a review, Electrophoresis 39 (21) (2018) 2642–2654.

[330] Ø. Bleka, R. Just, J. Le, P. Gill, Automation of High Volume MPS mixture interpretation using CaseSolver, Forensic Science International: Genetics Supplement Series (2019).

[331] G.P. Consortium, et al., A global reference for human genetic variation, Nature 526 (7571) (2015) 68.

[332] C. Phillips, Forensic genetic analysis of bio-geographical ancestry, Forensic Science International: Genetics 18 (2015) 49–65.

[333] A. Möller, E. Meyer, B. Brinkmann, Different types of structural variation in STRs: HumFES/FPS, HumVWA and HumD21S11, International Journal of Legal Medicine 106 (6) (1994) 319–323.

[334] K.B. Gettings, D. Ballard, M. Bodner, L.A. Borsuk, J.L. King, W. Parson, et al., Report from the STRAND Working Group on the 2019 STR sequence nomenclature meeting, Forensic Science International: Genetics 43 (2019) 102165.

[335] K.B. Gettings, L.A. Borsuk, D. Ballard, M. Bodner, B. Budowle, L. Devesse, et al., STRSeq: a catalog of sequence diversity at human identification Short Tandem Repeat loci, Forensic Science International: Genetics 31 (2017) 111–117.

[336] J.L. King, F.R. Wendt, J. Sun, B. Budowle, STRait Razor v2s: advancing sequence-based STR allele reporting and beyond to other marker systems, Forensic Science International: Genetics 29 (2017) 21–28.

[337] J.M. Butler, Y. Shen, B.R. McCord, et al., The development of reduced size STR amplicons as tools for analysis of degraded DNA, Journal of Forensic Sciences 48 (5) (2003) 1054–1064.

[338] P.M. Schneider, K. Bender, W.R. Mayr, W. Parson, B. Hoste, R. Decorte, et al., STR analysis of artificially degraded DNA - results of a collaborative European exercise, Forensic Science International 139 (2–3) (2004) 123–134.

[339] M.J. Ludeman, C. Zhong, J.J. Mulero, R.E. Lagacé, L.K. Hennessy, M.L. Short, et al., Developmental validation of GlobalFiler^{TM} PCR amplification kit: a 6-dye multiplex assay designed for amplification of casework samples, International Journal of Legal Medicine 132 (6) (2018) 1555–1573.

[340] K.B. Gettings, L.A. Borsuk, C.R. Steffen, K.M. Kiesler, P.M. Vallone, Sequence-based US population data for 27 autosomal STR loci, Forensic Science International: Genetics 37 (2018) 106–115.

[341] J. Hoogenboom, K.J. van der Gaag, R.H. de Leeuw, T. Sijen, P. de Knijff, J.F. Laros, FDSTools: a software package for analysis of massively parallel sequencing data with the ability to recognise and correct STR stutter and other PCR or sequencing noise, Forensic Science International: Genetics 27 (2017) 27–40.

[342] R. Just, J. Le, J. Irwin, LUS+: extension of the LUS designator concept to differentiate most sequence alleles for 27 STR loci, Forensic Science International: Reports (2020) 100059.

[343] R. Li, R. Wu, H. Li, Y. Zhang, D. Peng, N. Wang, et al., Characterizing stutter variants in forensic STRs with massively parallel sequencing, Forensic Science International: Genetics 45 (2020) 102225.

[344] K.J. van der Gaag, R.H. de Leeuw, J. Hoogenboom, J. Patel, D.R. Storts, J.F. Laros, et al., Massively parallel sequencing of short tandem repeats—population data and mixture analysis results for the PowerSeq^{TM} system, Forensic Science International: Genetics 24 (2016) 86–96.

[345] S.B. Vilsen, T. Tvedebrink, P.S. Eriksen, C. Børsting, C. Hussing, H.S. Mogensen, et al., Stutter analysis of complex STR MPS data, Forensic Science International: Genetics 35 (2018) 107–112.

[346] A. Woerner, J. King, B. Budowle, Flanking variation influences rates of stutter in simple repeats, Genes 8 (11) (2017) 329.

[347] L.I. Moreno, M.B. Galusha, R. Just, A closer look at Verogen's Forenseq^{TM} DNA Signature Prep kit autosomal and Y-STR data for streamlined analysis of routine reference samples, Electrophoresis 39 (21) (2018) 2685–2693.

[348] S.Y. Anvar, K.J. van der Gaag, J.W. van der Heijden, M.H. Veltrop, R.H. Vossen, R.H. de Leeuw, et al., TSSV: a tool for characterization of complex allelic variants in pure and mixed genomes, Bioinformatics 30 (12) (2014) 1651–1659.

[349] J. Hoogenboom, K.J. van der Gaag, T. Sijen, STRNaming: standardised STR sequence allele naming to simplify MPS data analysis and interpretation, Forensic Science International: Genetics Supplement Series 7 (1) (2019) 346–437.

[350] J.E. Dennis, R.B. Schnabel, Numerical methods for nonlinear equations and unconstrained optimization, Classics in Applied Mathematics 16 (1983).

[351] R.B. Schnabel, J.E. Koonatz, B.E. Weiss, A modular system of algorithms for unconstrained minimization, ACM Transactions on Mathematical Software (TOMS) 11 (4) (1985) 419–440.

[352] C. Liu, Q. Liu, Marginal likelihood calculation for the Gelfand–Dey and Chib methods, Economics Letters 115 (2) (2012) 200–203.

[353] D.M. Ommen, C.P. Saunders, C. Neumann, The characterization of Monte Carlo errors for the quantification of the value of forensic evidence, Journal of Statistical Computation and Simulation 87 (8) (2017) 1608–1643.

[354] A. Gelman, W.R. Gilks, G.O. Roberts, Weak convergence and optimal scaling of random walk Metropolis algorithms, Annals of Applied Probability 7 (1) (1997) 110–120.

[355] A. van den Hout, I. Alberink, Posterior distributions for likelihood ratios in forensic science, Science & Justice 56 (5) (2016) 397–401.

[356] C.E.H. Berger, K. Slooten, The LR does not exist, Science & Justice 56 (5) (2016) 388–391.

[357] A. Biedermann, S. Bozza, F. Taroni, C. Aitken, Reframing the debate: a question of probability, not of likelihood ratio, Science & Justice 56 (5) (2016) 392–396.

[358] K.A. Martire, G. Edmond, D.N. Navarro, B.R. Newell, On the likelihood of 'encapsulating all uncertainty', Science & Justice 57 (1) (2016) 76–79.

[359] G.S. Morrison, Special issue on measuring and reporing the precision of forensic likelihood ratios: introduction to the debate, Science & Justice 56 (5) (2016) 371–373.

[360] M.J. Sjerps, I. Alberink, A. Bolck, R.D. Stoel, P. Vergeer, J.H. van Zanten, Uncertainty and LR: to integrate or not to integrate, that's the question, Law, Probability and Risk 15 (1) (2015) 23–29.

[361] K. Slooten, C.E.H. Berger, Response paper to 'the likelihood of encapsulating all uncertainty': the relevance of additional information for the LR, Science & Justice 57 (6) (2017) 468–471.

[362] D. Taylor, T. Hicks, C. Champod, Using sensitivity analysis in Bayesian networks to highlight the impact of data paucity and direct future analysis: a contribution to the debate on measuring and reporting the precision of likelihood ratios, Science & Justice 56 (5) (2016) 402–410.

Index

A

Akaike information criterion (AIC), 248, 335

Alleles

  designations, 3, 43, 60, 67, 226, 242, 393, 428, 434

  drop-out, 56, 60, 89, 91, 96, 107, 111, 112, 127, 134, 240, 294

    probability, 97, 99, 104, 107, 119, 134–136

  frequencies, 7, 35, 39, 141, 198, 212, 282, 285, 361, 420, 427, 440

    databases, 10, 285

  masking, 407

  microvariant, 63

  peak heights, 48, 55, 56, 60, 67, 95, 103, 124, 149, 181, 191, 204, 222, 229, 237

  probabilities, 8, 27, 31, 38, 194

  proportion, 77, 78, 82, 186, 187, 365

  rare, 2, 10, 41, 47, 141, 318, 345, 351

  sequences, 428, 433, 444

  simulation, 186, 188, 192

  spurious, 127

  stutter, 229, 263, 267, 282, 441, 446

Alternate

  contributors, 26

  genotype combination, 27

  major genotype, 75

  propositions, 130, 156, 173, 196, 241, 263

Amelogenin locus, 75

AmpFlSTR Identifiler, 430

AmpFlSTR SGM plus multiplex, 111

Analysis

  kinship, 46, 47

  sensitivity, 157

  short tandem repeat, 2, 3

Analytical threshold, 201, 235

Automated tests

  for *DNAxs*, 323

B

Binomial probability, 124

Block repeats, 433

  longest uninterrupted sequence (LUS), 433

C

Calibration, 299

CaseSolver, 178, 351, 356–358, 380, 382, 431

Casework

  forensic, 3, 52, 144, 281, 309, 310, 314, 358

Charged coupled device (CCD), 126

Clayton guidelines, 70, 181

CODIS, 5, 314, 347–349, 430

  core loci, 5, 344

  database searches, 346, 348, 349

Combined stutter/degradation

  model, 226

Common ancestry, 32

Compound repeats, 428

Conditioned

  genotype, 120, 203, 237

    combinations, 205

  known contributors, 274

  minor genotype, 74

  probabilities, 13–15, 19, 387

  suspect, 196, 261

  victim, 27

Conservative value, 317

Contributors

  minimum number, 15, 17, 73, 74, 167, 175, 251, 264, 274, 278, 358, 394, 421, 422, 425

  parameters, 204

Conventional STRs, 420, 429

Cosmopolitan populations, 30, 35, 38, 42

Cumulative probability, 254, 305, 321, 340

D

Database

  CODIS, 344

  European, 45

  population, 34, 285, 286

  searches, 115, 165, 339–341, 351, 358, 381, 399, 400

  size, 339, 340, 346

  STRseq, 437

Deconvolution, 76, 82, 88, 212, 239, 255, 257, 358, 367

  spreadsheet, 215

Defense

  proposition, 14, 18, 21, 100, 195, 240, 345, 352, 387

498 Index

Degradation, 123, 215
  characteristics, 123
  index, 123
  model, 232, 305, 316, 317, 322, 332, 337, 362,
    364, 421
  parameter, 124, 126, 128, 278
  probability, 126
  slope, 318
Denominator, 14
Detection threshold, 202, 240, 242, 254, 263, 282,
    294, 317, 318, 320, 321, 332, 337, 361,
    362, 420
DNA
  database searches, 347, 348, 350
  databases, 4, 312, 342, 344, 374, 393, 427
  evidence, 111, 131, 258, 376, 396, 401, 408, 411
  mixture, 52, 153, 277, 345, 346, 351, 356, 385,
    392, 404, 405, 411
  profile, 17, 18, 60, 73, 94, 112, 114, 129, 130,
    153, 274, 317, 327, 343, 363, 390, 391,
    393
DNAmatch2, 380, 382
DNAStatistX, 305, 309, 315, 316, 332
DNAxs, 310, 328, 332
Drop-in, 133, 134, 153
  model, 235
  probability, 156
Drop-out, 91–93, 95, 133, 134, 150, 153, 158, 205
  alleles, 56, 60, 89, 91, 96, 107, 111, 112, 127,
    134, 240, 294
  analysis, 105
  estimation, 346
  extreme, 95
  locus, 112
  parameter, 134, 135, 140, 205, 237, 360, 421
  probability, 96, 97, 99, 102, 106, 109, 135, 156,
    158, 205, 206, 352, 360
    parameter, 156–158, 161, 354
    per-donor, 156
  threshold, 207

E

Elimination databases, 116, 381, 382
ENFSI, 11, 38, 42, 55, 116, 241
  DNA database management, 116
  study, 45
  verbal scale, 449
Error
  false negative, 286, 287

  false positive, 286, 288, 290
ESS loci, 5, 343, 430
EuroForMix, 282, 286–288, 354, 356, 357, 360,
    361, 378, 380, 420, 421, 437, 440
  analysis, 261, 266, 444
  for database searching, 354
  implementation, 221
  model, 221, 232, 233, 264, 286, 440
    validation, 322
  software, 214, 215, 239
  theory, 239
European
  database, 45
  loci, 343
  multiplexes, 6
  populations, 11, 42, 420
European DNA profiling group (EDNAP), 4
European standard set of loci (ESS), 5, 42, 343
Evaluative reporting, 341, 342, 376, 389, 400, 401
Excess contributors
  effect, 267, 407, 422, 425

F

Fallacy, 398, 400
  prosecutor's, 18, 167, 395–399, 401, 404, 416
False
  negative
    error, 286, 287
    results, 293
  positive
    error, 286, 288, 290
    results, 290
Forensic
  casework, 3, 52, 144, 281, 309, 310, 314, 358
  database, 37, 45
Forensic Science Service (FSS), 4
Forward
  stutter, 62, 64, 66, 67, 234, 240, 285, 298, 299,
    334, 335, 435
  model, 273, 282
Frequency database, 40, 354, 381
  population, 408, 420

G

Gamma distribution, 199
Gamma model, 199
GDA software, 45
GeneMapper stutter filter, 297, 299
GeneMarker, 321
Genetic data analysis (GDA), 44

Genetic drift, 31, 35
GenoProof mixture, 52
Genotype
  alternatives, 207
  combinations, 27
  conditioned, 120, 203, 237
  contributors, 28, 182, 189, 195, 237, 446
  frequencies, 8, 31, 33, 141
  heterozygote, 8, 94, 97, 120, 134–136, 141–143, 239, 409
  homozygote, 34, 95, 120, 134–136, 141, 240
  probabilities, 7, 10, 26, 35, 48, 133, 137, 141, 143, 145–147, 194, 195, 198, 361
    for multiple contributors, 39
  replicates, 120
GlobalFiler, 358, 361, 363
  allele frequencies, 374
  kit, 364

H

Hardy–Weinberg
  equilibrium, 6–9, 11, 52
  tests, 43
Heterozygote, 10, 16, 23, 26, 31, 33, 34, 37, 38, 43, 66, 73, 77, 82, 88, 94, 95, 97, 101, 102, 190
  alleles, 56
  balance, 49, 55, 56, 59–62, 70, 89, 92, 189, 237
    calculations, 86
    expectations, 93
    thresholds, 195, 311, 337
  contributors, 77, 82
  drop-out, 121
  genotype, 8, 94, 97, 120, 134–136, 141–143, 239, 409
  imbalance, 56, 60, 71, 72, 91, 107, 112, 127, 205
  states, 94
Homozygote, 10, 16, 17, 23, 26, 33, 37, 38, 43, 73, 77, 82, 94, 95, 97, 98, 100, 115, 119–121, 134, 206, 243, 334, 409
  contributors, 82
  drop-out, 421
  genotype, 34, 95, 120, 134–136, 141, 240
  phenotypic, 101
  probabilities, 31
  threshold, 93
Human genome databases, 1
Human populations, 141

HW
  expectations, 11, 27, 31, 32, 34, 35, 72
  tests, 44

I

Identity by state (IBS) threshold, 368
Identity by descent (IBD), 32, 143
Independence
  across replicates, 134
  alleles, 35
  tests, 9
Information gain, 434–436, 446–449, 451
Inter-locus balance, 55
Interpretation, 239, 390
Intra-locus and inter-locus balance, 60
Inverse match probability (IMP), 176
Investigative
  reporting, 339, 341, 359, 376
ISFG DNA commission, 2, 49, 102, 107, 173, 174, 196, 251, 339, 385, 388, 389, 392, 399, 400, 402, 404, 407, 414, 415, 429
Isolated
  populations, 31, 45
  sub-populations, 31, 40

J

Joint
  probability, 119, 129, 131, 135, 150, 176, 213
    replicate, 147

K

Kinship analysis, 46, 47

L

Likelihood ratio, 14, 20, 21, 27, 41, 49, 52, 137, 299, 386, 387
  estimation, 6
  framework, 387
  maximum, 415
  threshold, 349
Loci
  autosomal, 30, 430
  DNA, 5
  European, 343
  STRs, 4, 42, 71, 113, 345, 428, 430
LoCIM, 310, 328
  inference, 314
  information, 327
Locus
  drop-out, 112

500 Index

heterozygote, 112
specific stutter filters, 317, 333
STR system, 4
Log likelihood, 198, 199, 205, 211, 219, 226, 275, 277, 278, 319
values, 226, 232, 267, 275
Logistic regression, 104
Longest uninterrupted sequence (LUS), 379, 431
LRmix, 129, 133, 149, 286, 288, 316, 344, 357, 359, 360, 382, 420, 421
model, 149, 358
LRmix Studio, 153, 178, 282, 286–288

M

Marginal probabilities, 213, 214, 258
Marker, 62, 63, 67, 86, 97, 107, 254, 314, 318, 321
names, 60–62, 67, 86
Markov chain Monte Carlo (MCMC), 50, 254
Masking
alleles, 88, 209
effect, 73, 74, 82
Massively parallel sequencing (MPS), 3, 65, 86, 122, 419, 420
MasterMix, 185
Matching allele
comparison, 354
count, 361, 373
Maximum
allele count, 74, 327, 407, 421
likelihood estimation, 109, 185, 196, 315
Microvariant alleles, 63
Migration, 30
Minimum number
of contributors, 15, 17, 73, 74, 167, 175, 251, 264, 274, 278, 358, 394, 421, 422, 425
Mixture
analysis, 420, 425, 427
contributors, 77
DNA, 52, 153, 277, 345, 346, 351, 356, 385, 392, 404, 405, 411
genotype combinations, 181, 185
interpretation, 12, 49, 65
models, 410
profiles, 270, 288, 290, 291, 361, 375
proportion, 49, 75, 181, 182, 186, 222, 237, 239, 246, 268, 305, 318, 331, 423, 436
from allele peak heights, 198
parameter, 183, 193, 201
per contributor, 203, 204

ratio, 74, 75, 77, 88, 420
simple, 70
Model
combined stutter/degradation, 226
degradation, 232, 305, 316, 317, 322, 332, 337, 362, 364, 421
EuroForMix, 221, 232, 233, 264, 286, 440
for one contributor, 200
forward stutter, 273, 282
LRmix, 149, 358
probabilistic, 98, 118, 127, 129, 130, 133, 191, 196, 237, 240, 376
qualitative, 149, 153, 178, 237, 287, 303, 357, 376, 422
quantitative, 178, 181, 258, 287, 307, 357, 359, 376, 407, 421
stutter, 220, 221, 223, 226, 284, 298, 317, 337, 362
validation, 239, 251, 252, 278, 279, 316, 321, 322, 331, 338
Multiplexes, 4, 42, 43, 112, 430
Mutation, 30

N

National DNA database, 3, 4, 94, 95, 102, 178, 339, 343, 344, 356, 373, 375, 379, 382, 389, 399, 400, 428, 429
Netherlands Forensic Institute (NFI), 178, 304, 309
New generation sequencing (NGS), 12
Non-contributor, 132, 164, 285, 286, 288, 291, 300, 302, 308, 322, 346, 378, 408–410, 412, 422
tests, 163, 164, 166–168, 171, 172, 175, 178, 407, 409, 414, 417, 421
Normal distribution model, 192
Numerator, 14

P

Peak area, 55
Peak height
alleles, 48, 55, 56, 60, 67, 95, 103, 124, 149, 181, 191, 192, 204, 222, 229, 237
average, 56, 60
expectation, 82, 201–204, 221–223, 226, 229, 230, 246, 318
model fitted, 255
probabilistic assessment, 199
proportions, 77, 78, 182, 192, 222, 264
threshold, 313

Population
  allele frequencies, 141
  common ancestry, 32, 52
  database, 34, 285, 286
  frequency
    database, 408
  genetics, 6, 42, 52, 429
  movement, 30
  size, 30, 397
  structure, 32, 52
  sub-structuring, 38, 44, 129, 141, 144, 150
    effect, 29, 141
  surveys, 37, 52
Posterior drop-out probability, 354
Posterior probability, 302, 396
PowerPlex Fusion 6C, 270, 305, 317, 318, 321, 322, 430
Probabilistic
  approach, 150
  calculations, 82, 99, 120, 184, 367
  definitions, 98
  expectations, 7
  genotyping, 70, 76, 195, 308, 442, 450
    methods, 49, 304, 386, 392, 404, 420
    software, 48, 113, 304, 382, 406, 429, 450, 451
  model, 98, 118, 127, 129, 130, 133, 191, 196, 237, 240, 376
  software, 198, 379
  weights, 191, 192, 237
Probability
  cumulative, 254, 305, 321, 340
  degradation, 126
  density, 200
    distributions, 203
    function, 193, 199
  distribution, 117
  drop-out, 96, 99, 102, 106, 109, 156, 158, 205, 206, 352, 360
    parameter, 156–158, 161, 354
  error, 399
  genotype combinations, 195
  joint, 119, 129, 131, 135, 150, 176, 213
  marginal, 213, 214, 258
  posterior, 74, 302, 396
    drop-out, 354
  propositions, 399
  replicates, 132–137, 147, 148
  threshold, 252

Promega PowerPlex Fusion 6C, 282, 307
Proportion
  mixture, 49, 75, 181, 182, 186, 222, 237, 239, 246, 268, 305, 318, 331, 423, 436
    from allele peak heights, 198
    parameter, 183, 193, 201
    per contributor, 203, 204
  peak height, 182
  stutter, 62, 222, 226, 239, 318, 435
Propositions, 14
  activity level, 391, 394
  alternate, 130, 156, 173, 196, 241, 263
  defense, 14, 18, 21, 100, 195, 240, 345, 352, 387
  hierarchy, 390
  offense level, 391
  probability, 399
  prosecution, 14, 18, 19, 100, 161, 194, 199, 240, 258, 352, 387
  source level, 391
  sub-source level, 390
  sub-sub-source level, 391
Prüm
  inclusion rules, 343
  matching rules, 343
  software, 343

Q

Qualitative model, 149, 153, 178, 237, 287, 303, 356, 357, 376, 422
Quantitative
  model, 178, 181, 258, 287, 307, 357, 359, 376, 407, 421, 425
  threshold, 366

R

Random
  DNA profiles, 159
  genotypes, 39
  man, 164, 408
  matching profiles, 339, 340
  mating, 30, 38
  sampling, 31, 35
  unknown individuals, 178
Random man not excluded (RMNE), 49, 304, 385, 386
  calculation, 386
Rare alleles, 2, 10, 41, 47, 141, 318, 345, 351
  frequency, 156, 331, 352
Receiver operating characteristic (ROC), 296
Relatedness, 46, 140, 143, 144, 146, 177, 406, 417

502 Index

calculations, 178, 268, 270
effect, 46, 406
formulae, 143, 146
in mixtures, 146
sub-populations, 286
tests, 291
Relative fluorescence units (RFU), 239
Repeats
complete, 427
compound, 428
consecutive, 63
LUS, 451
per allele, 427
simple, 428
singleton, 434
STRs, 63
Replicates, 284
analyses, 118, 130, 150, 175, 305, 306
probability, 132–137, 147, 148
theory, 176
tests, 127, 130
Reporting threshold
for casework, 288, 305
Residual sum squared (RSS), 79, 183

S

Sampling effects, 9, 44
Sensitivity analysis
LRmix Studio, 157
Sensitivity test
EuroForMix, 254, 275
Short tandem repeat (STR), 2, 3, 52, 239
Sibling, 46–48, 140, 143, 178, 268, 271, 285, 291, 307, 406
genotypes, 352
Simple repeats, 428
SmartRank, 310, 314, 344, 345, 347, 348, 350, 380, 382
analysis, 348
DNA database search, 351
exercises, 352
performance, 346
software, 344, 350
SNP, 420, 425
allele frequencies, 420
analysis, 420
markers, 86
mixtures, 421

Software
approaches, 49
developers, 324
development, 323
DNAxs, 310, 327
EuroForMix, 214, 215, 239
implementation, 278, 282
list, 49
models for complex stutters, 337
probabilistic
genotyping, 113, 304, 382, 406, 429, 451
programs, 304, 318, 322
SmartRank, 350
validation, 278, 281, 282, 307
Spurious alleles, 127
Stochastic effects, 66, 69, 71, 91, 107, 113, 119, 127, 175, 284
Stochastic threshold, 55, 56, 71, 88, 93, 95, 97, 100, 102, 107, 167, 313
STR-validator, 60, 61, 66, 68, 91
STRs, 2, 4
loci, 4, 42, 71, 113, 345, 428, 430
STRseq
BioProject, 430
database, 429, 437
Stutter, 62, 65, 66, 220
alleles, 446
analysis, 431
calculation, 67
characteristics, 435, 436
filter, 65, 66, 240, 284, 285, 362, 435, 446
effect, 446, 449
threshold, 440
formation, 64, 65
guidelines, 70
impact, 223
model, 220, 221, 223, 226, 284, 298, 317, 337, 362
noise expectations, 436
parameter, 220, 232
prediction, 431, 434, 435
proportion, 62, 222, 223, 226, 239, 318, 435
rates, 69
ratio, 55, 62, 64, 66–68
STR-MPS, 431
variants, 431
Stuttermark, 436, 443, 444
Stuttermodel, 436, 443

Sub-populations
  allele
    diversity, 45
    frequencies, 36
  boundaries, 30
  relatedness, 286
  structuring, 39
Sub-source
  level, 390–392
  propositions, 393, 395
Sub-sub-source level, 392

T

Tandem repeats, 282, 427
Tests
  Hardy–Weinberg equilibrium (HW), 6
  Fisher's exact, 9
  kinship, 53
  non-contributor, 163, 164, 166–168, 171, 172, 175, 178, 407, 409, 414, 417, 421
  relatedness, 291
  replicates, 127, 130
Threshold
  drop-out, 207, 222
  homozygote, 93

stutter filter, 440
tests
  for heterozygote balance, 190
Total allele count (TAC), 327, 407
Triallelic loci, 71
Turing expectation, 300, 408, 410

U

Universal analysis software (UAS), 86, 437
  stutter filter thresholds, 441

V

Validation, 277
  conceptual, 279
  model, 239, 251, 252, 278, 279, 316, 321, 322, 331, 338
  operational, 280
  software, 281, 307
Verbal scale, 261, 305, 401, 402
Virtual genotypes, 345

W

Wahlund effect, 8, 31, 33, 37
Weak evidence effect, 401

Made in United States
North Haven, CT
02 December 2024

61532557R00291